COOK'S

ILLUSTRATED

～ 2002 ～

$29.95

Copyright 2002 © by The Editors of *Cook's Illustrated*
All rights reserved, including the right of reproduction in
whole or in part in any form.

Published by
Boston Common Press Limited Partnership
17 Station Street
Brookline, MA 02445

ISBN: 0-936184-62-0
ISSN: 1068-2821

To get home delivery of *Cook's Illustrated*, call 800-526-8442 inside the U.S., or 515-247-7571 if calling from outside the U.S., or subscribe online at http://www.cooksillustrated.com.

In addition to the Annual Hardbound Editions, *Cook's Illustrated* offers the following publications:

The Best Recipe Series
The Best Recipe
Grilling & Barbecue
Soups & Stews
American Classics
Italian Classics

The America's Test Kitchen Series (companion cookbooks to our hit public television series)
The America's Test Kitchen Cookbook
    (2002 season cookbook)
Here in America's Test Kitchen
    (2003 season cookbook)

Additional books from the editors of
Cook's Illustrated magazine
The Cook's Bible
The Yellow Farmhouse Cookbook
The Dessert Bible
The Cook's Illustrated Complete Book of Poultry
The Cook's Illustrated Complete Book of Pasta & Noodles
365 Quick Tips
1993–2002 Master Index

The How To Cook Master Series
How to Make a Pie
How to Make an American Layer Cake
How to Stir-Fry
How to Make Ice Cream
How to Make Pizza
How to Make Holiday Desserts
How to Make Pasta Sauce
How to Make Salad
How to Grill
How to Make Simple Fruit Desserts
How to Make Cookie Jar Favorites
How to Cook Holiday Roasts and Birds
How to Make Stew
How to Cook Shrimp and Other Shellfish
How to Barbecue and Roast on the Grill
How to Cook Garden Vegetables
How to Make Casseroles and Pot Pies
How to Make Soup
How to Saute
How to Cook Potatoes
How to Make Quick Appetizers
How to Make Sauces & Gravies
How to Cook Chinese Favorites
How to Make Muffins, Biscuits, and Scones
How to Cook Chicken Breasts

To order any of our cookbooks listed above, give us a call at 800-611-0759 inside the U.S., or at 515-246-6911 if calling from outside the U.S.

You can order subscriptions, gift subscriptions, and any of our books by visiting our online store at:

www.cooksillustrated.com

NUMBER FIFTY-FOUR

JANUARY & FEBRUARY 2002

COOK'S
ILLUSTRATED

Rating
Large Saucepans
8 Contestants, 3 Winners

Weeknight
Pork Cutlets
Tender, Crisp, and Quick

Pantry Pasta Sauces

Chicken Taste-Off
Kosher Bird Beats Free-Range

20-Minute
Stroganoff

Spring Rolls
Light, Fresh, and Easy

Soft, Chewy
Molasses Cookies

Caramelizing Onions
New Uses for Parchment Paper
Chicken Vesuvio
Braising Belgian Endive
Profiteroles Simplified

www.cooksillustrated.com

$4.95 U.S./$6.95 CANADA

02>

62805

0 232817 1

CONTENTS

January & February 2002

COOK'S ILLUSTRATED

Home of America's Test Kitchen
www.cooksillustrated.com

PUBLISHER AND EDITOR
Christopher Kimball

SENIOR EDITOR
Jack Bishop

MANAGING EDITOR
Dawn Yanagihara

SENIOR WRITER
Adam Ried

EDITORIAL MANAGER
Barbara Bourassa

ART DIRECTOR
Amy Klee

TEST KITCHEN DIRECTOR
Bridget Lancaster

ASSISTANT TEST KITCHEN DIRECTOR
Erin McMurrer

ASSOCIATE EDITORS
Raquel Pelzel
Julia Collin

COPY EDITOR
India Koopman

MANAGING EDITOR,
BOOKS AND WEB SITE
Becky Hays

ASSISTANT EDITOR, WEB SITE
Shona Simkin

TEST COOKS
Shannon Blaisdell
Matthew Card
Meg Suzuki

CONSULTING EDITORS
Jasper White
Robert L. Wolke

PROOFREADER
Jana Branch

VICE PRESIDENT MARKETING
David Mack

SALES REPRESENTATIVE
Jason Geller

CIRCULATION RETAIL SALES MANAGER
Jonathan Venier

MARKETING ASSISTANT
Connie Forbes

CIRCULATION MANAGER
Larisa Greiner

PRODUCTS MANAGER
Steven Browall

DIRECT MAIL MANAGER
Robert Lee

CUSTOMER SERVICE MANAGER
Jacqueline Valerio

INBOUND MARKETING REPRESENTATIVE
Adam Dardeck

VICE PRESIDENT OPERATIONS
AND TECHNOLOGY
James McCormack

PRODUCTION MANAGER
Jessica Quirk

PRODUCTION COORDINATOR
Mary Connelly

PRODUCTION ASSISTANTS
Ron Bilodeau
Jennifer McCreary

SYSTEMS ADMINISTRATOR
Richard Cassidy

WEBMASTER
Nicole Morris

CHIEF FINANCIAL OFFICER
Sharyn Chabot

CONTROLLER
Mandy Shito

OFFICE MANAGER
Juliet Nusbaum

RECEPTIONIST
Henrietta Murray

PUBLICITY
Deborah Broide

For list rental information, contact The SpecialLISTS, 1200 Harbor Blvd. 9th Floor, Weehawken, NJ 07087; 201-865-5800; fax 201-867-2450. Editorial office: 17 Station Street, Brookline, MA 02445; 617-232-1000; fax 617-232-1572. Editorial contributions should be sent to: Editor, *Cook's Illustrated*. We cannot assume responsibility for manuscripts submitted to us. Submissions will be returned only if accompanied by a large self-addressed stamped envelope. Postmaster: Send all new orders, subscription inquiries, and change of address notices to: *Cook's Illustrated*, P.O. Box 7446, Red Oak, IA 51591-0446. PRINTED IN THE USA.

BLUE CHEESES Blue cheeses gain their renowned qualities from *Penicillium roqueforti,* a mold added to the milk at the beginning of the cheese-making process. In the ripening stage, the cheese is pierced with skewers, exposing the mold to oxygen, which makes it turn blue. Cow's milk is used to produce most blue cheeses, including Maytag Blue, Stilton, Shropshire Blue, Fourme d'Ambert, Bleu de Gex, Bleu de Termignon, and Gorgonzola (available in two styles—mild dolce and sharper naturale). A few blue cheeses are made with sheep's milk (such as Roquefort Papillon), goat's milk (Bleu de Basques), or a combination of all three milks (Cabrales and Picon, although the latter is sometimes made with only cow's milk). The characteristics of a blue cheese depend on many factors, including the type of milk used (cheeses made from goat's or sheep's milk are generally more pungent) and the extent of aging (the longer the aging, the more crumbly the texture).

COVER (*Potatoes*): ELIZABETH BRANDON, BACK COVER (*Blue Cheeses*): JOHN BURGOYNE

IT HAPPENED ONE DAY

In the country, disaster comes in many forms—an overturned tractor, a barn fire, or a bucking chainsaw—and over time, we learn to take precautions. I always park my pickup facing home when logging in the woods (if you are injured, you have a better chance of driving out), I don't change gears on a loaded tractor when going downhill (if the brakes fail, you're done for), and I don't stack green hay in a barn since it can spontaneously burst into flames. I've met locals with one arm, parents who have lost children in haying accidents, and more than one mill worker down at Miles Lumber who is at least one finger short. One of my most vivid memories as a child was watching Colonel Vaughn's barn burn from the top of Swearing Hill. At first it looked like a small brush fire, and then I realized that this was a day I would never forget, the smoke curling up into the sky, dark and sinister, as if left by an invading army.

In the country, there are many signs of a well-regulated universe: sap running, hay growing, the arrival of hunters with out-of-state plates, and early morning gossip and doughnuts at the Wayside Country Store. Even potato bugs, Japanese beetles, and gypsy moths play their parts in this cycle, evidence that disaster is as predictable as a heavy frost in September. Over time, we can get used to news of droughts, fires, even car crashes—events that creep into our notion of daily life. Still, some news is beyond our capacity for assimilation—reality overtakes imagination—

and then our first cup of coffee never tastes quite the same.

Charlie Bentley, our last local farmer and a respected selectman, was injured this past spring in a tractor accident. He was working under a disk harrow, and, when the tractor started up, the harrow dropped suddenly and caught him by the neck. He was dragged through the field, face-down, until the tractor could be stopped. He survived—Vermont farmers are hardy folk—but as he is the last upstanding representative of the town's past, the event shook us all.

Within days, a neighbor organized a pancake breakfast fundraiser. I cooked 35 pounds of homemade sausage, others made vats of pancake batter, the country store sent along gallons of orange juice, and locals donated items for a silent auction: watercolors, quilts, toy tractors, jam, cookies, bluebird houses—even a phone in the shape of a duck. On a crisp spring morning in June, 250 kids, farmers, carpenters, plumbers, truckers, and dairymen raised more than $10,000—not much by city standards—but an impressive sum for a small mountain town.

The rest of that summer never regained its rhythm, so my wife and I decided to hold a covered-dish supper over Labor Day weekend. Neighbors brought molasses-laced baked beans, ambrosia, three-bean salad, macaroni-chili

Christopher Kimball

casserole, vegetable lasagna, honey cake, and cherry pie, along with their folding lawn chairs. We stacked bales of hay for a table, boiled 150 ears of sweet corn, and served up 60 pounds of barbecued beef. As night came, we turned on the strings of construction lights hanging from the trees, and the kids scattered into the nearby cornfield, playing hide-and-seek. Charlie Bentley showed up and did his part, tucking into seconds, casting an eager eye toward the softer, more brightly colored desserts.

Everything finally seemed back to normal that evening as we sat together in tattered lawn chairs drawn in a circle under an ancient maple tree, listening to a distant thunderstorm that was slowly moving up the valley. A column of boys paraded smartly around the gathering with sticks held stiffly over narrow shoulders, lightning flashed in the distance like approaching artillery, and groups of locals slowly dissolved into the night, enveloped by pear trees and darkness. Just then, as twilight surrendered and the distant thunder was upon us, we awoke from thoughts of the coming storm and listened to the sound of the children in the cornfield. In our darkest hour, they called out to us from the heart of America, reminding us that every small town is a great nation, and each child is a nation unto himself.

FOR MORE INFORMATION

www.cooksillustrated.com

At the *Cook's Illustrated* Web site you can order a book, give a gift subscription to *Cook's Illustrated* magazine, sign up for our free e-newsletter, subscribe to the magazine, or check the status of your subscription. Join the Web site and you'll have access to our searchable databases of recipes, cookware ratings, ingredient tastings, quick tips, cookbook reviews, and more.

The Web site also features free recipes, techniques, and answers to cooking questions; original editorial material not found in the magazine; a question-and-answer message board; and a list of upcoming appearances by editor and publisher Christopher Kimball.

Have questions about your subscription? Visit our customer service page, where you can change your address, renew your subscription, pay your bill, or read answers to frequently asked questions.

COOK'S ILLUSTRATED Magazine

Cook's Illustrated (ISSN 1068-2821) magazine is published bimonthly (6 issues per year) by Boston Common Press Limited Partnership, 17 Station Street, Brookline, MA 02445. Copyright 2002 Boston Common Press Limited Partnership. Periodical postage paid at Boston, Mass., and additional mailing offices, USPS #012487.

A one-year subscription is $29.70, two years is $55, and three years is $75. Add $6 postage per year for Canadian subscriptions and $12 per year for all other countries outside the U.S. To order

subscriptions in the U.S. call 800-526-8442; from outside the U.S. call 515-247-7571. Gift subscriptions are available for $24.95 each. Postmaster: Send all new orders, subscription inquiries, and change-of-address notices to Cook's Illustrated, P.O. Box 7446, Red Oak, IA 51591-0446, or call 800-526-8442 inside the U.S.; from outside the U.S. call 515-247-7571.

AMERICA'S TEST KITCHEN Television Series

Look for our television series on public television. For program times in your area, recipes, and details about the shows, or to order the companion book to the second season of the series, *The America's Test Kitchen Cookbook*, visit http://www.americastestkitchen.com.

COOKBOOKS

To order any of the following books, as well as *The America's Test Kitchen Cookbook*, call 800-611-0759 inside the U.S. or 515-246-6911 from outside the U.S.

➤ **The Best Recipe Series** Includes *The Best Recipe* as well as *The Best Recipe: Grilling & Barbecue* and *The Best Recipe: Soups & Stews.*

➤ **The How to Cook Master Series** A collection of 25 single-subject cookbooks covering topics such as quick appetizers, simple fruit desserts, and sauces.

➤ **The Annual Series** Annual hardbound editions of the magazine as well as a nine-year (1993–2001) reference index.

Commercial Chicken Broths

What kind of chicken is used to make canned chicken broth? And what's the role of all those other ingredients you see on can labels?

BETH BLOOMBERG
SHELBURNE, VT.

➤ In our March/April 2000 issue, we conducted a blind tasting of 13 brands of chicken broth and found that products made by Swanson and Campbell's took the top four spots, although none could compete with homemade stock. When the results came in, we asked the Campbell Soup Company, parent company of Swanson, about the ingredients in an effort to determine what gave these products their edge. "One thing that distinguishes our broth," said Cindy Ayers, Campbell's vice president of global consumer food communications, "is its balanced combination of flavors; these flavors give our broth added depth." She then added, "When we develop or enhance our flavors, we use the flavors of a homemade broth as our gold standard."

This sounded reasonable, but we wondered exactly how the broth is made. We decided to press on and talked to Dr. T. C. Chen, professor of poultry product technology at Mississippi State University. He noted that the main quality differentiator is the kind of bird used to make broth. Yet the bird rarely makes it to the plant where the broth is made. Instead, many soup companies, including Campbell's, order concentrated broth from a supplier. Chen also noted that it is common for soup companies to add flavor enhancers to the concentrated broth gel. But what are these flavor enhancers, and where do they come from?

To find out, we contacted Sara Risch, consultant to the Institute of Food Technologists, who said that one of the ways companies add flavor to products like chicken broth is to add so-called reaction flavors. Reaction flavors are produced by heating various combinations of sugars and amino acids (the building blocks of protein). Depending on the combination, anything from a chocolate-like to a popcorn-like to a chicken-like flavor can be developed. If reaction flavors are part of Campbell's secret recipe, said Risch, chances are the company is using an outside source to create that chicken flavor. "Very often a company that makes the broth doesn't make the flavor. It would go to a flavor company," she said.

Typical flavoring materials include meat and seafood extracts and flavors, cheese powders, hydrolyzed vegetable protein, yeast extracts, and vegetable purees. As it turns out, many of these ingredients show up on the labels of commercial chicken broth. In addition, the *Cook's* test kitchen noted that the top two broths in our tasting contained the highest levels of sodium and that both contained monosodium glutamate.

In the end, it seems that commercial chicken broth is made by means of a complex process that has little in common with the task of making homemade stock; all the two share are a few base ingredients. This may explain why even the best commercial broths can't compete with the real thing in a blind tasting.

Cooking Today's Leaner, Meaner Pork

Most of the pork chops I bring home from the market end up dry and tough after being cooked. Is this inevitable?

BARBARA SUTTON
SOMERVILLE, MASS.

➤ Today's pig is the result of the pork industry's efforts to meet consumers' desire for lower-fat foods. It has an average of 50 percent less fat than its counterpart in the 1950s. But today's pork is not only leaner, it's meaner—that is, less forgiving when cooked. Fat adds flavor to meat, and it also helps to keep it juicy and tender when cooked.

Compounding these problems, according to Steven Meyer, staff economist at the National Pork Board, is the consumer's inclination to overcook pork out of concern that it may be contaminated with the trichinosis parasite. But this concern is now largely baseless since there are a small number of cases per year and many of these come from wild game. The Pork Board recommends cooking pork until it is just slightly rosy in the center and registers 150 degrees Fahrenheit on an instant-read thermometer. The *Cook's* test kitchen suggests a final temperature of 145 degrees, keeping in mind that larger cuts of pork can be removed from the oven at roughly 135 degrees, covered, and allowed to rest, during which time the temperature will rise by at least 10 degrees. (Be sure to check the final temperature before serving to make certain that it reaches 145 degrees.)

In an effort to keep customers happy and pork juicy even if it's been somewhat overcooked, pork producers have introduced a product called "enhanced pork" to the market. Enhanced pork is injected with a solution of water, salt, and sodium phosphate, all of which are among the ingredients used to cure pork when making bacon. The objective is to both season the pork from within and to make it more resistant to drying out when cooked. The process is similar to that used by some turkey producers in an effort to keep the breast meat from drying out during cooking.

Curious about enhanced pork, we purchased two packages of center-cut boneless pork chops at local markets, one of which was labeled "enhanced." (According to David Meisinger, director of pork quality at the National Pork Board, all enhanced pork must be so labeled and must indicate the amount of enhancement solution used as a percentage of the meat's weight. The label on the package we purchased, for example, indicated that "tenderness and juiciness" were "enhanced with up to 10 percent of a solution containing water, salt, and sodium phosphate.")

We sautéed the chops, cooking them to a temperature of 145 degrees, then let them sit, covered, for five minutes to let the juices redistribute themselves throughout the meat. The results? Most tasters did indeed find the enhanced pork to be juicier and more tender. But while the unenhanced pork was found to be drier and tougher to chew, it was also described by some tasters as having a more natural pork flavor, which they preferred to the somewhat salty taste of the enhanced pork.

Our recommendation? Try the enhanced pork yourself and see if you prefer it to unenhanced pork, bearing in mind that cooking the pork just until done is especially important if you are to get satisfying results with the latter.

Baking Powders with and without Aluminum

I recently saw an aluminum-free baking powder in my supermarket. Does this mean regular baking powder contains aluminum? Are these products interchangeable?

FRANCIS HSAI
EXTON, PA.

➤ The formulas used to make baking powders today are much more carefully calibrated than when this leavener was first packaged for home cooks nearly 200 years ago, but the chemistry remains the same. Baking powders depend on the inclination of an alkaline substance (sodium bicarbonate, or baking soda) and an acid (originally cream of tartar, but today there are more options) to react and produce carbon dioxide gas bubbles, thereby leavening batters for muffins, cakes, and other baked goods that need a quicker rise than can be provided by yeast.

Baking soda has always been a pretty good buy, while cream of tartar, a byproduct of wine making, has never come cheap. It was first used in prepared baking powders in 1835, but by the 1850s a cheaper alternative, monocalcium phosphate (MCP), was introduced, and it continues to be used in baking powders today. MCP is similar to cream of tartar in that it reacts with baking soda immediately when the two are combined with water. (Cornstarch is a component of all baking powders. It absorbs moisture, thereby helping to keep the acid and the baking soda from interacting during storage; it also helps to disperse the acid and baking soda evenly throughout a batter.) What this immediate reaction means in professional baker's terms is that MCP gives a batter more bench rise (the leavening that takes place before a batter goes into the oven) than oven rise (the leavening that takes place in the oven). This is not necessarily a bad thing, but it does require the cook to get the batter into the oven fairly quickly; if not, the baking powder will exhaust much of its leavening power on the bench, and the muffin or cake will not rise as much as it could or should in the oven.

Enter the acidic leavener sodium aluminum sulfate (SAS), added to many baking powders since the beginning of the 20th century. SAS and a compound used interchangeably with it today, sodium aluminum phosphate (SALP), don't react with baking soda and water at room temperature. It's only in the oven, when the temperature rises above 120 degrees Fahrenheit, that their leavening power goes to work. Several top-selling brands of baking powder—including Calumet, Clabber Girl, and Davis—make use of both MCP and one of the aluminum compounds as a kind of insurance so the home cook gets both good bench rise and good oven rise. (Another popular brand, Rumford, uses only MCP with no aluminum compounds.) The MCP goes to work as soon as liquid is added to the dry ingredients, and the SAS or SALP kicks in when exposed to the heat of the oven. In most such formulations, about one-third of the leavening takes place on the bench and the balance in the oven. These baking powders are all referred to as double-acting, in reference to the fact that the leavening action takes place twice—once outside the oven, once inside the oven.

Does any of this make any difference in the kitchen? To answer this question, we made biscuits, scones, and yellow cake with the aluminum-free Rumford and baking powders containing SAS or SALP. We then compared the results. Both types of baking powders performed well in terms of creating a good rise; thus, the brands containing aluminum do not guarantee more oven rise as long as the mixed batter made with aluminum-free baking powder isn't left to sit around before baking. (Hulman and Company, maker of Rumford, considers its baking powder double-acting because it does provide both bench rise and oven rise, about two-thirds on the bench and one-third in the oven, the reverse proportion of most other double-acting powders. The company recommends that batters made with Rumford go into the oven directly after mixing.) The other issue is taste. Critics of baking powders containing SAS or SALP state that these compounds give baked goods a slight but unpleasant metallic flavor. A couple of our tasters could indeed detect a very slight metallic flavor in each baked good made with the baking powders containing aluminum, but most tasters could not discern a difference.

The answer? Aluminum-free baking powders such as Rumford work just as well as brands made with aluminum compounds. If you have a keen palate that is highly sensitive to metallic flavors or if you wish to limit your ingestion of aluminum, then Rumford is for you.

Best Way to Restore a Rusty Cast–Iron Pan

I discovered an old, rusty cast-iron skillet while helping my elderly aunt clean out her cellar. Is there any way to restore it?

JEAN MARTIN
ANDOVER, MASS.

➤ We realized that years—perhaps decades—worth of rust present more of a challenge than a

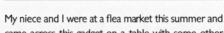

WHAT IS IT?

My niece and I were at a flea market this summer and came across this gadget on a table with some other kitchen odds and ends. Is it some sort of can opener?

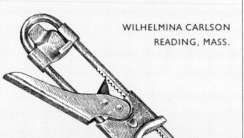

WILHELMINA CARLSON
READING, MASS.

You were on the right track when you suggested that this item might be a can opener. It turns out that it's a jar or bottle opener. A bow tie–shaped grip with tiny metal teeth is affixed to one end of the U-shaped tool (at bottom in illustration), and another, similarly fashioned grip is attached to a plate that slides up and down the entire length of the tool. To use the opener, you position the two bow tie–shaped grips on opposite sides of a jar or bottle lid and then squeeze the lever attached to the sliding metal plate flush to the tool. This locks the sliding plate and attached grips in place. You then hold onto the rounded end of the tool to get some leverage and twist to easily open the lid. Or at least the lid should open easily. In trying to use this gadget we found that the grips often failed to take hold of the lid, slip-sliding this way and that instead. While we did get it to work—and it worked best on the scored lid of a pickle jar—it was only after an unreasonable amount of effort.

splotch or two when one of our test cooks brought in a couple of small, rusty old skillets that she'd found for $5 each at a yard sale. To remove this serious sort of rust, the sources we consulted recommended vigorous rubs with sandpaper (from fine to coarse), emery cloth (often used in metal polishing), fine steel wool, or salt. We got unsatisfactory results when we tried a few different grades of sandpaper and the emery cloth. They seemed to scratch and mar the pans, and they were uncomfortably square and stiff to work with, not conforming to the pans' shape. Fine steel wool was much easier to use and removed a good portion of the rust. The best approach was to scrub, then dust out the loosened particles of rust with a cloth to see what progress had been made, then scrub some more. This was fine as far as it went, which was to leave a thin but stubborn film of rust on the pans.

This is where salt came in. A member of our staff had recommended a combination of salt and hot oil to remove less serious cases of rust, and we thought we might try this now that most of the rust had been removed. We wiped the interior of the pans as clean as possible with a cloth and then took them to the stovetop. Into one pan, we poured enough vegetable oil to heavily coat the pan bottom, then turned the heat to medium-low and let the pan heat up for about five minutes (until the handle was too hot to touch). We then added enough salt to form a liquidy paste and began to scrub with a thick wad of heavy-duty paper towels, holding the pan steady with a potholder. One such treatment was all that was needed for this pan. We tossed out the salt, gave the pan a quick wash with warm, sudsy water to remove any traces of rust, dirt, and salt, and then dried it thoroughly. The finish on the surface of the pan was now slick and black. On the second pan we had to go through the heat-and-scrub part of the routine three times, each time replenishing with clean oil and fresh salt so we could judge our progress. The pan was then washed and dried, with results not quite as handsome as with the first pan but still impressive.

The real test of our efforts didn't come until the next morning, when we fried eggs lightly over in each pan with butter. The eggs flipped and then slipped out of each pan and onto plates without even a hint of sticking—and they tasted pretty good, too.

Pennsylvania–Grown Saffron

The results of our saffron tasting, reported in the Kitchen Notes section of our November/December 2001 issue, prompted a number of readers to write in to find out exactly where they could purchase the surprise winner, grown and processed in not Spain or India but Pennsylvania. The saffron can be ordered from PA General Store (800-545-4891; www.pageneralstore.com).

Quick Tips

Regulating Electric Burner Temperature

Electric burners take longer than gas burners to respond to temperature setting adjustments. When he has to reduce the heat to bring a pot of soup or stew from a rolling boil down to a gentle simmer, Matt Walker of Santa Rosa, Calif., eliminates the time lag by using two burners.

As the food approaches the point of a rolling boil, turn a second burner on to low heat. Once the food reaches a boil, move the pot to the burner with the lower setting, and the food will immediately settle down to a simmer. Don't forget to switch off the first burner once you've moved the pot.

Extra Grip for Tongs

In the January/February 2001 article "Uncommon Uses for Common Kitchen Tools," we recommended the use of tongs to remove ramekins of custard from a water bath. Cooks who may worry about the ramekins slipping in the tongs can try this tip from Cyndy Carroll of Tabernacle, N.J. She slips rubber bands around each of the two tong pincers, and the sticky rubber provides a surer grip.

Making the Most of the Polder Timer/Thermometer

The Polder Timer/Thermometer, with its built-in temperature alarm, is one of our favorite cooking tools. It constantly monitors the internal temperature of roasts and breads and sounds an audible alarm when the food reaches the precise temperature that was programmed in. Though we think of using the Polder when baking or roasting in the oven or cooking on the grill, Dolores Palomi of Seattle, Wash., has integrated it into her stovetop cooking.

A. For the best cup of coffee, the water should be heated to just below a boil. To get the temperature just right, set the alarm on the Polder to 200 or 205 degrees and insert the probe into the pouring spout of the kettle. Be careful not to scorch the wire on the burner.

B. Many soup and stew recipes call for bringing the contents of the pot to a boil before bringing it down to a simmer. In these cases, set the Polder to sound at about 200 or 205 degrees. The signal will warn you in time to turn down the heat before the food boils too hard. Reset the Polder for 180 degrees to make sure the contents won't fall below or rise above the temperature of an ideal simmer.

Shortcut for Juicing Limes and Lemons

Faced with a pile of tiny Key limes to juice for a pie and unable to locate his citrus juicer, Bruce Ryden of Centerville, Minn., came up with a quick, easy way to squeeze all that citrus: Place two or three quartered limes in the hopper of a potato ricer and squeeze the handles together. This method also works for standard supermarket-variety limes and lemons.

Instant Counter Space

No matter the size of the kitchen, a little extra counter space for resting bowls, platters, or cooling racks never hurts. Margaret Trevino of San Antonio, Texas, crafts extra space by opening a drawer and resting a cutting board across the top.

Moving Many Small Containers at Once

Many cooks like to freeze small portions of homemade stocks and soups in individual containers such as recycled yogurt cups. But if your freezer is more than a few steps away from the stovetop—say in the garage or basement—it may be hard to get the containers to the freezer without spilling a cup or two. Having dropped one too many containers of stock, Maggie Fisher of Seattle, Wash. now places a container in each cup of a muffin tin and carries the whole lot with ease.

New and Improved Cushion for Water Bath

Many recipes for baked individual custards—including our own Classic Crème Brûlèe recipe in the November/December 2001 issue—recommend lining the bottom of the water bath pan with a kitchen towel to both insulate and cushion the ramekins. Of course, this leaves you with a sopping wet towel at the end of cooking. Bridget Nan Dwyer of Seattle, Wash., decided to try her nonstick baking mat (called a Silpat) instead. The mat kept the ramekins firmly in place, and there was no wet towel to wring out when the custard was done. Managing editor Dawn Yanagihara pointed out that it would also be a good idea to use the mat to steady the bowl while preparing the custard mixture.

Send Us Your Tip We will provide a complimentary one-year subscription for each tip we print. Send your tip, name, address, and daytime telephone number to Quick Tips, Cook's Illustrated, P.O. Box 470589, Brookline, MA 02447.

Cleaning a Waffle Iron

Many new waffle irons feature nonstick cooking surfaces, which are easy to clean. Even so, some residue is occasionally left in the ridges. Seth Swoboda of Astoria, N.Y., found that cotton swabs are well suited to this cleaning task.

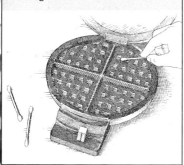

Safe Knife Transport, Redux

The July/August 2001 tip about inserting a knife blade into a paper towel roll for safe transport inspired Mark Perrette of Jamaica Plain, Mass., to share his own trick for traveling with knives. He cuts a slit in a thick piece of corrugated cardboard and slips the knife into the opening.

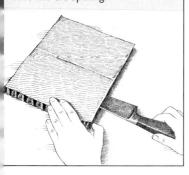

Impromptu Pot Covers

Many skillets are sold without covers, yet it is occasionally useful to have one on hand. Instead of buying a cover separately, which can be expensive, both Miri Spiro of Toronto, Ontario, and Peter Harvey of Salt Lake City, Utah, have come up with some alternatives, including a large, heatproof plate and an inexpensive, 12- or 16-inch pizza pan.

Safest Garlic Peeling

One effective method for peeling garlic cloves is to crush them using the broad side of a knife blade. While this method is perfectly safe if you treat the knife blade with care, some cooks, including John Swartz of Washington, D.C., and Joan Slomanson of New York, N.Y., would rather skip the knife altogether. Here are their methods.

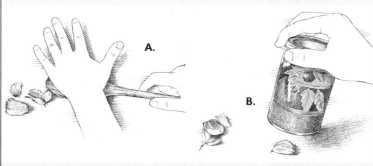

A. Cover the garlic clove with the concave side of a wooden spoon and press down hard. The cup of the spoon prevents the garlic clove from shooting out across the work surface.

B. Alternatively, whack the clove with the bottom of a can. The weight of the contents helps crush the clove, and the lip at the bottom of the can keeps the clove neatly in place on the work surface.

Drying Dishes Quickly

Many cooks who wash dishes by hand would prefer to wash, dry, and put away the dishes in one fell swoop. Rather than waiting for them to air-dry and putting them away later, Suzanne Shier of Halifax, Nova Scotia, props up a small table fan level with the dishes in the rack and directs the air flow onto the dishes, which dry in record time.

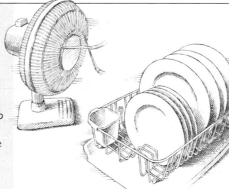

Easy Seasoning

Stews, braises, and sautés always taste best when any meat, poultry, or fish they contain is well seasoned before being cooked. But sprinkling salt and pepper evenly over any more than a couple of pieces can be tedious—and messy to boot. Karen Sato of Vancouver, British Columbia, found a way to simplify and clean up the process.

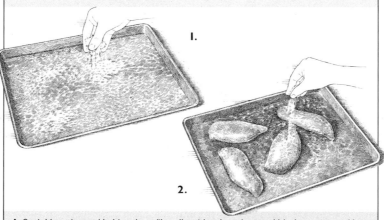

1. Sprinkle a rimmed baking sheet liberally with salt and ground black pepper and lay the pieces of meat, poultry, or fish on the seasoning-covered surface. Press each piece lightly to make sure the seasonings adhere to the bottom, and jiggle the pan so that the portions slide over any loose seasoning.

2. Season the tops, and you are ready to proceed with the recipe.

Space-Saving Cutting Board and Baking Sheet Storage

Beth Krishtalka of Lawrence, Kan., is loathe to waste kitchen storage space by laying cutting boards and baking sheets flat. Beth found the perfect solution at her local office supply store. An inexpensive metal vertical file holder is ideal for storing cutting boards and baking sheets. They not only take up less space but are easy to grab when you need one.

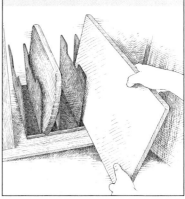

Securing Small Items in the Dishwasher

It's easy for small kitchen utensils such as cake testers or trussing needles to fall through the slots in the dishwasher cutlery container. To keep utensils where they belong, follow this tip from Daphne Gray-Grant of Vancouver, British Columbia.

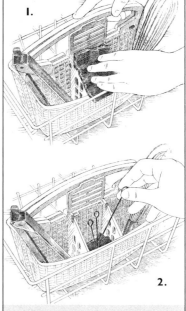

1. Stuff a small nylon pot scrubber into the bottom of the cutlery container.

2. Secure small items by sticking them into the pot scrubber. The scrubber will prevent anything from falling through.

Homemade Spring Rolls

Restaurant spring rolls often feature gummy noodles, soggy rice paper, and saccharine peanut dipping sauce. We set out to produce light, fresh, and easy-to-make spring rolls.

⇒ BY BECKY HAYS AND BRIDGET LANCASTER ⇐

Southeast Asian spring rolls (not the deep-fried Chinese variety) are made with translucent rice paper wrappers that have been softened in water and then filled with cool rice vermicelli, raw vegetables, and fragrant herbs. A popular menu item, they offer a textural symphony (soft wrapper, toothsome noodles, and crunchy vegetables) as well as stark but appealing contrasts in flavor (mint, basil, cilantro, chiles, peanuts, and fish sauce). But spring rolls can be disappointing, as lesser establishments use gummy noodles, iceberg lettuce, soggy rice paper, shriveled herbs, and saccharine "peanut" sauces that taste not a whit like peanuts. Given that they require only a short list of fresh ingredients and no cooking other than boiling noodles, it occurred to us that a home cook could easily produce a four-star spring roll worthy of the best Asian restaurant.

We began our investigation with the wrapper. Wrappers come out of the package hard and inedible and so must be soaked in water before use. It quickly became apparent that timing was crucial here. When soaked too long (more than 30 seconds), the wrappers simply disintegrated; when soaked for just two or three seconds, the wrappers remained stiff. We found the ideal soak time to be 10 seconds.

Even after just 10 seconds of soaking, however, the wrappers are so delicate that they fall apart if simply placed on a kitchen counter for rolling. The trick, we discovered, is to use a damp kitchen towel, which supports the wrappers without sticking to them. We also found it best to make the rolls one at a time and to cover them with a second damp towel once finished to keep the wrappers moist and pliable.

With the wrappers taken care of, we turned to the filling, starting with the noodles. Thin vermicelli-style rice noodles are cooked just like American or Italian pasta. However, we did note that the thickness ranges from brand to brand, which affects cooking time. It's best to taste the noodles every minute or so during cooking until they are tender. A rinse under cold water is then needed to stop the cooking and keep these starchy noodles from congealing into an inseparable mass.

As for the vegetables, we tried jícama, a root

Southeast Asian spring rolls contain fresh herbs, cucumbers, carrots, and rice noodles. For easy eating, wrap a lettuce leaf around each roll.

vegetable, which had a nice crunch but was too sweet, and daikon, an Asian radish, which was good but hard to find. These two possibilities were out. Two more possibilities were carrot and cucumber. Carrot contributed a pleasantly sweet flavor and nice texture when grated. We tried grating cucumber as well but ended up with watery, soggy rolls. When sliced into substantial planks, however, the cucumber added significant crunch without dampening the wrappers. We also liked its cool, subtle flavor.

For the herbs, fragrant cilantro and Thai basil (we found that mint can be used as a substitute for the latter) sparkle when used in tandem, and their frilly leaves are a visual bonus. We ran into trouble, though, when we inadvertently got a few whole large basil leaves in a single bite. The solution was twofold: tear large leaves into

pieces before using and sprinkle them over the inner section of the rice paper before rolling (rather than piling them up, as most recipes suggest).

Despite our liberal dose of herbs, the rolls remained bland. We went back to our library of cookbooks and discovered spring roll recipes that included an acidic marinade for the vegetables and noodles that adds both flavor and moisture. The liquid ingredients for the marinade included a few typical Southeast Asian flavorings: lime juice, rice vinegar, and fish sauce (a pungent liquid made from fermented fish). We settled on a simple mixture based on fish sauce and lime juice. A teaspoon of sugar and some chopped fresh chiles balanced the acidity and gave the rolls a sweet-hot punch, while chopped peanuts added substance.

As for the dipping sauce, we began with a standard recipe for peanut sauce made with hoisin sauce, sugar, peanut butter, and water and tested a dozen variations. We decided to eliminate the sugar, giving the peanut flavor center stage, and then cut back on the hoisin sauce, which is also quite sweet. Next we added garlic, chili sauce, and hot red pepper flakes to bring up the heat. Tomato paste is an authentic addition that imparted a pleasing color. The resulting sauce was gently sweet and spicy. As for serving, we found that a leaf of lettuce makes a fresh-tasting, bright-colored wrap for the finished spring roll.

Now we finally had flavorful spring rolls that could be made easily and quickly at home. They are so good, in fact, that we won't be ordering them off a menu anytime soon.

STEP-BY-STEP | SLICING THE CUCUMBER

1. Cut peeled cucumber in half crosswise. Cut ¼-inch planks from outermost part of each cucumber half, leaving seeds behind.

2. Cut each plank into five ⅛-inch strips. You should have about 40 strips of cucumber.

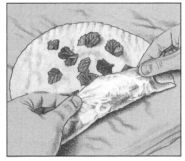

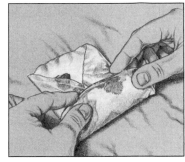

1. Lay herbs and cucumber on wrapper, followed by carrot mixture and noodles.

2. Fold up bottom 2-inch border of wrapper over filling.

3. Fold left, then right edge of wrapper over filling.

4. Roll filling to top edge of wrapper to form tight cylinder.

SOUTHEAST ASIAN–STYLE SPRING ROLLS
MAKES 8 SPRING ROLLS

If you can't find Thai basil, do not substitute regular basil; its flavor is too gentle to stand up to the other, more assertive flavors in the filling. Mint makes a better substitute. (For more information on Thai basil, see Kitchen Notes, page 30.) If you are unable to obtain fish sauce, substitute an equal amount of rice vinegar plus ¼ teaspoon salt. Spring rolls are best eaten immediately, but they can be held for up to 4 hours in the refrigerator, covered with a clean, damp kitchen towel.

1	teaspoon sugar
1½	tablespoons fish sauce
2½	tablespoons juice from 1 lime
1	teaspoon salt
3	ounces rice vermicelli
1	large carrot, peeled and grated on large holes of box grater (about ½ cup)
⅓	cup coarsely chopped roasted unsalted peanuts
1	medium jalapeño or 2 Thai chiles, stemmed, seeded, and minced, or ½ teaspoon red pepper flakes
1	large cucumber (about 12 ounces), peeled and cut according to illustrations on page 6
4	large leaves red leaf or Boston lettuce, halved lengthwise
8	round rice paper wrappers (8 inches in diameter)
½	cup loosely packed fresh Thai basil leaves or mint leaves, small leaves left whole, medium and large leaves torn into ½-inch pieces
½	cup loosely packed fresh cilantro leaves Peanut Dipping Sauce (recipe follows)

1. Combine sugar, fish sauce, and lime juice in small bowl; set aside.

2. Bring 2 quarts water to boil in medium saucepan. Stir in salt and rice vermicelli. Cook until noodles are tender but not mushy, 3 to 4 minutes. Drain noodles and rinse under cold running water until cool. Drain again and transfer to medium bowl; toss 2 tablespoons fish sauce mixture with noodles and set aside.

3. Combine carrot, peanuts, and jalapeño in small bowl. Add 1 tablespoon fish sauce mixture; toss to combine. Toss cucumber in remaining 1 tablespoon fish sauce mixture.

4. Place lettuce on platter. Spread clean, damp kitchen towel on work surface. Fill 9-inch pie plate with 1 inch room-temperature water. Working one at a time, immerse each wrapper in water until just pliable, about 10 seconds; lay softened wrapper on towel. Scatter 6 Thai basil leaves and 6 cilantro leaves over wrapper. Arrange 5 cucumber sticks horizontally on wrapper (see illustration 1, above); top with 1 tablespoon carrot mixture, then arrange about 2½ tablespoons noodles on top of carrot mixture. Wrap spring roll according to illustrations 2 through 4; set on 1 lettuce piece on platter. Cover with second damp kitchen towel; repeat with remaining wrappers and filling. Serve with dipping sauce, wrapping lettuce around exterior of each roll.

SOUTHEAST ASIAN–STYLE SPRING ROLLS WITH SHRIMP

Peel and remove tails from 8 ounces medium (31/35 count) shrimp. Follow recipe for Southeast Asian–Style Spring Rolls, adding shrimp to boiling water along with salt in step 2; cook until shrimp are opaque, about 3 minutes. Using slotted spoon, transfer shrimp to small bowl; use water to cook rice vermicelli as in step 2. When cool enough to handle, coarsely chop shrimp. When assembling spring rolls, place about 2 tablespoons chopped shrimp on top of noodles.

PEANUT DIPPING SAUCE
MAKES ABOUT ¾ CUP

The sauce can be refrigerated in an airtight container for up to 3 days. Serve at room temperature.

¼	cup smooth peanut butter
¼	cup hoisin sauce
¼	cup water
2	tablespoons tomato paste
1	teaspoon Asian chili sauce (optional)
2	teaspoons peanut or vegetable oil
2	medium garlic cloves, minced or pressed through garlic press
1	teaspoon red pepper flakes

Whisk peanut butter, hoisin sauce, water, tomato paste, and chili sauce, if using, in small bowl. Heat oil, garlic, and red pepper flakes in small saucepan over medium heat until fragrant, 1 to 2 minutes. Stir in peanut butter mixture; bring to simmer, then reduce heat to medium-low and cook, stirring occasionally, until flavors blend, about 3 minutes. (Sauce should have ketchup-like consistency; if too thick, add water, 1 teaspoon at a time, until proper consistency is reached.) Transfer to bowl; cool to room temperature.

Under Wraps

Spring roll wrappers are the traditional choice for Vietnamese and Thai spring rolls. Made from a paste of rice flour and water that is stamped into bamboo mats and dried, rice paper wrappers are translucent, brittle, and delicate—meaning they can be difficult to work with. On trips to Asian markets we also noticed wrappers made from wheat flour or ground tapioca. We bought all three kinds and went back to the kitchen to test them.

The wrappers made from wheat flour were thick and opaque, too firm for the delicate spring roll, and their distinct wheat flavor muddied the bright flavors of the vegetables. At the opposite end of the spectrum, the wrappers made from tapioca flour were nearly transparent and very fragile. Their texture was too flimsy and sticky for many tasters. The rice paper wrappers proved the most neutral of casings. Tender, yet structurally sound enough to hold the fillings, the rice paper wrappers were also neutral in flavor, allowing us to fully appreciate the bright mix of flavors within the roll. —B.L.

Discovering Chicken Vesuvio

We solve the problems of this Chicago chicken and potatoes classic: dull meat, soggy skin, tasteless potatoes, and a bitter sauce.

⇒ BY RAQUEL PELZEL ⇐

Indigenous to Chicago's Italian restaurants, chicken Vesuvio is steeped in local history. Seeking an authentic replication, I prepared a handful of recipes in the *Cook's* test kitchen. With their flabby skin, bland meat, mealy potatoes, and bitter, greasy sauces, these versions bore little resemblance to the classic restaurant dish I remembered. A Chicago native myself, I was determined to duplicate the best restaurant-style Vesuvio—with its heady flavor and interplay of crisp skin and tender meat—for the home kitchen.

Chicken First, Then Potatoes

Tradition dictates that this dish contain chicken and wedged potatoes, both of which are first browned on top of the stove and then baked in the oven with garlic, white wine, and herbs. The problem is that as the chicken sits in liquid in the oven, the skin becomes soggy. Hoping to avoid the issue altogether, I tried a batch with skinless chicken. But without the skin to protect the meat when seared on the stovetop, the chicken came out tough and dry. I concluded that skin-on chicken was a must.

Next I decided to layer the chicken, skin-side up, on top of the potatoes (which rested in the broth). This preserved the crispy skin, but the chicken lost the moistness and rich flavor it acquired when sitting in liquid. I modified the layering procedure, placing the chicken on the floor of the pan first, with the potatoes on top, then switching the positions of the chicken and potatoes midway through baking (see illustrations on page 9). This did the trick. Both the potatoes and chicken benefited from the gutsy-flavored sauce and I had crispy skin to boot.

Although the potato wedges had great flavor from the broth, they were grainy and mealy. Thinking that my choice of russet potatoes was a mistake, I tested them against two other, less starchy varieties: the all-purpose white potato and the Yukon Gold potato (the red potato's rotund shape made the wedges too wide and stout for consideration). The white all-purpose potatoes didn't fare much better than the russets, but the Yukon Golds were perfect. They had a buttery flavor and a smooth, firm texture, and they browned beautifully.

Because the potatoes are partially cooked before going into the oven, getting a fully tender wedge was simply a matter of matching the right oven temperature with the right-size potato wedge. I

With crispy-skinned chicken, bronzed potatoes, and a fiery garlic, herb, and wine sauce, chicken Vesuvio is a welcome diversion from the ordinary baked chicken dinner.

tested a variety of temperatures—I wanted the chicken to cook as quickly as possible while also properly cooking the potatoes—and finally decided on 400 degrees. At this temperature, the potato wedges should be cut ¾ inch thick.

Getting the Sauce Right

The backbone of this sauce is the pan drippings, or *fond*. They negate the need to add stock or chicken broth to achieve depth of flavor—the fond left in

the pan after frying the chicken and potatoes serves this purpose. The problem, I soon discovered, was that most of the sauces were bitter tasting. To break the cycle, I examined two potentially problematic components: the drippings and the garlic.

After the chicken was fried and the potatoes browned, my pan had been over the medium-high flame for about 20 minutes; although the fond had not burned, it definitely had dark patches. So instead of searing the chicken and potatoes over a medium-high flame the entire time, I started the chicken at medium-high, reduced the heat to medium when I flipped the chicken, and then reduced the heat to medium-low once the potatoes were ready to be turned. I was pleased—my fond stayed golden, with no dark spots. And although this new trilevel flame cooking method took a few more minutes on the stovetop, the end result was worth the wait—the sauce was rich but not bitter.

If Vesuvio's heart is the sauce, then its soul is the garlic, which is added to the pan after the chicken and potatoes have been sautéed and removed. After a few rounds of testing, I discovered that I needed to let the pan cool for a couple of minutes before adding the garlic. The residual heat of the pan bloomed the garlic perfectly without the

---

Why Does Chicken Skin Stick to the Pan?

While testing chicken Vesuvio, I noticed that sometimes the chicken skin would stick to the pan, whereas other times it browned nicely without sticking. Curious as to what was causing the sticking, I called Sarah Birkhold, an assistant professor in poultry science at Texas A & M University. She explained that one possible cause could be the temperature at which the bird was scalded during processing.

To quickly remove chicken feathers from the carcass, producers briefly submerge the chicken in very hot water. (Kosher chickens, which are submerged in cold water, are an exception. See page 26 for more information on kosher chickens.) If the water is too hot, says Birkhold, the natural wax in the chicken's skin is removed. Wax acts as a shield between the skin and the hot oil; if the wax is absent, the chicken skin is more likely to stick to the pan.

How can you tell if the skin is protected? Birkhold says that if the skin has a yellowish tinge, it's a good sign that the cuticle, where the wax is found, is intact, because it's within the cuticle that pigment is retained. Another indication is evident when you blot the chicken dry with paper towels before pan-searing; if the paper towels stick like glue to the skin, it has more than likely lost its cuticle. If you can't tell whether there is a waxy coating on your chicken skin or if you suspect that the cuticle has been removed, just be sure to preheat your pan and the fat for the full two minutes (or three minutes for a Le Creuset pan) as directed in the recipe to ensure that the chicken skin sticks to the chicken, not the pan.

---

danger of overbrowning, and deglazing the pan with the wine once the garlic became aromatic stopped the garlic from developing too much color. After testing amounts of garlic from two cloves to two heads, I settled on one head of garlic, minced by hand, pressed through a garlic press, or minced in a food processor (for more information on how the method of garlic preparation affects its flavor, see "Flavorful Garlic," right).

To provide enough sauce for four servings, I needed to use 1 cup of wine. I also added fresh lemon juice to the sauce before pouring it over the chicken; it lifted the sauce's profile, harmonizing the individual components. After a quick shower of fresh-chopped parsley (for color as well as fresh herb flavor) this dish was good to go—home, that is. And the next time I get a craving for Vesuvio, I'll only have to travel to the kitchen—not Chicago—to get my fix.

CHICKEN VESUVIO
(CHICKEN AND POTATOES WITH GARLIC AND WHITE WINE)
SERVES 4

An equal weight of bone-in, skin-on chicken thighs, legs (separated into thigh and drumstick pieces), or split breasts (each breast halved lengthwise) may be substituted for the whole chicken. If you don't care for chicken skin, simply remove it after pan-frying and before baking. A large, 8-quart Dutch oven with a diameter of 12 inches serves this dish well. If using a Le Creuset Dutch oven, heat the oil for an extra minute.

- 2 tablespoons olive oil
- 1 whole chicken (about 3½ pounds), giblets and wings discarded; chicken cut into 8 pieces (2 each of thighs and drumsticks, with breast cut into quarters)
- ¾ teaspoon salt
- ½ teaspoon ground black pepper
- 3 Yukon Gold potatoes (about 8 ounces each), peeled and cut lengthwise into 8 wedges about ¾ inch thick
- 2½ tablespoons minced or pressed garlic (8 to 12 medium cloves)
- 1 cup dry white wine
- 2 sprigs fresh oregano
- 2 sprigs fresh thyme
- 1 sprig fresh rosemary
- 2 tablespoons juice from 1 lemon
- 2 tablespoons minced fresh parsley leaves

1. Adjust oven rack to lower-middle position; heat oven to 400 degrees. Line rimmed baking sheet with paper towels.

2. Heat 1 tablespoon oil in large, heavy-bottomed Dutch oven over medium-high heat until hot and shimmering, but not smoking, about 2 minutes. Meanwhile, thoroughly pat chicken dry with paper towels and sprinkle pieces with ½ teaspoon salt and ¼ teaspoon pepper. Place chicken pieces skin-side down in single layer in pot and cook without moving them until uniformly golden brown and crisp, 4 to 6 minutes (if chicken is browning too quickly, reduce heat). Reduce heat to medium; using tongs, turn chicken pieces over and cook until uniformly golden brown and crisp on second side, 8 to 10 minutes longer. Transfer chicken, skin-side up, to prepared baking sheet.

3. Add remaining 1 tablespoon oil to pot. Add potatoes, arranging them in single layer with one flat side of each wedge against bottom of pot; cook until golden brown, 6 to 8 minutes. Reduce heat to medium-low and turn potatoes; cook until golden brown on all sides, 8 to 10 minutes longer. Transfer potatoes to baking sheet with chicken.

4. Remove pot from burner and cool 2 minutes. Add all but 1 teaspoon garlic and cook, using pot's residual heat, until garlic is fragrant, about 30 seconds; add wine, oregano, thyme, rosemary, and remaining ¼ teaspoon each salt and pepper. Return chicken pieces skin-side up to pot, then arrange potatoes on top.

5. Bake uncovered 10 minutes; using tongs, rearrange so chicken is on top of potatoes and facing skin-side up (see illustration below). Bake until instant-read thermometer inserted into thickest part of breast pieces registers 160 degrees, 8 to 10 minutes longer; remove breast pieces to serving dish and tent loosely with foil. Return pot with thighs, drumsticks, and potatoes to oven and cook until instant-read thermometer inserted into thickest part of thigh registers 175 degrees, 5 to 10 minutes longer. Arrange chicken and potatoes in serving dish; discard herb stems. Stir remaining 1 teaspoon garlic and lemon juice into liquid in pot; pour sauce over chicken and potatoes, sprinkle with parsley, and serve.

Flavorful Garlic

More garlic does not necessarily equal more flavor. The fiery flavor of garlic is unleashed only when garlic is cut or crushed. When the cell walls are broken, the enzyme alliinase is released and acts on the compound alliin to produce allicin and other, similar compounds; these compounds give garlic its characteristic bite. The more a clove of garlic is cut or minced, the more enzyme is released, and the more intense the flavor. Garlic mellows in flavor when cooked (as when unpeeled cloves are toasted in a dry skillet until slightly colored or when whole heads are wrapped in foil and roasted until very soft), because allicin and like compounds are transformed into yet another group of compounds, known as allyl disulfides, which are more mild in flavor and even a bit sweet. Use the chart below to adjust garlic flavor to your taste.

	Type of Garlic	Characteristics
Most Intense	**PRESSED** through a garlic press	Somewhat textureless. Fiery, robust, and harsh.
	MINCED in a food processor	Pungent and rounded with a uniform texture.
	MINCED by hand	Full and rounded without being too harsh.
	SLIVERED	Perfumed and mild, with the occasional burst of garlic flavor.
	TOASTED whole cloves	Sweet, mellow, and slightly nutty.
Least Intense	**ROASTED** whole head	Very mild, caramel-like, and sweet.

TECHNIQUE | LAYERING THE CHICKEN AND POTATOES

The best way to achieve crisp chicken skin, moist and flavorful meat, and tender, flavorful potatoes is to start the chicken on the bottom of the pan so it soaks up flavor and moisture from the sauce (see illustration at left); midway through the baking time, reverse the order in which the chicken and potatoes are layered so that the chicken no longer sits in the broth and the skin can crisp (see illustration at right).

Secrets of Caramelized Onions

Caramelized onions can take hours to make and often turn out stringy, dry, or charred. Here's how to produce this simple but universal condiment in just 45 minutes.

≥ BY JULIA COLLIN ≤

Raw onions will nearly fill a 12-inch skillet (left). After five minutes over high heat, the onions will soften and release some moisture (center). Reduce the heat to medium and cook until the onions are glossy, soft, and deeply browned, about 40 minutes longer (right).

Sweet, glossy, with complex flavor, caramelized onions have a pedigree far superior to the mongrel side dish offered at your local steakhouse. Made with only four ingredients (not counting salt, pepper, and water) and featuring the most common of all pantry staples, caramelized onions easily play a wide range of culinary roles, from condiment for burgers to sauce for roast chicken. Caramelized onions can also team up with bacon and sour cream to make a classic dip or be used on their own as a topping for steak.

As simple as caramelized onions are, I soon discovered that poor technique can yield onions that are dried out, burnt, bland, gummy, and/or greasy. Among the half dozen recipes I tried, some produced onions that were much too sweet, while others seemed barely cooked. One recipe produced a sticky mass of onion-flavored goo that tasters had a hard time identifying. What I was looking for were soft yet lightly toothsome onions with a deep, complex character and a lustrous, dark golden hue.

To start, I tried several different methods of caramelizing onions: in a roasting pan in the oven as well as on top of the stove in a regular skillet, a nonstick skillet, and a Dutch oven. The oven dried out the onions before they had a chance to fully caramelize, whereas on the stovetop the onions were easier to regulate throughout the cooking process. In terms of the pan used, the high sides of the Dutch oven encouraged condensation, causing the reduction and caramelization process to take about 15 minutes longer with no discernible difference in flavor or texture. The low-sided skillets caramelized the onions more quickly. When it came to choosing between regular and nonstick, I decided on the slippery, nonstick surface. This pan was easier to clean, and the flavorful juices did not cling to the pan but were instead forced to mingle with the onions.

Release the Moisture

After this first round of tests, I realized that the process of caramelization cannot begin until the onions start to release their juices. This release of moisture is an indication that cell walls are breaking down, turning complex starches within the cells into simple sugars. These sugars then caramelize and, owing to a series of chemical reactions, turn darker and add a variety of complex flavors. The question was how to get this process started as soon as possible.

The recipes consulted employed a variety of techniques. Some added salt and sugar at the beginning of the cooking process, some started cooking the onions under a lid, while others noted the importance of cutting the onion with the "grain" (slicing stem to root), which is said to encourage the release of juices. I tested all three methods and found that while adding salt and sugar at the outset did not encourage faster caramelization, it did give the resulting onions a fuller, more impressive flavor. Using a lid for all or

even part of the caramelizing process did speed things up, but the resulting onions had a stale, steamed flavor that tasters didn't like. Slicing with or against the grain made absolutely no difference. After much additional testing, I finally discovered the secret to jumpstarting caramelization: Start the onions off over a high flame for five minutes to quickly release their moisture.

The next question was what to do with the flame after the initial five-minute blast. Several cookbooks note the importance of cooking the onions over low heat to allow the sugars to caramelize slowly, while others call for high heat, claiming that caramelization will take only 15 minutes. To test these theories, I took three pans of onions through the initial five-minute blast, then put one over a very low flame, another over a medium flame, and left the last over the high flame. The results were as expected: The onions cooked over a low flame took nearly two hours to fully caramelize, those cooked over a medium flame took a total of 45 minutes, and those blasted over high heat took about 20 minutes. The differences in flavor were as dramatic as the cooking times. The slowly cooked onions were extremely sweet, with a stringy, dried-out texture. The quickly cooked onions were invitingly dark and glossy but had a shallow, slightly charred flavor. The moderately cooked onions, on the other hand, were perfect. With varying shades of brown, these onions had a complex, multilayered flavor and struck the perfect balance between toothsome and yielding.

What Fat?

Making four batches, I tested olive oil, vegetable oil, butter, and a combination of vegetable oil and butter. The olive oil was overpowering, with a slightly bitter edge. The vegetable oil allowed for a clean, onion flavor, while the butter tasted extremely round and muted. The combination of vegetable oil and butter was the winner, releasing a clean, well-defined onion flavor lightly tempered with the rich taste of butter.

Finally, I tried adding flavorings such as stock, wine, and vinegar, but tasters preferred the flavor of the onions with the help of only a little light brown sugar (it brought out a heartier flavor than granulated sugar), salt, and black pepper. One tablespoon of water gathered up the drops of caramelized onion juice from around the edges of the pan without diminishing the flavor or texture of the onions. Now I had a simple recipe for caramelized onions that lived up to its pedigree.

CARAMELIZED ONIONS
MAKES 1 CUP

Caramelized onions are easily added to most any meal. Try them in an omelet, frittata, or strata or with scrambled eggs and home fries. They taste fantastic on grilled cheese sandwiches, BLTs, and burgers or thrown into pasta, potato, or green salads. Add them to stuffings, gratins, casseroles, and savory tarts or sprinkle them over bruschetta, focaccia, or pizza. They spiff up baked and mashed potatoes, rice, risotto, and polenta. Last, try caramelized onions with apples and a good cheese for dessert.

- 1   tablespoon unsalted butter
- 1   tablespoon vegetable oil
- ½   teaspoon salt
- 1   teaspoon light brown sugar
- 2   pounds onions (see "Do You Know Your Supermarket Onions?"), peeled and sliced ¼ inch thick (see illustration, above right)
- 1   tablespoon water
    Ground black pepper

Heat butter and oil in 12-inch nonstick skillet over high heat; when foam subsides, stir in salt and sugar. Add onions and stir to coat; cook, stirring occasionally, until onions begin to soften and release some moisture, about 5 minutes. Reduce heat to medium and cook, stirring frequently, until onions are deeply browned and slightly sticky, about 40 minutes longer. (If onions are sizzling or scorching, reduce heat. If onions are not browning after 15 to 20 minutes, raise heat.) Off heat, stir in water; season to taste with pepper. (Can be refrigerated in airtight container for up to 7 days.)

BACON, SCALLION, AND CARAMELIZED ONION DIP
MAKES ABOUT 1½ CUPS

This recipe uses only ½ cup—or a half recipe—of caramelized onions.

1. Fry 3 slices (about 3 ounces) bacon, cut into ¼-inch pieces, in small skillet over medium heat until crisp, about 5 minutes; remove with slotted spoon to paper towel–lined plate and set aside.

2. Combine ½ cup caramelized onions, 2 scallions, minced, ½ teaspoon cider vinegar, ¾ cup sour cream, and bacon in medium bowl. Season to taste with salt and pepper and serve. (Can be refrigerated in airtight container for up to 3 days.)

CARAMELIZED ONION SAUCE WITH WHITE WINE
MAKES ABOUT 2 CUPS

This sauce is an excellent accompaniment to a simple pork roast or roast chicken.

Follow recipe for Caramelized Onions, adding 1 medium garlic clove, minced, and 1 small shallot, minced, to onions when onions are deeply browned and slightly sticky; cook until fragrant, about 1 minute. Stir in 1 cup canned low-sodium chicken broth and ½ cup dry white wine; simmer until mixture reduces to about 2 cups, 2 to 3 minutes. Omit water. Off heat, whisk in 3 tablespoons cold butter, 1 tablespoon at a time; adjust seasoning with salt and pepper. Use immediately.

TECHNIQUE |
SLICING THE ONIONS

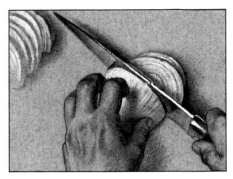

Cut off root end of onion; halve onion pole to pole, then peel. Place flat side down on cutting board; slice onion into ¼-inch-thick slices across the grain.

CARAMELIZED ONION JAM WITH DARK RUM
MAKES ABOUT 1 CUP

Spread this jam on a sandwich with cream cheese, or serve it on a platter with cheese and crackers.

Follow recipe for Caramelized Onions, substituting 2 tablespoons dark rum for water. Off heat, wave lit match over skillet until rum ignites; shake skillet until flames subside. Transfer onions to food processor along with 1 teaspoon minced fresh thyme and 1 tablespoon light brown sugar. Pulse to jam-like consistency, about five 1-second pulses. Transfer to medium bowl; stir in ½ teaspoon cider vinegar and salt and pepper to taste. (Can be refrigerated in airtight container for up to 7 days.)

Do You Know Your Supermarket Onions?

The type of onion you choose for this recipe has a tremendous effect on flavor. Although the caramelizing times of these various onions are consistent, our tasters' preferences were not. Some liked a sweeter, more mellow flavor, while others liked their onions with more bite. Tasters with a sweet tooth gravitated to the white and Vidalia onions (the latter being the sweeter of the two). Those who preferred a heartier onion flavor with only moderate sweetness were drawn to Spanish onions.

YELLOW ONION
Tasters found this onion to strike a "good balance between savory and sweet," with a "mild onion flavor" and "beautiful color." A few found it unpleasantly "gummy," with a "bitter finish." Nobody loved it; nobody hated it.

WHITE ONION
This controversial onion was rated both at the top and the bottom of the tasters' charts. Some liked its simple, "sugary," "mellow" flavor, while others found it "too sweet" and "one-dimensional," with "no texture."

SPANISH ONION
Most tasters liked this onion for its "deep and complex" flavor and "meaty" texture. While its "heartiness," tempered only by a "moderate sweetness," ranked highly with some, it was considered a bit "harsh" by others.

RED ONION
When caramelized, this onion turned very dark. Its flavor ranked neither high nor low. Tasters found it "pleasantly sweet," with a "good onion flavor," despite its "sticky" and "jammy" consistency.

VIDALIA ONION
It came as no surprise that the Vidalia—a notably sweet variety similar to Maui and Walla Walla— was the sweetest sample. Its texture was less pleasing, however, deemed both a bit "chalky" and "gummy."

Improving Stroganoff

This retro "Russian" dish may look like a stew, but it's actually a quick sauté
that can be on the table in 20 minutes.

> BY THE COOK'S ILLUSTRATED TEST KITCHEN <

Don't be timid about getting the pan hot—this dish derives its flavor from well-browned meat and mushrooms.

Beef stroganoff—the classic marriage of beef, mushrooms, onions, and sour cream served with egg noodles—may look and taste like a stew, but it is actually a quick pan sauté joined in holy matrimony with an even quicker pan sauce. A well-made stroganoff exhibits tender meat, a velvety sauce, and a surprising amount of flavor given its short cooking time. A bad beef stroganoff—and there are plenty of them—has an almost desperate "anything goes" feeling; a hodgepodge list of ingredients such as prepared mustard, paprika, Worcestershire sauce, cider vinegar, tomato paste, brown sugar, brandy, and sherry ultimately leads to divorce.

The essential problem with stroganoff derives from its basic cooking method. Because it is made with a pan sauce—not as a slow braise or stew—it is a light proposition that doesn't have time to develop flavor. Although our first impulse, like everyone else's, was to use as many flavor-building ingredients as possible, we hoped to solve the mystery of beef stroganoff using a combination of flavor-enhancing cooking methods paired with a more limited shopping list.

The first test was the cut of beef. Although we knew that beef tenderloin was favored in stroganoff because it is so tender, we thought that other, albeit tougher, steak cuts might bring more flavor to the pan. Toward that end, we made stroganoffs with strips of sirloin, rib-eye, and blade steak and compared them with a recipe made with tenderloin. Our assumption proved faulty. While the improved flavor of fattier cuts is striking in many applications, it was altogether lost in a sauce rich with dairy. In addition, all cuts but the tenderloin were unpleasantly chewy and at odds with the notion of a soft, plush main course blanketed in sauce and caressed by hot buttery noodles.

Although tenderloin was the clear winner in the texture department, it did come at a price in terms of flavor. We were surprised to find that, at least in this dish, wide strips of tenderloin tasted, in the words of one taster, "a bit like canned dog food." We solved this problem by using thinner strips of meat and reducing the total amount of meat in the recipe. (The thinner strips sautéed faster and hotter, yielding better flavor than thicker strips, which tended to steam.) Now we had both good flavor and texture.

Many recipes flour the meat to promote browning and thicken the sauce, but the flour prevented the beef from browning properly and formed a thick, gummy coating on the meat. A better approach was to add a single tablespoon of flour to the pan along with the sauce ingredients. As for the mushrooms, we knew they would benefit from hot, dry heat, which would brown their edges and leave their insides silky and flavorful. This cooking method was vastly superior to the lazy man's approach: slicing and then simply simmering them in the sauce. This recipe needed flavor, and this was one place to find it.

With flavor in mind, we wondered if something other than the common button mushroom (the choice in almost every recipe we uncovered) would be worth the added expense. After testing several possibilities, we found the answer was no. In this recipe, the way the mushrooms are cooked (in this case, browning) is more responsible for flavor development than the choice of mushrooms. Button mushrooms, if properly cooked, are just fine. We did discover that it's essential to leave the mushrooms in large pieces rather than slicing them thin. Halved or quartered mushrooms (depending on their initial size) have a textural presence equal to that of the beef.

We knew that the *fond*, or browned bits left in the pan after sautéing, would be critical to a flavorful sauce and that the sequence of the sauté would be key. (However, since we are committed to testing everything, we also threw a batch of meat into a skillet with no attention to browning. Sure enough, it looked just like the stroganoff we had seen in hotel chafing dishes—pale, tasteless, and lackluster.) When we sautéed the beef first, removed it from the pan, and then browned the mushrooms, the fond in the pan burned. We found it was better to start with the mushrooms (which, by the time they were finished, had barely colored the pan bottom), remove them from the pan, and then sauté the beef. Once the beef had been sautéed and set aside with the mushrooms, a beautiful brown film covered the pan. It needed only to be lifted from the pan with a little liquid, or deglazed.

The obvious choices for deglazing the pan were canned beef broth, canned chicken broth, and wine (most recipes called for white, but we saw some with red). We bet that a combination of broth and wine would prove to be the winner but tested every possible pairing of beef broth, chicken broth, red wine, and white wine.

Tasters quickly dismissed red wine because it

did not meld well with the dairy that was eventually added to the dish. On the other hand, everyone in the kitchen thought white wine added brightness and sweetness that balanced the dairy nicely. As for the broth, canned chicken and beef broths tasted bland on their own but were complex and flavorful when used together. We settled on a half cup each of white wine, chicken broth, and beef broth, choosing the beef broth to deglaze the pan. We then poured it into the bowl with the browned beef and mushrooms and started to build our sauce.

Onions were tested head to head with shallots and, to our great surprise, the bright flavor of the onions won out. Next we tested the long list of pantry staples mentioned at the beginning of this story. The only survivors were 1 teaspoon of tomato paste and 1½ teaspoons of dark brown sugar.

We added the splash of chicken broth and white wine and now needed only some dairy to bring this dish home. Some sources suggested heavy cream, but we found it made sauces that were too sweet and bland. A big spoonful of sour cream added complexity and tartness to the dish. This at last was stroganoff—quick, but full of flavor, and when in the company of a bowl of hot, buttered noodles, pretty irresistible.

BEEF STROGANOFF
SERVES 4

Sour cream can curdle if added directly to hot liquid. (For more information on this phenomenon, see page 30.) To prevent curdling, temper the sour cream by stirring a little of the hot liquid into it and then adding the warmed sour cream mixture to the pan. Buttered egg noodles (see the box at right for details of our tasting) are the classic accompaniment to this recipe. Add noodles to boiling water at the same time the onion goes into the pan in step 4, so that the noodles and stroganoff will be done at about the same time.

1½	tablespoons vegetable oil
12	ounces white button mushrooms, wiped clean and halved if small, quartered if medium, cut into sixths if large
	Salt and ground black pepper
¾	pound beef tenderloin (about 2 filets), cut into ⅛-inch strips (see illustrations above)
½	cup canned low-sodium beef broth
1	tablespoon unsalted butter
1	small onion, minced (½ cup)
1	teaspoon tomato paste
1½	teaspoons dark brown sugar
1	tablespoon all-purpose flour
½	cup canned low-sodium chicken broth
½	cup dry white wine
⅓	cup sour cream
8	ounces egg noodles, cooked in salted water, drained, and tossed with 2 tablespoons butter

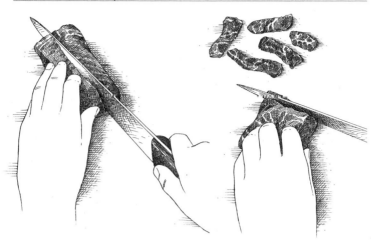

1. Turn filet on its side and cut in half to yield two ½-inch-thick medallions.

2. Cut medallions across grain into ⅛-inch strips.

1. Heat 1 tablespoon oil in heavy-bottomed 12-inch skillet over medium-high heat until hot and shimmering, but not smoking, about 2 minutes; swirl to coat pan. Add mushrooms and cook over high heat without stirring for 30 seconds; season with salt and pepper and continue to cook, stirring occasionally, until mushrooms are lightly browned, about 4 minutes longer. Transfer to medium bowl.

2. Return skillet to high heat, add remaining ½ tablespoon oil; swirl to coat pan. Place tenderloin strips in skillet. Using tongs, spread the meat into single layer, making sure that strips do not touch, and cook without turning until well-browned on first side, 2 minutes. Turn strips and cook on second side until well-browned, about 1 minute longer. Season with salt and pepper to taste and transfer to bowl with mushrooms.

3. Add beef broth to skillet, scraping up browned bits on pan bottom with wooden spoon; simmer until broth is reduced to ¼ cup, about 3 to 4 minutes. Transfer broth to bowl with mushrooms and beef, scraping skillet clean with rubber spatula.

4. Return skillet to medium-low heat and add butter; when butter foams, add onion, tomato paste, and brown sugar. Cook, stirring frequently, until onion is lightly browned and softened, about 6 minutes; stir in flour until incorporated. Gradually whisk in chicken broth and wine; increase heat to medium-high and bring to boil, whisking occasionally, then reduce heat to medium-low and simmer until thickened, about 2 minutes. Whisk liquid from mushrooms and beef into sauce and simmer to incorporate. Stir about ½ cup of hot sauce into sour cream, then stir mixture back into sauce. Add mushrooms and beef; heat to warm through, about 1 minute. Adjust seasonings with salt and pepper and serve over buttered egg noodles.

TASTING: **Egg Noodles**

Egg noodles are the traditional accompaniment to stroganoff. In our tests, we found that wider noodles work better with the substantial pieces of beef and mushroom in this dish, but we wondered if there were significant differences between brands. So we went shopping and brought back just about as many brands of wide egg noodles as we could find for a blind tasting in the test kitchen.

The noodle lineup included six leading brands—Manischewitz, Pennsylvania Dutch, Barilla, Light 'n Fluffy, Mueller's, DaVinci—and Black Forest Girl, an imported German brand found in the ethnic food aisle of a local supermarket. Tasters assessed the flavor, texture, and color of the noodles straight from the pot, drained but unadorned. There was no landslide victor—the top three brands came within points of each other—but the differences between the winners and the losers were dramatic.

Manischewitz, Barilla, and DaVinci were all tough, gummy, and pasty, with unpleasant off-flavors. Manischewitz and Barilla had slightly fishy, somewhat metallic flavors, while DaVinci tasted more like cardboard. Mueller's maintained a neutral position throughout the tasting, receiving neither harsh criticism nor accolades. Pennsylvania Dutch got slightly higher marks; these substantial, ruffled noodles had a "clean" taste.

The top-rated brands were Light 'n Fluffy and Black Forest Girl. Light 'n Fluffy noodles were just that, but they also had a balanced buttery flavor. Black Forest Girl noodles were sturdy and full-bodied, with a fresh, wheaty flavor. Neither of these brands was too starchy or gummy. They are the perfect match for stroganoff or most any stew. —Shannon Blaisdell

THE BEST NOODLES

The Best Breaded Pork Cutlets

Tender cutlets in a crisp crust—rather than greasy disks—are a sure thing when you know the two keys to pan-frying: enough oil and enough heat.

⇒ BY ADAM RIED ⇐

To many Americans, a pork dinner usually means chops or a roast. But denizens of the midwestern heartland, particularly Iowa, Indiana, and Missouri, might think instead of pan-fried breaded pork cutlets. Or they might think of tough disks of meat shrouded in a greasy, pale crust, which is how these cutlets can turn out if they're not cooked properly. If things go well, though, the pork is tender and the breading crisp, golden, and substantial.

Testing started with the basics: the pork itself. The two suitable cuts of pork we found in the supermarket, boneless loin chops and tenderloin, were also the two cuts cited most consistently in the recipes we researched. Naturally, we tried both and tasters favored cutlets from the tenderloin by a wide margin. They were remarkably tender and mildly flavored.

The next issue was thickness. When the cutlets were too thick, the breading overbrowned by the time the interior cooked through; when too thin, the meat was done long before the breading had taken on enough color. We ended up preferring cutlets pounded to a thickness of ½ inch. They were thick enough to offer some chew and a cushion against overcooking as the crust developed to a deep, even, golden brown. At first, we simply cut the tenderloin crosswise into ½-inch slices. But the tenderloin is a slender muscle, so these slices were rarely more than 2½ inches in diameter (and often smaller), making a skimpy presentation indeed. Our solution—to divide the tenderloin into six pieces (about 2 inches each in thickness) and then pound them to the desired thickness—both increased the diameter of the cutlets so they looked more attractive and standardized the yield of the recipe. One tenderloin now yielded six broad cutlets, enough for three servings.

As we often do in the test kitchen, we tried brining the cutlets—soaking them in a solution of water, salt, and sugar—to make them more juicy and flavorful when cooked. After several tests and considerable debate, we decided to skip this step since it did not improve the texture of the meat (pork tenderloin is almost always tender and supple unless overcooked). Seasoning the cutlets with salt and pepper was a much easier way to add flavor. To provide a good baseline flavor, liberal doses of salt and ground black pepper on the cutlets themselves were essential; experiments with seasoning only

Breaded pork cutlets make an excellent sandwich when layered with lettuce, tomato, and mayonnaise in a soft bun, roll, or white sandwich bread.

the breading components with different herb and spice combinations were less effective.

Many classic midwestern recipes call for a cornmeal coating mixture. Here our tasters broke with tradition, selecting a thick coat of fresh bread crumbs (made by grinding high-quality white sandwich bread in the food processor) over a cornmeal–flour combination, dried bread crumbs, Japanese panko crumbs, and crushed cracker crumbs. The homemade bread crumbs were light, crisp, and flavorful, whereas the cornmeal was gritty, the dried crumbs stale, the panko supercrisp but too neutral in flavor, and the crackers pasty. A thin coat of beaten egg (with a bit of oil added to help it slide off the meat more easily) acted as glue between the meat and crumbs, and

a sheer film of flour applied to the meat just beforehand allowed the egg to cling. We tried to do without the initial flour coating, but the egg would not adhere to the meat without it, leading to a flimsy coating.

The glory of these cutlets is the crust, which is, alas, the component that can most easily go awry. One bad habit of many cooks we know—skimping on the oil when they pan-fry—deals the crust a fatal blow. We tried cooking a batch of cutlets in just 4 tablespoons of oil, and the result—poor, splotchy browning—confirmed our hunch that using enough oil is critical. To develop their hallmark golden, crunchy crust, the cutlets must be pan-fried in oil that reaches roughly halfway up their sides, about ½ cup per batch in a 12-inch skillet.

Heat, or lack thereof, is another problem that most cooks encounter when pan-frying. When we failed to heat the oil enough before adding the cutlets to the skillet, several problems arose. First, the breading absorbed too much oil, so the finished cutlets were greasy. Second, the breading took too long to brown properly, and that extended stay in the pan caused the meat to toughen slightly. These pitfalls are avoided easily enough, though, if the oil is hot enough for the cutlets to sizzle briskly upon entering the pan and to then continue cooking at a moderate pace that allows the breading to brown evenly without burning at the edges. We found that the pan must be preheated over medium-high heat until the oil starts to shimmer—about 2½ minutes. (Time may vary depending on your particular pan and stovetop.) Taking care not to overcrowd the skillet with more than three cutlets per batch, we tested cooking times and learned that 2½ minutes per side browned the breading to a gorgeous golden hue without overcooking the meat within.

So if you don't skimp on either the oil or the heat, you can produce beautifully browned pork cutlets that are crisp on the outside and tender and juicy on the inside. And they make great sandwiches to boot.

CRISP BREADED PORK CUTLETS
SERVES 3

Pork tenderloins, which are sometimes sold in pairs, can weigh anywhere from 12 to 24 ounces. For this recipe, it is best to use a tenderloin that weighs at least 16 ounces. If you have two skillets, you can use both at once to cut the time it takes to fry. Our favorite accompaniments for breaded pork cutlets are applesauce, mashed potatoes, or coleslaw. If your cutlets are destined for a sandwich, check out "Sandwich Trimmings," at right, for garnish ideas.

- 6 slices high-quality white bread, such as Pepperidge Farm, crusts removed and torn into rough 1½-inch pieces
- ½ cup all-purpose flour
- 2 large eggs
- 1 tablespoon plus 1 cup vegetable oil
- 1 pork tenderloin (about 1 pound), trimmed of silver skin, cut crosswise into 6 pieces, and pounded to thickness of ½ inch, following illustrations 1–4, below
  Salt and ground black pepper

1. Process bread in food processor until evenly fine-textured, 10 to 15 seconds (you should have about 3 cups fresh bread crumbs); transfer crumbs to pie plate or shallow baking dish.

2. Adjust oven rack to lower-middle position, set large heatproof plate on rack, and heat oven to 200 degrees. Spread flour in second pie plate. Beat eggs with 1 tablespoon oil in third pie plate. Position flour, egg, and bread crumb plates in row on work surface.

Sandwich Trimmings
Pork cutlet sandwiches take well to a range of garnishes, traditional and not. Try any combination of the following: lettuce, thin-sliced tomato or red onion (raw or pickled), coleslaw, mustard, barbecue sauce, tartar sauce, pickle relish, or prepared chutney. Mayonnaise is also traditional: if you feel adventurous, flavor it by mixing ½ cup mayonnaise with 1 minced anchovy fillet (about ½ teaspoon) or 1 small minced chipotle chile en adobo (about 1 teaspoon). For an Asian-inspired mayo, add 2 teaspoons soy sauce and ½ teaspoon each grated ginger and minced garlic. Soft white sandwich bread and hamburger buns are the breads of choice.

3. Blot cutlets dry with paper towels and sprinkle thoroughly with salt and pepper. Working one at a time, dredge cutlets thoroughly in flour, shaking off excess. Using tongs, dip both sides of cutlets in egg mixture, allowing excess to drip back into pie plate to ensure very thin coating. Dip both sides of cutlets in breadcrumbs, pressing crumbs with fingers to form even, cohesive coat. Place breaded cutlets in single layer on wire rack set over baking sheet and allow coating to dry about 5 minutes.

4. Meanwhile, heat ½ cup oil in heavy-bottomed 12-inch nonstick skillet over medium-high heat until shimmering but not smoking, about 2½ minutes. Lay 3 cutlets in skillet; fry until deep golden brown and crisp on first side, gently pressing down on cutlets with wide metal spatula to help ensure even browning and checking browning partway through, about 2½ minutes (smaller cutlets from tail end of tenderloin may cook faster). Using tongs, flip cutlets, reduce heat to medium, and continue to cook until meat feels firm when pressed gently and second side is deep golden brown and crisp, again checking browning partway through, about 2½ minutes

longer. Line warmed plate with double layer of paper towels and set cutlets on top; return plate to oven.

5. Discard oil in skillet and wipe skillet clean using tongs and large wad paper towels. Repeat step 4 using remaining ½ cup oil and now-clean skillet and preheating oil just 2 minutes to cook remaining 3 cutlets.

JAPANESE-STYLE CRISP BREADED PORK CUTLETS (TONKATSU)

In Japanese restaurants, fried pork cutlets called *tonkatsu* are popular. Tonkatsu are much like our own pork cutlets but are even easier to make. First, because the meat is meant to have some chew, boneless loin chops can be used, thus eliminating the need to butcher a tenderloin. Neither is there a need to make fresh bread crumbs; use Japanese panko bread crumbs instead. Tonkatsu are served with a simple sauce made from American pantry ingredients (recipe follows).

Follow recipe for Crisp Breaded Pork Cutlets, making the following changes: Substitute 6 boneless center-cut pork loin chops, trimmed of silver skin and fat, for pork tenderloin, and pound to between ½ and ¼ inch thick, substitute equal amount cornstarch for flour and panko for fresh bread crumbs. To serve, slice cutlets into ¾-inch-wide strips and drizzle with Tonkatsu Sauce.

TONKATSU SAUCE
MAKES ABOUT ½ CUP

- ½ cup ketchup
- 2 tablespoons Worcestershire sauce
- 2 teaspoons soy sauce
- ½ teaspoon dry mustard powder, mixed with 1 teaspoon water until smooth

Mix all ingredients thoroughly in small bowl.

STEP-BY-STEP | TURNING ONE TENDERLOIN INTO SIX CUTLETS

 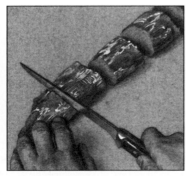  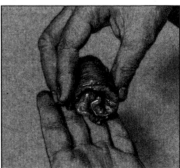

1. Slip knife under silver skin, angle it slightly upward, and use gentle sawing motion to remove silver skin.

2. Cut tenderloin crosswise into six equal pieces, including tapered tail end.

3. Place one piece of tenderloin on cut side on piece of plastic or parchment, cover with second piece, and pound gently to even thickness of ½ inch.

4. To produce cutlet from thin tail-piece, fold tip of tail under cut side and pound between two sheets of plastic or parchment.

Parchment Paper: Kitchen Workhorse

We use parchment paper every day in the test kitchen, not only for baking but for many other tasks. Here's how to take parchment paper beyond the cookie sheet.

BY SHANNON BLAISDELL

Parchment sold for kitchen use is paper that has been treated with sulfuric acid and coated with silicone. Sulfuric acid turns the paper's surface sleek and smooth, but, more important, it makes the paper impervious to grease and moisture and enormously resistant to high temperatures. The silicone coating goes one step further to make the surface of the paper nonstick.

Strong and tough, parchment paper comes in a variety of forms: sheets, rolls, bleached, unbleached, and combinations thereof. Though we buy large commercial sheets in bulk for the test kitchen, our favorite retail brand is Reynolds (see Kitchen Notes, page 30, for testing results).

Parchment Paper versus Wax Paper

Parchment paper is not the same as wax paper. Invented by Thomas Edison, wax paper is tissue paper that's been coated with paraffin on both sides, making it resistant (but not impervious) to grease and moisture. Wax paper is easily compromised by liquid, it is prone to tearing, and it is not heatproof (the wax begins to melt at relatively low temperatures). Wax paper can be used in the oven only if the paper is completely covered and protected from direct heat. You can line a cake pan with wax paper (the batter will cover and protect the paper), but don't line a cookie sheet with wax paper (the exposed portions will smoke and char).

Parchment is slightly more expensive than wax paper, but you get a lot of value for your money. Parchment can do everything that wax paper can do and more, and it can sometimes be reused. The same sheet can often be used several times to line cookie sheets, for instance.

ADDING DRY INGREDIENTS

We often use parchment paper rolled into the shape of a funnel to add dry ingredients to mixing bowls or food processor workbowls when making cake batter or bread dough. This means one less dirty bowl to wash. Flour can also be sifted directly onto parchment.

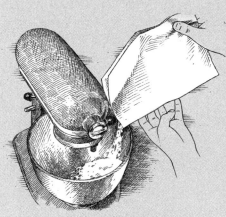

Left: Measure flour, spices, leaveners, and other dry ingredients onto a piece of parchment paper, then fold the parchment in half and pour the dry ingredients into the mixing bowl.

Right: Many food processor bread recipes call for adding flour in small increments. Instead of hovering over the food processor as you slowly add the flour, make a paper funnel using a doubled piece of parchment and place it in the feed tube. The flour will flow slowly and steadily into the bowl.

MEASURING AND REFILLING SPICES

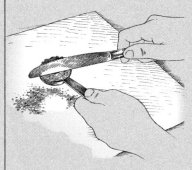

1. Measure ingredients such as spices, leaveners, and salt over a piece of parchment, not over the mixing bowl, to ensure accuracy.

SPLATTER-FREE MIXING

Hand-held mixers can get the job done but often cause an excessive amount of splashing, especially when you are beating a thin, liquid batter or whipping cream. Here's how we keep the mess under control.

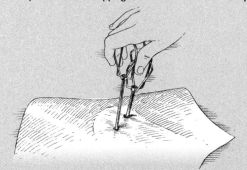

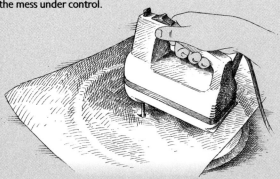

1. On a piece of parchment cut larger than the size of your mixing bowl, make two holes, spaced as far apart as the beater openings on your mixer. Insert the beater stems through the holes and into the beater base.

2. While you're mixing, the parchment will cover the bowl, preventing the contents from splattering onto the counter or walls.

2. Spills can easily be poured back into their containers. Use this technique to fill salt shakers and pepper mills as well.

Illustration: John Burgoyne

READY TO ROLL

Pie, pizza, and cookie dough are all easier to handle when parchment is in the picture.

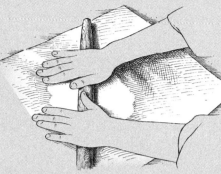

Pie Dough

Constantly reflouring a countertop to keep pie dough from sticking is a nuisance. And adding too much flour can make the dough dry and tough. In the test kitchen, we like to roll the dough between two sheets of parchment. (This also works with pizza dough.)

Pizza Dough

Getting a sticky pizza dough to slide off of a pizza peel can be tricky. If you roll out and sauce the pizza on parchment paper, you can slide the pizza, trimmed paper and all, onto the peel and into and out of the oven with ease. The parchment won't burn, and it easily falls away from the baked pie.

Icebox Cookies

After rolling the cookie dough into a log, lift the dough onto a piece of parchment and roll to seal. Refrigerate the parchment-wrapped dough until it is cold and firm. When you want to bake the cookies, unroll and slice the dough.

IN THE FREEZER

Wouldn't it be nice to freeze chops, steaks, or shaped burgers in one bag and then pull out just a few as needed? To avoid thawing unwanted meat because the block is frozen solid, we separate chops, steaks, and burgers with sheets of parchment, place the meat in freezer bags, and freeze as usual. The paper between the meat makes it much easier to pull individual pieces from the frozen package. This technique works with flour and corn tortillas as well as crêpes.

LINING CAKE PANS

Parchment paper ensures that cakes won't stick to pans. Here's how to get a perfect fit.

I. Trace the bottom of your cake pan roughly in the center of a sheet of parchment (use two sheets if using two pans).

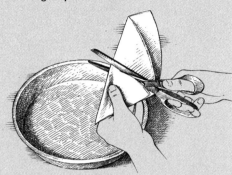

2. Fold the traced circle in half, in half again, and then in half again. Cut along the inside edge of the tracing. Unfold and fit the paper in the pan.

KEEPING THE CAKE PLATE CLEAN

I. Using four rectangular pieces of parchment, form an empty square on top of the cake platter, leaving an overhang. Place the cake layers in the center of the empty parchment square, frost, and decorate.

2. Once the frosting has had a chance to set slightly, carefully pull the sheets from beneath the cake, leaving behind a perfectly clean plate.

PARCHMENT SLING FOR BROWNIES AND BAR COOKIES

It can be difficult to extract brownies and bars from baking pans. Parchment solves this problem, prevents sticking, and makes cleanup a breeze.

I. Place two parchment sheets perpendicular to each other in the pan. Scrape the batter into the pan, pushing it into the corners.

2. After the brownies or bars have been baked and cooled, use the parchment to transfer them to a cutting board, and then slice into individual portions.

Pantry Pasta Sauces with Tuna

Follow these simple steps to transform canned tuna and a few other staples into a quick, highly flavored pasta dinner.

⋽ BY THE COOK'S ILLUSTRATED TEST KITCHEN ⋸

What cook hasn't come home from a long day, tired and hungry, to find the refrigerator bare, offering poor prospects for a good, quick dinner? Yet a simple can of tuna paired with a box of dried pasta can come to the rescue even faster than the pizza delivery guy. The trick is to choose the right can of tuna and use it properly to make a fast, satisfying dinner; otherwise the sauce can be murky, mealy, and unappetizing.

A side-by-side tasting of different types of tuna made into sauces got us going. The lineup comprised water-packed solid white StarKist (which won the *Cook's* July/August 1998 canned tuna tasting), its vegetable oil–packed counterpart, and a tuna packed in olive oil (after the Italian style), which, like the other tunas, is available on many supermarket shelves. The surprise winner was the water-packed tuna, preferred for its toothsome texture and light, clear flavor. Several dissenters favored the rich flavor of the tuna packed in olive oil, but everyone frowned upon the off flavor and mushy texture of the tuna packed in vegetable oil. (If you like the stronger flavor of tuna packed in olive oil, we found it best to drain the tuna and use fresh oil to make pasta sauces.)

Draining the tuna well prevents it from tasting waterlogged and diluting the sauce. We also found it useful to use our fingers to shred large chunks to a fine and uniform texture, thereby ensuring even distribution of the tuna. These techniques add but a minute to the preparation time yet make real improvements to the overall consistency of the final dish. We wondered about the right time to add the tuna to the other sauce ingredients and found that adding it late in the game was best. If sautéed from the start, the tuna dried out and became gritty, dragging the texture of the whole dish down with it. If the tuna is added to the sauce at the last minute and allowed to just heat through, it remains moist and tender.

Because these sauces are relatively thick, we pair

For sauces with the best flavor and texture, drain the tuna thoroughly, break up any chunks with your fingers, and don't let the tuna cook for more than a minute.

them with stubby, open, or tubular pasta shapes that can trap the sauce effectively. Penne, fusilli, radiatore, and gemelli are particularly good choices.

PASTA AND GARLIC-LEMON TUNA SAUCE WITH CAPERS AND PARSLEY
SERVES 4 TO 6

- 3   tablespoons olive oil
- 6   medium garlic cloves, minced or pressed through garlic press (about 2 tablespoons)
- ½   teaspoon red pepper flakes
- 3   tablespoons capers, rinsed and drained
- ½   cup dry white wine
- 2   cans (6 ounces each) solid white tuna in water, drained well and chunks broken up with fingers
     Salt
- ¼   cup chopped fresh parsley leaves
- 1   teaspoon grated zest from 1 lemon
- 3   tablespoons unsalted butter, cut into 6 pieces
- 1   pound penne or fusilli, cooked until al dente and drained, ¼ cup pasta cooking water reserved
     Ground black pepper

1. Heat oil, 1 tablespoon garlic, red pepper flakes, and capers in 12-inch skillet over medium-high heat, stirring frequently, until fragrant and sizzling but not browned, 1 to 2 minutes. Add wine and bring to simmer; simmer until aroma bears no trace of alcohol, about 1 minute. Add tuna and 2 teaspoons salt and cook, stirring frequently, until tuna is heated through, about 1 minute.

2. Toss tuna mixture, remaining garlic, parsley, zest, butter, cooked pasta, and reserved pasta water to coat in warm serving bowl. Adjust seasonings with salt and pepper to taste; serve immediately.

PASTA AND TOMATO TUNA SAUCE WITH GARLIC AND MINT
SERVES 4 TO 6

- 4   tablespoons olive oil
- 6   medium garlic cloves, minced or pressed through garlic press (about 2 tablespoons)
- 1   can (28 ounces) diced tomatoes, drained
- ½   cup dry red wine
- 2   cans (6 ounces each) solid white tuna in water, drained well and chunks broken up with fingers
     Salt
- 1   tablespoon balsamic vinegar
- 2   tablespoons chopped fresh mint or parsley leaves
- 1   pound penne or fusilli, cooked until al dente and drained, ¼ cup pasta cooking water reserved
     Ground black pepper

1. Heat 2 tablespoons oil and 1 tablespoon garlic in 12-inch skillet over medium-high heat, stirring frequently, until fragrant and sizzling but not browned, 1 to 2 minutes. Add tomatoes and cook, stirring constantly, until combined, about 30 seconds. Add wine and bring to simmer; simmer until aroma bears no trace of alcohol, about 1 minute. Add tuna and 2 teaspoons salt and cook, stirring frequently, until tuna is heated through, about 1 minute.

2. Toss tuna mixture, remaining oil and garlic, vinegar, mint, cooked pasta, and reserved pasta water to coat in warm serving bowl. Adjust seasoning with salt and pepper to taste; serve immediately.

PASTA AND RED PEPPER TUNA SAUCE WITH ANCHOVIES, GARLIC, AND BASIL

SERVES 4 TO 6

6	tablespoons olive oil
6	medium garlic cloves, minced or pressed through garlic press (about 2 tablespoons)
½	teaspoon red pepper flakes
2	anchovy fillets, minced
1	cup (about 7 ounces) jarred roasted red bell peppers, cut into ½-inch pieces
½	cup dry white wine
2	cans (6 ounces each) solid white tuna in water, drained well and chunks broken up with fingers Salt
1	tablespoon juice from 1 lemon
2	tablespoons chopped fresh basil or parsley leaves
1	pound penne or fusilli, cooked until al dente and drained, ¼ cup pasta cooking water reserved Ground black pepper

1. Heat 3 tablespoons oil, 1 tablespoon garlic, and red pepper flakes in 12-inch skillet over medium-high heat, stirring frequently, until fragrant and sizzling but not browned, 1 to 2 minutes. Add anchovies and roasted red peppers and cook, stirring constantly, until slightly dry, about 30 seconds. Add wine and bring to simmer; simmer until aroma bears no trace of alcohol, about 1 minute. Add tuna and 2 teaspoons salt and cook, stirring frequently, until tuna is heated through, about 1 minute.

2. Toss tuna mixture, remaining oil and garlic, lemon juice, basil, cooked pasta, and reserved pasta water to coat in warm serving bowl. Adjust seasoning with salt and pepper to taste; serve immediately.

PASTA AND SICILIAN-STYLE TUNA SAUCE WITH RAISINS, GREEN OLIVES, AND BASIL

SERVES 4 TO 6

3	tablespoons olive oil
6	medium garlic cloves, minced or pressed through garlic press (about 2 tablespoons)
½	cup pitted green olives, slivered (about 15 large olives, or 2 ounces)
½	cup dark raisins
¼	cup dry red wine
5	tablespoons balsamic vinegar
2	tablespoons sugar
2	cans (6 ounces each) solid white tuna in water, drained well and chunks broken up with fingers Salt
2	tablespoons chopped fresh basil leaves
3	tablespoons unsalted butter, cut into 6 pieces
1	pound penne or fusilli, cooked until al dente and drained, ¼ cup pasta cooking water reserved Ground black pepper

1. Heat oil and 1 tablespoon garlic in 12-inch skillet over medium-high heat, stirring frequently, until fragrant and sizzling but not browned, 1 to 2 minutes. Add olives and raisins and cook, stirring frequently, until heated through, about 30 seconds. Add wine, 4 tablespoons vinegar, and sugar and bring to simmer; simmer until aroma bears no trace of alcohol, about 1 minute. Add tuna and 2 teaspoons salt and cook, stirring frequently, until tuna is heated through, about 1 minute.

2. Toss tuna mixture, remaining garlic and 1 tablespoon vinegar, basil, butter, cooked pasta, and reserved pasta water to coat in warm serving bowl. Adjust seasoning with salt and pepper to taste; serve immediately.

TESTING EQUIPMENT: Manual Can Openers

Like many gadgets, a can opener isn't something most cooks give much thought to until they're using one. But with several new types on the market, all boasting superior operation and safety features, we wanted to see if there were notable differences among leading brands.

We purchased four "safety" can openers and six standard can openers with varying grips and features. Prices ranged from $6.99 to $24.95. A standard can opener attaches to the side of the can and punctures the lid just inside the rim. When you are done, both the lid and the edges of the can are often jagged and rough. A safety can opener attaches to the top of the can and punctures the outside of the can just below the rim. When you are done, both the lid and the edges of the can are perfectly smooth.

We tested all 10 models on standard 14½-ounce cans of beans and 6-ounce cans of tuna. We judged each opener on its comfort, ease of operation, and safety.

COMFORT In terms of comfort, we took into account both the grip and the turning mechanism. Can openers with an ergonomic grip and a comfortable turning mechanism were preferred over models that pinched our fingers or forced an uncomfortable hand angle.

EASE OF OPERATION Ease of operation hinged on time—if more than one rotation around the can was necessary, or if we had to pause and restart turning, the opener was downgraded.

SAFETY Determining safety was clear-cut. If the opened can had smooth edges and little handling of sharp-edged tops was necessary, the opener earned the top rating. If the operation endangered fingers or produced ragged edges on the can or its top, the opener received a lower rating.

RESULTS In the end, our testers preferred the standard can openers to the safety models. Perhaps it was our life-long use of standard can openers, but we simply could not get used to the different hand position required, the two-part operation, or the locking handles on the safety openers. Many of the safety can openers were stiff and difficult to operate, and all caused liquid to spill out of the side of the can because the entire top was removed. Standard models may not result in perfectly smooth edges, but we are willing to use a bit of extra caution in exchange for ease, speed, and comfort.

Our favorite standard can openers were the Oxo Good Grips ($9.95), with a great grip and comfortable turning mechanism, and the Swing Away ($6.99), a classic stainless steel opener with plastic-coated handles for extra comfort. If safety is your prime concern, our testers had the best luck with the Culinare MagiCan Auto Release ($9.99). —Shona Simkin

BEST STANDARD CAN OPENERS

OXO Good Grips
This model earned top marks for its great plastic grip and comfortable turning mechanism. Operation was fast, easy, and secure.

SWING AWAY
This is probably what your grandmother has in her drawer. The plastic-coated handles are especially easy on your hands.

BEST SAFETY CAN OPENER

CULINARE MagiCan Auto Release
This all-plastic option is exceedingly safe, but liquid spills from cans while opening them. Friendly for lefties as well as righties.

How to Braise Belgian Endive

Add a pinch of sugar and stick to the stovetop for tender braised endive with multidimensional flavor.

⇉ BY ADAM RIED AND MATTHEW CARD ⇇

Raw Belgian endive, with its sharp and pleasantly bitter flavor, may be an acquired taste. The right cooking method, however, transforms endive into a vegetable side dish of uncommonly complex flavor—at once mellow, sweet, and rich, yet still faintly bitter. According to generations of French and Belgian cooks, braising is the cooking method of choice. Just try to find a classic French cookbook without a braised endive recipe, along with the suggestion that it accompany a simple roast chicken, veal, or pork supper.

Most recipes for braised endive follow the same protocol: Brown the endive in fat, then finish cooking it, covered, in a small amount of liquid over low heat. The challenge is to develop the deep flavor, richness, and gentle sweetness necessary to balance the endive's natural bite.

Available year-round, Belgian endive heads should have tightly packed leaves and a torpedo-like shape. The white leaves, essentially devoid of color because they are grown in the dark, are tinged slightly with yellow at the tip. It is said that if the yellow tinge is particularly deep, the endive will taste more bitter than usual. Our observations confirmed that notion when we tasted the endive raw, but we noted no effect on the flavor once the endive had been braised.

The first question was whether the endive really had to be browned before being braised. None of our tasters was impressed with the sharp, shallow flavor of endive that had not been browned, so we kept that step. We tested both butter and olive oil, and the former won hands down—the milk solids in the butter turn an appealing nut-brown as they cook, and, overall, the butter adds a deeper, richer flavor. We took this notion one step further and lightly caramelized the endive using the butter and a pinch of sugar. The butter and sugar provided rich, sweet undertones that complemented the endive's bitterness nicely, without overpowering it. We added extra dimension to the flavor with some minced fresh herbs (tasters preferred thyme and parsley) and a small amount of fresh lemon juice for brightness.

The braising liquid also had a considerable impact on the flavor of the dish. Water, a common choice, had few supporters among our tasters. Cream was too rich and cider too seasonal for a year-round recipe. White wine made the dish too acidic, and while chicken broth tasted deep and round, it obscured the flavor of the endive. The ideal balance resided in a mixture of equal parts white wine and chicken broth, which produced deep yet brightly flavored endive that retained a hint of its own bitterness, something we wanted to preserve. We made the most of the braising liquid by reducing it to make a light sauce after the endive finished cooking, thereby concentrating its sweetness and richness.

Our last question concerned the cooking process. Classic technique dictates that endive be covered with a piece of buttered parchment, then cooked in a warm oven for a long period. In our tests, however, we achieved excellent flavor and texture simply by leaving the endive in a single layer in the same skillet used to brown it and braising on the stovetop with the pan's lid in place of the parchment. This method was not only straightforward but quick—the endive became completely tender within 15 minutes. Stovetop cooking also left plenty of room in the oven for a roast to complete the meal.

BRAISED BELGIAN ENDIVE
SERVES 4

To avoid discoloration, do not cut the endive far in advance of cooking. Delicate endive can fall apart easily if not handled gently. Move the halved endive in the pan by grasping the curved sides gingerly with tongs and supporting the cut sides with a spatula while lifting and turning. You will need a skillet with a tight-fitting lid for this recipe.

- 3 tablespoons unsalted butter
- ½ teaspoon sugar
  Salt
- 4 medium Belgian endive (about 4 ounces each), wilted or bruised outer leaves discarded and each endive halved lengthwise
- ¼ cup dry white wine
- ¼ cup canned low-sodium chicken broth
- ½ teaspoon minced fresh thyme leaves
- 1 teaspoon juice from 1 lemon
- 1 tablespoon minced fresh parsley leaves
  Ground black pepper

1. Heat 2 tablespoons butter in 12-inch heavy-bottomed skillet over medium-high heat; when foam subsides, sprinkle sugar and ¼ teaspoon salt evenly over skillet and set endive cut-sides down in a single layer. Cook, shaking skillet occasionally to prevent sticking and adjusting burner if browning too quickly, until golden brown, about 5 minutes. Turn endive over and cook until curved sides are golden brown, about 3 minutes longer. Carefully turn endive cut-sides down. Add wine, broth, and thyme; reduce heat to low, cover skillet tightly, and simmer, checking occasionally and adding 2 tablespoons water if pan appears dry, until leaves open up slightly and endive are tender throughout when pierced with tip of paring knife, 13 to 15 minutes. Transfer endive to warmed serving platter; set aside.

2. Increase heat to medium-high to bring liquid in skillet to boil; simmer until reduced to syrupy consistency, 1 to 2 minutes. Off heat, whisk in remaining tablespoon butter, lemon juice, and parsley. Adjust seasoning with salt and pepper, spoon sauce over endive, and serve immediately.

BRAISED BELGIAN ENDIVE
WITH BACON AND CREAM

Fry 3 slices (about 3 ounces) bacon, cut into ¼-inch pieces, in 12-inch heavy-bottomed skillet over medium heat until crisp, about 5 minutes; remove with slotted spoon to paper towel–lined plate and set aside. Follow recipe for Braised Belgian Endive, using bacon fat in skillet instead of butter to brown endive in step 1, substituting 2 tablespoons heavy cream for butter in step 2, and omitting lemon juice. Sprinkle sauced endive with reserved bacon and serve.

CIDER-BRAISED BELGIAN ENDIVE
WITH APPLES

Because the apples absorb some of the braising liquid, more cider is added to the pan before the sauce is reduced.

Follow recipe for Braised Belgian Endive, sautéing 1 medium Granny Smith apple, peeled, cored, and cut into ¼-inch-thick wedges, along with endive, and substituting ½ cup apple cider for chicken stock and wine. Remove apples from skillet along with endive, add another 2 tablespoons cider to skillet, and continue with recipe from step 2, omitting lemon juice.

Profiteroles at Home

Bad profiteroles are misshapen, underrisen, soggy affairs. Great profiteroles are crisp and delicate—and they can be made at home in just 90 minutes.

≥ BY DAWN YANAGIHARA ≤

P rofiteroles might just be the most perfect dessert in existence: crisp, tender, and airy pastry encasing cold, creamy ice cream and napped by dark, luxurious chocolate sauce. Unfortunately, perfect profiteroles are often enjoyed only in the abstract, as those served in many restaurants are dismal representations. Stale and indelicate, with a texture somewhere between damp cardboard and Styrofoam, these prefabbed pastries must be cut with a knife, and the accompanying sauce only hints at bittersweet chocolate flavor. Having multiple components and a high-maintenance look, profiteroles might seem beyond the reach of a home cook looking for a tempting dinner party dessert. But in this case, looks are deceiving. Profiteroles can be made at home inside of 90 minutes and well in advance of serving (save for the last-minute assembly). With store-bought ice cream and a simple homemade chocolate sauce, profiteroles are, well, a piece of cake and easier than pie.

Choux Maker

Pâte à choux is the most basic French pastry, the first lesson in classic French cookery. It has both sweet and savory applications but is most familiar when filled with pastry cream to make éclairs or cream puffs, also called profiteroles. (Filled with ice cream and served with chocolate sauce, this pastry becomes the subject of this article.) Pâte à choux should bake into light, airy, well-puffed pastry with a delicately crisp crust. Split one open and the inside should be primarily hollow, with a soft, custardy webbing lining the interior walls. But beware the pitfalls of bad pâte à choux. The dough will spread on the baking sheet if too soft, and it may not rise properly. It may bake up lopsided, it is subject to collapse after baking, and, finally, the most common problem, it can turn soggy as it cools.

The ingredients in pâte à choux are standard, and so, for the most part, are the proportions. The traditional technique of making pâte à choux is to bring water or milk, salt, and butter to a boil in a saucepan. When the mixture reaches a rolling boil, the flour is stirred in to make a paste, the

Profiteroles start with crisp, light cream puffs that are then filled with ice cream and napped with a simple homemade bittersweet chocolate sauce.

saucepan is returned to low heat, and the paste is cooked. During cooking, the paste is stirred constantly, stimulating the development of gluten, the protein that gives bread doughs elasticity. Gluten provides for a better, stronger rise in the oven. Then the eggs are beaten in one by one. The pâte à choux is then ready to be piped onto a sheet pan and baked.

To determine how long the paste really needs to be cooked, I made four batches of pâte à choux and cooked each to a different degree—from not at all up to five minutes—over low heat. The uncooked batch and the one cooked for only a minute failed to attain much height with baking. The batches made from paste cooked for three and five minutes, however, both baked into voluminous puffs. Because neither I nor my tasters could detect a significant difference between these two, I opted for three minutes of cooking. Since stovetops undoubtedly vary, I took the temperature of the paste and used this as an additional measure of doneness.

The traditional method of introducing the eggs is to do so gradually and to stir vigorously after each addition. It's an arduous task, to say the least. If added in a single large addition, the eggs splash about and require the patience of Job and the arm of Hercules to be incorporated into the

dough. I discovered, however, that all of this grunt work was entirely unnecessary. The cooked paste can be transferred to a standing mixer or a food processor and the eggs incorporated swiftly, with nary one turn of a wooden spoon. Best of all, both machines produced pastry superior to one made by hand—the puffs were lighter, puffier, and well-risen. It was the food processor, though, that brought the paste together with mercurial speed, making it the machine of choice. (Rose Levy Beranbaum introduced this method in *The Pie and Pastry Bible,* Scribner, 1998.) The hot paste is whirled around for a few seconds to cool it slightly, then, with the machine running, the eggs are added in a steady stream. Pâte à choux has never gone together more quickly and easily—and without a fatigued arm.

Puffed Up

With my technique set, I focused next on the ingredients, beginning with the liquid. Pastry made exclusively with milk was gloriously golden but disappointingly soft; one with only water was ashen and wan yet pleasantly light and crisp. Neither appealed. With equal parts milk and water, the pastry browned nicely, but its texture remained faintly soft. Seventy-five percent water and 25 percent milk made a pastry that both colored and crisped agreeably.

Eggs next. Whole eggs are the norm, but both Shirley Corriher, in *Cookwise* (Morrow, 1997), and Beranbaum promote a partial replacement of whole eggs by egg whites, explaining that the whites make incredibly light, crisp pastry. To test this premise, I made pastries with whole eggs only and got puffs that, though golden from the yolks, were soft, stalwart, and breadlike. On the other end of the spectrum, an excess of whites made the puffs firm, brittle, and dry, with an unappealing pallor and texture. With the right balance of whole eggs to egg whites (in this case, 2 whole eggs to 1 egg white), the pastry was crisp and delicate, well-risen, light, airy, and well-colored. It was also the perfect consistency for piping—thick, but soft enough to fall in great globs from a spoon.

Butter is added to pâte à choux not only for flavor but texture; it makes the pastry tender. Three tablespoons yielded flavor-deprived pastry that had a stale, chewy texture, while 4 tablespoons delivered good results. But with 5 tablespoons the pastry was much improved: delicately crisp, with an impeccably rich flavor.

As for flour, a good number of recipes indicated that bread flour benefits pâte à choux because its higher protein content means that more gluten can be developed when the paste is made, and a glutinous, elastic paste can achieve greater expansion and height in the oven. What these recipes failed to reveal was what I found in my testing: Bread flour also makes tougher, crunchier (not crispier), less delicate pastry. I stuck with all-purpose flour, trying both unbleached and bleached. Not surprisingly, unbleached flour was favored for its nuttier, toastier flavor, traits that the bleaching process seems to remove.

The last ingredients to consider were salt and sugar. Salt heightened flavor, while sugar encouraged browning and added a bit of sweetness.

Bad Puffs, Good Puffs

If removed from the oven too early, puffs collapse as they cool (left). Proper baking ensures crisp, well-risen puffs (right).

Pipe Down

To determine the size of the puff best suited to profiteroles, I sought the opinions of colleagues. We agreed that a single large puff was inelegant, two medium puffs were not visually pleasing on a plate, while three smaller puffs were just right.

The next step was placing shapely portions of dough on a baking sheet. While some recipes suggest that a pastry bag can be sidestepped and the pâte à choux simply dropped onto the baking sheet like cookie dough, I had no success with this technique; the baked puffs were uneven and unattractive. Turning to a pastry bag fitted with a plain tip (½-inch size), I piped the neatest, roundest mounds possible onto a greased and parchment-lined baking sheet. (I found the "grease" necessary to hold the parchment in place; without it, the parchment lifted as I tried to pull the pastry bag away.) Some recipes suggested using the back of a teaspoon dipped in water to smooth the surface and even out the shape of the mound, and this technique proved useful.

The proper baking of pâte à choux is as key to the pastry's success as are proper cooking techniques and ingredients. The browning and doneness must be synchronized. If the puffs are soft and underdone but removed from the oven because they are brown, they will collapse before your very eyes. The puffs are leavened by steam pushing up from the interior, so, as you might imagine, they require a hit of heat to get them going. A 400-degree oven proved too cool, and the pâte à choux sprouted to a size no larger than button mushrooms. A 425-degree oven, however, was too hot, and the pastry was brown before it was done. With a little more experimentation, I hit upon the right temperature and time combination: 425 degrees for 15 minutes, then down to 375 degrees for another 8 to 10 minutes.

Recipes often warn that an overcrowded baking sheet can cause the puffs to collapse. I found this to be true: There should be at least an inch of space between piped mounds of pâte à choux. A large baking sheet (12 by 18 inches, or a half-sheet pan) thus works best. Recipes also often call for sprinkling the baking sheet with water just before baking. (The water, they claim, converts to steam in the oven, which prevents the exterior of the pastry from setting too quickly, affording the puffs more time to rise higher.) When tested, this method proved bogus—the resulting puffs were not improved at all.

After being baked, the pastry may be crisp externally, but the inside remains moist with residual steam. If it is allowed, the moisture will be absorbed into the pastry, making it soggy. This means that immediately following baking the puffs must be slit to release steam and be returned to a turned-off, propped-open oven where they can dry out for about 45 minutes to ensure crispness. Once dry and crisp and finally cooled, the puffs can stay at room temperature for a day or be stored in a zipper-lock plastic bag and thrown into the freezer for a month or so. Just a brief warm-up in the oven to rejuvenate them (a crucial step often overlooked in restaurants, where profiteroles are sometimes frozen already assembled with the ice cream filling), and they are ready to go. This is part of the beauty of pâte à choux.

Some Assembly Required

To serve six (the yield of the pâte à choux recipe), I used an assembly-line method to plate the profiteroles, splitting all of them open on their plates, then filling and saucing them all at once. However, by the time that I plopped the final scoop of rapidly softening ice cream on the final pastry bottom, the first scoops were beginning to melt. The solution was to line a baking sheet with parchment paper and chill it in the freezer, then scoop the ice cream and place the scoops on the chilled sheet. I then returned the baking sheet to the freezer (this, by the way, can be done days in advance). When the pastry was ready to be filled, I quickly dropped the ice cream into place, pressed the tops on, and sauced the profiteroles. Much quicker, neater, and easier.

All that was needed now was chocolate sauce, but not the watery, tasteless, saccharine chocolate sauces available in grocery stores. The profiteroles required the unfettered, intense flavor of pure, dark chocolate. Enter our Bittersweet Chocolate Sauce from September/October 2001. It goes together in the blink of an eye (10 minutes) and can be made well in advance and warmed for serving.

Crisp, cold, sweet, warm, bitter, chocolatey, and rich—here at long last was profiterole perfection.

PÂTE À CHOUX (CREAM PUFF PASTE)
MAKES ABOUT 24 TWO-INCH PUFFS

A serving of profiteroles consists of three baked puffs filled with ice cream and topped with sauce. This recipe makes 24 puffs, technically enough to serve 8, but inevitably a few bake up too awkwardly shaped to serve to guests. Refer to the illustrations on page 23 when making and piping the paste.

- 2 large eggs plus 1 large egg white
- 5 tablespoons unsalted butter, cut into 10 pieces
- 1 ounce (2 tablespoons) whole milk
- 3 ounces (6 tablespoons) water
- 1½ teaspoons sugar
- ¼ teaspoon salt
- 2½ ounces (½ cup) unbleached all-purpose flour, sifted

1. Adjust oven rack to middle position and heat oven to 425 degrees. Spray large (12 by 18-inch) baking sheet with nonstick cooking spray and line with parchment paper; set aside. Beat eggs and egg white in measuring cup or small bowl; you should have ½ cup (discard excess). Set aside.

2. Bring butter, milk, water, sugar, and salt to boil in small saucepan over medium heat, stirring once or twice. When mixture reaches full boil (butter should be fully melted), immediately remove saucepan from heat and stir in flour with heatproof spatula or wooden spoon until combined and mixture clears sides of pan. Return saucepan to low heat and cook, stirring constantly, using smearing motion, for 3 minutes, until mixture is slightly shiny with wet-sand appearance and tiny beads of fat appear on bottom of saucepan (temperature of paste should register 175 to 180 degrees on instant-read thermometer).

3. Immediately transfer mixture to food processor and process with feed tube open for 10 seconds to cool slightly. With machine running, gradually add eggs in steady stream. When all eggs have been added, scrape down sides of bowl, then process for 30 seconds until smooth, thick, sticky paste forms. (If not using immediately, transfer paste to medium bowl, cover surface flush with sheet of plastic wrap sprayed lightly with nonstick cooking spray, and store at room temperature for up to 2 hours.)

4. Fold down top 3 or 4 inches of 14- or 16-inch pastry bag fitted with ½-inch plain tip to form a cuff. Hold bag open with one hand in cuff and fill bag with paste. Unfold cuff, lay bag on work surface, and, using hands or bench scraper, push paste into lower portion of pastry bag. Twist top of bag and pipe paste into 1¼- to 1½-inch mounds on prepared baking sheet, spacing them about 1 to 1¼ inches apart (you should be able to fit about 24 mounds on baking sheet).

5. Use back of teaspoon dipped in bowl of cold water to smooth shape and surface of piped mounds. Bake 15 minutes (do not open oven door), then reduce oven temperature to 375 degrees and continue to bake until golden brown and fairly firm (puffs should not be soft and squishy), 8 to 10 minutes longer. Remove baking sheet from oven. With paring knife, cut ¾-inch slit into side of each puff to release steam; return puffs to oven, turn off oven, and prop oven door open with handle of wooden spoon. Dry puffs in turned-off oven until centers are just moist (not wet) and puffs are crisp, about 45 minutes. Transfer puffs to wire rack to cool. (Cooled puffs can be stored at room temperature for up to 24 hours or frozen in zipper-lock plastic bag for up to 1 month. Before serving, crisp room temperature puffs in 300-degree oven 5 to 8 minutes, or 8 to 10 minutes for frozen puffs.)

STEP-BY-STEP | MAKING THE PASTE

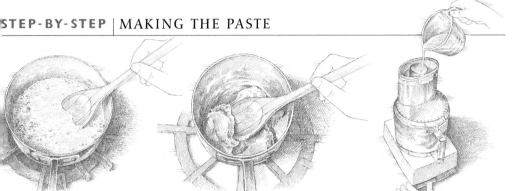

1. Occasionally stir butter mixture until it comes to full boil. Remove pan from heat.

2. Add flour, return pan to low heat, and cook paste for 3 minutes, stirring constantly and using smearing motion.

3. With feed tube open, process paste 10 seconds, then add eggs in steady stream.

STEP-BY-STEP | PIPING THE PASTE

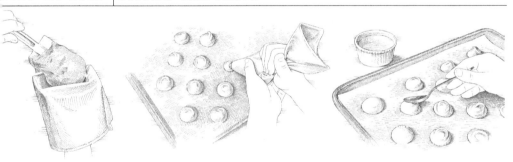

1. Fill pastry bag with paste, push paste to bottom of bag using hands or bench scraper, and twist top of bag to seal.

2. Pipe paste into 1¼- to 1½-inch mounds on prepared baking sheet.

3. Use back of teaspoon dipped in water to even out shape and smooth surface of mounds.

STEP-BY-STEP | ASSEMBLING THE PROFITEROLES

1. Scoop ice cream onto prepared baking sheet, freeze until firm, and cover with plastic wrap.

2. Use paring knife to split puffs about ⅜ inch from bottom. Set three bottoms on each dessert plate.

3. Place scoop of ice cream on each bottom and press tops into ice cream. Pour sauce over profiteroles.

BITTERSWEET CHOCOLATE SAUCE
MAKES 1½ CUPS

Whisk the sauce gently so as not to create tiny air bubbles that can mar its appearance.

- ¾ cup heavy cream
- 3 tablespoons light corn syrup
- 3 tablespoons unsalted butter, cut into three pieces
  Salt
- 6 ounces bittersweet chocolate, chopped fine

Bring heavy cream, corn syrup, butter, and salt to boil in small nonreactive saucepan over medium-high heat. Off heat, add chocolate while gently swirling saucepan. Cover pan and let stand until chocolate is melted, about 5 minutes. Uncover and whisk gently until combined. (Can be cooled to room temperature, placed in airtight container, and refrigerated for up to 3 weeks. To reheat, transfer sauce to heatproof bowl set over saucepan of simmering water. Alternatively, microwave at 50 percent power, stirring once or twice, 1 to 3 minutes.)

PROFITEROLES
SERVES 6

For profiteroles, the smooth, dense texture and rich flavor of a high-quality custard-style ice cream is preferable to the light, fluffy texture and milky flavor of Philadelphia-style ice cream, which is made without eggs. In our September/October 2001 vanilla ice cream tasting, Edy's Dreamery came out on top. If you're serving several guests, prescooping the ice cream makes serving quick and neat, but if you're assembling only a couple servings or your freezer lacks space, you can skip the prescooping step. Refer to illustrations at left when assembling profiteroles.

- 18 cream puffs
- 1 quart custard-style vanilla or coffee ice cream
- 1 recipe Bittersweet Chocolate Sauce (warmed if made ahead)

1. Line baking sheet with parchment paper; freeze until cold, about 20 minutes. Using 2-inch ice cream scoop (about same diameter as puffs), scoop ice cream onto cold baking sheet and freeze until firm, then cover with plastic wrap; keep frozen until ready to serve. (Ice cream can be scooped and frozen for up to 1 week.)

2. When ready to serve, use paring knife to split open puffs about ⅜ inch from bottom; set 3 bottoms on each dessert plate. Place scoop of ice cream on each bottom and gently press tops into ice cream. Pour sauce over profiteroles and serve immediately.

Soft, Chewy Molasses Spice Cookies

Dry, tasteless molasses cookies belong on a Christmas tree, not in a cookie jar.
We made more than 50 batches to find the best recipe for an uncommonly
soft, chewy cookie with a warm, tingling spiciness.

⇒ BY DAWN YANAGIHARA ⇐

Molasses cookies are the cookie pariahs, the dowdy group in the cookie crowd, permanently out of style and hopelessly old-fashioned. But I've come to appreciate good molasses cookies for their honesty and simplicity. On the outside, their cracks and crinkles give them a humble, charming countenance. Inside, an uncommonly moist, soft yet chewy, tooth-sinking texture is half the appeal; the other is a warm, tingling spiciness paired with the dark, bittersweet flavor of molasses. But molasses spice cookies are often miserable specimens, no more than flat, tasteless cardboard rounds of gingerbread. They can be dry and cakey without the requisite chew; others are timidly flavored with molasses and are either recklessly or vacantly spiced.

I started by testing a half dozen different recipes, using a variety of fats, flours, and mixing methods. Although these early experiments yielded vastly different cookies in terms of both flavor and appearance, a few things were clear. The full, rich flavor of butter was in, flat-tasting shortening was out. Flour required little thought—unbleached all-purpose flour was perfectly suited to the task. The mixing technique was a standard one: Cream the butter and sugar, add any eggs, then the molasses, and, finally, stir in the dry ingredients. Now I had a solid working recipe that I could use as a basis for further testing.

Molasses is at the core of these cookies. Enough must be used to give the cookies a dark, smoky, bittersweet flavor, but a surfeit of molasses created a sticky, unworkable dough. For the amount of butter (12 tablespoons) and flour (2¼ cups) I was using, the molasses ceiling was ½ cup. Up to this point I had been using mild (also called light) molasses. In an attempt to boost flavor, I baked batches with dark and blackstrap molasses. (See "The Best Molasses for Cookies," page 25.)

Molasses alone cannot supply the cookies with enough sweetness, so either granulated or brown sugar is required. Dark brown sugar (I chose dark over light for its stronger flavor) yielded cookies that were surprisingly puffy and cakey, and they spread too little on the baking sheet. Granulated sugar yielded cookies that were pale both in color and flavor. A combination of granulated and brown sugars was the ticket. The brown sugar fortified the molasses flavor, while the granulated

Sugar infused with orange zest gives a variation on our chewy molasses cookies a frosted appearance.

sugar, a spreading agent, allowed the cookies to attain a good, even thickness in the oven without much puff.

Most molasses cookie recipes call for a single egg to bind things together. The white of a whole egg—harmless as it may seem—made the dough sticky. The difference was subtle, but the white also caused the baked cookies to have a slightly cakelike crumb and a firmer, drier feel than I cared for. A single yolk was all the cookies wanted.

Molasses is a mildly acidic ingredient, so baking soda, an alkali that reacts with acid to provide lift, was the logical leavener for these cookies. In my testing, cookies with too little baking soda were flat and failed to develop those attractive fault lines. Instead, they looked vaguely scarred. The proper amount of baking soda (1 teaspoon) gave the cookies nice height—a pleasure to

sink your teeth into—and a winsome appearance, with large, meandering fissures.

It was time to refine the flavor of the cookies. A teaspoon of vanilla extract complemented generous amounts of sharp, spicy ground ginger and warm, soothing cinnamon. Cloves, rich and fragrant, and allspice, sweet and mysterious, were added, but in more judicious quantities. Finely and freshly ground black pepper added some intrigue, a soupçon of heat against the deep, bittersweet flavor of the molasses.

To shape the molasses cookies, I rolled generous heaping tablespoons of dough into balls, coating them with granulated sugar, which, after baking, gave the cookies a frosted sparkle. At a too-high temperature—400 degrees—the surface and edges of the cookies took on a tough, overbaked quality. At 350 degrees, the cookies had a uniformly soft texture, which was OK but uninteresting. Cookies baked in a 375-degree oven were perfect, the edges slightly crisped and the interiors soft and chewy. Because cookies baked on the lower rack inevitably ended up puffed and smooth rather than craggy and cracked, I determined that they were best baked one sheet at a time.

Most important, I noted—and you should, too—that the cookies must come out of the oven when they appear substantially underdone; otherwise their soft, moist, chewy texture will harden on cooling. Whisk them out of the heat when the edges are hardly set, the centers are still soft and puffy, and the dough looks shiny and raw between the cracks. The cookies finish baking with residual heat, so don't shortchange them of a five-minute repose on the baking sheet before removal to the cooling rack. Then, while the warm, spicy aroma lingers in the kitchen, be the first to bite into a warm, soft, chewy molasses spice cookie that may be out of style but is definitely not out of favor.

SOFT AND CHEWY MOLASSES SPICE COOKIES
MAKES ABOUT 22 COOKIES

Measure the molasses in a liquid measuring cup. If you find that the dough sticks to your palms as you shape the balls, moisten your hands occasionally in a bowl filled with cold water and shake off the excess. Bake the cookies one sheet at a time. If baked two sheets at a time, the cookies started on the bottom rack won't develop the attractive cracks. The cookies should look slightly raw and underbaked when removed from the oven. If you plan to glaze the cookies (see recipe below), save the parchment paper used to bake them.

- ⅓ cup (about 2½ ounces) granulated sugar, plus ½ cup for dipping
- 2¼ cups (11¼ ounces) unbleached all-purpose flour
- 1 teaspoon baking soda
- 1½ teaspoons ground cinnamon
- 1½ teaspoons ground ginger
- ½ teaspoon ground cloves
- ¼ teaspoon ground allspice
- ¼ teaspoon finely ground black pepper
- ¼ teaspoon salt
- 12 tablespoons (1½ sticks) unsalted butter, softened but still cool
- ⅓ cup (about 2½ ounces) packed dark brown sugar
- 1 large egg yolk
- 1 teaspoon vanilla extract
- ½ cup (about 6 ounces) light or dark molasses (see box, right)

1. Adjust oven rack to middle position and heat oven to 375 degrees. Line 2 baking sheets with parchment paper. Place ½ cup sugar for dipping in 8- or 9-inch cake pan.

2. Whisk flour, baking soda, spices, and salt in medium bowl until thoroughly combined; set aside.

3. In standing mixer fitted with paddle attachment, beat butter with brown and granulated sugars at medium-high speed until light and fluffy, about 3 minutes. Reduce speed to medium-low and add yolk and vanilla; increase speed to medium and beat until incorporated, about 20 seconds. Reduce speed to medium-low and add molasses; beat until fully incorporated, about 20 seconds, scraping bottom and sides of bowl once with rubber spatula. Reduce speed to lowest setting; add flour mixture and beat until just incorporated, about 30 seconds, scraping bowl down once. Give dough final stir with rubber spatula to ensure that no pockets of flour remain at bottom. Dough will be soft.

4. Using tablespoon measure, scoop heaping tablespoon of dough and roll between palms into 1½-inch ball; drop ball into cake pan with sugar and repeat to form about 4 balls. Toss balls in sugar to coat and set on prepared baking sheet,

spacing them about 2 inches apart. Repeat with remaining dough. Bake 1 sheet at a time until cookies are browned, still puffy, and edges have begun to set but centers are still soft (cookies will look raw between cracks and seem underdone), about 11 minutes, rotating baking sheet halfway through baking. Do not overbake.

5. Cool cookies on baking sheet 5 minutes, then use wide metal spatula to transfer cookies to wire rack; cool cookies to room temperature and serve. (Can be stored at room temperature in airtight container or zipper-lock plastic bag up to 5 days.)

MOLASSES SPICE COOKIES WITH DARK RUM GLAZE

For the glaze, start by adding the smaller amount of rum; if the glaze is too thick to drizzle, whisk in up to an additional ½ tablespoon rum.

Follow recipe for Soft and Chewy Molasses Spice Cookies. When completely cool, return cookies to cooled parchment-lined baking sheets. Whisk 1 cup confectioners' sugar (about 4½ ounces) and 2½ to 3 tablespoons dark rum in medium bowl until smooth. Dip spoon into glaze and then move spoon over cookies so that glaze drizzles down onto them; repeat as necessary. Transfer cookies to wire rack and allow glaze to dry, 10 to 15 minutes.

MOLASSES SPICE COOKIES WITH ORANGE ESSENCE

The orange zest in the sugar coating causes the sugar to become sticky and take on a light orange hue; the baked cookies have a unique frosty look.

In workbowl of food processor, process ⅔ cup granulated sugar and 2 teaspoons grated orange zest until pale orange, about 10 seconds; transfer sugar to 8- or 9-inch cake pan and set aside. Follow recipe for Soft and Chewy Molasses Spice cookies, adding 1 teaspoon grated orange zest to butter and sugars along with molasses in step 3 and substituting orange sugar for granulated sugar when coating dough balls in step 4.

TASTING: The Best Molasses for Cookies

Molasses is a byproduct of the cane sugar–refining process. It is the liquid that is drawn off after the cane juice has been boiled and undergone crystallization. The resulting molasses is then subjected to two subsequent boilings. With each boiling, the molasses grows increasingly dark, bitter, and potent as more sugar is extracted.

There are three different types of molasses. Light, or mild, molasses comes from the first boiling, dark molasses from the second, and blackstrap from the third. In the past, sulfur dioxide was often added to molasses to clarify it. Although this process made molasses look more attractive, it added an unappealing flavor. Today, most, if not all, molasses on the market is unsulfured.

Grocery store shelves are not packed with molasses options. Grandma's is the baseline offering, and Brer Rabbit brand can be found in well-stocked supermarkets nationwide. Blackstrap molasses is commonly available in natural foods stores. We made cookies with five different bottles of molasses. Tasters liked both brands of light and dark molasses but found blackstrap molasses too overpowering in a cookie. The moral of the story: Buy either light or dark molasses based on your preference for a mellow or intense molasses flavor.

- **Grandma's Mild Flavor** Cookies made with this molasses had a warm bronze color. The molasses flavor was solid, decently rich, and "nicely balanced." Good for those who like molasses flavor but not its bitterness.
- **Grandma's Robust Flavor** This molasses filled the cookies with both dark color (akin to a chocolate cookie) and deep flavor. They were criticized as "too strong" by one taster but touted as "spicy and rich" by another.
- **Brer Rabbit Mild Flavor** Noteworthy was the lovely sepia color of the cookies made with this molasses. The cookies garnered comments such as "complex and nuanced" and "fruity" with a "clean finish."
- **Brer Rabbit Full Flavor** These cookies had an even richer sepia color than those made with mild Brer Rabbit. "Straight-up" and "smooth" molasses flavor without even so much as a trace of bitterness.
- **Plantation Blackstrap** A couple of tasters admired the potent molasses flavor, but most others remarked that the molasses was so overwhelming that the spices could hardly be tasted. User discretion advised.

Kosher Bird Wins Chicken Tasting

Many factors influence the taste and texture of commercially raised chickens, but salting or brining the bird is the key to success.

⇒ BY RAQUEL PELZEL ⇐

Picking out a quality chicken at the supermarket is a guessing game. The terms *fresh, organic, free-range, all natural,* and *lean* rarely indicate good flavor or texture, and neither does price. In our 1994 chicken tasting, the only dependable sign of quality we found was brand, with Bell & Evans and Empire taking top honors. Eight years later, we wondered if these companies would win a second tasting and if, at long last, we could find a reliable, non-branded measure of quality.

Down on the Farm

We identified and investigated a long list of genetic and environmental factors that might help consumers purchase a high-quality, tasty bird. Our first stop was genetic engineering, through which birds are bred to meet the goals of a particular producer. Murray's chickens, for example, are engineered for a high yield of breast meat and a low yield of fat. (Tasters found them "tough" and "dry.") Perdue chickens are bred for a high ratio of meat to bone. (We found this means big breasts and scrawny legs.) But it seemed to us that few, if any, producers were engineering birds for flavor.

Next we examined a wide range of environmental factors, including feed and living conditions.

Some birds dine on feed that is free of animal byproducts and animal fats, but our tasters could not detect a difference in flavor or texture based on the presence or absence of animal byproducts in the feed. A low-stress environment is supposed to produce more tender meat, says Tom Stone, director of marketing for Bell & Evans. Although the Bell & Evans facility I visited in Pennsylvania appeared relatively stress-free—clean and with good natural light—this theory was impossible to confirm or deny.

A chicken's age can also have an effect on flavor. The older the chicken (an older broiler/fryer is seven to nine weeks old rather than the more typical six to seven weeks), the more distinct its flavor is thought to be. Free-range chickens are usually older than indoor chickens when processed because they take longer to reach their proper weight. (Because free-range chickens have unrestricted access to the outdoors, it is virtually impossible to prevent them from eating random grasses and insects. Consequently, their diet is a mix of these elements as well as feed, and they gain weight more slowly.) Nonetheless, we found the "free-range" moniker to be no indication of superior flavor. The two free-range birds we tasted, Eberly and D'Artagnan, had both fans and critics.

Does Processing Method Matter?

Processing factors that can affect the flavor and appearance of a chicken include how the chicken was rinsed and chilled prior to being packaged. Antimicrobial agents, such as sodium triphosphate, are sometimes added to the rinse water to cut down contamination by bacteria like salmonella. (Some tasters can detect traces of this chemical. It is usually described as "metallic.") Some rinsing methods inadvertently add excess water under the skin, leading to a shriveled appearance after cooking. After being slaughtered and rinsed, the chickens are quickly chilled to a temperature of about 28 degrees Fahrenheit, or just above their freezing point. If the chickens are chilled too quickly, their meat can get spongy and watery. If chilled too slowly, the meat can dry out and develop an off color. None of these effects could be confirmed in our tasting because we could not be certain about how a particular bird was processed.

Our first solid clue to any possible connection between processing method and flavor emerged when we discovered that Empire, the only kosher chicken in our tasting, was also the best tasting. Both Empire and Murray birds are hand-slaughtered rather than killed by machine, which ensures both a clean kill and a quick and efficient "bleed-out." (Murray birds are not kosher but are processed under similar conditions in accordance with Muslim law.) Industry experts indicated that machine-processed chickens are more likely to be subject to improper slaughtering, which can cause blood to clot, resulting in tough meat or a livery flavor.

Because tasters far preferred the Empire chicken to Murray's, however, it followed that more was at work here than slaughtering technique. For one thing, kosher chickens like Empire's are dunked in cold water to remove feathers after slaughter. Cold water firms both the skin and the fat layer beneath it. In contrast, most other producers scald birds in hot water to remove the feathers. The experts we talked to said that scalding can "solubilize" the chicken's fat, leading to excessive moisture loss and a wrinkled appearance in the chicken skin after cooking. Uneven scalding can also cause "barking," or a blotchy appearance in the skin.

Appearance aside, perhaps the most noticeable difference between the Empire bird and the others we sampled was that the Empire bird tasted juicy and well-seasoned. To remove as many impurities as possible, the chickens are buried in salt for one hour and then rinsed off with cold spring water. The combination of salt and water acts like a brine, encouraging the fibers in the meat to open and trap the salt and water, leading to a juicier, more flavorful bird. This single factor, more than any other, seems to have put the Empire bird ahead of the pack.

If you are looking for advice on purchasing a high-quality chicken, we recommend kosher. All the other adjectives—free-range, natural, lean, organic, and the like—don't necessarily translate into a better-tasting chicken. Empire, the brand that won our current contest, was followed by Bell & Evans, winner of our 1994 tasting. You can't go wrong with either. Tyson, a mass-produced bird that costs $1.29 per pound, came in third, ahead of birds costing twice as much. One last word of advice. Out of nine birds in the tasting, Perdue finished dead last. This is one brand to avoid if possible. If a Perdue bird is your only choice, however, see "Home Brining: Turning Losers into Winners," at left.

Home Brining: Turning Losers into Winners

Because the winning bird in our tasting is packed in salt and then rinsed, we wondered what would happen if we brined the runner-up, Bell & Evans, as well as the last-place Perdue chicken, tasting them alongside the first-place Empire bird. To find out, we put three more chickens into the oven. The Empire and Bell & Evans birds still finished on top, but the Perdue chicken wasn't far behind. The brined Perdue chicken was milder and less toothsome than the other two birds, but it was certainly acceptable. Our conclusion: If your local market doesn't carry kosher chickens, you can use a quick saltwater soak to improve the quality of just about any chicken.

Brining a 3½- to 4-pound chicken:

Combine 1 gallon cold water, 1 cup table salt (or 2 cups kosher salt), and 2 cups sugar in a large pot. Add the chicken and let soak in the refrigerator for 3½ to 4 hours (or one hour per pound).

TASTING CHICKENS

For this tasting, we gathered nine widely available brands of chicken. We chose broiler/fryers that weighed from 3½ to 4 pounds. The birds were roasted without additional seasonings to an internal temperature of 160 degrees at the breast and 170 degrees at the leg/thigh and were served to 30 members of the *Cook's* staff. Tasters were asked to evaluate the chicken for overall appearance and for the flavor and texture of both white and dark meat.

HIGHLY RECOMMENDED

EMPIRE KOSHER Broiler Chicken
PENNSYLVANIA
$2.29/lb.

Many tasters found this bird to be the most flavorful of the tasting, calling it "perfectly seasoned" and "well balanced." The meat tasted "natural" and "sweet," while the texture was "firm," "moist," and "tender." During processing the Empire bird is covered with salt to draw out impurities in the meat, so it never needs to be brined in a saltwater solution to pump up the flavor or juiciness of the meat

RECOMMENDED

BELL & EVANS Fresh Young Chicken
PENNSYLVANIA
$2.69/lb.

Tasters found the Bell & Evans chicken to be "pretty," as well as flavorful, with its meat tasting "clean," "fresh," and "natural." The texture of the white meat was called "firm" and "moist," whereas the dark meat was described as "moist" and "tender." This bird is fed an all-vegetable diet that contains no animal byproducts or antibiotics.

TYSON Fresh Young Chicken
ARKANSAS HEADQUARTERS
$1.29/lb.

One taster said this "tastes like chicken," while another found it lacking in flavor. Its white meat was described as "firm," albeit slightly "mealy," while its dark meat was well liked for its tenderness. Tyson was downgraded by some tasters for the "uneven" color of its skin.

D'ARTAGNAN Fresh Free Range Certified Organic Young Natural Chicken
PENNSYLVANIA
$3.00/lb.

Described as "golden," "glossy," and "archetypically beautiful," this free-range bird wowed tasters with its good looks. Although the white meat was called "dry" and "stringy," tasters felt it had a "natural flavor." The dark meat was called "moist" and "tender," although some panelists thought it had "livery" undertones.

EBERLY'S Free Range Young Natural Chicken
PENNSYLVANIA
$2.49/lb.

Tasters described this free-range bird as "golden and gorgeous," but many thought the white meat was "stringy." "Bland" and "boring" to some, others loved its "natural" and "buttery" flavor. Separated by just one point, the D'Artagnan and Eberly's chickens are actually the exact same bird. Eberly's raises all of its chickens on an organic, all-vegetable feed free of antibiotics; some, however, receive the D'Artagnan sticker, while others get the Eberly's label.

NOT RECOMMENDED

MURRAY'S Fresh Young Lean Chicken
NEW YORK
$1.99/lb.

With an impressive 44 percent less fat than other commercial chickens, the Murray's chicken is the only bird that the U.S. Department of Agriculture allows to be labeled as "low-fat." While this may be a benefit to those who count calories and fat grams, our tasters thought the chicken was somewhat "bland" and generally "unremarkable." The skin was described as "golden" and "speckled," while the meat was "slightly metallic," "tough," "dry," and "chewy." This chicken is raised on an all-vegetable, antibiotic-free feed.

FOSTER FARMS Fresh Young Chicken
CALIFORNIA
$0.99/lb.

The dark meat tasted "gamey" and "livery," the white meat "off" and "metallic." Both dark and white meat were "overly moist." The bird itself appeared to have "puffed and deflated," leaving it with "wrinkled" skin.

ROCKY JUNIOR Frying Chicken
CALIFORNIA
$2.29/lb.

Tasters described this sample as being "bland" and "tasteless," with "gamey" dark meat; its texture was called "chewy," "wet," and "stringy." Tasters also objected to its "anemic" appearance. This bird is raised on an all-vegetable, antibiotic-free feed.

PERDUE Fresh All Natural Chicken
MARYLAND HEADQUARTERS
$1.49/lb.

Tasters objected to the look, texture, and flavor of this chicken. They described the skin as "shriveled." The texture was "pithy," "chalky," and "stringy." The flavor was "a bit off," with a "sour quality that kicks in at the end." Perdue breeds its birds for a high meat-to-bone ratio, giving them large breasts, scrawny legs, and a more compact look than the other, more leggy birds in the tasting.

The Saucepan That Saved Dinner

Most large saucepans will get the job done, but some can actually make up for your mistakes.

≥ BY ADAM RIED ≤

We recently asked a number of home cooks which pot or pan they used the most, and the answer was surprisingly consistent: "My big saucepan." Many of us here in the test kitchen might have said the same thing. Whether we are blanching vegetables, cooking beans, or making a double batch of rice to accompany a staff lunch, we reach for a large—by which we mean three- to four-quart—saucepan.

Clearly, the large saucepan is a kitchen workhorse that should handle everyday tasks with aplomb. Which begs the question: Does the brand matter? With prices for large saucepans ranging from just $24.99 (for a Revere stainless steel model with thin copper cladding at the base) up to $140 (for an All-Clad pan with a complete aluminum core, stainless steel interior, and exterior cladding), there's a lot of money riding on the answer. To offer some guidance, we tested eight models, all between three and four quarts in size, from well-known cookware manufacturers.

Unlike many *Cook's* tests of pots and pans, this one does not include models with nonstick finishes. Nonstick pans do an acceptable job of browning food but fall short when it comes to developing *fond,* the brown, sticky, caramelized film that forms on the pan bottom and eventually imparts deep flavor to the dish you're building. Many of the dishes prepared in a large saucepan, from chowder to chili, derive part of their savory backbone from the fond, so we decided that nonstick finishes were out.

The tests we performed were based on common cooking tasks and designed to highlight specific characteristics of the pans' performance. Sautéing chopped onion illustrated the pace at which the pan heats up and sautés. Cooking white rice provided a good indication of the pans' ability to heat evenly, as well as how tightly the lid sealed. Making pastry cream let us know how "user-friendly" the pan was. Was it shaped such that a whisk could reach into the corners without trouble, was it comfortable to pick up, and could we pour liquid from it neatly? These traits can make a real difference when you use a pan day in and day out.

Important Differences

Of the tests we performed, sautéing onions was the most telling. In our view, onions should soften reliably and evenly (and with minimal attention and stirring) when sautéed over medium heat. In this regard, the All-Clad, Calphalon, KitchenAid, and Sitram pans all delivered. The Chantal and Cuisinart pans sautéed slightly faster, necessitating a little more attention from the cook, but still well within acceptable bounds. Only the Revere and Farberware Millennium sautéed at a pace fast enough to be considered problematic.

So what's the big deal about sautéing on the fast side? Ostensibly, very little, as long as you focus on what you are doing. When we conduct tests, our focus is keen, but in real life, few cooks enjoy that luxury. Whether from a calling child or a ringing phone, most cooks face distractions while they work. This is precisely the time when a medium sauté pace might save dinner because it can prevent the food from burning for a short while when you turn away. We confirmed this by leaving sautéing onions unattended in the medium-paced All-Clad and the quicker-paced Revere for six minutes. The All-Clad onions overbrowned a little,

The Saucepans We Tested

RECOMMENDED

All-Clad Stainless Steel
Performed beautifully, but why not include a rolled lip for neat pouring?

Calphalon Commercial
Performed well in tests but has minor design shortcomings.

KitchenAid Stainless Steel
Some users questioned the balance when lifting this solid performer.

RECOMMENDED WITH RESERVATIONS

Chantal
Arguably, the beauty of the group. Aside from a slightly fast sauté speed, it performed well.

Sitram Professional Induction
The lid is a weak or, more accurately, lightweight feature. Otherwise, a decent pan.

Cuisinart Everyday Stainless
Nice heft and handle, though the handle gets hot near the base.

NOT RECOMMENDED

Revere Stainless Steel Copper Clad Bottom
Performance shortcomings outweigh a few nice design touches.

Farberware Millennium
Turned out dry rice and overbrowned onions.

RATING LARGE SAUCEPANS

RATINGS

★★★
GOOD
★★
FAIR
★
POOR

Eight large saucepans, each with a capacity of three to four quarts and available in open stock, were tested and evaluated according to the following criteria. All stovetop cooking tests were performed over 10,000 BTU gas burners on the KitchenAid ranges in our test kitchen.

PRICE: Prices paid at Boston-area retail or national mail-order outlets. You may encounter different prices depending on the outlet.
MATERIALS: Materials that go into the pan itself as well as into the lid and handle. Stainless steel is abbreviated as SS, aluminum as AL.
WEIGHT: Measured with the lid.
HANDLE: Handles that remained cool from the base to the tip during the sauté test were rated good. Handles that became uncomfortable to touch at the base were rated fair.
SAUTÉ SPEED: We started with a cold pan and sautéed 1 cup chopped onions in 2 tablespoons vegetable oil over medium heat for 10 minutes. Pans that produced soft, pale gold onions with no burnt edges were rated good; pans that produced onions that were barely colored and retained notable crunch were rated fair; and pans that produced onions that were dark brown, crisp, or burnt at the edges were rated poor.
RICE: We prepared a double batch of long-grain white rice by bringing 3 cups water to boil, adding 1 teaspoon salt and 2 cups rice, returning to a boil, simmering covered over lowest heat for 15 minutes, and resting undisturbed off heat for 15 minutes longer. Pans that turned out evenly cooked, fully tender grains were rated good; if the grains were slightly undercooked or there was slight browning or notable sticking of the rice to the pan bottom, the pan was rated fair.
PASTRY CREAM: We scalded half-and-half in each pan and then cooked pastry cream (following the recipe in the July/August 2001 issue of *Cook's*) until it registered 180 degrees on an instant-read thermometer. All pans were able to turn out perfect pastry cream without browning or sticking and were rated good.
TESTERS' COMMENTS: These comments augment the information on the chart with observations about unusual or noteworthy aspects of the pans and their performance.

Brand	Price	Materials	Weight	Handle	Sauté Speed	Rice	Pastry Cream	Testers' Comments
FAVORITE **All-Clad** Stainless Steel 3 Quart	$139.99	SS w/ complete AL core; SS lid, handle	3 lb. 10 oz.	★★★	★★★	★★★	★★★	Long, indented handle helps cook attain a secure grip when lifting and pouring. If this pan had a rolled lip, it could be the perfect pan.
RECOMMENDED **Calphalon** Commercial Hard-Anodized 3½ Quart	$110.99	Anodized AL pan, lid; SS handle	4 lb. 3 oz.	★★★	★★★	★★★	★★★	The bruiser of the group—are we cooking or weight-training here? May be a challenge to lift for some cooks. Lip is not rolled, which makes pouring from pan a messy proposition.
KitchenAid Stainless Steel 3 Quart	$119.00	SS w/ complete AL core; SS lid, handle	3 lb. 7 oz.	★★★	★★★	★★★	★★★	Rolled lip makes for neat pouring, but handle is too short for some.
RECOMMENDED WITH RESERVATIONS **Chantal** Saucepan #35-200S 3 Quart	$89.99	Enameled carbon steel; glass lid; SS handle	3 lb. 6 oz.	★★★	★★	★★★	★★★	Sautés slightly fast, so it requires a bit of extra attention. Nothing unacceptable, however.
Sitram Professional Induction 3.17 Quart	$56.90	SS w/ AL base; SS lid, handle	3 lb. 11 oz.	★★	★★★	★★	★★★	Especially light lid allowed quite a bit of steam to escape, so rice began to stick to pan bottom.
Cuisinart Everyday Stainless 3¾ Quart, Model 919-20	$79.99	SS w/ copper sandwich bottom; SS lid, handle	3 lb. 4 oz.	★★	★★	★★★	★★★	Have to watch the sauté speed, which is a little faster than we like. Other than that, a very serviceable saucepan.
NOT RECOMMENDED **Revere** Stainless Steel Copper Clad Bottom 3 Quart	$24.99	SS w/ copper-clad bottom; SS lid; phenolic handle	1 lb. 10 oz.	★★★	★	★★	★★★	The team featherweight heats up and sautés exceptionally fast, so it can be difficult to control. Lid allowed significant steam to escape as rice cooked, so the rice browned and stuck a bit.
Farberware Millennium 3 Quart	$44.99	SS w/ AL sandwich bottom; SS lid, handle	2 lb. 6 oz.	★★	★	★★	★★★	The heft was comfortable, the handle hot at the base, and the performance far from ideal.

but the Revere onions burned.

The Revere and Farberware pans that sautéed onions faster than we'd like are the lightest of the bunch, weighing only 1 pound 10 ounces and 2 pounds 6 ounces, respectively. This indicates that they are made from thinner metal, which is one reason they heat quickly. We found, however, that too heavy a pan, such as the 4-pound Calphalon, could be uncomfortable to lift when full. We found the ideal weight to be about 3½ pounds; pans within a few ounces of this weight, including the All-Clad, KitchenAid, Chantal, Sitram, and Cuisinart, balance good heft with easy maneuverability.

While none of the pans failed the rice test outright, there were performance differences. In the Sitram, Revere, and Farberware pans the rice stuck and dried out at the bottom, if only a little bit. Although this did not greatly affect the texture, flavor, or ease of cleanup, we'd still choose a pan for which this is not an issue.

Every pan in the group turned out perfect pastry cream. During this test, we did observe one design element that made it easy to pour liquid from the pan neatly, without dribbles and spills. A rolled lip that flares slightly at the top of the pan helps control the pour. Only two pans in the group do not have a rolled lip—the All-Clad and the Calphalon.

While handles on skillets and sauté pans must be able to withstand high oven temperatures, most saucepan handles see only the top of the stove. A saucepan handle should, however, remain cool enough to grasp easily during stovetop cooking, as did the handles on all the pans we tested, for the most part. On the Sitram, Cuisinart, and Farberware, the base of the handle (where it attaches to the pan body) got too hot to touch after 10 minutes over medium heat, but the end of the handle stayed cooler.

Winner's Circle

Which pan should you buy? That depends largely on two things: your budget and your attention as a cook. Based on our tests, we'd advise against really inexpensive pans—those that cost less than $50. For somewhere between $50 and $100, you can get a perfectly competent pan, including any of those in the Recommended with Reservations category of the above chart. The only caveat is that you may have to watch them carefully to avoid overcooking certain foods; they offer less margin of error than the pans in the Recommended category. The most expensive pans in the group, the All-Clad, Calphalon, and KitchenAid, were not flawless: The Calphalon is heavy, both it and the All-Clad lack rolled lips, and the KitchenAid has a relatively short, curved handle. That being said, these three pans can save your dinner, providing moderate, steady heat, even when you're distracted.

≥ BY BRIDGET LANCASTER ≤

Beau Thai

During the recipe development for our Southeast Asian–Style Spring Rolls (page 6), we discovered that most recipes called for Thai basil. Wondering if this special breed of basil would indeed make a difference, we pitted it head-to-head (or, in this case, roll-to-roll) against the more commonly found sweet basil (also called Italian basil).

The differences were as subtle as a sledgehammer. Thai basil has a distinctive flavor, with hints of mint, licorice, and cinnamon that tasters found "authentic" to the spring rolls, "clean," and "refreshing." The sweet basil was described as having a more mellow, grassy flavor, which tasters thought "better suited to a tomato sauce" and "inauthentic to the spring rolls."

We highly recommend Thai basil for spring rolls. If you cannot find Thai basil in your supermarket, use mint, which is a better substitute than sweet basil.

Endive Primer

Have you wondered why the Belgian endive in your shopping cart is so expensive? Considering the effort that goes into growing this vegetable, it's no wonder that Belgians refer to endive as white gold. Belgian endive is cultivated using a lengthy process called forcing, which occurs over a period of several months. During the first growing period, in late spring, chicory seeds are planted and allowed to grow until the roots are well developed and small leaves appear above the ground. In autumn, the roots are pulled out of the ground and the leaves are removed. The roots are inspected for disease and proper size and then placed in a cold room or under refrigeration for anywhere from a few days to several months. In effect, the root is being forced into controlled dormancy.

When the farmer desires, the dormant chicory roots are replanted, but this time they are grown in complete darkness to discourage the greening of the plant, which can produce a bitter flavor. The other secret of superior endive is the use of warm soil (never below 60 degrees), which promotes the delicate flavor of good endive. Eventually, endive buds, called *chicons,* appear above ground. The chicons should be ghostly white in appearance, with just the faintest tinge of yellow appearing on the tips of the leaves. When they reach the proper size, the chicons are harvested and immediately packed between sheets of dark paper to prevent discoloration or blemishing during shipping.

So the next time you wonder about the high price of endive, remember that it took nearly a year (and sometimes longer) for it to go from the ground to your table, and be thankful to enjoy it at any cost.

Kitchen Therapy

Ever wanted a multipurpose kitchen tool that also serves as a stress reliever? Then look no further than your local hardware store. The rubber mallet—the kind you might put to use in a woodworking shop—sees plenty of action in the test kitchen. With a heavy head and great leverage, a rubber mallet takes the work out of pounding chicken breasts paper thin, smashes heads of garlic with one hit, and can even flatten a 14-pound turkey into submission. Yes, the looks we get when swinging this mighty tool are a bit peculiar, but considering that the average price of a mallet is about $6, therapy has never been so cheap.

Curds and Whey

Let's be honest. Who among us hasn't been responsible for a broken sauce? In our Beef Stroganoff recipe (page 12), we use a method called tempering to introduce sour cream into the hot sauce. Tempering prevents the sour cream from breaking, or splitting (the sauce separates into clumps of particles floating in a watery liquid). How exactly does tempering work?

Sour cream is a cultured dairy product, which means it has been exposed to (unharmful) bacteria cultures. The bacteria perform two functions: (1) They produce acid that gives the cream its characteristically sour tang, and (2) the acid causes the chief proteins in cream, referred to as casein proteins (also in milk), to clot, causing the mixture to thicken.

The casein proteins are still stable at this point, but they can tolerate little more trauma. A blast of heat is all that is needed to cause the proteins to continue clotting to the point at which they squeeze together so tightly that they expel liquid, called whey. The result is a watery mess.

By tempering the sour cream with a little of the hot sauce, thereby raising the temperature gradually, it is possible to introduce the sour cream to a hot sauce without causing it to separate.

EQUIPMENT: **Parchment Performance**

Best Brand: Reynolds

In the test kitchen we use large (16⅜ by 24⅜ inches) commercial-grade sheets of parchment paper that we order by the case from professional kitchen supply stores. Because most home cooks are stuck with retail-grade parchment, we decided to compare a few popular brands. Included were Fox Run Craftsmen (flat sheets), Beyond Gourmet (unbleached roll), and Reynolds (bleached roll), as well as a sheet of Super Parchment (a washable and reusable product). We tested these products using two of our recipes: Thin and Crispy Chocolate Chip Cookies (March/April 2001) and Thin-Crust Pizza (January/February 2001).

For the cookie test, we lined baking sheets with each type of parchment paper. After 12 minutes in a 375-degree oven, all brands performed well, displaying little browning and no charring at all. Release was also good with all brands; the cookies slid off their respective parchment sheets with ease. Beyond Gourmet and Reynolds—the two brands that come in a roll—tended to curl up at the edges, but this problem was easily solved by placing the sheets with their curled edges down. The weight of the dough kept the parchment paper flat.

With all brands performing well with cookies, we moved on to a more stressful test with our Thin-Crust Pizza. (Pizza dough is rolled into a 14-inch circle between floured sheets of parchment and plastic wrap. The plastic is removed, the dough is topped with sauce and cheese, and excess parchment is trimmed. The pizza, still on the parchment, is then slid onto a preheated pizza stone in a 500-degree oven and baked for 12 minutes.) Once again, none of the brands burned. However, size mattered. Reynolds was the only brand wide enough to handle a 14-inch pizza. (Using two sheets of the other brands to make a larger area yielded a pizza with slightly undercooked dough. Of course, this wasn't an option with the reusable 13 by 17-inch sheet of Super Parchment.) Reynolds is available nationwide in 30-square-foot rolls that retail for approximately $2.50.

Letters from the Kitchen

Culinary newsletters preach, inform, entertain, and educate, but which ones are worth the price of a subscription? BY CHRISTOPHER KIMBALL

Culinary newsletters are much like Christmas cards—they can be heartfelt, businesslike, pithy, discursive, chatty, philosophical, or merely historical. Some are casual, throwing recipes about as if they were at a covered dish supper, while others are elitist, hard on the trail of a rare Robiola cheese from southern Piedmont. Here are five of the better-known culinary newsletters and my thoughts on whether they are worth the paper and postage.

COOK AND TELL, Karyl Bannister
16/year, 10 issues; Love's Cove, P.O. Box 363, Southport, ME 04576
www.cookandtell.com

➢ This 12-page, digest-size letter is the most homespun of the lot. Preceded by a personal essay are a dozen or so recipes that would be at home in a good community cookbook. The recipes come from readers, friends, cookbooks, restaurants, and magazines and feel like the fare found in mass market women's magazines: Betty's Easy Fish Fillets, Quick-Lunch Hummus Rollup, and Cathy's Reliable Chocolate Cake. In effect, *Cook and Tell* is a postcard from mom with selections from her recipe box. Of the five recipes we tested, three were winners and two were certainly acceptable.) This is unpretentious Tuesday night cooking, a hodgepodge of food one serves to family and friends—the sort of folks who still own a lunchbox, know how to start a chainsaw, and make Halloween costumes by hand.

THE CURMUDGEON'S HOME COMPANION
Dan Goldberg
18/year, 12 issues; P.O. Box 3312, Yountville, CA 94599
www.curmudgeon.com

➢ I am partial to curmudgeons, being one myself, so I was taken with the name of this four-page monthly newsletter. Unlike *Cook and Tell, The Curmudgeon's Home Companion* is more discourse than recipes, with Dan Goldberg offering lengthy opinions on everything from mayonnaise to global warming. This is not terribly insightful speculation (I am not sure he needs to opine on household clutter), rather, it is the type of dinner conversation

one might have at a Chinese restaurant in a shopping mall—relaxed, informal, and fun, but leaving one with a hunger for something more substantial. Goldberg usually runs half a dozen recipes in each issue, most of which are sophisticated but simple. We made an excellent Peach and Onion Salad, an interesting Basil-Lemon Liqueur, and a good Peach Clafouti. Perfect Sesame Noodles were hardly that—even the test kitchen dogs kept their distance—and Polenta Casserole was lackluster.

DREADED BROCCOLI, Barbara Haspel and Tamar Haspel
$14/year, 4 issues; 235 West End Avenue, #6C, New York, NY 10023
www.dreadedbroccoli.com

➢ This 12-page newsletter has a bit more gravitas and depth than either *Cook and Tell* or *Curmudgeon*. It offers a handful of recipes often accompanied by detailed notes about the ingredients, a column on nutrition (why organic produce, for example, is often no better for you than conventional vegetables), a timeline, and restaurant reviews. The Haspels, like their fellow newsletter editors Dan Goldberg and Karyl Bannister, begin each quarterly letter with a personal essay, but they stick closer to the subject of food, a plus if you prefer M.F.K. Fisher to a Hallmark card. The recipes were a mixed bag. The Indian Pudding curdled and the Peach Cake was bland and soupy on top. However, Mushroom Barley Ragout was top-notch, Lobster Salad was a keeper, and Winesicles were odd but good.

SIMPLE COOKING, John Thorne and Matt Lewis Thorne
$24/year, 6 issues; P.O. Box 778, Northampton, MA 01061
www.outlawcook.com

➢ John Thorne is an eclectic, serious food writer, one who is far beyond the world of church socials but still has at least one foot in Smalltown, USA. *Simple Cooking,* an 8-page bimonthly newsletter that he publishes with his wife, Matt Lewis Thorne, digs deep into its subject. More than half of a recent issue was devoted to satays, serving up history, terminology, cooking techniques, equipment, and, of course, recipes. The Thornes are more editors than

reporters, often quoting from books and using far-flung correspondents. They also include book reviews, letters from readers, essays on such food-related topics as grill cooks, and the occasional bit of food fiction. Their approach to food is intellectual, yet they marry their cerebral appetite with a well-fed lust for good food, which, as they would agree, makes them more food philosophers than scientists. (I have to admire anyone who prints a recipe for a bologna sandwich alongside one for homemade scallion pancakes.) The recipes tested ranged from a spectacular bagna cauda to a tasty chocolate/hazelnut torte with sketchy directions (except for the impractical instruction to whisk egg whites by hand for 15 minutes). A pasta dish with zucchini and sausage was very good, and an Israeli salad was perfect. One loser was a confusing recipe for eggs in tomato sauce.

THE ART OF EATING, Edward Behr
$36/year, 4 issues; P.O. Box 242, Peacham, VT 05862
www.artofeating.com

➢ Edward Behr is a culinary elitist, a term that he would wear without a hint of shame. He is an intrepid reporter and researcher, traveling around the world to seek out the truth about such culinary mysteries as "saison" beer in Belgium, sauternes, and Modena balsamic vinegar. This 32-page publication is less a newsletter than a travel magazine, replete with black-and-white photos taken by the author. What sets *The Art of Eating* apart from its fellow newsletters is Behr's relentless quest for the truth. He takes nothing at face value and trusts no one. Where *Cook and Tell* might run a quick and easy satay recipe and *Simple Cooking* presented a comprehensive compilation of terms, recipes, and techniques, Behr would go where the action is, tasting satays from street vendors in Jakarta. This singlemindedness applies to the construct of the issues as well; they are single-subject, covering narrow topics within wine, food, or travel. Behr also includes a lot of useful resource material. His notes on where to eat and what to buy are by themselves worth the price of the subscription. *The Art of Eating* is light on recipes, however; some issues may have only two or three. Of the six we tested, Bread and Zucchini Soup, Polenta with Pork and Cabbage, Potato Cakes, and Marinated Flank Steak were excellent, while a chicken roasted in butter and a traditional ragu left us wishing for clearer directions and something else for dinner.

RESOURCES

Most of the ingredients and materials necessary for the recipes in this issue are available at your local supermarket, gourmet store, or kitchen supply shop. The following are mail-order sources for particular items. Prices listed below were current at press time and do not include shipping or handling unless otherwise indicated. We suggest that you contact companies directly to confirm up-to-date prices and availability.

Chicken Tasting

For information on the availability of Empire chickens, go to the company's Web site at **www.empirekosher.com** and select Distribution by State. When you click your state, a list will pop up that includes all available stores, arranged by city, complete with addresses and phone numbers. Or call Empire at **800-233-7177.** The best way to find Bell & Evans chickens is to use the store locator service offered on the company Web site, **www.bellandevans.com.** Just supply your postal and e-mail address and the company will contact you with information on the nearest source. You can also call the company at **717-865-6626.**

Large Saucepan Testing

In our testing of large saucepans on page 28, we measured the performance of 3- to 4-quart saucepans by sautéing onions, steaming rice, and making pastry cream. The All-Clad Stainless Steel 3 Quart Saucepan came out on top. **Kitchen Etc. (32 Industrial Drive, Exeter, NH 03833; 800-232-4070; www.kitchenetc.com)** carries the pan, item #161871, for $139.99. Kitchen Etc. also carries the recommended Calphalon Commercial Hard-Anodized 3½ Quart Saucepan, item #586834, for $110.99. The KitchenAid Stainless Steel 3 Quart Covered Sauce Pan can be ordered from **A Cook's Wares (211 37th Street, Beaver Falls, PA 15010; 800-915-9788; www.cookswares.com),** item #KA103, for $119.

Molasses Spice Cookies

Molasses is the core flavor ingredient in the molasses spice cookies on page 25. Of the three different kinds of molasses that exist—light (sometimes called mild), dark (sometimes called full or robust), and blackstrap—our tasters preferred cookies made with light or dark, depending on their preference for mellow or intense molasses flavor. The choice is yours. We found the brands Grandma's and Brer Rabbit to be excellent choices. Both are available in supermarkets, although Brer Rabbit is not as widely available. You can purchase 24-ounce jars of Brer Rabbit Molasses, dark or light, from **Rafal Spice Company (2521 Russell Street, Detroit, MI 48207; 800-228-4276),** item #441314 (dark) and #431318 (light), for $5.99 each.

Spring Rolls

Southeast Asian–Style Spring Rolls (page 7) are easy to make at home, and, given the many ethnic markets in cities nationwide, rounding up the ingredients shouldn't be too difficult. If need be, however, rice paper rounds and rice vermicelli can be mail-ordered.

A 12-ounce pack of 8-inch Rice Paper Rounds, item #TVTI540, is $3.95 from **Adriana's Caravan (321 Grand Central Terminal, New York, NY 10017; 800-316-0820; www.adrianascaravan.com).** When shopping for the rice vermicelli, make sure you don't pick up thin cellophane noodles (also labeled "vermicelli") made from mung beans. In our tests, cellophane noodles cooked up gummy and rubbery. The rice variety is the right choice for this recipe; though soft, they have a bit of a bite. You can order a 16-ounce package of dried rice vermicelli from **Thai Grocer (2961 North Sheridan Road, Chicago, IL 60657; 773-988-8424; www.thaigrocer.com),** item #ND0104, for $1.39.

Chicken Vesuvio

If you are a garlic lover, the recipe for Chicken Vesuvio on page 9 will be right up your alley. The recipe calls for a full head of garlic, minced in a manner of your choice. Garlic passed through a press is the most intense—the garlic for the true garlic lover. Our favorite press is the Zyliss Susi DeLuxe. If you can't find one in your favorite kitchen store, order it from **Cook's Corner (836 South 8th Street, Manitowoc, WI 54220; 800-236-2433; www.cookscorner.com),** item #12018, for $14.99.

Oil splatters are a concern when the chicken and potatoes for chicken Vesuvio are browned. You can minimize the mess by drying the chicken pieces thoroughly, as directed (excess moisture will cause the hot oil to splatter). Putting a screen over the Dutch oven to contain the splatters is also a good idea. This way your stovetop will need less attention at the end of the day. You can order a large, 13-inch splatter screen, item #321583, from **Kitchen Etc.** for $3.99.

Pâte à Choux

The best tool to use when stirring hot pâte à choux is a heatproof spatula. It is in no danger of melting, and it is the perfect shape to achieve the smearing motion called for in the recipe instructions. In a test of spatulas conducted for our Web site, the winner was the Williams-Sonoma large Clear Silicone Spatula. You can find it in stores or order it from **Williams-Sonoma (P.O. Box 7456, San Francisco, CA, 94120-7456; 800-541-2233; www.williams-sonoma.com),** item #2210680, for $9. When piping the choux puffs, we like to use a 14-inch pastry bag fitted with a ½-inch tip. **Kitchen Krafts (P.O. Box 442, Waukon, IA 52172-0442; 800-776-0575)** sells a 14-inch pastry bag, item #CD0014, for $3.30. The bag is made of a superpliable nylon fabric that is coated inside with polyurethane to prevent leaking. The pastry bag is easy to handle and to clean; just wash it in hot water and dry. Kitchen Krafts also sells the ½-inch plain pastry tube (or tip) we use in piping, item #DT0806, for $1.45.

United States Postal Service

Statement of Ownership, Management, and Circulation

1. Publication Title	2. Publication Number	3. Filing Date
Cook's Illustrated	1068-2821	10/1/01
4. Issue Frequency	5. Number of Issues Published Annually	6. Annual Subscription Price
Bi-Monthly	6	$29.70

7. Complete Mailing Address of Known Office of Publication (Not printer) (Street, city, county, state, and ZIP+4)
Boston Common Press
17 Station Street, Brookline, MA 02445
Contact Person
Telephone 617-232-1000

8. Complete Mailing Address of Headquarters or General Business Office of Publisher (Not printer)
Same as above.

9. Full Names and Complete Mailing Addresses of Publisher, Editor, and Managing Editor (Do not leave blank)
Publisher (Name and complete mailing address)
Christopher Kimball, Boston Common Press
17 Station Street, Brookline, MA 02445
Editor (Name and complete mailing address)
Same as publisher.
Managing Editor (Name and complete mailing address)
Barbara Bourassa, Boston Common Press
17 Station Street, Brookline, MA 02445

10. Owner (Do not leave blank. If the publication is owned by a corporation, give the name and address of the corporation immediately followed by the names and addresses of all stockholders owning or holding 1 percent or more of the total amount of stock. If not owned by a corporation, give the names and addresses of the individual owners. If owned by a partnership or other unincorporated firm, give its name and address as well as those of each individual owner. If the publication is published by a nonprofit organization, give its name and address.)

Full Name	Complete Mailing Address
Boston Common Press	17 Station Street
Limited Partnership	Brookline, MA 02445
(Christopher Kimball)	

11. Known Bondholders, Mortgagees, and Other Security Holders Owning or Holding 1 Percent or More of Total Amount of Bonds, Mortgages, or Other Securities. If none, check box ▶ ☐ None

Full Name	Complete Mailing Address
N/A	

12. Tax Status (For completion by nonprofit organizations authorized to mail at nonprofit rates) (Check one)
The purpose, function, and nonprofit status of this organization and the exempt status for federal income tax purposes:
☐ Has Not Changed During Preceding 12 Months
☐ Has Changed During Preceding 12 Months (Publisher must submit explanation of change with this statement)

PS Form 3526, October 1999 (See Instructions on Reverse)

13. Publication Title: Cook's Illustrated
14. Issue Date for Circulation Data Below: September/October 2001

15. Extent and Nature of Circulation		Average No. Copies Each Issue During Preceding 12 Months	No. Copies of Single Issue Published Nearest to Filing Date
a. Total Number of Copies (Net press run)		526,539	548,930
b. Paid and/or Requested Circulation	(1) Paid/Requested Outside-County Mail Subscriptions Stated on Form 3541. (Include advertiser's proof and exchange copies)	401,039	418,811
	(2) Paid In-County Subscriptions Stated on Form 3541 (Include advertiser's proof and exchange copies)	0	0
	(3) Sales Through Dealers and Carriers, Street Vendors, Counter Sales, and Other Non-USPS Paid Distribution	60,021	62,000
	(4) Other Classes Mailed Through the USPS	0	0
c. Total Paid and/or Requested Circulation [Sum of 15b. (1), (2),(3),and (4)] ▶		461,061	480,811
d. Free Distribution by Mail (Samples, compliment ary, and other free)	(1) Outside-County as Stated on Form 3541	3,286	3,036
	(2) In-County as Stated on Form 3541	0	0
	(3) Other Classes Mailed Through the USPS	0	0
e. Free Distribution Outside the Mail (Carriers or other means)		688	590
f. Total Free Distribution (Sum of 15d. and 15e.) ▶		3,974	3,626
g. Total Distribution (Sum of 15c. and 15f) ▶		465,035	484,437
h. Copies not Distributed		61,504	64,493
i. Total (Sum of 15g. and h.) ▶		526,539	548,930
j. Percent Paid and/or Requested Circulation (15c. divided by 15g. times 100)		99.1%	99.3%

16. Publication of Statement of Ownership
☐ Publication required. Will be printed in the Jan/Feb 2002 issue of this publication. ☐ Publication not required.

17. Signature and Title of Editor, Publisher, Business Manager, or Owner
Date 10/1/01

I certify that all information furnished on this form is true and complete. I understand that anyone who furnishes false or misleading information on this form or who omits material or information requested on the form may be subject to criminal sanctions (including fines and imprisonment) and/or civil sanctions (including civil penalties).

Instructions to Publishers

1. Complete and file one copy of this form with your postmaster annually on or before October 1. Keep a copy of the completed form for your records.
2. In cases where the stockholder or security holder is a trustee, include in items 10 and 11 the name of the person or corporation for whom the trustee is acting. Also include the names and addresses of individuals who are stockholders who own or hold 1 percent or more of the total amount of bonds, mortgages, or other securities of the publishing corporation. In item 11, if none, check the box. Use blank sheets if more space is required.
3. Be sure to furnish all circulation information called for in item 15. Free circulation must be shown in items 15d, e, and f.
4. Item 15h., Copies not Distributed, must include (1) newsstand copies originally stated on Form 3541, and returned to the publisher, (2) estimated returns from news agents, and (3), copies for office use, leftovers, spoiled, and all other copies not distributed.
5. If the publication had Periodicals authorization as a general or requester publication, this Statement of Ownership, Management, and Circulation must be published; it must be printed in any issue in October or, if the publication is not published during October, the first issue printed after October.
6. In item 16, indicate the date of the issue in which this Statement of Ownership will be published.
7. Item 17 must be signed.

Failure to file or publish a statement of ownership may lead to suspension of Periodicals authorization.

PS Form 3526, October 1999 (Reverse)

RECIPES
January & February 2002

Beef Stroganoff

Crisp Breaded Pork Cutlet Sandwich

Southeast Asian–Style Spring Rolls

Caramelized Onions atop Focaccia

Chicken Vesuvio

PHOTOGRAPHY: CARL TREMBLAY

http://www.cooksillustrated.com

If you enjoy *Cook's Illustrated* magazine, you should visit our Web site. Simply log on at http://www.cooksillustrated.com. Although much of the information is free, database searches are for site subscribers only. *Cook's Illustrated* subscribers are offered a 20 percent discount.

Here are some of the things you can do on our site:

Search Our Recipes: We have a searchable database of all the recipes from *Cook's Illustrated*.

Search Tastings and Cookware Ratings: You will find all of our reviews (cookware, food, wine, cookbooks) plus new material created exclusively for the Web site.

Find Your Favorite Quick Tips.

Check Your Subscription: Check the status of your subscription, pay a bill, or give gift subscriptions online.

Visit Our Bookstore: You can purchase any of our cookbooks, hardbound annual editions of the magazine, or posters online.

Subscribe to *e-Notes*: Our free e-mail companion to the magazine offers cooking advice, test results, buying tips, and recipes about a single topic each month.

AMERICA'S TEST KITCHEN

Join the legions of cooks who watch our show, *America's Test Kitchen*, on public television each week. For more information, including recipes from the show and a schedule of program times in your area, visit http://www.americastestkitchen.com.

Braised Belgian Endive

Pasta and Red Pepper Tuna Sauce

Molasses Spice Cookies with Orange Essence

Profiteroles

Piron

Roquefort Papillon

Stilton

Gorgonzola Dolce

Fourme d'Ambert

Bleu de Termignon

Maytag Blue

Cabrales

Shropshire Blue

Bleu de Basques

Bleu de Gex

Gorgonzola Naturale

BLUE CHEESES

NUMBER FIFTY-FIVE

MARCH & APRIL 2002

Home of **AMERICA'S TEST KITCHEN**

COOK'S
ILLUSTRATED

New York–Style
Cheesecake

Perfect Pot Roast
The Secret to Fork-Tender Meat

Spaghetti Puttanesca
In Just 11 Minutes

Chicken Paprikash
Which Paprika Is Best?

Rating Supermarket
Cheddars
Does Price Matter?

Testing Oven
Thermometers
Why Every Oven Needs One

Lemon Pound Cake
Made Easy

Blue-Ribbon Cheddar Soup
Pan-Roasting Halibut
Wilted Spinach Salads
Best Cauliflower Gratin

www.cooksillustrated.com

$4.95 U.S./$6.95 CANADA

CONTENTS
March & April 2002

COOK'S
ILLUSTRATED
Home of America's Test Kitchen
www.cooksillustrated.com

PUBLISHER AND EDITOR
Christopher Kimball

SENIOR EDITOR
Jack Bishop

MANAGING EDITOR
Dawn Yanagihara

SENIOR WRITER
Adam Ried

EDITORIAL MANAGER
Barbara Bourassa

ART DIRECTOR
Amy Klee

TEST KITCHEN DIRECTOR
Bridget Lancaster

ASSISTANT TEST KITCHEN DIRECTOR
Erin McMurrer

ASSOCIATE EDITORS
Raquel Pelzel
Julia Collin

COPY EDITOR
India Koopman

MANAGING EDITOR,
BOOKS AND WEB SITE
Rebecca Hays

TEST COOKS
Shannon Blaisdell
Matthew Card
Meg Suzuki

CONSULTING EDITORS
Shirley Corriher
Elizabeth Germain
Jasper White
Robert L. Wolke

TEST KITCHEN INTERN
Merrill Stubbs

ASSISTANT TO THE PUBLISHER
Sumantha Selvakumar

PROOFREADER
Jana Branch

VICE PRESIDENT MARKETING
David Mack

RETAIL SALES MANAGER
Jason Geller

CIRCULATION RETAIL SALES MANAGER
Jonathan Venier

MARKETING ASSISTANT
Connie Forbes

CIRCULATION MANAGER
Larisa Greiner

PRODUCTS MANAGER
Steven Browall

DIRECT MAIL MANAGER
Robert Lee

CUSTOMER SERVICE MANAGER
Jacqueline Valerio

INBOUND MARKETING REPRESENTATIVE
Adam Dardeck

VICE PRESIDENT OPERATIONS
AND TECHNOLOGY
James McCormack

PRODUCTION MANAGER
Jessica Quirk

PRODUCTION COORDINATOR
Mary Connelly

PRODUCTION ASSISTANTS
Ron Bilodeau
Jennifer McCreary

SYSTEMS ADMINISTRATOR
Richard Cassidy

WEBMASTER
Nicole Morris

CHIEF FINANCIAL OFFICER
Sharyn Chabot

CONTROLLER
Mandy Shito

OFFICE MANAGER
Juliet Nusbaum

RECEPTIONIST
Henrietta Murray

PUBLICITY
Deborah Broide

For list rental information, contact The SpeciaLISTS, 1200
Harbor Blvd, 9th Floor, Weehawken, NJ 07087; 201-865-
5800; fax 201-867-2450. Editorial office: 17 Station Street,
Brookline, MA 02445; 617-232-1000; fax 617-232-1572.
Editorial contributions should be sent to: Editor, *Cook's
Illustrated*. We cannot assume responsibility for manuscripts
submitted to us. Submissions will be returned only if accompanied by a large self-addressed envelope. Postmaster: Send all
new orders, subscription inquiries, and change of address
notices to: *Cook's Illustrated*, P.O. Box 7446, Red Oak, IA
51591-0446. PRINTED IN THE USA.

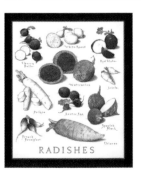

RADISHES

RADISHES Cruciferous plants related to turnips and horseradish, radishes can be divided into two main categories: spring (Red Globe, Watermelon, Icicle, French Breakfast, Easter Egg, Cherry Belle, White Round) and winter (Daikon, Chinese, Spanish Black). As their seasonal groupings suggest, spring radishes are harvested young and are therefore small, while winter radishes are gathered later in the season and can grow to a size of 2 feet or more. The common Red Globe radish has a notably peppery flavor and is most often used in salads or as a garnish. Specialty varieties of spring radishes, such as French Breakfast and Icicle, have a delicate, mild bite and are best eaten in salads or enjoyed in the French style—slathered in butter, sprinkled with salt, and sandwiched in crusty bread. Daikon radishes usually appear alongside sushi in long, crisp ribbons. Chinese radishes are pickled, stir-fried, or used in decorative carvings. Spanish Black radishes are robust and taste best sautéed or braised.

COVER (*Ramps*): ELIZABETH BRANDON, BACK COVER (*Radishes*): JOHN BURGOYNE

THE HORSE WHISPERER

Last summer, my wife and I set out to purchase a couple of older horses, the type that won't shy at a barking dog, crow-hop at the sound of a gunshot, or sit their rear end in a ditch because they're lazy. Vermonters, always free with conflicting advice, told us how to inspect the hocks, keep an eye out for strangles (a common infection), listen for respiratory ills, and check the teeth to guess the age, a technique that is akin to inspecting wooly bears to predict the severity of winter. In short, we were easy marks for any half-decent horse trader.

There is a man called Harry O'Rourke, Jr., whose family owns Pond Hill Ranch in Castleton, Vt. He has more than 500 horses there in the winter on 3,000 acres, the ranch having been cobbled together by his grandfather during the Great Depression. Harry runs rodeos in the summer, selling hot dogs and sodas to the pickup crowd. (My favorite pickup bumper sticker: "Possum—The other white meat.") The crowd looks on as cowboys barrel-race, rope steers, and ride bucking broncos for a share of the modest prize money. Predictable, perhaps, but nonetheless this mix of rugged individualism and Americana quickly overshadows any thoughts of white-collar sophistication. At rodeos, you laugh at the clown, never at the cowboys.

Horse traders have a poor but well-deserved reputation (drugging wild horses to calm them during a sale is not uncommon), but I'd heard good things about Harry. He is middle-aged, with time having settled kindly into his face, as if he knows how to turn the years to his advantage, daring them to make something of it. He walks bow-legged, like a determined retriever headed toward

a half-gnawed bone. Like any seasoned farmer or horseman, he doesn't waste energy. He speaks plainly, without elaboration, and somehow gets to the point without ever being direct. Harry buys his horses through auctions out West, the sort that feature animals trail-ridden by city-slicker buckaroos at dude ranches in Montana and Wyoming. He leases most of them out in the summer to riding stables in New England but also sells horses when he can for extra cash.

Now a horse whisperer is a man or woman who talks to horses. They've been known to break a wild horse in under an hour. Their secret is listening. They know that each animal is different, and by looking a horse in the eye, they can sense what a horse wants and fears. Harry is no official whisperer, but watching him around a horse is like watching an old married couple do chores together: They never get in each other's way.

One Saturday in early August, we drove up to Pond Hill to test-drive some of the stock. It was a hot day, and Pond Hill was dusty owing to a long-standing drought. While our four kids drank grape sodas and played under the only shade tree in sight, my wife and I rode quarter horses, palominos, and an assorted bunch of breeds in between. Both my rear end and my pride were damaged (one pony got the better of me, and we ended up in the barn instead of on the trail), and what had been intended as a quick visit started to turn into an all-day affair. It was

Christopher Kimball

hot, the watering hole was covered in green muck, the manure was thick on the ground, the flies were fierce, and by midafternoon the children were restless, picking fights and chucking rocks. Waves of brightly plumed tourists came and went for their one-hour trail rides, sitting upright on their mounts like bankers on tractors. We finally settled on a chestnut and an appaloosa, and Harry and I walked over to his office to do the paperwork.

A few minutes later, I came out to discover that the family van was locked, thanks to Caroline, my 11-year-old, and the keys were inside. Well, after six hours in the sun I was thirsty, tired, and done in, so I gave her a good tongue-lashing in full view of a bench full of cowboys. Harry walked over, looked me in the eye, smiled, and said he'd call for the gas station guy to come up and slip the lock. He handed out hard candy to each of the kids and then invited us all back to the office for a cold soda. The kids tamely played with the dog, my wife and I took a chair, and Harry spun a few stories about horse trading. The time passed quickly, and, soon enough, the car was fixed, the kids were asleep on the back seat, and we were on our way home.

I was thinking about how well Harry handled horses, wondering if he could be a real horse whisperer. I turned to my wife and said, "Harry sure does know a lot about horses." She looked at me curiously, laughed to herself, and replied, "Yeah, and a fair amount about people, too."

FOR MORE INFORMATION

www.cooksillustrated.com

At the *Cook's Illustrated* Web site you can order a book, give a gift subscription to *Cook's Illustrated* magazine, sign up for our free e-newsletter, subscribe to the magazine, or check the status of your subscription. Join the Web site and you'll have access to our searchable databases of recipes, cookware ratings, ingredient tastings, quick tips, cookbook reviews, and more.

The Web site also features free recipes, techniques, and answers to cooking questions; original editorial material not found in the magazine; a question-and-answer message board; and a list of upcoming appearances by editor and publisher Christopher Kimball.

Have questions about your subscription? Visit our customer service page, where you can change your address, renew your subscription, pay your bill, or read answers to frequently asked questions.

COOK'S ILLUSTRATED Magazine

Cook's Illustrated (ISSN 1068-2821) magazine is published bimonthly (6 issues per year) by Boston Common Press Limited Partnership, 17 Station Street, Brookline, MA 02445. Copyright 2002 Boston Common Press Limited Partnership. Periodical postage paid at Boston, Mass., and additional mailing offices, USPS #012487.

A one-year subscription is $29.70, two years is $55, and three years is $75. Add $6 postage per year for Canadian subscriptions and $12 per year for all other countries outside the U.S. To order subscriptions in the U.S. call 800-526-8442; from outside the U.S. call 515-247-7571. Gift subscriptions are available for $24.95 each. Postmaster: Send all new orders, subscription inquiries, and change-of-address notices to Cook's Illustrated, P.O. Box 7446, Red Oak, IA 51591-0446, or call 800-526-8442 inside the U.S.; from outside the U.S. call 515-247-7571.

COOKBOOKS

The following books, as well as *The America's Test Kitchen Cookbook*, are available by calling 800-611-0759 inside the U.S. or 515-246-6911 from outside the U.S.

➤ **The Best Recipe Series** Includes *The Best Recipe* as well as *The Best Recipe: Grilling & Barbecue* and *The Best Recipe: Soups & Stews.*

➤ **The How to Cook Master Series** A collection of 25 single-subject cookbooks covering topics such as quick appetizers, simple fruit desserts, and sauces.

➤ **The Annual Series** Annual hardbound editions of the magazine as well as a nine-year (1993–2001) reference index.

AMERICA'S TEST KITCHEN Television Series

Look for our television series on public television. For program times in your area, recipes, and details about the shows, or to order the companion book to the 2002 series, *The America's Test Kitchen Cookbook*, visit http://www.americastestkitchen.com.

Chasing Rainbows

A couple of my pots and pans have splotches of rainbow-like discoloration that I can't seem to remove no matter how hard I scrub. What causes the discoloration? Is there any way to get rid of it? If not, should I continue to cook with these pans?

VAL DELL
CORNING, N.Y.

➤ While some sources we checked suggest that rainbowing is the result of minerals left behind by hard water or simply a bad job of dishwashing, Hugh Rushing, executive vice president of the Cookware Manufacturers Association in Mountain Brook, Ala., said the most likely cause is heat. Rainbowing, also known as heat tint or heat mottling, can occur in stainless steel cookware when it is heated to a temperature above 500 degrees, a situation that might arise, for example, when a pan is left sitting empty on a burner for too long. Most stovetop cooking takes place between temperatures of 300 and 400 degrees.

What is it about stainless steel that causes it to rainbow? Stainless steel cookware acquires the valuable properties we associate with it—shine, strength, resistance to corrosion—by virtue of the chromium and nickel added to the steel (or iron) during processing. (Better-quality cookware is often labeled "18/10 stainless." This indicates a chromium content of 18 percent and a nickel content of 10 percent.) The element likely reacting to the intense heat to produce rainbowing, says Rushing, is chromium, a metal whose name, coincidentally enough, is derived from *chroma*, the Greek word for color.

To see whether and how rainbowing might be removed from a pan, we talked to Chris Sommer, a consumer service representative at cookware manufacturer All-Clad. Sommer told us that rainbowing can be removed, even though its presence in a pot or pan won't interfere with cooking, and that All-Clad recommends two products: Bar Keepers Friend, a powdered cleanser available in supermarkets, and Chef's Stainless Steel Liquid Cleaner, available only through catalog and Web retailer Chef's Catalog. We picked up two more brands of cleanser—Cameo and Bon Ami—at the supermarket and also decided to try a couple of home remedies we'd heard of: vinegar and a rub with kosher salt and lemon juice.

We found a few mildly rainbowed pans in the test kitchen, and each of the four commercial cleansers did a good job of cleaning them. Neither the vinegar nor the salt/lemon rub did a whit of good. Looking for a more challenging case, we turned to associate editor Julia Collin, who had for some time been complaining of two heat-damaged pans she had at home. The interior of one, a large braisier, was thoroughly rainbowed. We again applied our six treatments and came up with the same results as above; only the home remedies failed to work. The real challenge, however, was a small saucepan that had been discolored well beyond rainbowing. Julia had on two occasions put water on to boil in the pan and forgot about it. Each time the pan boiled dry and proceeded to develop a coppery/brownish tint that repeated scrubbing had failed to remove. Again the home remedies failed, but this time one of the four commercial contenders fell out, too. After being rubbed as directed on a different spot on the bottom of the pan for 30 seconds, Cameo, the Chef's cleanser, and Bar Keepers Friend worked their way through the tainted surface to reveal the shiny stainless steel below. Bon Ami failed to make any progress.

Which cleanser do we recommend? While Cameo, Bar Keepers Friend, and the Chef's liquid cleaner all performed well, the first two are more easily found and, at prices of $1.29 for 10 ounces and $2.19 for 12 ounces, respectively, are a better buy. A 12-ounce container of Chef's Stainless Steel Liquid Cleaner can be purchased at www.chefscatalog.com for $5.99.

The Short of It

Once or twice I've seen the word *short* used in articles on baking, as in adding "shortness" to pastry. Can you tell me what this means?

CAROLYN CASAGRANDE
MONTPELIER, VT.

➤ Bakers must be nothing if not precise, and so it should come as no surprise that they have a term reserved for a particularly important aspect of pastry: its tenderness. When bakers talk about shortening a pastry, they're essentially talking about increasing its tenderness, making it more crumbly. A shortbread cookie is a perfect example of shortness; it is so tender, so crumbly, so short that it nearly melts in your mouth.

To find out how the term *short* entered the baker's vocabulary, we turned to Ben Fortson, senior lexicographer at the Boston-based *American Heritage Dictionary*. He told us that one of the original meanings of *short* was "friable," as in easily crumbled or crushed into powder. The first documented use of *short* as applied to baking was in a cookbook in England around 1430, Fortson said, while the term *shortening* as we know it in baking first appeared in America in 1796. Yet another, certainly less pleasant (though no less useful) application of *short* in this sense of crumbly or friable showed up in England in 1618, when farmers were in the habit of adding straw to manure to make it break up more easily when used as a fertilizer. They called their creation short manure or short muck.

Powdered versus "Real" Buttermilk

What do you know about powdered buttermilk? I'm curious to try it in place of real buttermilk in baking because I find that whenever I bring home a quart from the dairy case, I end up using a cup or so and then letting the rest sit in my refrigerator until it spoils.

GRETA HENRY
SWAMPSCOTT, MASS.

➤ Powdered buttermilk is a staple of commercial baking, but your question prompted us to see what's out there for consumers. What we found is a product called Buttermilk Blend, manufactured by Saco Foods of Middleton, Wis. Your question, as well as Saco's description of its product, also caused us to consider what is the closest thing to "real" buttermilk these days.

As explained in Notes from Readers in the July/August 2001 issue of *Cook's*, the buttermilk found in the dairy case today is not your grandmother's buttermilk, a tangy, watery substance left over once cream had been churned into butter. The liquid buttermilk available today is made more after the fashion of yogurt, in which harmless bacteria are added to milk to break down the milk sugar (lactose) and in the process create lactic acid, which thickens the milk and helps to produce a tangy flavor. According to information on Saco's Web site (www.sacofoods.com), its powdered buttermilk is made from the byproduct of butter-making at nearby dairies—basically, your grandmother's buttermilk minus the water. Eager to see if we preferred one of these products over the other—and how the usual stand-in for buttermilk, soured milk, would fare—we baked up three batches of biscuits and three chocolate cakes and held a blind tasting.

Tasters generally found the powdered-buttermilk and soured-milk biscuits to be lighter and fluffier than the liquid buttermilk biscuits, and several tasters preferred the flavor of the biscuits made with soured milk (soured by adding 1 tablespoon white vinegar to 1 cup whole milk), describing them as "more buttery." Nonetheless, each batch of biscuits was palatable. All three batches had a pleasingly tender texture, and they all browned and rose nicely.

When it came to chocolate cake, tasters found

the powdered-buttermilk cake to have the fluffi-est, most even texture and the most mellow flavor. Tasters detected a slightly sour tang in the cake made with liquid buttermilk, and they actually preferred this fuller flavor. The soured-milk cake was liked least of all, with several tasters finding it flat-tasting and overly moist. Still, these differences were small in scale. As one taster said of the three cakes, "I wouldn't refuse any of them."

All in all, do we recommend Saco's Buttermilk Blend as a replacement for liquid cultured buttermilk in baking? Yes. It's easy to use (the powder is added to the recipe along with the dry ingredients, and water is added when the liquid buttermilk is called for). It has a longer shelf life than liquid buttermilk (one year refrigerated after opening, as opposed to about one month). And it's also cheaper when purchased in a 16-ounce container (which gives you the equivalent of 5 quarts of liquid buttermilk for $3.29; the product is also available in 3.2-ounce boxes of four packets, the equivalent of a liquid quart, for $1.29, about the same price as a quart of buttermilk from the dairy case). Then again, in a pinch, a cup of milk and a tablespoon of vinegar don't do such a bad job either.

Plastic Wrap in the Microwave

I've noticed that some plastic wraps claim to be formulated for use in the microwave, some for wrapping and storing food. What's the difference?

JEREMIAH WHITTEN
MINNEAPOLIS, MINN.

➤ Concerns that plasticizers, softening agents added to some plastic wraps to promote clingability, migrate to some foods when exposed to heat have contributed to the development of wraps formulated for use in the microwave. To see what we could observe in terms of differences in performance in wraps advertised as suitable for the microwave and wraps advertised as suitable for wrapping and storing food (that is, promoting clingability), we purchased six different wraps at the grocery store and put them through a couple of simple tests. In one test, we melted in the microwave 4 tablespoons of butter placed in a small bowl and covered with plastic wrap. In another test, we placed a bunch of grapes in a bowl, covered the bowl with wrap, and turned it upside down to see if the wrap remained in place.

Two types of Saran Wrap are on the market, Saran Original (formerly called Saran Classic), which is intended for microwave use, and Saran Cling Plus (formerly Handi-Wrap), which is largely intended for storing prepared food and leftovers but, according to instructions on the box, is also microwave-safe. Of all the wraps tested, Saran Original was the sturdiest. It is heavier, tougher, and stiffer than the other five wraps tested. It held up very well in the microwave and, as might be expected based on

WHAT IS IT?

My mother used this "ovenette" to bake potatoes when I was growing up in the 1950s. Can you tell me anything about it? Does it have other purposes?

CAROL VORHEES
DETROIT, MICH.

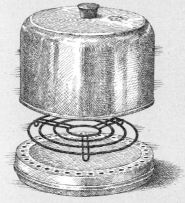

One of our editors recognized your ovenette right away, having also grown up with one, and went to her mother's house to see if it was still there. What she found tucked away in her mother's basement was an ovenette manufactured by West Bend, which continues to manufacture small home appliances from its headquarters in West Bend, Wis. West Bend still had a copy of the instructions it sent out with the ovenette years ago and was happy to fax us a copy.

The West Bend ovenette is about 6½ inches high and 10½ inches in diameter, large enough, we discovered, to bake four good-sized Idaho potatoes. But the ovenette was designed to do a lot more than bake potatoes. This simple piece of cookware, which has a thermometer built into the top of the cover, was meant to be used for all sorts of stovetop baking and roasting when the oven was otherwise occupied. The metal base of the ovenette sits on a stovetop burner, which can be adjusted as needed, to cook foods placed on a rack inside the main chamber. The instructions for the West Bend ovenette demonstrate its versatility, including recipes for a rolled rib roast, tuna-noodle casserole, cornmeal muffins, and apple pie. After our success with baked potatoes, we roasted some chicken legs (juicy on the inside, though the skin could have been crispier), baked some cornmeal muffins (which browned and domed perfectly and were moist and tender to boot), and even tried an apple pie (only here were the results truly disappointing; our pie was piled high with apples, and the moisture they released turned the ovenette into a steamer, so the crust failed to crisp and brown).

It turns out, then, that your mother's ovenette still might come in handy around the holidays or whenever there's a crowd coming for dinner and oven space is at a premium.

its recommended use, did not do well in the clingability test: The grapes fell out of the bowl. Saran Cling Plus passed the grapes-in-the-bowl test with flying colors, and it also held up in the microwave, showing no signs of melting.

Glad ClingWrap is advertised as a dual-purpose wrap, and we found that it was: It held up in the microwave and showed good cling (the grapes remained in the bowl).

Unlike the boxes for Saran Original and Glad Cling Wrap, the box for Reynolds Plastic Wrap makes no mention of its suitability for the microwave, but the company Web site does recommend it for microwave use. Reynolds Wrap passed the grapes-in-the-bowl test, but it showed slight signs of melting in the microwave.

The final two wraps tested were a grocery store brand, one recommended for wrapping and storing leftovers, the other for the microwave. Both passed the grapes-in-the-bowl test, but, oddly, the wrap supposedly formulated for the microwave showed signs of melting, whereas the other did not.

Government scientists have done preliminary testing of several brands of plastic wrap for the migration of softening agents to food. While as a matter of policy they will not disclose the brands tested, one researcher did say that "for the plastics we tested, whenever they were advertised for microwave use, they caused less migration." He also cautioned against the use of cheap

"off" brands (like the supermarket brand we tested), as they generally showed the most migration. The results of the government tests also concur with other sources stating that fatty foods heated in the microwave are most susceptible to migration, especially if the wrap is in direct contact with the food. To minimize migration, leave an inch of space between the food and the wrap and leave a corner of the wrap open to allow steam to escape.

Which wrap should you buy? If you want to keep just one wrap in your kitchen, Glad ClingWrap or Saran Cling Plus are your best choices based on our tests. If microwave performance (without clingability) is your top concern, Saran Original was the sturdiest wrap tested.

Where to Find DaVinci Olive Oil

➤ Several readers have written in to say they've had trouble tracking down DaVinci Extra Virgin Olive Oil, the most highly rated brand sampled in the olive oil tasting we conducted for the March/April 2001 issue. DaVinci can be purchased online at www.efoodpantries.com. Click Specialty Food Pantry, then go to the Imported Italian Products category and click the link for DaVinci products. A 17-ounce bottle of DaVinci's Extra Virgin Olive oil is available for $3.75, plus $4.94 for shipping. The cost of shipping relative to the price of the oil goes down as you order more bottles.

Quick Tips

Cutting Hard Cheese Safely

Sometimes it's handy to cut a smaller piece from a large chunk of hard cheese, as when, for instance, you want to pass cheese to grate over pasta or risotto at the table. Because hard cheese is difficult to cut through, many cooks often place one hand over the top of their chef's knife blade and the other over the handle to put their weight into the cut. When using this technique, Ashley Robinson of Brighton, Mass., adds an extra measure of safety and comfort by putting a folded dish towel between her hand and the blade.

Easy-Reach Kitchen Tools

Many cooks keep measuring cups and spoons in a drawer, where they can get buried deep among other utensils. Patricia Ryan Madson of El Granada, Calif., has a way to keep these small items within easy reach. She mounted a simple hardware store key holder near her work space and, instead of using it to safeguard keys, hangs measuring spoons and cups from it.

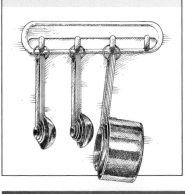

Stabilizing Coffee Filters

When using a manual drip coffee maker, the grounds can spill down into the pot because the paper filter folds over on itself when the water is poured into it. To avoid this problem, Carol Green-Bovest of Boxford, Mass., barely dampens the paper filter and presses it against the sides of the plastic cone. When she adds the coffee and pours the water through, the filter adheres to the cone.

Double Duty for Pot Lids

Most stews start with browning the protein component, which is then removed from the pan so other ingredients can be browned, and is added back later to finish cooking with the cover in place. When she makes a stew, Bobbie Love of Kapaa, Hawaii, uses the following shortcut to avoid dirtying extra dishes. Instead of transferring the browned meat to a bowl, invert the lid of the pan in which you're cooking over a bowl or another pot. The lid, which you would have to wash anyway, now serves as both a spoon rest and receptacle for the sautéed food.

Plastic Produce Bag Storage

Many home kitchens sport a drawer filled to the gills with crumpled plastic produce bags. Determined to reclaim her drawer, Susan Denton of Kelowna, British Columbia, fashioned a new system for storing plastic bags by stuffing them into an empty tissue box. A box will accommodate many, many bags, which are then easy to remove one at a time when the need arises.

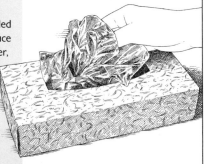

Disposing of Oil Neatly

Deep-fried foods are a real treat, but cleaning up after frying is not. Disposing of the spent oil neatly and safely is a particular challenge, which Edythe Cardon of Bethesda, Md., has met by using the following method. Make a quadruple- or quintuple-layered bag using four or five leftover plastic grocery bags. With someone holding the bag open over a sink or in an outdoor area, carefully pour the cooled frying oil from the pot into the innermost bag. Tie the bag handles shut before disposing of the oil.

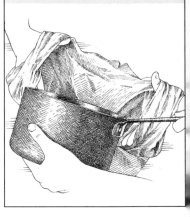

Grip for Instant-Read Thermometer

The sheathes that house many instant-read thermometers are designed for use as holders so that cooks can keep their hands safely away from hot liquids when measuring their temperatures. But if you are like us, it's not long before the sheath disappears into the kitchen junk drawer, never to be seen again. In the absence of a sheath, Nancy Sorrells of Great Falls, Va., has developed an alternative thermometer holder. Insert the thermometer through one hole of a slotted cooking spoon, then simply hold onto the spoon handle to dip the thermometer tip into the liquid.

Send Us Your Tip We will provide a complimentary one-year subscription for each tip we print. Send your tip, name, address, and daytime telephone number to Quick Tips, Cook's Illustrated, P.O. Box 470589, Brookline, MA 02447.

Cooking Instructions Always at the Ready

Many thrifty cooks save money by purchasing staple ingredients in bulk. As she transferred her bulk-purchased foods into storage containers, Cheryl Vanni of Eugene, Ore., had an idea that would make it easier for the younger and less experienced cooks in her household to prepare these foods. While packaging items such as rice, polenta, or pancake mix, write instructions for preparing that food on a mailing label and stick it to the container. Cheryl, for instance, can now ask her son to make the rice for dinner, knowing the instructions are right there.

Thin Slicing Simplified

Many recipes call for thinly slicing a boneless cut of meat, such as a chicken or pork cutlet. Of course, fresh meat can be slippery and hard to grasp, which can make cutting thin slices a challenge. To make the job a little easier, follow this advice from Tom Ryan of Elgin, Ill., and Ann Bever of Dallas, Texas. Place the meat in the freezer for about 20 minutes. The meat will firm up but not freeze, making it easier to slice or trim. Alternatively, if the meat has already been frozen solid, slice or trim it before it has thawed completely.

Guaranteed Chill for Gibsons

In *Cook's* January/February 2001 recipe for Beef Burgundy, we suggest substituting frozen pearl onions for fresh to garnish the stew. In the midst of preparing the frozen onions, Lee Bernstein of Oakland, Calif., thought of another excellent way to put frozen onions to use. Garnish a Gibson (a martini garnished with onions instead of olives) with two frozen onions instead of the traditional pickled onions. The frozen onions help keep the cocktail chilled while also imparting the ideal essence of onion.

Stabilizing Stuffed Peppers

The *Cook's* March/April 2001 article on stuffed peppers inspired several readers to share their methods for dealing with a common problem: how to keep the peppers upright in the pan as they cook. In addition to the two tips listed in the September/October 2001 Quick Tips, Michael Kaloyanides of Bethany, Conn., Julia White of Savannah, Ga., and Veronica Johnson of Seattle, Wash., offered the following methods.

A. Season thick wedges of potato with olive oil, salt, and ground black pepper and place them with one cut side down next to the peppers to prop them up. By gently tucking the tip of a potato wedge between the bottom of a pepper and the pan, you provide the peppers with extra support—and you get crisp roasted potatoes out of the deal as well.

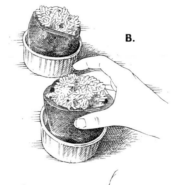

B. Place each pepper in an individual ovenproof custard cup. This is also a great system when you want to cook only a couple of peppers, instead of a whole batch.

C. Reserve the tops of the peppers, which you have cut off to open the peppers for stuffing, and insert them between the stuffed peppers in the pan for added stability.

Elevating a Measuring Cup

Resting a liquid measuring cup with its contents on a flat surface is essential to obtaining an accurate measurement. To avoid having to crouch down to read the measurement from a cup sitting on a countertop or table, try this tip from Laurie Latour of Jacksonville Beach, Fla. Invert a large mixing bowl on the counter and place the measuring cup on the bowl.

Spinning Greens Even Drier

Salad spinners go a long way toward drying clean, wet salad greens. But in our September/October 1998 test of salad spinners, we found that greens still benefit from a post-spin blotting with paper towels before they see the salad bowl. Aileen Sharma of Tantallon, Nova Scotia, combines the two processes by spinning two or three paper towels with the greens.

Keeping Foods Submerged in Liquid

Dried mushrooms, tomatoes, and chiles are so light that they often bob to the surface of the water being used to hydrate them. This can cause the pieces to soften unevenly. To keep the pieces evenly submerged, Karen Sato of Vancouver, British Columbia, uses a pot with its own steamer insert.

Place the liquid and the ingredients to be hydrated in the pot, and then position the steamer insert over them to keep the food submerged in the liquid. Make sure the water level rises above the holes in the bottom of the steamer insert.

Pan-Roasting Halibut

Is it possible to cook halibut steaks that have plenty of flavor and are both tender and moist—and do it quickly?

≥ BY ADAM RIED AND MEG SUZUKI ≤

Tuna, salmon, and swordfish are the fish steaks most American home cooks know best, but halibut also deserves its share of the limelight. With its naturally lean, firm texture and clean, mild flavor, halibut is often preferred braised rather than roasted or sautéed because this moist-heat cooking technique keeps the fish from drying out. The downside, however, is that braising does not develop as much flavor as other methods, producing fish the test kitchen considers lackluster. So we set out to discover a cooking method that not only added flavor but also produced a perfectly cooked, moist, and tender piece of fish.

Steak Out

Before addressing the questions of technique and sauce, we took to the supermarkets and fishmongers to settle on the best cut of halibut with which to proceed. Fillets, we learned, come from smaller fish and are rare, so we ruled them out. By virtue of availability, halibut steaks were a better choice. But steaks vary considerably in size depending on the weight of the particular fish, which typically ranges from 15 to 50 pounds but can reach up to 300 pounds.

After buying more than 40 pounds of halibut, our advice is this: Inspect the steaks in the fish case and choose the two that are closest in size. This approach ensures that the steaks will cook at the same rate, thus avoiding the problem of overcooking the smaller one. We found the best size steak for the home cook to be between 10 and 12 inches in length and roughly 1¼ inches thick (see "Three Kinds of Halibut Steak" on page 7). (We did test thinner and thicker steaks, adjusting the cooking time as necessary, and had success on both counts.) We also tried halibut steaks that we purchased frozen. The flavor matched that of the fresh fish, but tasters were disappointed in the texture, which they found mushy and fibrous.

Keeping in mind that we wanted to brown the fish to develop flavor, we tested two different techniques: skillet-cooking on the stovetop and roasting in the oven at 500 degrees. Neither was

Turning halibut steaks requires two metal spatulas. Gently lift one long side of the steak and, supporting it with the other spatula, flip so the browned side is down.

ideal. The skillet-seared fish browned nicely but became a little dry. The roasted sample was moist and evenly cooked, but it barely browned and had little flavor—we craved some of the browning from the skillet to intensify the flavor. To achieve this, we chose a common restaurant technique and combined the methods.

First we seared the fish in a heavy-duty, ovenproof skillet on the stovetop, and then we put the whole thing—pan and fish—into the oven to finish cooking. This approach was an improvement, but we still had a problem. Our efforts to brown the fish sufficiently to enhance flavor usually caused it to overcook.

After much additional testing, we finally hit on the solution. Instead of sautéing the fish on both sides, we seared it on one side only, flipped it in the pan, and then placed it in the oven to finish with the seared side up. This worked beautifully, combining the enhanced flavor of browned fish with the moist interior that came from finishing in the oven's even heat. Finally, moist fish with great sautéed flavor.

Next we explored a few refinements. All home cooks know that fish sticks to the pan, and a

nonstick skillet is the common solution to this problem. In this case, however, we feared that many nonstick skillets would not be truly oven-worthy, so we had to solve the sticking problem that came with use of a traditional skillet. We knew that success would lie in a well-preheated pan. In a skillet preheated over high heat for just one minute, the fish stuck like crazy. After two minutes, it stuck a little bit. What did the trick was 2½ minutes of preheating over high heat.

We also tried searing in different fats. Butter burned badly, even when combined with oil. The best choice was pure olive oil, the richness of which tasters welcomed over vegetable oil.

Temperature and Time

Oven temperatures were up next for testing, and we tried four settings: 425, 450, 475, and 500 degrees. Finding no discernible difference in the fish roasted at any of these temperatures, we opted for 425 degrees because it offered the greatest margin for error. (The slower the oven, the longer the window of time for doneness.) Timing was another key to moist, perfectly cooked fish. For the type and thickness of steaks we were using, we found that six minutes of oven time left the fish a bit underdone. At roughly nine minutes the flakes were opaque, but they had not sacrificed any moisture or tenderness.

In addition to timing, we wanted to determine if there were other reliable clues as to when the fish was done properly. Evie Hansen, director of marketing for National Seafood Educators and author of several seafood cookbooks, noted that for health safety reasons, the U.S. Food and Drug Administration suggests a final internal temperature of 140 degrees on an instant-read thermometer. We tested this suggested temperature and concur.

With the fish seared and roasted properly, all we needed was a sauce or two to accompany it. Though we usually think of making an easy sauce from the drippings left in the pan, in this case that was not an option because the pan was

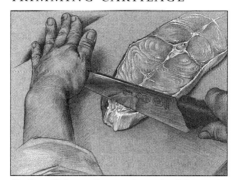

Cutting off the cartilage at the ends of the steaks ensures that they will fit neatly in the pan and diminishes the likelihood that the small bones located there will end up on your dinner plate.

overheated from the hot oven. After trying a variety of relishes, salsas, flavored butters, and vinaigrettes, tasters all agreed that they preferred a sauce with some richness (that is, fat) to complement the lean fish. Flavored butters were easy to prepare and fit the bill in terms of richness, as did vinaigrette because of its olive oil.

PAN-ROASTED HALIBUT STEAKS
SERVES 4 TO 6

This recipe calls for a heavy ovenproof skillet. If you plan to serve the fish with one of the flavored butters or sauces below, prepare it before cooking the fish. Even well-dried fish can cause the hot oil in the pan to splatter. You can minimize splattering by laying the halibut steaks in the pan gently and putting the edge closest to you in the pan first so the far edge falls away from you.

- 2   tablespoons olive oil
- 2   (full) halibut steaks (see right), each about 1¼ inches thick and 10 to 12 inches long (about 2½ pounds total), gently rinsed, dried well with paper towels, and trimmed of cartilage at both ends (see illustration above)
  Salt and ground black pepper

1. Adjust oven rack to middle position and heat oven to 425 degrees. When oven reaches 425 degrees, heat oil in 12-inch, heavy-bottomed, ovenproof skillet over high heat until oil just begins to smoke, about 2½ minutes.

2. Meanwhile, sprinkle both sides of both halibut steaks generously with salt and pepper. Reduce heat to medium-high, swirl oil in pan to distribute; carefully lay steaks in pan and sear, without moving them, until spotty brown, about 4 minutes (if steak is thinner than 1¼ inches, check browning at 3½ minutes; thicker steaks of 1½ inches may require extra time, so check at 4½ minutes). Off heat, flip steaks over

in pan using two thin-bladed metal spatulas (see photo on page 6).

3. Transfer skillet to oven and roast until instant-read thermometer inserted into steaks reads 140 degrees, flakes loosen, and flesh is opaque when checked with tip of paring knife, about 9 minutes (thicker steaks may take up to 10 minutes). Remove skillet from oven and, following illustration at right, separate skin and bones from fish with spatula. Transfer fish to warm platter and serve immediately, with flavored butter or sauce, if desired (recipes follow).

CHIPOTLE-GARLIC BUTTER WITH LIME AND CILANTRO
MAKES ABOUT 4 TABLESPOONS

- 4   tablespoons (½ stick) unsalted butter, softened
- 1   medium chipotle chile en adobo, seeded and minced, with 1 teaspoon adobo sauce
- 1   medium garlic clove, pressed through garlic press or minced to paste (about 1 teaspoon)
- 1   teaspoon honey
- 1   teaspoon grated zest from 1 lime
- 2   teaspoons minced fresh cilantro leaves
- ½   teaspoon salt

Beat butter with fork until light and fluffy; stir in remaining ingredients until thoroughly combined. Dollop a portion of butter over pieces of cooked fish, allowing butter to melt; serve immediately.

ANCHOVY-GARLIC BUTTER WITH LEMON AND PARSLEY
MAKES ABOUT 4 TABLESPOONS

- 4   tablespoons (½ stick) unsalted butter, softened
- 1   anchovy fillet, minced to paste
- 1   medium garlic clove, pressed through garlic press or minced to paste (about 1 teaspoon)
- 1½ teaspoons juice from 1 lemon
- 2   tablespoons minced fresh parsley leaves
- ½   teaspoon salt

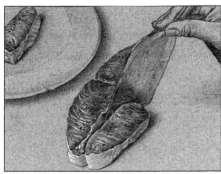

Remove the skin from the cooked steaks and separate each quadrant of meat from the bones by slipping a spatula gently between them. Transfer the pieces of meat to a warm serving platter.

Beat butter with fork until light and fluffy; stir in remaining ingredients until thoroughly combined. Dollop a portion of butter over pieces of cooked fish, allowing butter to melt; serve immediately.

CHUNKY CHERRY TOMATO–BASIL VINAIGRETTE
MAKES 1½ CUPS

- ½   pint cherry or grape tomatoes, each tomato quartered (about 1 cup)
- ¼   teaspoon salt
- ¼   teaspoon ground black pepper
- 2   medium shallots, minced (about 3 tablespoons)
- 2   tablespoons minced fresh basil leaves
- 3   tablespoons juice from 1 lemon
- 6   tablespoons extra-virgin olive oil

Mix tomatoes with salt and pepper in medium mixing bowl; let stand until juicy and seasoned, about 10 minutes. Whisk shallots, basil, lemon juice, and oil in small mixing bowl; add to tomatoes and toss to combine. Pour vinaigrette over pieces of cooked fish and serve immediately.

Three Kinds of Halibut Steak

FULL STEAK: 4 SECTIONS   BELLY CUT: 2 SECTIONS   BONELESS STEAK: 1 SECTION

Most halibut steaks consist of four pieces of meat attached to a central bone (left). It is not uncommon, however, to encounter a steak with just two pieces, both located on the same side of the center bone (center). These steaks were cut from the center of the halibut, adjacent to the belly cavity. The belly, in effect, separates the two halves. We slightly preferred full steaks with four meat sections; each full steak serves two or three people. If you can find only the belly steaks, you will have to purchase four steaks instead of two to make the recipe. Avoid very small, boneless steaks (right) cut entirely free from the bone and each other. Most boneless steaks won't serve even one person.

Chicken Paprikash

The secret to this simple chicken braise? Choose the right paprika, and use it wisely.

⇒ BY ELIZABETH GERMAIN ⇐

Chicken paprikash is a simple chicken stew whose name comes not from its essential spice, paprika, but from the Hungarian word for a dish with browned meat and sour cream. The traditional version *(paprikás csirke* in Hungarian) calls for browning chicken and onion in bacon drippings, braising the meat in chicken stock and paprika, and then making a sauce from the liquid using sour cream. In this country, however, paprikash has been thrown helter-skelter into the melting pot, often resulting in dry chicken, muddled flavors, mile-long ingredient lists, flabby skin, and gluey sauce. I was looking for a rendition that could be made easily at home and would produce succulent chicken, a nice balance of heat, spice, and aromatics, and a rich, flavorful sauce that could by no means double as wallpaper paste.

Building the Stew

Many paprikash recipes call for browning a whole cut-up chicken. Although the skin was crisp and flavorful after being browned, it became soft and unappealing after being stewed. In addition, the breast meat dried out and the wings were unappetizing. The solution was to replace the whole cut-up chicken with eight thighs. (Dark meat remains moist and tender when cooked.) I wondered if the thighs were best cooked skin-off or skin-on. Tests proved that the skin is necessary to keep the outer layer of meat from drying out during browning. Browning with the skin on also enhances the chicken flavor; the browned bits stick to the bottom of the pan, are dislodged during deglazing, and add depth of flavor and color to the sauce. Because cooking chicken in liquid quickly turns crisp skin flabby, I added a simple step: Remove the skin after browning but before the thighs are stewed.

Next came the aromatics and vegetables. Onions are a must. Their pungent flavor balances the sweetness of the paprika. Tasters also found both red and green peppers to be welcome additions that offset the spiciness of the paprika. Long strips of pepper felt out of place in this dish, so I cut each pepper in half before slicing it thin. (These shorter strips soften nicely and are easier to

Sautéing the paprika for one minute releases its full flavor. With longer cooking the spice burns and turns bitter.

eat.) Tasters rejected carrots and mushrooms (no surprise), but I was caught off-guard when it turned out that tomatoes brought a proper balance between sweet and acidic components in the paprikash. Tomato paste muddied the colors and flavors, but tasters responded favorably to diced canned tomatoes. Draining the tomatoes kept them from overpowering the other flavors.

Most paprikash recipes call for deglazing the pan with wine once the vegetables have been cooked. I found red wine too harsh; white wine complemented the other flavors nicely while also adding complexity. By comparison, chicken stock, the liquid of choice in classic recipes, was bland.

Next I explored seasonings. Garlic seemed out of place with the mellow, sweet flavors now gracing the dish. A little dried marjoram is traditional, and tasters felt it was a worthy addition. I also added some flour to help thicken the liquid. A tablespoon provided just enough thickening power; more flour and the sauce became pasty.

My paprikash was now ready to be stewed. Stovetop simmering produced inconsistent results. In some cases, the chicken was done in

just 25 minutes, in others, the cooking time lengthened to 40 minutes, despite the consistent flame used throughout testing. The oven was a much more reliable source of heat than the stovetop. A 300-degree oven cooked the stew perfectly in 30 minutes every time.

Just before serving, sour cream is traditionally added to the liquid to create a more luxurious sauce. Some Americanized recipes called for heavy cream instead. Although the cream made the sauce velvety and smooth, tasters missed the tang of the sour cream. I tested various amounts and settled on a modest ⅓ cup, which must be tempered to avoid curdling the sauce. The best method was to stir some of the hot sauce with the cold sour cream in a small bowl and then add the warmed sour cream to the pot.

Unlocking the Flavor of Paprika

Chicken paprikash may not derive its name from paprika, but that spice is certainly its defining flavor. There are paprikas on the market from Hungary, Spain, and the United States, but the first thing to pay attention to when shopping is whether the paprika is hot or sweet, as hot paprika is known for its bitterness. The winner of our tasting was a Hungarian sweet paprika, the spice traditionally used in paprikash (see "Picking Paprika" on page 9).

One big question still remained. What is the best method of using paprika in this dish—that is, what technique will bring out the most and best flavor this spice has to offer? With a nod to its historical use—as a preservative for uncooked meat—my first thought was to use the paprika to season the uncooked chicken, along with salt and pepper. The results were disappointing. Although the kitchen initially filled with the wonderful aroma of paprika, it soon turned to the smell of singed peppers. The flavor of the finished dish was bitter, and the color had faded from a warm rusty red to burnt sienna.

Next I tried the conventional approach of sautéing the spice to release its full flavor and aroma. Sure enough, adding the paprika to the sautéed vegetables just prior to deglazing infused the stew with paprika's sweet scent and taste. A minute was all the time needed for the flavor of the paprika to blossom.

Now it was finally time to add the crucial finishing touch to the dish—the sour cream. Here I came across an unexpected problem: The sour cream seemed to dull the flavor of the paprika, which had definitely lost some of its potency. I tried increasing the volume of paprika added to the pan for sautéing, but when I added the sour cream, the flavor of the sauce remained too mellow. The remedy turned out to be fairly simple. By reserving some of the paprika and blending it with the sour cream, I got great results. The paprika added with the sour cream brought another dimension to the dish, intensifying the flavor of the paprika.

At last I had found the secret to great home-made chicken paprikash. Briefly sautéing the tasters' choice of Hungarian sweet paprika with onions and peppers helped to unlock its flavor, and adding a bit of uncooked paprika just before serving created complexity and brought some intensity to the finished dish. Best of all, I had discovered that this seemingly sophisticated dish was actually quite simple, one that could easily be made on any weeknight.

CHICKEN PAPRIKASH
SERVES 4

The stew can be made in advance through step 2. To keep the sour cream from separating from the sauce, it's best added to the reheated stew just before serving. Rice or mashed potatoes are good accompaniments, but buttered egg noodles were tasters' favorite. If you want to try them, cook 8 ounces of egg noodles, then drain and toss them with 2 tablespoons butter.

- 8 bone-in chicken thighs (about 3 pounds), trimmed of excess skin and fat
  Salt and ground black pepper
- 1 teaspoon vegetable oil
- 1 large onion, halved and sliced thin
- 1 large red bell pepper, stemmed, seeded, halved widthwise, and cut into ¼-inch strips
- 1 large green bell pepper, stemmed, seeded, halved widthwise, and cut into ¼-inch strips
- 3½ tablespoons sweet paprika
- ¼ teaspoon dried marjoram
- 1 tablespoon all-purpose flour
- ½ cup dry white wine
- 1 (14½-ounce) can diced tomatoes, drained
- ⅓ cup sour cream
- 2 tablespoons chopped fresh parsley leaves

1. Adjust oven rack to lower-middle position; heat oven to 300 degrees. Season both sides of chicken liberally with salt and pepper. Heat oil in large Dutch oven over medium-high heat until shimmering but not smoking, about 2 minutes. Add 4 chicken thighs, skin-side down, and cook without moving them until skin is crisp and well-browned, about 5 minutes. Using tongs, turn chicken pieces and brown on second side, about 5 minutes longer; transfer to large plate. Repeat with remaining chicken thighs and transfer to plate; set aside. When chicken has cooled, remove and discard skin (see illustration at

TASTING: Picking Paprika

The brilliant red powder we call paprika comes from the dried pods (fruit) of the plant species *Capsicum annuum L.*, the clan of peppers that ranges from sweet bells to the very hottest chiles. Several varieties of *Capsicum annuum L.* are used to produce paprika; there is no one specific "paprika pepper." Pods differ in shape and size and vary in degree of potency. Some are round, others are elongated. Some show no pungency, others are fairly hot.

The best paprika is thought to come from Hungary and Spain. In the United States, California and Texas are the main producers. Most European paprika pods are set out to dry naturally in the sun, a process that takes up to 25 days. Domestically grown paprika pods are oven-dried in about 30 hours.

Paprikas can be hot, sweet, or somewhere in between. The differences in pungency, color, and flavor relate to the proportion of mesocarp (fruit wall), placenta (the white veins), and seeds that are ground together. Sweet paprika is made mostly from peppers' mesocarp, while hot paprika is a product of the placenta and seeds. The latter are ground to yield a spicy powder with an orange-brown color and, some spice experts say, poor flavor. It is almost as pungent as common chile powders and cayenne pepper.

The problem with all of this information is that except for allowing you to choose intelligently between sweet and hot paprika, it does you little practical good at the supermarket. In stores and catalogs we uncovered six choices: McCormick's (from California), Whole Foods Organic (also California), Penzeys Hungary Sweet, Szeged Hungarian Hot, Pendery's Spanish, and Igo Basque Piment d'Espelette (also from Spain). The Pendery's Spanish paprika had the deepest red color. Tasters likened the color of the rest to "Crayola-orange," "saffron," or "brick."

Tasters enjoyed the robust but balanced flavor of Penzeys Hungary Sweet (left) and gave this paprika top scores. Pendery's Spanish (center) took second place—hailed for its deep color and rich flavor. McCormick's (right) earned third place in the tasting and is widely available in supermarkets.

Once the paprikas were in the stews, there were equally diverse comments on flavor. Penzeys Hungary Sweet emerged as the overall favorite, hailed for its "roasty," "bold," and "balanced" flavor. The spice did not overpower the stew, but it had plenty of depth. Pendery's Spanish was the runner-up. It had an "earthy" quality and very rich flavor (though not as rich as our winner), with fruity notes. McCormick's finished in third place and was touted for its "lush," "big red pepper" flavor. Stews made with the other three paprikas received less favorable comments. Szeged Hungarian Hot was deemed intense and slightly bitter, the Whole Foods paprika was judged bland and uninteresting, and the Basque Piment d'Espelette was so hot that it was hard to detect any flavor (tasters liked this paprika the least).

Our conclusion? Chicken paprikash is best flavored with Hungarian sweet paprika. Other sweet paprikas (from Spain or California) can deliver good results, but don't use hot paprika in this dish. —Shannon Blaisdell

right). Discard all but 1 tablespoon fat from pan.

2. Add onion to fat in Dutch oven and cook, stirring occasionally, over medium heat until softened, about 5 minutes. Add red and green peppers and cook, stirring occasionally, until onions are browned and peppers are softened, about 3 minutes. Stir in 3 tablespoons paprika, marjoram, and flour; cook, stirring constantly, until fragrant, about 1 minute. Add wine, scraping pot bottom with wooden spoon to loosen browned bits; stir in tomatoes and 1 teaspoon salt. Add chicken pieces and accumulated juices, submerging them in vegetables; bring to a simmer, then cover and place pot in oven. Cook until chicken is no longer pink when cut into with paring knife, about 30 minutes. Remove pot from oven. (At this point, stew can be cooled to room temperature, transferred to an airtight container, and refrigerated for up to 3 days. Bring to simmer over medium-low heat before proceeding.)

3. Combine sour cream and remaining ½ tablespoon paprika in small bowl. Place chicken on individual plates. Stir a few tablespoons of

hot sauce into sour cream, then stir mixture back into sauce in pot. Spoon enriched sauce and peppers over chicken, sprinkle with parsley, and serve immediately.

TECHNIQUE | SKINNING
BROWNED CHICKEN

Once the chicken thighs have been browned and cooled, grasp the skin from one end and pull to separate it from the meat. Discard skin.

Really Good Cheddar Soup

Bad cheddar soup is oily, stringy, and gummy. Really good cheddar soup takes only 20 minutes to prepare and is silky and elegant enough for company.

⇒ BY JULIA COLLIN ⇐

At its finest, cheddar soup is elegant and silky, with the distinct character of cheddar balanced amid a whirl of supporting flavors. At its worst, cheddar soup is little different from that fluorescent, overly processed cheesefood that shimmies and shakes out of a can. For most of us, though, cheddar soup is a thick and oily first course with a stringy, gummy texture. Success, if I could find it, would depend on taming the texture of melted cheddar while balancing its flavor with that of the other ingredients.

For starters I tried two cookbook recipes. The first was simple: Add flour to melted butter and cook (thereby creating a roux, or a paste of butter and flour), simmer with milk, and finish with cheese. The second recipe was slightly more complicated. It called for sautéing onions, carrots, and celery in butter, sprinkling with flour to create a roux, then simmering with milk, chicken broth, and herbs; the soup was pureed in a blender, with cheese added at the end of the process. The results were predictable. The simpleton soup of roux, milk, and cheese had a shallow dairy flavor and gluey texture. While the second soup was more interesting, it lacked a good cheddar punch, and the texture was fibrous and mealy. From these tests, I learned that vegetables and chicken broth would be necessary to keep the soup from tasting one-dimensional and that I needed to work on the cheese flavor and texture.

Making the Soup Base

Focusing on the base of the soup, I set the other components aside and questioned the importance of the roux, which is usually used for its thickening ability. I wondered why most recipes included this classic French mixture of butter and flour rather than letting the cheese thicken the soup. Making two batches, with and without roux, I found that the rouxless batch separated. Stringy clumps of cheese gathered on the bottom of the pot, and an oil slick formed on the surface. Curious, I spoke with several of our food science experts, who offered an explanation. Cheddar soup is essentially an emulsion of fat and liquid in which many, many tiny droplets of fat are evenly dispersed throughout the liquid. The stability of the emulsion depends directly on this even dispersal of fat. The emulsion breaks, or separates, when the droplets of fat begin to touch. A domino effect begins as one droplet of fat after another starts to cling and separate out of the emulsion. This is where the roux comes in. When coated in butter, the individual granules of flour mix uniformly into the cheese, thereby thickening the liquid and stabilizing the emulsion. Understanding why the roux was necessary, I moved on to the other ingredients in the soup base.

I tried replacing the milk with half-and-half and found the soup improved greatly. The extra fat made the soup lush without tasting decadent.

The minced vegetables (onion, carrot, and celery) had already proven themselves as flavor enhancers, but I was disappointed with the texture of the soup when they were pureed with the other ingredients before the cheese was added. Avoiding the blender altogether, I tested straining the vegetables from the base versus leaving them in the soup unprocessed. Although the strained soup was smooth, it had less flavor than the soup with small, tasty bites of vegetable. Along with the vegetables, I found a pinch of cayenne, a sprinkle of fresh thyme, and a drizzle of dry sherry elevated the soup base from humdrum to almost ethereal.

Adding the Cheese

With the soup base in place, I focused next on how to add enough cheese to provide depth of flavor without ruining the texture. Working with 5 cups of soup base, I added cheddar to the pot 1 ounce at a time. At 12 ounces (most recipes call for 6 to 8 ounces), the soup had an undeniable core flavor of cheddar that was neither overpowering nor heavy. I tried a variety of supermarket cheddars and found the extra-sharp too piquant, the mild too bland, and the preshredded generic and flavorless. I decided to steer a middle course and use a sharp cheddar, shredding it myself. Owing to the amount of cheese used, the soup heavily reflects its flavor, whatever the quality or brand chosen. (For information on selecting cheddar, see pages 28–29.)

Although 12 ounces of cheddar added tremendous flavor, it also created a problem. The texture was glutinous, just the thing that I had been trying to avoid. The solution was to adjust the strength of the roux. After much testing, I found that 2 tablespoons of flour to 3 tablespoons of butter made a delicate roux able to stabilize the soup without turning it thick or gummy. Still, I found that this soup easily broke its emulsion when brought to a simmer. The problem was that most recipes call for adding the cheese to a hot soup base. I found it safer to remove the pot from the heat and allow it to cool for a minute. Off heat, the shredded cheese could be stirred into the base without a problem. With help from this simple technique, 12 ounces of cheddar, a minimum of roux, and a carefully constructed soup base, this cheddar soup has a velvety, lithe texture and an honest, elegant flavor.

CHEDDAR SOUP
MAKES ABOUT 7 CUPS, SERVING 4 TO 6

This soup isn't the best candidate for making in advance. Reheat the soup in a saucepan over low heat, whisking gently to prevent the soup from separating. Do not bring above a bare simmer.

- 3 tablespoons unsalted butter
- 1 medium onion, minced (about 1 cup)
- 1 medium carrot, minced (about 1/3 cup)
- 1 small celery rib, minced (about 1/4 cup)
- 1 medium garlic clove, minced
- 2 tablespoons all-purpose flour
- 2 1/2 cups canned low-sodium chicken broth
- 2 1/2 cups half-and-half
- 1 bay leaf
- Pinch cayenne
- 3 tablespoons dry sherry
- 12 ounces sharp cheddar cheese, shredded (about 3 cups)
- 1 tablespoon minced fresh thyme leaves
- Salt and ground black pepper

1. Heat butter in large heavy-bottomed Dutch oven over medium heat until foaming; add onion and cook, stirring occasionally, until softened, about 4 minutes. Add carrot, celery, and garlic; cook until garlic is fragrant, about 1 minute. Add flour and cook, stirring to coat vegetables, until mixture begins to brown on bottom of pot, about 2 minutes. Gradually whisk in chicken broth and half-and-half and add bay leaf. Increase heat to medium-high and bring to boil; reduce heat to medium-low and simmer until vegetables soften, about 10 minutes.

2. Off heat, add cayenne and sherry; cool soup for 1 minute. Slowly whisk in cheese and thyme; season with salt and pepper and serve immediately.

How to Cook Pot Roast

We cooked more than 100 pounds of beef to find the answer to tender, moist, flavorful pot roast. What's the secret? Cook it until it is done—and then keep on cooking.

> BY BRIDGET LANCASTER

Pot roast, a slow-food survivor of generations past, has stubbornly remained in the repertoire of Sunday-night cookery, but with few good reasons. The meat is often tough and stringy and so dry that it must be drowned with the merciful sauce that accompanies the dish.

A *good* pot roast by definition entails the transformation of a tough (read cheap), nearly unpalatable cut of meat into a tender, rich, flavorful main course by means of a slow, moist cooking process called braising. It should not be sliceable; rather, the tension of a stern gaze should be enough to break it apart. Nor should it be pink or rosy in the middle—save that for prime rib or steak.

Choice Cut

The meat for pot roast should be well marbled with fat and connective tissue to provide the dish with the necessary flavor and moisture. Recipes typically call for roasts from the sirloin (or rump), round (leg), or chuck (shoulder). When all was said and done, I cooked a dozen cuts of meat to find the right one.

The sirloin roasts tested—the bottom rump roast and top sirloin—were the leanest of the cuts and needed a longer cooking period to break down the meat to a palatable texture. The round cuts—top round, bottom round, and eye of round—had more fat running through them than the sirloin cuts, but the meat was chewy. The chuck cuts—shoulder roast, boneless chuck roast, cross rib, chuck mock tender, seven-bone roast, top-blade roast, and chuck-eye roast—cooked up the most tender, although I gave preference to three of these cuts (see "My Three Chucks" on page 12). The high proportion of fat and connective tissue in these chuck cuts gave the meat much-needed moisture and superior flavor.

Brown and Braise

Tough meat can benefit from the low, dry heat of oven roasting, and it can be boiled. With pot roast, however, the introduction of moisture by means of a braising liquid is thought to be integral to the breakdown of the tough muscle fibers. (We also tried dry-roasting and boiling pot roast just to make sure. See page 12 to find out why braising was the winner.) It was time to find out what kind of liquid and how much was needed to best cook the roast and supply a good sauce.

For a complete meal of meat, vegetables, and sauce, add carrots, potatoes, and parsnips near the end of the cooking time.

Before I began the testing, I needed to deal with the aesthetics of the dish. Because pot roast is traditionally cooked with liquid at a low temperature, the exterior of the meat will not brown sufficiently unless it is first sautéed in a Dutch oven on the stovetop. High heat and a little oil were all that were needed to caramelize the exterior of the beef and boost both the flavor and appearance of the dish.

Using water as the braising medium, I started with a modest ¼ cup, as suggested in a few recipes. This produced a roast that was unacceptably fibrous, even after hours of cooking. After increasing the amount of liquid incrementally, I found the moistest meat was produced when I added liquid halfway up the sides of the roast (depending on the cut, this amount could be between two and four cups). The larger amount of liquid also accelerated the cooking process, shaving nearly one hour off the cooking time needed for a roast cooked in just ¼ cup of liquid. Naively assuming that more is always better, I continued to increase the amount of water but to no better effect. I also found that it was necessary to cover the Dutch oven with a piece of foil before placing the lid on top. The added seal of the foil kept the liquid from escaping (in the form of steam) through the cracks of a loose-fitting lid and eliminated any need to add more liquid to the pot.

Next I tested different liquids, hoping to add flavor to the roast and sauce. Along with my old standby, water, I tested red wine, low-sodium canned chicken broth, and low-sodium canned beef broth. Red wine had the most startling effect on the meat, penetrating it with a potent wine flavor that most tasters agreed was "good, but not traditional pot roast." However, tasters did like the flavor of a little red wine added to the sauce after the pot roast was removed from the pan. Each of the broths on

Roasting versus Braising

A distinctive pattern of fat and connective tissue runs through the meat of a chuck roast (left). When cooked in dry heat, or roasted (middle), the fat and sinew do not break down sufficiently, even after many hours in the oven. Cooking the meat in moist heat, or braising (right), promotes a more complete breakdown of the fat and connective tissue, yielding very tender meat.

The Mystery of Braising

Braising—searing meat, partially submerging it in liquid in a sealed pot, and then cooking it until fork-tender—is a classic technique used with tough cuts of meat. A variety of cooks have put forward theories about why and how braising works (as opposed to roasting or boiling). We set out to devise a series of experiments that would explain the mystery of braising.

Before kitchen testing began, we researched the meat itself to better understand how it cooks. Meat (muscle) is made up of two major components: muscle fibers, the long thin strands visible as the "grain" of meat, and connective tissue, the membranous, translucent film that covers the bundles of muscle fiber and gives them structure and support. Muscle fiber is tender because of its high water content (up to 78 percent). Once meat is heated beyond about 120 degrees, the long strands of muscle fiber contract and coil, expelling moisture in much the same way that it's wrung out of a towel. In contrast, connective tissue is tough because it is composed primarily of collagen, a sturdy protein that is in everything from the cow's muscle tendons to its hooves. When collagen is cooked at temperatures exceeding 140 degrees, it starts to break down to gelatin, the protein responsible for the tender meat, thick sauces, and rich mouthfeel of braised dishes.

In essence, then, meat both dries out as it cooks (meat fibers lose moisture) and becomes softer (the collagen melts). That is why (depending on the cut) meat is best either when cooked rare or pot-roasted—cooked to the point at which the collagen dissolves completely. Anything in between is dry and tough, the worst of both worlds.

This brings us to why braising is an effective cooking technique for tough cuts of meat. To determine the relative advantages of roasting, braising, and boiling, we constructed a simple test. One roast was cooked in a 250-degree oven, one was braised, and one was simmered in enough liquid to cover it. The results were startling. The roast never reached an internal temperature of more than 175 degrees, even after four hours, and the meat was tough and dry (see "Roasting versus Braising" on page 11). To our great surprise, both the braised and boiled roasts cooked in about the same amount of time, and the results were almost identical. Cutting the roasts in half revealed little difference—both exhibited nearly full melting of the thick bands of connective tissue. As far as the taste and texture of the meat, tasters were hard pressed to find any substantial differences between the two. Both roasts yielded meat that was exceedingly tender, moist, and infused with rich gelatin.

The conclusion? Dry heat (roasting) is ineffective because the meat never gets hot enough. It does not appear that steam heat (braising) enjoys any special ability to soften meat over boiling. Braising has one advantage over simmering or boiling, however—half a pot of liquid reduces to a sauce much faster than a full pot. –Matthew Card

---

their own failed to win tasters over completely—the chicken broth was rich but gave the dish a characteristic poultry flavor, while the beef broth tasted sour when added solo. In the end, I found an equal proportion of each did the job, with the beef broth boosting the depth of flavor and chicken broth tempering any sourness. Because different amounts of liquid would have to be added to the pot depending on the size and shape of each individual roast, I chose to be consistent in the amount of chicken and beef broth used—1 cup each—and to vary the amount of water to bring the liquid level halfway up the roast.

Trying to boost the flavor of the sauce even more, I added the basic vegetables—carrot, celery, onion, garlic—to the pot as the meat braised. Unfortunately, the addition of raw vegetables made the pot roast taste more like a vegetable stew. I then tried sautéing them until golden brown and found that the caramelized flavor of the vegetables added another layer of flavor to the sauce. Tomato paste, an ingredient found in several recipes, was not a welcome addition. Tasters appreciated the sweetness it added but not the "tinny" flavor. A little sugar (2 teaspoons) added to the vegetables as they cooked gave the sauce the sweetness tasters were looking for.

Some recipes thicken the sauce with a mixture of equal parts butter and flour (*beurre manié*); others use a slurry of cornstarch mixed with a little braising liquid. Both techniques made the sauce more gravy-like than I preferred, and I didn't care for the dilution of flavor. I chose to remove the roast from the pot, then reduce the liquid over high heat until the flavors were well concentrated and the texture more substantial.

Time, Temperature, and Error

When it comes to how to cook the roast, the schools of thought are divided neatly into two camps: on the stove or in the oven. After a few rounds of stovetop cooking, I felt that it was too difficult to maintain a steady, low temperature, so I began pot-roasting in the oven, starting out at 250 degrees. This method required no supervision, just a turn of the meat every 30 to 40 minutes to ensure even cooking. I then tested higher temperatures to reduce the cooking time. Heat levels above 350 degrees boiled the meat to a stringy, dry texture because the exterior of the roast overcooked before the interior was cooked and tender. The magic temperature turned out to be 300 degrees—enough heat to keep the meat at a low simmer while high enough to shave a few more minutes off the cooking time.

As expressed before, pot roast is well-done meat—meat cooked to an internal temperature above 165 degrees. Up to this point, I was bringing the meat to an internal temperature of 200 to 210 degrees, the point at which the fat and connective tissue begin to melt. In a 300-degree oven, I found that the roast came up to that temperature in a neat 2½ hours, certainly by no means a quick meal but still a relatively short time in which to cook a pot roast. But I still had not achieved the desired fall-apart-tender pot roast, so I went back and reviewed my prior testing to see what I might have missed.

Once in a great while in the test kitchen we happen upon a true "Eureka!" moment, when a chance test result leads to a breakthrough cooking technique. Some days before, I had forgotten to remove one of the roasts from the oven, allowing it to cook one hour longer than intended. Racing to the kitchen with my instant-read thermometer, I found the internal temperature of the roast was still 210 degrees, but the meat had a substantially different appearance and texture. The roast was so tender that it was starting to separate along its muscle lines. A fork poked into the meat met with no resistance and nearly disappeared into the flesh. I took the roast

---

My Three Chucks

The seven-bone roast (left) is a well-marbled cut with an incredibly beefy flavor. It gets its name from the bone found in the roast, which is shaped like the number seven. Because it is only 2 inches thick, less liquid and less time are needed to braise the roast. Do not buy a seven-bone roast that weighs more than 3½ pounds, as it will not fit into a Dutch oven. This roast is also sometimes referred to as a seven-bone steak.

The top-blade roast (middle) is also well-marbled with fat and connective tissue, which make this roast very juicy and flavorful. Even after thorough braising, this roast retains a distinctive strip of connective tissue, which is not unpleasant to eat. This roast may also be sold as a blade roast.

The chuck-eye roast (right) is the fattiest of the three roasts and the most commonly available. The high proportion of fat gives pot roast great flavor and tenderness. Because of its thicker size, this roast takes the longest to cook.

SEVEN-BONE POT ROAST TOP-BLADE POT ROAST CHUCK-EYE ROAST

out of the pot and "sliced" into it. Nearly all the fat and connective tissue had dissolved into the meat, giving each bite a soft, silky texture and rich, succulent flavor. I "overcooked" several more roasts. Each roast had the same great texture. The conclusion? Not only do you have to cook pot roast until it reaches 210 degrees internally, but the meat has to remain at that temperature for a full hour. In other words, cook the pot roast until it's done—and then keep on cooking!

SIMPLE POT ROAST
SERVES 6 TO 8

For pot roast, we recommend a chuck-eye roast. Most markets sell this roast with twine tied around the center (see photo on page 12). If necessary, do this yourself. Seven-bone and top-blade roasts are also good choices for this recipe. Remember to add only enough water to come halfway up the sides of these thinner roasts, and begin checking for doneness after 2 hours. If using a top-blade roast, tie it before cooking (see illustrations at right) to keep it from falling apart. Mashed or boiled potatoes are good accompaniments to pot roast.

1	boneless chuck-eye roast (about 3½ pounds)
	Salt and ground black pepper
2	tablespoons vegetable oil
1	medium onion, chopped medium
1	small carrot, chopped medium
1	small celery rib, chopped medium
2	medium garlic cloves, minced
2	teaspoons sugar
1	cup canned low-sodium chicken broth
1	cup canned low-sodium beef broth
1	sprig fresh thyme
1–1½	cups water
¼	cup dry red wine

1. Adjust oven rack to middle position and heat oven to 300 degrees. Thoroughly pat roast dry with paper towels; sprinkle generously with salt and pepper.

2. Heat oil in large heavy-bottomed Dutch oven over medium-high heat until shimmering but not smoking. Brown roast thoroughly on all sides, reducing heat if fat begins to smoke, 8 to 10 minutes. Transfer roast to large plate; set aside. Reduce heat to medium; add onion, carrot, and celery to pot and cook, stirring occasionally, until beginning to brown, 6 to 8 minutes. Add garlic and sugar; cook until fragrant, about 30 seconds. Add chicken and beef broths and thyme, scraping bottom of pan with wooden spoon to loosen browned bits. Return roast and any accumulated juices to pot; add enough water to come halfway up sides of roast. Bring liquid to simmer over medium heat, then place large piece of foil over pot and cover tightly with lid; transfer pot to oven. Cook, turning roast every 30 minutes, until

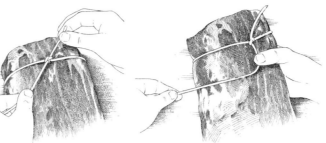

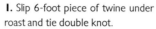

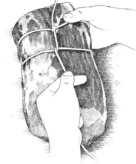

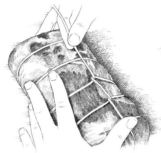

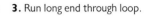

1. Slip 6-foot piece of twine under roast and tie double knot.

2. Hold twine against meat, and loop long end under and around roast.

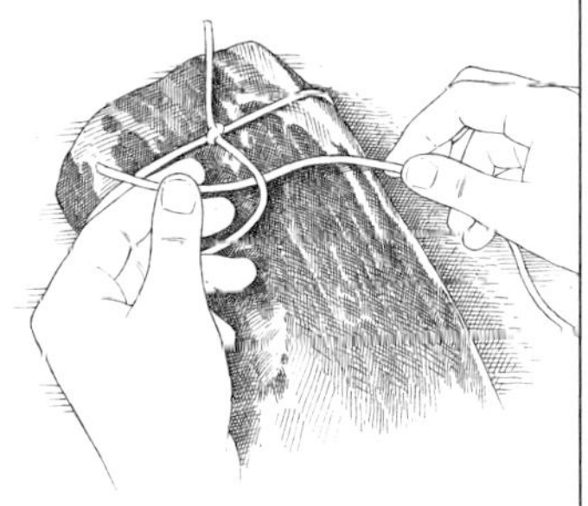

3. Run long end through loop.

4. Repeat procedure down length of roast.

5. Roll roast over and run twine under and around each loop.

6. Wrap twine around end of roast, flip roast, and tie to original knot.

fully tender and meat fork or sharp knife easily slips in and out of meat, 3½ to 4 hours.

3. Transfer roast to carving board; tent with foil to keep warm. Allow liquid in pot to settle about 5 minutes, then use wide spoon to skim fat off surface; discard thyme sprig. Boil over high heat until reduced to about 1½ cups, about 8 minutes. Add red wine and reduce again to 1½ cups, about 2 minutes. Season to taste with salt and pepper.

4. Using chef's or carving knife, cut meat into ½-inch-thick slices, or pull apart into large pieces; transfer meat to warmed serving platter and pour about ½ cup sauce over meat. Serve, passing remaining sauce separately.

POT ROAST WITH ROOT VEGETABLES

In this variation, the vegetables—carrots, potatoes, and parsnips—are added near the end of cooking.

1. Follow recipe for Simple Pot Roast. In step 2, when roast is almost tender (sharp knife should meet little resistance), add 1½ pounds (about 8 medium) carrots, sliced ½ inch thick (about 3 cups); 1½ pounds small red potatoes, halved if larger than 1½ inches in diameter (about 5 cups); and 1 pound (about 5 large) parsnips, sliced ½ inch thick (about 3 cups) to Dutch oven, submerging them in liquid. Continue to cook until vegetables are almost tender, 20 to 30 minutes.

2. Transfer roast to carving board; tent with foil to keep warm. Allow liquid in pot to settle about 5 minutes, then use wide spoon to skim

fat off surface; discard thyme sprig. Add wine and salt and pepper to taste; boil over high heat until vegetables are fully tender, 5 to 10 minutes. Using slotted spoon, transfer vegetables to warmed serving bowl or platter. Using chef's or carving knife, cut meat into ½-inch-thick slices or pull apart into large pieces; transfer to bowl or platter with vegetables and pour about ½ cup sauce over meat and vegetables. Serve, passing remaining sauce separately.

POT ROAST WITH MUSHROOMS, TOMATOES, AND RED WINE

This recipe is based on *stracotto*, an Italian pot roast with tomatoes and red wine.

1. Follow recipe for Simple Pot Roast, adding 10 ounces white button mushrooms, cleaned and quartered, to Dutch oven along with onion, carrot, and celery in step 2. Decrease chicken and beef broths to ½ cup each and add ½ cup dry red wine and 1 can (14½ ounces) diced tomatoes, with juice, along with broths.

2. After skimming fat off liquid in step 3, add 1 sprig fresh rosemary; omit red wine. Boil liquid over high heat until reduced to 1½ cups; discard rosemary and thyme sprigs. Season to taste with salt and pepper.

3. Using chef's or carving knife, cut meat into ½-inch-thick slices or pull apart into large pieces; transfer meat to warmed serving platter or bowl, pour sauce and vegetables over meat, and serve.

Wilted Spinach Salads

For a salad with bright flavors and a lilting texture, go easy on the oil and heavy on the seasonings, and use a light hand to dress the greens.

⇒ BY THE COOK'S ILLUSTRATED TEST KITCHEN ⇐

When properly wilted, the leaf edges soften slightly, but the spinach retains some crunch.

Many cooks consider wilted spinach salad—in which a warm, fragrant dressing gently wilts fresh spinach leaves—to be a restaurant indulgence. While these elegant salads are surprisingly easy to make at home, there are potential problems. After sampling several recipes in the test kitchen, tasters concurred that these salads can disappoint in two major ways—with greasy, dull-tasting dressings and with spinach reduced to mush in puddles of dressing as deep as a fish pond.

First we wanted to identify the best type of oil to use in these salads. Though dressings made with pure olive oil were fine—use it if that's what you have on hand—the flavor nuances of extra-virgin oil gave the dressings more depth and dimension.

When it came to the acidic component, tasters generally favored fresh lemon juice for its bright, tangy flavor, though balsamic vinegar fared well in a dressing made with smoky bacon and sweet red onion. We discovered that dressings in which the acidic component was added early and heated through lacked brightness. The punch was restored when we swirled in the lemon juice or vinegar after the oil and other ingredients had been heated.

We also tested the ratio of oil to acid. The ratio we use for most vinaigrettes, 4 parts oil to 1 part acid, produced greasy dressings. Mindful that we didn't want too much oil overpowering the tender

spinach, we scaled back the ratio to 3 parts oil and 1 part acid. A little extra acid made the dressings sharp and fresh-tasting.

Several of us in the test kitchen had in the past encountered wilted salads swimming in dressing, which gave the greens a decidedly drowned, slimy texture. After tasting salads tossed with various quantities of dressing, our tasters settled on just ¼ cup of dressing for 6 cups of greens. The ¼ cup coated the greens generously yet allowed them to retain enough structural integrity to leave these wilted salads with a slight but satisfying crunch. Serve these salads without delay to enjoy the best of their singular texture.

WILTED SPINACH SALAD WITH BACON AND BALSAMIC VINAIGRETTE

SERVES 4 AS A FIRST COURSE

We prefer the ease of prewashed baby spinach, sold in 5-ounce packages in most supermarkets. If you choose to use bunched baby spinach instead, make sure to wash and dry the leaves well.

- 5 ounces baby spinach, about 6 cups
- 2 slices bacon (about 2 ounces), cut into ¼-inch pieces
- 1 tablespoon extra-virgin olive oil
- ½ small red onion, minced (about ½ cup)
- ¼ teaspoon salt
- ⅛ teaspoon ground black pepper
- ⅛ teaspoon sugar
- 1 tablespoon balsamic vinegar

Place spinach in large bowl. Fry bacon in small skillet over medium heat until crisp, about 5 minutes; transfer with slotted spoon to paper towel–lined plate, leaving fat in skillet. Return skillet to medium heat and add oil, onion, salt, pepper, and sugar. Cook, stirring occasionally, until onion is slightly softened, 2 to 3 minutes. Add balsamic vinegar; swirl to incorporate. Pour warm dressing over spinach and toss gently to wilt. Sprinkle bacon over spinach; serve immediately.

WILTED SPINACH SALAD WITH FETA, OLIVES, AND LEMON VINAIGRETTE

- 5 ounces baby spinach, about 6 cups
- 3 tablespoons extra-virgin olive oil

- 1 medium shallot, minced (about 2 tablespoons)
- 1 medium garlic clove, minced (about 1 teaspoon)
- 1 teaspoon minced fresh oregano leaves
- ¼ teaspoon salt
- ⅛ teaspoon ground black pepper
- ⅛ teaspoon sugar
- 1 tablespoon juice from 1 lemon
- 2 ounces feta cheese, crumbled (about ¼ cup)
- 6 black olives, sliced thin (about 2 tablespoons)

Place spinach in large bowl. Add oil, shallot, garlic, oregano, salt, pepper, and sugar to small skillet and cook over medium heat until shallot is slightly softened, 2 to 3 minutes. Add lemon juice; swirl to incorporate. Pour warm dressing over spinach, add feta and olives, and toss gently to wilt. Serve immediately.

WILTED SPINACH SALAD WITH ORANGES, RADISHES, AND CITRUS VINAIGRETTE

To cut neat orange sections free of membrane and pith, slice off the peel and pith using a very sharp paring knife and following the contour of the fruit. Then, holding the orange over a bowl and working section by section, slip the knife between the membrane and section and slice to the center. Turn the blade and slide it along the membrane on the second side of the section to completely free the section.

- 5 ounces baby spinach, about 6 cups
- 3 tablespoons extra-virgin olive oil
- 1 medium shallot, minced (about 2 tablespoons)
- ¼ teaspoon grated zest and segments from 2 medium oranges
- ¼ teaspoon salt
- ⅛ teaspoon ground black pepper
- ⅛ teaspoon sugar
- 1 tablespoon juice from 1 lemon
- 4 medium radishes, grated on large holes of box grater (about ⅓ cup)

Place spinach in large bowl. Add oil, shallot, orange zest, salt, pepper, and sugar to small skillet and cook over medium heat until shallot is slightly softened, 2 to 3 minutes. Add lemon juice; swirl to incorporate. Pour warm dressing over spinach; add orange segments and grated radishes, and toss gently to wilt. Serve immediately.

Spaghetti Puttanesca in 11 Minutes

In the time it takes to boil spaghetti, you can make this simple, gutsy sauce.

⊃ BY SHANNON BLAISDELL ⊂

Said to have been created by Neapolitan ladies of the night, puttanesca is a pasta sauce with attitude. Most home cooks buy this lusty sauce by the jar or know it as restaurant fare: a slow-cooked tomato sauce with garlic, crushed red pepper, anchovies, capers, and black olives tossed with spaghetti. But those of us familiar with puttanesca are often disappointed. Chock-full of high-impact ingredients, puttanesca is often overpowered by one flavor—too fishy, too garlicky, too briny, or just plain salty and acidic. It can also be unduly heavy and stew-like or dull and monochromatic. I was searching for a simple, satisfying sauce with aggressive but well-balanced flavors.

The Pungent Trio

I started my testing by tossing all of the ingredients—minced garlic, minced olives, whole capers, minced anchovies, and red pepper flakes—into a base of canned tomatoes and simmered the lot for 25 minutes. The result was a dull-witted sauce with undeveloped flavors. My first revision began with sautéing the garlic in olive oil to deepen the garlic flavor, but, as I found out, the garlic should not be allowed to brown; when it did, the sauce quickly became bitter. To rectify the problem, I mixed a bit of water with the garlic before it went into the pan. The water slowed the cooking, making the garlic less likely to brown and burn.

Deciding how to prepare and cook the olives was my next task. After several tests, I decided to toss coarsely chopped olives into the sauce at the very last minute, allowing the residual heat of the tomatoes to warm them. This preserved their flavor, their texture, and their independence. As for which olives worked best, I started with Neapolitan Gaeta olives—small, black, earthy, and herbaceous. For good measure I also tested Alfonso, Kalamata, and canned black olives in place of the Gaetas. Tasters unanimously rejected the "insipid," "springy" canned olives but liked

both the Alfonso and Kalamata olives for their "soft," "melting" qualities.

Capers were the least of my worries. Of all the ingredients, they were the most resilient, well able to retain their shape, texture, and flavor. Rinsing them thoroughly, whether salt- or brine-cured, and adding them at the end of cooking along with the olives proved best.

Fish, Fire, and Tomatoes

Up to this point, the anchovies in my sauce, added along with the tomatoes to simmer, tasted flat and salty and gave the sauce a funky, fishy taste. I tried mashing whole fillets into the oil with a fork and found the process tedious and ineffective; stray chunks were left behind and inevitably ended up offending an anchovy-sensitive taster. What worked best in the end was to mince the anchovies to a fine paste and add them to the oil in the pan with the garlic. In two or three minutes, the anchovies melted into the oil on their own (no fork necessary) and their characteristically full, rich flavor blossomed.

"Blooming" an ingredient in oil is a technique often used to develop flavor. Since it had worked so well with the garlic and anchovies, I decided to try it with the red pepper flakes instead of simmering them with the tomatoes, as I had in the original test. As they cooked with the garlic and anchovies, their flavor permeated the oil.

As for the tomatoes, I tested crushed tomatoes, canned whole tomatoes (chopped by hand), canned diced tomatoes, and fresh. The canned diced tomatoes were the winner. They had a sweet flavor and clung nicely to the pasta. But I still wasn't sure whether I should use the diced tomatoes along with their juices or not. Testing the two options head to head made my choice easy. When cooked with tomatoes and their juices, the sauce took 25 minutes to cook down to the right consistency; when cooked with the diced tomatoes alone, it reached the optimal consistency in a mere eight minutes. Tasters were also unanimously in favor of the lightly cooked sauce, finding its flavor fresh and "less stewed" as well as "sweet." They also liked the "meaty texture" and firm bite of the tomatoes in this version of the sauce.

One last discovery improved the sauce still further. In the test kitchen, we are in the habit of reserving a little pasta cooking water to toss with the finished pasta to keep the sauce from drying out. On a whim, I decided to substitute some of the drained tomato juice for the water, which gave the sauce a brighter, more lively flavor.

After simple preparation and a mere 11 minutes on the stove, the time in which it takes to boil the pasta, my puttanesca had become assertive, pungent, and extremely fresh-tasting. The secret was in quick, minimal cooking that allowed each ingredient to maintain its identity. Sometimes quick cooking actually means more flavor.

SPAGHETTI PUTTANESCA
SERVES 4

The pasta and sauce cook in just about the same amount of time. If you like the fruitiness of extra-virgin olive oil, toss 1 tablespoon into the sauced pasta before serving.

- 4 medium garlic cloves, minced to paste or pressed through garlic press (1 packed tablespoon)
  Salt
- 1 pound spaghetti
- 2 tablespoons olive oil
- 1 teaspoon red pepper flakes
- 4 teaspoons minced anchovies (about 8 fillets)
- 1 (28-ounce) can diced tomatoes, drained, ½ cup juice reserved
- 3 tablespoons capers, rinsed
- ½ cup black olives (such as Gaeta, Alfonso, or Kalamata), pitted and chopped coarse
- ¼ cup minced fresh parsley leaves

1. Bring 4 quarts water to rolling boil in large Dutch oven or stockpot. Meanwhile, mix garlic with 1 tablespoon water in small bowl; set aside. When water is boiling, add 1 tablespoon salt and pasta; stir to separate pasta. Immediately heat oil, garlic mixture, red pepper flakes, and anchovies in large skillet over medium heat; cook, stirring frequently, until garlic is fragrant but not brown, 2 to 3 minutes. Stir in tomatoes and simmer until slightly thickened, about 8 minutes.

2. Cook pasta until al dente. Drain, then return pasta to pot; add ¼ cup reserved tomato juice and toss to combine.

3. Stir capers, olives, and parsley into sauce. Pour sauce over pasta and toss to combine, adding more tomato juice to moisten if necessary. Adjust seasonings with salt; serve immediately.

Minced versus Chopped Olives

Minced olives (left) produced a muddy sauce with purple spaghetti. Coarsely chopped olives (right) won't dye the pasta and taste better.

Artichokes Made Easy

How to choose, clean, and cook this hard-to-handle spring vegetable.

BY MATTHEW CARD

CHOOSING ARTICHOKES

Artichokes are a perennial belonging to the sunflower family, with the edible portion of the plant being an immature thistle. The plants grow quite large, reaching up to 6 feet in diameter and 3 to 4 feet in height. While available off and on throughout the year, the high season for artichokes is the spring, when there are plenty on the market and their price is generally low.

Artichokes are commonly sold in three sizes: small, medium, and large. Surprisingly, different-sized artichokes bud simultaneously on the same plant; the artichokes that grow on the plant's center stalk are the largest, while the smallest grow at the juncture between the plant's leaves and outer stems. After preparing, cooking, and eating all three sizes, we found that we preferred the small and medium artichokes to the large, which can be tough and fibrous.

When selecting fresh artichokes at the market, you can follow a few rules of thumb. The artichokes should be tight and compact, like a flower blossom (which is what they are), their color should be an unblemished bright green, and they should "squeak" when you rub the leaves together—evidence that the artichoke still retains much of its moisture. If you tug at a leaf, it should cleanly snap off; if it bends, it's old. Also be on guard for leaves that look dried out and feathery at the edges—a sure sign of an over-the-hill artichoke.

A small artichoke (left) is the size of a chicken egg and weighs between 2 and 4 ounces. A medium artichoke (right) is the size of an orange and weighs between 8 and 10 ounces.

TRIMMING ARTICHOKES

There are two basic approaches to preparing artichokes. You can leave them whole (with minimal trimming before cooking) and let your guests eat them leaf by leaf at the table, or you can trim them to the heart before cooking (removing all inedible portions) and let your guests reap the benefits of your labor. Medium artichokes can be left whole or trimmed to the heart. Small artichokes are best trimmed to the heart.

Whether you are working with small or medium artichokes, leaving them whole or trimming them, artichokes will turn brown almost as soon as they are cut. It is crucial to submerge them in acidulated water, which neutralizes the enzymes responsible for the browning, or oxidation. We tried a variety of acids to prevent oxidation, including white wine vinegar, apple cider vinegar, and lemon juice, and were most pleased with lemon juice because of its bright yet neutral flavor. Simply add the juice of ½ lemon to 1 quart of water, then use the juiced lemon half to rub the cut portions of the artichokes to keep them from browning as you trim them. Once cleaned, the artichokes can be dropped into the bowl of acidulated water.

WHAT'S EDIBLE AND WHAT'S NOT

Much of an artichoke is inedible, including the entire exterior as well as the fuzzy choke and tiny inner leaves in the center. (Although in small artichokes the choke is so undeveloped it can be ignored.) Only the heart, stem, and bottom portions of the inner leaves become meaty and tender when cooked. The cooked heart can be eaten with a knife and fork. The edible portion at the bottom of the leaves is best scraped off with your teeth. A full-sized leaf, with a dotted line separating the edible portion from the inedible, is shown below at left.

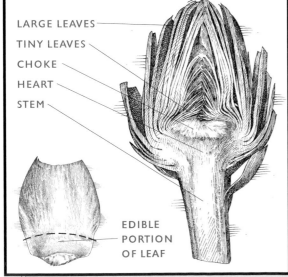

LARGE LEAVES
TINY LEAVES
CHOKE
HEART
STEM

EDIBLE PORTION OF LEAF

ROASTING SMALL ARTICHOKE HEARTS

Small, or "baby," artichokes are simpler to prepare than medium artichokes because you do not have to remove the choke. Roasting, which concentrates their delicate flavor and lightly crisps their exterior, is our favorite way to cook small artichoke hearts. Plan on roughly four artichokes per serving.

1. Cut off the top quarter and snap off the fibrous outer leaves until you reach the yellow leaves.

2. With a paring knife, trim the dark green exterior from the base of the artichoke as well as the exterior of the stem. Trim a thin slice from the end of the stem, then cut the artichoke in half, slicing from tip to stem. Drop the trimmed artichoke into a bowl of acidulated water until ready to cook.

3. Drain the trimmed artichokes and toss with enough olive oil to coat lightly. Season with salt and pepper to taste and place cut-side down on a rimmed baking sheet. Roast in a 400-degree oven, turning after 15 minutes, until artichokes can be easily pierced with a skewer, about 25 minutes total. While still hot, sprinkle with lemon juice and more salt to taste.

STEAMING WHOLE MEDIUM ARTICHOKES

Medium artichokes are our favorite for serving whole. Easy to prepare (see illustrations 1 to 3 at right), each artichoke conveniently serves one person. After experimenting with a variety of cooking methods, including boiling, roasting, steaming, and microwaving, we concluded that steamed artichokes had the deepest, most pronounced flavor. We discovered that artichokes steam nicely set on top of thick-sliced onion rings (see illustration 4 at right), which keeps them from becoming waterlogged. If you do not have onions on hand, a steaming rack also works.

Fill a pot with lightly salted water to ½ inch below the top of the onion rings, and set one artichoke, stem-side down, on each onion ring. Bring the water to a boil over medium-high heat and cook, covered. Once the water is boiling, medium artichokes will cook in about 30 minutes. Check the pot periodically to make sure the water has not boiled dry. You'll know the artichokes are done when an outer leaf releases easily when pulled.

After steaming, cool the artichokes for at least 15 minutes before serving. Artichokes are dense, and they retain a lot of heat, so it is easy to burn your fingers. Steamed artichokes can also be chilled and eaten cool.

1. Removing the pin-sharp thorns at the tips of the leaves makes for easier handling and a more attractive presentation. Grasp the artichoke by the stem and hold it horizontal to your body. Using kitchen shears, trim the tips off the leaves row by row, skipping the top two rows.

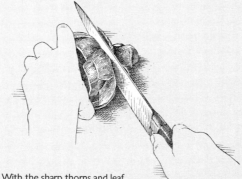

3. With the sharp thorns and leaf tips removed, the stem can now be cut flush with the base of the bulb. Drop the trimmed artichoke in a bowl of acidulated water until ready to cook.

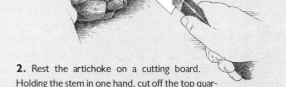

2. Rest the artichoke on a cutting board. Holding the stem in one hand, cut off the top quarter (the top two rows) of the artichoke with a sharp chef's knife.

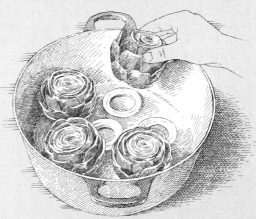

4. Cut very thick slices (about 1½ inches) from medium onions and use your fingers to pop out the outer three or four rings from the rest of the slice. Space the onion rings evenly across the bottom of a Dutch oven, and set one trimmed artichoke on each ring.

PREPARING MEDIUM ARTICHOKE HEARTS FOR COOKING

If you remove all inedible portions before cooking, artichoke hearts can be prepared in almost any fashion, including steaming, braising, sautéing, and grilling. Leave trimmed artichoke hearts as is (in halves) if serving as a side dish; thinly slice the artichoke halves to use them in pasta sauces or rice dishes.

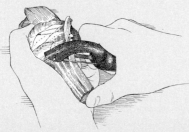

1. Holding the artichoke by the stem, bend back and snap off the thick outer leaves, leaving the bottom portion of each leaf attached. Continue snapping off the leaves until you reach the light yellow cone at the center.

2. With a paring knife, trim off the dark outer layer from the bottom—this is the base of the leaves you've already snapped off.

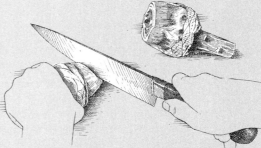

3. Cut off the dark, purplish tip from the yellow cone of artichoke leaves.

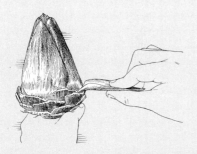

4. With a vegetable peeler, peel off the fibrous, dark green exterior of the stem. After peeling, cut off the bottom ½ inch of the stem.

5. Cut the artichoke in half, slicing from tip to stem.

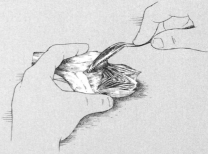

6. Scrape out the small purple leaves and the fuzzy choke with a grapefruit spoon or tomato corer. Drop the trimmed artichoke into a bowl of acidulated water until ready to cook.

The Best Cauliflower Gratin

Poorly made cauliflower gratin is a gruesome merger of floury sauce and mealy cauliflower sitting under a damp carpet of bread crumbs. Here is our take on how to do it right.

⇒ BY JULIA COLLIN ⇐

Usually reserved for salad bars and crudités, cauliflower is often overlooked because of its eccentric texture and unusual flavor. But when sprinkled with a little cream and broiled under a thin sheet of buttery crumbs, these earthy flavored, milky white florets shine in the form of a classic French gratin.

Quite often, though, this simple gratin falls flat, with mealy bits of cauliflower drowned in a thick, fatty sauce. At the other extreme, raw florets float in a soupy, spa-inspired milk broth. More disappointing than badly cooked cauliflower or an ailing sauce, however, is a pale, damp crust. But under the alluring, toasted upper crust of a good gratin lie perfectly cooked pieces of cauliflower, both tender to the bite and well seasoned, and lightly dressed in a smooth, creamy sauce. Taking note of recipes that produced both extremes, I broke this simple dish into its three components—cauliflower, sauce, and bread crumb topping—focusing on each individually before combining them in the oven.

A Perfect Bite in Every Floret

"Cauliflower is nothing but cabbage with a college education," said Mark Twain, though it barely resembles its leafy, potent-flavored relative. With small, dense clusters of firmly packed florets protected by large, stiff outer leaves, this vegetable demands agile knife work to yield attractive, fork-sized pieces. I determined that ¾-inch florets with 1-inch stems were the perfect size.

The first problem with cauliflower gratin is ensuring that the florets are properly cooked—toothsome, but neither mealy nor crunchy. Because cauliflower is a dry, dense vegetable that requires an ample amount of moisture and heat to cook through properly, parcooking is necessary. Cooking three separate batches, I tried steaming, microwaving, and boiling florets.

Steaming was simple and quick, although the cauliflower turned out bland yet tainted with an unappealing cabbage-like flavor. (Could this be how cauliflower was cooked in the Twain household?) With the lid left on, volatile acids became trapped inside the steaming pot, infusing the cauliflower with that unpleasantly familiar flavor. Microwaving the cauliflower in a bowl with some water worked, but the rate of cooking was difficult to monitor, increasing the chance of overcooking.

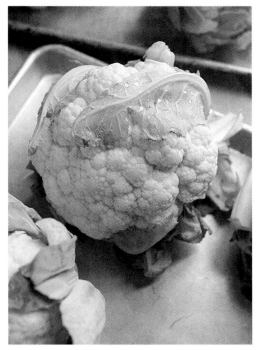

For the best flavor and texture, cook cauliflower in salted boiling water and then rinse it under cold water.

Cooking the cauliflower in salted boiling water, a technique known as blanching, worked best. The cooking rate was easy to monitor, while the salted water washed away and diluted any volatile acids. The resulting cauliflower not only had a clean, uncorrupted flavor but was lightly (yet thoroughly) seasoned. This was a simple but interesting discovery. Although boiling vegetables is out of fashion in some circles, this method has a huge advantage over steaming—the salt in the water seasons the cauliflower as it cooks.

I found that the ¾-inch florets cooked in three to four minutes, yielding a tender exterior with a slightly crunchy core. To prevent further cooking, I ran them under cold water.

Getting Saucy

The classic sauce used in cauliflower gratin is a smooth, creamy, cheese-rich Mornay (milk thickened with a mixture of butter and flour known as a roux). It is seasoned with fresh thyme, onions, nutmeg, and Parmesan or Gruyère cheese. Modern recipes use a similar technique but alter the amounts of roux and milk while adding a variety of flavorings, from cayenne pepper to goat cheese. Wanting to steer clear of thick or watery sauces that would either suffocate or flood the florets, I began to tinker with ingredients and ratios.

To start, I tested three sauces, one made with cream, one with half-and-half, and one with milk. While the sauces required various amounts of roux to attain the same consistency, I was slightly surprised at the tasters' preference for heavy cream. Because its thicker viscosity required less roux (and therefore less flour), the sauce tasted fresh and clean. By comparison, sauces made with milk or half-and-half required more roux and tasted dull, with a glutinous mouthfeel.

I found that ½ cup Parmesan cheese was enough to flavor the lightly thickened cream without being overpowering. Gruyère and cheddar also worked well, while Swiss and goat cheese (commonly found in other recipes) had the wrong texture when melted. Along with fresh thyme and nutmeg, I preferred the perfumed flavor of shallot to the usual onion. Although this French classic generally does not contain garlic or cayenne, tasters liked them both.

The Browning of the Crumbs

Despite perfectly cooked florets and a delicate cream sauce, it is the gratin's toasty brown top that is the defining feature of this dish—and the one most difficult to master. Many gratin recipes produce a lifeless carpet of tasteless, soggy crumbs, just the thing to remind one of bad frozen dinners. My tests began with store-bought bread crumbs, but their fine texture made a heavy, soggy coating that tasted stale and processed. Instead, I found it best to throw a few slices of bread into the food processor with some softened butter. These fresh, buttery crumbs browned evenly and emerged with a light, crisp texture. I tested various types of bread and found that high-quality sandwich bread worked best. While a baguette produced hard, sharp shards, the crumb of cheap sandwich bread was simply too weak and insubstantial. High-quality sandwich bread had a pliable crust and a sturdy crumb that processed and toasted without problem.

The biggest breakthrough, however, came in the selection of the baking dish. (See "Gratin Dishes," page 19.) A high-sided, narrow baking dish produced poorly browned, overcooked cauliflower, whereas a wide, shallow dish allowed the gratin to heat through quickly and yielded a perfectly toasted upper crust. Many recipes called for the broiler, but I found that a high-heat oven worked even better. With heat radiating throughout, the cream and cauliflower became bubbling hot as the crumbs browned nicely on top. Using a 450-degree oven, the gratin was done in about 10 minutes, turning this classic French vegetable preparation into a modern side dish simple enough for your weekday repertoire.

CAULIFLOWER GRATIN
SERVES 6

Although this dish goes together quickly, you can prepare the topping and blanch the cauliflower (steps 1 and 2) an hour or two in advance. Don't prepare the sauce or bake the gratin until just before serving.

Bread Crumb Topping
- 4 slices sandwich bread with crusts, each slice torn into quarters
- 2 tablespoons unsalted butter, softened
- ¼ teaspoon salt
- ⅛ teaspoon ground black pepper

Filling
- Salt
- 1 large head cauliflower (about 3 pounds), trimmed into ¾-inch florets (see illustrations, below)
- 2 tablespoons unsalted butter
- 1 medium shallot, minced (about 2 tablespoons)
- 1 garlic clove, minced
- 1 tablespoon all-purpose flour
- 1½ cups heavy cream
- Pinch fresh ground nutmeg
- Pinch cayenne
- ⅛ teaspoon ground black pepper
- 1 teaspoon minced fresh thyme leaves
- ½ cup (2 ounces) plus 2 tablespoons grated Parmesan cheese

1. **FOR THE TOPPING:** Pulse bread, butter, salt, and pepper in food processor until mixture resembles coarse crumbs, about ten 1-second pulses; set aside.

2. **FOR THE FILLING:** Adjust oven rack to middle position; heat oven to 450 degrees. Bring 4 quarts water to boil in Dutch oven or stockpot over high heat. Add 1 tablespoon salt and cauliflower; cook until outsides are tender but insides are still slightly crunchy, 3 to 4 minutes. Drain cauliflower in colander and rinse under cold running tap water until no longer hot. Leave cauliflower in colander to drain.

3. Heat butter in large skillet over medium heat; when foam subsides, add shallot and cook until softened, about 2 minutes. Add garlic and cook until fragrant, about 30 seconds; stir in flour until combined, about 1 minute. Whisk in cream and bring to boil. Stir in nutmeg, cayenne, ¼ teaspoon salt, pepper, thyme, and ½ cup cheese until incorporated. Off heat, gently stir in cauliflower until evenly combined. Transfer mixture to 11 by 7-inch (2-quart) gratin dish. Sprinkle remaining 2 tablespoons cheese evenly over surface, then sprinkle evenly with bread crumb topping. Bake until golden brown and sauce is bubbling around edges, 10 to 12 minutes. Serve immediately.

CAULIFLOWER GRATIN WITH LEEKS AND GRUYÈRE

Halve 3 small leeks lengthwise, using white and light green parts only, and rinse well; slice crosswise into ¼-inch pieces (you should have about 1 cup). Follow recipe for Cauliflower Gratin, cooking leeks along with shallot until softened, about 4 minutes, and substituting an equal amount Gruyère for Parmesan.

CAULIFLOWER GRATIN WITH HAM AND CHEDDAR CHEESE

Cut 6 ounces ham steak into ½-inch cubes (you should have 1 cup). Follow recipe for Cauliflower Gratin, cooking cubed ham along with shallot and substituting an equal amount sharp cheddar cheese for Parmesan.

TESTING EQUIPMENT: **Gratin Dishes**
A wide, shallow dish maximizes the gratin's surface area while giving the heat easy access to the crumbs on top. I found eight possible options, priced from $7 to $160, including several specifically labeled "gratin dishes" as well as some sold as "casserole dishes" or "oval dishes." Using the recipe for Cauliflower Gratin, I tested these eight dishes to see what differences, if any, I could find.

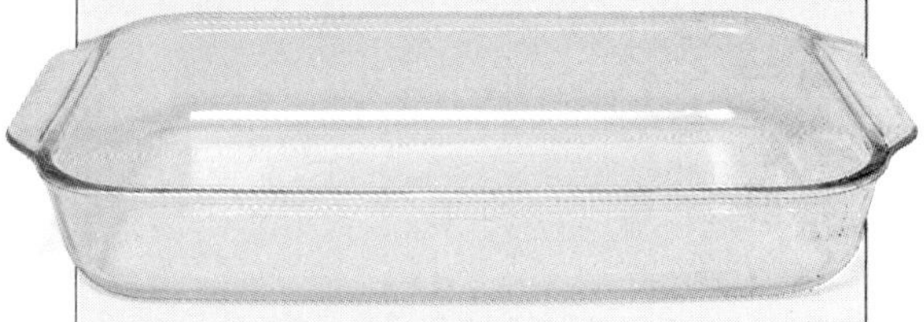

BEST BUY:
Pyrex 2-Quart Casserole Dish, $7

BEST LOOKING:
All-Clad Stainless Au Gratin, $160

Matching the surface area of the dish with the Cauliflower Gratin recipe, I found the dishes ranging from 70 to 100 square inches to be optimal for achieving an even blanket of crumbs. The 59-square-inch Corning Ware 2½-quart oval dish ($19.99) forced me to pack the crumbs on top of one another, creating a thick layer that never browned. On the other hand, the 117-square-inch Pyrex 3-quart casserole dish ($7) scattered the crumbs too widely. These two dishes might work with other recipes, but not this one.

The depth of the dish was also important. The 4-inch-high sides of the Corning Ware 4-quart oval roaster ($21.99) cast a shadow over the gratin that prevented the edges from browning. Most dishes have shallower sides (I found 2 inches to be ideal) that promote better browning. This applies to all gratins, not just this recipe.

Another factor is material. Le Creuset's 14-inch oval dish is made of enameled cast iron, which heats up slowly. The cauliflower and sauce made in this dish were still cool by the time the crust had toasted. Lighter, faster-heating materials, such as glass, porcelain, and stainless steel, are better choices.

Which dish should you buy? I produced hot, nicely browned gratins in several dishes: the Pyrex 2-quart casserole dish ($7), the Emile Henry 13-inch oval dish ($35), the Apilco #14 oval au gratin dish ($68), and the All-Clad Stainless oval au gratin dish ($160). More money might buy better looks but not better performance. —J.C.

STEP-BY-STEP | CUTTING CAULIFLOWER INTO FLORETS

1. Trim stem near base of head. Cut around core to remove; discard core.

2. Using paring knife, cut individual florets from inner stem.

3. Cut florets in halves or quarters to yield ¾-inch pieces.

Simplifying Lemon Pound Cake

Although made from only a handful of ingredients, pound cake can be a finicky, disappointing dessert prone to disaster. We set out to construct a foolproof recipe.

≥ BY RAQUEL PELZEL ≤

Making a wedding cake is hard. Making a multi-layered Dobos torte out of génoise sponge cake and buttercream is daunting. But lemon pound cake? Well, that's easy, isn't it? After all, it's made only of eggs, butter, sugar, flour, and lemon mixed together and baked in a loaf pan. But if it's so easy, why do pound cakes often turn out spongy, rubbery, heavy, and dry rather than fine-crumbed, rich, moist, and buttery? In addition, most pound cake recipes call for creaming the batter, a tricky method that demands the ingredients be at just the right temperature to achieve a silken cake batter. So my goal was twofold: Produce a superior pound cake while making the process as simple and foolproof as possible.

I started with a pound cake recipe developed in the *Cook's* test kitchen in 1994 that was known for being excellent in its results but finicky in its preparation. The cake was top-notch, with a submissive crumb and a golden, buttery interior. In fact, it was everything I wanted from a pound cake except for one thing—the preparation method was anything but foolproof. Made in the traditional style of creaming the butter and sugar until fluffy and pale, the method was so exacting that even the smallest diversion sent the batter over the edge into a curdled abyss. To achieve perfection, the ingredients had to be at an unforgiving 67 degrees, the butter and sugar beaten together for exactly five minutes to aerate, and the eggs drizzled into the batter over a period of 3 to 5 minutes. All of these precautions were advised to eliminate the danger of "breaking" the batter (a pound cake has so many eggs that keeping them in emulsion can be tricky when using the creaming method), which can make the crust look mottled and leave the cake's interior dense and tough.

Machine Age

I turned to other cake recipes for ideas. First I tried cutting softened butter into flour using a standing mixer. After the butter and flour resembled knobby crumbs, I added some of the eggs, beat the mixture until cohesive, then added the rest of

Before applying the lemon glaze, poke the cake's top and sides with a toothpick. The perforations allow the glaze to seep into the center of the cake.

the eggs and beat the batter further until thick, fluffy, and lush. We often favor this method for cakes because it produces a velvety texture and a superfine crumb. Although the pound cake batter assembled this way looked great, the baked cake was too open-grained and tender, more like a yellow cake than a pound cake.

Next I tried melting the butter, a method often used in making quick breads. The liquids are combined and the dry ingredients then mixed into the wet by hand. This method was quick and easy. Melting the butter eliminated all of the temperature issues associated with creaming. Best of all, the batter could be pulled together and put into the oven in five minutes.

With a tight grain, a perfect swell and split in its center, and a nice, browned exterior, this cake showed promise. When I made it a second time, however, it sagged in the center. Additional tests yielded varying results. The problem may have been in the mixing method; perhaps inconsistent mixing produced inconsistent cakes. The solution? A food processor would do a better job of emulsification and also standardize the process. I

added the eggs, sugar, and vanilla to the food processor bowl, combining them enough to integrate the sugar and eggs, and then I drizzled the melted butter in through the feed tube. I transferred the watery base to a large bowl, added lemon zest, and sifted in cake flour and salt, whisking these ingredients in by hand.

The method was a success. The cake had a split dome that afforded a peek inside at the marvelously yellow color of its interior. Just to be sure, I made the cake again and again, with the same results. Recognizing that some home cooks don't have a food processor, I tried the method in a blender. Although the cake was a bit more dense, the differences were so minimal that I recommend either approach. With my method determined, I focused on the cake's texture and flavor.

A Modern Pound Cake

My objective was to make the cake just a bit lighter, but not so light as to resemble a yellow cake. (Pound cakes are by definition heavier and more dense than layer cakes.) When I tested cake flour against all-purpose, the former was superior, making the cake more tender. But the cake still needed more lift and less sponginess.

I was at this point using two sticks of melted butter. Thinking that more butter might improve the texture, I increased the amount, but the cake

Doorstop or Cake? You Decide.

Pound cake has been around since the 1700s, originally created as an alternative to more time-intensive yeasted fruitcakes like babka and stollen. It was traditionally made from 1 pound each of eggs, butter, sugar, and flour. To get a better sense of the taste and texture of an original pound cake, I made one according to the classic recipe.

To my surprise, the batter was dreamy, much like a thick and fluffy buttercream icing. The cakes (this amount of batter provided me with enough to fill two loaf pans comfortably) baked up beautifully at 350 degrees, coming out of the oven with picture-perfect fissures and perfectly tanned crusts.

Beauty aside, though, it's easy to see why modern cooks have veered away from the historic recipe. Tasters described the texture as "leaden" and the flavor akin to an "underbaked sugar cookie." This recipe reads better than it tastes. —R.P.

turned out greasy. Next I turned to the eggs. The original *Cook's* recipe called for 3 eggs plus 3 yolks, so I tried 4 whole eggs instead (an equivalent liquid amount), thinking that the additional white might add some lift. The cake was better but still on the dense side. Without success, I tried adding cream (this cake turned out heavy) and reducing the flour (this one was greasy). Four whole eggs had gotten me close, but the texture was still not ideal.

In the oldest of recipes (from the 1700s), eggs were the only ingredient in pound cake that gave it lift. In the 1850s, however, many cooks began adding the new wonder ingredient—baking powder—to achieve a lighter texture and a higher rise. Although traditionalists might scoff at the addition of chemical leavening, I was willing to give it a try. With just 1 teaspoon, I instilled enough breath into the cake to produce a consistent, perfect crumb. Now that I had simplified the method and achieved the right texture, it was time to concentrate on lemon flavor.

Lemon Laws

In all of my prior tests, I had experienced difficulty keeping the lemon zest afloat. In cake after cake, the zest came together in large yellow clumps. The solution turned out to be simple. When the lemon zest was pulsed with the sugar before the eggs were added to the food processor bowl, the baked cake came out evenly dotted throughout with perfect specks of zest. I also added lemon juice to the batter to boost flavor.

While some prefer their lemon pound cake plain, or with only a simple shower of confectioners' sugar, I like a blast of lemon flavor. A quick glaze—made by bringing sugar and lemon juice to a boil—tasted great in the pan but failed to migrate into the nooks and crannies of the cake's crumb when simply brushed on top. I used an old trick to help the glaze on its way, poking small perforations through the cake's top crust and sides with a toothpick. The glaze now penetrated to the interior of the cake, distributing plenty of lemon flavor. Finally, I had a quick, foolproof recipe that delivered a great crumb and plenty of lemon flavor. Pound for pound, this cake's a winner.

LEMON POUND CAKE
MAKES ONE 9 BY 5-INCH CAKE, SERVING 8

You can use a blender instead of a food processor to mix the batter. To add the butter, remove the center cap of the lid so it can be drizzled into the whirling blender with minimal splattering. This batter looks almost like a thick pancake batter and is very fluid.

16	tablespoons (2 sticks) unsalted butter, plus
	1 tablespoon, softened, for greasing pan
1 ½	cups (6 ounces) cake flour, plus 1 tablespoon
	for dusting pan
1	teaspoon baking powder
½	teaspoon salt
1 ¼	cups (8 ¾ ounces) sugar
2	tablespoons grated zest plus 2 teaspoons juice
	from 2 medium lemons
4	large eggs
1 ½	teaspoons vanilla extract

1. Adjust oven rack to middle position and heat oven to 350 degrees. Grease 9 by 5-inch loaf pan with 1 tablespoon softened butter; dust with 1 tablespoon cake flour, tapping out excess. In medium bowl, whisk together flour, baking powder, and salt; set aside.

2. In glass measuring cup or microwave-safe bowl, microwave butter, covered with plastic wrap, at full power until melted, 1 to 2 minutes. (Alternatively, melt butter in small saucepan over medium heat.) Whisk melted butter thoroughly to reincorporate any separated milk solids.

3. In food processor, process sugar and zest until combined, about five 1-second pulses. Add lemon juice, eggs, and vanilla; process until combined, about 5 seconds. With machine running, add melted butter through feed tube in steady stream (this should take about 20 seconds). Transfer mixture to large bowl. Sift flour mixture over eggs in three steps, whisking gently after each addition until just combined.

4. Pour batter into prepared pan and bake 15 minutes. Reduce oven temperature to 325 degrees and continue to bake until deep golden brown and skewer inserted in center comes out clean, about 35 minutes, rotating pan halfway through baking time. Cool in pan for 10 minutes, then turn onto wire rack and brush on Lemon Glaze, if desired. Cool to room temperature, at least 1 hour. (Cooled cake can be wrapped tightly in plastic wrap and stored at room temperature for up to 5 days.)

LEMON GLAZE
ENOUGH TO GLAZE ONE 9 BY 5-INCH CAKE

Brush this glaze onto the warm cake to give it a fresh sweet-tart lemon kick.

| ½ | cup (3 ½ ounces) sugar |
| ¼ | cup juice from 1 or 2 medium lemons |

While cake is cooling, bring sugar and lemon juice to boil in small nonreactive saucepan, stirring occasionally to dissolve sugar. Reduce heat to low and simmer until thickened slightly, about 2 minutes. Apply glaze as shown in illustrations below.

LEMON–POPPY SEED POUND CAKE

Follow recipe for Lemon Pound Cake through step 1. Toss 1 tablespoon flour mixture with ⅓ cup poppy seeds in small bowl; set aside. Continue with recipe from step 2, folding poppy seed mixture into batter after flour is incorporated.

Creaming Method versus Food Processor Method

CREAMING METHOD
➤ **TOTAL TIME (MAKING AND BAKING): 3 hours and 15 minutes**
Although it produces a lovely cake batter and a very nice-looking pound cake, the creaming method is laborious and time-consuming, in part because you must wait for the ingredients to come to room temperature.

FOOD PROCESSOR METHOD
➤ **TOTAL TIME (MAKING AND BAKING): 1 hour, plus or minus 5 minutes**
We like the food processor method because it's easy, it's fast, and it produces a pound cake just as tasty (and nearly as attractive) as one made by the creaming method. Because this method relies on melted butter, you can have the cake in the oven 10 minutes after walking into the kitchen.

1. After removing cake from pan, poke entire top with toothpick.

2. Poke cake on all sides with toothpick.

3. Brush top and sides of cake with glaze. Cool to room temperature.

STEP-BY-STEP | GLAZING POUND CAKE

Perfecting New York–Style Cheesecake

What's the secret to the perfect New York cheesecake? It's a character trait that most New Yorkers would never admit to—restraint.

≳ BY DAWN YANAGIHARA ≲

Cheesecake has taken a tawdry twist these days, sullied by ice cream–style flavors such as Irish coffee, cappuccino crunch, and Key lime. We all know that the only true cheesecake—the one with unimpeachable credentials—is the New York cheesecake. It is a subtle orchestration of different textures made sublime by a rare and welcome exercise in restraint. Rejecting the Ben and Jerry school of everything-but-the-kitchen-sink concoctions, the ideal New York cheesecake is timeless in its adherence to simplicity. It should be a tall, bronze-skinned, and dense affair. At the core, it should be cool, thick, smooth, satiny, and creamy. Radiating outward, it goes gradually from velvet to suede, then, finally, about the edges, it becomes cake-like and fine-pored. The flavor should be pure and minimalist, sweet and tangy, and rich to boot. This cheesecake should not taste citrusy or vanilla-laden, nor should it be fluffy, mousse-like, leaden, gummy, chewy, or starchy. A well-made cheesecake should not be so dry as to make you gag, and it definitely should not bake up with a fault line as large as the San Andreas (we're talking New York, after all).

There is no shortage of New York cheesecake recipes in cookbooks or magazines or on the Internet. I selected five promising recipes to sample. One turned out looking and tasting more like a gargantuan round of goat cheese than a cheesecake. The other four were good, but tasters cited each for some sort of infraction—an overabundance of orange zest, a taste of raw flour, a pasty mouthfeel, or a texture too light for New York cheesecake—that made every one of them less than great. I wanted a cheesecake far simpler and purer in flavor, with a flawless texture. With this lucid vision of New York cheesecake and a fierce appetite, I embarked on a long journey.

Crust Counts

Some recipes claim that a pastry crust was the crust of choice for the original New York cheesecake, so I tried one. That effort, though, resulted only in a crust that became soggy beneath the filling. Most recipes forgo the pastry crust for a crumb crust—cookie or cracker crumbs are tasty and more practical options. Every taster, including myself, considered a mere dusting of crumbs on the bottom of the cheesecake insufficient. We wanted a crust with more presence.

Great New York cheesecake is smooth, satiny, and dense, with a bronzed top and a crisp graham cracker crust.

A graham cracker crust—made with 1 cup of crumbs, some sugar, and melted butter, pressed into the bottom of a springform pan, and pre-baked until fragrant and browning around the edges—was ideal at a thickness of about 3/8 inch. If served within a day of being baked, it retained its crispness. (When held for a couple of days, the crust softened, but tasters still appreciated its sweet toasty flavor, and the texture was superior to a gummy pastry crust.) Brown sugar and ground cinnamon did not improve the crust. I also tried substituting gingersnaps and then chocolate wafers for the graham crackers. Although the former were overpowering, the latter worked well, remaining crisp even longer than the graham cracker crumbs. Nonetheless, most tasters preferred graham crackers, so the chocolate wafers are offered as an alternative.

Less Is More

A great New York cheesecake should be of great stature. One made with 2 pounds (four bars) of cream cheese was not tall enough. I threw in another half pound, reaching the springform pan's maximum capacity, and the cheesecake stood tall. The amount of sugar was quickly settled at 1½ cups. The cheesecake struck a perfect balance of sweet and tangy.

Cheesecakes require a dairy supplement to the cream cheese, such as heavy cream, sour cream, or sometimes both. I made a cheesecake without additional dairy and quickly discovered why it is necessary. Cream cheese on its own produces a pasty cake, akin to mortar—much like a bar of cream cheese straight out of its wrapper. Additional dairy loosens up the texture of the cream cheese, giving the cake a smoother, more luxurious texture. Although some recipes call for as much as 1½ cups of sour cream per 8 ounces of cream cheese, I found that 1/3 cup sour cream combined with 2½ pounds cream cheese was ideal. (Too much sour cream makes cheesecake taste sour and acidic.) As for heavy cream, another common addition, I found that amounts large enough to improve the texture of the cheesecake also dulled the flavor. So it was cream cheese and sour cream—and, once again, restraint was key.

Eggs help bind the cheesecake, make it cohesive, and give it structure. They also help create a smooth, creamy texture. Whole eggs alone are often called for in softer, airier cheesecakes of non–New York persuasions. Recipes for New York cheesecake, however, agree that a few yolks in addition to whole eggs help to produce the velvety, lush texture of a proper New York cheesecake. After much testing, I settled on 6 whole eggs plus 2 yolks, a combination that produced an agreeable texture: dense but not heavy, firm but not rigid, and perfectly rich.

Starch—usually either flour or cornstarch—helps make cheesecake thicker, but as evidenced by the half-dozen or so starch-laced cakes I made, even in amounts as small as a tablespoon, a gummy, starchy presence can be detected. Tasters much preferred the meltingly luxurious quality of a completely starch-free cheesecake.

Could it be possible that even good cooks might be better off simply defrosting a store-bought frozen cheesecake instead of baking a fresh one at home? We wanted to make sure our efforts (and possibly yours) weren't in vain, so we thawed four commercial cheesecakes and conducted a blind taste test, adding our homemade version as one of the contenders.

The commercial contestants were Sara Lee Original Cream Cheesecake ($6.69/16 ounces); The Ultimate New York Cheesecake from David Glass ($8.99/15 ounces),

a gourmet dessert company; Original Cheesecake from The Cheesecake Factory ($16.95/38 ounces), a chain of eateries featuring more than 30 flavors of cheesecake; and Trader Joe's New York Style Cheesecake ($3.69/18 ounces).

It was a landslide, with the *Cook's* cheesecake winning easily. Tasters prized its "fresh," "tangy" flavor and "crisp" crust with "true graham flavor." To our surprise, Sara Lee earned second place for its "soft," "smooth" texture, though a few tasters remarked that it left a "burning sensation" in the back of their throats. Sara

Lee easily beat out more expensive "gourmet" cheesecakes made by David Glass and The Cheesecake Factory. Tasters described the David Glass entry as "artificially vanilla," with an "overly cinnamony crust." The Cheesecake Factory cake was deemed "acidic and sour." Each and every taster put the Trader Joe's cheesecake in last place, uniformly rejecting it as "pasty," "floury," and "absolutely tasteless."

The lesson here is clear: Don't be lured by the ease of store-bought cheesecake. Take the time to make it at home, and you won't be disappointed. —Becky Hays

SURPRISE WINNER
Sara Lee beat out "gourmet" options, but
it couldn't compare to homemade.

NOT WORTH THE CALORIES OR THE MONEY
These cakes were deemed "artificial" tasting, "sour," or "pasty."
From left: David Glass, The Cheesecake Factory, Trader Joe's.

Perfecting the flavor was, to me, a weighty issue, but an easy one to work through. Tasters moaned that orange zest makes cheesecake taste like a Creamsicle, so it was out of there in a New York minute. Next to go was lemon zest because its flavor was distracting. A couple teaspoons of lemon juice, however, perked things up without adding a distinctively lemon flavor. Just a bit of salt (sodium is already part of cream cheese) and a couple teaspoons of vanilla extract rounded out the flavors. Thankfully, my tasters and I were on the same page. We all appreciated a minimalist cheesecake.

Bake High and Low

One reason cheesecake is well loved by cooks is that it goes together easily. Even so, I noted that care must be used when mixing the ingredients lest the batter end up with small nodules of unmixed cream cheese that mar the smoothness of the baked cake. Frequent and thorough scraping of the bowl during mixing is key to ensuring that every bit of cream cheese is incorporated. It's also helpful to start with semi-softened cream cheese. It doesn't need to be at room temperature, and it definitely doesn't need to be microwaved. Simply cutting the cream cheese into chunks and letting it stand while preparing the crust and assembling the other ingredients—30 to 45 minutes—makes mixing easier. (When icebox-cold, the cream cheese resists being mixed. It clings to the beaters and bowl in firm, waxy chunks and requires much scraping and beating before it will cooperate.)

There are many ways to bake a cheesecake—in a moderate oven, in a low oven, in a water bath, or in the New York fashion, in which the cake bakes at 500 degrees for about 10 minutes and then at 200 degrees for about an hour. I tried them all, but

the New York method was the only one that yielded the attractive nut-brown surface I was after. This supersimple, no-water-bath (no leaking pans, layers of foil prophylactics, or boiling water), dual-temperature baking method also produced a lovely graded texture—soft and creamy at the center and firm and dry at the periphery.

The New York baking method was not without flaws, however. After an hour at 200 degrees, the very center of the cheesecake—even after chilling—was loose and slurpy, the result of underbaking. Some recipes leave the cheesecake in the still-warm, turned-off, propped-open oven for about 30 minutes to finish setting up. When I tried this, the cheesecake was marginally better but still insufficiently baked.

Next I extended the hour-long oven time to 90 minutes, baking the cheesecake to an internal temperature of about 150 degrees. Once chilled, it was cheesecake perfection. With a cleanly set center rather than a wet and sloppy one, it sliced into neat slabs. And though each slice kept its shape, every bite was satiny on the tongue. (Because all ovens bake differently, it's important to guard against overbaking the cheesecake. Taken to internal temperatures of more than 160 degrees, my test cheesecakes were hopelessly cracked—see "The Conundrum of the Crack" on page 24. To avoid this problem, use an instant-read thermometer. It is the most reliable means of judging the doneness of the cheesecake.)

Cheesecake is also well loved (by the sweet tooth, not the waistline) because it lasts longer in the refrigerator than a dessert should. After a day or two, the crust is a little soggy, but the cake tastes every bit as good. For breakfast, forget the bagel. Go for the cheesecake.

TECHNIQUE | PATTING
THE CRUST INTO PLACE

1. Use bottom of ramekin or drinking glass to press crumbs into bottom of buttered springform pan. Press crumbs as far as possible into edges of pan.

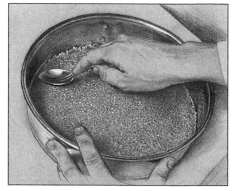

2. Use teaspoon to neatly press crumbs into circumference of pan to create clean edge.

For the crust, chocolate wafers (Nabisco Famous) can be substituted for graham crackers; you will need about 14 wafers. The flavor and texture of the cheesecake is best if the cake is allowed to stand at room temperature for 30 minutes before serving. When cutting the cake, have a pitcher of hot tap water nearby; dipping the blade of the knife into the water and wiping it clean with a kitchen towel after each cut helps make neat slices.

Graham Cracker Crust
- 1 cup (4 ounces) graham cracker crumbs (8 whole crackers, broken into rough pieces and processed in food processor until uniformly fine)
- 1 tablespoon sugar
- 5 tablespoons unsalted butter, melted, plus additional 1 tablespoon melted butter for greasing pan

Cheesecake Filling
- 2½ pounds cream cheese, cut into rough 1-inch chunks and left to stand at room temperature for 30 to 45 minutes
- ⅛ teaspoon salt
- 1½ cups (10½ ounces) sugar
- ⅓ cup (2½ ounces) sour cream
- 2 teaspoons juice from 1 lemon
- 2 teaspoons vanilla extract
- 2 large egg yolks plus 6 large whole eggs

1. **FOR THE CRUST:** Adjust oven rack to lower-middle position and heat oven to 325 degrees. Combine graham cracker crumbs and sugar in medium bowl; add 5 tablespoons melted butter and toss with fork until evenly moistened. Brush bottom and sides of 9-inch springform pan with most of remaining melted butter, making sure to leave enough to brush pan in step 3. Empty crumbs into springform pan and, following illustrations on page 23, press evenly into pan bottom. Bake until fragrant and beginning to brown around edges, about 13 minutes. Cool on wire rack while making filling.

2. **FOR THE CHEESECAKE FILLING:** Increase oven temperature to 500 degrees. In standing mixer fitted with paddle attachment, beat cream cheese at medium-low speed to break up and soften slightly, about 1 minute. Scrape beater and bottom and sides of bowl well with rubber spatula; add salt and about half of sugar and beat at medium-low speed until combined, about 1 minute. Scrape bowl; beat in remaining sugar until combined, about 1 minute. Scrape bowl; add sour cream, lemon juice, and vanilla, and beat at low speed until combined, about 1 minute. Scrape bowl; add yolks and beat at medium-low speed until thoroughly combined, about 1 minute. Scrape bowl; add whole eggs two at a time, beating until thoroughly combined, about 1 minute, and scraping bowl between additions.

3. Brush sides of springform pan with remaining melted butter. Set springform pan on rimmed baking sheet (to catch any spills if springform pan leaks). Pour filling into cooled crust and bake 10 minutes; without opening oven door, reduce oven temperature to 200 degrees and continue to bake until instant-read thermometer inserted into center of cheesecake registers about 150 degrees, about 1½ hours. Transfer cake to wire rack and cool 5 minutes; run paring knife between cake and side of springform pan. Cool until barely warm, 2½ to 3 hours. Wrap tightly in plastic wrap and refrigerate until cold, at least 3 hours. (Cake can be refrigerated up to 4 days.)

4. To unmold cheesecake, remove sides of pan. Slide thin metal spatula between crust and pan bottom to loosen, then slide cake onto serving plate. Let cheesecake stand at room temperature about 30 minutes, then cut into wedges and serve.

The Conundrum of the Crack

Some cooks use the crack to gauge when a cheesecake is done. I say if it's cracked, it's overdone, not to mention unsightly. Exactly what happens, you may ask, that causes the cheesecake to form a fault line?

What I learned from two months of baking was that when the internal temperature of a cheesecake rose beyond 160 degrees, it almost always cracked. The best way to prevent cheesecake from cracking is to use an instant-read thermometer to test its doneness. Take it out of the oven when it reaches 150 degrees at the center to avoid overbaking.

That said, there is a second opportunity for the cheesecake to crack, this time outside of the oven. During my testing, a perfectly good-looking cake cracked as it sat on the cooling rack—the cake shrank during cooling and clung to the sides of the springform pan. If the cake clings tenaciously enough, it splits at its weakest point, the center. To avoid this type of late cracking, cool the cheesecake for only a few minutes, then free it from the sides of the pan with a paring knife before allowing it to cool fully. —D.Y.

To Top It Off

The dense, creamy richness of a New York cheesecake makes it the perfect candidate for some kind of fruity foil. A ruby-colored, glazed strawberry topping is the classic fruit accompaniment to New York cheesecake.

I tried to make one out of frozen strawberries, but, once thawed, the berries looked ragged and unattractive. I tried gently poaching fresh slivered berries in sugar syrup, but the syrup was weak in flavor and color. I tried cooking berries with sugar until they released their juices, but they never released enough to make much of a sauce, so I supplemented their juices with strawberry liqueur and thickened the liquid with cornstarch. Sadly, the strawberry flavor from the liqueur was not pure, and the heat killed the fresh flavor and texture of the berries, making them shaggy and dull.

I shifted gears. This time I macerated slivered berries in some sugar and a pinch of salt for about 30 minutes to soften them and cause them to exude some of their juices. I then pureed a cup of strawberry jam in a food processor until it was smooth. The pureeing made the jam frothy, so I simmered it for a few minutes until it was again dark, clear, and free of froth. I stirred in some lemon juice to add liveliness, then poured the molten mixture over the berries, tossed them, and chilled them for a few hours. The maceration and the heat of the jam gave the berries just enough coaxing to transform them from their raw rigid state to a yielding texture. The syrup they sat in had a clean strawberry flavor and draped nicely over a slice of cheesecake. —D.Y.

FRESH STRAWBERRY TOPPING
MAKES ABOUT 1½ QUARTS

This accompaniment to cheesecake is best served the same day it is made.

- 2 pounds strawberries, cleaned, hulled, and cut lengthwise into ¼- to ⅛-inch slices
- ½ cup sugar
- Pinch salt
- 1 cup (about 11 ounces) strawberry jam
- 2 tablespoons juice from 1 lemon

1. Toss berries, sugar, and salt in medium bowl; let stand until berries have released juice and sugar has dissolved, about 30 minutes, tossing occasionally to combine.

2. Process jam in food processor until smooth, about 8 seconds; transfer to small saucepan. Bring jam to simmer over medium-high heat; simmer, stirring frequently, until dark and no longer frothy, about 3 minutes. Stir in lemon juice; pour warm liquid over strawberries and stir to combine. Let cool, then cover with plastic wrap and refrigerate until cold, at least 2 hours or up to 12 hours. To serve, spoon a portion of topping over each slice of cheesecake.

Can an Oven Thermometer Make You a Better Baker?

Inaccurate ovens produce burned soufflés and soggy cakes. Can an inexpensive oven thermometer come to the rescue?

≥ BY ADAM RIED ≤

Have you ever baked a cake or pie that was only half-done after the suggested cooking time? We have, and the reason often was a poorly calibrated oven. In fact, our research indicates that two different ovens set to the same temperature can differ in actual temperature by as much as 90 degrees (see "The Heat Is On . . . Or Is It?" below right). This means that the accuracy of your oven can spell the difference between disaster and culinary triumph.

Even the ovens here in our test kitchen often stray from reliability in between service calls from the professionals who recalibrate them. Recently, for example, we found that the ovens in our double wall oven unit differed from each other by 30 degrees when set to the same temperature. That's why we often use an oven thermometer to tell us what's really going on. In fact, we consider the oven thermometer such an important tool that we rounded up eight popular models to test. With our ovens freshly calibrated and a computerized, supersensitive thermometer (the ChartScan Portable Data Recorder) to accurately monitor oven temperatures, we set out to assess the various models based on readability, accuracy, and stability.

But First, a Word about Your Oven

Cooking in an oven is not as straightforward a process as you might think. In fact, three different dynamics of heat transfer are simultaneously in play. Radiation is the heat energy (generated by the heating element) carried through the air inside the oven cavity. Convection is the movement of the hot air itself; think of the fan inside a convection oven. Last is conduction, which is the transfer of energy from one hot surface to another; think of a piece of meat browning while in contact with the surface of a hot pan. Of these three dynamics, radiation from the heating element is responsible for the lion's share of browning that occurs when you bake or roast in the oven.

Conversations with David Anderson, senior product manager at Whirlpool, revealed that the average oven designed for home use does not simply heat up to the temperature set on the dial and then stay there. Anderson noted that an oven's heating elements are either on at full power or off—with no middle ground. To maintain the desired temperature, the heating elements cycle within a manufacturer-determined tolerance, heating up and cooling down to temperatures just above and below the desired temperature. The precise temperature tolerances and timing of the cycles vary from manufacturer to manufacturer. For instance, Anderson said that Whirlpool uses one-minute intervals, so the elements will be on for one minute, then off for the next, then on again, and so forth as necessary. This cycling process is regulated by an internal temperature sensor located in the oven cavity.

We wanted to put this information to the test, so we hooked up our ChartScan Temperature Data Recorder to an electric oven in the test kitchen and programmed it to record the temperature once every 10 seconds for 1½ hours. We placed 15 temperature sensors, called thermocouples, at different locations up and down and side to side in the oven cavity and set the dial to 350 degrees. At the dead-center location in the oven, we found the temperature cycled within a range of roughly 25 degrees, from a low of about 335 degrees to a high of about 361 degrees. We analyzed a gas oven in the same manner and found the temperature spread to be somewhat narrower, between 343 and 359 degrees.

Uneven Heating

A careful look at the numbers generated by our ChartScan tests also confirmed the common assertion that the heat within an oven cavity is not

---

The Heat Is On . . . Or Is It?

We know from experience in our test kitchen that the calibration of most ovens—that is, their ability to reach and hold the temperature set on the dial—is far from perfect. We figured that the same must be true of home ovens, so, armed with our winning oven thermometer, we tested 16 ovens in the homes of staff and friends.

We were right. After setting each oven to 350 degrees and allowing a 30-minute preheating period, we found that several of them ran as much as 50 degrees low or 40 degrees high. That kind of inaccuracy can have a huge—and likely bad—effect on your cooking if you are not aware of it.

In fact, only two of the 16 ovens tested registered exactly 350 degrees. One of those two, incidentally, had been delivered brand new the week we tested it; this was but the second time it had ever been turned on, so it is no surprise that its calibration was good. Ten ovens ran cool, anywhere from 300 degrees—a whopping 50 degrees off the mark—to 340 degrees, while the remaining four ovens ran hot, from 360 degrees all the way up to 390 degrees, a substantial 40 degrees off.

So what's the moral of this story? There are three. First, do not assume that your oven is accurate, which means that you should begin checking baked goods for doneness well before the cooking time suggested in recipes. Second, buy an oven thermometer. A $13 investment could dramatically improve your baked goods. Third, if your oven runs very hot or very cool you might want to consider spending the money (about $100, in our experience) to have it calibrated. —A.R.

Testing Home Ovens

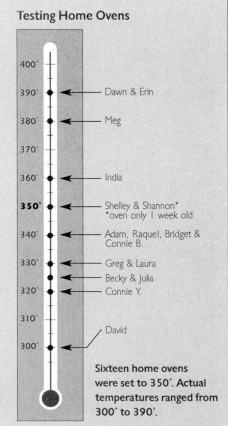

Sixteen home ovens were set to 350°. Actual temperatures ranged from 300° to 390°.

---

consistent; that, in effect, there are hot and cold spots. Though we might have suspected otherwise, we found that the bottom of our electric test oven tended to run hotter than the top, usually by between 5 and 15 degrees. We also found that the rear of our oven ran hotter than the front by roughly 5 to 10 degrees. There was also a stunning difference from right to left in our oven, with the right side sometimes running up to 50 degrees hotter than the left!

The uneven heat is the reason why many cookbook authors suggest rotating pans in the oven when you bake. We ran a simple test of baking sugar cookies to confirm this advice. Sure enough, the cookies were browned a little less evenly from one side of the pan to the other when we failed to turn the cookie sheet partway through the baking time.

Curious as to whether there was any truth to the common kitchen wisdom that electric ovens heat more evenly than gas ovens, we repeated the ChartScan tests on a gas range in the test kitchen. The temperatures recorded in our tests bore out some validity in this axiom. For instance, the temperature differential between the bottom and top of the cavity was closer to 50 degrees, where it had been just 5 to 15 degrees in the electric oven.

In an attempt to explain all of these temperature variations, many of our sources pointed to numerous factors that affect the way in which an oven heats up. Included among them are the size of the cavity; the number and position of the heating elements; the size, shape, and position of whatever you are cooking; and, in the case of double wall ovens, whether you are heating just one oven at a time or both simultaneously. Without performing extensive tests on different brands of ovens, we cannot comment on the desirability of different models; we can only strongly suggest that you use a good thermometer to investigate the performance of your own oven.

The Thermometers

An oven thermometer will give you a fighting chance in the guessing game of temperatures inside your oven. Widely available in stores from the local supermarket right up to fancy kitchenware emporia, we wondered if price—which ranged from a low of about $5 for the Pyrex model to a high of almost $32 for a mercury-based Taylor model—really mattered.

As awareness of mercury's toxic properties has increased, the mercury-based thermometers that were once common have become rare. In fact, the Taylor Serviceman's Folding Oven Test Thermometer was the only mercury-based model in our group of eight. In another Taylor model, the Classic Oven Guide Thermometer, blue-dyed alcohol took the place of mercury, but all of the other models were based on a bimetal coil. Engineers from Taylor Environmental Instruments explained that the bimetal coil,

Buying a Thermometer

Several *Cook's* editors had heard the same bit of advice about selecting an oven thermometer at the store: Select the thermometer that comes closest to the average temperature of the other thermometers on the shelf. (In other words, the thermometers in a store may vary slightly in their reading of room temperature, from say, 67 to 73 degrees, so you would want to choose a thermometer with a reading of 70 degrees.) We put this theory to the test with our winning thermometer, the Taylor Classic Oven Guide.

Among the 15 Taylor Oven Guides at the store, we found a variation of about 10 degrees. We bought the one which read closest to an average of all the others and brought it back to the test kitchen to compare it with three we had purchased previously. In a pleasant bit of anticlimax, they all registered exactly the same temperature in our oven tests. Even though the readings varied slightly at room temperature, they were consistent at higher oven temperatures. —A.R.

mounted inside the thermometer and attached at one end to the pointer on the dial, is made from two types of metal, bonded together, which have different rates of expansion and contraction when subjected to changes in temperature. When the temperature increases or decreases, the coil changes length, which causes

---

The Oven Thermometers We Tested

OUR FAVORITE

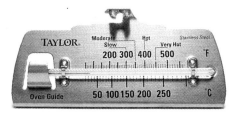

Taylor Classic Oven Guide
Perfect accuracy and exceptional stability make this thermometer a winner.

Component
Stable, readable, and reasonably accurate.

Cooper
Its stability is nowhere near as good as its accuracy.

Pyrex
A champ when it comes to readability, but suffers from flimsy construction.

Hoan
Respectable accuracy, but falls through the oven rack easily.

Taylor Serviceman's
The most expensive thermometer by far and not widely available. The only one to employ mercury.

Taylor Classic Oven Dial
Very easy to read if it sits on the oven shelf, but very difficult to read if it hangs.

Polder
Unexceptional in every way, from readability to stability.

RATING OVEN THERMOMETERS

RATINGS
★★★
GOOD
★★
FAIR
★
POOR

We rated eight oven thermometers and evaluated them according to the following criteria. Tests were performed in the same, freshly calibrated KitchenAid Superba Selectra 27 electric oven in the *Cook's Illustrated* test kitchen.

PRICE: Prices paid in Boston-area stores, in national mail-order catalogs, or on the Web.

READABILITY: Thermometers with large, bold-print numbers and relatively large faces of 2 inches or more were the easiest to read and therefore preferred.

ACCURACY: The thermometers' accuracy was mea-sured against readings from a sophisticated temperature sensor called the ChartScan Portable Data Recorder, in the same test kitchen oven, heated to 200, 350, and 500 degrees. Temperature-sensing thermocouples were attached to the oven rack adjacent to the thermometers, then connected to the data recorder, which was in turn connected to a laptop computer. This setup recorded the precise temperature of that spot inside the oven every 10 seconds, and when it registered our target temperatures exactly, we took a reading of the oven thermometer being tested. Thermometers that registered all three temperatures correctly or that were off by no more than 8 degrees were rated good, those off by 9 to 17 degrees were rated fair, and those off by 18 to 25 degrees (25 degrees was the maximum variation) were rated poor.

TEMPERATURE RANGE/INCREMENTS: All thermometers tested cover the usual range of oven temperatures. A thermometer that marks temperature in 10-degree increments is more precise than one that registers temperature in 25-degree increments.

TESTERS' COMMENTS: This category encompasses disparate factors that can make the thermometers easier or more difficult to use. All the thermometers could either hang from an oven rack or sit on it, but some were more stable than others. Stable thermometers, which were difficult to knock over if hit accidentally with a pan being placed in or removed from the oven, were preferred.

Brand	Price	Readability	Accuracy at 500°	Accuracy at 350°	Accuracy at 200°	Range/ Increments	Testers' Comments
FAVORITE **Taylor** Classic Oven Guide Thermometer, Model 5921	$12.99	★★★	★★★	★★★	★★★	50° to 550° in 10° increments	Temperature readings were spot on, and this Taylor passed our knock-over test with flying colors. The most stable thermometer of the group, in part because of its 4-inch length.
Component Design Magnet Mounted Oven Thermometer, Model MOT1	$7.99	★★★	★★★	★★	★★	100° to 600° in 25° increments	The magnet mounted on the back of the dial is a boon to stability. That, and the uncluttered dial graphics, earned the Component a second-place rating.
Cooper Oven Thermometer, Model 24HP	$7.95	★★	★★★	★★★	★★	200° to 600° in 25° increments	The bold numbers on its compact face provide average readability.
Pyrex Accessories Oven Thermometer, #16416	$4.99	★★★	★★	★★	★★★	100° to 600° in 25° increments	Excellent readability owing to its large, uncluttered, stark white dial face with clear, simple graphics. No Celsius scale.
Hoan Stainless Steel Oven Thermometer, Style No. 43460	$6.99	★★★	★★	★★	★★★	200° to 500° in 20° increments	Bold numbers with red markers every 50° make this thermometer easy to read despite its small dial face. No Celsius scale.
Taylor Serviceman's Folding Oven Test Thermometer, Model 5903	$31.50	★★★	★	★★	★★★	100° to 600° in 25° increments	Arrived with neither instructions nor a hook, so we could not hang it from the rack. Very easy to read, and it's stable if you place it diagonally on the oven rack. No Celsius scale.
Taylor Classic Oven Dial Thermometer, Model 5931	$5.99	★★★	★	★	★★★	175° to 515° in 5° increments	Bold-face numbers help readability, but the poor design of the hanger hinders readability because it causes the dial face to tilt downward. No Celsius scale.
Polder Oven Thermometer	$7.95	★★	★	★★	★★	50° to 500° in 10° increments	Get out your reading glasses—you'll need them to decipher the crowded dial face. Two complete scales for Fahrenheit and Celsius are the culprits.

the pointer on the dial face to rotate to indicate the temperature.

According to our tests at moderate to high oven temperatures, most of the thermometers were pretty accurate, but only one model, the Taylor Classic Oven Guide Thermometer, was spot-on at all temperatures we tested. On the other hand, only three models—the Taylor Serviceman's Folding Oven Test Thermometer (with the mercury), the Taylor Classic Oven Dial Thermometer, and the Polder—produced readings that were more than about 18 degrees off, which was the limit of our tolerance (see chart above for more information).

During the testing, we also noted that two models in particular, the Cooper and the Polder, could be difficult to read owing to small dial faces that are overstuffed with graphics. When you shop, look for an uncluttered thermometer face with bold numbers for good readability.

The last issue that affects everyday use is stability. All of the thermometers can either sit on the oven shelf or hang from it. Either way, unfortunately, it is easy to knock over the thermometer while maneuvering a pan in or out of the oven. Even more irritating is when the thermometer falls through the wires of the rack to the bottom of the cavity. Both instances occasion a clumsy retrieval process with a hand shod in a bulky oven mitt. Two of the thermometers, the Taylor Classic Oven Guide, with its extrawide, 4-inch base, and the Component Design, with its built-in magnet, minimized such antics; they were exceptionally stable in our knock tests. At the same time, the Taylor Oven Guide and the Component Design are each only 2 inches tall, so it was easy to maneuver pans up and over without disturbing them.

All in all, most of the thermometers performed acceptably, but one, the moderately priced Taylor Classic Oven Guide, shone especially bright in every test. Though it was not the least expensive of the contestants, its readability, stability, and accuracy represent a good value as far as we're concerned. In fact, we may just buy one for each of the 10 ovens in our test kitchen.

Supermarket Cheddar Fails to Excite Tasters

Supermarket cheddar cheeses are pale imitations of authentic farmhouse cheddars, but they are cheap and widely available. Some are even worth eating.

⇒ BY RAQUEL PELZEL ⇐

A great farmhouse cheddar cheese is hard, fine-textured, and flaky, with a sharp, tangy edge that's a little sweet, nutty, slightly bitter, and herbaceous. These various flavors come together to create a well-balanced, complex, and rewarding taste experience. The bad news is that farmhouse cheddars are expensive ($11 to $19 per pound) and often hard to find. Supermarket cheddars, on the other hand, can be one-dimensional, sour, and unbalanced, exhibiting textures that are rubbery and homogenous rather than flaky and fine-grained.

That said, because supermarket cheddars are so easy to find and afford, we were interested in exploring their merits. We organized a blind tasting of eight common brands to find out which ones were best fresh out of the package and which fared best in a grilled cheese sandwich.

Cheddar in Name Only

Before conducting the tasting, we were keen to find out what sort of cheese qualifies as cheddar. Unlike other great cheeses, such as Parmigiano-Reggiano and Stilton, cheddar is not name-protected. Anyone can make cheddar cheese anywhere and any way. Although the U.S. Food and Drug Administration (FDA) regulates cheddar cheese as a final product (it must have no less than 50 percent milk fat solids and no more than 39 percent moisture), the means by which manufacturers produce the cheese are ungoverned. This is why there is so much variation in flavor between one cheddar and another and why even within the "sharp" category we found some cheeses as mild as mozzarella and others as robust as Parmesan.

The traditional way to make cheddar cheese is called cheddaring. During cheddaring, the curd (made by adding acid-producing cultures and clotting agents to unpasteurized whole milk) is cut into slabs, then stacked, cut, pressed, and stacked again. Along the way a large amount of liquid, called whey, is extracted from the curd base. The remaining compacted curd is what gives farmhouse cheddars their hard and fine-grained characteristics.

The quicker, safer, more cost-effective way to make cheddar, employed by most manufacturers to meet the ever-increasing demand of the mass market for cheese, is called the stirred-curd method. Instead of being stacked and weighted, as in the cheddaring process, the curd is stirred and then pressed against the sides of a large vat to remove the whey. This shortcut slightly changes the texture of the curd, producing a softer, more pliable cheese. Is stirred-curd cheese still technically a cheddar cheese even though it's not cheddared? According to the FDA, it is—as long as it meets the composition requirements for milk fat solids and moisture.

Grafton Village (number four in the tasting) is one of the only companies in the tasting that still hand-cheddars its cheese (although it uses pasteurized milk and ages the cheese in the package). This was evident to our tasters, who overwhelmingly described Grafton's cheddar as "flaky" and "crumbly," just like a farmhouse cheddar. Brands made with the stirred-curd method were universally described as even-textured and smooth. To our surprise, tasters did not automatically mark down brands with a smooth texture. In fact, Cabot, Tillamook, and Cracker Barrel, all made using the stirred-curd method, rated higher than Grafton Village's hand-cheddared cheese.

The Well-Balanced Cheese

One of the great surprises of our tasting was the success of Cracker Barrel, which, at a mere $3.29 for 10 ounces, outpolled Organic Valley cheddar, which sells for $10.59 per pound and is made with raw milk. Part of the reason for Organic Valley's low rating was its performance in a grilled cheese sandwich. When melted, Organic Valley cheddar became greasy as the fat separated from the milk solids in the cheese. Melted Cracker Barrel, on the other hand, was described by

---

Farmhouse Cheddars

Farmhouse cheddar cheese is made by small creameries that start with unpasteurized milk, hand-cheddar the curd, and then wrap and age the cheese in a cloth. To see just how good these cheeses really are, we organized a tasting, rounding up three farmhouse cheddars from England and one from Vermont. We also included Cabot, our top-ranked supermarket cheddar, for comparison.

With a price range of about $11 to $19 per pound, farmhouse cheddars are neither cheap nor widely available (see Resources on page 32 for ordering information). But if you live near a specialty foods or cheese store, we strongly recommend that you try them. Even in the grilled cheese sandwich, all four of the farmhouse cheddars beat the pants off of Cabot. Whereas Cabot was merely "mellow" and "bland," the farmhouse brands were described as "honey-like," "grassy," and "laced with horseradish." Overall, the farmhouse brands provided a more exciting and enjoyable cheddar experience. Here are some comments on the four farmhouse cheddars tasted, with cheeses listed in order of preference. All four cheeses are highly recommended.

KEEN'S Farmhouse Cheddar SOMERSET, ENGLAND
➤ **$17.95 for 1 pound:** Tangy, nutty, and rich.

BURROUGH'S Farmhouse Cheddar SOMERSET, ENGLAND
➤ **$18.95 for 1 pound:** Balanced, sharp, and intense.

MONTGOMERY'S Farmhouse Cheddar SOMERSET, ENGLAND
➤ **$17.95 for 1 pound:** Herbaceous, earthy, and sharp.

SHELBURNE FARMS Farmhouse Cheddar SHELBURNE, VT.
➤ **$10.95 for 1 pound:** Nutty and delicate; like Parmigiano-Reggiano in both flavor and texture.

The tasters' favorite:
KEEN'S FARMHOUSE CHEDDAR

tasters as both "smooth" and "cohesive." We discovered that the difference lies in the chemistry of cheese.

According to Harold McGee in his book *On Food and Cooking* (Simon & Schuster, 1984), cheeses that have been aged longer have shorter protein chains and can therefore tolerate higher temperatures without separating. While this explains why a younger cheese may become greasy in a grilled cheese sandwich, what about an older cheese that separates, such as Organic Valley, which is aged for 10 months? In addition, why didn't other young cheeses, like Cracker Barrel, which is aged for only two months, separate? Food scientist and cheese expert Barry Swanson explained that a well-balanced cheese won't separate. But if there is too much fat, water, or lactic acid in a cheese, whether young or old, it risks separation.

Tasters also found that the Organic Valley cheddar tasted sour. Just as an unbalanced cheese may separate when heated, this lack of balance (for example, too much lactic acid) can also produce sourness. At the other end of the spectrum, lack of flavor, as was noted with the Heluva Good cheddar, can be the result of a culture that doesn't produce enough acid. Another possible cause could be the milk itself—if it is low in protein, there isn't enough food for the added culture to consume. In fact, protein is so vital to making a quality cheese that some manufacturers, like the highly rated Cabot and Tillamook brands, pay farmers a premium for milk with a higher-than-average protein content.

A Good "Barnyard" Cheese

Finally, we had to confront the proclivities of our own palates. Because most of us were raised on lower-quality supermarket cheddars, we aren't used to "barnyard" flavors, such as those found in the Horizon Organic and Organic Valley brands. This "unclean" flavor occurs when the cultures that break down the protein in cheese produce specific ammonia-like compounds during aging. At first, we thought that our rejection of these flavors was merely a lack of sophistication, but this notion was quickly set aside when we tasted authentic farmhouse cheddars that were full-flavored but also sweet, nutty, and herbaceous. When these stronger flavors are exhibited in a well-made and well-balanced cheese, they are easily appreciated by just about anyone. In short, we loved them.

What should you buy? Supermarket cheddars such as Cabot, Tillamook, Cracker Barrel, and Grafton Village offer relatively "clean" flavors and good performance when melted. (The sharpness of the flavor varies.) For a first-class cheddar experience, however, you may well want to seek out a real farmhouse cheese that offers a more complex taste and texture (see "Farmhouse Cheddars" on page 28).

TASTING CHEDDAR CHEESE

We collected a group of nationally available cheddar cheeses from local supermarkets and natural foods stores. We limited the tasting to "sharp" cheddars, which are aged from 60 days up to a year. Cheeses were tasted cubed and in grilled cheese sandwiches. Twenty-eight *Cook's Illustrated* staff members rated the cheddars for flavor and texture. Cheeses are listed in order of preference based on their combined scores when sampled raw and in sandwiches.

RECOMMENDED

CABOT Sharp Vermont Cheddar Cheese

➤ **$2.29 for 8 ounces**, AGED 5 TO 8 MONTHS

This cheese came in first place in both the grilled cheese and the raw cheese tastings. Tasters liked its approachable flavor, described as "sharp," "clean," and "tangy." In a grilled cheese sandwich, it was "buttery" and "mellow" without being even the slightest bit greasy.

TILLAMOOK Sharp Cheddar Cheese

➤ **$6.99 for 1 pound**, AGED 9 MONTHS

As the only annatto-colored cheese in the tasting (meaning that the cheese is orange rather than white), raw Tillamook cheddar stood out not only for its color but for its "tangy" and "piquant" characteristics. Tasters liked the Tillamook cheese less in the grilled cheese sandwich, where it was criticized for "sweet" and "sour" flavors.

CRACKER BARREL Sharp White Cheddar Cheese

➤ **$3.29 for 10 ounces**, AGED 2 MONTHS

Called "flavorful and easy," Cracker Barrel won over tasters with its "mellow," "clean" flavor. In the grilled cheese sandwich, it was described as "good and generic," with a "smooth" and "cohesive" texture.

GRAFTON VILLAGE CHEESE COMPANY Premium Vermont Cheddar Cheese

➤ **$3.89 for 8 ounces**, AGED 1 YEAR

This hybrid balances traditional cheddar-making methods, such as hand-cheddaring the curd, with modern cheddar-making practices, such as using pasteurized milk and aging the cheese in its package. Grafton's crumbly texture and pungent flavor earned top scores among many tasters. Some, however, found it too "pungent" and "sour."

RECOMMENDED WITH RESERVATIONS

HORIZON Organic Cheddar Cheese

➤ **$3.99 for 8 ounces**, AGED 6 TO 9 MONTHS

Many tasters commented that Horizon Organic cheddar "didn't taste like cheddar"—that it was too potent. While some liked its strength, others called it "stinky" and "barnyardy." Most tasters found the cheese too "runny" and too "sharp" when melted in a grilled cheese sandwich.

LAND O LAKES Sharp Cheddar Cheese

(Called Lake to Lake Cheddar Cheese on the West Coast)

➤ **$1.99 for 8 ounces**, AGED 6 TO 12 MONTHS

"This cheese is like the kind on a supermarket deli platter," commented one taster, with other tasters agreeing, calling it "bland," "boring," and "rubbery" when eaten out of hand. In the grilled cheese sandwich, some called it "dull," but others liked the "classic grilled cheese" flavor.

NOT RECOMMENDED

ORGANIC VALLEY Organic Raw Milk Sharp Cheddar

➤ **$10.59 for 1 pound**, AGED 10 MONTHS

Described as "buttermilky" and "sour," this unpasteurized cheddar didn't find many fans. Its texture was described as "rubbery" and "gummy" when raw and "greasy" and "oozy" when melted.

HELUVA GOOD Sharp Cheddar Cheese

➤ **$2.19 for 8 ounces**, AGED 2 TO 9 MONTHS

"This cheese tastes like mozzarella," said one taster, while another called it "completely one-dimensional." Most found it "tasteless" and "rubbery" both when eaten raw and when melted in a grilled cheese sandwich.

A Rule to Cook By

Wondering why that cake didn't rise properly? Or why those cookies ran together? Are the steaks over-cooked? Possibly one of the most overlooked but valuable kitchen tools is the standard measuring ruler. It can prove that the 8-inch cake pan you are using is actually 9 inches, that the cookies have been spaced together too closely, and that the supposedly 1-inch-thick steak the butcher sold you is only ½ inch thick. Here in the test kitchen, we reach for our trusty 18-inch stainless steel rulers, which can be thrown right into the dishwasher. They can be purchased at any office supply store for about $4.

Rigor Mortis Pot Roast?

While the paradigms of cooking state that pot roast is best when cooked low and slow, we were intrigued to find quite a few recipes referring to pot roast cooked partially or entirely in the microwave (yes, we have a few microwave cookbooks in our library). We even found reference in a food science book to the superiority of a microwave when it comes to cooking tough cuts of meat. Science aside (gasp!), and to appease our curiosity, we put the palates of the *Cook's* staff to the test and offered up some electromagnetically prepared pot roast.

From all outward appearances, the microwave-cooked pot roast was indistinguishable from its traditionally cooked brethren. It was well browned (this was accomplished on the stovetop to give it at least a fighting chance) and fork-tender (a texture obtained in less than two hours—quick but not speedy), and it produced a beautifully rich sauce to boot. However, after tasting the roast, most tasters noticed a resilient, chewy texture that was not present in the oven-cooked pot roast. Moreover, as the roast sat on the carving board, the meat fibers began to seize up and harden until they took on the texture of a tight beef jerky. So if you

can eat a 3½-pound roast in about 15 minutes, go right ahead and use the microwave. Just be sure to throw the leftovers to the dog.

Flipping Over Fish

Fretting about flipping fragile fish? Don't get frustrated—there is a tool designed to lift and turn large pieces of cooked fish (such as the halibut in our recipe on page 7). This spatula features an extrawide, perforated head that provides support along the entire length of the fish and also allows liquid to drain through. For availability, see Resources, page 32.

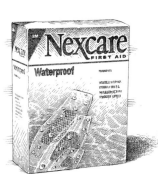

Cover That Pot

By the time 1 quart of water or milk comes to a boil, it can lose more than ⅛ cup in volume through steam if left uncovered. While this might not seem like much, it's just enough to throw off a recipe for chocolate cake, make a pastry cream more like pasty cream, or turn the simplest boiled rice gummy and undercooked. So the next time the recipe calls for boiling

a precise amount of liquid, put a lid on it.

The Whole Tomato

After working on batch 20 or so of Spaghetti Puttanesca (page 15), we ran out of 28-ounce cans of diced tomatoes. Noticing the cans of whole tomatoes in the pantry, we drained the tomatoes, diced them—approximating the size found in the already diced tomatoes—and used them in our recipe. The difference was amazing.

This batch of puttanesca had a completely anemic tomato presence. Perplexed, we picked up a few cans each of the diced and whole tomatoes. We drained the diced tomatoes to weigh and measure the tomato solids. Before weighing and measuring the whole tomatoes, we drained and then diced them to approximate the size of the chunks in the canned diced tomatoes.

We found that the can of diced tomatoes contained 2½ cups (about 15½ ounces) of drained tomato solids. The can of whole tomatoes contained a scant 1¾ cups (about 12¾ ounces) of tomato solids. Both types of tomatoes come in 28-ounce

cans; the difference in weight is made up in the tomato juice. By adding the whole tomatoes that we had diced ourselves, we were cheating the recipe of ¾ cup tomatoes. No wonder the lack of tomato flavor.

Wine and Artichokes

So you're planning a dinner party at which you'll be serving a lovely appetizer of artichokes. Better think twice about what beverage to serve. Many sources warn against serving wine with artichokes, claiming that this vegetable can make an expensive Chardonnay taste like Welch's grape juice. In fact, artichokes contain a unique acid called cynarin that can stimulate sweetness receptors in the mouth and make anything consumed immediately afterward taste sweet.

To test this proposition, 18 members of the *Cook's* staff tasted steamed artichokes followed by plain water. Two tasters (or about 11 percent) reported that the water tasted distinctly sweet after sampling artichokes. Sensitivity to cynarin is genetically determined. The best way to find out if you're included in this group is to run a test yourself.

TESTING EQUIPMENT: Bandage Badinage

Along with the joys of cooking comes the occasional boo-boo. This means that a well-stocked kitchen should be equipped not only with a battery of pots and pans but with a first-aid kit—including bandages. But what good is a bandage if it falls off while you're doing the dishes? Although we always cover our bandages with rubber gloves, we wanted to see if there was a waterproof bandage that lives up to its claims, so we put a few national brands to the test.

The testing included Band-Aid Brand Adhesive Bandage Water Block Plus, Curad Aqua-Protect, Nexcare First Aid Waterproof Bandage by 3M, and New Skin Liquid Bandage, a liquid that dries to form a protective film after being applied to the wound. After mummifying ourselves with bandages, we went about our daily duties, which involve chopping, cooking, baking, and—the toughest test for a bandage—washing dishes. When the day was over and our hands were chafed and chapped, we examined the bandages that survived (some failed before the test was complete) to evaluate their tenacity and ability to keep skin dry.

3M Nexcare Bandage

The first to fail our test was the Band-Aid Brand, which fell off within the first hour. The New Skin Liquid Bandage, although promising at first, started to peel away after scrubbing a few pots and pans. The Curad Aqua-Protect clung feverishly to our hands up to hour number six, when the ends started to curl away; eventually, the bandage allowed water to seep in. By far the best was the 3M brand Nexcare Waterproof Bandage. Even after its vigorous all-day workout, the bandage stuck to the skin for dear life. At the end of the day, we peeled away the bandage to find the skin underneath undisturbed. Nexcare bandages can be found at most drugstores in an assorted box of 30. We purchased ours at a local drugstore for $3.39.

Pastry Chefs Come Home

Two acclaimed pastry chefs—one from Canada, the other from France—write for a home audience, with largely sweet results. BY CHRISTOPHER KIMBALL

IN THE SWEET KITCHEN
Regan Daley
Artisan, 692 pages, $35

Any book that promises to be "The Definitive Baker's Companion" has a lot to prove given the wealth of really good baking books published in the last dozen years—Julia Child's *Baking with Julia,* Rose Levy Beranbaum's two tomes, *The Cake Bible* and *The Pie and Pastry Bible,* and Richard Sax's *Classic Home Desserts,* to name just a few. On one level, at least, Regan Daley must be awarded the term *definitive* in that the first 374 pages of her book contain no recipes, only advice about tools, techniques, and ingredients. In addition, this information has the refreshing glow of firsthand experience, even in discussions of seemingly obscure items such as pumpkin seeds. Daley has obviously cooked with them. The book is large, simply but nicely designed, and it has a modest 16 pages of extremely well-executed color photographs. It feels like a keeper.

PROS: This is a very personal cookbook, one that has unique, appealing recipes. Daley is clearly a restaurant pastry chef, but her creations are a nice mix of homey recipes (such as Deep Chocolate Pudding) and interesting but manageable adventures into baking (such as White Coffee Pots de Crème). The author doesn't feel the need to provide culinary fireworks at every turn, although the recipes have plenty to satisfy even the most seasoned home cook.

CONS: The selection in this book is not comprehensive; there are only 150 or so recipes. There is no crisp, for example, the only oatmeal cookie is part of an ice cream sandwich, and if you are looking for a basic custard, forget about it. You'll find four custards in the index, none of which is anything like what grandma used to make. In addition, some recipes are a bit beyond the pale for average home cooks, including Hazelnut Crème Brûlée with a Crushed Praline Crust.

RECIPE TESTING: Daley's recipes work. Not only are they well tested, but they are interesting and well reasoned. The slam-dunk winners were Oven-Roasted Pears with Red Wine and a Gratin of Goat Cheese (simple, sophisticated, and sensational), Oven-Roasted Figs with Honey and Orange

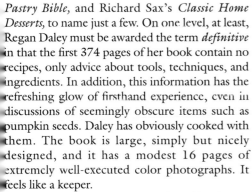

(simple, quick, and elegant), and the Sweet Potato Cornbread (Daley includes a chapter on sweetened breads) that many of us served for Thanksgiving last year. There were a few disappointments along the way. The crust for the Cazuela Pie (made with pumpkin, sweet potato, and coconut milk) was tough and brittle, even though the filling was fantastic. (Her pie pastry recipe is a bit short on fat.) Butter-Toffee Crunch Shortbread was well liked, although the toffee itself became tacky and tough to chew after baking. The chocolate chip cookies drew mixed reactions, with some tasters noting that they were a bit too chocolatey and cloying; however, getting 10 people to agree on the perfect chocolate chip cookie is close to impossible. Toasted Hazelnut Pound Cake was quite good if a bit dry, and a biscotti recipe was marked down for its overpowering crunch, although the flavors (pine nuts, polenta, and currants) were interesting. All in all, Daley gets high marks for creativity and a very good, but not outstanding, grade for execution.

CHOCOLATE DESSERTS
Pierre Hermé with Dorie Greenspan
Little, Brown, 288 pages, $40

Pear and Fresh Mint Tempura with Chocolate Rice Pudding. White Chocolate and Rhubarb Charlotte. Faubourg Pavé. Now do you get it? This book is a peek inside the mind of a four-star French pastry chef, the kind of guy who tries to make even hot chocolate with attitude. The introduction to this book attempts to broaden the appeal of the contents by singing the praises of the simpler recipes—the brownie, rice pudding, a few cookies—but don't be fooled. If you are not willing to take your confections seriously, and if you don't have at least a modicum of dessert-making experience, you will find this book akin to gazing at Gwyneth Paltrow. You can admire her from a distance, but only a fool would be confident about the chances for an intimate encounter. For the paparazzi out there, however, the

photographs and recipes, even if never consummated, may be worth the price of admission.

PROS: The good news is that Pierre Hermé is a master pastry chef, the book is well produced, and the photographs are rich and inviting. When he is good, he is very, very good. What other cookbook offers a Chocolate, Coffee, and Whiskey Cappuccino made with coffee granité, chocolate cream, whipped cream, and Rice Krispies! (It sounds horrible, but it tasted great.) In addition, Dorie Greenspan really knows how to write a recipe, so her instructions are clear and easy to follow, making even the four-part recipes manageable.

CONS: This book is a slick production and there is a bit too much fawning over the brilliance of the Chocolate Zen Master. It's probably deserved, but humility was not central to the planning of this volume. There are many superb recipes here, but when Hermé fails, he falls head over heels. That being said, he does deliver many recipes that are *épatant* (amazing). Simply put, caveat emptor.

RECIPE TESTING: The great recipes are both unique and real showstoppers. Among them were the cappuccino recipe mentioned above, Chocolate-Covered Crunchy Hazelnut Cookies (crunchy, nutty, and elegant), Hot Chocolate with Coffee (also great ice-cold), Chocolate-Caramel Truffles (quick, easy, and decadent), and Chocolate Macaroons (crispy on the outside, chewy on the inside). However, there was more than a smattering of losers. The Warm Chocolate Croquettes in Cold Coconut-Milk Tapioca Soup was the sort of dessert one might order at a trendy New York restaurant, but its pairing of fried coconut, cream, and tapioca left our dinner guests reaching for the Pepto-Bismol. The Chocolate Rice Pudding was more like a bowl of fudge than pudding; the Spiced Hot Chocolate was good but a bit like a liquid chocolate bar (the Aztecs would have liked it); and Pistachio Waffles with Chocolate Cream had tasty components, but the combination was a bit of a culinary reach. Moist and Nutty Brownies were the latter but not the former (and they weren't chocolatey enough, either), the Chocolate and Lemon Madeleines were fair, and Suzy's Cake, a one-layer decadent chocolate cake, was easy to make and tasted great, but it was, in one taster's opinion, a bit too soft.

Most of the ingredients and materials necessary for the recipes in this issue are available at your local supermarket, gourmet store, or kitchen supply shop. The following are mail-order sources for particular items. Prices listed below were current at press time and do not include shipping or handling unless otherwise indicated. We suggest that you contact companies directly to confirm up-to-date prices and availability.

Oven Thermometers

Of all the oven thermometers tested on page 25, the Taylor Classic Oven Guide Thermometer, model 5921, was our winner. It was the most accurate and most stable thermometer of the group. **Kitchen Etc. (32 Industrial Drive, Exeter, NH 03833; 800-232-4070; www.kitchenetc.com)** carries this oven thermometer, item #176204, for $12.99.

Farmhouse Cheddars

If you are a cheese lover, we recommend spending a little extra on farmhouse cheddars. Tasted against conventional cheddars, there is just no comparison. **Formaggio Kitchen (244 Huron Avenue, Cambridge, MA 02138; 888-212-3224; www.formaggiokitchen.com)**, our favorite local purveyor of fine cheeses, meats, condiments, and other delicacies, carries all four of the farmhouse cheddars we tasted—and then some. See page 28 for tasting notes. Shelburne Farms farmhouse cheddar, made in Vermont, is a raw milk cheddar, made exclusively with milk from purebred Brown Swiss cows, that is aged for a minimum of one year. It sells for $10.95 per pound. Formaggio also carries the three cheddars we tasted from dairies located in Somerset, England: Montgomery's ($17.95 per pound), Keen's ($17.95 per pound), and Burrough's ($18.95 per pound). All three produce outstanding cheddars.

Cheddar Soup

Whisking the chicken broth and half-and-half into the roux in our Cheddar Soup (page 10) is perhaps the most important step in the recipe. Steady, even whisking with an effective whisk will help you attain the same velvety, lithe texture we did in the test kitchen. In a recent testing of whisks, we found the Rösle Stainless Steel "Jug" Whisk to be our favorite. While it may be a bit on the expensive side, it is a sturdy and well-balanced performer that should last a lifetime. The 12½-inch whisk is the perfect size for a variety of tasks, including making this soup. **A Cook's Wares (211 37th Street, Beaver Falls, PA 15010; 800-915-9788; www.cookswares.com)** sells our favorite Rösle whisk, item #RS26, for $21.

Puttanesca

Our Spaghetti Puttanesca (page 15) takes only 11 minutes to cook, so why spend any more time than that preparing it for the pan? If you don't have an olive (or cherry) pitter to pit the ½ cup olives called for in the recipe, you just might have to spend that extra time. It is extremely hard to pit olives by hand while effectively collecting all of the olive's meat, which generally likes to stick to the pit in chunks. By using an olive pitter, however, you can blast the pits out of the olive with one quick squeeze. You can get a triple-plated, chrome-over-zinc (it will never rust) olive pitter from **Williams-Sonoma (P.O. Box 7456, San Francisco, CA 94120-7456; 800-541-2233; www.williams-sonoma.com)** for $12.50 (item #83-1341288) that will get the job done with speed and efficacy.

Cauliflower Gratin

Cauliflower gratin is the perfect side dish: It is easy to make as well as delicious, and it goes from oven to table in the dish in which it is baked. We baked our gratin (see page 18) in a range of characteristically shallow (between 1 and 2 inches in height) gratin and casserole dishes to gauge differences in their performance. The cheapest dish of the group produced a gratin just as tasty as the most expensive dish. Pyrex 2-quart casserole dishes, which cost about $7, are widely available in grocery, hardware, and kitchen stores, but if you are looking to splurge on a dish with a sleeker look, we suggest the All-Clad 12-inch Stainless Oval Au Gratin pan. It is a beauty. **Northwestern Cutlery (160 Kelly Street, Elk Grove, IL 60007; 800-650-9866; www.cutleryandmore.com)** carries the Au Gratin, item #5812, for $159.95.

Lemon Pound Cake

With a few of our favorite pieces of kitchen equipment on hand, turning out a pound cake (see page 20) with a moist, lush texture and a rich, buttery, lemony flavor is a cinch. Ekco Baker's Secret Non-Stick Large Loaf Pan was the top performer in our September/October 2000 loaf pan testing, revered for its practical design, even browning capability, and ease of release and cleaning. At a suggested retail price of a mere $3.99, there is no reason not to have one—or two—in your kitchen. This pan is great for our pound cake as well as for other cakes and breads. The pan is made of tinned steel with a nonstick coating and has easy-to-grip handles. It is available at most discount and grocery stores. You can call customer service at the manufacturer, **World Kitchen**, at **800-367-3526**, to find the retailer nearest you that carries Ekco products. Also handy was the soft-bristled pastry brush we used to glaze the pound cake. **Kitchen Etc.** carries a Sparta 2-inch pastry brush, item #592626, for $7.99, that is perfect for the job.

New York–Style Cheesecake

We had great success baking the cheesecake on page 22 in Kaiser's La Forme 9-inch leakproof springform pan. The cheesecake came out of the oven tall, tanned, smooth, and creamy every time. Commercial-weight steel provides even and gentle heat distribution, and the nonstick surface allows for effortless release and removal. You can find the Kaiser springform pan, item #730035, for $35.95 at **Chef's Resource (2844 Rounsevel Terrace, Laguna Beach, CA 92651; 866-765-2433; www.chefsresource.com)**.

Pan–Roasted Halibut

Because of its odd shape and delicate texture, halibut (see page 6) is the perfect candidate for a fish spatula. Although a thin, flexible, tapered spatula is traditionally used with fish, we found a spatula with a wide, broad, perforated head to be more suitable for a fish steak with the heft and size of halibut. **Williams-Sonoma** sells a stainless-steel fish (and asparagus) spatula, item #83-2083756, for $15, that will have you turning the fish with aplomb.

Chicken Paprikash

If you want to make your paprikash (see page 8) a bit more special, we suggest getting your hands on Penzeys Hungarian Sweet Kulonlege Paprika. Compared with standard supermarket brands, this paprika adds more depth of flavor and imparts a deeper, more vibrant color to the stew. You can order a 2.4-ounce glass jar of Hungarian sweet paprika from **Penzeys Spices (P.O. Box 924, Brookfield, WI 53008-0924; 800-741-7787; www.penzeys.com)**, item #47551 for $3.39. We also like the intensely deep red Spanish paprika from **Pendery's (1221 Manufacturing Street, Dallas, TX 75207; 800-533-1870; www.penderys.com)**. A 2.64-ounce jar item #00112-25, is $3.25.

Kitchen Ruler

Ask most seasoned cooks if they have a "kitchen ruler" at home and they will answer yes. How else do you measure the thickness of a steak or the size of a pan? **BossOnline.com (1127 South Mannheim Road, Westchester, IL 60154; 800-444-2677; www.bossonline.com)** carries the perfect 18-inch stainless steel ruler, item #ACM-10417 for $4.17.

RECIPES
March & April 2002

Chicken Paprikash, 9

Cauliflower Gratin, 19

Wilted Spinach Salad, 14

Pan-Roasted Halibut with Chipotle Butter, 7

Pot Roast with Root Vegetables, 13

PHOTOGRAPHY: CARL TREMBLAY

http://www.cooksillustrated.com

If you enjoy *Cook's Illustrated* magazine, you should visit our Web site. Simply log on at http://www.cooksillustrated.com. Although much of the information is free, database searches are for site subscribers only. *Cook's Illustrated* subscribers are offered a 20 percent discount.

Here are some of the things you can do on our site:

Search Our Recipes: We have a searchable database of all the recipes from *Cook's Illustrated*.

Search Tastings and Cookware Ratings: You will find all of our reviews (cookware, food, wine, cookbooks) plus new material created exclusively for the Web site.

Find Your Favorite Quick Tips.

Check Your Subscription: Check the status of your subscription, pay a bill, or give gift subscriptions online.

Visit Our Bookstore: You can purchase any of our cookbooks, hardbound annual editions of the magazine, or posters online.

Subscribe to *e-Notes:* Our free e-mail companion to the magazine offers cooking advice, test results, buying tips, and recipes about a single topic each month.

AMERICA'S TEST KITCHEN

Join the millions of cooks who watch our show, *America's Test Kitchen*, on public television each week. For more information, including recipes from the show and a schedule of program times in your area, visit http://www.americastestkitchen.com.

Spaghetti Puttanesca, 15

Cheddar Soup, 10

New York–Style Cheesecake, 24

Lemon Pound Cake, 21

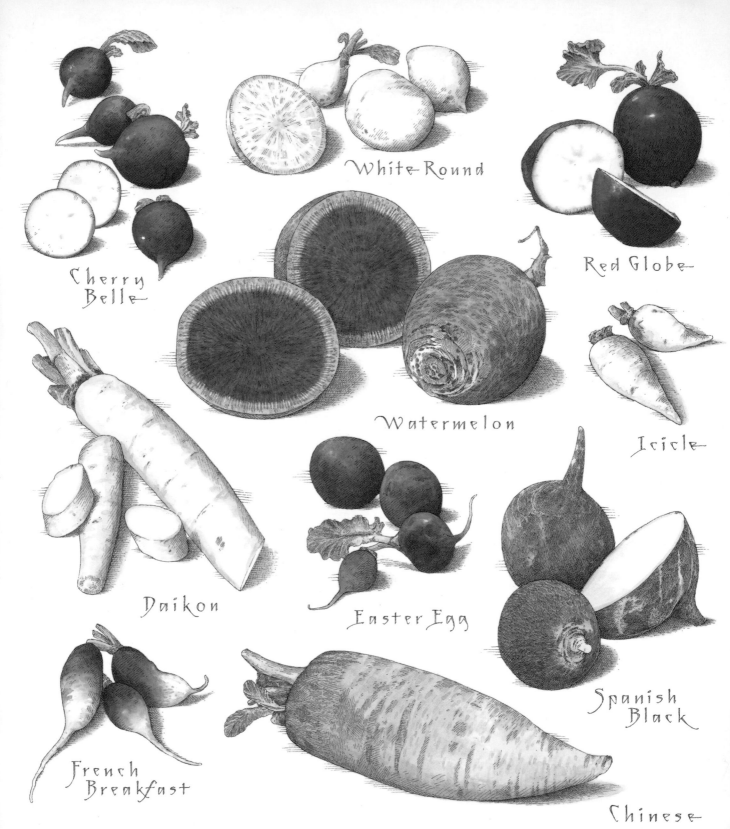

White Round

Red Globe

Cherry Belle

Watermelon

Icicle

Daikon

Easter Egg

Spanish Black

French Breakfast

Chinese

RADISHES

NUMBER FIFTY-SIX

MAY & JUNE 2002

Home of **AMERICA'S TEST KITCHEN**

COOK'S
ILLUSTRATED

Grilling Pork Chops
Seared Outside, Juicy Inside

Quick and Easy Cinnamon Buns

Ground Beef Tacos
Turning Junk Food into Good Food

Chicken Caesar Salad

Rating Charcoal Grills
Do You Need to Spend $400?

Hot Fudge Pudding Cake

French Roast Coffee Taste Test
Starbucks vs. Chock Full o' Nuts

Fruit Smoothies
Vegetable Stir-Fries
Jambalaya Simplified
Spinach Dip
Garlic-Lemon Potatoes

www.cooksillustrated.com
$4.95 U.S./$6.95 CANADA

CONTENTS

May & June 2002

COOK'S ILLUSTRATED

Home of America's Test Kitchen
www.cooksillustrated.com

PUBLISHER AND EDITOR
Christopher Kimball

EXECUTIVE EDITOR
Jack Bishop

SENIOR EDITOR
Dawn Yanagihara

SENIOR WRITER
Adam Ried

EDITORIAL MANAGER
Barbara Bourassa

ART DIRECTOR
Amy Klee

TEST KITCHEN DIRECTOR
Bridget Lancaster

ASSISTANT TEST KITCHEN DIRECTOR
Erin McMurrer

ASSOCIATE EDITORS
Raquel Pelzel
Julia Collin

COPY EDITOR
India Koopman

MANAGING EDITOR,
BOOKS AND WEB SITE
Rebecca Hays

TEST COOKS
Shannon Blaisdell
Matthew Card
Meg Suzuki

CONTRIBUTING EDITOR
Elizabeth Germain

CONSULTING EDITORS
Shirley Corriher
Jasper White
Robert L. Wolke

TEST KITCHEN INTERN
Merrill Stubbs

ASSISTANT TO THE PUBLISHER
Sumantha Selvakumar

PROOFREADER
Jana Branch

VICE PRESIDENT MARKETING
David Mack

RETAIL SALES MANAGER
Jason Geller

CIRCULATION RETAIL SALES MANAGER
Jonathan Venier

SALES REPRESENTATIVE
Shekinah Cohn

MARKETING ASSISTANT
Connie Forbes

CIRCULATION MANAGER
Larisa Greiner

PRODUCTS MANAGER
Steven Browall

DIRECT MAIL MANAGER
Robert Lee

CUSTOMER SERVICE MANAGER
Jacqueline Valerio

CUSTOMER SERVICE REPRESENTATIVE
Kate Caccamo

VICE PRESIDENT OPERATIONS
AND TECHNOLOGY
James McCormack

PRODUCTION MANAGER
Jessica Quirk

PRODUCTION COORDINATOR
Mary Connelly

PRODUCTION ASSISTANTS
Ron Bilodeau
Jennifer McCreary

PRODUCTION INTERNS
Mike Haggerty
Sarah Lorimer

SYSTEMS ADMINISTRATOR
Richard Cassidy

WEBMASTER
Nicole Morris

CHIEF FINANCIAL OFFICER
Sharyn Chabot

CONTROLLER
Mandy Shito

OFFICE MANAGER
Juliet Nusbaum

RECEPTIONIST
Henrietta Murray

PUBLICITY
Deborah Broide

For list rental information, contact The SpeciaLISTS, 1200 Harbor Blvd. 9th Floor, Weehawken, NJ 07087; 201-865-5800; fax 201-867-2450. Editorial office: 17 Station Street, Brookline, MA 02445; 617-232-1000; fax 617-232-1572. Editorial contributions should be sent to: Editor, *Cook's Illustrated*. We cannot assume responsibility for manuscripts submitted to us. Submissions will be returned only if accompanied by a large self-addressed envelope. Postmaster: Send all new orders, subscription inquiries, and change of address notices to: *Cook's Illustrated*, P.O. Box 7446, Red Oak, IA 51591-0446. PRINTED IN THE USA.

FRESH BEANS

FRESH BEANS Beans can be eaten at three stages of their growth. Snap beans are eaten, pod and all, while still immature. As the tiny seeds in the pods grow, they become shell beans. The fully formed but still soft beans are removed from their shells and cooked briefly for eating. Dried beans are left on the plant until they rattle in their pods, which are discarded. The beans can be stored indefinitely. Yellow wax, dragon tongue, and haricot vert are eaten at the snap bean stage. They all boast a crisp, tender texture and sweet flavor; Chinese long beans are more pliable. Romanos are consumed as both snap and shell beans. Fava and cranberry beans are harvested as shell and dry beans. As shell beans, favas have a buttery texture and bittersweet flavor, while cranberry beans have a distinctive nutlike flavor. Sea beans (not really beans at all) grow along the seashore. Salty and crisp when fresh, they can also be steamed or sautéed and are often pickled.

COVER (*Lettuce & Radishes*): ELIZABETH BRANDON, BACK COVER (*Fresh Beans*): JOHN BURGOYNE

WHAT LIES BENEATH

Any Vermont town that has facing mountains named Swearing Hill and Minister Hill must have an interesting past. I just didn't know how interesting when my family built a small cabin up on Southeast Corners Road in 1955 on 20 acres that were part of the old Ford farm. My sister and I slept in the loft along with the mice, we watched summer storms blow in over the Woodcock place, and I spent hours trying to catch crawfish in Tidd Brook and shoot partridge with a .22— my single-shot 12-gauge just about knocked me down every time I pulled the trigger.

It's hard to ignore the past when you come across abandoned farms at the tops of mountains where snowshoe hares and bobcats live, stone walls at 3,000 feet where you least expect them, and cellar holes on top of Egg Mountain, where Colonel Shea hid out in the 1780s. Like West Virginia, the town is full of hollows and ridges, so there are plenty of places to hide. Perhaps that is why there are dark stories about our town. I've heard tales of bodies buried up in Beartown, the story of how the hanging tree got its name, and rumors of influenza epidemics so bad that victims were laid out by the side of the road like cordwood, ready to be picked up in wagons for mass burial. And don't think for a minute that the woods still don't hold other secrets—moonshine, jacked deer, and ghosts.

It's true enough that many of our town's outlaws are gone, along with the Woodcocks' doghouse (the one with the TV antenna on top). On Tuesday nights, the town hall is used for yoga classes (T-shirts and cut-offs for the ladies), and someone organized a feminist drumming group that is part girls' night out and part encounter group. You can now buy a cappuccino down at the country store, although "No Trespassing" signs are still posted for liberals and real estate agents. And, yes, Doug Wright just sold the only filling station in town, taking with him the secret to his success, a photo album of topless biker women from Daytona. He went down every year to update his collection.

But some things never change. Every year we have a Buck Board, in which all the hunters ante up a dollar in a pool for the season's biggest deer (which weighed in at 198 pounds last year), the Fourth of July parade is still horse-drawn, and the Christmas party is given in the town hall, complete with Santa Claus, vegetarian lasagna, and frosted sheet cake. Last summer, I rode by my neighbors' place in midafternoon and found the two of them sitting buck naked by the side of the road, cooling off after a sauna and waving to traffic. Although many of the houses are now freshly painted (one neighbor still has tar paper on the front of his house to get a lower tax assessment), up in the hollows and in the camps you'll find a place that couldn't care less about the march of time. That's why so many of us love this town. It just never really took to civilization.

So, last summer, I went searching for the town's last great mystery, the monks. Rumors abound about the Carthusians, a small group of monks who built a monastery on top of Red Mountain. They are a silent order, wear brown habits, and have no contact with the town other than to ask for advice on sugaring or farming through a hired man. I set out with a rough set of directions ("turn by the waterfall and stay to your right"), a sandwich, and a pair of good boots.

After a couple hours of hiking and two dead

Christopher Kimball

ends, I came to a small pasture, where I stopped for lunch. I ate my sandwich and apple in a sea of timothy and rye peppered with ochre Indian paintbrushes and black-eyed Susans. I walked some more and then, as the afternoon grew long, I heard bells coming from a grove of ash and birch. It sounded like a call to prayer. Suddenly, monks appeared from the woods in pairs, older men walking with younger acolytes. They wore coarse, wide-brimmed hats, the sort found, I would guess, in the Middle Ages. They smiled but didn't speak. They walked slowly down into the grove and disappeared.

I stood and listened to the last of the bells, the pine woods transformed into a shrine, the light filtering down onto a carpet of leaves and needles and speckled, hoary tree trunks. I slowly turned and headed home, back past the small swamps, the bear sign, the thatches of blackberry bushes, and the stands of young birches.

When I walked in the door, my oldest daughter asked, "Did you find them, Daddy?"

I thought for a minute about the monks who had appeared suddenly out of the woods, called to prayer by unseen bells. Then I wondered about the bodies in Beartown and the murder committed at the hanging tree.

"No, just went for a hike," I replied.

Let my children grow up where the hollows are haunted, the woods bury their dead, and an afternoon walk might end high above the valley in a place where ghosts still walk side by side in a silent grove. It's a privilege, I thought, to live in the last town in America that knows how to keep its secrets.

FOR MORE INFORMATION

www.cooksillustrated.com

At the *Cook's Illustrated* Web site you can order a book, give a gift subscription to *Cook's Illustrated* magazine, sign up for our free e-newsletter, subscribe to the magazine, or check the status of your subscription. Join the Web site and you'll have access to our searchable databases of recipes, cookware ratings, ingredient tastings, quick tips, cookbook reviews, and more.

COOK'S ILLUSTRATED Magazine

Cook's Illustrated (ISSN 1068-2821) magazine is published bimonthly (6 issues per year) by Boston Common Press Limited Partnership, 17 Station Street, Brookline, MA 02445. Copyright 2002 Boston Common Press Limited Partnership. Periodical postage paid at Boston, Mass., and additional mailing offices, USPS #012487.

A one-year subscription is $29.70, two years is $55, and three years is $75. Add $6 postage per year for Canadian subscriptions and $12 per year for all other countries outside the U.S. To order subscriptions in the U.S. call 800-526-8442. Gift subscriptions are available for $24.95 each. Postmaster: Send all new orders, subscription inquiries, and change-of-address notices to Cook's Illustrated, P.O. Box 7446, Red Oak, IA 51591-0446, or call 800-526-8442 inside the U.S. and 515-247-7571 outside the U.S.

COOKBOOKS

You can order the following books, as well as *The America's Test Kitchen Cookbook*, by calling 800-611-0759 inside the U.S. and 515-246-6911 outside the U.S.

➤ **The Best Recipe Series** Includes *The Best Recipe* as well as *Grilling & Barbecue, Soups & Stews,* and *American Classics.*

➤ **The How to Cook Master Series** A collection of 25 single-subject cookbooks.

➤ **The Annual Series** Annual hardbound editions of the magazine as well as a nine-year (1993–2001) reference index.

AMERICA'S TEST KITCHEN Television Show

Look for our television series on public television. For program times in your area, recipes, and details about the shows, or to order the companion book to the second series, *The America's Test Kitchen Cookbook*, go to http://www.americastestkitchen.com.

Heavy Cream versus Whipping Cream

What is the difference between whipping cream and heavy cream? When should I use one versus the other?

DORIS WHITTEN
HARVARD, MASS.

➤ According to the U.S. government's Code of Federal Regulations, heavy cream must consist of at least 36 percent milk fat, whipping cream (sometimes also called light whipping cream) at least 30 percent but no more than 36 percent. This may not sound like much of a difference, but after whipping up more than a few bowls of cream and talking to some experts in the dairy industry, we learned that it can be.

We set out to purchase a pint of whipping cream and a pint of heavy cream, whip them up, and assess their performance in five categories: time to whip to stiff peaks, volume, staying power (how long the whipped cream would hold its shape), texture, and flavor. What we brought back to the test kitchen, however, were three pints of cream. We found just one kind of whipping cream in the dairy case but two kinds of heavy cream.

One type of heavy cream listed additives on its label and described their functions as follows: to help "put air into the cream as it is whipped" (mono- and diglycerides) and to help "hold the whipped cream peaks" (carrageenan). The whipping cream listed these additives, too, as well as another intended to help "create stiff peaks" (polysorbate 80). Both this heavy cream and the whipping cream were also ultrapasteurized, a process that extends shelf life (up to 60 days, unopened) while also destroying some of the proteins in the cream that promote whipping.

The other type of heavy cream that we found had no additives and listed just one ingredient—cream—and it was pasteurized, a process that is like ultrapasteurization in that it kills pathogenic microbes but does less damage to the proteins that promote whipping. (In pasteurization, which extends shelf life to only about 20 days, cream is generally heated to 145 degrees or 161 degrees, depending on the particular process used. In ultrapasteurization, cream is heated to 280 degrees or higher.) The pasteurized heavy cream also contained more fat than the ultrapasteurized heavy cream, 6 grams per tablespoons versus 5 grams per tablespoon, respectively, which translates to a fat content of 40 percent versus about 36 percent.

With our three creams in the kitchen, we took out our hand mixer and got to work. The first category up was whipping time, and here the whipping cream was the winner by a long shot, taking just under three minutes to reach stiff peaks. The heavy creams reached stiff peaks after about five minutes. In terms of volume, all three creams doubled from 1 cup liquid to about 2 cups whipped. As for staying power, the lower-fat whipping cream lost its peaks and became watery after just a few hours in the refrigerator. The heavy creams were fine for up to a day.

Tasters found the freshly whipped whipping cream to be lighter and more airy than either of the heavy creams. It was also more fleeting, melting in your mouth almost as soon as you were able to taste it (no doubt because of the lower fat content). Of the two heavy creams, the higher fat, pasteurized cream was judged the thickest as well as the best-tasting. It was sweeter and more buttery than either the ultrapasteurized heavy cream or the whipping cream. Evidently, the additives, as well as the process of ultrapasteurization, compromise the sweet, delicate flavor of cream.

Why do manufacturers use the additives? The emulsifiers and stabilizing agents in the whipping cream and the ultrapasteurized heavy cream help compensate for the relative lack of fat. It's cheaper for a manufacturer to use a lower-fat cream with additives than a higher-fat cream without additives.

Wanting to test the creams' performance in cooking, we decided to use each one in a simple reduction sauce with chicken broth. All three creams thickened upon reduction without breaking, but the sauce with the pasteurized, highest fat cream was by far the most appealing—velvety smooth and pleasant tasting.

All told, then, pasteurized heavy cream, with a fat content of 40 percent (or 6 grams per tablespoon), is the best all-purpose cream to have on hand if you can find it. If not, the next best choice is ultrapasteurized heavy cream. We don't recommend whipping cream.

Allergic to Shrimp or Not?

When I clean shrimp my hands get red and itchy, which makes me think I might be allergic. But I seem to have no reaction when I eat cooked shrimp. Have you heard of this problem?

HARRIET GRANT
PALO ALTO, CALIF.

➤ As a matter of fact, when the recipe for jambalaya (see page 10) was being developed and many pounds of shrimp were cleaned in the test kitchen, a couple of test cooks and an editor complained of reddened, itchy hands. The reaction faded fairly quickly (within 30 minutes), however, and these members of our staff thoroughly enjoyed eating the cooked shrimp in the jambalaya. After doing a little research, we came up with several explanations for this unusual reaction.

Iodine was one possibility. Certain people are allergic to iodine, and some shrimp are thought to feed on algae with a high concentration of iodine. Another was sulfites, which are commonly used to keep shrimp from developing black spots. Yet another possibility was a protein in the shrimp that is broken down during cooking or digestion and so rendered harmless before entering the bloodstream. In most food allergies, the body is reacting to a protein that is not broken down during cooking or digestion. In the case of the classic shrimp allergy, in which people develop allergic symptoms upon eating raw or cooked shrimp, that protein is typically tropomyosin.

Several scientists we spoke to were familiar with this phenomenon, but none knew of a study conducted for the purpose of finding out just what causes some people's hands to turn red and itchy on contact with raw shrimp. However, with the help of one food scientist, Steve Taylor, professor and head of the department of food science and technology at the University of Nebraska at Lincoln, we were able to narrow the field by making a few deductions.

The chance that the reaction is caused by iodine or sulfites is small, according to Taylor, who believes the most likely candidate is a protein in the shrimp that is destroyed by heat. A similar reaction is known to occur among some people when they peel potatoes, Taylor said. These people can eat cooked potato because the protein that causes the reaction when handling raw potatoes, called patatin, is broken down during cooking. Although scientists have not identified a similar protein in shrimp, Taylor thinks this is the most likely culprit. To avoid itchy skin when cleaning shrimp, our sensitive test cooks simply wear rubber gloves.

How Much Shallot Is One Shallot?

When a recipe calls for one shallot, what, exactly, is called for—one entire shallot or one section, or clove, from one shallot?

DEBORAH FIRST
DULUTH, MINN.

➤ We found little consensus about this question in the cookbooks we checked. Even in the test kitchen, different cooks held different opinions. After some debate, we agreed that the following argument made the most sense. A shallot may consist of one, two, three, or even four irregularly sized cloves, unlike a head of garlic, whose cloves are many and fairly regular in size. In contrast, most shallots (whether they have one clove or four) are approximately the same size. For this reason, it's more accurate to write recipes that use an entire shallot, not a single clove, as the equivalent of "one shallot." Of course, for maximum accuracy, it's best to measure the shallot when minced. In the test kitchen, we consider one medium shallot to equal 3 tablespoons minced.

Food Mills versus Ricers

What is the difference between a food mill and a ricer?

SAWAKO FUKUSHIMA
PORTLAND, ORE.

☞ Ricers are most often used to make smooth, creamy mashed potatoes. The peeled, cooked potato is put in the basket of the ricer's lower half and forced through small holes when the upper handle is closed, thereby mashing—actually, pureeing—the potato. While we have come across a ricer that contains two interchangeable plates, one for a coarse puree, one for a fine puree, ricers usually come with a fixed basket that has holes of only one size.

A food mill purees food and strains it at the same time. Food is placed in the hopper and a hand-crank mechanism turns a conical blade in the hopper against a perforated disk, forcing the food through the disk. Most food mills have three interchangeable disks with various-sized holes. A food mill can thus not only make mashed potatoes but can make them from unpeeled potatoes, forcing the flesh through the holes in the disk while holding back the skins. Food mills can also puree butternut squash for soup while holding back the skin, seeds, and stringy pith; puree apples to make flawlessly smooth applesauce with no need for the cook to have peeled and cored the apples; and puree cooked tomatoes, removing the skin and bitter seeds for you.

While some cooks swear by the ricer for making superior-quality mashed potatoes (there's less likelihood that the potatoes' starch cells will be ruptured, which can make for gluey potatoes), if you're looking for one kitchen tool that will mash potatoes and make all sorts of other purees, the food mill is the way to go.

Cooking versus Preparation Times

I made your Beef Stroganoff from the January/February 2002 issue, and the recipe took longer than the 20 minutes promised in the story. Just the cooking times in the recipe added up to 20 minutes.

JIM SHINE
IPSWICH, MASS.

☞ In the story, we wrote that this "dish may look like a stew, but it's actually a quick sauté that can be on the table in 20 minutes." We mentioned cooking time because many cooks wrongly assume that stroganoff must simmer for hours, like any true stew. As you indicate, our recipe calls

for 20 minutes of stovetop cooking. However, this time does not account for the preparation of ingredients. We estimate that it will take most home cooks an additional 20 minutes to prepare the mushrooms, slice the beef, mince the onion, and measure out the other ingredients. With this in mind, we should have said that it will take about 40 minutes total to put the stroganoff on the table. We apologize for the confusion.

WHAT IS IT?

While at my parent's home recently I went searching through the kitchen drawers for a corkscrew and came across this curious-looking gadget. I thought you might know what it is.

PAUL V. STEWART
HILTON HEAD, S.C.

☞ At first, we thought this might be someone's slightly odd variation on a traditional egg slicer but ultimately learned that what you have is a tomato slicer. These slicers have a row of thin, evenly spaced, serrated blades (usually 11 of them) that are typically 4 to 5 inches long and attached to a plastic, wooden, or metal (like yours) handle. According to one of our source books on kitchen gadgets, *Cook's Tools* (William Morrow, 1980) by Susan Campbell, the preferred technique for slicing is to push the tomato through the blades rather than using the blades to slice through the tomato, as you would do with a knife. Some tomato slicers, according to Campbell, are even sold with a "pusher," a small square of flat plastic with a handle that can be used to push the top of the tomato through the slicer so fingers don't come in contact with the sharp blades.

Tomato slicers are still sold today, and we purchased one for $9.99 to see how it worked. A couple of bloody fingers later, we well appreciated the need for the plastic pusher, which was not included with our tomato slicer. The gadget did produce neatly cut slices of tomato, but a sawing motion and some force had to be applied to push the tomato through the blades, which were sharp enough to nick the fingertips of one editor as she tried to use it.

What the designer of this device did get right was the use of narrow serrated blades. Our tool of choice for cutting tomatoes is a bread knife, whose serrated edge cuts right through the skin without tearing it and then continues right through the delicate flesh without marring or crushing it. So, even if you can find a tomato slicer that comes with a pusher, we still recommend a serrated knife, which is up to many kitchen tasks, not just one.

Is There an Easier Way to Clean Shrimp?

I noticed a device in a kitchen store that claims to make the job of cleaning shrimp easier. It's called the Shrimp Butler and costs about $40. Does it work? Is it worth the money?

RON URBANOVITCH
CITY OF SEMINOLE, FLA.

☞ The Shrimp Butler measures 9 inches tall and 8 inches long at the base, and it's made entirely of plastic except for a small, razor-sharp blade safely affixed to the inside of the casing. Shrimp are fed into a slot at the top of the machine and conveyed past the blade and out the bottom of the machine by means of a ridged wheel, the sides of which tighten to hold the shrimp steady when the lever that moves the wheel is pulled. The procedure, then, is to place a shrimp on the wheel, pull the lever, watch the shrimp come flying out of a chute, and then push the lever back up so you can start the whole process again. Each shrimp pops out with its back sliced neatly open, clearly revealing the vein, if any, that runs just under the back of the shell.

If you plan to shell and devein your shrimp before cooking them, the Shrimp Butler will not do this for you. It does certainly facilitate the task of deveining (by revealing the vein) and shelling (by giving you a good place to start from when peeling), but is this assistance worth its price of $39.99?

To answer this question, we recorded the time it took the same staff member (not a test cook) to shell and devein 1 pound of medium-large shrimp prepped by the Shrimp Butler and the time it took to do the job entirely by hand. The staff member took a total of 14 minutes, 10 seconds, to shell and devein the shrimp by hand and 10 minutes, 50 seconds, with assistance from the Shrimp Butler, for a time savings of 3 minutes, 20 seconds.

Do we recommend the Shrimp Butler? While it does make deveining and shelling easier, the degree to which it does so—saving our shrimp cleaner about 3 minutes per pound of shrimp—doesn't seem worth the expense. The Shrimp Butler must also be taken apart and washed thoroughly, a process that takes several minutes. Washing a paring knife and your hands is much quicker.

Errata

☞ The note about cheeses on the contents page of our January/February 2002 issue mistakenly identifies Bleu de Basques as a goat's milk cheese when it is in fact made from sheep's milk.

☞ We made two errors in our story about cheddar cheese in the March/April 2002 issue. Grafton Village uses unpasteurized milk in its cheese. The company also ages its cheese in vacuum-sealed 42-pound blocks, not in its retail packaging, as readers may have been led to believe.

Quick Tips

Spreading Napkins

Stacks of paper napkins appear at almost every informal social gathering. No doubt many a partygoer has noticed how difficult it can be to pick up just one paper napkin at a time, since they tend to cling to each other. Nicole McNeel of Coral Gables, Fla., uses this simple trick to make it easier for her guests to grab one napkin at a time.

Make a fist and press down on the stack of napkins. Apply pressure in short, sharp motions, rotating your fist clockwise a quarter turn each time. With each turn, the napkins will fan out slightly, and after a few turns the stack will have formed a spiral that exposes an edge of each napkin, making it possible to grab one at a time.

Removing Pinbones from Salmon

Locating and removing the pinbones from a side of salmon, or even a couple of fillets, can be tricky. Running your fingers along the flesh is one way to locate them, but Gina Di Palma of Coquitlam, British Columbia, has found an even better method. She inverts a size-appropriate mixing bowl on a work surface and drapes the salmon over it, flesh-side up. The curvature of the bowl forces the pinbones to stick up and out, so they are easier to spot, grasp with pliers, and remove.

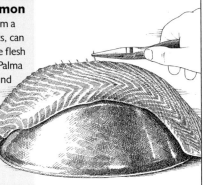

Retrieving a Fallen Oven Thermometer

In our testing of oven thermometers (*Cook's*, March/April 2002), we found that they often topple over in a hot oven, necessitating awkward retrieval with a hand protected by a bulky oven mitt. Brian Bauhs of Jamaica Plain, Mass., devised a better way. Whether the thermometer falls over on the oven rack or right through it to the oven floor, tongs are the perfect tool for retrieving and repositioning it. Tongs keep your hands a safe distance away from the hot rack while enabling dexterity that's not possible with your hand clad in an oven mitt.

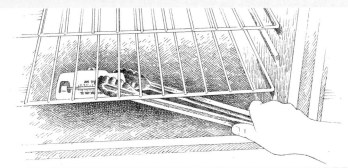

Preventing the Vegetable Vanishing Act

Cooks who have a garbage disposal installed in their sink often peel and pare vegetables and fruit right over the sink. Of course, this likely means they have at some point also dropped the item they were paring and watched in dismay as it vanished down the wide drain hole into the disposal. Corinne Livesay of Grant, Minn., avoids this problem by positioning a small funnel in the drain hole. The funnel, with a diameter just slightly larger than that of the drain opening, catches the desirable pieces of food, especially things like new potatoes, kiwis, and strawberries.

Faux Gastrique for Fruit Salad

The July/August 2001 issue of *Cook's* offered recipes for *gastriques*, sweet/tart dressings that make a tasty foil for fresh fruit salad. Although gastriques take just 15 minutes to prepare, Linda Sanders of Walnut Creek, Calif., found a way to shave 14 minutes off the process by using a reasonable and very simple facsimile of a gastrique: a couple of tablespoons of slightly thawed frozen limeade or lemonade concentrate. When tossed with the fruit, the concentrate contributes a sweet/tart flavor similar to that of a true gastrique.

The Pan Flip That Stops Drips

Pouring melted butter, warm oil, sauce, or almost any liquid from a pan often creates a drip down the outside of the pan. This not only makes a mess on the pan's exterior but can burn onto the pan bottom if you place the pan back on a hot burner. Kimiko Bush of Turbotville, Pa., has figured out how to prevent the drip with a simple flick of her wrist. Instead of immediately turning the pan right-side up after pouring out the contents, she continues to turn the pan in the direction of the pour, through one full rotation, until it eventually ends right-side up. This forces the liquid to run back into the pan instead of down its side.

Send Us Your Tip We will provide a complimentary one-year subscription for each tip we print. Send your tip, name, address, and daytime telephone number to Quick Tips, Cook's Illustrated, P.O. Box 470589, Brookline, MA 02447.

Salad on the Go

Lunchtime thoughts often turn to salad, even for those who pack their own lunch to eat at work. But salads present a problem when prepared early and eaten later in the day. Many cut items dry out, and the dressing causes the greens to turn limp. Marilyn Godfrey of Ventura, Calif., and Michelle Blain of Allston, Mass., have figured out how to solve these problems.

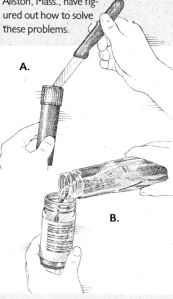

A. If the salad is to include juicy items, such as tomatoes, or items that might dry out if pre-cut, such as cheese, bring them intact and pack a paring knife, nestled safely inside of a plastic travel toothbrush holder.
B. To transport a small amount of dressing, use one of the jars in which dry spices are packed. Their small size and tight seal are perfect for the job.

Combating Odoriferous Ingredients

After working with pungent ingredients such as garlic, onions, or fish, many cooks use a little lemon juice to wash away any lingering odors from their hands. But sometimes the smell is stronger than the citrus. For those tough cases, Joan Grace of Bath, Maine, recommends washing your hands with a couple of tablespoons of mouthwash. Any inexpensive brand is fine.

Organizing Pot Lids

Many cooks store their pans and lids in a single drawer. To keep the lids from sliding around and under the pans, Lynn Miller of Houston, Texas, installed a slender expansion curtain rod at the front of her drawer. The lids stand up straight between the front of the drawer and the curtain rod, always within sight and reach.

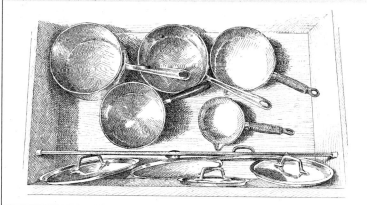

Two Simple Racks for Spice Drawers

It is best to store spices away from heat and light (not on the counter in a spice rack), but if your chosen spot is a drawer, then you have to either label the lid or lift up the jar to determine its contents. Tired of this irritating routine, Barbara Gard of Somerville, Mass., and Marilyn Fausti of Edgewater, Fla., each fashioned spice racks that fit right into a kitchen drawer. These racks hold spice bottles at an angle so their labels are visible at a glance.
A. For a wide drawer of 24 inches or more, Barbara Gard fits two or three expansion curtain rods, like the one used in the pot-lid drawer organizer tip above, into the drawer and leans the spice bottles against them.

B. For a drawer that is too narrow to fit an expansion curtain rod, try this trick from Marilyn Fausti.
1. Cut three pieces from a ¼-inch-diameter wooden dowel to the width of the drawer. Cut two pieces of corrugated cardboard to the depth and length of the drawer, then cut three small X's in each, at 2½-inch lengths, to hold the dowels in place.
2. Place one piece of cardboard against each sidewall of the drawer. Position the dowels across the drawer and insert them into the small X's.
3. Lean the spice bottles against the dowels in the drawer, with the labels facing up.

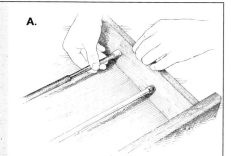
A.

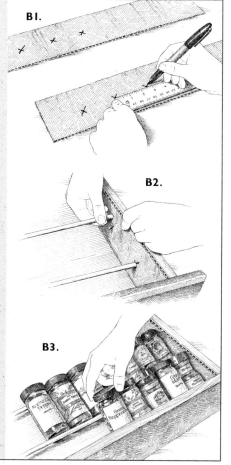
B1.

B2.

B3.

Controlling the Mess of a Lobster Dinner

Whether eaten at home or in a restaurant, lobster dinners inevitably make a sticky mess as fluid escapes in gushes and geysers from the shells as you crack them to get to the meat. Laurie Shapiro of Sudbury, Mass., has found an easy way to stem this tide. Using tongs, hold the cooked lobster by the tail above the cooking pot, so the claws are pointing down into the pot. Then use kitchen shears to cut about ¼ inch off the tip of each claw and continue holding the lobster as the water in its shell drains back into the pot through the holes in the claws.

Nonstick Coating for Your Food Processor

It's easy to shred semisoft cheeses such as mozzarella or cheddar in the food processor—until, of course, a big chunk sticks in the feed tube or gums up the shredding disk. Donna Schueller of Peosta, Iowa, avoids this problem by spraying the feed tube, disk, and workbowl of her food processor with a light coating of nonstick cooking spray before she begins.

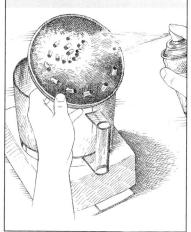

Grilling Thick Pork Chops

Is it possible to grill thick-cut pork chops that are seared and crispy outside and juicy and perfectly cooked inside? Yes, but it all starts with buying the right chop.

⊰ BY BRIDGET LANCASTER ⊱

Burgers and chicken are predictable grilling fare, but throw a thick, juicy pork chop on the fire and you have something exceptional, at least in theory. The reality of many a grilled pork chop is a burnt exterior, raw interior, tough meat, nary a hint of flavor—the list goes on. I was looking for perfection: a plump, Rubenesque chop with a seared crust reminiscent of chiaroscuro and an interior that would be juicy and flavorful all the way to the bone. I wanted a chop that looked and tasted so good that it transcended the far reaches of backyard grilling and became art.

Choosing the Chop

Thick pork chops usually come from the loin of the pig, which runs from the shoulder to the hip (see "Shopping for Chops," page 7). To determine which cut would be best, I conducted a blind taste test with four different chops, starting with the blade chop, which is from the shoulder end, or front, of the loin. Because the shoulder region of the loin has the most fat and is riddled with connective tissue, tasters found the blade chops to be full of flavor but also tough and chewy. At the hip end of the loin are the sirloin chops. These were dry, somewhat tasteless, and a bit tough. Moving on to the center of the loin, I tested the center-cut chop and the rib chop. Although both were tender and flavorful, tasters preferred the rib chops, which were juicy and well marbled with fat.

Pumping Up the Flavor

Although rib chops are flavorful on their own, I wanted to see if I could boost their flavor by using a spice rub, marinade, or brine. I tested two types of rub: dry and wet. The wet rubs, made with spices and a liquid, gave the chops good flavor but also caused their exteriors to turn syrupy. Tasters preferred the dry rubs, which combine potent dried spices with sugar to create big flavor and a crisp crust.

Next I tried marinating the chops in an acidic oil mixture flavored with herbs and garlic. While the marinade succeeded in flavoring the exterior

A spice rub (made in five minutes with pantry items) boosts the flavor of these pork chops and helps create an especially crisp crust.

of the chops, it did little for the interior. Moreover, the meat took on a slimy texture that prohibited formation of a good crust.

Finally, I tried brining, a method we often turn to here at *Cook's,* in which lean cuts of meat (usually pork or poultry) are soaked in a solution of water and salt and sometimes sugar. (Brining yields moist, well-seasoned meat and poultry that are hard to overcook, an important factor when grilling.) The brined chops were well seasoned throughout, not just on the surface. They were also extremely juicy—each bite was full of moist, seasoned pork flavor.

Discovering Fire

As a preliminary test, I pitted hardwood charcoal against the more traditional charcoal briquettes. After grilling a few chops over each, I found I preferred the hardwood for its intensely hot fire and slightly smoky flavor. As for the fire itself, I always begin testing with a single-level fire—that is, a fire of even and generally high heat made by spreading coals evenly across the grill. I threw the chops over the fire and watched as they browned

to a beautiful bronze within minutes. But when I pulled the chops off the grill and cut into one, it was rare at the bone. Moderating the temperature of the fire only drew out the cooking time and sacrificed the deep, caramelized crust that I had achieved over the high heat.

Moving next to a two-level fire, which is achieved by banking more hot coals on one side of the grill than on the other, I tried a multitude of temperature combinations, each time starting the chops over high heat to develop a nicely browned crust. Moving the chops from high to medium, high to low, and high to no heat were all tested, but none of these combinations produced a thoroughly cooked interior in a reasonable amount of time. Throwing the grill lid back on after the initial sear cooked the chops all the way through—a breakthrough to be sure—but the flavor of the meat was adversely affected. (The inside of most grill covers is coated with a charcoal residue that readily imparts bitter, spent flavors to foods.) Seizing on the notion of covering the chops for part of the cooking time, I turned to a handy disposable aluminum roasting pan to solve the problem. I threw the pan over the chops after searing them over high heat and moving them to the cooler part of the grill. This time I had a crisp crust, juicy meat, and no off flavors.

In my eagerness to serve these perfect chops, I cut into them right off the grill and watched as the juices ran out onto the plate. I allowed the next round of chops to sit covered under the foil pan for five minutes. When I cut into the chops this time, only a little of the juice was expelled. I was surprised, however, to find that these chops were slightly tougher than the chops that did not rest. I took the internal temperature and found that it was now nearly 165 degrees—overcooked in my book. (At 145 degrees, pork is cooked, safe to eat, and still juicy. Temperatures above 150 degrees yield dry, tough meat.) I cooked one more batch of chops and this time took them off the grill earlier, once they had reached an internal temperature of 135 degrees, and let them sit under the foil pan for a good five minutes. Thanks to the residual heat left in the bone, the temperature shot

A Bone Worth Picking

To find out how boneless chops would fare on the grill, we removed the bones from several rib chops, grilled them, and compared them with their bone-in counterparts in a blind taste test. (We took the meat off the grilled bone-in chops and then sliced the meat from both chops so as not to tip off tasters.) The results were clear. Every taster preferred the meat that had been cooked on the bone. It was much more juicy and had more pork flavor than the meat cooked without the bone. We contacted several food scientists, who offered a few explanations.

First, because bone is a poor conductor of heat, the meat located next to the bone doesn't cook as quickly as the rest. Although this factor doesn't alter the cooking time significantly, having a section of the pork chop cook at a slightly slower rate contributes to a juicier end product.

The bone also insulates the muscle closest to it, protecting it from exposure to the air. In a boneless chop, a larger area of muscle is exposed, so more of the flavorful juices evaporate during grilling.

Finally, fat is a crucial source of flavor, and, as it melts during cooking, it also increases the perceived juiciness. In certain cuts, especially ribs and chops, deposits of fat are located next to the bone. When the bone is removed, some fat is removed as well. With less fat, the boneless chops cooked up with less pork flavor and seemed drier. –Meg Suzuki

up an average of 10 to 15 degrees, bringing the meat into that desirable range of 145 to 150. Magic. Or perhaps this was art.

CHARCOAL-GRILLED PORK CHOPS
SERVES 4

Rib loin chops are our top choice for their big flavor and juiciness. Spice rubs add a lot of flavor for very little effort, but the chops can also be seasoned with pepper alone just before grilling.

- ³/₄ cup kosher salt or 6 tablespoons table salt
- 6 tablespoons sugar
- 4 bone-in rib loin pork chops or center-cut loin chops, each 1¹/₂ inches thick (about 3 pounds total)
- 1 recipe spice rub or ground black pepper

1. Dissolve salt and sugar in 3 quarts cold water in 2-gallon zipper-lock plastic bag. Add chops and seal bag, pressing out as much air as possible. (Alternatively, divide brine and chops evenly between two 1-gallon zipper-lock bags.) Refrigerate, turning bag once, until fully seasoned, about 1 hour. Remove chops from brine and dry thoroughly with paper towels. Coat chops with spice rub or season generously with pepper.

2. Ignite large chimney starter filled with hardwood charcoal (about 2¹/₂ pounds) and burn until charcoal is covered with layer of fine gray ash. Build

a two-level fire by stacking most of coals on one side of grill and arranging remaining coals in single layer on other side. Set cooking grate in place, cover grill with lid, and let grate heat up, about 5 minutes. Use wire brush to scrape cooking grate clean.

3. Cook chops, uncovered, over hotter part of grill until browned on each side, 2¹/₂ to 3 minutes per side. Move chops to cooler part of grill and cover with disposable aluminum roasting pan. Continue grilling, turning once, until instant-read thermometer inserted through side of chop and away from bone registers 135 degrees, 7 to 9 minutes longer. Transfer chops to platter; cover with foil pan, and let rest 5 minutes. Internal temperature should rise to 145 degrees. Serve immediately.

GAS-GRILLED PORK CHOPS

Because gas grill lids don't build up a residue that can impart an off flavor to foods (as charcoal grills do), they can be used to concentrate heat.

Follow step 1 of Charcoal-Grilled Pork Chops. Light grill and turn all burners to high; cover and heat grill 15 minutes. Use wire brush to scrape cooking grate clean. Turn off all but one burner. Place chops over hotter part of grill, cover, and cook until browned on each side, 3 to 4 minutes per side. Move chops to cooler side of grill. Cover and continue cooking, turning once, until instant-read thermometer inserted through side of chop and away from bone registers 135 degrees, 7 to 9 minutes longer. Transfer chops to platter, tent loosely with foil, and let rest 5 minutes. Internal temperature should rise to 145 degrees. Serve immediately.

BASIC SPICE RUB FOR PORK CHOPS
MAKES ¹/₄ CUP, ENOUGH FOR 4 CHOPS

- 1 tablespoon ground cumin
- 1 tablespoon chili powder
- 1 tablespoon curry powder
- 1 teaspoon ground black pepper
- 2 teaspoons brown sugar

Combine all ingredients in small bowl.

INDIAN SPICE RUB FOR PORK CHOPS
MAKES SCANT ¹/₄ CUP, ENOUGH FOR 4 CHOPS

- 1 tablespoon fennel seeds
- 1 tablespoon ground cumin
- 1 teaspoon ground coriander
- 1 teaspoon ground cardamom
- 1 teaspoon dry mustard
- ¹/₂ teaspoon ground cinnamon
- ¹/₄ teaspoon ground cloves
- 2 teaspoons brown sugar

Grind fennel seeds to powder in spice grinder. Mix with remaining ingredients in small bowl.

TASTING: Shopping for Chops

Pork chops come from the loin of the pig. A whole pork loin (shown below) weighs 14 to 17 pounds and can be cut into blade chops, rib chops, center-cut chops, and sirloin chops. The loin muscle runs the entire length of the backbone (muscle is obscured by bones in the photo). Starting midway back, the tenderloin muscle runs along the opposite side of the backbone (this muscle is visible in the photo). Center-cut and sirloin chops contain both kinds of muscle. We found that the tenderloin cooks more quickly than the loin and can dry out. This is one reason why we prefer rib chops, which contain only loin meat. Following are tasters' impressions after sampling four different chops cut from the loin. Rib chops were tasters' top choice, followed by center-cut chops.

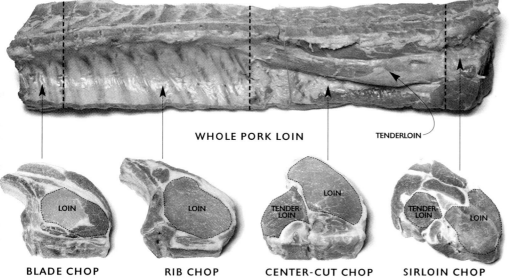

WHOLE PORK LOIN   TENDERLOIN

BLADE CHOP
Fattiest, toughest, juiciest, most flavor

RIB CHOP
Some fat, relatively tender, juicy, great flavor

CENTER-CUT CHOP
Little fat, relatively tender, less juicy, good flavor

SIRLOIN CHOP
Tough, quite dry, little flavor

Ground Beef Tacos

Forget the seasoning packets and prefab taco shells. The best tacos are homemade.

≥ BY THE COOK'S ILLUSTRATED TEST KITCHEN ≤

So maybe they're not authentic Mexican. They're Tex-Mex . . . maybe even gringo. But ground beef tacos have earned a special place in the palates of at least a couple of generations of Americans. We recall our mothers ripping open the seasoning packet, the colorful array of toppings in mismatched bowls that cluttered the tabletop, and, of course, the first bite that cracked the shell and sent a trickle of orange grease running down the wrist. Indeed, there is something appealing about the silly taco. It's a mix of spicy ground beef, shredded cheese, sweet chopped tomatoes (or, as some would have it, jarred salsa), and cool iceberg lettuce. Those in favor of more toppings can always add chopped onions, diced avocado, and sour cream. All this contained in a crisp and corny taco shell. Seems hard to go wrong.

But when we sampled a few tacos made from supermarket kits in the test kitchen, our happy memories faded. The fillings tasted flat and stale, reeking of dried oregano and onion powder. The store-bought shells tasted greasy and junky—too much like unwholesome snack food to be served at the dinner table. There's no denying that these seasoning packets, along with prefab taco shells, make taco-making ridiculously easy, but with only a little more effort we thought we could produce a fiery, flavorful filling and crisp, toasty taco shells . . . tacos that even adults could enjoy.

Inside Out

We began by trying fillings made according to the few cookbook recipes we uncovered. There were two approaches. The first had us brown ground beef in a skillet, add spices, sometimes chopped onion and garlic, and water, and then simmer. The second directed us to sauté the onion and garlic before adding the beef to the pan, and this is the technique we preferred. Sautéing the onion softened its texture and made its flavor full and sweet, while a quick minute of cooking helped bring out the garlic's flavor. For a pound of ground beef, a small chopped onion was enough; as for garlic, we liked the wallop of a tablespoon, minced.

For burgers we prefer the relatively fatty 80 percent lean ground chuck, and we expected we would like the same for the taco filling. After tasting them all, though, we were surprised to learn that our tastes leaned toward the leaner types. Anything fattier than 90 percent lean ground beef cooked into a slick, greasy mess.

The labels on taco seasoning packets indicate a

For taco shells with great flavor and an authentic, homey appearance, set aside just 20 minutes and fry corn tortillas yourself.

hodgepodge of ingredients, including dehydrated onion and/or garlic, MSG, mysterious "spices," and even soy sauce. They all include chili powder, however, so that's where we started to fashion our own mixture, beginning with 1 tablespoon and quickly increasing it to 2 tablespoons for more kick. A teaspoon each of ground cumin and ground coriander added savory, complex flavors. Dried oregano in a more modest amount—½ teaspoon—provided herbal notes. For a little heat, we added cayenne.

The flavors were bold, but we wanted to make them fuller and rounder. From past experience we knew that heating spices on the stovetop, as is often done in various types of ethnic cooking, makes their flavors blossom, so we tried this technique with our taco filling. In one batch we simply sprinkled the spices over the beef as it simmered, and in the second we added the spices to the sautéed onion along with the garlic and gave them a minute to cook. The difference was marked. The second batch was richly and deeply flavored, and the spices permeated the beef, whereas the flavors in the first batch seemed to

merely sit in the liquid that surrounded the meat, and the beef itself tasted rather dull.

Because the meat was lean and we needed a sauce to carry the flavors of the spices, the filling required some liquid. Many recipes call only for water, but water produced a thin, hollow-tasting mixture. We tried canned chicken broth, canned plain tomato sauce, and a combination of the two, and the combination was best.

The final flavor adjustments to the filling came in the form of sweet and sour. A teaspoon of brown sugar expanded and enriched the flavor of the spices. Two teaspoons of cider vinegar picked up where the tomato sauce left off by adding just enough acidity to activate all the taste buds. Our taco filling was now, in the words of one taster, "perfect." We moved on to the shells.

No Fear of Frying

A tasting of store-bought taco shells (see "Shell Shocked," page 9) was quick to move us in search of something better. While the convenience of these ready-to-eat shells is obviously a huge draw for many home cooks, we wondered if it would be worth the trouble to purchase corn tortillas that could be fried at home, thereby producing a superior shell for our taco filling. The flavor of the first home-fried shells we tried was a revelation, so we went on to perfect a technique.

Because corn tortillas are like thin pancakes—they will not hold a shape—the question was how to fry them into the traditional wedge shape used for tacos. The method we settled on was simple enough. We fried one half of the tortilla until it stiffened, holding onto the other half with tongs. Next, the other half was submerged in the oil while we kept the shell mouth open (about 2 inches wide), again using the tongs. Finally, we slipped the first half back into the oil to finish cooking. Each shell took about 2½ minutes, not an unreasonable investment of time given the huge improvement in taste and texture that homemade taco shells offer.

Toppings

Of course, what goes into the toppings for tacos is largely a matter of choice. Shredded cheese, however, is required, and Monterey Jack and cheddar were the obvious picks. We bypassed jarred salsa in favor of some simple chopped tomato and onions because we preferred their fresher, brighter flavors and textures. Shredded iceberg lettuce was favored over romaine for its crispier crunch. Sour cream and diced avocado were also on the shortlist of toppings. Finally, chopped fresh cilantro—never an option on our mothers' tables—was also welcomed. It helped to drag the tacos out of the past and into the present. These were tacos that tasted better than we remembered.

BEEF TACOS
MAKES 8 TACOS, SERVING 4

Tomato sauce is sold in cans in the same aisle that carries canned whole tomatoes. Do not use jarred pasta sauce in its place. We prefer to let diners top their own tacos with whatever fillings they prefer. There's no need to prepare all of the toppings listed below, but cheese, lettuce, and tomatoes are, in our opinion, essential.

Beef Filling

- 2   teaspoons corn or vegetable oil
- 1   small onion, chopped small (about ⅔ cup)
- 3   medium garlic cloves, minced or pressed through garlic press (about 1 tablespoon)
- 2   tablespoons chili powder
- 1   teaspoon ground cumin
- 1   teaspoon ground coriander
- ½   teaspoon dried oregano
- ¼   teaspoon cayenne pepper
       Salt
- 1   pound 90 percent lean (or leaner) ground beef
- ½   cup canned tomato sauce
- ½   cup canned low-sodium chicken broth
- 1   teaspoon brown sugar
- 2   teaspoons vinegar, preferably cider vinegar
       Ground black pepper

Shells and Toppings

- 8   Home-Fried Taco Shells (recipe follows) or store-bought shells (warmed according to package instructions)
- 1   cup (4 ounces) shredded cheddar or Monterey Jack cheese
- 2   cups shredded iceberg lettuce
- 2   small tomatoes, chopped small
- ½   cup sour cream
- 1   avocado, diced medium
- 1   small onion, chopped small
- 2   tablespoons chopped fresh cilantro leaves
       Hot pepper sauce, such as Tabasco

1. Heat oil in medium skillet over medium heat until hot and shimmering but not smoking, about 2 minutes; add onion and cook, stirring occasionally, until softened, about 4 minutes. Add garlic, spices, and ½ teaspoon salt; cook, stirring constantly, until fragrant, about 1 minute. Add ground beef and cook, breaking meat up with wooden spoon and scraping pan bottom to prevent scorching, until beef is no longer pink, about 5 minutes. Add tomato sauce, chicken broth, brown sugar, and vinegar; bring to simmer. Reduce heat to medium-low and simmer, uncovered, stirring frequently and breaking meat up so that no chunks remain, until liquid has reduced and thickened (mixture should not be completely dry), about 10 minutes. Adjust seasonings with salt and pepper.

2. Using wide, shallow spoon, divide filling evenly among taco shells; place two tacos on individual plates. Serve immediately, passing toppings separately.

STEP-BY-STEP | MAKING YOUR OWN TACO SHELLS

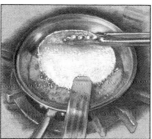  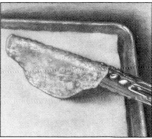

1. Using tongs to hold tortilla, slip half of tortilla into hot oil. With metal spatula in other hand, keep half of tortilla submerged in oil. Fry until just set, but not brown, about 30 seconds.

2. Flip tortilla; hold tortilla open about 2 inches while keeping bottom submerged in oil. Fry until golden brown, about 1½ minutes. Flip again and fry other side until golden brown, about 30 seconds.

3. Transfer shell upside down to prepared baking sheet to drain. Repeat with remaining tortillas, adjusting heat as necessary to keep oil between 350 and 375 degrees.

HOME-FRIED TACO SHELLS

The taco shells can be fried before you make the filling and rewarmed in a 200-degree oven for about 10 minutes before serving.

- ¾   cup corn, vegetable, or canola oil
- 8   (6-inch) corn tortillas

1. Heat oil in 8-inch heavy-bottomed skillet over medium heat to 350 degrees, about 5 minutes (oil should bubble when small piece of tortilla is dropped in; tortilla piece should rise to surface in 2 seconds and be light golden brown in about 1½ minutes). Meanwhile, line rimmed baking sheet with double thickness of paper towels.

2. Follow illustrations above to fry shells.

TASTING: Shell Shocked

Prefab taco shells simplify the process of taco-making, but we wondered if all shells were created equal. We conducted a tasting to find out, trying six brands of store-bought taco shells (warmed according to package directions) as well as home-fried shells. The runaway winner was the home-fried shells. Uneven and imperfect, they looked charming and real, not manufactured (see photo on page 8). Most important, tasters preferred their clean, toasty corn flavor and crisp yet sturdy texture. One taster noted that the home-fried shells brought flavor and texture to the assembled taco, whereas most other taco shells seemed no more than convenient containers.

Rating the rest seemed more a matter of choosing the lesser of evils. **Old El Paso Taco Shells** finished a distant second. They were described as "dry," and some tasters picked up "plastic" and "chemical" flavors, but a few appreciated their crispness and faint corny sweetness. **El Rio Taco Shells** and **Ortega Taco Shells** tied for third. The former were crisp but "too delicate" and "absolutely tasteless"; the latter were hard, dry, and tough, but some liked the "well-seasoned" corn flavor. Fourth place **Taco Bell Taco Shells** were bland, with a decidedly stale texture. **Bearitos Taco Shells**, made with organically grown blue corn and costing almost a dollar more than some other brands, took fifth. Their color was off-putting and their texture too brittle and delicate to support the taco filling. **Old El Paso White Corn Taco Shells** came in sixth place, disliked for a rancid flavor and a stale texture.

We tested six brands of supermarket taco shells, but none could compare with shells we fried ourselves using store-bought corn tortillas.

Taking the Jumble Out of Jambalaya

Most recipes ask a lot from the home cook and provide no more than mushy rice, rubbery shrimp, and dry chicken in return. We wanted great jambalaya in one hour.

≥ BY RAQUEL PELZEL WITH SHANNON BLAISDELL ≤

With chicken, sausage, shrimp, rice, tomatoes, and a laundry list of herbs and spices, jambalaya may sound more like a weekend project than a weeknight dinner. But done right, jambalaya is a one-pot meal that can be on the table in about an hour. Like New Orleans, the city from which it came, jambalaya's combination of sweet, spice, and smoke makes it a standout. But when poorly executed, jambalaya is no better than the Vegas version of New Orleans: a thin-flavored imposter with gummy rice, overcooked shrimp, and tough, dry chicken.

We started by testing a half-dozen recipes, all of which followed the same protocol: In a large Dutch oven, brown the chicken and remove; brown the sausage and remove; sauté the vegetables; add the cooking liquid, tomatoes, seasonings, and rice; return the chicken and sausage to the pot; and, finally, add the shrimp when the rice is about half done. Our conclusion? We wanted fluffier rice, more succulent chicken, more delicate shrimp, a more modest amount of tomato, and fresher flavors. In addition, we wanted a streamlined method that would come together easily in a home kitchen.

One Step at a Time

Although most jambalaya recipes call for a whole chicken cut up into parts, we opted to use chicken thighs instead. We knew this would save us the time it takes to cut up a chicken, but we also thought that using thighs, which are composed of relatively fatty dark meat, might solve the problem of dry chicken, since white meat is more apt to dry out.

We started by searing both sides of the chicken (with the skin on to provide extra fat to flavor the dish) in just 2 teaspoons of hot vegetable oil, then removed it from the pot, set it aside to cool, and peeled off the skin (chicken skin becomes soggy and unappetizing when cooked in liquid). Rice and liquid went into the pot, followed by the chicken, and, after just 25 minutes, the chicken and rice were perfectly cooked through. But there was something clumsy about eating the chicken

This New Orleans specialty blends perfectly cooked rice with shrimp, sausage, and chicken.

off the bone. For our next test, we tried cooking the chicken in exactly the same way, but instead of serving the thighs whole, we shredded them. Now the dish looked and tasted much more appealing, offering a bite of chicken in every forkful and no cumbersome bone to deal with.

Next we took on the sausage. After comparing the classic choice, andouille, with tasso, chorizo, and linguiça, we decided that nothing tastes like andouille—a Cajun sausage that infuses spice and smoke into the rest of the ingredients in the pot (see "Pick Your Pork" on page 11). We browned ¼-inch pieces of andouille in the chicken fat and then set them aside, planning to add them back to the pot along with the liquid, rice, and chicken.

Vegetables were the next item on our roster. Because the trio of minced bell pepper, onion, and celery is key to Cajun cooking, we included all three in our recipe. However, after testing bitter-tasting green peppers (the classic choice) against red, we unabashedly chose the reds, which were sweet. We also decided to add 2 tablespoons of minced garlic to give the jambalaya more punch. Most recipes use artificial-tasting

garlic powder or too little fresh garlic to make much of an impact.

Now approaching our tenth test, we began to dread the task of chopping and mincing the vegetables and garlic. It just took too much time. So we took out the food processor and gave the vegetables a whirl. What a difference! Not only did the food processor get the job done in seconds, but the vegetables were cut into smaller pieces than when hand-chopped and so sautéed more quickly in the pan and contributed more flavor.

Rice and Shine

For the rice, we started with 2 cups of water to 1 cup of long-grain white rice, the liquid ratio recommended on the back of the rice box. But our rice turned out gummy, and there wasn't enough to serve four to six people. We decided to increase the rice to 1½ cups, using only 2¼ cups water instead of the traditional 3 cups. The rice was now too dry, so we bumped up the water to 2¾ cups. This rice was the perfect compromise between fluffy pilaf (too light for jambalaya) and sticky risotto (too heavy).

Most jambalaya recipes call for homemade chicken stock, but we found that canned chicken broth was fine given the other strong flavors in the dish. We also tried combining clam juice with the chicken broth, hoping that it might bring out the sweetness of the shrimp. Although the clam juice/chicken broth duo was pleasing and delicate, the rice needed more punch. In an effort to boost the flavor of the rice, we substituted ¼ cup of tomato juice (from a can of diced tomatoes) for an equal amount of water. Now the rice was perfect: flavorful and cohesive without being gummy, heavy, or sticky.

The next step was to find a way to keep the shrimp tender and sweet. We seared the shrimp in a hot pan, set them aside, and then added them back to the jambalaya when the chicken was halfway done. This batch was a failure. The shrimp were tough, and they took on a smoky flavor from the searing that provided little contrast with the andouille. For the next test, we added the raw shrimp just five minutes before the chicken and rice were finished. After removing the lid, we could see that the shrimp were perfectly cooked to a blushing pink, still tender and succulently sweet.

This jambalaya was smoky and sweet, spicy and

TASTING: **Pick Your Pork**

Andouille, a seasoned smoked sausage, is the most authentic choice for jambalaya, with tasso, also known as Cajun ham, a close second. (Tasso is a lean chunk of highly seasoned pork or sometimes beef that is cured and then smoked.) Since andouille and tasso can sometimes be hard to find in supermarkets, we tested the two against chorizo and linguiça (Spanish and Portuguese sausages, respectively), which are more widely available.

After making a batch of jambalaya with each sausage, tasters agreed there ain't nothing like the real thing. Andouille was perfection. It had intense heat and the bold flavor of garlic and herbs, and it imparted a noticeable yet manageable amount of smokiness to the dish. While well-seasoned and flavorful, tasso was ultrasmoky and had a strange, gristly texture that no one liked. Linguiça was bland and added little heat to the finished product; chorizo was slightly more piquant, but still dull.

TASSO

ANDOUILLE

Tasso has great flavor, but tasters did not like its gristly texture and found its smokiness overpowering. Andouille is a better choice for jambalaya: spicy, bold, smoky, *and* perfectly textured.

Andouille is clearly the best choice for jambalaya, but we wondered if all andouille were created equal. So we gathered five brands available nationally in supermarkets and by mail-order (see Resources on page 32) and put them to the test. Here are the results, brands listed in order of preference:

CHEF PAUL'S REGULAR (sometimes called "mild") andouille took the crown, one vote shy of a sweep. Its "smoky," "rich," and "earthy" flavors and "balanced heat level," are the perfect accompaniment to the other big flavors in jambalaya.
JACOB'S andouille was big, dark, and jerky-esque, with a strange muscled grain. Despite its aesthetic shortcomings, Jacob's andouille was our runner-up. It had a "deeply smoky," almost sweet flavor.
CHEF PAUL'S HOT andouille was so spicy it masked the sausage's other flavors.
POCHE'S andouille had little flavor to offer, and its texture was "chewy," "rubbery," and "tough."
NORTH COUNTRY SMOKEHOUSE andouille was excessively spicy and had a strange "tinny" flavor.

The conclusion is clear: If you can find Chef Paul's regular andouille, buy it. —Shannon Blaisdell

savory, with perfectly tender shrimp, moist chicken, flavorful sausage, and rice cooked just so. You'd never have guessed we were eating it in our Boston test kitchen and not on Bourbon Street.

CHICKEN AND SHRIMP JAMBALAYA
SERVES 4 TO 6

Because andouille varies in spiciness, we suggest tasting a piece of the cooked sausage and then adjusting the amount of cayenne in the jambalaya to suit your taste. If you can't find andouille, try tasso, chorizo, or linguiça; if using chorizo or linguiça, consider doubling the amount of cayenne. The onion, celery, bell pepper, and garlic can be chopped by hand instead of in the food processor. The shrimp don't need to be deveined, but you can do so if you prefer. If you're serving only four people, you may choose to skip the shredding step and serve the chicken on the bone.

1	medium onion, peeled, ends trimmed, and quartered lengthwise
1	medium celery rib, cut crosswise into quarters
1	medium red bell pepper, stem removed, seeded, and quartered lengthwise
5	medium garlic cloves, peeled
2	teaspoons vegetable oil
4	bone-in, skin-on chicken thighs
8	ounces andouille sausage, halved lengthwise and cut into 1/4-inch pieces
1 1/2	cups (10 ounces) long-grain white rice
1	teaspoon salt
1/2	teaspoon minced fresh thyme leaves
1/4	teaspoon cayenne pepper (see note)
1	(14 1/2-ounce) can diced tomatoes, drained, 1/4 cup juice reserved
1	cup bottled clam juice
1 1/2	cups canned low-sodium chicken broth
2	large bay leaves
1	pound medium-large shrimp (31 to 35 shrimp per pound), shelled
2	tablespoons minced fresh parsley leaves

1. In food processor, pulse onion, celery, red pepper, and garlic until chopped fine, about six 1-second pulses, scraping down sides of bowl once or twice. Do not overprocess; vegetables should not be pureed (see illustration at right).

2. Heat oil in large heavy-bottomed Dutch oven over medium-high heat until shimmering but not smoking, about 2 minutes. Add chicken, skin-side down, and cook until golden brown, about 5 minutes. Using tongs, turn chicken and cook until golden brown on second side, about 3 minutes longer. Transfer chicken to plate and set aside. Reduce heat to medium and add andouille; cook, stirring frequently, until browned, about 3 minutes. Using slotted spoon, transfer sausage to paper towel–lined plate and set aside.

3. Reduce heat to medium-low, add vegetables, and cook, stirring occasionally and scraping

TECHNIQUE |

SHREDDING CHICKEN

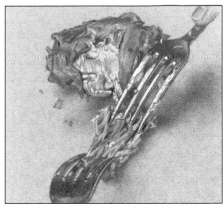

Hold one fork in each hand, with the prongs down and facing toward each other. Insert the prongs into the chicken meat and gently pull the forks away from each other, breaking the meat apart and into long, thin strands.

bottom of pot with wooden spoon, until vegetables have softened, about 4 minutes. Add rice, salt, thyme, and cayenne; cook, stirring frequently, until rice is coated with fat, about 1 minute. Add tomatoes, reserved tomato juice, clam juice, chicken broth, bay leaves, and browned sausage to pot; stir to combine. Remove and discard skin from chicken; place chicken, skinned-side down, on rice. Bring to boil, reduce heat to low, cover, and simmer for 15 minutes. Stir once, keeping chicken on top, skinned-side down. Replace cover and continue to simmer until chicken is no longer pink when cut into with paring knife, about 10 minutes more; transfer chicken to clean plate and set aside. Scatter shrimp over rice, cover, and continue to cook until rice is fully tender and shrimp are opaque and cooked through, about 5 minutes more.

4. While shrimp are cooking, shred chicken (see illustration above). When shrimp are cooked, discard bay leaves; off heat, stir in parsley and shredded chicken, and serve immediately.

Properly Cut Vegetables

Using the pulse button on the food processor yields finely chopped vegetables in seconds. Don't overprocess or puree the vegetables—they should remain in distinct pieces.

The New Classic Chicken Caesar Salad

To balance the flavors in this classic salad, skip the ersatz ingredients and look to tradition for the dressing.

≽ BY THE COOK'S ILLUSTRATED TEST KITCHEN ≼

Since its invention in the 1920s, Caesar salad has suffered at the hands of chefs and home cooks alike. The Caesar was conceived as a salad of whole lettuce leaves, cloaked with a rich dressing made from such unlikely partners as egg, Worcestershire sauce, lemon juice, garlic, and Parmesan cheese and garnished with garlic croutons. Over time it has been subjected to such oddball additions as chickpeas, palm hearts, and barbecued ribs, and the dressing has been adulterated with everything from Asian fish sauce to pickled chiles. Aside from anchovies, a hotly debated but common ingredient, such transgressions ruin this unusual but undeniably successful marriage of ingredients.

We wanted to bring Caesar salad back to its roots, rediscovering a dressing that is both unique and sublime. We were struck, however, by the not inconsiderable effort required to make the salad. Given this investment of time and effort, we decided to make our Caesar not a first course but a light main dish by adding one untraditional (but now familiar) ingredient: sliced chicken breast. We wanted the chicken to add heft to the salad without disturbing the underlying magic of the dressing.

All Dressed Up

Most Caesar salad dressings have at least one of two common problems. The first is texture, which should be thick and smooth, not thin or gluey. The second is lack of balance among the dressing's key flavors—lemon, Worcestershire, and garlic (and often anchovies)—which are frequently so out of whack that they assault your palate with a biting surplus of garlic or lip-sucking profusion of lemon.

We took on texture first. The classic thickening agent in this olive oil–based dressing is egg, which is either added raw or simmered in the shell very briefly in a process called coddling. The recipes we dug up in our research also included dressings that relied on mayonnaise and sour cream for thickening, but tasters summarily rejected both, finding that the former seemed better suited to a sandwich topping and the latter a party dip. In

Take Caesar salad to new heights with homemade garlic croutons and broiled chicken that's been brined for extra juiciness.

side-by-side tests of raw and coddled eggs, tasters preferred the noticeably smoother consistency of the coddled-egg dressing. The brief exposure to heat caused the yolk to thicken slightly, thereby giving the dressing a creamier texture. Many tasters wanted the dressing to be thicker still, so we decided to discard the egg white, which contributed extra liquid, and to double the number of yolks to two. Keep in mind, however, that such a brief exposure to heat does not render the egg as safe as if it were cooked fully; you are still essentially consuming raw egg, which may be of concern to some diners.

A series of tests focused on minor adjustments to ingredient amounts led us to a well-balanced dressing. Based on an oil quantity of ⅓ cup and our two coddled yolks, tasters favored just under 2 tablespoons of lemon juice and a modest teaspoon each of Worcestershire sauce and garlic. The last touch was anchovy, which tasters felt gave the dressing a welcome flavor dimension.

As for the lettuce, romaine is the standard choice. Our tasters stuck to it for its pleasantly sweet flavor and crunchy texture.

Beefing It Up—with Chicken

The chicken added to Caesar salad in restaurants is often dry and leathery. For our Caesar, we wanted chicken that was moist, well seasoned, and quick and easy to prepare.

Skinless, boneless breasts were the overwhelming choice of tasters, who felt that dark meat tasted out of place. With our eye cocked toward speed and ease, we tested three cooking methods: grilling, sautéing, and broiling. Grilling was too much work for a simple salad. Sautéing was eliminated because it required an extra step (flouring the chicken) and produced (believe it or not) chicken that was too flavorful for this purpose. Broiling, on the other hand, gave us what we wanted—a quick, simple cooking method and chicken that would blend right into the landscape of an already full-flavored salad.

With the chicken positioned about 6 inches beneath the broiler element, broiling took just eight largely unattended minutes. Unfortunately, the outer layer of chicken dried out a bit under the broiler, so we subjected the chicken to a quick, 30-minute brine (a soak in a solution of water, salt, and sugar that would season the chicken and help it retain moisture during cooking). While the chicken brined, we prepared the croutons and dressing.

And Don't Forget the Croutons

The garlicky croutons were the last element of the salad to examine. We tried store-bought croutons, but they were described by tasters as "stale" and "artificial tasting." From there we tried various types of white bread and determined that any type made without sweetener tasted fine. Buy a baguette or country white loaf instead of sliced sandwich bread, as the latter usually contains added sugar.

We tested three different methods of making croutons, including toasting, sautéing, and baking the bread cubes, and we tried each method with and without oil and garlic. We quickly learned that infusing olive oil with garlic flavor—rather than using minced garlic—was a key step. Whereas the minced garlic became burnt and bitter in the oven, allowing raw garlic to steep in olive oil for 20 minutes produced a

TESTING EQUIPMENT: **The Fat-Fighting Foreman**

Set foot in any cookware or discount store these days and you will inevitably come face-to-face with a huge display of George Foreman's Lean Mean Fat Reducing Grilling Machines. They are everywhere, so in our quest for a quick, easy way to dispatch chicken breasts for the chicken Caesar salad, we decided to give the Foreman grill a whirl.

The Foreman is an indoor electric grill. The cooking surface is nonstick-coated and ridged to create the semblance of grill marks on the food, and it's angled so that fat from the cooking food will drain out the front of the grill and into a small pan beneath it. The food is sandwiched between top and bottom grilling plates, which hinge closed clamshell-style, and both grilling plates contain heating elements so both sides of the food cook at once. Needless to say, there is no smoke or fire involved.

After cooking salmon fillets, grilled cheese sandwiches, chicken cutlets, hamburgers, and bone-in pork chops, we quickly discovered that this Foreman doesn't deliver a knockout punch. The salmon and the grilled cheese sandwiches (the outsides of which we brushed with melted butter before cooking) were our most successful tests, both forming attractive crusts and cooking through quickly. The chicken breasts looked better than they tasted because most of the flavorful, caramelized crust that formed stuck to the grilling plates instead of the meat, and the hamburgers and chops would have been better cooked in a skillet.

So, has this Foreman earned its place in the culinary ring? No, it doesn't even win a decision on points. While the Foreman did produce very good grilled cheese and respectable salmon, we prefer a nonstick skillet as the more effective, versatile kitchen tool. —Adam Ried

FOREMAN GRILL
This Foreman isn't a champ.

pleasantly garlicky flavor. In the end, we simply tossed raw bread cubes with the seasoned oil and baked them until crisp and golden.

Our chicken Caesar salad proves the old adage that everything old becomes new again. The croutons have been restored to their original glory—crisp, garlicky, and familiar—and the dressing once again embodies a careful balance of classic flavors accented with the more modern addition of anchovies. Last but not least, the broiled chicken turns this dish into an easy but classic main course.

CHICKEN CAESAR SALAD
SERVES 4 AS A LIGHT MAIN DISH

For efficiency, several components of the salad can be prepared at the same time. Start by preparing the flavored oil for the croutons. While the oil infuses, prepare the brine and brine the chicken. Once the chicken is brining, finish the croutons and prepare the dressing. If you follow these steps, all the components will be ready to come together when the chicken is cooked. Or, if you prefer to work in advance, both the croutons and the dressing can be made one day ahead.

Garlic Croutons
- 2 large garlic cloves, minced fine or pressed through garlic press
- 1/4 teaspoon salt
- 3 tablespoons extra-virgin olive oil
- 3 cups 3/4-inch bread cubes from 1 baguette or country loaf

Broiled Chicken Breasts
- 6 tablespoons kosher salt or 3 tablespoons table salt
- 3 tablespoons sugar
- 4 boneless, skinless chicken breast halves (about 6 ounces each), trimmed of excess fat
  Ground black pepper

Caesar Dressing
- 2 large eggs
- 1 tablespoon plus 2 teaspoons juice from 1 lemon
- 1 teaspoon Worcestershire sauce
- 1/4 teaspoon salt
- 1/8 teaspoon ground black pepper
- 1 medium garlic clove, minced fine or pressed through garlic press (about 1 teaspoon)
- 4 flat anchovy fillets, minced (about 1 1/2 teaspoons)
- 1/3 cup extra-virgin olive oil

Salad
- 2 medium heads romaine lettuce (large outer leaves removed) or 2 large romaine hearts; washed, dried, and torn into 1 1/2-inch pieces (about 10 cups lightly packed)
- 1/3 cup grated Parmesan cheese

1. FOR THE CROUTONS: Adjust oven rack to middle position and heat oven to 350 degrees. Mix garlic, salt, and oil in small bowl; let stand 20 minutes to infuse flavors, then pour through fine-mesh strainer into medium bowl. Add bread cubes and toss to coat. Spread bread cubes in even layer on rimmed baking sheet; bake, stirring occasionally, until golden, 12 to 15 minutes. Cool croutons on baking sheet to room temperature. (Can be covered and stored at room temperature up to 24 hours.)

2. FOR THE CHICKEN: Dissolve salt and sugar in 1 1/2 quarts cold water in gallon-sized zipper-lock bag or plastic container. Add chicken and seal bag, pressing out as much air as possible; refrigerate 30 minutes until fully seasoned. Remove chicken from brine, dry thoroughly with paper towels, and season with pepper.

3. Meanwhile, adjust oven rack to upper-middle position (should be about 6 inches away from heating element) and heat broiler. Spray broiler pan top lightly with nonstick cooking spray and position over pan bottom. Place chicken on pan; broil until spotty brown and firm to the touch, about 8 minutes, turning chicken halfway through cooking. Transfer chicken to plate and set aside.

4. FOR THE DRESSING: Bring 2 inches water to boil in small saucepan over high heat. Lower eggs into water and cook 45 seconds; remove with slotted spoon. When cool enough to handle, crack eggs open; reserve yolks in small bowl and discard whites. Add lemon juice, Worcestershire, salt, pepper, garlic, and anchovies to yolks; whisk until smooth. Whisking constantly, add oil in slow, steady stream. Adjust seasonings with salt and pepper. (Dressing can be refrigerated in airtight container up to 1 day; shake before using.)

5. TO FINISH THE SALAD: In large bowl, toss lettuce, Parmesan, and about two-thirds of dressing to coat; divide evenly among individual plates. Remove tenderloins from chicken breasts; place in bowl used to dress lettuce, along with remaining dressing. Cut chicken breasts crosswise into 1/2-inch slices, add to bowl, and toss to coat. Divide dressed chicken evenly among plates, arranging slices on lettuce. Sprinkle each plate with a portion of croutons and serve immediately.

TECHNIQUE | CODDLING EGGS

1. Use slotted spoon to lower eggs into simmering water. Cook 45 seconds, then transfer eggs with slotted spoon to bowl.

2. When eggs are cool enough to handle, crack each in half and gently transfer yolks from shell to shell, letting whites fall through to bowl below. Transfer yolks to separate bowl; discard whites.

Thai-Style Stir-Fried Vegetables

A simple homemade sauce is paired with supermarket ingredients to produce quick stir-fries with complex flavor.

⇒ BY THE COOK'S ILLUSTRATED TEST KITCHEN ⇐

Thai cooking is often distinguished by a combination of four simple flavors: salt, sour, sweet, and hot. This quartet provides the foundation for many dishes, while other ingredients, such as curry paste, coconut milk, and fresh herbs, are added to flesh out the structure. We set out to develop a rudimentary mixture of these four flavors that could be prepared with supermarket ingredients and made to serve as a base for a wide variety of Thai-style vegetable stir-fries.

The first essential flavor—salt—comes from fish sauce. Made from salted, fermented fish or prawns, fish sauce has a powerful fishy aroma, but it actually tastes more salty than it does fishy. Tasters chose a fairly generous 3 tablespoons for a distinct but not overpowering pungency.

Limes often give Thai dishes their sour note. We tried lime juice alone, but tasters called for a deeper, more resonant lime flavor. So we added grated lime zest to the juice. The combination provided a one-two punch of lime that was both bright and deep.

From there we moved on to the sweet flavor, traditionally provided by palm sugar. A little less sweet than cane sugar, palm sugar comes from several types of palm trees. With no palm sugar to be had in most supermarkets, we tested granulated, light, and dark brown sugars, maple syrup, molasses, and honey. Light brown sugar was the tasters' favorite.

Initial tests determined that tasters wanted just a suggestion of heat, not outright spiciness. Hot sauces were rejected for the vinegar most of them contain. Tasters selected red pepper flakes, which offered reliable, uncomplicated heat.

Whether you choose a dish made with garlic sauce, peanut sauce, or curry sauce from the recipes that follow, our easy, multidimensional sauce base will give it complexity and a recognizable Thai flavor profile. Jasmine rice makes an authentic accompaniment to all of these stir-fries, but any long-grain white rice will do. With its rice accompaniment, each recipe could serve as many as six to eight as part of a multicourse Thai meal.

THAI SAUCE BASE

- 3 tablespoons fish sauce
- 1 tablespoon juice plus 1 teaspoon grated zest from 1 lime
- 1 tablespoon light brown sugar
- 1/8 teaspoon red pepper flakes

Mix all ingredients in small bowl until sugar is dissolved; set aside.

STIR-FRIED EGGPLANT WITH GARLIC AND BASIL SAUCE

SERVES 4 TO 6 AS A MAIN DISH WITH RICE

- 1 tablespoon plus 1 teaspoon peanut oil
- 1 large eggplant (about 1 pound), cut into 3/4-inch cubes (6 to 7 cups)
- 6 medium cloves garlic, minced or pressed through garlic press (about 2 tablespoons)
- 1 (3/4-inch) piece fresh ginger, peeled and minced (about 1 tablespoon)
- 1 recipe Thai Sauce Base
- 2 scallions, white and green parts, sliced thin
- 1/2 cup fresh basil leaves, torn into rough 1/2-inch pieces

Heat 1 tablespoon oil in 12-inch nonstick skillet over high heat until shimmering, 2 to 3 minutes. Add eggplant and cook, stirring every 10 to 15 seconds, until browned and tender, 4 to 5 minutes. Push eggplant to sides of skillet, clearing center of pan. Add remaining teaspoon oil, garlic, and ginger to center of pan and mash with back of spoon; cook until fragrant, 30 to 45 seconds, then stir mixture into eggplant. Add Thai Sauce Base and stir until combined. Off heat, stir in scallions and basil; serve immediately.

STIR-FRIED BROCCOLI AND RED PEPPERS WITH PEANUT SAUCE

SERVES 4 TO 6 AS A MAIN DISH WITH RICE

- 1 recipe Thai Sauce Base
- 3/4 cup coconut milk
- 1/4 cup water
- 3 tablespoons smooth peanut butter
- 1 tablespoon plus 1 teaspoon peanut oil
- 1 large red bell pepper (about 8 ounces), cut lengthwise into 1/2-inch strips
- 9 ounces broccoli, cut into even 1-inch florets (about 4 cups)
- 2 medium cloves garlic, minced or pressed through garlic press (about 2 teaspoons)
- 1 (1/4-inch) piece fresh ginger, peeled and minced (about 1 teaspoon)

1. Whisk Thai Sauce Base, coconut milk, water, and peanut butter in small bowl until smooth; set aside.

2. Heat 1 tablespoon oil in 12-inch nonstick skillet over high heat until shimmering, 2 to 3 minutes. Add red pepper and broccoli; cook, stirring every 10 to 15 seconds, until just barely tender, about 2 minutes. Push vegetables to sides of skillet, clearing center of pan. Add remaining teaspoon oil, garlic, and ginger to center of pan and mash with back of spoon; cook until fragrant, about 30 seconds, then stir mixture into vegetables. Reduce heat to medium-low and stir in sauce mixture. Simmer to heat through and blend flavors, about 1 minute; serve immediately.

STIR-FRIED CAULIFLOWER WITH THAI RED CURRY SAUCE

SERVES 4 TO 6 AS A MAIN DISH WITH RICE

- 1 recipe Thai Sauce Base
- 1 cup coconut milk
- 2 teaspoons Thai-style red curry paste
- 1 tablespoon plus 1 teaspoon peanut oil
- 3 pounds cauliflower (about 1 large head), cut into even 3/4-inch florets (about 4 cups)
- 2 medium cloves garlic, minced or pressed through garlic press (about 2 teaspoons)
- 1 (1/4-inch) piece fresh ginger, peeled and minced (about 1 teaspoon)
- 6 ounces snow peas, strings removed (about 2 cups)
- 2 tablespoons minced fresh basil leaves

1. Whisk Thai Sauce Base, coconut milk, and curry paste in small bowl until smooth; set aside.

2. Heat 1 tablespoon oil in 12-inch nonstick skillet over high heat until shimmering, 2 to 3 minutes. Add cauliflower and cook, stirring every 10 to 15 seconds, until just barely tender, about 3 minutes. Push cauliflower to sides of skillet, clearing center of pan. Add remaining teaspoon oil, garlic, and ginger to center of pan and mash with back of spoon; cook until fragrant, about 30 seconds, then stir mixture into vegetables. Reduce heat to medium-high; stir in sauce mixture. Simmer, stirring occasionally, until cauliflower is tender, about 2 minutes; add snow peas and continue to simmer until cauliflower is fully tender, about 3 minutes longer. Sprinkle with basil; serve immediately.

Rediscovering Spinach Dip

This lackluster 1950s relic was long overdue for a face-lift.
The solution turned out to be surprisingly easy.

≥ BY SHANNON BLAISDELL ≤

In 1954 the world was introduced to what would become our most popular party fare: Lipton's onion soup mix combined with sour cream. Spinach dip—made with vegetable soup mix, sour cream, and frozen spinach—was hot on its heels. Fifty years later, most spinach dips are still based on soup mixes, and the flavors are still flat, exorbitantly salty, and nothing near fresh. Yet a good spinach dip can be made easily enough with just a few fresh ingredients, a couple of kitchen tools, and no more than 30 minutes of preparation. It should be rich, thick, and creamy—perfectly dippable—and brimming with big, bold flavors, especially the flavor of spinach. I set out to renovate spinach dip without compromising its quick and easy appeal.

I started my testing with the obvious: the spinach. I gathered four varieties of fresh spinach: curly (or crinkly), flat (or smooth), semi-savoy (a hybrid of the two), and baby. For the sake of comparison, I also included frozen spinach. I trimmed, washed, chopped, and wilted the fresh spinaches in hot pots (I simply thawed the frozen spinach), made the dips, chilled them to set (cool and thicken), and then let tasters dig in. I had to look twice at the tallied results. Frozen spinach was the victor. Tasters liked its "familiar," "intense" flavor and even used the word "fresh" to describe it. The fresh varieties were too "meek," their flavor lost among the other ingredients. After a few more tests to determine consistency, I found that 20 to 30 seconds in the food processor chopped the thawed frozen spinach into small, manageable bits and made the dip smooth and creamy.

The '50s were creeping their way back into my recipe—frozen spinach, no cooking (so far), and speedy preparation—but I wasn't about to backtrack on flavor. Armed with a host of fresh herbs and other pungent ingredients, I began developing the flavor components for the dip, sans soup mix. Among the herbs, parsley and dill were by and large the standards, and they worked appealingly well when combined.

Onions and shallots were problematic, as they required cooking to mellow their astringency and soften their crunch. I wasn't cooking the spinach, so I thought it would be a waste of time and effort to start pulling out pots and pans now. In the end, a combination of raw scallion whites and one clove of garlic added the perfect amount of bite and pungency. With just a dash of hot pepper sauce for a kick of heat and some salt and pepper, the dip came out of the processor light, fresh, and full of bold flavors—far better than the soup mix recipe and not much more work.

The problem was that the dip, which took only about 15 minutes to make, took almost two hours to chill. I wanted to skip this polar timeout, and the solution was simple enough. Instead of thawing the spinach completely, all I had to do was to thaw it partially. Before processing, I microwaved the frozen block for three minutes on low, broke it into icy chunks, and squeezed each one with all my might, extracting a surprising amount of liquid. The chunks were still ice cold and thoroughly cooled the dip as they broke down in the processor. Though my hands were slightly numb, the dip was thick, creamy, and cool enough for immediate service.

So I didn't complicate spinach dip after all; frozen spinach and a food processor kept it simple. Soup mix was out. Flavor was in.

CREAMY HERBED SPINACH DIP
MAKES ABOUT 1½ CUPS

Partial thawing of the spinach produces a cold dip that can be served without further chilling. If you don't own a microwave, the frozen spinach can be thawed at room temperature for 1½ hours then squeezed of excess liquid. The garlic must be minced or pressed before going into the food processor; otherwise the dip will contain large chunks of garlic.

- 10 ounces frozen chopped spinach
- ½ cup sour cream
- ½ cup mayonnaise
- 2 tablespoons thinly sliced scallions, white parts only, from 3 medium scallions
- 1 tablespoon chopped fresh dill leaves
- ½ cup packed flat-leaf parsley leaves
- 1 small garlic clove, minced or pressed through garlic press (about 1 teaspoon)
- ¼ teaspoon hot pepper sauce, such as Tabasco
- ½ teaspoon salt
- ¼ teaspoon ground black pepper
- ½ medium red bell pepper, diced fine (about ¼ cup)

1. Thaw spinach in microwave for 3 minutes at 40 percent power. (Edges should be thawed but not warm; center should be soft enough to be broken apart into icy chunks.) Squeeze partially frozen spinach of excess water.

2. In food processor, process spinach, sour cream, mayonnaise, scallions, dill, parsley, garlic, hot pepper sauce, salt, and pepper until smooth and creamy, about 30 seconds. Transfer mixture to medium bowl and stir in bell pepper; serve. (Dip can be covered with plastic wrap and refrigerated up to 2 days.)

SPINACH DIP WITH BLUE CHEESE AND BACON

If making this dip in advance, hold off on sprinkling the bacon over it until just before serving.

Cut 3 slices bacon into ¼-inch pieces and fry in small skillet over medium-high heat until crisp and browned, about 5 minutes; using slotted spoon, transfer to paper towel–lined plate and set aside. Follow recipe for Creamy Herbed Spinach Dip, omitting dill, hot pepper sauce, salt, and red bell pepper and processing 1½ ounces crumbled blue cheese (about ⅓ cup) along with spinach. Adjust seasoning with salt; before serving, sprinkle bacon over dip.

SPINACH DIP WITH FETA, LEMON, AND OREGANO

Follow recipe for Creamy Herbed Spinach Dip, omitting hot pepper sauce, salt, and red bell pepper and processing 2 tablespoons fresh oregano leaves, 2 ounces crumbled feta cheese (about ½ cup), and 1 tablespoon lemon juice plus 1 teaspoon grated lemon zest along with spinach. Adjust seasoning with salt.

CILANTRO-LIME SPINACH DIP WITH CHIPOTLE CHILES

This dip is good served with tortilla chips.

Follow recipe for Creamy Herbed Spinach Dip, omitting hot pepper sauce and red bell pepper and processing ¼ cup packed cilantro leaves, 1 tablespoon seeded and minced chipotle chiles in adobo sauce (about 2 medium chiles), 1 tablespoon lime juice plus ½ teaspoon grated lime zest, ½ teaspoon light brown sugar, and ⅛ teaspoon ground cumin along with spinach.

Trimming and Tying Meat and Poultry

A few simple butcher's tricks will make your meats and poultry look and taste their very best. BY MATTHEW CARD

TRIMMING BASICS

Our two favorite knives for cutting meat are a standard 8-inch chef's knife and a thin-bladed, flexible boning knife that can negotiate the tight spots a chef's knife cannot. (For our rating of leading boning knives, see "Choosing a Boning Knife" on page 17). For some cuts, either knife will suffice, but some tasks, such as removing chicken cutlets from the breast, require the dexterity of a boning knife.

Before trimming meat or poultry, make sure that your knives are sharp. Dull knives are dangerous and will make sloppy, imprecise cuts. We usually sharpen our knives just before cutting meat. If we are doing a lot of cutting, we re-steel our knives halfway through the job to ensure a keen edge and consistent cuts from beginning to end.

In another nod to safety, it is a good practice to dry the meat or poultry with paper towels prior to trimming. A good drying will keep it from slipping about on the cutting board.

Trimming Beef or Pork Tenderloin

While we generally purchase whole beef tenderloins already trimmed, uncleaned tenderloins are often available for steeply discounted prices. While most cooks know to remove the white, opaque fat encasing the meat, the silver skin—the shiny, fibrous connective tissue beneath the fat—must also come off because it toughens and shrinks as it cooks, making for a misshapen, unevenly cooked roast. A pork tenderloin (shown below) is always sold with the thin, membranous silver skin attached, but it is quick work to remove it with the same technique used for the beef tenderloin.

After cutting off the extraneous fat, slip the tip of a boning knife underneath the silver skin, angle it slightly upward, and, using a gentle sawing motion, cut the silver skin from the roast, keeping it taut against the knife's blade. Repeat the process until you have removed the silver skin from the entire roast.

Trimming Cutlets from a Whole Chicken Breast

You can save money by slicing your own cutlets from a whole chicken breast instead of purchasing boneless, skinless cutlets.

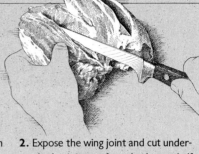

1. Using a boning knife, cut along both sides of the breastbone, starting at the tail end, following the rib cage down, and separating the meat from the bone.

2. Expose the wing joint and cut underneath the joint to free the breast half from the rib cage. Repeat on the other side of the breastbone.

Trimming Fat and Tendons from Chicken Cutlets

Boneless, skinless chicken breasts are appealing for many reasons, including the fact that they are recipe-ready. Well, almost. It is well worth taking an extra minute or two to trim them of excess fat and the tough tendon running down the center of the tenderloin.

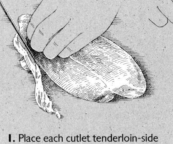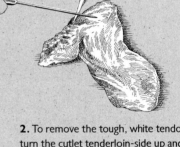

1. Place each cutlet tenderloin-side down (the tenderloin is that floppy, thin piece of meat attached to the breast), and smooth the top with your fingers. Any yellow fat will slide to the periphery, where it can be trimmed away.

2. To remove the tough, white tendon, turn the cutlet tenderloin-side up and peel back the thick half of the tenderloin so it lies top-down on the work surface. Use the point of a paring or boning knife to cut around the tip of the tendon to expose it, then scrape the tendon free with the knife.

Trimming Meat for Kebabs

Because of its heavy marbling, rich flavor, and low price, top blade steak is our favorite cut for beef kebabs. However, there is a thick ribbon of gristle running through the steak that must be removed. Once the gristle is excised, the two halves are easily cubed. Large cubes are harder to overcook than small cubes, but they do not readily absorb a marinade's flavor. We found that butterflying large cubes allows the flavor of the marinade to penetrate the meat more deeply. After marinating, the meat is skewered as if it were still one large cube.

1. Halve the steak, leaving the gristle attached to one side.

2. Cut the gristle away from the half to which it is still attached.

3. Cut the meat into 1¼-inch cubes, then cut each cube almost through at the center to butterfly it.

TYING BASICS

Tying cuts of meat keeps them compact and ensures even cooking. While we prefer butcher's twine because it is thick and easy to work with, any kitchen twine will do the job in a pinch. Make sure to use all-natural cotton or linen twine, which won't taint the meat or burn in the oven.

Tying a Butcher's Knot

This basic knot can be made without a spare finger to hold the string in place.

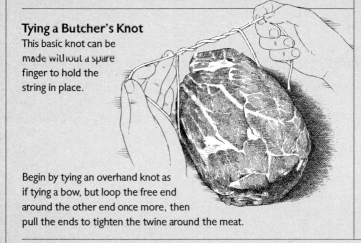

Begin by tying an overhand knot as if tying a bow, but loop the free end around the other end once more, then pull the ends to tighten the twine around the meat.

Tying a Beef Tenderloin

Because the tenderloin narrows at one end, the thin portion must be tucked under itself and tied so that it will cook at the same rate as the rest of the roast.

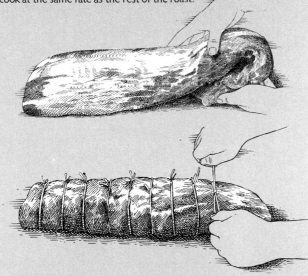

1. Tuck the skinny end portion, about the last 6 inches, underneath the tenderloin and secure with a 12-inch length of twine.

2. Tie off the rest of the roast at 1½-inch intervals. The twine should be tied firmly but not too tight, in which case it will squeeze out the meat's juices.

Tying Medallions and Other Steaks

Round, boneless steaks such as tenderloin and rib-eye will hold their shape better during cooking if tied first. A slice of bacon can be wrapped around lean cuts of beef before they are tied. We also like to bind veal and lamb shanks before cooking so that the meat remains attached to the bone.

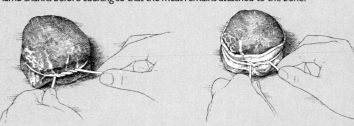

Wrap a 12-inch piece of twine firmly around the steak's circumference and secure it with a butcher's knot. If using bacon, wrap it around the steak before the twine.

Tying a Standing Rib Roast

If left untied, the outer layer of meat on a standing rib roast tends to separate from the rib-eye muscle as it cooks, making for an unappealing presentation. The solution is easy: Tie a piece of twine around both ends of the roast, running the twine between the bones.

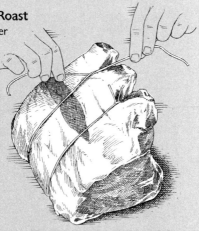

TESTING EQUIPMENT: CHOOSING A BONING KNIFE

The slim, flexible blade of a boning knife may look eccentric, but it is perfectly designed to slide nimbly through joints, between bones, and under silver skin. It is an essential tool for such tasks as removing cutlets from a whole chicken breast and can also be used to remove fat and silver skin (see illustrations on page 16).

Because most home cooks are likely to use a boning knife infrequently, we wondered if a cheaper knife would do. To find out, we tested six leading knives with blades between 5 and 7 inches long and prices between $9 and $71. Both large- and small-handed testers used each knife to butcher a whole chicken and to trim beef ribs of fat and silver skin. Each knife was evaluated for handle comfort, slipperiness (hands become very greasy when butchering), agility (including flexibility), and sharpness.

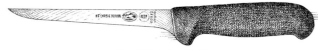

Best Boning Knife

An extremely narrow blade makes the Forschner Fibrox especially agile.

The winning Forschner Fibrox, priced at $18, received high marks for its uniquely designed ergonomic handle as well as its slim, highly maneuverable blade and razor-sharp edge. The plastic handle nestled comfortably into both large and small hands, and it stayed there even when our hands became slick with fat. The blade was the narrowest of the lot, which made it very agile. And while all the knives arrived with razor-sharp edges, the Forschner seemed exceptionally keen, gliding effortlessly through tough tendon and thick skin.

TESTERS' COMMENTS ON THE KNIVES (listed in order of preference)

➤ **Forschner (Victorinox) Fibrox: $17.90**

COMMENTS: Comfortable, "easy-to-grip" handle and narrow blade impressed all comers. "Great flexibility around bones." "Amazing" sharpness out of the box.

➤ **J. A. Henckels Professional S: $49.99**

COMMENTS: Finished a close second with a blade "nearly as agile as the Forschner" but lost points for its "slippery" handle.

➤ **Wüsthof-Trident Grand Prix: $54**

COMMENTS: Handle fit "like a glove" but turned slippery when coated in chicken fat. "Fiendishly sharp" blade is wider than most and not as agile as the top choices.

➤ **Global: $70.99**

COMMENTS: The textured metal handle received very mixed reviews. The narrowness of the bolster (the piece of metal couched between the blade and the handle) felt "dangerous," although the blade was "quite agile."

➤ **Chicago Cutlery: $14.99**

COMMENTS: Testers complained that the handle felt "boxy" and the long blade was "hard to control."

➤ **Farberware Professional: $8.99**

COMMENTS: Very awkward, ill-designed handle fit neither large nor small hands. The blade felt "flimsy" during use.

Introducing Greek-Style Garlic-Lemon Potatoes

Twenty minutes and a skillet are all it takes to transform potatoes, lemon, and garlic into a gutsy side dish.

≥ BY ADAM RIED AND MEG SUZUKI ≤

As sure as you'll find a huge picture of the Parthenon on the wall at your local Greek diner, you'll also find Greek-style garlic-lemon potatoes on the menu. Often cut in small cubes and either baked in the oven or sautéed on a huge griddle, these popular potatoes are at once tangy with lemon, sharp with garlic, and earthy with oregano. Served alongside every meal from breakfast through dinner, they can accompany an omelet or a simple roast chicken with authority. Done well, the potatoes are crusty, well browned, and accented by a full (but not overpowering) lemon flavor and plenty of garlic bite. If things go wrong, though, they turn out soggy and sour.

Cooking Them Right

Most of the recipes we found revealed that the standard home-cooking technique for Greek potatoes is to cube raw potatoes, toss them in a baking dish with a mixture of lemon juice, garlic, oregano, and oil, add a little water, and then bake them until the water has evaporated and the potatoes have absorbed the flavors of the seasoning mixture. A number of recipes demanded what seemed to us an unreasonably long baking time of 90 minutes as well as constant monitoring and stirring of the potatoes near the end of cooking. As we discovered when we made the potatoes according to this traditional method, they didn't turn out even close to perfect anyway. The texture was downright soggy, and most tasters felt that the lemon flavor was harsh and acidic. Worse yet was the total absence of the crisp, browned crust we wanted on the potatoes. We decided our first task would be reducing the cooking time.

More research turned up two possible solutions: oven-roasting without the seasonings and stovetop cooking in a skillet. Oven-roasting the potatoes and then adding a lemon-garlic-herb mixture when they emerged from the oven made for a huge improvement. These simple steps cut the cooking time in half, to 45 minutes, while also producing a flavorful, caramelized crust. The results we got from the skillet method were even better. With the intense heat of the hot pan

To keep the flavor of these skillet-browned potatoes fresh and lively, add the lemon, garlic, and oregano just before serving.

over a medium-high flame, the potatoes developed a gorgeous, flavorful, mahogany brown crust in just 11 minutes. Although perfect on the outside, the potatoes were not completely cooked on the inside. After a number of tests, we found that simply covering the skillet and allowing the browned potatoes to cook for an additional 5 minutes gave them a tender and velvety interior. Now we had cut the time down from 90 minutes to less than 20, and the results were crisp and flavorful rather than soggy and acidic.

We tested different skillets and found a heavy-bottomed, 12-inch nonstick model best suited to the task. The heavy construction translates into even heat distribution, which reduces the risk of burning and maximizes browning. And don't skimp on size: The large diameter provided enough space to arrange the potatoes in a single layer for optimal browning. Finally, while the nonstick finish made cleanup a breeze, it is not essential. We successfully cooked the potatoes in a conventional pan (without a nonstick coating), but the pan required a fair amount of elbow grease to clean. In the course of testing, we learned to use only four potatoes, so as not to compromise the browning by crowding the pan, and to make sure the potatoes were evenly sized, so all the pieces would cook at the same rate.

In terms of the cooking medium, we liked the flavor of extra-virgin olive oil, but using it over high heat destroyed its delicate fruitiness. Next we tried pure olive oil and then vegetable oil, and tasters found the flavor differences to be minimal (we chose vegetable oil since it is a pantry staple). Some butter was necessary to boost the flavor of the oil. Finally, because we wanted the flavor of extra-virgin olive oil, we decided to add some to the cooked potatoes along with the seasonings.

Which Potatoes Are Best?

We were surprised that few recipes specified what type of potato to use. Surely there would be differences between high-starch/low-moisture potatoes such as russets (commonly used for baking), medium-starch potatoes such as all-purpose or Yukon Gold, and low-starch/high-moisture potatoes such as Red Bliss, which are often used for roasting and boiling. After testing representatives from the three categories, our tasters consistently favored Yukon Golds for their appealing blend of smooth, velvety texture, rich yellow hue, and buttery flavor. Red Bliss potatoes took a close second for their supple, creamy texture. Russets were rejected because the pieces broke apart easily and were mealy. With regard to preparing the Yukon Golds, tasters preferred peeled potatoes cut into wedges ¾ inch thick as opposed to thicker wedges, slices, or cubes.

Lemon and Garlic

Lemon, garlic, and oregano give this dish its character. Most of the recipes we consulted called for lemon juice, some as little as 2 tablespoons and others as much as ½ cup. Throughout our testing, tasters agreed that potatoes flavored with lemon juice alone tasted sharp, shallow, and acidic. So we tried adding some grated lemon zest to impart a deeper lemon flavor. Indeed it did; tasters responded well to batches made with a full tablespoon of grated zest per 2 pounds of potatoes, along with a modest 2 tablespoons of juice for brightness and moderate acidity.

Garlic is another key flavoring. At first we thought that raw garlic might have too much bite for the dish, but tasters dismissed our attempts to tame the garlic flavor by toasting the whole cloves or cooking the minced garlic in oil until it was sweet and mellow. Judging the flavor of these batches too "docile" and "wimpy," they agreed that raw garlic was the way to go. One clove, two cloves, and even three cloves were deemed too weak. We were shocked when tasters chose the batch of potatoes with four cloves of minced raw garlic, describing it as "bright, fresh, and gutsy." Last, we replaced the dusty-tasting dried oregano used in so many recipes with fresh, and all the tasters approved.

Potatoes Done Right

Don't cut the potatoes into haphazardly shaped pieces or crowd the pan (top). For even cooking and proper browning, the potatoes should be sliced evenly and cooked in a single layer (bottom).

The only thing left was to determine the optimum amount of time for the potatoes and seasonings to get acquainted. Testing showed that adding the lemon, garlic, and herbs to the pan midway through the potatoes' cooking time (or any earlier) not only diminished their flavor but also increased the risk of burning the garlic. Instead, we mixed the seasonings into the potatoes once they were fully cooked, which provided the strong hits of flavor that our tasters demanded.

Now that these classic potatoes are so quick and easy to make, chances are you can get them on the table at home in less time than it would take you to drive to the nearest diner.

GREEK-STYLE GARLIC-LEMON POTATOES
SERVES 4

If your potatoes are larger than the size we recommend, you may have to increase the covered cooking time by up to 4 minutes. Though a nonstick pan makes cleanup easier, it is not essential.

1	tablespoon vegetable oil
1	tablespoon unsalted butter
4	medium Yukon Gold potatoes (7 to 8 ounces each, about 2 pounds total), peeled and cut lengthwise into 8 wedges (see illustration above)
4	medium garlic cloves, minced or pressed through garlic press (about 1 heaping tablespoon)
1	tablespoon extra-virgin olive oil
2	tablespoons juice plus 1 tablespoon grated zest from 2 lemons
2	tablespoons minced fresh oregano leaves
1	teaspoon salt
½	teaspoon ground black pepper
2	tablespoons minced fresh parsley leaves

1. Heat vegetable oil and butter in heavy-bottomed 12-inch nonstick skillet over medium-high heat until butter melts and foaming subsides, swirling pan occasionally. Add potatoes in single layer; cook until golden brown (pan should sizzle but not smoke), about 6 minutes. Using tongs, turn potatoes so second cut sides are down; cook until deep golden brown on second side, about 5 minutes longer. Reduce heat to medium-low, cover tightly, and cook until potatoes are tender when pierced with tip of paring knife, about 5 minutes.

2. While potatoes cook, combine garlic, olive oil, lemon juice and zest, and oregano in small bowl. When potatoes are tender, add garlic-lemon mixture, salt, and pepper; stir carefully (so as not to break potato wedges) to distribute. Cook, uncovered, until seasoning mixture is heated through and fragrant, 1 to 2 minutes. Sprinkle potatoes with parsley, stir gently to distribute; serve immediately.

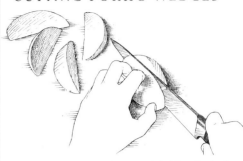

Halve the potato lengthwise and, holding the knife perpendicular to the board, cut each half in half lengthwise to make quarters. Holding the knife at 45 degrees to the board, cut each quarter in half lengthwise, dividing the potato into a total of eight equal-sized wedges.

GREEK-STYLE GARLIC-LEMON POTATOES WITH OLIVES AND FETA

Follow recipe for Greek-Style Garlic-Lemon Potatoes, adding 3 ounces crumbled feta cheese (about ⅓ cup) and 8 Kalamata (or other black, brine-cured) olives, pitted and sliced (about ¼ cup), along with parsley.

GREEK-STYLE GARLIC-LEMON POTATOES WITH SPINACH AND ANCHOVIES

If you don't fancy anchovies, this dish can be made without them.

Follow recipe for Greek-Style Garlic-Lemon Potatoes, adding 1 teaspoon minced anchovies (about 3 fillets) along with garlic-lemon mixture; stir mixture into potatoes, then add 2½ ounces clean baby spinach leaves (about 3 cups), and gently stir mixture again to distribute. Omit parsley.

SPICY GREEK-STYLE GARLIC-LEMON POTATOES

In keeping with the bold flavors of the dish, this variation is very spicy.

Follow recipe for Greek-Style Garlic-Lemon Potatoes, adding 2 small jalapeño chiles, cut into ¼-inch slices (with seeds and membranes), to pan just before covering skillet in step 1.

GREEK-STYLE GARLIC-LEMON POTATOES WITH SUN-DRIED TOMATOES AND SCALLIONS

Follow recipe for Greek-Style Garlic-Lemon Potatoes, adding 1 ounce oil-packed sun-dried tomatoes, sliced (about ¼ cup), and 2 medium scallions, sliced (about ¼ cup), along with garlic-lemon mixture.

Really Good Fruit Smoothies

For a smoothie with knock-your-socks-off flavor, replace the usual yogurt with milk, add juice for freshness, and then fill the blender with a lot of fruit.

⇒ BY JULIA COLLIN ⇐

For the best flavor, use 3½ cups of fruit for every cup of liquid and chill the fruit to reduce the amount of ice needed.

Blurring the line between health food and junk food, smoothies are everywhere, from convenience stores to donut shops and drive-thrus. But these expensive, generically flavored, candy-sweet concoctions are far removed from the smoothies of 20 years ago. Originally made with ingredients like flaxseed, oat bran, and soy protein powder, early smoothies were holistic healthshakes spruced up with a handful of berries and a little ice. Yet a good idea lurks somewhere between these junk food and health food extremes—a smoothie that is icy, fruity, slightly sweet, lightly creamy, and thick but straw-friendly. A good smoothie should be satisfying and rejuvenating without tasting like a sweet milkshake or a fruity glass of Metamucil.

Although smoothies are easy to make, they are difficult to make well. After giving some initial recipes a whirl, I found their textures ranged from that of a 7-Eleven Slurpee to something like milk of magnesia, and none offered much fruit flavor. The problem with these smoothies was not with how they were made but with what they were made of. Besides fruit and ice, the ingredients included a wide range of fillers and flavorings, from the obvious yogurt to the more obscure tofu and instant lemonade mix. To help organize a list of ingredients for further testing, I categorized all reasonable possibilities into four groups: dairy and liquids, sweeteners and flavorings, fruit, and ice. I also decided it would be easiest to develop the recipe using strawberries (their texture is neither too watery nor too fibrous) before trying other fruits.

Back to Basics

A basic smoothie is a blend of fruit, ice, and some sort of dairy. Without dairy, the fruit and ice make something akin to a slushy. Using a big handful of strawberries and several cubes of ice, I tested a range of dairy-aisle possibilities, including yogurt, milk, half-and-half, cream, tofu, buttermilk, and soy milk. I was slightly surprised when whole milk won the tasting. Everyone in the test kitchen liked its clean, mellow flavor; it added just enough fat and protein to keep the smoothie from becoming a slushy. Although yogurt is the most common dairy component, tasters found its sour tang overwhelmed the more delicate flavor of the fruit. Among the other contestants, buttermilk was too tart, half-and-half and heavy cream too rich, and soy milk and tofu just too strange in both flavor and texture. I tried replacing the whole milk with skim milk and 2 percent milk but found the reduced fat content left these smoothies watery and hollow tasting.

To keep the dairy in check, most recipes also add juice. My tasters, too, preferred smoothies made with both milk and juice. Prepared this way, the fruit flavors were cleaner, brighter, and more potent. By comparison, the juiceless batch tasted mellow and, for lack of a better word, milky. I tested apple, orange, grape, white grape, cranberry, and white cranberry juice as well as fruit punch. The mild, easy flavor of apple juice came in second place to the unanimous winner, white cranberry juice. With an elegantly perfumed flavor, the white cranberry juice added complexity and nuance that enhanced the flavor of the fruit rather than overwhelming it (see "Colorless Cranberry Juice," below). Red cranberry juice was just too potent and tart, orange juice tasted bitter and acidic, and the grape juices and fruit punch made the smoothie taste like candy. I played with the ratio of milk to juice and found that a 50/50 blend was optimal.

Sweeteners and Flavorings

Throughout the testing, it had become obvious that sugar was necessary to boost the fruit flavor. I tested other sweeteners, such as honey, maple syrup, and brown sugar, but their earthiness muted the flavor of the fruit. Lemon juice, on the other hand, helped define the flavor of the fruit, making the smoothie taste clean and crisp. Owing to the variety and ripeness of each fruit, it was impossible to measure the sugar and lemon juice in exact amounts beyond a range of 2 to 6 teaspoons. Out of curiosity, I tried adding vanilla extract, but tasters gagged on it. A simple pinch of salt, on the other hand, helped bring out the flavor of even the blandest berries.

Next I tried adding a banana to the mix. Most recipes add banana for flavor and sweetness as

Colorless Cranberry Juice

How does Ocean Spray make its white cranberry juice white? The company uses immature, blond berries harvested a few weeks early. Because they haven't been on the vine as long as their older, red siblings, they haven't had the chance to develop the deep crimson color or a full flavor profile. When compared with the classic cranberry cocktail, white cranberry juice (which is mixed with white grape juice concentrate) has almost no tint and a sweet, perfumed, easygoing flavor, which we liked both straight up and in our smoothies. –J.C.

How Much Fruit Do I Need?

We found that 3½ cups of prepared fruit are needed to make four smoothies. Here's how to shop for fruit so that once you remove any hulls, skins, seeds, pits, or cores you'll have the right amount.

Fruit	How Much to Buy
BERRIES	16 ounces
CANTALOUPE	1 small melon (2½ pounds)
HONEYDEW	½ large melon (2½ pounds)
MANGO	2 large mangoes (1¼ pounds each)
PAPAYA	2 small papayas (1¼ pounds each)
PINEAPPLE	½ large pineapple (3 pounds)
WATERMELON	2-pound piece

well as its creamy, mouth-coating texture. With the banana included, tasters admitted that my blended fruit drink had finally turned the corner and become an honest-to-goodness smoothie.

The Fruit

Wanting the smoothie to have a strong fruit flavor, I made several batches, increasing the amount of fruit per cup of smoothie base (milk, juice, sugar, lemon juice, and salt). Although most recipes call for 1 cup of fruit for every cup of base, I ended up adding 3½ cups of strawberries per cup of base. (Beyond 3½ cups, the mixture turned fibrous and mealy.) This unbelievably high ratio not only drove home the fruit flavor but also helped bulk up the consistency. Most commercial smoothies use second-rate fruit and try to make up for it with excessive dairy and funky flavorings. It is this elementary discovery that draws the distinction between a great smoothie and a bland wannabe (perhaps an obvious observation—ripe fruit made great smoothies, unripe fruit made bland ones).

Having developed the recipe using strawberries, it was time to test other fruits. I was aware that watery fruits, such as watermelon, and thick fruits, such as mangoes, might require variations in the ratio of fruit to liquid, so I organized the fruit into three categories: berries, melons, and tropical fruits. All types of berries blended into the recipe with ease, but melons did best with a little less liquid. Thick tropical fruits, such as pineapple and mango, required a bit more. Although I found that frozen fruit does work when fresh, ripe fruit is unavailable, the smoothie won't taste as fresh. I got best results when allowing the fruit to defrost fully in the refrigerator.

TESTING EQUIPMENT: **The King of Blenders**

If you've ever ordered a smoothie at a juice bar or coffee house, it was probably made in a Vita-Mix. With a powerful motor and a price tag of about $400, the Vita-Mix is both the ultimate blender and the trophy appliance in any well-equipped kitchen. But how does this souped-up blender compare with the $40 Osterizer, which won our blender testing (see the May/June 2000 issue)? I set up a strenuous course of blending exercises to see just what this machine could do.

The Vita-Mix quickly ground 4 cups of roasted peanuts into 2 cups of smooth peanut butter, while the Osterizer choked, its overworked motor spewing out fumes, and produced only finely chopped peanuts. With the Vita-Mix, I was able to blend 1 pound whole frozen strawberries along with 2 cups ice, ½ cup sugar, and 1 cup half-and-half into soft-serve ice cream. The blades of the Osterizer simply got stuck and refused to cut anything. Both machines were able to produce fine crumbs from several slices of bread, but only the 249-mile-per-hour blade tips of the Vita-Mix could produce hot fondue from cold ingredients in a mere four minutes.

A powerful 2-horsepower motor is behind the Vita-Mix's superior capabilities. To put its brawn into perspective, consider that an average food processor runs at 1 horsepower, a chainsaw at 3 to 4 horsepower, and a push lawn mower at 4 to 6 horsepower. Running at 0.60 horsepower, the Osterizer simply didn't have enough power to compete in the tough tests I had designed. But, then again, the Osterizer costs a tenth of what the Vita-Mix costs, and it works just fine when making smoothies and handling other tasks you expect of a (mere mortal) blender. —J.C.

The Vita-Mix has more than three times the horsepower of a standard kitchen blender, but it doesn't make a better smoothie.

The Big Chill

To cool off the smoothie, I began adding ice to the blender. Three cubes were the limit; any more ice made the mixture taste watery. But the smoothie was not cold enough for most tasters. Frozen bananas cooled things off nicely, but they took a long time to freeze through—too long, if you wanted to make a spur-of-the-moment smoothie. A good alternative was to chill all of the fruit (including the banana) by laying it out on a baking sheet and freezing it for 10 minutes. These partially frozen pieces of fruit easily blended into a frosty and rejuvenating drink. This was no sugary shake or fibrous frappe—this was a really good fruit smoothie.

BERRY SMOOTHIES
MAKES 4½ CUPS, ENOUGH FOR 4 SERVINGS

Vary the amounts of sugar and lemon juice depending on the ripeness of the fruit.

1	medium ripe banana (about 4 ounces), peeled and cut crosswise into eight pieces
3½	cups berries (about 16 ounces)
½	cup whole milk
½	cup white cranberry or apple juice
	Pinch salt
3–6	teaspoons sugar
2–3	teaspoons lemon juice
3	ice cubes (about 1½ ounces total)

Line rimmed baking sheet with parchment paper; arrange banana and berries in single layer on baking sheet. Freeze fruit until very cold, but not frozen, about 10 minutes. In blender, puree cold fruit, milk, juice, salt, 1 tablespoon sugar, 1 teaspoon lemon juice, and ice until uniformly smooth, 10 to 15 seconds. Taste for sugar and lemon; if desired, add more sugar or lemon and blend until combined, about 2 seconds longer. Serve immediately.

MELON SMOOTHIES

Make sure the melon is absolutely ripe, if not overripe. Underripe melon yields bland smoothies that taste, if anything, like cardboard.

Follow recipe for Berry Smoothies, replacing berries with equal amount of peeled, seeded, and cubed watermelon, cantaloupe, or honeydew (1- to 2-inch pieces are fine) and reducing amounts of milk and juice to ⅓ cup each.

TROPICAL FRUIT SMOOTHIES

Follow recipe for Berry Smoothies, replacing berries with equal amount of peeled, cored or seeded, and diced pineapple, papaya, or mango (1- to 2-inch pieces) and increasing amounts of milk and juice to ⅔ cup each.

Quick and Easy Cinnamon Buns

Yeasted cinnamon buns take hours to make, and store-bought are dreadful. Could we transform a recipe for baking-powder biscuits into quick, high-rise breakfast buns?

⇒ BY RAQUEL PELZEL ⇐

Cinnamon buns are quick to please: You bite into one, and you're happy. The bun is tender and fluffy, the filling is sweet and spicy, and the glaze is sinful, encouraging even the well-bred to lick the gooey remnants from their fingers. It's a shame, then, that making cinnamon buns at home can try the patience of the most devoted cooks. Most recipes call for yeast, which means they also call for a lot of time and skill as well as a standing mixer (or powerful biceps). The alternative is to make cinnamon buns from a tube or a box, options that produce inferior buns whose flavor lies somewhere between chemicals and cardboard. My aim was to put cinnamon buns back in the home kitchen in good time, sacrificing neither flavor nor fluffiness for speed. In short, I wanted great buns without the hassle.

You're not dreaming. Homemade cinnamon buns can be ready to eat less than an hour after you wake up.

The Power in Powder

I started with a tasting of our own yeasted cinnamon buns (*The Best Recipe: American Classics*, 2002). With a soft and resilient texture and a bready, open crumb, the texture of these buns was top-notch, and the combination of cinnamon and yeast produced a grown-up flavor. Unfortunately, the start-to-finish time was nearly five hours. Now I knew what texture and flavor I wanted from cinnamon buns. I just wanted it quicker and easier.

Toward this end, the first decision I made was to work from recipes leavened with baking powder rather than yeast. The next step was to determine the best method for incorporating the fat into the other ingredients. First I tried the classic mixing method of cutting cold butter into dry ingredients, as is done for pie dough. This method turned out cinnamon buns that were dense, flaky, and craggy rather than tender, light, and fluffy.

The next mixing method I tried called for combining melted butter with the liquid ingredients in a food processor, then adding the dry ingredients. While I hoped that the food

processor would make the mixing process easier, these baked-off buns weren't worth the effort. The dough was very sticky, making it difficult to work with.

The last method I tried was the *Cook's* quick cream biscuit method (from the May/June 2000 issue), in which heavy cream is added to flour, sugar, baking powder, and salt. What makes this dough unique is its complete lack of butter. The

dough relies entirely on the heavy cream for tenderness and flavor. Still better, the dough can be mixed in a minute using just one bowl. This process was by far the fastest and easiest, and I wanted to go with it, but a few refinements would be required before it produced really good cinnamon buns.

Add Butter, Forgo Milk

To make the dough more tender, my first thought was to switch all-purpose flour for the more delicate, lower-protein cake flour. But low-protein cake flour turned the dough into a sticky mess that was hard to roll out.

My next inclination was to test whole or skim milk in place of heavy cream, but whole milk made the buns too heavy, and skim milk made them tough and bland. I increased the amount of baking powder to achieve lightness but ended up with metallic-tasting buns. I then tested buttermilk, a common ingredient in biscuit doughs, and had some success. (I also added ½ teaspoon of baking soda to balance the acidity of the buttermilk. Baking soda reacts with the acid in buttermilk to produce carbon dioxide gas, which causes lift.) The acid in the buttermilk gave the buns a more complex flavor and tenderized the gluten in the dough, making the interior airy and light.

But now the dough was too lean for my taste (owing to the buttermilk, most of which is made by adding acidic cultures to skim or partially skimmed milk). I arrived at the solution when I added 2 tablespoons of melted butter to the buttermilk. Just as I had hoped, the dough was tender, complex, and rich.

TASTING: Supermarket Cinnamon Buns

We sampled four supermarket cinnamon buns in a blind tasting and found none of them to be palatable. Here's what tasters had to say:

PILLSBURY
Home-Baked Classics

"Filling is aggressive and one-dimensional;" texture is "gummy and tough."

PILLSBURY
Canned Cinnamon Buns

"Vaguely bitter" with a "chemical" aftertaste; "like eating a sponge."

SARA LEE
Delux Cinnamon Buns

"Strange," "plastic," "artificial vanilla" flavor and a "shocking saffron" color.

PEPPERIDGE FARM
Cinnamon Buns

Tastes like "melted plastic." "This bun is infinitely horrible."

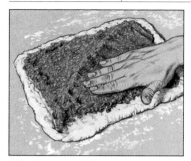

1. Brush dough with 2 tablespoons melted butter. Sprinkle evenly with filling, leaving ½-inch border of plain dough around edges. Press filling firmly into dough.

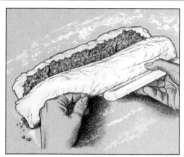

2. Using bench scraper or metal spatula, loosen dough from work surface. Starting at long side, roll dough, pressing lightly, to form a tight log. Pinch seam to seal.

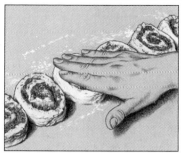

3. Roll log seam-side down and cut evenly into eight pieces. With hand, slightly flatten each piece of dough to seal open edges and keep filling in place.

4. Place one roll in center of prepared nonstick pan, then place remaining seven rolls around perimeter of pan.

Filling and Finishing

Whereas most recipes instruct bakers to roll out the dough, I found it easier to pat the dough into a rough-shaped rectangle, thus making the recipe even simpler. For the cinnamon-sugar filling I decided on a union of brown sugar, white sugar, cinnamon, cloves, and salt. Before sprinkling the filling on the dough, I brushed it with 2 tablespoons of melted butter to help the filling cling to the dough. Because the cinnamon mixture was loose and dry, however, it was still apt to fall away from the dough when the buns were cut and transferred to the baking pan. The easy solution was to add 1 tablespoon of melted butter to the dry ingredients, which made the mixture the consistency of wet sand, allowing me to press it into the dough easily. This time the filling stayed put.

Next I tackled the rolls' appearance. Instead of rising to the occasion in the oven, they were slouching in their seats. I reviewed the article on quick cream biscuits to see if I might find the source of the problem there. Sure enough, the recipe stated that if the dough wasn't kneaded before being shaped, it didn't rise nicely in the oven. I made two batches of dough, kneading one and not the other, and was surprised to find that just a quick 30-second knead solved the problem. Contrary to what one might think, the short knead didn't toughen the buns; it just provided the dough with enough strength to take in a big breath and hold it.

To finish the buns, I tried a host of different glazes, all based on a quick confectioners' sugar and water glaze, which is inherently pasty and grainy. After a few trials, I found a way to sufficiently mask the graininess and pasty flavor by combining buttermilk and cream cheese, then sifting the confectioners' sugar over the paste (if the sugar is not sifted, the glaze will be lumpy). This glaze was smooth, thick, and pleasantly tangy, although it does add one more ingredient to the shopping list for the buns: cream cheese.

As for what to bake the buns in, I tried muffin tins, pie plates, cookie sheets, springform pans,

glass baking dishes, and cake pans. With its straight sides, round shape, and perfect size, I chose a 9-inch nonstick cake pan. I started baking at 425 degrees and got lucky the first time out. The buns baked in 25 minutes, rose and browned nicely, and were cooked all the way through.

Now the moment of truth had come. It was time for a blind tasting of my quick cinnamon buns head-to-head with our yeasted cinnamon buns. The quick buns got a quick nod of approval, with many tasters even preferring them to the more sophisticated and elegantly flavored yeasted buns. Best of all, these shortcut cinnamon buns can be on the table in an hour—a fact you may very well choose to keep to yourself.

QUICK CINNAMON BUNS WITH BUTTERMILK ICING

MAKES 8 BUNS

Melted butter is used in both the filling and the dough and to grease the pan; it's easiest to melt the total amount (8 tablespoons) at once and measure it out as you need it. The finished buns are best eaten warm, but they hold reasonably well for up to 2 hours.

    1 tablespoon unsalted butter, melted, for pan

Cinnamon-Sugar Filling
    ¾ cup (5¼ ounces) packed dark brown sugar
    ¼ cup (1¾ ounces) granulated sugar
    2 teaspoons cinnamon
    ⅛ teaspoon cloves
    ⅛ teaspoon salt
    1 tablespoon unsalted butter, melted

Biscuit Dough
    2½ cups (12½ ounces) unbleached all-purpose flour, plus additional flour for work surface
    2 tablespoons granulated sugar
    1¼ teaspoons baking powder
    ½ teaspoon baking soda
    ½ teaspoon salt

    1¼ cups buttermilk
    6 tablespoons unsalted butter, melted

Icing
    2 tablespoons cream cheese, softened
    2 tablespoons buttermilk
    1 cup (4 ounces) confectioners' sugar

1. Adjust oven rack to upper-middle position and heat oven to 425 degrees. Pour 1 tablespoon melted butter in 9-inch nonstick cake pan; brush to coat pan. Spray wire rack with nonstick cooking spray; set aside.

2. TO MAKE CINNAMON-SUGAR FILLING: Combine sugars, spices, and salt in small bowl. Add 1 tablespoon melted butter and stir with fork or fingers until mixture resembles wet sand; set filling mixture aside.

3. TO MAKE BISCUIT DOUGH: Whisk flour, sugar, baking powder, baking soda, and salt in large bowl. Whisk buttermilk and 2 tablespoons melted butter in measuring cup or small bowl. Add liquid to dry ingredients and stir with wooden spoon until liquid is absorbed (dough will look very shaggy), about 30 seconds. Transfer dough to lightly floured work surface and knead until just smooth and no longer shaggy.

4. Pat dough with hands into 12 by 9-inch rectangle. Following illustrations above, fill, roll, cut, and arrange buns in buttered cake pan. Brush with 2 tablespoons remaining melted butter. Bake until edges are golden brown, 23 to 25 minutes. Use offset metal spatula to loosen buns from pan; without separating, slide buns out of pan onto greased cooling rack. Cool about 5 minutes before icing.

5. TO MAKE ICING AND FINISH BUNS: While buns are cooling, line rimmed baking sheet with parchment paper (for easy cleanup); set rack with buns over baking sheet. Whisk cream cheese and buttermilk in large nonreactive bowl until thick and smooth (mixture will look like cottage cheese at first). Sift confectioners' sugar over; whisk until smooth glaze forms, about 30 seconds. Spoon glaze evenly over buns; serve immediately.

Easiest Hot Fudge Pudding Cake

Here's how to make a homey, no-fuss chocolate cake with hot fudge sauce—baked together in one dish.

⇒ BY THE COOK'S ILLUSTRATED TEST KITCHEN ⇐

Hot fudge pudding cake has several aliases: Denver pudding cake, chocolate upside-down cake, brownie pudding cake, or sometimes simply chocolate pudding cake. This 1950s community cookbook recipe may be a bit dated, but it's a boon to the cook looking for a simple baked dessert that requires no creaming or whipping. Hot fudge pudding cake is definitely not a dessert for entertaining; it does not impress with its looks. It's a humble, homely dessert with bumps, lumps, and cracks, an easy one to turn up your nose at. But those who have eaten hot fudge pudding cake know its charms: unpretentious, moist, brownie-like chocolate cake sitting on a pool of thick, chocolate pudding–like sauce, baked together in one dish, as if by magic. Served warm with vanilla ice cream, this cake more than makes up for its lack of looks.

In the matter of pudding cakes, there are two distinct styles. The fussier version requires beaten egg whites rather than chemical leaveners for lift and a hot water bath to produce a soufflé-like cake above a custard-like sauce. Then there's the absurdly simple hot fudge pudding cake that resembles a chemically leavened brownie and can be made by a rookie baker equipped with only a few bowls and a whisk. It was the latter style that we were pursuing, so we gathered a few recipes and tried them. All were disappointing. Instead of deep and chocolatey, they tasted dull and mild. Instead of providing enough spoon-coating sauce to accompany the cake, some were dry, with a disproportionate amount of cake, while the others were soupy, with a wet, sticky, underdone cake.

For those who aren't familiar with the magic of pudding cakes, here's how they work. The batter is made in the manner of a brownie batter, but with milk added. After the batter goes in the baking dish, things take an unusual turn. A mixture of sugar and cocoa is sprinkled over the batter, then liquid is poured on top, and the mess goes into the oven. (Depending on the recipe, the cocoa and sugar may first be dissolved in hot water, then poured over.) The step of pouring liquid over the batter is so odd that the cook making a hot fudge pudding cake for the first time quickly becomes skeptical. With baking, however, what looks to be a mistake is transformed into a dessert. The cake rises to the surface, and the liquid that started out on top sinks

Dutch-processed cocoa and semisweet chocolate give this humble-looking dessert a potent punch. Top off each portion with a scoop of vanilla ice cream.

to the bottom, taking the sugar and cocoa with it, becoming the "hot fudge sauce."

Go Dutch

With a working recipe cobbled together, our first goal was to pump up the chocolate flavor, suspecting that the problem was that most recipes call for cocoa rather than chocolate. In our experience, cocoa alone carries potent—sometimes acrid—chocolate flavor, but it cannot deliver the complexity or richness of chocolate. We tried adding different amounts of bittersweet chocolate to the pudding cake. Two ounces in addition to the 1/3 cup of cocoa was the ideal amount to obtain fuller flavor. More chocolate and the cake was too wicked with chocolate and its texture became sodden.

We also thought to try regular "natural" cocoa versus Dutch-processed cocoa. The former is lighter in color and more acidic than the latter. In a side-by-side tasting, we were stunned by the

difference. The "natural" cocoa version tasted sharp and harsh, but the one made with Dutch-processed cocoa (we used Droste, a brand widely available in supermarkets) tasted smooth, round, and full. It was unanimous. Every person who tasted the two cakes vastly preferred the one made with Dutch-processed cocoa. To sweeten the cake and counter the bitterness of the cocoa, 2/3 cup of sugar was required. We tried substituting some brown sugar for granulated but found it a nuisance because of the way it clumps (not a problem if the butter and sugar were being creamed together, but this cake was too easy for that). Besides, the brown sugar added no significant flavor benefit.

The next issue we needed to settle was that of the egg. There seemed to be two styles of hot fudge pudding cake in this regard: those that contained egg and those that didn't. The eggless cakes were mushy and crumbly. Their crumb lacked structural integrity, and, because they were soft and mushy, there seemed to be little distinction between what was supposed to be cake and what was supposed to be hot fudge. We tried as many as two whole eggs, but our preference was for a pudding cake made with just one yolk. It was brownie-like, with a nice, tooth-sinking crumb. Cakes made with whole eggs were drier and slightly rubbery.

So far, we had been using 1 cup of unbleached all-purpose flour, but the cake layer was a tad too thick. We tried smaller amounts of flour, hoping that the texture wouldn't suffer as a consequence. The good news was that we actually preferred the cake with 3/4 cup of flour. It tasted more richly of chocolate and had a more moist, brownie-like texture. And with a little less height, the amount of cake was a better match for the amount of sauce.

The butter in hot fudge pudding cake is always melted, never creamed. (This cake requires a heavy-duty leavener, such as baking powder, to force the cake layer up through the sludge that becomes the sauce. Although creaming is one way to provide lift, in this case the contribution made by aerated butter would be minimal and not worth the effort.) With only 4 tablespoons of melted butter, the cake tasted lean and dry. With 8, it was leaden and greasy. Six tablespoons was the ideal amount. Like most other cakes, hot fudge pudding cakes contain some dairy, usually milk. We tried heavy cream and half-and-half to see if either had desirable effects. Heavy cream made a slick, greasy, fat-laden cake. With half-and-half, the cake was somewhat greasy and a little too rich. Milk was the way to go.

For lift, we relied on baking powder. One recipe called for 2 tablespoons per cup of flour ("chemical warfare" was one taster's term for this mixture). Two teaspoons of baking powder was just fine. To heighten flavor, we added ¼ teaspoon salt and 1 tablespoon vanilla (there was a lot of chocolate flavor to contend with).

From Top to Bottom

As previously mentioned, there are two ways to add the ingredients destined to become the fudge sauce. A mixture of cocoa and sugar can be sprinkled on the batter and water then poured over it, creating what looks like a pan-full of river sludge. Alternatively, the cocoa and sugar can first be dissolved in boiling water. We compared two such pudding cakes. The one with the sprinkled cocoa/sugar mixture baked up with crisp edges and a faintly crisp crust that we preferred over the uniformly soft, cakey surface of the other. It was as if some of the sugar, moistened by the water, remained at the surface even after the liquid seeped to the bottom, and then caramelized to form a pleasing crust.

We tried different amounts of cocoa in the sauce-to-be and landed at ⅓ cup, the same amount we put in the cake. A mixture made with all granulated sugar resulted in a toffee-like crust, rather sticky and tough, with one-dimensional sweetness. We preferred a mix of granulated sugar and brown sugar, with the molasses flavor of the latter producing a full, round taste.

The amount of water poured over the cake determines the amount of sauce at the bottom. One and one-half cups—a little more than what most recipes call for—was ideal, yielding an ample amount of sauce with the right consistency. Some hot fudge pudding cake recipes suggest using coffee instead of water. Indeed, we thought the coffee was a nice addition. It didn't interfere with the chocolate flavor but nicely complemented it, cutting through some of the cake's cloying qualities and enriching the flavor. For ease, we took to using 2 teaspoons of instant coffee mixed into the water, but cold, brewed coffee cut with a little water works too.

We tested different oven temperatures and baking times. While most recipes indicated 350 degrees for about 35 minutes, we preferred 325 degrees for 45 minutes. The lower temperature helped keep the sauce from rapidly bubbling, a phenomenon that can cause spillage if left unchecked. In addition, the slightly longer baking time promoted a nicer crust. We noted that this cake combined lots of pleasing textures: a silky sauce, a moist, cakey crumb, and a thin, brittle crust, especially around the edges.

When attacked with a spoon straight from the oven, the hot fudge pudding cake revealed a thin, blistering-hot sauce and a sodden cake. If allowed to cool for 20 to 30 minutes, however, the sauce became pudding-like and the cake brownie-like. The warm cake cries out to be served with vanilla or coffee ice cream (whipped cream just isn't serious enough). For serving to guests, we adapted the recipe to bake in individual ramekins so that apologies for the cake's dowdy appearance need not be made so profusely. Leftovers reheat well in the zap of a microwave, but don't count on having any.

HOT FUDGE PUDDING CAKE
SERVES 8

If you have cold, brewed coffee on hand, it can be used in place of the instant coffee and water, but to make sure it isn't too strong, use 1 cup of cold coffee mixed with ½ cup of water. Serve the cake warm with vanilla or coffee ice cream. Leftovers can be reheated, covered with plastic wrap, in a microwave oven.

2	teaspoons instant coffee
1½	cups water
⅔	cup (2½ ounces) Dutch-processed cocoa
⅓	cup (1¾ ounces) packed brown sugar
1	cup (7 ounces) granulated sugar
6	tablespoons unsalted butter
2	ounces semisweet or bittersweet chocolate, chopped
¾	cup (3¾ ounces) unbleached all-purpose flour
2	teaspoons baking powder
1	tablespoon vanilla extract
⅓	cup whole milk
¼	teaspoon salt
1	large egg yolk

1. Adjust oven rack to lower-middle position and heat oven to 325 degrees. Lightly spray 8-inch square glass or ceramic baking dish with nonstick cooking spray. Stir instant coffee into water; set aside to dissolve. Stir together ⅓ cup cocoa, brown sugar, and ⅓ cup granulated sugar in small bowl, breaking up large clumps with fingers; set aside. Melt butter, remaining ⅓ cup cocoa, and chocolate in small bowl set over saucepan of barely simmering water; whisk until smooth and set aside to cool slightly. Whisk flour and baking powder in small bowl to combine; set aside. Whisk remaining ⅔ cup sugar, vanilla, milk, and salt in medium bowl until combined; whisk in yolk. Add chocolate mixture and whisk to combine. Add flour mixture and whisk until batter is evenly moistened.

2. Pour batter into prepared baking dish and spread evenly to sides and corners. Sprinkle cocoa/sugar mixture evenly over batter (cocoa mixture should cover entire surface of batter); pour coffee mixture gently over cocoa mixture. Bake until cake is puffed and bubbling and just beginning to pull away from sides of baking dish, about 45 minutes. (Do not overbake.) Cool cake in dish on wire rack about 25 minutes before serving.

INDIVIDUAL HOT FUDGE PUDDING CAKES

Follow recipe for Hot Fudge Pudding Cake, heating oven to 400 degrees and lightly spraying eight 6- to 8-ounce ramekins with nonstick cooking spray; set ramekins on baking sheet. Divide batter evenly among ramekins (about ¼ cup per ramekin) and level with back of spoon; sprinkle about 2 tablespoons cocoa/sugar mixture over batter in each ramekin. Pour 3 tablespoons coffee mixture over cocoa/sugar mixture in each ramekin. Bake until puffed and bubbling, about 20 minutes. (Do not overbake.) Cool ramekins about 15 minutes before serving (cakes will fall).

STEP-BY-STEP | PUDDING CAKE 1-2-3

1. Pour batter into prepared baking dish and spread evenly into sides and corners with rubber spatula.

2. Sprinkle cocoa/sugar mixture evenly over batter. Mixture should cover entire surface of batter.

3. Pour coffee mixture gently over cocoa mixture, and put baking dish in oven.

The Truth about French Roast Coffee

French roast, darling of the Starbucks crowd, may not be what you think. Here's why.

≥ BY ANNA KASABIAN AND RAQUEL PELZEL ≤

You order a large coffee from your local coffee bar and, on any particular day, the beans might come from one of a dozen different countries—Sumatra, Costa Rica, Guatemala. But one thing is likely: The beans have been dark-roasted. They may even be French roast beans. Of course, all coffee beans are roasted before being ground and brewed, but a French roast is dark—very dark—and, thanks to Starbucks and other specialty retailers, it is also very popular. It seemed to us, then, that the obvious question for the consumer was, Which brand of French roast beans is best?

Just like wine, coffee gets its flavor by many means. There is the type of bean, the place where the beans are grown (even the same type of bean grown in different locales in the same country will develop different flavors), and the time of harvest. And then there is the processing method, the mix of beans in a particular blend, the length of time the beans are roasted, the type of grind, the quality of the water used, and the coffee-making process. (The latter is not insignificant. Great beans produce lousy coffee when brewed incorrectly.)

All Beans Are Not Created Equal

Given this confusing wealth of factors, many consumers focus on the type of bean, something that experts find hard to explain. Arabica, the most popular bean at the moment, is so popular that even McDonald's promotes its use in the coffee sold under the golden arches. But the arabica bean comes in many varieties, the best of which are grown in climates with relatively cool evening temperatures. In other words, some arabica beans are good and some are not.

But if the bean itself isn't a reliable indicator of quality (even the country of origin doesn't make one coffee good and another bad), what should the consumer consider when choosing a coffee from the supermarket shelf? The only choices left are the brand and the type of roast. Using the popular French roast as our reference point, we conducted a tasting of nine supermarket brands and the results were, well, shocking. Chock Full o' Nuts squeaked by Starbucks for first-place honors in the first round of tastings, indicating that price (Starbucks costs more than twice as much as Chock Full o' Nuts) is no guarantee of satisfaction. Noting that the ratings were close for all brands, we repeated the tasting. The second time around the results were just as close, but the rankings were

different. We did note, however, that some tasters preferred a darker roast and others a lighter roast, a key factor that contributed to the odd results. In other words, tasters were not responding to quality per se, they were simply expressing a preference as to what degree the beans were roasted. Is it possible, then, that all French roasts—no matter the type of bean—are not created equal? To try to settle the matter, we decided to turn to some experts and set out for the Excellent Coffee Company, a coffee roaster in Pawtucket, R.I.

Measuring Darkness

We took our nine brands on the road and this time subjected them to an Agtron reading, which measures the amount of light reflected from particles of ground coffee. A very dark roast has an Agtron reading of 19, a very light roast a reading of 75. According to common industry standards, a French roast usually falls in the range of 20 to 30. Based on their Agtron readings, only four of the nine coffees we tested were true French roasts. Two qualified as Italian roasts, with readings under 20, and three qualified as Viennese roasts, with readings over 30. So brand does make a difference. The beans in brands advertised as French roast are in fact roasted to very different degrees. Coffee drinkers who favor that charred, heavily roasted flavor should go for Starbucks, but if you like a lighter, more subtle cup of coffee, you might choose Chock Full o' Nuts or Eight O'Clock.

But what about French roast itself? Despite its popularity, the confusing taste test results made us wonder if the roasting process somehow camouflaged the quality of the beans, thus making brand recognition difficult. We turned to Kevin Knox of Allegro coffee, one-time Starbucks quality-control man and coauthor with Julie Sheldon Huffaker of *Coffee Basics* (John Wiley & Sons, 1996). He sums up French roast by saying, "It's just burnt coffee."

The Roasting Rules

To understand just what Knox means, it's necessary to know a bit about the coffee-roasting process. Beans can be roasted from light (American) to medium (Full City) to dark (Viennese, French, and Italian, the darkest roast). Although these are imprecise terms, the method is simple enough.

Beans are roasted by hot air and then cooled. They can be roasted slowly or quickly, and the cooling method can vary as well, and variations in both factors affect flavor. The reason French roast beans are often considered burnt is that they are roasted until many of their carbohydrates (sugar and cellulose) are converted to carbon (that is, incinerated), causing the beans to lose up to 20 percent of their weight in the process. Thus many experts believe French roasting destroys flavors, rendering the differences between high- and low-quality beans meaningless. Forget about the subtle flavor of honeysuckle in Kenyan beans or the bittersweet chocolate taste of Guatemalan Antigua.

To test this theory, we did a tasting at Excellent Coffee of both high-quality and mediocre beans roasted to both light and dark stages. While expert and staff tasters could tell which bean was which when the beans were lightly roasted, the differences between the high-quality and low-quality beans were harder to detect when the beans were darkly roasted; in fact, some tasters preferred the lower-quality dark roast beans to the higher-quality dark roast beans. Knowing that character flaws and nuances in flavor can be masked by dark roasting, professionals "cup," or taste, coffee brewed from very lightly roasted beans.

We also asked the Excellent Coffee experts to blind-taste French roast Starbucks against Chock Full o' Nuts. The result? They preferred the cheaper Chock Full o' Nuts, a lighter roast that

How Dark Is That Bean?

To quantify the differences between roasts, industry experts use Agtron readings, which measure the amount of light the ground coffee particles reflect. The scale runs from 15 (the darkest possible roast) to 80 (the lightest). Below are commonly accepted values for various popular roasts.

Agtron Reading	Coffee Roast
BELOW 20	Italian
20 TO 30	French
30 TO 40	Viennese
40 TO 50	Full City
50 TO 60	Hotel/Restaurant
ABOVE 60	American

TASTING FRENCH ROAST COFFEE

To gather the samples for our supermarket whole bean French roast coffee tasting, we consulted recent grocery store sales data to determine the most popular brands in the category. We also included some nationally available natural foods store brands and one organic brand. All beans were ground using the same technique in the same blade grinder (the Capresso Cool Grind, one of the winners in our November/December 2001 testing of coffee grinders). The coffee was brewed in brand new Krups ProAroma coffee makers (winner of our November/December 1998 testing of coffee makers) and served within minutes of brewing. We tasted the coffee on three occasions; the notes include the most popular comments made in all three tastings. Tasters were asked to evaluate the coffee for aroma, body, flavor, and acidity. We have also included an Agtron reading (a measurement of how much light is reflected from particles of ground coffee) for each coffee; the lower the number, the darker the roast. Coffees are listed in order from darkest to lightest roast.

STARBUCKS French Roast Coffee
- $8.49 for 12 ounces
- AGTRON READING: 16.8

Our tasters either loved the "smoky," "burnt" flavor of Starbucks or they hated it. To some it was "mysterious" and "nutty," with "mild cocoa" undertones; but to others it tasted "charred" and "dirty." Its aroma had a strong "roasted" and "toasty" presence, and its acidity was definitely "sharp."

365 EVERY DAY VALUE Whole Foods Market French Roast Coffee
- $9.99 for 24 ounces
- AGTRON READING: 16.9

This "tastes like I just smoked a cigarette," said one panelist; another thought the coffee tasted "like rubber." Others enjoyed its "roasted" aroma and "smoky," "bitter" qualities. With a "full" body and "sharp" acidity, this coffee is definitely not for those who like a mellow brew.

ALLEGRO Organic French Roast Coffee
- $8.99 for 12 ounces
- AGTRON READING: 20.1

The aroma of Allegro's coffee was described as "rich" and "toasty." One taster found its flavor "refreshing," with a "smoky" twang; others, however, criticized the coffee for being "thin" and its flavor "fleeting." Its acidity was "sharp" but fell "flat" quickly.

MILLSTONE French Roast Coffee
- $7.99 for 10 ounces
- AGTRON READING: 20.1

Millstone was one of the only coffees in the tasting that consistently ranked at the bottom of the charts. Disliked for its "bitter," "bland," and "boring" flavor, this coffee was described by tasters as "very middle of the road," "nothing special," and even "truly awful."

GREEN MOUNTAIN Coffee, French Roast
- $5.99 for 10 ounces
- AGTRON READING: 25.6

Although Green Mountain was criticized for its "acrid aftertaste," tasters were still fond of the "tangy" and "bitter" qualities that "nicely balanced" each other. Some tasters called its aroma "burnt" and "harsh," while others described it as "toasty" and "nutty," with a "sour" kick.

DON FRANCISCO'S French Roast Coffee
- $6.60 for 12 ounces
- AGTRON READING: 26.9

Although its flavor was deemed "smoky" and "tangy," some tasters found this coffee to be "flat" and "one-dimensional." Its body, however, was pleasantly "full" and its acidity on the "medium" side.

CHOCK FULL O' NUTS Cafe Blend French Roast Coffee
- $3.99 for 12 ounces
- AGTRON READING: 31.0

We consistently liked Chock Full o' Nuts. Tasters described it as "complex, fruity, and interesting," with a "super chocolate background and great acidity." Its flavor was likened to "caramel," balanced with a "sour" and "sharp" edge. Tasters also favored this "medium-bodied" coffee for its "bright" acidity.

FOLGERS French Roast Coffee
- $3.29 for 11 ounces
- AGTRON READING: 34.8

Although the Folgers brew smelled "rich," "toasty," and "roasted," tasters couldn't overcome its "overwhelming bitterness" and "acrid" components; some even likened the flavor to "bad citrus." Its acidity was too "sharp," "potent," and "strong" for our tasters.

EIGHT O'CLOCK Bean Coffee, French Roast
- $3.29 for 12 ounces
- AGTRON READING: 38.1

This coffee was considered "pleasant and drinkable but not incredibly complex." Although tasters described its flavor as "balanced" and "earthy," a number of them concurred that the Eight O'Clock coffee just "didn't have enough personality." Its aroma was marked down for "dull" and "stale" attributes.

---

they found "mild and sweet," opposed to the dark roast Starbucks, which they found "smoky and sharply acidic." (The tasters did comment, however, that they could discern a higher-quality bean in the Starbucks coffee than in the Chock Full o' Nuts, although they didn't care for the burnt taste of the roasting.)

So the best question to ask when it comes to supermarket French roast coffees isn't "Which brand is best?" Even though Starbucks uses high-quality beans, its coffee doesn't have much on Folgers or Eight O'Clock when the beans are French roasted. George Howell, founder of the Coffee Connection, goes so far as to say that "taste can wind up having little to do with quality." What is certain is that for dark roast coffees, the roasting process has a bigger impact on flavor than bean quality.

What *is* the best question to ask when selecting a French roast coffee? Probably, "How do you like your coffee?" As Howell points out, if given French roast, the person who prefers light roast "will feel like he is walking into a dark room. It's all thickness and no clarity." Meanwhile, someone who favors dark roast but is given light roast "feels like he is being attacked by the corrosive rays of the sun." So forget about beans, price, and country of origin and simply use the notes above to help you choose the brand of French roast best suited to your palate. We've organized the coffees in order from the darkest to the lightest roasts. Keep in mind that how you drink your coffee may also influence your choice. Black coffee drinkers may prefer a lighter roast, whereas those who add milk and sugar might find the darker roasts more appealing.

Anna Kasabian, coauthor of *Cooking Spaces* (Rockport, 2000), is at work on her eighth book.

Is a $399 Charcoal Grill Really Necessary?

Even the $99 model performed well in our tests and has plenty of great features. Does more money add value?

≥ BY ADAM RIED ≤

Flicking a switch to light a gas grill may be convenient, but for many die-hard grillers nothing beats cooking over a live charcoal fire. The pleasure is utterly visceral: the glowing, red-hot coals, the smoke, the intense sizzle, the interplay of food and flame, and the aroma of searing meat. And, of course, there is the flavor. Charcoal-fueled fires infuse food with characteristic notes of wood and smoke that no gas fire can match.

Yet deciding which charcoal grill to buy is not so straightforward. They come in different shapes and sizes, with different features, and at vastly different prices. We chose six grills from five manufacturers that ran the gamut—from round to rectangular, bare-bones to fully loaded, smaller to larger, and less than $50 to more than 10 times

that amount—and pressed them into service in the alley behind the test kitchen for evaluation. A few weeks of grilling steaks, hamburgers, bone-in chicken breasts, and ribs led us to some interesting observations and a couple of decent choices but not, alas, to a grill that is perfect in all respects.

Grill Configuration

Grilling a mountain of food over two weeks revealed very little difference in cooking performance in our grills. Each developed a fire hot enough to sear the food, which is what charcoal grilling is all about. Each also offers vents to control airflow—and thereby the intensity of the fire—but I was not able to detect any advantages or disadvantages based on the number or position of the vents. It was possible, however, to identify

two important design factors: the size of the grill and the depth of the grill cover.

After years of grilling on a small portable grill, I can speak personally about the benefits of upsizing. (The cooking surface on smaller grills runs 18 inches square or 21 inches round; the cooking area on the largest grill was 18 by 26 inches.) A large surface area is essential if you cook for large groups (and useful even when you don't) because it affords the opportunity to easily grill some extra food alongside tonight's dinner. For instance, I rarely grill a meal without covering every available inch of grill space with vegetables to have on hand for tomorrow's antipasto, pizza, or pasta salad. It is also easier to build a two-level fire (hot on one side and cooler on the other) in a large grill. In short, size matters. Among the grills tested, the New Braunfels Santa Fe was the size champ, with 468 square inches of grilling space.

While at *Cook's* we generally don't use the cover when grilling over high heat, it is necessary when grill-roasting large cuts, such as a turkey or prime rib, over lower heat. To trap heat and contain any flavorful smoke generated from wood chunks or chips, the grill cover must fit comfortably over the food and form a tight seal with the grill bottom. We recommend 12- to 14-pound turkeys for grill-roasting, and the New Braunfels and Sunbeam grills were the only ones with covers that closed over a 14-pounder (set on a V-rack to promote even cooking). All of the grills in the group, except for the Thermos, swallowed the 12-pounder.

Features, Functional and Frivolous

In some respects, charcoal grills are a little like cars. Any new car will get you from point A to point B, but extra features like traction control or anti-lock brakes make the car easier to drive, and goodies like a sunroof or heated seats help you enjoy the ride more. Likewise, all charcoal grills will cook your food, but several features can make the process easier and more enjoyable.

Though I never would have guessed it, the presence of an attached table made a huge difference. After years of precariously balancing platters on deck railings and chair arms, it was a welcome relief to have a secure, accessible place to put dishes and utensils. The New Braunfels doubled the pleasure with two large tables on opposite ends of the grill. Score another point for New

The Charcoal Grills We Tested

New Braunfels Santa Fe
Maybe not perfect, but an excellent value with lots of features for a very reasonable price.

Weber Performer
Luxo-version of the classic kettle grill. The Weber One-Touch Platinum (which was not tested) drops some of the less valuable features and is cheaper by $150.

Sunbeam Portable Charcoal Grill
Earns honorable mention as a good rock-bottom budget choice.

The Cajun Grill
Some details are beautifully designed; others fall short. Too expensive to forgive flaws.

Weber One-Touch Silver
The archetypal kettle grill that could stand to offer more features for the money.

Thermos Kettle Grill
Failing the turkey test was the kiss of death for this otherwise reasonably good grill.

RATING CHARCOAL GRILLS

RATINGS

★★★
GOOD

★★
FAIR

★
POOR

We rated six charcoal grills and evaluated them according to the following criteria. The grills were tested by pressing them into daily service for recipe development in the test kitchen.

PRICE: Paid in Boston-area stores, in catalogs, and on the Web.

COOKING AREA: The larger, the better.

TURKEY TEST: Grills should accommodate a small turkey or other large cuts with the lid down and shut tight for grill-roasting. If we could close the lid completely over a 14-pound turkey, the grill was rated good. If we could close the lid completely over only a smaller 12-pound turkey, the grill was rated fair. If the lid would not close fully over the 12-pound turkey, the grill was rated poor.

TABLES: Grills with two tables, or one exceptionally large table, were rated good. Grills with a single average-sized table were rated fair, and grills with no table at all were rated poor.

ADJUSTABILITY: Grills on which either the charcoal rack or the cooking grate was adjustable were preferred and rated good. If there was no means of adjusting either the rack or the grate, the grill was rated fair. There was no poor rating in this category.

EXTRA FEATURES: Other features on the grill.

TESTERS' COMMENTS: Observations on features that were especially useful or superfluous, design flaws, and overall structural integrity.

Brand	Price	Cooking Area	Turkey Test	Tables	Adjustability	Extra Features	Testers' Comments
BEST BUY **New Braunfels** Santa Fe, Model 01308725	$99.00	468 sq. in. 18" x 26"	★★★	★★★	★★★	Built-in thermometer, door to charcoal rack for fire tending and ash removal, lower storage shelf	A user-friendly grill with better features than structural integrity. Huge cooking surface, two wide side tables, and a door into the charcoal area are all great features. We did, however, have to revisit this grill with the wrench to keep it fit and tight.
RECOMMENDED WITH RESERVATIONS **Weber** Performer	$399.00	363 sq. in. 21½" diam.	★★	★★★	★★	Gas ignition, thermometer, storage shelf, charcoal bin, ash catcher, hinged cooking grate, lid holder, tool hooks	Its many nice touches include a thermometer with real numbers, large table, hinged cooking grate, and overall solid construction. Gas ignition is useful but utterly inessential. With so many thoughtful features, why didn't Weber make the cooking grate or the charcoal rack adjustable?
Sunbeam 22-Inch Square Portable Charcoal Grill	$49.96	342 sq. in. 18½" x 18½"	★★★	★★	★★★	Hinged lid	A very nice grill but for three major flaws: a relatively small cooking area, a cooking grate that slides around whenever you move the food on it, and a flimsy overall feel. Otherwise, not bad if you have just a few dollars and only a couple of people to feed.
The Cajun Grill Model PG200	$519.00	442 sq. in. 18" x 26"	★★	★★	★★★	Ash-catcher tray	So heavy and solid it feels like it could weather a cyclone. Best charcoal rack adjustment system encountered, yet the rack itself is too narrow to provide even heat over 100 percent of the cooking surface. No way to add charcoal to the fire without removing the cooking grate.
Weber One-Touch Silver	$99.00	363 sq. in. 21½" diam.	★★	★	★★	Open ash-catcher pan	Solid and competent but with no frills. The handles on the cooking grate are the only "extra."
Thermos 22½-Inch Kettle Grill	$59.99	363 sq. in. 21½" diam.	★	★	★★★	Ash catcher, lower storage shelf	Thoughtfully featured and fine to grill on, but too small. Because most home cooks have just one charcoal grill, we'd bypass this model, which is too shallow to accommodate large cuts for grill-roasting.

Braunfels. Among our group, only the Weber One-Touch Silver and the Thermos lacked tables of any kind.

If you plan to barbecue or grill-roast (both methods entail long cooking over a relatively low fire), some means of easily adding charcoal to the fire is useful. Once again, the New Braunfels offered the perfect solution—a small door to the charcoal rack, which made it a breeze to tend the fire and add fuel. The Webers offer a different solution—cooking grates, which are either hinged or open at the ends so you can slip in the charcoal. If you have to add fuel to any of the other grills, you must endure the aggravation of removing the food and the cooking grate to get to the fire.

Another thoughtful feature is some means of adjusting the height of either the charcoal rack or the cooking grate. If given no respite from a hot fire, many foods, such as thick steaks, pork chops, and chicken breasts, will burn on the outside before cooking through on the inside. So they must be finished over a cooler fire. This is easy to accomplish if you can adjust the charcoal rack down away from the cooking grate, as is the case with the New Braunfels, the Cajun, and the Thermos. On the Sunbeam, the charcoal rack is fixed, but you can adjust the height of the cooking grate, so the effect is the same. Still, the ability to adjust the charcoal rack or cooking grate is not essential. On the Webers, which do not offer such adjustability, you can build a two-level fire that is hot on one side and cool on the other to achieve the same effect. This simply takes a little extra knowledge on the part of the griller. It is easier, though, if you can change the level of the fire with the shift of a lever or the turn of a dial.

Several other features fell into the nice but not necessary category. Notable among them was the gas ignition on the Weber Performer, which did its job well but added expense and weight. A chimney starter is so easy to use that I would happily forgo the gas ignition. On the other hand, an ash catcher—a container attached to the bottom of the grill to trap ashes—makes life easier when it comes time to clean out the grill. When you barbecue or grill-roast, a built-in thermometer is handy, though you can always put a grill thermometer through the lid vents.

The Winning Formula

In the end, value—which I define as the balance of size, features, and price—determined my recommendations. This formula makes the New Braunfels look pretty good, with its impressive size and host of features, and at a cost of just $99. But it's not perfect. The charcoal rack adjustment system is limited to three positions, and the whole unit struck me as flimsy, especially when compared with the solid, well-designed, seven-position system on the Cajun Grill. The New Braunfels grill's structural integrity also failed to impress me. I had to tighten its nuts and bolts several times throughout the testing.

Though the Weber Performer does not offer an adjustment system for moving the charcoal rack and I viewed its gas ignition system as superfluous, it is solid and extremely well outfitted. The caveat here is price—nearly $400, or four times that of the New Braunfels. (Weber does offer a similar model, the One-Touch Platinum, which comes with an ash catcher and a large attached table but does not include a gas ignition system or thermometer, for about $249. This grill strikes me as a better value than the Performer because it has all of the Performer's important features but none of the bells and whistles that add mightily to its price tag.)

In the end, I'd say the general guideline is to buy the largest, best-outfitted grill your budget will allow. And, silly as it may sound, whatever you do, make sure there is a table attached.

⇒ BY BRIDGET LANCASTER ⇐

New Knife in the Block

It's sad, but the boning knife is often the most neglected knife in the block. Sure, it's great for boning cuts of meat, and when it comes to removing the silver skin from pork tenderloin (check out the illustration on page 16), there's nothing better. But we found that the long, paper-thin blade also makes quick work of removing the peel from citrus fruits such as oranges and grapefruit. Flexibility is the key here, and the knife's flexible blade takes the curve of the fruit nicely, with little marring of the inner flesh. In addition, the thin blade is perfect for removing sections of citrus fruit every time.

Freeze Out

We know that freezing can have a detrimental impact on meat. We've all seen the pool of liquid left behind by defrosted meat, pointing to a less flavorful and less juicy eating experience. Would the same thing happen to brined meat? To find out, we left a batch of brined (and drained) pork chops in the freezer for a week (properly wrapped, of course). Then we defrosted them overnight in the fridge, fired up the grill, and compared them with just-brined chops that hadn't been frozen.

The previously frozen chops had a somewhat strange, although not completely unpleasant texture (described as almost spongelike by one taster), while the freshly brined chops retained their meaty texture. And although the frozen chops did exude quite a bit of liquid during defrosting, they were still amazingly juicy, almost as good as the fresh chops. The moral of the story? While we don't advocate the practice of freezing meat, we'll sink our chops into brined pork chops—formerly frozen or not—any day.

Attention Carmen Miranda!

It may not be a pressing matter for most people, but here in the test kitchen we wanted to know if all supermarket pineapples are created equal. After all, we've fallen victim to the sweet smell of these tropical beauties only to find our palates puckering from the sour fruit.

A survey of local supermarkets produced pineapple of two origins: Hawaii and Costa Rica (easily identified by their attached tags). The chosen pineapples (four from each growing region) were similar in ripeness. All yielded slightly when touched, were golden in color (green pineapples are underripe), and carried that familiar heady pineapple aroma. We tasted the fruit both straight up and in a smoothie.

The fruit from Hawaii was astoundingly astringent. Tasters could only un-pucker their mouths long enough to exclaim "bitter" and "sour." Smoothies made with this fruit were rather flavorless. The Costa Rican pineapple (sometimes labeled "extra-sweet" or "gold") triumphed in the tasting. Both straight up and in a smoothie, this fruit was packed with an ultrasweet, honeylike flavor that one taster called "pumped-up pineapple." There are no doubt some bad Costa Rican pineapples for sale as well as some better Hawaiian fruit, but in our experience, it pays to check a pineapple's origins.

Mellowing with Age

Did you know that squeezing a lemon too far in advance can have a big impact on its flavor? That's just what we found out when we tested day-old lemon juice against freshly squeezed juice in a head-to-head test. After making two batches of lemon curd, one made with day-old juice and the other with fresh juice, we called in tasters to see if they could detect a difference. Could they ever!

The curd made with day-old lemon juice was much mellower—it lacked the tongue-tingling impact found in the curd made with just-squeezed juice. Some tasters also noted a faint off-flavor in the curd made with day-old juice, but most could not pick up this flavor. Oddly enough, tasters were split on which curd they preferred. Some liked the buffered lemon flavor of the previously squeezed juice, saying that the fresh juice produced a curd that was too harsh. Others liked the full, bright lemon flavor of the curd made with fresh juice. So if you want big lemon flavor, squeeze it at the last minute, but if you are averse to acidity, squeeze and let it sit.

TASTING: **Something's Fishy**

To some, anchovies are those "stinky little fish" that adorn (or curse) the tops of pizzas. But to us, those little fish are a pantry mainstay, invaluable to the flavor of many sauces. But are all anchovies the same?

All preserved anchovies—small silver-skinned fish usually caught in warm Mediterranean waters—have been cured in salt, but they come to the market in two forms, packed in olive oil (we've all seen those flat, little tins) or in salt. The salt-packed variety are the least processed, having only their heads and some entrails removed, leaving the filleting and rinsing to the home cook. Oil-packed anchovies have been filleted at the factory and are ready-to-use. We purchased four brands of oil-packed anchovies—Ortiz (from Spain), Pastene and Flott (from Morocco), and Rustichella D'Abruzzo (from Italy)—along with Flott salt-packed anchovies (from Italy). An anchovy paste made by Flott was included in the tasting as well.

We tasted the anchovies in our Caesar dressing and straight up (yes, I said straight up). We found that the Spanish (Ortiz) fishies were the favorite for their salty and pleasantly fishy flavor as well as for their firm and "meaty" texture. The salt-packed Flott anchovies took second place and were well liked for their clean flavor and "solid" texture, while the Rustichella D'Abruzzo were found to be a bit more "harsh" and more salty. The two brands from Morocco fell to last place. Both were disliked for their "mushy" texture and "flat" flavor. As for the anchovy paste, let's see . . . "vile," "heinous," "gritty, bony, and salty." Well, you be the judge.

Although food snobs may insist that salt-packed anchovies are the only way to go, our tasters found that the right oil-packed anchovies can be just as good.

1st PLACE
ORTIZ Oil Packed

2nd PLACE
FLOTT Salt Packed

3rd PLACE
RUSTICHELLA D'ABRUZZO
Oil Packed

4th PLACE
PASTENE Oil Packed

5th PLACE
FLOTT Oil Packed

6th PLACE
FLOTT Paste

On the Road to Paris

Can coquilles St. Jacques taste just as good in Skokie as in Paris? Two chefs offer the promise of real French cooking in American kitchens. BY CHRISTOPHER KIMBALL

 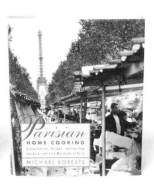

My favorite Paris bistro is Chez George. It's narrow and crowded, has a limited menu, and everyone smokes. On my last trip I had a mixed green salad, *steak de canard* served with lentils, and fresh mixed berries with whipped cream, all topped off with an espresso and a bill that didn't make me wish I had bought a Renault instead. I have tried to reproduce this meal at home, but the salad is always lackluster, the lentils tasteless, the duck second-rate, the berries better looking than tasting, and the whipped cream flavorless relative to what you get in France—that is, about as exciting as the Weather Channel. So when Patricia Wells, a resident Parisian for 20 years, and Michael Roberts, a frequent visitor, offered to solve the longstanding problems of translating modern French food into the American vernacular, we were all ears.

THE PARIS COOKBOOK
Patricia Wells
HarperCollins, 320 pages, $30

Patricia Wells knows the culinary side of Paris better than any American alive and has put that information to good use in her food lover's guides to France and Paris. *The Paris Cookbook* (2001) is, on the face of it, another brilliant idea. Select the best, most adaptable recipes from the most beloved restaurants in Paris, and whip them into shape for an American audience. One might wonder if this project is doomed to failure given the shortcomings of the ingredients on our side of the Atlantic. Still, even reasonable facsimiles of great Parisian recipes would be more than welcome.

PROS: This book is nicely designed, including the cover, which manages to use the tired image of the Eiffel Tower in a fresh, appealing manner. Each recipe is attributed to a restaurant, which is listed along with its address, phone and fax numbers, and Métro stop. Wells has done a great service by including recipes from wine bars, bistros, cafés, and, yes, even the famed Taillevent, a mix that is extremely appealing.

CONS: The recipes sound interesting, but once you get into the kitchen the results are decidedly mixed. Part of the problem is that the recipes often needed better editing. We wondered if 2 tablespoons of salt should have been 2 teaspoons, plodded through instructions that could have been more concise (and precise), and found some techniques that produced lackluster results. We also felt that some of the recipes ran to alarming excess, such as when Wells instructs the cook to boil pasta in 3 quarts of milk and then to throw out the milk! Likewise, a chicken fricassee calls for $20 worth of morels, 2 cups of wine, and a cup of cream without delivering the rich, satisfying sauce we expected. To be fair, however, if you choose carefully, Wells delivers quite a few authentic, first-class recipes.

RECIPE TESTING: The good news is that 10 of the 17 recipes we tested were worth a second shot and a handful were spectacular, the sort of recipes that belong in the home cook's repertoire. In this latter category were Gallopin's Green Bean, Mushroom, and Hazelnut Salad; Penne with Mustard and Chives; and La Cagouille's Sea Scallops with Warm Vinaigrette—all simple and delicious, reflecting the essence of good Parisian cooking. Unfortunately, many recipes did not reach these high standards. With a bit of editing, some turned out good food such as Chez Henri's Sautéed Potatoes, which needed to cook much longer than indicated, and Frédéric Anton's Twice-Cooked Mushrooms, which would have been just fine if sautéed only once. Other recipes were problematic. Benoît Guichard's Macaroni Gratin (in which one boils penne in milk and then discards the milk) produced undercooked pasta. Flora's Polenta Fries tasted great but stuck to the bottom of the pan. Brasserie Balzar's Midnight Onion Soup was bland at best. Les Bookinistes's Fresh Cod Brandade used a whopping 2 tablespoons of salt, which made it virtually inedible. And Flora's Spicy Spareribs were covered with foil as they baked, which made the sauce watery tasting.

PARISIAN HOME COOKING
Michael Roberts
Morrow, 335 pages, $25

Michael Roberts, one of the founding fathers of California cuisine (for many years he was the chef at Trumps restaurant in Los Angeles), turned his literary guns on friends and merchants who often cook in small, poorly equipped Parisian apartments. This voyeuristic adventure promises simplicity, full flavor, and a bit of armchair traveling as well, as you are invited into the homes of real Parisians, a rare treat indeed. *Parisian Home Cooking* (1999) is nicely designed, containing casual black-and-white shots of markets and economy kitchens (you know, the ones without $25,000 granite countertops and $15,000 stoves). Hey, if Parisians can turn out great food in tiny kitchens, so can we!

PROS: The idea behind this book is enormously appealing, since few authors have written about what real Parisians cook at home. The recipes sound simple, look simple, and have that special French touch: poached eggs for dinner, a broccoli rabe gratin, Roquefort sauce over steak. Perhaps Roberts will uncover a bit of that French magic and make it accessible to the rest of us.

CONS: Although they looked great and seemed simple enough in print, many of the recipes gave us trouble in the kitchen. Baking and cooking times were frequently off, a mushroom loaf collapsed when unmolded, pastry dough was hard to roll out, and many directions were confusing. (Why call for a heavy-lidded skillet if you don't cook with the lid on?) The recipes needed more testing.

RECIPE TESTING: We tested 15 recipes but found only seven worth making again. The two big winners were Sauerkraut and Brussels Sprout Soup and Fennel and Onions Baked with Vermouth. Both were simple and spectacular. Pan-Roasted Turkey Breast with Onion Marmalade was good, although the skin was on the soggy side; Beef Tenderloin Steaks with Roquefort Sauce were rich but delicious; a chicken pan-fried in butter was fine, although the sauce was lackluster; and the Leek and Potato Soup was simple enough and satisfying. The Chestnut Cake and the Pot-Roasted Turkey Thighs, Endive, and Mushrooms needed a kitchen doctor who makes house calls. Several other recipes were fine as far as they went but not worth adding to the home cook's repertoire.

Most of the ingredients and materials necessary for the recipes in this issue are available at your local supermarket, gourmet store, or kitchen supply shop. The following are mail-order sources for particular items. Prices listed below were current at press time and do not include shipping or handling unless otherwise indicated. We suggest that you contact companies directly to confirm up-to-date prices and availability.

Charcoal Grills

The New Braunfels Smoker Company Santa Fe grill, model #01308725, was the winner of our grill test on page 28, largely because of its ample grilling surface and adjustable charcoal rack. Other helpful features include a charcoal filler drawer that makes for easy refilling of the charcoal rack while grilling and wood-slatted shelves on both sides for holding grilling paraphernalia. The grill is $99 and widely available in hardware and discount stores, including **Home Depot, Kmart, Lowe's, Sears, Target,** and **Wal-Mart.** To find the dealer nearest you, contact the **New Braunfels Smoker Company** directly at **800-232-3398.**

Blenders

Used by coffee and juice bars to concoct frothy, aerated beverages, the Vita-Mix blender (page 21) is in a league of its own, with a price tag to match. In addition to working wonders on smoothies, it can make peanut butter, soft-serve yogurt, and fondue. The Vita-Mix 5000 is available for $399 with both a "classic white" base, item #1203, and a "classic black" base, item #1204, directly from the **Vita-Mix Corporation, Household Division (8615 Usher Road, Cleveland, OH 44138; 800-848-2649; www.vita-mix.com).**

The Oster 12-Speed Glass Blender, the winner of our May/June 2000 blender testing, showed off its merits again during recipe development for fruit smoothies (page 20). Its high-speed blade and easy-to-operate controls made quick work of all of the smoothies we tried. The Oster, item #630038, is available for $39.99 from **Kitchen Etc. (32 Industrial Drive, Exeter, NH 03833; 800-232-4070; www.kitchenetc.com).**

Boning Knives

Price is not everything when it comes to knives. We tested six boning knives, varying in price from $9 to $71, and found that an $18 knife outperformed the rest of the field. The Forschner "Fibrox" boning knife was the testers' favorite for its sure grip, ergonomic handle, well-designed blade, and keen edge. The Forschner 6-inch flexible boning knife, item #WFV112, is available for $17.90 from **Professional Cutlery Direct (242 Branford Road, North Branford, CT 06471; 800-859-6994; www.cutlery.com).** The other top-scoring knives are also available from Professional Cutlery Direct. The Wüsthof-Trident Grand Prix (5-inch blade), item #WWU208, is $54, and the Henckels Professional S (5½-inch blade), item #WHNPS6BF, is $49.99.

Coffee Beans

While all of the French roast coffees in our tasting (see page 26) are available in supermarkets nationwide, in some parts of the East Coast, **Don Francisco** can be hard to find. If your local market doesn't carry it, you can order directly from the company at **www.don-francisco.com** or **800-697-5282.** The whole-bean French roast is available in 12-ounce bags for $6.60 and 5-pound bags for $34.50.

Coffee Gear

To grind coffee for our tasting, we relied on the Capresso coffee grinder, winner of our test of inexpensive coffee grinders (see the November/December 2001 issue). The Capresso Coffee Grinder, item #23385, is available for $19.95 from **Sur La Table (1765 Sixth Avenue, Seattle, WA 98134-1608; 800-243-0852; www.surlatable.com).**

To brew coffee, we turned to the winner of our test of six coffee makers (see the November/December 1998 issue). With such features as electronic timing and a built-in water filter, the Krups ProAroma 12 Time with NaturActiv filter, model 453, consistently produced the best-tasting cup of coffee. It is also available at **Sur La Table** in white, item #25006, and black, item #25007, for $99.99.

Tongs

Tongs can be your best friend in the kitchen. From flipping meat on the grill and turning sautéing vegetables to stirring pasta, they do it all. For frying taco shells, they keep your hands a safe distance from the perils of hot oil. While they are available in a variety of lengths, we prefer 12-inch tongs for all-purpose kitchen use. The test kitchen is stocked with heavy-duty, stainless steel tongs made by Amco, item #573445. They are available for $6.50 from **Kitchen Etc.**

Chili Powder

Chili powder gives the meat filling for tacos much of its distinctive flavor. In our September/October 2000 chili powder tasting, Spice Island Chili Powder won tasters' accolades as the best of the bunch. Its "big flavor" stood out compared with the others, and tasters liked its "smoky character" and "lingering heat." While it is available in most supermarkets on the West Coast, it can be harder to find in the East, although some Kmart stores across the country do carry it. To find out if a store near you carries the chili powder, call **Kmart** at **800-635-6278.** Spice Islands Chili Powder can also be mail-ordered from **Edge Distributing** at **800-373-3726.** The chili powder is available only in cases of six 2.4-ounce jars for $23.77. El Paso Chile Company's Chili Spices and Fixin's Powder finished on the heels of Spice Island. Tasters found it "deep yet sweet and complex—slightly smoky." You can order a pack of two ½-ounce pouches for $2.95, item #FECSP01, from **El Paso Chile Company (909 Texas Avenue, El Paso, TX 79901; 800-274-7468; www.elpasochile.com).**

Andouille Sausage

While many supermarkets carry at least one brand of andouille, the highly seasoned pork sausage that gives jambalaya its robust kick, not all andouille are created equal. In a side-by-side comparison (see page 11), we found that these sausages vary greatly in flavor and texture from brand to brand. The tasters' favorite proved to be from Paul Prudhomme, the chef who has done more than anyone to popularize Cajun cooking. His sausage has a balanced flavor and bracing spiciness. Twelve-ounce packages can be ordered for $4.70 each, with a minimum of five packages per order, from **Chef Paul's Magic Seasonings (P.O. Box 23342, New Orleans, LA 70183-0342; 800-457-2857; www.chefpaul.com).** The sausage is available in both regular, item #R12, and hot, item #H12.

Nonstick Cake Pans

A nonstick cake pan made unmolding the gooey cinnamon buns on page 23 a snap. The caramelized sugar, usually stubbornly sticky, slid right from the pan. The Ekco Baker's Secret nonstick round cake pan, which costs a mere $4, took top honors in our cake pan testing (see the November/December 1999 issue), squeaking past the $80 All-Clad Bonded Bakeware. The Ekco is made of tin-plated steel sealed with a nonstick surface, while the All-Clad consists of triple layers of aluminum with two outer layers of stainless steel bonded to a nonstick surface. Unlike any of the other pans tested, both the Ekco and the All-Clad have handles affixed to the sides, a handy feature that makes it easy to get the pans in and out of a hot oven and reduces the risk of marring batter or the fragile edges of freshly baked cakes—and sticky buns. To purchase the Ekco pan from the dealer nearest you, contact the manufacturer, **World Kitchen,** at **800-367-3526.** The All-Clad pan, product #24070, is available from **Sur La Table.**

RECIPES

May & June 2002

Charcoal-Grilled Pork Chop, 7

Beef Tacos with Home-Fried Shells, 9

PHOTOGRAPHY: CARL TREMBLAY

Stir-Fried Broccoli and Red Peppers with Peanut Sauce, 14

Chicken and Shrimp Jambalaya, 11

Cilantro-Lime Spinach Dip with Chipotle Chiles, 15

Chicken Caesar Salad, 13

Greek-Style Garlic-Lemon Potatoes, 19

Fruit Smoothies, 21

http://www.cooksillustrated.com

If you enjoy *Cook's Illustrated* magazine, you should visit our Web site. Simply log on at http://www.cooksillustrated.com. Although much of the information is free, database searches are for site subscribers only. *Cook's Illustrated* subscribers are offered a 20 percent discount.

Here are some of the things you can do on our site:

Search Our Recipes: We have a searchable database of all the recipes from *Cook's Illustrated*.

Search Tastings and Cookware Ratings: You will find all of our reviews (cookware, food, wine, cookbooks) plus new material created exclusively for the Web.

Find Your Favorite Quick Tips.

Check Your Subscription: Check the status of your subscription, pay a bill, or give a gift subscription online.

Visit Our Bookstore: You can purchase any of our cookbooks, hardbound annual editions of the magazine, or posters online.

Subscribe to *e-Notes*: Our free e-mail companion to the magazine offers cooking advice, test results, buying tips, and recipes about a single topic each month.

AMERICA'S TEST KITCHEN

Join the millions of cooks who watch our show, *America's Test Kitchen*, on public television each week. For more information, including recipes from the show and a schedule of program times in your area, visit http://www.americastestkitchen.com.

Individual Hot Fudge Pudding Cake, 25

Quick Cinnamon Buns with Buttermilk Icing, 23

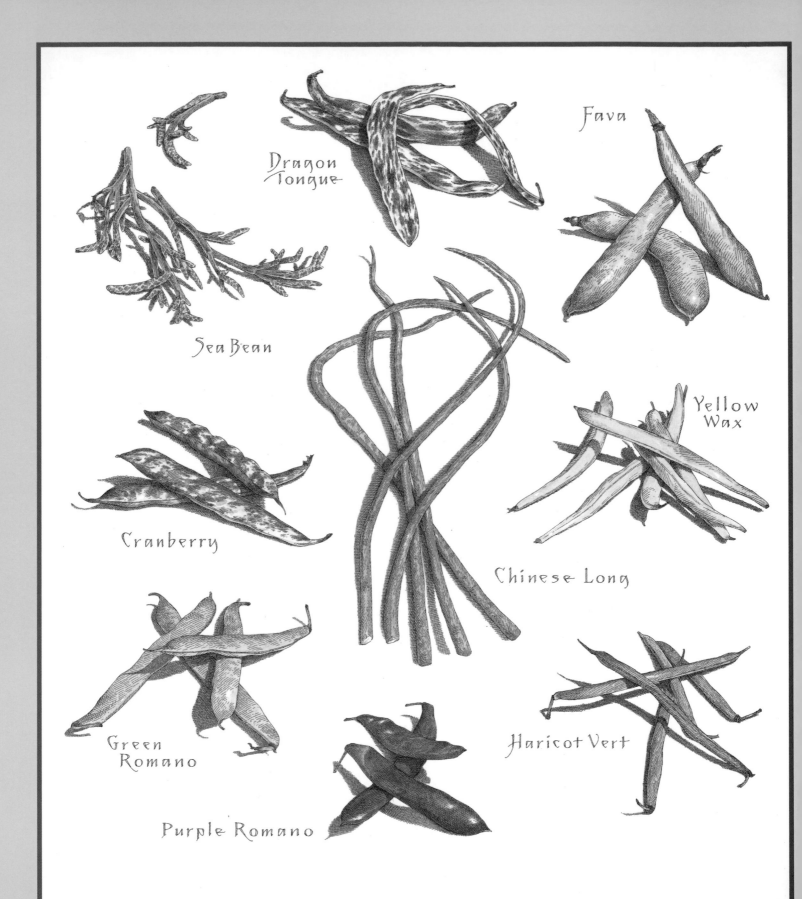

Dragon Tongue

Fava

Sea Bean

Yellow Wax

Cranberry

Chinese Long

Green Romano

Haricot Vert

Purple Romano

FRESH BEANS

NUMBER FIFTY-SEVEN

JULY & AUGUST 2002

Home of **AMERICA'S TEST KITCHEN**

COOK'S
ILLUSTRATED

Best Blueberry Cobbler

BBQ Ribs
Tender, Moist, and Smoky

Testing "Vegomatics"
Do Choppers/Shredders Really Work?

Nachos Done Right

Tuscan Grilled Steak
Transform a T-Bone with
Lemon and Olive Oil

Buttermilk Coleslaw
Pickle-Crisp and Creamy

Rating Tortilla Chips
Doritos Beats Boutique Brands

Ice Cream Sandwiches
New Quick Method

Leafy Salads 101
Spice Rubs for Chicken
Pad Thai at Home
French Potato Salad
Better Salade Niçoise

www.cooksillustrated.com

$4.95 U.S./$6.95 CANADA

CONTENTS

July & August 2002

COOK'S
ILLUSTRATED

Home of America's Test Kitchen
www.cooksillustrated.com

PUBLISHER AND EDITOR
Christopher Kimball
EXECUTIVE EDITOR
Jack Bishop
SENIOR EDITORS
Dawn Yanagihara
Adam Ried
EDITORIAL MANAGER
Barbara Bourassa
ART DIRECTOR
Amy Klee
TEST KITCHEN DIRECTOR
Erin McMurrer
SENIOR WRITERS
Bridget Lancaster
Sally Sampson
ASSOCIATE EDITOR
Julia Collin
COPY EDITOR
India Koopman
MANAGING EDITOR,
BOOKS AND WEB SITE
Rebecca Hays
TEST COOKS
Shannon Blaisdell
Matthew Card
Meg Suzuki
CONTRIBUTING EDITOR
Elizabeth Germain
CONSULTING EDITORS
Shirley Corriher
Jasper White
Robert L. Wolke
KITCHEN ASSISTANT
Rochelle Rashotsky
TEST KITCHEN INTERNS
Rajeev Samantrai
Merrill Stubbs
Nina West
ASSISTANT TO THE PUBLISHER
Samantha Selvakumar
PROOFREADER
Jana Branch
FACT CHECKER
Amanda Read
VICE PRESIDENT MARKETING
David Mack
RETAIL SALES MANAGER
Jason Geller
CIRCULATION RETAIL SALES MANAGER
Jonathan Venier
SALES REPRESENTATIVE
Shekinah Cohn
MARKETING ASSISTANT
Connie Forbes
CIRCULATION MANAGER
Larisa Greiner
PRODUCTS MANAGER
Steven Browall
DIRECT MAIL MANAGER
Robert Lee
CUSTOMER SERVICE MANAGER
Jacqueline Valerio
CUSTOMER SERVICE REPRESENTATIVE
Kate Caccamo
VICE PRESIDENT OPERATIONS
AND TECHNOLOGY
James McCormack
PRODUCTION MANAGER
Jessica Quirk
PRODUCTION COORDINATOR
Mary Connelly
PRODUCTION ASSISTANTS
Ron Bilodeau
Jennifer McCreary
PRODUCTION INTERNS
Mike Haggerty
Sarah Lorimer
SYSTEMS ADMINISTRATOR
Richard Cassidy
WEBMASTER
Nicole Morris
CHIEF FINANCIAL OFFICER
Sharyn Chabot
CONTROLLER
Mandy Shito
OFFICE MANAGER
Juliet Nusbaum
RECEPTIONIST
Henrietta Murray
PUBLICITY
Deborah Broide

For list rental information, contact The SpecialLISTS, 1200 Harbor
Blvd. 9th Floor, Weehawken, NJ 07087, 201-865-5800, fax 201-
867-2450. Editorial office: 17 Station Street, Brookline, MA
02445, 617-232-1000; fax 617-232-1572. Editorial contributions
should be sent to: Editor, *Cook's Illustrated*. We cannot assume
responsibility for manuscripts submitted to us. Submissions will be
returned only if accompanied by a large self-addressed envelope.
Postmaster: Send all new orders, subscription inquiries, and change
of address notices to: *Cook's Illustrated*, P.O. Box 7446, Red
Oak, IA 51591-0446. PRINTED IN THE USA.

PEACHES AND
NECTARINES

PEACHES AND NECTARINES Peaches have thin, velvety skin of various yellow hues, some with
crimson accents that, contrary to popular opinion, are not a mark of ripeness but of genetics. The
smooth-skinned nectarine is descended from the downy peach. While peaches and nectarines are
generally yellow-fleshed (as are the Halford Cling and Elberta peaches and the Flamekist nectarine) or white-fleshed (the Babcock peach and the Arctic Rose nectarine), a few varieties have
red flesh (as does the Indian Blood peach) or even flesh with a tinge of green (the Honeydew nectarine). Yellow Saturn peaches have a distinctively compressed shape, a flavor that is sweet and
mild, and a texture that is tender, almost melting. All nectarines and most peaches are freestones,
meaning that the pits are easily removed. Clingstone peaches, such as the Halford, are used for
canning because the pits are best removed by machine.

COVER (*Cherries*): ELIZABETH BRANDON, BACK COVER (*Peaches and Nectarines*): JOHN BURGOYNE

REAL VERMONTERS DON'T WEAR SUNGLASSES

Real Vermonters don't wear sunglasses, because sunglasses are as frivolous as answering machines, front doors that lock, and radar detectors. Real Vermonters don't walk in the woods without a gun, they don't own pets they can't eat (except for hunting dogs and cows), and they never buy a new hat—they get them for free at Agway, Grimm, or the local mill. They never use fireplaces (lose too much heat), cell phones, or Kleenex, and I've never seen a real Vermonter pass a car, chew gum, or wear a ski parka. Old-time Vermonters wear pants of only one color (green) and think that watching sap boil is pretty good entertainment (sugaring is on a par with NASCAR). If you ask a Vermonter to tell you a story, he won't say a word, but if you tell him one of your own, you'll be in for an earful. The last president real Vermonters think was worth a damn was native son Calvin Coolidge, and they tell plenty of stories about old Cal.

Real Vermonters chew Skoal and eat Slim Jims, luncheon meats, and potatoes any way you can cook them. They are perfectly happy with any sort of meat on the dinner plate, including squirrel, rabbit, woodchuck, moose, venison, even bear. (A dinner plate without meat is like a shotgun without shells.) The only kind of pasta salad they've eaten is macaroni. Dinner is served at noon; supper is what you eat after work.

Real Vermonters just show up when you need help, like when your pickup is axle-deep in March mud or when the beefer gets loose and heads down the valley. They'll pull out your truck, find your cattle, fix your evaporator, restart your furnace, plow your snow, or chainsaw your dead tree for free. If you offer to pay them, they won't speak to you for a month. If you build a new house and hire help from the next town, they won't speak to you for a year.

Vermonters complain about taxes, weather, hunting, sap, local politics, taxes, neighbors, and taxes. Not too long ago, the state had more deer, better snow cover, fewer real estate agents, and lower taxes. Real Vermonters know that the world is getting smaller because there are more No Hunting signs. One leaves town only to check out a horse, attend a farm auction, or get a tractor fixed. Someone who moves to the next town might as well have left for Afghanistan. They are spoken of in the past tense.

For entertainment, real Vermonters go visiting. They'll drop in and watch you eat your supper (they eat early), muck your barn, or clean your gun. Although real Vermonters drink only Nestea and Country Time Lemonade, most younger Vermonters will, if offered, take a beer or two. The brands of choice are Genny (Gennessee) and Pabst, and, in hard times, their purchases are made one can at a time. Foster's "Oil Cans" (the 24½-ounce variety) are reserved for special occasions such as weddings, sugaring season, or the day your son gets his first deer.

Some Vermonters still go to church, but they don't sing much; they don't like standing out from the crowd. The collection plate is viewed with as much enthusiasm as a federal tax, yet when any members of the congregation need help, Vermonters will cook for them, drive them to the clinic, feed their chickens, and help with the haying. Vermonters were born to volunteer as long as it's their idea. Trying to organize a bunch of Vermonters is like trying to herd pigs.

Vermonters shop at Price Chopper, NAPA

Christopher Kimball

Auto Parts, and the state liquor store. They prefer to barter rather than pay cash, but they prefer cash to credit cards. They don't drink coffee with funny flavors like hazelnut, and they'd rather be found standing stark naked on Main Street than caught sipping a cappuccino. Any Vermont man would give one arm and his best rabbit dog to spend an evening with Reba McEntire. Real Vermonters fish with worms, not flies, and they don't understand the point of "catch and release." They fish for meat.

Real Vermonters don't read newspapers, unless you count the *Vermont News Guide* and the *Auto Hunter*. Vermonters don't talk about national politics or sex, the first being irrelevant and the latter infrequent. Ask a Vermonter about a "race" and he thinks you are talking about four wheels and an internal combustion engine. Vermonters don't take vacations, because they don't wear bathing suits, travel in groups, or go anyplace where they can't be useful.

Most of all, Vermonters still remember how this country got built in the first place. They can diskharrow a field, change a clutch, pour a foundation, use a crockpot, drive a backhoe, patch a spare, mend a fence, and dress out a six-pointer. When the rest of us have used up our last shreds of dignity and common sense, I know of a small state that will still have a generous supply of both. You can see it every time you look into the eyes of a Vermonter. After all, real Vermonters don't wear sunglasses.

➤ *My apologies to Calvin Coolidge for paraphrasing his speech "Vermont Is a State I Love."*

FOR MORE INFORMATION

www.cooksillustrated.com

At the *Cook's Illustrated* Web site you can order a book, give a gift subscription to *Cook's Illustrated* magazine, sign up for our free e-newsletter, subscribe to the magazine, or check the status of your subscription. Join the Web site and you'll have access to our searchable databases of recipes, cookware ratings, ingredient tastings, quick tips, cookbook reviews, and more.

COOK'S ILLUSTRATED Magazine

Cook's Illustrated (ISSN 1068-2821) magazine is published bimonthly (6 issues per year) by Boston Common Press Limited Partnership, 17 Station Street, Brookline, MA 02445. Copyright 2002 Boston Common Press Limited Partnership. Periodical postage paid at Boston, Mass., and additional mailing offices, USPS #012487.

A one-year subscription is $29.70, two years is $55, and three years is $75. Add $6 postage per year for Canadian subscriptions and $12 per year for all other countries outside the U.S. To order subscriptions in the U.S. call 800-526-8442. Gift subscriptions are available for $24.95 each. Postmaster: Send all new orders, subscription inquiries, and change-of-address notices to *Cook's*

Illustrated, P.O. Box 7446, Red Oak, IA 51591-0446, or call 800-526-8442 inside the U.S. and 515-247-7571 outside the U.S.

COOKBOOKS

You can order the following books, as well as *The America's Test Kitchen Cookbook*, by calling 800-611-0759 inside the U.S. and 515-246-6911 outside the U.S.

➤ **The Best Recipe Series** Includes *The Best Recipe* as well as *Grilling & Barbecue, Soups & Stews*, and *American Classics*.

➤ **The How to Cook Master Series** A collection of 25 single-subject cookbooks.

➤ **The Annual Series** Annual hardbound editions of the magazine as well as a nine-year (1993–2001) reference index.

AMERICA'S TEST KITCHEN Television Show

Look for our television series on public television. Visit http://www.americastestkitchen.com for program times in your area, recipes, and details about the shows, or to order the companion book to the second series, *The America's Test Kitchen Cookbook*.

What Is Self–Rising Flour?

I've noticed bags of "self-rising flour" on the same shelf with the usual 5-pound bags of all-purpose flour. What is self-rising flour, and what is it used for?

SANDY BAIRD
NEWTON, MASS.

☛ Self-rising flour is something we'd never used in the test kitchen until we came across the cookbooks reviewed in this issue (see page 31), two of which were published in the United Kingdom and one in Australia, and all of which contain recipes that call for self-rising flour (or, as those speaking the Queen's English call it, self-*raising* flour). In these countries, self-rising flour is apparently in wider use than it is in the United States. Still, self-rising flour is available here (it is popular in the South), and it has several distinguishing characteristics. It contains a leavener (baking powder, approximately 1½ teaspoons per cup) and salt (½ teaspoon per cup) and is made from a soft flour that brings it closer to cake flour than to all-purpose. Most all-purpose flour has a protein content of 10 to 11 percent, whereas self-rising flour and cake flour have protein contents of 8 to 9 percent. Less protein generally translates into more tender baked goods.

To find out how self-rising flour performs in the kitchen, we selected three recipes from the cookbooks reviewed in this issue. We also wanted to see how these three recipes would fare when made with substitutes that American home cooks are likely to have on hand: cake flour and all-purpose flour, plus the requisite amounts of baking powder and salt per cup of flour.

We first tried a cookie—Chocolate Almond Crunchies—from Delia Smith's *How to Cook* (DK Publishing, 2001). Packed with oats and nuts but just a modicum of flour, all three batches of these cookies baked up well. Those made with all-purpose were a little tougher to bite into than those made with the softer self-rising and cake flours, but, in terms of flavor, the cookies were pretty much the same.

Next up were No-Fuss Blueberry Muffins from Donna Hay's *Off the Shelf* (Morrow, 2001). Here, too, the texture of the muffins made with all-purpose flour was less tender than that of the other two batches.

Finally, we tried the three flours in a simple cake recipe unadulterated with nuts, oats, chocolate, or fruit. This recipe, called Victoria Sponge, is from Nigella Lawson's *How to Be a Domestic Goddess* (Hyperion, 2001). This time several tasters favored the cake made with cake flour: It was the most tender and had the finest crumb. The cake made with all-purpose flour was much less tender, while the cake made with self-rising flour was slightly less tender.

Why do flour millers like King Arthur and Gold Medal bother to make self-rising flour? One reason is that self-rising flour, because of its fairly low protein content, makes baked goods (especially cakes, muffins, and biscuits) that are more tender than those made with all-purpose flour. However, cake flour offers the same advantage (it did even better than self-rising flour in our cake test), and it is more widely available. Yes, with cake flour you need to measure out baking powder and salt yourself, but the "convenience" of self-rising flour seems pretty minor. Therefore, we recommend using cake flour in recipes that call for self-rising flour and just adding the baking powder and salt yourself. The generally agreed upon formula is 1½ teaspoons baking powder and ½ teaspoon salt for every cup of flour, which worked in the three recipes we tested.

Open and Closed Crumbs

I've seen articles on baking that mention the desirability of a "closed crumb" versus an "open crumb." What, exactly, are bakers talking about when they talk about "crumb"?

EDITH CARLSON
BANGOR, MAINE

BRIOCHE
A closed crumb

SOURDOUGH BREAD
An open crumb

☛ Bakers use the terms *closed* (or *tight*) and *open* (or *loose*) to describe the texture of a baked good, often in reference to its aeration, or the relative size and concentration of the air pockets. A comparison to knitting isn't a bad one. A very tightly knit sweater with small stitches that lets little air through (and so keeps you warm) would be comparable to a pound cake or the piece of brioche shown here. A shawl with a very open pattern would be comparable to the open crumb that's typical of an English muffin or the piece of sourdough bread shown here. Crumb is affected by nearly everything that goes into a cake or bread: the type of flour, the amount of yeast or chemical leavener, and the amount of liquid. In general, tenderness is characteristic of a fine, tight crumb, while chewiness goes along with the open crumb of artisan breads such as sourdough.

Making Crème Fraîche at Home

Occasionally a recipe calls for crème fraîche. What's the best substitute if I can't find the real thing?

FRANK MACALUSO
MIAMI, FLA.

☛ We searched cookbooks and the Internet for a formula that would approximate the silky smooth, almost cream-cheesey texture, and rich, faintly sour yet slightly sweet and nutty taste of the authentic crème fraîche some editors and test cooks have sampled in France. The traditional way of making crème fraîche in France is simply to let heavy cream sit out at room temperature while the lactic bacteria inherent to cream do their job of thickening it and blooming its flavor.

Most of the recipes we found called for adding a small amount of cultured dairy product (usually 1 tablespoon buttermilk or sour cream, occasionally yogurt) to the heavy cream (1 cup) to speed things up some. But we still would have to wait—at least 12 hours, probably more like 24, or better still, according to some recipes, even 36 to 48 hours. A couple of recipes also suggested heating the mixture—to anywhere from 80 to 100 degrees—to speed things up a bit more. We also came across a couple of recipes that involved no waiting at all: Just mix and eat. One called for equal parts heavy cream and sour cream, blended with a whisk, the other for 3 parts heavy cream and 1 part sour cream, whipped to soft peaks.

The first thing we learned was that heating the mixtures of buttermilk, sour cream, or yogurt and cream wasn't helpful. The three samples that we heated (to 90 degrees) never thickened as much as the unheated mixtures merely set out at room temperature (about 72 degrees). All three of these room-temperature mixtures thickened to the consistency of sour cream in 24 hours. The flavor of the cream mixed with yogurt was unpalatable—harshly sour. Tasters rejected it immediately. The mixture made with sour cream was less sour but still a bit too strong. The mixture with buttermilk was preferred by most tasters, who liked its cleaner, milder flavor.

What about the two "mix and eat" recipes? While a couple of tasters thought the whipped heavy and sour cream might make a nice dessert topping, it was really not at all like crème fraîche. The half sour cream/half heavy cream mixture came closer to crème fraîche, but not as close as the mixture with buttermilk that had been allowed to sit at room temperature for a day. All of that said, when tasters were presented with "real" crème fraîche, one from a company in Vermont, the other from France, each and every one preferred them over all of the homemade versions.

Our conclusion? If you can't find crème fraîche and have at least 24 hours before you plan to use it, the best approximation of the real thing is a mix of 1 tablespoon buttermilk and 1 cup heavy cream. If you can't wait a day and want to serve something milder and sweeter than sour cream but more tangy than whipped cream, then try the formula of 1 part sour cream and 1 part heavy cream; letting it sit out for even an hour or two helps to thicken the mixture and meld the flavors.

We found that in each of these cases, pasteurized heavy cream with a high milk fat content (40 percent, or 6 grams of fat per tablespoon of cream) outdoes ultrapasteurized heavy cream with a slightly lower milk fat content (36 percent, about 5 grams per tablespoon). The former made for a more lush and silky texture as well as a richer flavor.

The buttermilk/heavy cream version of crème fraîche can be refrigerated after sitting at room temperature for 24 hours or so (although we found that leaving the mixture out, covered, over the weekend, further developed the flavor). Once refrigerated, the crème fraîche will thicken still further. It can be kept refrigerated for about two weeks.

"Must Have" Pots and Pans

I can get a better deal buying a boxed set of cookware than I can the individual pieces you recommend in your equipment ratings, but I'm not sure if the pots and pans in the set are really what I need. What would you recommend as a good base for a pot and pan collection?

TED BRUCKER
DENVER, COLO.

➤ You're right to be suspicious about buying cookware sets. They often contain some pans that are not terribly useful. You may think you are saving money by buying a boxed set, but if you don't use some of the pots in the set and then need to go out and buy extra pieces to cover basic needs, you will spend more money in the long run.

What pots and pans are really essential? To answer your question, we asked our test cooks and editors which pots and pans they would choose to have in their home kitchen if they could have only four. On almost everyone's list was a nonstick skillet, which can be used for everything from frying or scrambling eggs to making omelets and hash browns or sautéing fish. An ovensafe nonstick pan (with a heat-resistant handle) can also be used to make frittatas or other dishes that must go from the stovetop to the oven or broiler. A 10-inch pan is the most useful size.

Our test cooks and editors believe that a 12-inch ovensafe conventional skillet is also essential. We use this pan to sauté foods that we want to brown, such as chicken cutlets and steaks. Crucial to the development of a flavorful sauce is the creation of *fond*, the brown bits of caramelized food that stick to the pan during cooking; a nonstick skillet by its very nature inhibits the development of fond and tends to produce less flavorful sauces. A large conventional skillet can also be used to make quick tomato sauces.

The next most popular items were a Dutch oven, traditionally used for braises and stews but also handy for deep-frying, and a saucepan, which can be used to cook everything from rice to potatoes to spinach to chocolate sauce. Choose a Dutch oven that is at least 6 quarts and preferably 8 quarts. Given just one saucepan, most of our test cooks and editors settled on a 3- or 4-quart size. A few soup makers insisted on having their stockpot for making chicken, beef, vegetable, and fish stocks. Note that most soup recipes, however, can be prepared in a large Dutch oven, and this pot is much more versatile than a stockpot.

Just about everyone in the test kitchen agreed that you should focus on durable, high-quality albeit expensive pans. You may pay a lot for such a pan, but you will pay only once, and you'll get a lifetime's worth of very good cooking out of it.

Do Lemon Juice and Whipped Cream Mix?

I've read that a few drops of lemon juice added to cream before whipping can prolong the life of the whipped cream. Does it work?

KELLIE DEJON
CAMBRIDGE, MASS.

➤ We've come across this theory before and so decided to test it by adding 5 drops of lemon juice—about 1/16 teaspoon, the usual amount suggested—to 1 cup of heavy cream before whipping it. The cream whipped up nicely to stiff peaks that stood up to those in a bowl of cream whipped without lemon juice. In fact, the lemon juice may have added stiffness and body to the cream by coagulating some of its protein (casein) to form solid curds. The citric acid in lemon juice is surprisingly strong, and even at 5 drops of juice per cup, the acidity (according to the food scientist we spoke with) is more than enough to coagulate casein.

But the lemon-whipped cream didn't stand the test of time. If anything, it deteriorated more quickly. In this and past tests we've found that heavy cream will maintain its whip for about 24 hours. At 24 hours, the cream with lemon juice showed more seepage of liquid. This can be attributed to the fact that proteins have a stabilizing effect on foams by reinforcing the walls around the pockets of trapped air. Because the lemon-treated cream contained less free protein, it broke down more quickly than the cream without lemon juice.

WHAT IS IT?

I purchased this mold at an antique store and am at a loss as to just what one would use it for.

MRS. K. KEITH
CEDARBURG, WIS.

➤ What you've found is a mold for a *bombe glacée*, or simply bombe. While the elliptical, creased football shape of your mold is now typical of this frozen dessert, earlier molds were smooth and spherical in shape and so were named after old-style bombs. The date of the original bombe is hard to pinpoint, but this dessert is listed in *The Complete Guide to the Art of Modern Cookery*, published in 1903 by French chef Auguste Escoffier. These traditional bombes were layered desserts made from ice cream and "a bombe mixture," a mousse- or custard-like preparation usually flavored with syrups and liqueurs. The outer layer of ice cream, usually vanilla, is spread evenly and thinly—perhaps 1/2 inch or so in depth—around the inside of the mold and frozen. Once the ice cream has hardened, the mold is removed from the freezer and the bombe mixture poured inside and filled to the rim. A sheet of paper (today wax or parchment paper) is placed over the filled mold and the lid secured on top. Once the entire dessert is frozen, it is unmolded—coaxed out of its shell by first dipping it in hot water or wrapping it briefly in a hot, wet towel—and inverted on a plate. When the finished dessert is sliced into, you can see the attractive effect of the layering.

While a stainless steel bowl can be used to prepare most bombes, an attractive melon-shaped mold of tinned steel with a 5-cup capacity, similar to that pictured, can be ordered for $14.99 from Fante's Kitchen Wares Shop at 1006 S. Ninth Street, Philadelphia, PA 19147-4798, 215-922-5557 or 800-44-FANTE. Go to http://fantes.com/ice_cream.htm#bombe to get to the listing for the bombe mold on Fante's Web site.

Quick Tips

Easy Decorations for Ice Cream Sandwiches

Though the homemade ice cream sandwiches on page 23 are extraordinary with no embellishment at all, it is fun and easy to dress them up a little. Spread sprinkles, toasted shredded coconut, toasted chopped nuts, or mini chocolate chips on a plate and dip the edges of the ice cream sandwiches into it. Press down firmly yet gently to make sure the decoration adheres to the ice cream.

Impromptu Basting Brush, Redux

In our July/August 2001 issue, John Abbattemateo of Pembroke, Mass., shared his tip for using a lettuce leaf to baste food on the grill with sauce when there's no brush on hand. Les Murray of Euless, Texas, uses a juiced lemon half. Spear a fork into the pointed end of the spent half-lemon, and use the cut side to apply the sauce to the food. Of course, this is even better when you have a lemony sauce.

More Kitchen Equipment Improvisations

Inspired by a collection of tips in the July/August 2001 issue for coping with a poorly equipped kitchen (such as you might find in a summer rental), several readers have offered new ideas.

A. When Shinei Tsukamoto of Walnut Creek, Calif., couldn't find a colander in the kitchen of his rental, he used a folding steamer basket. Just be sure to pour slowly and carefully because the sides are not as high as that of a regular colander.

B. Marcia O'Neil of Cedar Crest, N.M., could not find a citrus juicer or reamer in the kitchen where she was working. Desperate to squeeze several lemons for a dish, she picked up one of the beaters from a hand-held mixer and found it reamed the lemon halves beautifully.

C. Kerry Bittler of Portland, Ore., didn't have a splatter screen handy, so he came up with this solution. Cover the pan with an overturned wire mesh strainer of an appropriate diameter.

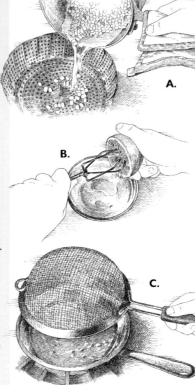

Quick and Easy Single Scoops of Ice Cream

Some home refrigerators freeze ice cream so hard that the ice cream has to sit on the counter to soften before it can be scooped. To children, especially, this can feel like a very long wait. Rather than making her small children wait when they want ice cream, Sarah Cushing of Hamburg, N.Y., uses this method to portion it out in advance.

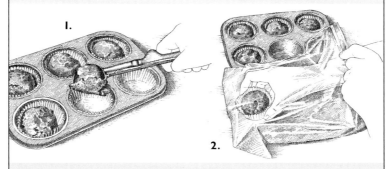

1. Scoop ice cream or frozen yogurt into a muffin tin lined with muffin papers, and then freeze.
2. Once frozen, the paper-lined portions can be stored in a plastic bag in the freezer for easy, ready-when-you-are servings. Just peel off the paper and place the ice cream in a bowl. This is also a great method for quickly firming up homemade ice cream, which is notoriously soft when it comes out of the machine.

Keep Dishes Spotless between Uses

Many home kitchen pantries, especially the oversized butler's pantries in older houses, feature open storage for platters and serving dishes. The downside of this system is that open shelves allow the dishes to get dusty between uses. But that's not a problem for Heather Seligman of Watertown, Mass., who keeps everything clean by wrapping the dishes tightly with plastic wrap before storing them.

Keeping Kitchen Utensils within Easy Reach

Inspired by the March/April 2002 tip to hang measuring spoons and other small utensils from a key rack so they will be easily accessible, Rose Kish of Beacon, N.Y., took the same notion a step further. This is her means of keeping both small and large utensils out of cluttered drawers and at the ready.

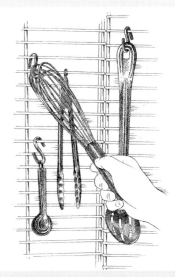

Mount a large piece of plastic-covered grating (available at home improvement and discount stores) on the wall in a convenient spot. Then simply use S-hooks to hang all kinds of kitchen utensils from it. If you would rather not mount the grate permanently, just set one edge on a counter and lean the grate against the wall. This way, it can be moved easily as the need arises.

Send Us Your Tip We will provide a complimentary one-year subscription for each tip we print. Send your tip, name, address, and daytime telephone number to Quick Tips, *Cook's Illustrated*, P.O. Box 470589, Brookline, MA 02447.

Handy Scissors for Clipping Summer Herbs

What a pleasure it is to have an herb garden to raid for summer cooking, and what a frustration it is when you forget to bring along your clipping scissors. Tired of trekking back into the house for her scissors, Jane Ashworth of Beavercreek, Ore., devised this trick to keep scissors handy in her garden all the time. Bend a wire coat hanger or heavy floral wire into the shape seen below, and stick it into the soil. Hang a small pair of inexpensive stainless steel scissors on it, and they'll be there whenever you are.

Nonstick Baking Sheet Liner Storage

Nonstick baking sheet liners are often stored flat. The problem is that other items often end up on top of them, making it difficult to retrieve one when you need it. Mary Ellen Johnson of Andover, Mass., has come up with an easy alternative storage method. She rolls each sheet liner tightly and stores it inside the tube from an empty paper towel roll. This cardboard tube protects the liner and ensures that it's always easy to get hold of. For liners of various sizes, just cut the cardboard tube to fit.

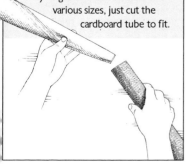

Grill-Marking Zucchini on Both Sides

Grill marks enhance both the appearance and the flavor of grilled vegetables. Typically when you grill zucchini, you halve them lengthwise, and the cut side of each half develops great grill marks while the skinned side does not. Gordon Brott of Camden, Maine, figured out a way to mark both sides.

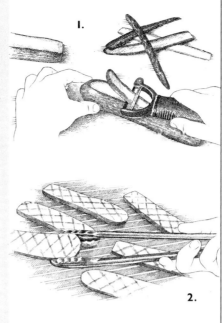

I. Cut a zucchini (or yellow summer squash) in half lengthwise and run a cheese plane or Y-shaped vegetable peeler over the skinned side a couple of times. This exposes some flesh and flattens the squash slightly for stability on the cooking grate.
2. The extra exposed flesh allows for grill marks on both sides of each squash half.

Protecting Cherished Recipes

To protect recipes from the splotches and splatters of usual kitchen duty, many cooks use plastic page protectors, available at office supply stores. Recently, Jeanette Frasca of Florence, Ore., and Elizabeth Zaring Davis of Wellston, Ohio, had to pinch-hit when they had no page protectors.

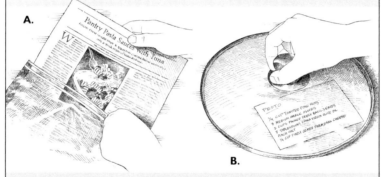

A. Zipper-lock bags serve the purpose admirably. Lay the zipper-lock bag flat on the counter, slide the sheet of paper right into it, and zip shut. Gallon-sized bags work nicely for 8½ by 11-inch sheets, while sandwich-sized bags work nicely for newspaper recipes mounted on index cards.

B. Clean, dry glass pot lids also do the job. Place the lid over the sheet of paper, or even over an open cookbook or magazine. The weight of the lid will keep it open.

Protecting Gas-Grill Controls

The ignition and burner control knobs on some gas grills can be persnickety if they get wet or dirty from exposure to the elements, especially if the grill is kept outdoors in the snow during the winter. Unable to find a cover for the entire grill, Tom Durkin of Victor, N.Y., came up with this impromptu solution. He inverts a disposable aluminum roasting pan over the control panel and tapes it in place on either end with duct or electrical tape.

Preventing Spice Rub Contamination

We geared our spice rub recipes for grilled chicken on page 20 to yield about a cup, so some will be left for the next session at the grill. To avoid contaminating the entire batch with raw food, portion out only as much spice rub as you'll need in a separate bowl, then seal and store the remaining spice rub. Now you can start rubbing the spices into the chicken.

Makeshift Sandwich Press

Toasted, pressed sandwiches such as croque monsieur, cubano, or grilled cheese with embellishments such as ham or roasted peppers take on a dense, luxurious texture and a deep, even crust when they are weighted in the pan or on the griddle. Typically, a heavy cast-iron sandwich press is used for this purpose, but most home cooks, of course, don't have a sandwich press handy. If you want to press a sandwich without the benefit of a true press, try this idea from Marc Healy of Chicago, Ill.

Fill your tea kettle with water and use it to weigh down the sandwiches as they cook. If you prefer, fill a saucepan with water and use it in the same manner. Remember to wipe the kettle or pan bottom before its next use.

Barbecued Baby Back Ribs

Ribs barbecued at home can be flavorless and dry. We wanted lots of smoky flavor and moist meat.

⇒ BY ERIN MCMURRER ⇐

On a hot summer's day, life doesn't get much better than devouring a big, juicy, smoky slab of spicy, mouth-watering ribs. But more often than not, baby back ribs cooked at home come out tasting like dry shoe leather on a bone. Given the expense (two slabs, enough to feed four people, run about $24) and time commitment (many recipes require half a day), bad ribs are a true culinary disaster. My goal was to produce flavorful, juicy, and tender ribs that would be well worth the time, money, and effort.

What Makes a Rib a Baby Back?

Purchasing pork ribs can be confusing. Some slabs are labeled "baby back ribs," while other, seemingly identical ribs are labeled "loin back ribs." After a bit of detective work, I learned that the only difference is weight. Both types of ribs are taken from the upper portion of a young hog's rib cage near the backbone (see the illustration below) and should have 11 to 13 bones. A slab (or rack) of loin back ribs generally comes from a larger pig and weighs more than 1¾ pounds; a slab of ribs weighing less is referred to as baby back ribs. (That being said, most restaurants don't follow this rule, using the term "baby back" no matter what they've got because it sounds better.) During testing, I came to prefer loin back ribs because they are meatier.

There is one other issue to consider. Beware of racks with bare bone peeking through the meat (along the center of the bones). This means that the butcher took off more meat than necessary, robbing you and your guests of full, meaty portions. Once you've purchased the ribs, there

Locating Baby Back Ribs

Baby back ribs (also referred to as loin back ribs) are cut from the section of the rib cage closest to the backbone (shaded dark in the drawing above). Lean center-cut roasts and chops come from the same part of the pig, which explains why baby back ribs can be expensive. Spareribs are cut closer to the belly of the pig, which is also where bacon comes from. Spareribs are larger and much fattier than baby back ribs.

Brining the ribs for just an hour keeps them moist as they cook over a low fire for four hours.

remains the question of whether the skin-like membrane located on the "bone side" of the ribs should be left on during cooking. One theory holds that it prevents smoke and spice from penetrating the meat, while some rib experts say that removing it robs the ribs of flavor and moistness. I found that the skin did not interfere with flavors; in fact, it helped to form a spicy, crispy crust.

Having a Good Smoke

Having worked in restaurant kitchens for many years, I have cooked hundreds of ribs indoors, in an oven, using low heat and slow cooking. In addition, the ribs were placed on a rack, over a sheet pan hold-

ing a shallow layer of water, and were tightly wrapped with foil to help keep them moist. These ribs were always tender, but they lacked smoky flavor. To get that flavor, I turned to outdoor grilling, but I was apprehensive about achieving the proper texture.

My first step was to research the range of grilling times and techniques offered by other recipes. Most cookbooks call for a total cooking time of 1½ to 3 hours. Some use a very hot grill, while others use a moderate grill. I tested all of these recipes and found the resulting ribs to be extremely tough. High-heat cooking was particularly troublesome, as it quickly dried out the meat. Ribs cooked over moderate heat for three hours were better, but they were still too tough.

I quickly reverted to the "low and slow" method from my restaurant days, this time substituting the dry heat of the grill for the moist heat of the oven. I built a two-level fire, in which only half of the grill is covered with charcoal, thinking it would be best to smoke the ribs indirectly—on the coal-less side of the grill—to prevent overcooking. (Two full racks of ribs fit on one side of a 22-inch grill.) To add flavor, I placed soaked wood chunks on the bed of coals and then put the cooking grate in place and laid down the spice-rubbed ribs. Finally, I put the grill cover in place, with the vent holes over the ribs to help draw heat and smoke past the meat, and turned my attention to cooking time and temperature.

I found that maintaining a temperature between 275 and 300 degrees for four hours produced ribs that were tasty and tender, with meat that fell off the bone. Decent ribs could be had in less time, but they weren't as tender as those cooked for a full four hours. It's easy to tell when the ribs are ready—the meat pulls away from the bone when the ribs are gently twisted.

The problem was that the dry heat of the grill produced ribs that were not as moist as those cooked in a steamy oven. My next test, then, was to cook the ribs halfway in an oven, using steam, and to finish them on the grill. These ribs were more moist, but now the problem was with the flavor; these ribs lacked the intense smokiness of those I had cooked entirely on the grill. Hoping to find another way to add moisture, I simmered the ribs in water for two hours. This robbed them of valuable pork flavor.

It then occurred to me that brining the ribs prior to cooking them might be the solution. I used our standard brining formula, which when applied to two 2-pound racks of ribs amounted to a two-hour immersion in 4 quarts of cold water mixed with 2 cups of kosher salt and 2 cups of sugar. This method produced, well, two very highly seasoned racks of ribs. Why? Ribs pack much more bone per pound than other cuts of meat, and all of the meat is right there on the exterior, so the brine doesn't have very far to go. I figured that a 2-pound rack of ribs must soak up the brine much more quickly than an equal-sized roast. I cut back the salt, sugar, and brining time by half, and the results were better, but the meat was still too sweet. I cut back the sugar by half once more, and this time the meat was both moist and perfectly seasoned.

These ribs were so good they didn't even need barbecue sauce! A quick rub with an easy-to-mix spice blend before going on the grill gave them just the right warm and savory touch.

BARBECUED BABY BACK RIBS FOR CHARCOAL GRILL
SERVES 4

For a potent spice flavor, brine and dry the ribs as directed, then coat them with the spice rub, wrap tightly in plastic, and refrigerate overnight before grilling. You will need two wood chunks, each about the size of a lemon, for this recipe.

Brine
- 1/2 cup table salt or 1 cup kosher salt
- 1/2 cup sugar
- 2 racks (about 2 pounds each) baby back or loin back ribs

Spice rub
- 1 tablespoon plus 1/2 teaspoon sweet paprika
- 1 1/2 teaspoons chili powder
- 1 3/4 teaspoons ground cumin
- 1 1/2 teaspoons dark brown sugar
- 3/4 teaspoon table salt or 1 1/2 teaspoons kosher salt
- 3/4 teaspoon dried oregano
- 3/4 teaspoon ground black pepper
- 1 teaspoon ground white pepper
- 1/2 teaspoon cayenne pepper

1. TO BRINE THE RIBS: Dissolve salt and sugar in 4 quarts cold water in stockpot or large plastic container. Submerge ribs in brine and refrigerate 1 hour until fully seasoned. Remove ribs from brine and thoroughly pat dry with paper towels.

2. While ribs are brining, cover two 3-inch wood chunks with water in medium bowl; soak wood chunks for 1 hour, then drain and set aside. Combine spice rub ingredients in small bowl. When ribs are out of brine and dried, rub each side of racks with 1 tablespoon spice rub; refrigerate racks 30 minutes.

3. TO BARBECUE THE RIBS: Open bottom vents on grill. Ignite about 4 1/2 quarts charcoal briquettes (3/4 large chimney-full, or about 65 briquettes) and burn until covered with thin coating of light gray ash, about 20 minutes. Empty coals onto one half of grill bottom, piling them 2 to 3 briquettes high; place soaked wood chunks on top of coals. Position cooking grate over coals, cover grill, open lid vents two-thirds of the way; heat grate 5 minutes, then scrape clean with wire brush.

4. Arrange ribs on cool side of grill parallel to fire; cover, positioning lid so that vents are opposite wood chunks to draw smoke through grill (grill temperature should register about 350 degrees on grill thermometer, but will soon start dropping). Cook for 2 hours, until grill temperature drops to about 250 degrees, flipping rib racks, switching their position so that rack that was nearest fire is on outside, and turning racks 180 degrees every 30 minutes; add 10 fresh briquettes to pile of coals. Continue to cook (grill temperature should register 275 to 300 degrees on grill thermometer), flipping, switching, and rotating ribs every 30 minutes, until meat easily pulls away from bone, 1 1/2 to 2 hours longer. Transfer ribs to cutting board, then cut between bones to separate ribs; serve.

BARBECUED BABY BACK RIBS FOR GAS GRILL

If you're using a gas grill, leaving one burner on and turning off the other(s) mimics the indirect heat method on a charcoal grill. Use wood chips instead of wood chunks and a disposable aluminum pan to hold them.

Follow recipe for Barbecued Baby Back Ribs for Charcoal Grill through step 3, making following changes: Cover 2 cups wood chips with water and soak 30 minutes, then drain. Place soaked wood chips in small disposable aluminum pan; set pan on burner that will remain on. Turn all burners to high, close lid, and heat grill until chips smoke heavily, about 20 minutes. (If chips ignite, extinguish flames with water from squirt bottle.) Scrape grill grate clean with wire brush; turn off burner(s) without wood chips. Arrange ribs on cool side of grill and cover (grill temperature should register about 275 degrees on grill thermometer). Cook for 4 hours, until meat easily pulls away from bone, flipping rib racks, switching their position so that rack that was nearest fire is on outside, and turning racks 180 degrees every 30 minutes. Transfer ribs to cutting board, then cut between bones to separate ribs; serve.

Is Wood Just Wood?

When choosing your smoking wood, choices probably seem limited, as most hardware stores stock and sell only the two most popular types: hickory and mesquite. But many grilling enthusiasts swear by harder-to-find, more exotic woods. I wondered if it was worth the bother (and expense) to find these woods. I also wondered about the differences between "chips" and "chunks."

It turns out that wood chips and wood chunks both have a place in the world of barbecue. Chunks, because of their larger size, burn considerably longer. More smoke means more flavor, so chunks are my choice for a charcoal grill. I soaked the chunks in water for an hour to promote smoking and avoid flaming, and then nestled them into the bed of burning coals. Unfortunately, when placed on the bottom of a gas grill, wood chunks do not get hot enough to smoke. On a gas grill, you must use wood chips, which should be soaked in water for a minimum of 30 minutes (so they smoke rather than ignite) and then placed in a disposable aluminum pan (to shield them from the lit burner).

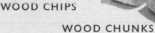

WOOD CHIPS

WOOD CHUNKS

With the basics under my belt, my search for rare wood began. I found a wide selection on Web sites that specialize in barbecuing. I chose eight different types and tested them for flavor differences while barbecuing baby back ribs. The ribs had been brined for 1 hour and were coated with spice rub. I wanted to see how each type of wood smoke would stand up to these big flavors.

I must admit, before testing these woods for differences in flavor, I doubted that I would find many. Isn't wood just wood? One by one, I was proved wrong. My tasters were shocked as well. Here are the eight woods I tested with comments about their flavor.

Apple and cherry woods produced slightly sweet and fruity smoke. **Peach** produced a slightly sweet and very woodsy flavored smoke. **Pecan,** the Southern cousin to hickory, is a bit more mellow but similar to hickory. **Maple**, a traditional choice with ham, produced a mellow, sweet smoke, which nicely balanced the spiciness of the ribs. **Oak** had a very perceptible but not unpleasant acidic note. **Hickory** produced a strong, pungent, hearty smoke that really stood up to the bold flavors of the spice rub. **Mesquite** is great for grilling because it burns very hot and lends a tangy smoke flavor to food over a short period of time. During the long, slow heat of barbecuing, however, I found the tanginess turned to bitterness.

In the end, tasters enjoyed ribs cooked over all of the woods tested, with the exception of mesquite. —E.M.

Building a Better Salade Niçoise

Seasoning each component independently is the key to a bright, full-flavored salad.

≥ BY ADAM RIED AND KAY RENTSCHLER ≤

The ingredients in salade Niçoise are simple, so they'd better be good. Use tender lettuce, ripe local tomatoes, garden-fresh green beans, and tuna packed in olive oil.

A long the French Riviera, salade Niçoise, the famous composed salad from the city of Nice, is commonplace. To many Americans, though, it seems just a bit fancy and exotic, if for no other reason than the ingredients are arranged separately on a platter, not tossed. More's the pity, then, that the rendition of salade Niçoise most of us encounter in this country is bland and lifeless—little more than a bed of lettuce on which lazily strewn piles of overcooked, underseasoned green beans and potatoes, off-ripe tomatoes, rubbery eggs, and soggy tuna drown in a sea of dull dressing.

The components of salade Niçoise seldom vary from the aforementioned lettuce, beans, potatoes, eggs, tomatoes, and tuna. These are joined by slivered red onion and piquant Mediterranean garnishes—always olives and sometimes capers and anchovies—as well as the occasional sweet pepper, cucumber, and artichoke heart and perhaps a few whole herb leaves. After trying a few salades Niçoise in the test kitchen, we dismissed those platters crowded by an unwieldy collection of ingredients and focused on three basic elements that we considered key (beyond the quality of the produce itself): the dressing, the manner

in which the salad components are dressed and assembled, and the tuna, which is what gives the dish its main-course status.

Dressing Details

Clearly, the dressing plays a crucial role in flavoring the salad, so we investigated it thoroughly. The importance of extra-virgin olive oil cannot be overstated here, and the fruitier the better. Our tasters preferred the tang of lemon juice over vinegar as the acidic element in the dressing and shallots over garlic to add a mild bite. A little mustard was also welcome in the vinaigrette for the depth of flavor it contributed, and, as another flavor boost, we replaced the standard parsley with the flavorful trio of fresh thyme, basil, and oregano.

Just as important as the ingredients in the dressing, we learned, was how we applied the dressing to the salad. Though we were rooting for the simplest approach—pouring the dressing carefully over the ingredients after they had been placed on the platter—this method won no fans. Because this salad is not tossed, the dressing was never perfectly distributed, so some bites were seasoned while others were not. At this point we took a cue from some classic French recipes in

which each ingredient is dressed individually before being added to the platter. Dressing the components separately really paid off, guaranteeing that every bite of each ingredient was fully and evenly seasoned. The downside of this method was the parade of bowls it occasioned—seven in all. After several experiments with the process, however, we decreased the number of bowls by three, and everyone here in the test kitchen agreed that they would happily wash four bowls to achieve such a harmonious salad.

Ingredients Survey

Many authorities consider tuna a defining element of salade Niçoise, so we tested several types. Tasters were enthusiastic about grilled fresh tuna, but not every cook would fire up the grill for this dish, so the fresh tuna is offered as a recipe variation. By way of canned tuna, we sampled it packed in olive oil (see "Tuna Packed in Olive Oil," page 9), vegetable oil, and water. Without exception, tasters preferred the tuna packed in olive oil for its rich flavor and meaty, silky texture. We were surprised, though, that the second choice was tuna packed in water, which tasted clean and allowed the flavors of the dressing through loud and clear. Tuna packed in vegetable oil, with its faded, faintly rancid flavor, was nobody's favorite.

We tested various ratios of the salad components and found them to be a matter of taste, provided they were in relative balance and were plentiful enough to afford every diner with a generous taste of each. What mattered more was the precise nature of the ingredients. For instance, butterhead lettuces such as Boston and Bibb were more tender than romaine, red leaf, or green leaf. And Red Bliss potatoes had better integrity and texture when boiled than russets.

Speaking of potatoes, the French often dress the potatoes while still hot from the pot, the theory being that warm potatoes absorb more dressing than cool ones. Our tests confirmed this: Potatoes dressed while warm tasted brighter and more fully seasoned than those that had been allowed to cool. Some French recipes go a step further by sprinkling them with extra wine or vermouth before adding the dressing. Indeed, this technique did enhance their flavor, and our tasters chose vermouth over white wine.

As we found in the end, this salad, when prepared with the right ingredients and some attention to detail, would give even a native Niçois a moment of pause.

SALADE NIÇOISE
SERVES 6 AS A LIGHT MAIN COURSE

Prepare all of the vegetables before you begin cooking the potatoes and this salad will come together very easily. The classic garnish of tiny, briny, piquant Niçoise olives is a hallmark of salade Niçoise. If they're not available, substitute another small, black, brined olive (do not use canned olives). Anchovies are another classic garnish, but they met with mixed reviews from our tasters, so they are optional. If you cannot find tuna packed in olive oil, substitute water-packed solid white tuna, not tuna packed in vegetable oil. (Among water-packed tunas, StarKist solid white took top honors in our tasting of 10 leading brands.) Compose the salad on your largest, widest, flattest serving platter. Do not blanket the bed of lettuce with the other ingredients; leave some space between the mounds of potatoes, tomatoes and onions, and beans so that leaves of lettuce peek through.

Vinaigrette
- ½ cup juice from 2 or 3 lemons
- ¾ cup extra-virgin olive oil
- 1 medium-large shallot, minced (about 3 tablespoons)
- 1 tablespoon minced fresh thyme leaves
- 2 tablespoons minced fresh basil leaves
- 2 teaspoons minced fresh oregano leaves
- 1 teaspoon Dijon mustard
  Salt and ground black pepper

Salad
- 4 large eggs
- 10 small new red potatoes (each about 2 inches in diameter, about 1¼ pounds total), each potato scrubbed and quartered
  Salt and ground black pepper
- 2 tablespoons dry vermouth
- 2 medium heads Boston or Bibb lettuce, leaves washed, dried, and torn into bite-sized pieces (about 8 cups loosely packed)
- 2 (6-ounce) cans olive oil–packed tuna (or three 4-ounce cans), drained
- 3 small vine-ripened tomatoes (about 14 ounces), each cored and cut into eighths
- 1 small red onion (about 4 ounces), sliced very thin
- 8 ounces green beans, stem ends trimmed and each bean halved crosswise
- ¼ cup Niçoise olives
- 10–12 anchovy fillets (optional)
- 2 tablespoons capers, rinsed (optional)

1. FOR THE VINAIGRETTE: Whisk lemon juice, oil, shallot, thyme, basil, oregano, and mustard in medium bowl; season to taste with salt and pepper and set aside.

2. FOR THE SALAD: Place eggs in small saucepan, cover by 1 inch with cold water, and bring to boil over high heat. Remove pan from heat, cover, and let stand 10 minutes. Meanwhile, fill medium bowl with 1 quart water and 1 tray ice cubes. With slotted spoon, transfer eggs to ice water; let stand 5 minutes. Peel eggs and quarter lengthwise; set aside (reserve ice water).

3. Meanwhile, bring potatoes and 4 quarts cold water to boil in large Dutch oven or stockpot over high heat. Add 1 tablespoon salt and cook until potatoes are tender when poked with paring knife, 5 to 8 minutes. With slotted spoon, gently transfer potatoes to medium bowl (do not discard boiling water). Toss warm potatoes with vermouth and salt and pepper to taste; let stand 1 minute. Toss in ¼ cup vinaigrette; set aside.

4. While potatoes cook, toss lettuce with ¼ cup vinaigrette in large bowl until coated. Arrange bed of lettuce on very large, flat serving platter. Place tuna in now-empty bowl and break up with fork. Add ½ cup vinaigrette and stir to combine; mound tuna in center of lettuce. Toss tomatoes, red onion, 3 tablespoons vinaigrette, and salt and pepper to taste in now-empty bowl; arrange tomato-onion mixture in mound at edge of lettuce bed. Arrange reserved potatoes in separate mound at edge of lettuce bed.

5. Return water to boil; add 1 tablespoon salt and green beans. Cook until tender but crisp, 3 to 5 minutes. Drain beans, transfer to reserved ice water, and let stand until just cool, about 30 seconds; dry beans well on triple layer of paper towels. Toss beans, 3 tablespoons vinaigrette, and salt and pepper to taste in now-empty bowl; arrange in separate mound at edge of lettuce bed.

6. Arrange reserved eggs, olives, and anchovies (if using) in separate mounds at edge of lettuce bed. Drizzle eggs with remaining 2 tablespoons dressing, sprinkle entire salad with capers (if using), and serve immediately.

SALADE NIÇOISE WITH GRILLED FRESH TUNA

1. Combine two 8-ounce tuna steaks, each about ¾ inch thick, with 2 tablespoons olive oil in gallon-sized zipper-lock bag; seal bag, place in refrigerator, and marinate, turning several times, for at least one hour or overnight. Remove tuna from bag, sprinkle with salt and pepper to taste, and set aside. Build very hot fire (you can hold your hand 5 inches above cooking grate for only 2 seconds); heat cooking grate thoroughly, scrape clean with wire brush, and wipe with small wad paper towels dipped in vegetable oil (hold wad with tongs). Grill tuna uncovered, turning once with thin metal spatula, to desired doneness, about 3 minutes total for rare and 4 minutes for well-done.

2. Follow recipe for Salade Niçoise, substituting grilled fresh tuna, cut into ½-inch thick slices, for canned tuna.

TASTING: Tuna Packed in Olive Oil

Given our preference for tuna packed in olive oil for salade Niçoise, we wondered if all brands are created equal. The six we found in grocery stores fell into three categories: light (made from bluefin, yellowfin, or skipjack tuna, or a mixture thereof), white (made from albacore tuna), and imported "white tuna" (made from bonito tuna).

As we found in an earlier tasting of tunas packed in water, our panel of tasters did not care for light tuna. The representative brands, Cento Solid Pack Light Tuna and Pastene Fancy Light Tuna, were thought to have "potent" and "metallic" flavors with a "bitter finish," as well as "chewed" and "unpleasant" textures. Surprisingly, our albacore contender, Dave's Albacore Fillets, came in dead last. "It's like eating nothing" was the comment that summed up all others.

The three best-tasting tunas were made by Ortiz, a small Spanish company. Ortiz cans primarily Northern bonito white tuna fished off the coast of Spain, a tuna not used by American packers. Europeans consider this tuna to be of highest quality because of its extremely white meat, tender texture, and full, clean flavor. The superior flavor is attributed to the migratory nature of the bonito tuna, a high-energy fish. High energy is equated with a high oil content, which in turn is equated with flavor—and lots of it. Although each of the three Ortiz tunas consists of the same ingredients—bonito del norte, olive oil, and salt—they have markedly different textures, and it was this characteristic that distinguished them and produced a winner. —Shannon Blaisdell

1st PLACE	2nd PLACE	3rd PLACE

ORTIZ Bonito del Norte "Ventresca"
➤ **$9.95 for a 3.88-ounce can**
Ventresca refers to the underside of the fish, where fat is more concentrated. These small fillets blew all other contenders out of the water with their "silky texture" and "fresh flavor."

ORTIZ Bonito del Norte (tinned)
➤ **$3.99 for a 3.95-ounce can**
The "flaky," "tender," and "pleasant" texture of this "intense and delicious" tuna was perfect for Niçoise.

ORTIZ Bonito del Norte (jarred)
➤ **$7.99 for a 7.76-ounce jar**
The large, dense chunks of tuna were somewhat "dry" and a tad "tough," but the flavor was great: "light," "clean," and "mild."

Pad Thai at Home

Ordered out, this Thai restaurant favorite is often greasy, soggy, and candy-sweet. Made at home, it can taste fresh and vibrant…and it cooks in minutes.

≥ BY DAWN YANAGIHARA ≤

Pad thai is a remedy for a dead, jaded palate. Hot, sweet, pungent Thai flavors tangled in an un-Western jumble of textures awaken all of the senses that have grown weary of the usual grub. I have downed numerous plate-fuls of pad thai, many from an excellent Thai restaurant only a few blocks away. What I noticed was that from one order to the next, pad thai prepared in the same reliable restaurant kitchen was inconsistent. If it was per-fect, it was a symphony of flavors and textures. It balanced sweet, sour, and spicy, and the tender, glutinous rice noodles ensnared curls of shrimp, crisp strands of bean sprouts, soft curds of fried egg, and sturdy bits of tofu. Sometimes, however, it tasted weak and flat, as if seasoned too timidly. At its worst, pad thai suffers from indis-criminate amounts of sugar, from slick, greasy noodles, or from bloated, sticky, lifeless strands that glom onto each other to form a chaotic skein.

I have become so enamored of pad thai and so tired of disappointment that I have attempted it several times at home with only moderate success, and that I attribute to luck. The recipes were unclear, ingredient lists were daunting, and I stumbled through the steps only to produce dry, undercooked noodles and unbalanced flavors. Happily, though, the home-cooked pad thai was loaded with plump, sweet shrimp (not the paltry four or five per restaurant order), and the flavors tasted clean and fresh. Despite my failures, my goal was to produce a consistently superlative pad thai at home.

In the Sticks

Rice sticks, the type of noodles used in pad thai, are often only partially cooked, particularly when used in stir-fries. I found three different methods of preparing them: soaking in room-temperature water, soaking in hot tap water, and boiling. I began with boiling and quickly realized that this was bad advice. Drained and waiting in the colan-der, the noodles glued themselves together.

Constant tossing while stir-frying the pad thai ensures even cooking and an even distribution of ingredients.

When I managed to stir-fry them, they wound up soggy and overdone. Noodles soaked in room-temperature water remained fairly stiff. After lengthy stir-frying, they eventually became ten-der, but longer cooking made this pad thai drier and stickier. Finally, I tried soaking the rice sticks in hot tap water for about 20 minutes. They "softened," turning limp and pliant, but were not fully tender. Drained, they were loose and sepa-rate, and they cooked through easily with stir-frying. The result? Noodles that were at once pleasantly tender and resilient.

Foreign Affairs

Sweet, salty, sour, and spicy are the flavor charac-teristics of pad thai, and none should dominate; they should coexist in harmony. Although the cooking time is short, the ingredient list isn't, and many components will appear foreign to some. Fish sauce supplies a salty-sweet pungency, sugar gives sweetness, the heat comes from ground chiles, vinegar provides acidity, and tamarind rounds out the dish with its fruity, earthy, sweet-tart molasses-tinged flavor. Garlic and sometimes shallots contribute their heady, robust flavors. Ketchup is called for in a couple of recipes (worth trying, but dubious) and soy sauce in another.

With these ingredients in hand, I set off to find out which ones were key to success and how much of each to use to achieve balanced flavor. For 8 ounces of rice sticks, 3 tablespoons of fish sauce and the same amount of sugar were ideal. Three-quarters of a teaspoon of cayenne (many recipes call for Thai chiles, but for the sake of simplicity, I opted not to use them) brought a low, even heat—not a searing burn—and 1 tablespoon of rice vinegar (pre-ferred in pad thai for its mild acidity and relatively complex fermented-grain flavor) greatly vivified the flavors.

Tasters liked the garlic at 1 tablespoon minced. Shallots had a surprising impact on flavor. Just one medium shallot (about 3 tablespoons minced) produced such a round, full sweetness and depth of flavor that we just couldn't say no. To coax the right character out of these two aromat-ics, I found that cooking them to the point of browning was critical; they tasted mellow, sweet, and mildly toasty.

Tamarind was the most enigmatic ingredient. Tamarind is a fruit that grows as a round brown pod about 5 inches long and is often sold as a paste (a hard, flat brick) or as a sticky concentrate. (For more information, see "Tamarind Options" on page 11.) Although we eschew hard-to-find ingredients at *Cook's*, I came to the conclusion that tamarind is central—if not essential—to the unique flavor of pad thai. Testing showed that tamarind paste has a fresher, brighter, fruitier flavor than concentrate, which tasted dull by comparison. For those who cannot obtain either tamarind paste or concentrate, I worked out a formula of equal parts lime juice and water as a stand-in. This mixture produces a less interesting and less authentic dish, but we polished off sev-eral such platefuls with no qualms.

I tried a little ketchup, but its sharp, vinegary tomato flavor was out of place. As for soy sauce, even just a mere tablespoon was a big bully—its assertive flavor didn't play nicely with the others.

The other ingredients in pad thai are sautéed

shrimp, scrambled eggs, chopped peanuts, bean sprouts, and scallions. For more textural intrigue and to achieve authentic pad thai flavor, dried shrimp and Thai salted preserved radish are worthy embellishments (both sold, of course, in Asian grocery stores). Dried shrimp are sweet, salty, and intensely shrimpy, and they add tiny bursts of incredible flavor. I used 2 tablespoons of the smallest dried shrimp I could find and chopped them up finer still, because tasters requested that their firm, chewy texture be mitigated. Thai salted preserved radish is brownish-yellow in color, dry, and a bit wrinkled, and it is sold in long sections (think daikon radish) folded into a flimsy plastic package. Two tablespoons of chopped salted radish added piquant, savory bits with a hard crunch.

Oddly, after consuming dozens of servings of pad thai I did not feel glutted. I was addicted. These days, if I order it in a restaurant, I prepare myself for disappointment. It's funny—pad thai is not unlike a chocolate chip cookie. It's always best homemade.

PAD THAI
SERVES 4 AS A MAIN DISH

A wok might be the implement of choice in restaurants and the old country, but a large 12-inch skillet (nonstick makes cleanup easy) is more practical for home cooks. Although pad thai cooks very quickly, the ingredient list is long, and everything must be prepared and within easy reach at the stovetop when you begin cooking. For maximum efficiency, use the time during which the tamarind and noodles soak to prepare the other ingredients. Tofu is a good and common addition to pad thai. If you like, add 4 ounces of extra-firm tofu or pressed tofu (available in Asian markets) cut into ½-inch cubes (about 1 cup) to the noodles along with the bean sprouts.

2 tablespoons tamarind paste or substitute (see "Tamarind Options" above)
¾ cup boiling water
3 tablespoons fish sauce
1 tablespoon rice vinegar
3 tablespoons sugar
¾ teaspoon cayenne pepper
4 tablespoons peanut or vegetable oil
8 ounces dried rice stick noodles, about ⅛ inch wide (the width of linguine)
2 large eggs
¼ teaspoon salt
12 ounces medium (31/35 count) shrimp, peeled and deveined, if desired
3 garlic cloves, pressed through garlic press or minced (1 tablespoon)
1 medium shallot, minced (about 3 tablespoons)
2 tablespoons dried shrimp, chopped fine (optional)
2 tablespoons chopped Thai salted preserved radish (optional)

6 tablespoons chopped roasted unsalted peanuts
3 cups (6 ounces) bean sprouts
5 medium scallions, green parts only, sliced thin on sharp bias
¼ cup loosely packed cilantro leaves (optional)
Lime wedges

1. Rehydrate tamarind paste in boiling water (see instructions in "Tamarind Options" above). Stir fish sauce, rice vinegar, sugar, cayenne, and 2 tablespoons oil into tamarind liquid and set aside.

2. Cover rice sticks with hot tap water in large bowl; soak until softened, pliable, and limp but not fully tender, about 20 minutes. Drain noodles and set aside. Beat eggs and ⅛ teaspoon salt in small bowl; set aside.

3. Heat 1 tablespoon oil in 12-inch skillet (preferably nonstick) over high heat until just beginning to smoke, about 2 minutes. Add shrimp and sprinkle with remaining ⅛ teaspoon salt; cook, tossing occasionally, until shrimp are opaque and browned about the edges, about 3 minutes. Transfer shrimp to plate and set aside.

4. Off heat, add remaining tablespoon oil to skillet and swirl to coat; add garlic and shallot, set skillet over medium heat and cook, stirring constantly, until light golden brown, about 1½ minutes; add eggs to skillet and stir vigorously with wooden spoon until scrambled and barely moist, about 20 seconds. Add noodles, dried shrimp, and salted radish (if using) to eggs; toss with 2 wooden spoons to combine. Pour fish sauce mixture over noodles, increase heat to high, and cook, tossing constantly, until noodles are evenly coated. Scatter ¼ cup peanuts, bean sprouts, all but ¼ cup scallions, and cooked shrimp over noodles; continue to cook, tossing constantly, until noodles are tender, about 2½ minutes (if not yet tender add 2 tablespoons water to skillet and continue to cook until tender).

5. Transfer noodles to serving platter, sprinkle with remaining scallions, 2 tablespoons peanuts, and cilantro; serve immediately, passing lime wedges separately.

Tamarind Options

Sweet-tart, dark brownish-red tamarind is a necessary ingredient for an authentic-looking and tasting pad thai. It's commonly sold in paste (also called pulp) and in concentrate form. But don't fret if neither is available—you can still make an excellent pad thai using the lime juice and water substitute below.

Tamarind Paste or Pulp
Tamarind paste, or pulp, is firm, sticky, and filled with seeds and fibers. We favored this product because it had the freshest, brightest flavor. To use it in the pad thai recipe, soak 2 tablespoons in ¾ cup boiling water for about 10 minutes, then push it through a mesh strainer to remove the seeds and fibers and extract as much pulp as possible.

TAMARIND PASTE

Tamarind Concentrate
Tamarind concentrate looks more like a scary pomade than foodstuff. It's black, thick, shiny, and gooey. Its flavor approximates that of tamarind paste, but it tastes less fruity and more "cooked," and it colors the pad thai a shade too dark. To use in the pad thai recipe, mix 1 tablespoon with ⅔ cup hot water.

TAMARIND CONCENTRATE

Lime Juice and Water Substitute
If tamarind is out of the question, combine ⅓ cup lime juice and ⅓ cup water and use it in its place; use light brown sugar instead of granulated to give the noodles some color and a faint molasses flavor. Because it will already contain a good hit of lime, do not serve this version with lime wedges.

LIME

Soaking Noodles

STIFF NOODLES
Soaking the rice sticks in room-temperature water yields hard noodles that take too long to stir-fry.

STICKY NOODLES
Fully cooking the rice sticks in boiling water results in soft, sticky, gummy, overdone noodles.

PERFECT NOODLES
Soaking the rice sticks in hot water yields softened noodles. When stir-fried, they are tender but resilient.

Grilling Steak, Tuscan Style

Transform the ordinary T-bone steak with peppery olive oil,
fresh-squeezed lemon juice, and a two-level fire.

⇒ BY ADAM RIED ⇐

When Americans garnish a steak, it's often with A.1. sauce. The French use a flavored compound butter. But the Italians have something even better (and arguably easier, too)—olive oil and lemon. *Bistecca alla Fiorentina,* as it is called in Tuscany, couldn't be simpler: a thick juicy steak grilled rare, sliced, and served with a drizzle of extra-virgin olive oil and a squeeze of lemon. For most of us here in the test kitchen, this unexpected combination was a revelation, and I expect that any steak lover who gives it a whirl will become a convert, too. The fruity, peppery olive oil amplifies the savory nature of the beef, while the lemon provides a bright counterpoint that cuts right through the richness to sharpen the other flavors.

In a dish this direct, good technique can mean the difference between mediocre and magical. So I recently grilled my way through more than 30 pounds of steak to perfect both the grilling technique and the details of the olive oil and lemon garnish—that is, when and how to introduce it.

Grill Right

Thick T-bone and porterhouse are the steaks recommended most often for bistecca alla Fiorentina. Both steaks feature a T-shaped bone with meat from the top loin (also known as the strip) on one side and from the tenderloin on the other side. The primary difference between the two is the size of the tenderloin piece, which is larger on the porterhouse. Of course I sampled both steaks and found them to be equally appealing—tender, with a robust, well-balanced flavor. There was no reason to test additional cuts. The suggested thickness, around 1¼ to 1½ inches, also worked out well, allowing for an appealing textural contrast between the smoky crust that formed on the outside of the steak and the rare, tender interior.

The flavor of that smoky, crisp, brown, caramelized crust is a primary reason to cook over a charcoal fire. A few rounds at the grill quickly

Steak Fiorentina is simply a perfectly grilled T-bone or porterhouse steak sliced, drizzled with olive oil, and served with lemon wedges.

proved that plenty of heat was necessary to achieve a sufficient crust. Anything cooler than medium-hot would not get the job done. But there was a problem: The interior had not cooked enough by the time the crust was perfectly done. Leaving the steak in place until the interior reached 120 degrees on an instant-read thermometer (rare) torched the exterior. Obviously, I needed a more reliable method.

A little pyro-experimentation helped solve the problem. I needed a two-level fire, with more coals on one side of the grill than on the other to create hotter and cooler areas. Starting the steaks over the hotter part of the fire allowed the exterior to sear deeply, and finishing them over the cooler area allowed the inside to cook through without charring the outside.

Garnish Right

The recipes I turned up in my research shared an odd sense of voodoo when it came to seasoning the steaks. Several recommended using the olive oil to marinate the raw steaks, a few more suggested rubbing the steaks with olive oil just before

grilling them, while one passionately declared that oiling the meat before cooking would cause it to "taste greasy and be nauseating." Another recipe insisted that the steaks be both salted and drizzled with olive oil after they had been cooked but before they were removed from the grill.

To see if any of these techniques could really work magic, I designed several tests. My tasting team and I evaluated steaks treated with oil in five different manners: marinated before grilling, brushed on the meat before grilling, brushed on the meat during grilling, drizzled on the whole cooked steaks before slicing, and drizzled over the sliced steak at serving time.

We preferred drizzling the oil over the sliced steak for a few reasons. It was the easiest, least fussy method; it flavored the meat more effectively, bringing the full fruity, peppery impact of the raw oil to the fore; and it guaranteed a hit of oil with each bite of steak. Although the steaks that had been oiled prior to or during grilling were not nauseating, as that one author had predicted, the heat of the grill did mitigate the nuances of the oil, in a sense deadening its flavor. The oiled steaks also caused more flare-ups on the grill. I tried both pure and extra-virgin olive oils, and the extra-virgin was far and away the best for its distinctive character and bold flavor. I went on to try a few different brands of extra-virgin oil and preferred those with bolder, fuller-bodied flavor over the milder oils. We also experimented with the lemon and found it easiest and best to squeeze it over the sliced steak at the last minute. Juicing the lemon and brushing the juice on the steaks any earlier relieved the lemon of some of its freshness and tang.

The use of garlic was a matter of some debate in the original recipes. Some included it, while others decried it as untraditional. The idea appealed to us nonetheless, so I tried four ways of working it into the program. I made a sauce with pureed fresh garlic, olive oil, and lemon juice and poured it over the sliced steak, but the garlic was overpowering. I tried rubbing both fresh and toasted garlic cloves over the cooked steak, but tasters were not impressed. Last, I rubbed a fresh-cut garlic clove over the bone, and then the meat, of the raw steak. The bone scraped up the garlic's surface, allowing small bits to cling to the meat. Once this steak was grilled, it had a faint suggestion of toasted garlic flavor that was a hit with the tasters. This became a variation on the basic recipe.

So next time you grill a steak, leave the A.1. sauce on the shelf and forget about the hassle of making a flavored butter. Garnishing a steak the Tuscan way is quick, easy, fresh, and more interesting by light years.

CHARCOAL-GRILLED TUSCAN STEAK WITH OLIVE OIL AND LEMON
(Bistecca alla Fiorentina)
SERVES 4

T-Bone and porterhouse steaks are large enough to serve two. We prefer to season the steaks with kosher salt because its coarse grains are easier to sprinkle evenly onto the meat than fine table salt. If you use charcoal briquettes instead of hardwood charcoal, one chimney-full will weigh close to 6 pounds. Also, you may have to increase the searing time by about 30 seconds on each side. There is no need to build a two-level fire if you can adjust the level of the charcoal rack on your grill; crank the rack up high to sear the steaks, then drop it down a couple of levels for less intense heat to finish cooking them.

- 2 T-bone or porterhouse steaks, each 1½ inches thick (about 3½ pounds total), patted dry
- 2 teaspoons kosher salt
- 1 teaspoon ground black pepper
- 3 tablespoons extra-virgin olive oil
  Lemon wedges for serving

1. Light large chimney starter filled with hardwood charcoal (about 2½ pounds) and burn until covered with layer of fine gray ash. Build two-level fire by stacking most of the coals on one side of grill and arranging remaining coals in single layer on other side. Set cooking grate in place, cover grill with lid, and let grate heat up, about 5 minutes. Use wire brush to scrape grate clean. Grill is ready when thicker layer of coals is medium-hot (you can hold your hand 5 inches above cooking grate for 3 to 4 seconds).

2. Meanwhile, sprinkle each side of steaks with ½ teaspoon salt and ¼ teaspoon pepper. Cook steaks, uncovered, over hotter part of grill until well-browned on each side, about 2½ minutes per side. (If steaks start to flame, move them to cooler side of fire and/or extinguish flames with squirt bottle). Move steaks to cooler side of grill and continue cooking, turning once, to desired doneness, 5 to 6 minutes more for rare (120 degrees on instant-read thermometer), 6 to 7 minutes for rare medium-rare (125 degrees), 7 to 8 minutes for medium medium-rare (130 degrees), or 8 to 9 minutes for medium (135 to 140 degrees).

3. Transfer steaks to cutting board and let rest 5 minutes. Following illustrations 1 through 3 (above), cut strip and tenderloin pieces off bones and slice crosswise about ½ inch thick. Arrange slices on platter, drizzle with olive oil, and serve immediately with lemon wedges.

GAS-GRILLED TUSCAN STEAK WITH OLIVE OIL AND LEMON

Turn all burners on gas grill to high, close lid, and heat until very hot, about 15 minutes. Scrape cooking grate clean with wire brush; leave one burner on high and turn other burner(s) down to medium. Follow recipe for Charcoal-Grilled Tuscan Steak with Olive Oil and Lemon, beginning with step 2.

GRILLED TUSCAN STEAK WITH GARLIC ESSENCE

Follow recipe for Charcoal- or Gas-Grilled Tuscan Steak with Olive Oil and Lemon, rubbing halved garlic clove over bone and meat on each side of steaks before seasoning with salt and pepper.

STEP-BY-STEP | SLICING T-BONE AND PORTERHOUSE STEAKS

1. Cut along bone to remove large top loin, or strip, section.

2. Cut smaller tenderloin section off bone.

3. Cut each large piece crosswise into ½-inch-thick slices for serving.

Choosing Charcoal

Charcoal is the carbonized remains of wood that has been burned in the absence of oxygen. Without oxygen, resins and moisture in the wood evaporate, leaving behind light, easily lit, combustible charcoal. Three types of charcoal dominate the market. They are hardwood charcoal (also called lump hardwood), which, like the wood used to make it, consists of irregularly shaped pieces and is additive-free; square, pillow-shaped briquettes made from scrap wood and sawdust that is burned and then compacted along with chemicals and other binders that help them both ignite and burn evenly; and a Kingsford product called Match Light, which consists of briquettes that have been permeated with lighter fluid and thereby promise to ignite with the touch of a lit match.

MATCH LIGHT   HARDWOOD   BRIQUETTE

Match Light charcoal (left) can impart a faint bitterness to delicate foods. Hardwood charcoal (center) burns a bit hotter than regular briquettes (right), making it the best choice for high-heat grilling.

We were anxious to test the common assertion that hardwood charcoal burns hotter and faster than briquettes, so we hooked up a sophisticated, high-range temperature sensor to the cooking grate above fires made from each of the three types of charcoal. We recorded temperatures after five minutes, 15 minutes, and 25 minutes to gauge the drop-off in heat. Sure enough, the hardwood fire was the hottest initially at just above 700 degrees, compared with 660 degrees for the briquettes and 550 degrees for the Match Light; the hardwood also dropped off the most dramatically—by almost 450 degrees—after 25 minutes.

We were also curious to see if we could detect flavor differences in foods grilled with the three types of charcoal, so we sampled steak (because it's hearty) and zucchini (because it's delicate). Though the hardwood charcoal fire formed the thickest, most deeply brown crust on the steaks, tasters did not detect any significant flavor differences in the three steaks. It was another story, however, with the zucchini. The zucchini grilled over hardwood charcoal colored the fastest and tasted smokier than the others. The briquette-grilled zucchini had the lightest grilled flavor (but no off flavors), and the Match Light–grilled sample demonstrated a faint but odd bitterness.

So where does this leave us? We'd just as soon avoid any off flavors in delicate foods, so we'll pass on the Match Light. For grill-roasting over a longer time period at a lower temperature, we'd opt for briquettes because they burn a little cooler and a lot longer than hardwood. But for straight-ahead grilling applications, especially when there's meat on the menu that cries out for a deep sear, we'll take hardwood. Grilling is all about high heat, and we'll take every extra degree that we can get. —A.R.

Nachos Done Right

Even this beleaguered staple of mall restaurants is worth doing well at home.

⇒ BY JULIA COLLIN ⇐

Common, inexpensive, and requiring little skill to make, nachos are not only far from haute cuisine, they are Homer Simpson's favorite repast, behind doughnuts. And Homer isn't alone. Nachos are a simple culinary pleasure many of us crave—crisp, warm tortilla chips mingling with melted cheese under a colorful banner of spicy salsa, luxurious guacamole, and a dollop of sour cream. Yet as elementary and popular as nachos are, finding a good plate of them can be hard. The worst examples appear at the snack counters of airports and large, discount marts where trays of chips that taste like cardboard are squirted with a few pumps of unnaturally fluid "cheese," doused with watery jarred salsa, and (if you're lucky) served with a minuscule portion of ready-made guacamole. My mission was simple: free nachos from the suffocating grasp of packaged ingredients and make them taste good again.

After sampling some local nacho fare and trying out a few recipes, I homed in on some key issues. First, the chips must be crisp and hot, not lukewarm, soggy, or charred. Second, there must be no shortage of cheese; a chip without cheese is just not a nacho. Third, there is no such thing as minimalist nachos. Good nachos require not only a hearty helping of cheese but also ample amounts of garnishes such as salsa, guacamole, sour cream, jalapeños, scallions, and so on. Finally, although it may seem blindingly obvious, I noted that fresh, quality ingredients make good nachos, while grim, overprocessed ingredients make airport nachos. Fortified by these insights, I was ready to create a good plate of nachos, and my tasters were already jockeying for position at the counter.

Chips and Cheese

Finding that 8 ounces of chips made enough nachos for four to six people (or two Homer Simpsons) and fit easily into a 13 by 9-inch baking dish, I made batches with increasing amounts of shredded cheese until my tasters called uncle. Four cups of shredded cheese turned out to be just right; lesser amounts left some chips neglected and more just about drowned them. To ensure an even distribution, it was necessary to toss the cheese with the chips before cooking. But the act of tossing, I quickly discovered, was brutal on the delicate chips, and some of the cheese was lost to the bottom of the baking dish. Instead, I tried building the nachos in layers—two layers of chips topped with cheese—which ensured even distribution. Not surprisingly,

Real nachos are more than just cheese and chips. With a quick tomato salsa and homemade guacamole, they are good, honest food.

these first few batches tasted far better than any nachos I had eaten elsewhere. The simple pairing of good-quality chips (see the tortilla chip tasting, page 26) with a generous amount of evenly distributed cheese had already made a huge difference.

Next I held a cheese tasting. Although most recipes call for cheddar or Monterey Jack, I wondered how tasters would react to other types of cheese, such as American, Havarti, Gouda, Muenster, or any of the jalapeño-studded varieties such as pepper cheddar, pepper Jack, and pepper Havarti. Cheddar turned out to be tasters' overall favorite, with a potent and true flavor, although Gouda was surprisingly good and garnered second place. To our great surprise, Monterey Jack was bland and tasteless, while American and every single one of the peppered cheeses tasted commercial and overprocessed. The other oddball contestants, Muenster and regular Havarti, had decent if unremarkable flavors but were quick to turn rubbery as they cooled. I tried using pre-shredded cheddar to save time but found the flavor to be dull and the texture dry. I got much better results by shredding a block of cheese in a food processor fitted with the shredding disk, which was easy enough and took little time.

I had been baking the nachos in a 350-degree oven for 20 minutes to melt the cheese and heat the chips through but wanted to experiment with speedier methods. The broiler caused the top layer of chips to burn before the inner layer of cheese had time to melt. Hot ovens set between 425 and 450 degrees produced chips with charred edges, but a 400-degree oven managed to both melt the cheese and warm the chips through to a lightly toasted crisp in merely 10 minutes. Not only was this a time saver, but the nachos tasted more fresh and less dried out than those baked for a longer period of time in a cooler oven.

Relishes and Garnishment

Chips and cheese may be the nacho plate's workhorses, but without salsa, guacamole, and sour cream, nachos look buck naked. And not just any old salsa or guacamole will do—they have to be fresh and lively tasting. Although salsa and guacamole are now conveniently sold in tubs and jars in the supermarket, most of these products are just about inedible (see "Is Store-Bought Guacamole an Option?" and "Fresh Salsa in a Flash"). Luckily, both can also be made at home in a few minutes, and the results are well worth the effort. When and where they are placed on the chips and cheese are also crucial to success. As for when, they must be added after the chips emerge from the oven to provide contrast in temperature, texture, and flavor. As for where, many recipes tell the cook to spread each topping evenly over each chip, but this instruction is both silly and time-consuming. I found that it's easier to simply dump a few scoops of salsa and guacamole on a small portion of the chips, off to the side, so that most of the chips remain unencumbered and easy to pick up.

Tasters liked the spicy addition of thinly sliced jalapeños, preferring them fresh rather than canned. They tasted best when sprinkled into the layers along with the cheese, which, when melted, helped the peppers adhere to the chips. Fresh, sliced scallions and wedges of lime—both added when the nachos emerge from the oven—were also welcome additions. The issue of spicy ground beef and refried beans—common additions to a nacho plate—provoked some controversy in the test kitchen. The result? I decided to use these ingredients in variations, as they quickly transform nachos into an indulgent, artery-clogging meal that begs for carbonation in a can and an all-night seat on the sofa in front of the television. This is not fancy French cuisine or exotic ethnic fare. This is simple American junk food, done right.

CHEESY NACHOS WITH GUACAMOLE AND SALSA

SERVES 4 TO 6

8	ounces tortilla chips (see tortilla chip tasting on page 26)
1	pound cheddar cheese, shredded (4 cups)
2	large jalapeño chiles (¾ ounce each), sliced thin (about ¼ cup)
2	scallions, sliced thin
1	recipe Fresh Guacamole (recipe follows)
½	cup (4 ounces) sour cream
1	recipe One-Minute Salsa (see recipe at right)
1	lime, cut into 6 wedges

Adjust oven rack to middle position and heat oven to 400 degrees. Spread half of chips in even layer in 13 by 9-inch baking dish or similar oven-proof platter; sprinkle evenly with 2 cups cheese and half of jalapeño slices. Repeat with remaining chips, cheese, and jalapeños. Bake until cheese is melted, 7 to 10 minutes. Remove nachos from oven, cool 2 minutes, then sprinkle with scallions. Along edge of nachos, drop scoops of guacamole, sour cream, and salsa. Serve immediately, passing lime wedges separately.

CHEESY NACHOS WITH REFRIED BEANS

Follow recipe for Cheesy Nachos with Guacamole and Salsa, dropping ¾ cup (about 6 ounces) refried beans in small spoonfuls on each chip layer before sprinkling with cheese.

CHEESY NACHOS WITH SPICY BEEF

2	teaspoons corn or vegetable oil
1	small onion, chopped fine
1	large garlic clove, minced or pressed through garlic press
1	tablespoon chili powder
¼	teaspoon dried oregano
½	teaspoon ground cumin
½	teaspoon ground coriander
¼	teaspoon cayenne pepper
⅛	teaspoon salt
½	pound 90 percent lean (or leaner) ground beef

1. Heat oil in medium skillet over medium heat until hot and shimmering, but not smoking, about 2 minutes. Add onion and cook, stirring

---

occasionally, until softened, about 4 minutes. Add garlic, spices, and salt; cook, stirring constantly, until fragrant and combined with onions, about 1 minute. Add ground beef and cook, breaking up meat with wooden spoon and scraping pan bottom to prevent scorching, until beef is no longer pink, about 5 minutes.

2. Follow recipe for Cheesy Nachos with Guacamole and Salsa, sprinkling half of beef mixture on each chip layer before sprinkling with cheese.

FRESH GUACAMOLE

MAKES ABOUT 1½ CUPS

2	small, ripe avocados (preferably Haas)
1	tablespoon minced red onion
1	small garlic clove, minced or pressed through garlic press
½	small jalapeño chile, minced (about 1½ teaspoons)
2	tablespoons minced fresh cilantro leaves
	Salt
1	tablespoon juice from 1 lime

1. Halve 1 avocado, remove pit, and scoop flesh into medium bowl. Using fork, mash lightly with onion, garlic, jalapeño, cilantro, and ⅛ teaspoon salt until just combined.

2. Halve and pit remaining avocado. Using a dinner knife, carefully make ½-inch cross-hatch incisions in flesh, cutting down to but not through skin. Using a soupspoon, gently scoop flesh from skin; transfer to bowl with mashed avocado mixture. Sprinkle lime juice over and mix lightly with fork until combined but still chunky. Adjust seasoning with salt, if necessary, and serve. (Can be covered with plastic wrap, pressed directly onto surface of mixture, and refrigerated up to 1 day. Return guacamole to room temperature, removing plastic wrap just before serving.)

TASTING: **Is Store-Bought Guacamole an Option?**

At the heart of any good guacamole is a ripe Haas avocado. Grown primarily in California and Mexico, these small, rough-skinned gems usually soften if left on the counter for a few days. But it can be hard to find fully ripened avocados for a spur-of-the-moment guacamole. Wondering if any of the ready-made guacamole at the supermarket would be an acceptable substitute, we tasted five leading brands to compare them with our own recipe.

At first glance, some of these guacamoles looked pretty good. But after sampling just a bite or two, tasters gagged, sealing the fate of these pretenders. The best of the lot, AvoClassic Guacamole, came out of a sealed plastic pouch and garnered comments such as "could be worse" and "not bad with some doctoring." The next best representative was Goya's Guacamole Dip, which had a "thin and mealy" texture and tasted "like nothing." Having increasingly negative reactions, tasters found the Trader Joe's and Calavo brands to be harsh and acidic, with flavors that "burned the back of the throat." Ranked at the very bottom was La Mexicana Guacamole, which drew comments such as "What is in this?" By comparison, our freshly made guacamole tasted almost angelic, with a pure, honest avocado flavor. So if you think the mood might strike, buy some avacados a few days ahead. —J.C.

Tasters were decidedly unimpressed with these ready-made guacamoles. AvoClassic Guacamole (far left) was the best of the lot but still not good enough to recommend.

Fresh Salsa in a Flash

After sampling 12 jarred salsas for the July/August 1997 issue of the magazine, tasters found commercially bottled salsas to be watery and sweet, with mushy vegetables and overprocessed flavors. For a snack as simple as nachos, I wondered if there was a way to make salsa that would taste better than the jarred stuff without the hassle of chopping multiple vegetables and herbs. Starting with *Cook's* favorite recipe for red salsa, I discovered a quick way to make fresh tomato salsa in a food processor. It takes merely a minute to produce and tastes far superior to anything you can buy at the store. Best of all, this salsa tastes just fine when made with canned diced tomatoes, so it can be made year-round.

ONE-MINUTE SALSA MAKES ABOUT 1 CUP

➤ This quick salsa can be made with either fresh or canned tomatoes, but if you're using fresh, make sure they are sweet, ripe, in-season tomatoes. If they aren't, canned tomatoes are a better choice.

½	small jalapeño chile or ½ chipotle chile in adobo sauce, minced
¼	small red onion, peeled and root end removed
1	small garlic clove, minced or pressed
2	tablespoons fresh cilantro leaves
¼	teaspoon salt
	Pinch ground black pepper
2	teaspoons juice from 1 lime
2	small ripe tomatoes (about ¾ pound), each cored and cut into eighths, or one (14-ounce) can diced tomatoes, drained

Pulse all ingredients except tomatoes in food processor until minced, about five 1-second pulses, scraping sides of bowl as necessary. Add tomatoes and pulse until roughly chopped, about two 1-second pulses.

Leafy Salads 101

Constructing the perfect salad is trickier than it seems. From battered greens to acidic vinaigrettes, simple salads can suffer from a variety of ills. Here's how to produce good salads every time. BY MATTHEW CARD

CLEANING GREENS

The first step in making any salad is cleaning the greens. (Unwashed greens should be carefully stowed away in the crisper and the rubber band or twist tie removed, as the constriction encourages rotting.) Nothing ruins a salad faster than gritty leaves. Our favorite way to wash small amounts of lettuce is in the bowl of a salad spinner; larger amounts require a sink. Make sure there is ample room to swish the leaves about and rid them of sand and dirt. The dirt will sink to the bottom. Exceptionally dirty greens (spinach and arugula often fall into this category) may take at least two changes of water. Do not run water directly from the faucet onto the greens as the force of the water can bruise them. When you are satisfied that the leaves are grit-free, spin them dry in a salad spinner. Greens must be quite dry, otherwise the vinaigrette will slide off and taste diluted.

1. Using your hands, gently move the greens about underwater to loosen grit, which should fall to the bottom of the salad spinner bowl.

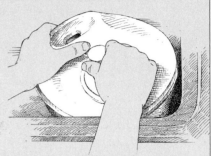

2. If you own a crank-style salad spinner, place it in the corner of your sink. This increases your leverage by pushing the spinner down to the sink floor and into the sink walls, thereby stabilizing it.

3. Line the empty salad spinner with paper towels, then layer in the greens, covering each layer with additional towels. In this manner, the greens will keep for at least two days.

4. For longer-term storage—up to a week—loosely roll the greens in a kitchen towel or paper towels and then place the rolled greens inside a large zipper-lock bag and seal it.

BEST SALAD SPINNERS

ZYLISS   OXO

When we tested eight salad spinners (September/October 1999), we had a two-way tie between spinners made by Zyliss and Oxo Good Grips. They both excelled at drying greens, though they had minor trade-offs: The Zyliss finished the task nominally faster, but the Oxo had a more ergonomic handle and a nonskid bottom, a big bonus. The design enhancements lifted the Oxo's price to $26, $5 more than the Zyliss.

PUREEING GARLIC FOR VINAIGRETTE

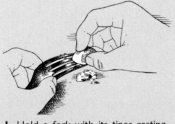

1. Hold a fork with its tines resting face-down on a cutting board. Rub a peeled clove of garlic rapidly back and forth against the tines, close to their points.

2. Once the clove has been forced through the tines, turn the fork over and mash any large chunks to make a smooth puree.

MINCING A SHALLOT FOR VINAIGRETTE

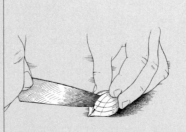

1. Place the peeled bulb flat-side down and make several slices parallel to the work surface, almost to (but not through) the root end. Then make a number of very closely spaced parallel cuts through the top of the shallot down to the work surface.

2. Finish the mincing by making very thin slices perpendicular to the lengthwise cuts.

ILLUSTRATION: JOHN BURGOYNE

MATCHING GREENS AND DRESSING

Most salad greens fall into one of three categories: mellow, spicy, or bitter. The following salads are representational pairings of each type of green and a vinaigrette that best matches its particular flavors. Feel free to mix and match greens from each category to change the flavor, color, and texture of each salad.

The vinaigrette recipes yield ½ cup dressing, or enough to dress 4 quarts of greens, about eight servings. When making smaller amounts of salad, figure on 2 tablespoons of dressing per quart of greens.

Whole fresh herb leaves, like parsley, basil, thyme, oregano, marjoram, and chervil, may also be added to any of these salads for a burst of flavor.

SALAD OF MELLOW GREENS WITH RED WINE VINAIGRETTE SERVES 8

➤ Mellow-flavored greens are the most common greens at the market and include lettuces such as Boston, bibb, red and green leaf, red oak, lolla rossa, and iceberg, as well as flat-leaf spinach. Their mild flavors are easily overpowered and are best complemented by a simple dressing, such as a classic red wine vinaigrette.

- 6 tablespoons extra-virgin olive oil
- 1½ tablespoons red wine vinegar
- ¼ teaspoon salt
- ⅛ teaspoon ground black pepper
- 4 quarts washed and dried mellow greens

Combine all dressing ingredients in jar, seal lid, and shake vigorously until emulsified, about 20 seconds. Dress greens (see right).

SALAD OF SPICY GREENS WITH MUSTARD AND BALSAMIC VINAIGRETTE SERVES 8

➤ Spicy greens include arugula, watercress, mizuna, and baby mustard. They easily stand up to strong flavors such as the mustard, shallots, and balsamic vinegar in this dressing.

- 6 tablespoons extra-virgin olive oil
- 1½ tablespoons balsamic vinegar
- 1 tablespoon Dijon mustard
- 1 teaspoon finely minced shallot (see illustrations on page 16)
- ¼ teaspoon salt
- ⅛ teaspoon ground black pepper
- 4 quarts washed and dried spicy greens

Combine all dressing ingredients in jar, seal lid, and shake vigorously until emulsified, about 20 seconds. Dress greens (see right).

SALAD OF BITTER GREENS WITH CREAMY GARLIC VINAIGRETTE SERVES 8

➤ Escarole, chicory, Belgian endive, radicchio, frisée, and young dandelion greens all fall into this category. A creamy, assertive vinaigrette tempers the astringency of the greens.

- ¼ cup extra-virgin olive oil
- 2 tablespoons sour cream or yogurt
- 1 tablespoon white wine vinegar
- 1 tablespoon juice from 1 lemon
- 2 teaspoons Dijon mustard
- 1 small garlic clove, pureed (see illustration on page 16)
- ¼ teaspoon salt
  Ground black pepper to taste
- 4 quarts washed and dried bitter greens

Combine all dressing ingredients in jar, seal lid, and shake vigorously until emulsified, about 20 seconds. Dress greens (see right).

TOSSING GREENS AND DRESSING

We found that an ideal salad bowl is wide-mouthed and relatively shallow, so that the greens become evenly coated with vinaigrette quickly. A wide bowl also facilitates gentle handling of the greens. The bowl should be roughly 50 percent larger than the amount of greens to make sure there is adequate room for tossing. For example, a salad with 4 quarts of greens should be tossed in a 6-quart bowl. Whatever utensils you choose to toss the salad—wooden spoons, hands (our favorite method), or tongs—a light touch is crucial. A roughly tossed salad will wilt much faster than a lightly tossed salad.

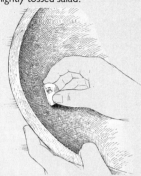

1. Add mild garlic flavor: Peel and cut a clove of garlic. With the cut-side down, rub the interior of your salad bowl.

2. Measure greens: Loosely pack the greens into a large measuring cup, figuring on 2 cups per serving.

3. Tear greens: If the greens are too large, gently tear them into manageable pieces with your hands just before serving the salad. If torn ahead of time, they will discolor and wilt.

4. Shake dressing: Just before adding the dressing, give it a quick shake to make sure that it is fully combined and that the solid ingredients, like shallots, are evenly dispersed.

5. Drizzle dressing: To prevent overdressed greens, add the dressing in small increments as you toss the salad.

6. Toss salad: Coat the greens by gently "fluffing" them, adding more vinaigrette only when certain the greens need it.

CHOOSING VINEGAR AND OIL

All vinegars are not created equal. Some, like red and white wine vinegars, have a searingly high acidity of 5 to 7 percent. Lemon juice, in comparison, is milder, about 4 percent. And depending on its age and quality, balsamic vinegar's acidity can vary a good deal (the cheap stuff being nothing more than caramel-colored red wine vinegar). We adjust the ratio of oil to vinegar to suit the vinegar's strength; the oil mellows the acidity. For example, a red wine–based vinaigrette requires 4 parts oil to 1 part vinegar, but a vinaigrette made with lemon juice requires just 3 parts oil to one part juice. Extra-virgin olive oil is our top choice for salads because it tastes good with all greens and vinegars.

French Potato Salad

Does your French potato salad recipe yield mangled bits of potatoes that taste dull and underseasoned? We set out in search of something better.

⊰ BY REBECCA HAYS WITH MEG SUZUKI ⊱

American-style potato salad, thickly dressed with mayonnaise and sweet pickle relish, is archetypal picnic fare and will always have a place on summer tables. But we've cooked (and eaten) piles of it over the years, and these days we're yearning for something lighter and fresher to serve with grilled fish, chicken, and even meat. In our minds, French potato salad is just the ticket. Having little in common with its American counterpart, French potato salad is served warm or at room temperature and is composed of sliced potatoes glistening with olive oil, white wine vinegar, and plenty of fresh herbs.

We expected quick success with this seemingly simple recipe—how hard could it be to boil a few potatoes and toss them in vinaigrette? We sliced the hot potatoes and then dressed them while they were still warm (warm potatoes are more absorbent than cool ones) and then served them up to our tasters. The salad looked mangled, as the warm potatoes consistently broke apart upon slicing. We chose not to peel the potatoes for the sake of convenience and beauty, but the potato skins inevitably tore, leaving unsightly streaks. And the salad didn't taste much better than it looked. Despite an assertively seasoned vinaigrette, the potatoes themselves were uniformly bland. Another irksome point was that it was hard to tell when the potatoes were done. Unevenly sized potatoes made it difficult to avoid some over- or undercooked potatoes in the finished dish. This wasn't going to be as easy as we thought.

Tattered Taters

Our first task was to put a stop to homely salads made from jagged, broken potatoes with ripped skins. We tried shocking the whole potatoes after cooking (reasoning that the ice cold water might somehow set the skin—it didn't), slicing the potatoes with a serrated knife (this helped a little bit, but the results were inconsistent), and starting the potatoes in boiling instead of cold water (this made absolutely no difference). It was proving impossible to slice a just-cooked potato without having it fall apart. What's more, the task was annoying. We kept burning our fingers on the boiling hot potatoes.

Up to this point, we were using low starch/high moisture red potatoes, the most common choice for salads. We backtracked, wondering if russet,

Thinly sliced potatoes cook in just five minutes and are ready to be dressed with mustard-herb vinaigrette and tossed with radishes and capers.

all-purpose, or Yukon Golds would be better-behaved. This lead was a dead end. None of the potatoes held together when sliced, nor could they compete with the sweet, earthy flavor and (potentially) good looks of the red potatoes. The russets were mealy and dry, the all-purpose were waxy and didn't soak up much dressing, and the Yukon Golds were grainy and soggy.

We reevaluated our cooking technique. We had been boiling the potatoes whole—generally the standard at *Cook's*, the idea being that the skins prevent potato starch from leaching out into the water—then slicing while warm. On a whim, we sliced some potatoes before cooking. This, surprisingly, did the trick. The potato slices emerged from the water unbroken and with their skins intact. They had a clean (not starchy) taste, were evenly cooked, and held together perfectly, unlike those that had been cooked whole before being sliced. (We still prefer boiling potatoes whole and in their skins for mashed potatoes because the starch retained produces a thick, creamy texture.) This one simple change in technique offered multiple benefits. First, the frustrating (and

sometimes painful) task of slicing hot potatoes was eliminated. Second, we now had no need to find uniformly sized potatoes to ensure even cooking. (We just needed to cut the potatoes into slices of uniform thickness.) Third, we found we could perfectly season the cut potatoes while they cooked by adding a hefty 2 tablespoons of salt to the cooking water.

Dressing Up

We shifted our focus to the vinaigrette and its usual suspects: olive oil, white wine vinegar, herbs, mustard, minced onion, chicken stock, and white wine. Because our initial tests had produced relatively dull salads, we decided to experiment with each component until we found a surefire way to pump up the flavor. The first improvement came by using slightly more vinegar than the test kitchen standard of 4 parts oil to 1 part vinegar. These bland potatoes could handle extra acid. We loved the sharp flavor notes added by champagne vinegar but found that white wine vinegar works well, too. As for the olive oil, both extra-virgin and pure olive oil make equally good bases for the dressing; tasters found little distinction between the two (the former being more flavorful than the latter), presumably because of the other potent ingredients in the vinaigrette. However, expensive fruity olive oils were rejected for their overpowering nature.

We liked the extra moisture and layer of complexity that chicken stock and wine added (salads made strictly with oil and vinegar were a tad dry), but it seemed wasteful to uncork a bottle or open a can only to use a few tablespoons. We found a solution to this problem and a revelation when we consulted Julia Child's *The Way to Cook* (Knopf, 1989). She suggests adding some of the potato cooking water to the vinaigrette, a quick and frugal solution that also added plenty of potato flavor and a nice touch of saltiness. Two teaspoonfuls of Dijon mustard and a sprinkle of freshly ground black pepper perked things up, while the gentle assertiveness of one minced shallot and a blanched garlic clove (raw garlic was too harsh) added even more depth. As for the fresh herbs, we made salads with all manner of them, including chives, dill, basil, parsley, tarragon, and chervil. But an inherently French fines herbes mixture seemed appropriate in theory and was heavenly in reality. Chives, parsley, tarragon, and chervil make up this classic quartet with anise undertones.

The last problem was how to toss the cooked, warm potatoes with the vinaigrette without damaging the slices. The solution was simple. We carefully laid the potatoes in a single layer on a baking sheet and then poured the vinaigrette over them. Spreading out the potatoes in this way also allowed them to cool off a bit, preventing residual cooking and potential mushiness. While we waited for the vinaigrette to soak into the potatoes, we had just enough time to chop the herbs and shallots before sprinkling them on the finished salad. Adding the herbs just before serving guards against wilting and darkening.

FRENCH POTATO SALAD WITH DIJON MUSTARD AND FINES HERBES
SERVES 6 AS A SIDE DISH

If fresh chervil isn't available, substitute an additional ½ tablespoon of minced parsley and an additional ½ teaspoon of tarragon. For best flavor, serve the salad warm, but to make ahead, follow the recipe through step 2, cover with plastic wrap, and refrigerate. Before serving, bring the salad to room temperature, then add the shallots and herbs.

- 2 pounds small (about 2-inch diameter) red potatoes, unpeeled, scrubbed, and cut into ¼-inch-thick slices
- 2 tablespoons salt
- 1 medium garlic clove, peeled and threaded on skewer
- 1½ tablespoons champagne vinegar or white wine vinegar
- 2 teaspoons Dijon mustard
- ¼ cup olive oil
- ½ teaspoon ground black pepper
- 1 small shallot, minced (about 2 tablespoons)
- 1 tablespoon minced fresh chervil leaves
- 1 tablespoon minced fresh parsley leaves
- 1 tablespoon minced fresh chives
- 1 teaspoon minced fresh tarragon leaves

1. Place potatoes, 6 cups cold tap water, and salt in large saucepan; bring to boil over high heat, then reduce heat to medium. Lower skewered garlic into simmering water and partially blanch, about 45 seconds. Immediately run garlic under cold tap water to stop cooking; remove garlic from skewer and set aside. Continue to simmer potatoes, uncovered, until tender but still firm (thin-bladed paring knife can be slipped into and

out of center of potato slice with no resistance), about 5 minutes. Drain potatoes, reserving ¼ cup cooking water. Arrange hot potatoes close together in single layer on rimmed baking sheet.

2. Press garlic through garlic press or mince by hand. Whisk garlic, reserved potato cooking water, vinegar, mustard, oil, and pepper in small bowl until combined. Drizzle dressing evenly over warm potatoes; let stand 10 minutes.

3. Toss shallot and herbs in small bowl. Transfer potatoes to large serving bowl; add shallot/herb mixture and mix gently with rubber spatula to combine. Serve immediately.

FRENCH POTATO SALAD WITH ARUGULA, ROQUEFORT, AND WALNUTS

Follow recipe for French Potato Salad with Dijon Mustard and Fines Herbes, omitting herbs and tossing dressed potatoes with ½ cup walnuts, toasted and coarsely chopped, 4 ounces Roquefort cheese, crumbled, and 1 small bunch arugula, washed, dried, and torn into bite-sized pieces (about 2½ cups) along with shallots in step 3.

FRENCH POTATO SALAD WITH FENNEL, TOMATO, AND OLIVES

When chopping the fennel fronds for this variation, use only the delicate wispy leaves, not the tough, fibrous stems to which they are attached.

1. Trim small fennel bulb of stalks and fronds; roughly chop fronds (you should have about ¼ cup). Halve bulb lengthwise; using paring knife, core one half of bulb, reserving second half for another use. Cut half crosswise into very thin slices.
2. Follow recipe for French Potato Salad with

After the potatoes have been thoroughly drained, spread them out on a rimmed baking sheet and drizzle evenly with vinaigrette.

Dijon Mustard and Fines Herbes, omitting chervil, chives, and tarragon, increasing parsley to 3 tablespoons, and tossing dressed potatoes with fennel, 1 medium tomato (about 6 ounces) peeled, seeded, and diced medium, and ¼ cup oil-cured black olives, pitted and quartered, along with shallots and parsley in step 3.

FRENCH POTATO SALAD WITH RADISHES, CORNICHONS, AND CAPERS

Follow recipe for French Potato Salad with Dijon Mustard and Fines Herbes, omitting herbs and substituting 2 tablespoons minced red onion for shallot. Toss dressed potatoes with 2 medium red radishes (about 1½ ounces), thinly sliced (about ⅓ cup), ¼ cup capers, rinsed and drained, and ¼ cup cornichons, thinly sliced, along with red onion in step 3.

SCIENCE: **Keeping Potato Salad Safe**

Mayonnaise has gotten a bad reputation, being blamed for spoiled potato salads and upset stomachs after many summer picnics and barbecues. You may think that switching from a mayonnaise-based dressing to a vinaigrette will protect your potato salad (and your family) from food poisoning. Think again.

The main ingredients in mayonnaise are raw eggs, vegetable oil, and an acid (usually vinegar or lemon juice). The eggs used in commercially made mayonnaise have been pasteurized to kill salmonella and other bacteria. Its high acidity is another safeguard; because bacteria do not fare well in acidic environments, the lemon juice or vinegar inhibits bacterial growth. Mayonnaise, even when homemade, is rarely the problem unless it contains very little acid. It's the potatoes that are more likely to go bad.

The bacteria usually responsible for spoiled potato salad are *Bacillus cereus* and *Staphylococcus aureus* (commonly known as staph). Both are found in soil and dust, and they thrive on starchy, low-acid foods like rice, pasta, and potatoes. If they find their way into your potato salad via an unwashed cutting board or contaminated hands, they can wreak havoc on your digestive system.

Most foodborne bacteria grow well at temperatures between 40 and 140 degrees Fahrenheit. This is known as the temperature danger zone, and if contaminated food remains in this zone for too long, the bacteria can produce enough toxins to make you sick. The U.S. Food and Drug Administration recommends refrigerating food within two hours of its preparation, or one hour if the room temperature is above 90 degrees. Heat from the sun is often what causes the trouble at summer picnics.

Although the high acid content of the vinaigrette for our French potato salad might slow bacteria growth, it's best to play it safe and follow the FDA's guideline. Don't leave the potato salad out for more than two hours; promptly refrigerate any leftovers. —M.S.

Spice Rubs for Grilled Chicken

Make-ahead spice blends provide deep flavor with little effort.

≥ BY SHANNON BLAISDELL ≤

Let's face it: Backyard barbecues and the spoils of the grill have become predictable. Purchased spice rubs are meant to liven things up, but we find many of them to be dull (with little spice flavor), overpowering (too much salt), and expensive to boot. Spice rubs should be savory, robust mixtures of spices and herbs that promote the development of deeply browned crusts filled with complex, concentrated flavors. The good news is that homemade rubs can handle this task nicely, are easy to make, and can be stored for months.

Although spice rubs can be used with many foods, I decided to concentrate on bone-in, skin-on, split chicken breasts. They are the perfect canvas for an invigorating rub: benign and mild. I brined the chicken, ensuring that it would be moist and well-seasoned, and then grilled the breasts using a two-level fire (a hot side for browning, a cooler side for cooking the breasts through) and a foil pan as a cover to produce crispy skin and succulent meat. (For more information on grilling chicken breasts, see the July/August 1997 issue of *Cook's*.)

Many experts tout the superiority of rubs made with whole spices toasted in a dry sauté pan and then ground in a mill. While these rubs don't require an enormous investment of time, I wanted to see if I could speed the process—without sacrificing too much flavor—by using pre-ground spices. As it turned out, the dry heat of the grill toasted the spices right on the chicken. I also discovered that pre-ground spices, which are so finely pulverized, have excellent sticking power—a real bonus. I proceeded to use pre-ground spices to develop four rubs with different flavor profiles.

Next I focused on the best way to get the rubs on the chicken. After rinsing the brined chicken and drying it with paper towels (drying helps to prevent charring that may result from the sugar in the brine), I tried oiling the meat before applying the rubs. This step wasn't necessary, though. All the rubs needed to adhere to the chicken was its natural moisture (there was still enough even after drying). Testing quickly showed that the only sane way to apply the rubs was to use my hands. This ensured even distribution over the skin and the underside of the breast and into every nook and cranny. (Thorough seasoning—including the underside—is important to help flavor the meat.) It is a messy task, but, like kneading dough, it's also fun. If you happen to find a spot where the skin is naturally detached from the breast, rub the flesh with the spices to further intensify the flavor. (But

don't pull the skin away from the flesh just to work the spice rub into the meat; it might flap and fall off or char during grilling.)

Once rubbed, the chicken breasts did well with a rest before being grilled. While the texture of the meat and skin didn't vary much whether the breasts rested or not, the flavor did. Letting the breasts sit in the refrigerator for one to eight hours gave the rub a chance to penetrate the meat; the longer the rest, the more intense the flavor.

Each of the spice rubs that follows makes enough to season about 16 breasts. If stored in airtight containers, the rubs will remain potent for up to three months—in other words, all summer long.

CAJUN SPICE RUB
MAKES ABOUT 1 CUP

- 1/2 cup sweet paprika
- 2 tablespoons kosher salt
- 2 tablespoons garlic powder
- 1 tablespoon dried thyme
- 2 teaspoons ground celery seed
- 2 teaspoons ground black pepper
- 2 teaspoons cayenne pepper

Combine all ingredients in small bowl.

JAMAICAN SPICE RUB
MAKES ABOUT 1 CUP

- 1/4 cup packed brown sugar
- 3 tablespoons kosher salt
- 3 tablespoons ground coriander
- 2 tablespoons ground ginger
- 2 tablespoons garlic powder
- 1 tablespoon ground allspice
- 1 tablespoon ground black pepper
- 2 teaspoons cayenne pepper
- 2 teaspoons ground nutmeg
- 1 1/2 teaspoons ground cinnamon

Combine all ingredients in small bowl.

TEX-MEX SPICE RUB
MAKES ABOUT 1 CUP

- 1/4 cup ground cumin
- 2 tablespoons chili powder
- 2 tablespoons ground coriander
- 2 tablespoons dried oregano
- 2 tablespoons garlic powder
- 4 teaspoons kosher salt

- 2 teaspoons cocoa
- 1 teaspoon cayenne pepper

Combine all ingredients in small bowl.

CURRY-CUMIN SPICE RUB
MAKES ABOUT 1 CUP

- 1/4 cup curry powder
- 1/4 cup ground cumin
- 1/4 cup chili powder
- 3 tablespoons ground black pepper
- 3 tablespoons packed brown sugar
- 1 tablespoon kosher salt

Combine all ingredients in small bowl.

GRILLED SPICE-RUBBED CHICKEN BREASTS

If you're using only a portion of the spice rub you've made, measure out and separate the amount you will need to make sure you don't contaminate the whole lot with fingers or utensils that have touched uncooked chicken.

1. TO BRINE AND SEASON CHICKEN BREASTS: For each pound of chicken breasts, dissolve 1/4 cup kosher salt (or 2 tablespoons table salt) and 2 tablespoons sugar in 1 quart cold tap water. Submerge chicken in brine and refrigerate 45 minutes, until fully seasoned. Remove chicken from brine, rinse under running water, dry thoroughly with paper towels, and rub all sides of each breast evenly with 1 tablespoon spice rub. Refrigerate chicken breasts, covered with plastic wrap, for at least 1 hour or up to 8 hours.

2. TO GRILL CHICKEN BREASTS: Build medium-hot fire (you can hold your hand 5 inches above grill surface for 3 to 4 seconds) on one side of grill. (If using gas grill, set one burner to high and other burner[s] to medium-low.) Grill chicken breasts, skin-side down, on hotter side of grill until well-browned on both sides, about 2 minutes per side. Move chicken, skin-side up, to cooler side of grill and cover with disposable aluminum roasting pan (or gas grill lid); continue to cook 10 minutes. Turn chicken skin-side down and cook 5 minutes longer until thickest part of chicken near bone is no longer pink when checked with tip of paring knife or internal temperature registers 160 degrees on instant-read thermometer. Transfer to serving platter; serve warm or at room temperature.

Buttermilk Coleslaw

Buttermilk coleslaw can be wilted and watery. Here's how to get
a pickle-crisp texture and a light but creamy dressing.

⇒ BY JULIA COLLIN ⇐

Order cornmeal-battered fish or deep-fried chicken from any authentic Southern eatery, and it will no doubt be accompanied by a side of buttermilk coleslaw. Unlike mayonnaise, buttermilk presents the opportunity for a coleslaw that is light, creamy, and refreshingly tart, with a mouthfeel that's neither too fatty nor too lean. The downside is that, also unlike mayonnaise which is thick and clingy, buttermilk is thin, so it presents the unappetizing possibility of thin, watery coleslaw. I may be a native Yank, but I do know that buttermilk coleslaw is bad when large, unevenly cut pieces of cabbage sit in a pool of unseasoned buttermilk. So my goal was clear: crisp, evenly cut pieces of cabbage lightly dressed with an authentic, flavorful buttermilk dressing that clings to the cabbage instead of collecting in the bottom of the bowl.

Tough and Squeaky

The tough, squeaky leaves and compact core of a cabbage head require both a sharp knife and a good game plan. I realized it is best to quarter and core the cabbage, then disassemble each quarter into stacks containing several layers of cabbage. These stacks can then be either laid flat on a cutting board and sliced with a chef's knife or rolled and fit into the feeder tube of a food processor fitted with the shredding disk.

As tempting as it is to toss freshly cut pieces of cabbage immediately with dressing, I found that such a hastily made coleslaw will weep within an hour, diluting the dressing into a puddle. To combat the weeping problem, I tried two popular methods of dealing with the prepped cabbage: ice water and salt. Soaking the sliced cabbage in ice water turned it temporarily plump and fresh, but the dressing didn't cling to it. In the end, the soaked cabbage just made for a bigger puddle of dressing. Salting the cabbage, on the other hand, worked perfectly. As the salt and cabbage sat, moisture was wicked out of the cabbage cells, wilting it to a pickle-crisp texture. To eliminate excess salt and water, the wilted cabbage needed a quick rinse and towel dry. (Left unrinsed and undried, the salty moisture trapped within the thatch of shredded cabbage ruined both the flavor and texture of the final coleslaw.) A mere teaspoon of salt was enough to draw the moisture out of half a head of cabbage.

Authentic Buttermilk Dressing

With my cabbage cut evenly and rid of excessive moisture, I needed to find a way to bulk up the buttermilk so that it would cling to the cabbage without losing its distinctively Southern twang. First, I tried mixing the buttermilk with increasing amounts of sour cream, but the dressing tasted overly sour by the time it was thick enough to coat. Switching to mayonnaise, I was able to make a dressing with good heft and adhesiveness, but I disliked the way the mayonnaise muted the buttermilk's characteristic zip. But when the buttermilk was both stiffened by mayonnaise and reinforced with sour cream, the dressing adhered well to the cabbage without tasting overly potent or losing its bite. I found that ½ cup buttermilk needed help from 2 tablespoons each of sour cream and mayonnaise to dress half a head of cabbage.

For finishing touches, I added a shredded carrot for both color and sweetness, which my tasters liked, and then tried celery, bell peppers, radishes, and red onions, all of which they did not like. The mild flavor of shallots was welcome, though, along with some parsley, and a pinch of sugar, mustard, and cider vinegar. The result? An authentic buttermilk coleslaw that will not weep whether it's accompanying food prepared north or south of the Mason-Dixon line.

Bad Slaw, Good Slaw

Unsalted cabbage is too crunchy and leaches moisture, which makes the coleslaw watery, left. Salted cabbage has already shed its moisture and makes coleslaw that is tender but not watery, right.

CREAMY BUTTERMILK COLESLAW
MAKES ABOUT 6 CUPS

If you are planning to serve the coleslaw immediately, rinse the salted cabbage in a large bowl of ice water, drain it in a colander, pick out any ice cubes, then pat the cabbage dry before dressing.

1	pound (about ½ medium head) red or green cabbage, shredded fine (6 cups)
	Salt
1	medium carrot, shredded on box grater
½	cup buttermilk
2	tablespoons mayonnaise
2	tablespoons sour cream
1	small shallot, minced (about 2 tablespoons)
2	tablespoons minced fresh parsley leaves
½	teaspoon cider vinegar
½	teaspoon sugar
¼	teaspoon Dijon mustard
⅛	teaspoon ground black pepper

1. Toss shredded cabbage and 1 teaspoon salt in colander or large mesh strainer set over medium bowl. Let stand until cabbage wilts, at least 1 hour or up to 4 hours. Rinse cabbage under cold running water. Press, but do not squeeze, to drain; pat dry with paper towels. Place wilted cabbage and carrot in large bowl.

2. Stir buttermilk, mayonnaise, sour cream, shallot, parsley, vinegar, sugar, mustard, ¼ teaspoon salt, and pepper together in small bowl. Pour dressing over cabbage and toss to combine; refrigerate until chilled, about 30 minutes. (Coleslaw can be refrigerated for up to 3 days.)

BUTTERMILK COLESLAW WITH GREEN ONIONS AND CILANTRO

Follow recipe for Creamy Buttermilk Coleslaw, omitting mustard, substituting 1 tablespoon minced cilantro for parsley and 1 teaspoon lime juice for cider vinegar, and adding 2 scallions, sliced thin, to dressing.

LEMONY BUTTERMILK COLESLAW

Follow recipe for Creamy Buttermilk Coleslaw, substituting 1 teaspoon lemon juice for vinegar and adding 1 teaspoon minced fresh thyme and 1 tablespoon minced fresh chives to dressing.

Ice Cream Sandwiches Made Easy

Why would you make an ice cream sandwich at home? Because it's easy, and it tastes a lot better than those flavorless sandwiches sold at the supermarket.

⇒ BY RAQUEL PELZEL ⇐

I don't know anyone who would turn down a fresh-from-the-freezer ice cream sandwich. Which is interesting, because most ice cream sandwiches are awful, made of flavorless, watery ice cream and bland and sticky chocolate cookies that, mysteriously, taste nothing like chocolate. There are good ice cream sandwiches to be found, but they are limited to gourmet restaurant menus, where one sandwich could cost you as much as a Big Mac, large fries, and three Happy Meals.

This made me wonder why more people don't make ice cream sandwiches at home. The cost is low—all you need is ice cream and cookie dough ingredients—and the payoff is high—you get an ice cream sandwich made with premium ice cream sandwiched between two intensely chocolate cookies. Perhaps it's the dearth of recipes. As I found out, there are but a handful of published recipes that tell you how to make an ice cream sandwich with real chocolate cookies, not chocolate chip or oatmeal cookie hybrids. With these recipes in hand, I decided to give the Good Humor man a run for his money.

After putting together several batches with disappointing results, I knew with certainty why smart people don't make ice cream sandwiches at home. First, dealing with ice cream, especially in hot summer weather, is an absolute melting nightmare—I ended up wearing more ice cream than the cookies. In addition, most recipes call for making cookie dough that must be rolled and cut, like sugar cookies. Rolling out a cookie dough that contains chocolate is a frustrating process that makes a sticky mess. So my goal of great, homemade ice cream sandwiches had been tempered by reality: the need for a quick and easy process (even in the middle of July) that produced both a substantial layer of ice cream and chocolatey, rich cookies that did not need to be rolled out like cookie dough.

Looking for Mr. Goodbar

To avoid rolling cookie dough, I decided to try a thick, brownie-like batter that could be spread into a rimmed, rectangular baking sheet. After baking, I would then unmold the giant rectangle

A combination of Dutch-processed cocoa powder and chocolate syrup gives the cookies great flavor and a strong, pliable texture.

cookie and cut out smaller rectangles.

I beat softened butter with sugar, eggs, and dry ingredients. But while I was beating the wet ingredients, too much air was incorporated into the batter, creating a cakey, spongy cookie rather than a dense one. Next I tried liquid fats—oil and melted butter. Although the texture was still not quite right, the butter won hands down—and now I could skip the step of beating it. To achieve a thinner cookie, I tried reducing the amount of flour (I had been using 1 cup), but the cookie became too brittle. The solution turned out to be simple; I reduced the leavener (baking soda) to a mere 1/8 teaspoon to achieve a thin layer of chocolate cookie. (I also tried the batter with no baking soda; it cooked up as hard as linoleum and not much better tasting.)

Now that the thickness of the cookie was just right, I focused on its chocolate punch. I tried adding melted chocolate to the batter, but it became sticky and difficult to spread in the parchment-lined pan. I then tried chocolate syrup, adding 1/4 cup to my batter. What a difference! The chocolate flavor was heightened, and the texture was pliable but strong, thanks to the hydrating and elasticizing effects of the corn syrup in the chocolate syrup.

I breathed a sigh of relief and moved on to my last chocolate test: Dutch-processed versus natural cocoa powder. With a lingering chocolate flavor and black-brown color, there was no contest—the Dutch-processed cocoa received a gold star.

Mastering the Ice Cream

Now that I had gotten a flat, pliable, super-chocolatey ice cream sandwich cookie, it was time to figure out how to outfit it with some ice cream. The most logical approach seemed to be to cut rectangular slabs of ice cream straight out of a rectangular-shaped half-gallon ice cream container. Easier said than done. Not only was it difficult to cut the ice cream exactly to the same size as the cookie, but I had to patch together the small rectangular slabs of ice cream in odd configurations, turning the ice cream sandwich assembly into a craft project. In addition, tasters didn't like the fluffy ice cream typically sold in half-gallon containers. They wanted a denser, creamier ice cream, which is typically sold in pints. So I tried letting the ice cream soften in the container for 15 minutes on the countertop before I spooned out portions and spread them onto the cookie base. But the ice cream had to be quite soft before it reached a spreadable consistency, and this made it difficult to sandwich two cookies together, as some ice cream always seemed to squish out the sides.

Choosing the Right Ice Cream

In my testing, I had the best results with rich, dense, and creamy custard-style ice cream (meaning that the ice cream contains eggs) with a low amount of overrun (meaning that the ice cream does not have a lot of air whipped into it during churning). Avoid chunky flavors; nuts and chips make cutting rounds difficult. As for brand recommendations, Edy's Dreamery won our September/October 2001 tasting of vanilla ice creams, followed by Double Rainbow. For our favorite chocolate ice cream, see page 23.

Chocolate Ice Cream

Vanilla ice cream is a classic for ice cream sandwiches, but the chocoholics in the test kitchen weren't satisfied until I sandwiched chocolate ice cream in between the two chocolate cookies. I decided to find out which brands taste best.

Of the seven brands tasted, the two that came out on top, Häagen-Dazs and Double Rainbow, were valued most for their "intense" chocolate flavor, "creamy" and "dense" texture, and "clean" finish. Brigham's, which took third place, was thought "refreshing" but too "sweet" and "airy." Coming in fourth and fifth were the Whole Foods Market house brand, 365 Every Day Value ice cream (noted for its "cocoa-powdery flavor"), and Turkey Hill ice cream (described as "too sweet" and "artificial"), respectively. The last two places were reserved for perhaps two of the most popular brands: Breyer's (which had a "mild chocolate flavor" that tasted like "cake batter") and Edy's Grand (which tasted like "chocolate milk" combined with "malt"). Edy's Grand should not be confused with Edy's higher-quality Dreamery line, which does not include plain chocolate ice cream. —R.P.

Häagen-Dazs and Double Rainbow (far left) easily scooped the competition.

I picked up on an idea to remove the ice cream completely from its container, beat it in a standing mixer to soften it, then spread it in another rimmed sheet pan. After refreezing the ice cream in the sheet pan, it would be the same size as the cookie—no spreading or jigsawing the ice cream together would be necessary. The problem was that the sheet pan with the ice cream took up a lot of freezer space. In addition, there was a lot of standing around and waiting for the ice cream to harden. I wanted a simpler method.

The obvious answer was to cut rounds of ice cream from round pint containers. However, the recipes that use this method also call for round cookies made from rolled cookie dough, an approach I had already nixed as too much work. Looking at my rectangular sheets of baked cookie dough, I wondered if there wasn't an easy way to turn them into circles. Finally, I had a brainstorm.

Why not use the stiff and sharp top of a Häagen-Dazs container to cut through the cookie dough? This worked well enough, but the finished sandwich cookies looked homely, even too homely to qualify as "rustic." (This method does work in a pinch.) The best solution was to use a round biscuit cutter that made perfect circles of both the cookie and the ice cream. Although some ice cream and baked chocolate cookie dough were wasted (most of the cookie scraps got gobbled up while I was assembling the sandwiches), I was more than happy that my sandwiches were easy to make and looked perfect. In fact, because the ice cream had exactly the same dimensions as the cookie, these sandwiches looked even better than those made from the more complicated recipes that called for rolling and cutting out cookie dough.

Chocolatey and pliant, these cookies didn't stick to my fingers, and the ice cream was thick and rich; it didn't melt away before I had a chance to sink my teeth into it. At the same time, the cookie is easy to make and the ice cream easy to manipulate. This sandwich has more than Good Humor, it has good taste.

THE BEST ICE CREAM SANDWICHES
MAKES EIGHT 3-INCH SANDWICHES

Dense, rich ice cream and smooth—not chunky—flavors make the best sandwiches. See page 4 for ways to dress up the sides of the ice cream sandwiches with shredded coconut, chopped nuts, sprinkles, or chocolate chips.

- 1 cup (5 ounces) unbleached all-purpose flour
- 1/2 cup (1 1/2 ounces) Dutch-processed cocoa powder
- 1/4 teaspoon salt
- 1/8 teaspoon baking soda
- 2 large eggs
- 2/3 cup (about 4 3/4 ounces) granulated sugar
- 1/4 cup (2 3/4 ounces) chocolate syrup
- 8 tablespoons (1 stick) unsalted butter, melted
- 2 pints vanilla, chocolate, or coffee ice cream (see note)

1. Adjust oven rack to middle position and heat to 350 degrees. Lightly spray 17 1/2 by 12-inch half-sheet pan or 17 by 11-inch jelly-roll pan with nonstick cooking spray and line with parchment paper (do not grease parchment).

2. Sift flour, cocoa, salt, and baking soda into medium bowl. Beat eggs, sugar, and chocolate syrup in large bowl until light brown. Add melted butter and whisk until fully incorporated.

3. Add dry ingredients to egg mixture. With rubber spatula, gradually incorporate dry ingredients into wet; stir until evenly moistened and no dry streaks remain. Pour batter into prepared baking sheet; using offset metal spatula, spread batter evenly in pan. Bake until cookie springs back when touched with finger, 10 to 12 minutes. Cool in pan on wire rack 5 minutes, then run paring knife around perimeter of baking sheet to loosen. Invert cookie onto work surface or large cutting board; carefully peel off parchment. Cool to room temperature, about 30 minutes.

4. Using 2 3/4- to 3-inch round biscuit cutter, follow illustration 1 to cut out 16 cookie rounds.

5. Following illustration 2, slice eight 3/4-inch-thick rounds from ice cream pints. Peel away and discard cardboard container. Following illustration 3, use same biscuit cutter to cut rounds from each slice. Assemble sandwiches. Serve immediately or place sandwiches on foil-lined baking sheet, cover tightly with second sheet foil, and freeze up to 3 hours. To store sandwiches longer, wrap individually in wax paper, then with foil; freeze up to 7 days. Let sandwiches frozen for more than 30 minutes stand at room temperature for 10 minutes before serving.

STEP-BY-STEP | ASSEMBLING ICE CREAM SANDWICHES

1. Using 2 3/4- to 3-inch biscuit cutter, cut 16 rounds from the baked cookie.

2. Using a serrated knife, slice away bottom of container. Dip knife in warm water, wipe clean, and cut four 3/4-inch-thick rounds, each time making small slice into pint then rotating container, eventually cutting through entire pint.

3. With same biscuit cutter used to cut cookie rounds, cut round out of each ice cream slice. Place cut ice cream round on cookie bottom, then top with another cookie, shiny side up.

Best Blueberry Cobbler

No-fuss drop biscuits and an unconventional baking method are the keys to a speedy, intensely flavored summer cobbler.

⇒ BY ERIN MCMURRER WITH MEG SUZUKI ⇐

We have always been huge fans of baked fruit desserts. What could be better than a hot and bubbly fruit filling matched with tender biscuits? As simple (and appealing) as this sounds, why do so many of us end up with a filling that is sickeningly sweet and over-spiced? Why is the filling so often runny, or, on the flip side, so thick and gloppy? Why are the biscuits, the most common choice of topping for cobblers, too dense, dry, and heavy? Our goal was to create a filling in which the berries were allowed to cook until lightly thickened. We wanted their natural sweetness to sing a cappella without being overshadowed by a symphony of sugar and spice. The biscuit should stand tall with structure, be crisp on the outside and light and buttery on the inside, and complement the filling. Most important, it had to be easy.

Our biscuit topping contains a little cornmeal for crunch and buttermilk for flavor.

The Filling Goes First

The basic ingredients found in most cobbler fillings are fruit, sugar, thickener (flour, arrowroot, cornstarch, potato starch, or tapioca), and flavorings (lemon zest, spices, etc.). The fruit and sugar are easy: Take fresh blueberries and add enough sugar such that the fruit neither remains puckery nor turns saccharine. For 6 cups of berries, we found ½ cup sugar to be ideal—and far less than the conventional amount of sugar, which in some recipes exceeds 2 cups.

Some recipes swear by one thickener and warn that other choices will ruin the filling. We found this to be partly true. Tasters were all in agreement that flour—the most common choice in recipes—gave the fruit filling an unappealing starchy texture. Most tasters agreed that tapioca thickened the berry juices nicely, but the soft beads of starch left in the fruit's juices knocked out this contender. (Also, when exposed to direct heat, as in a cobbler, the tapioca that remains near the surface of the fruit quickly turns as hard as Tic-Tacs.) Arrowroot worked beautifully, but this starch is far too expensive and can be difficult to find. Cornstarch and potato starch, the winners, proved to be interchangeable. They both thickened the juices without altering the blueberry flavor or leaving any visible traces of starch behind.

Lemon juice as well as grated lemon zest brightened the fruit flavor, and, as for spices, everyone preferred cinnamon. Other flavors simply got in the way.

Not Your Average Topping

For the topping, our guiding principle was ease of preparation. A biscuit topping is the way to go, and we had our choice of two types: dropped and rolled. Most rolled biscuit recipes call for cold butter cut into dry ingredients with a pastry blender, two knives, or sometimes a food processor, after which the dough is rolled and cut. The dropped biscuits looked more promising (translation: easier)—mix the dry ingredients, mix the wet ingredients, mix the two together, and drop (over fruit). Sounds good to us!

To be sure that our tasters agreed, we made two cobblers, one with rolled and one with dropped biscuits. The dropped biscuits, light and rustic in appearance, received the positive comments we were looking for but needed some work. To start, we had to fine-tune the ingredients, which included flour, sugar, leavener, milk, eggs, butter/shortening, and flavorings. We immediately eliminated eggs from the list because they made the

biscuits a tad heavy. As for dairy, heavy cream was too rich, whereas milk and half-and-half lacked depth of flavor. We finally tested buttermilk, which delivered a much-needed flavor boost as well as a lighter, fluffier texture. As for the choice of fat, butter was in and Crisco was out—butter tasted much better. Next we wanted to test melted butter versus cold butter. Although we had been using melted butter in the dropped biscuits, we wondered if cold butter would yield better results, as some sources suggested. We melted butter for one batch and cut cold butter into the dry ingredients (with a food processor) for another. The difference was nil, so melting, the easier method, was the winner.

We soon discovered that the big problem with drop biscuits is getting them to cook through. (The batter is wetter than rolled biscuit dough and therefore has a propensity for remaining doughy.) No matter how long we left the biscuits on the berry topping in a 400-degree oven, they never baked through, turning browner and browner on top while remaining doughy on the bottom. We realized that what the biscuits needed might be a blast of heat from below—that is, from the berries. We tried baking the berries alone in a moderate 375-degree oven for 25 minutes and then dropped and baked the biscuit dough on top. Bingo! The heat from the bubbling berries helped to cook the biscuits from underneath, while the dry heat of the oven cooked the biscuits from above.

There was one final detail to perfect. We wanted the biscuits to be more crisp on the outside and to have a deeper hue. This was easily achieved by bumping the oven to 425 degrees when we added the biscuits. A sprinkling of cinnamon-sugar on the dropped biscuit dough added just a bit more crunch.

BLUEBERRY COBBLER
SERVES 6 TO 8

While the blueberries are baking, prepare the ingredients for the biscuit topping, but do not stir the wet into the dry ingredients until just before the berries come out of the oven. A standard or deep-dish 9-inch pie pan works well; an 8-inch-square baking dish can also be used. Vanilla ice cream or lightly sweetened whipped cream is the perfect accompaniment. To reheat leftovers, put the cobbler in a 350-degree oven for 10 to 15 minutes, until heated through.

1. Place fruit mixture in pie plate, set plate on rimmed baking sheet, and bake until hot and bubbling around edges, about 25 minutes.

2. Pinch off eight equal-sized pieces biscuit dough and place on hot berry filling, spacing them at least ½ inch apart.

3. Sprinkle each mound of dough with cinnamon-sugar. Bake until biscuits are golden brown on top and cooked through, 15 to 18 minutes.

Filling

- ½ cup (3½ ounces) sugar
- 1 tablespoon cornstarch
  Pinch ground cinnamon
  Pinch salt
- 6 cups (30 ounces) fresh blueberries, picked over
- 1½ teaspoons grated zest plus 1 tablespoon juice from 1 lemon

Biscuit Topping

- 1 cup (5 ounces) unbleached all-purpose flour
- 2 tablespoons stone-ground cornmeal
- ¼ cup sugar, plus 2 teaspoons for sprinkling
- 2 teaspoons baking powder
- ¼ teaspoon baking soda
- ¼ teaspoon salt
- 4 tablespoons (½ stick) unsalted butter, melted
- ⅓ cup buttermilk
- ½ teaspoon vanilla extract
- ⅛ teaspoon ground cinnamon

1. Adjust oven rack to lower-middle position and heat oven to 375 degrees.

2. FOR THE FILLING: Stir sugar, cornstarch, cinnamon, and salt together in large bowl. Add berries and mix gently with rubber spatula until evenly coated; add lemon zest and juice and mix to combine. Transfer berry mixture to 9-inch glass pie pan, place pie pan on rimmed baking sheet, and bake until filling is hot and bubbling around edges, about 25 minutes.

3. FOR THE BISCUIT TOPPING: Whisk flour, cornmeal, ¼ cup sugar, baking powder, baking soda, and salt in large bowl to combine. Whisk melted butter, buttermilk, and vanilla in small bowl. Mix remaining 2 teaspoons sugar and cinnamon in second small bowl and set aside. One minute before berries come out of the oven, add wet ingredients to dry ingredients; stir with rubber spatula until just combined and no dry pockets remain.

4. TO ASSEMBLE AND BAKE COBBLER:

Remove berries from oven; increase oven temperature to 425 degrees. Pinch off 8 equal-sized pieces biscuit dough and place on hot berry filling, spacing them at least ½ inch apart (they should not touch). Sprinkle each mound of dough with cinnamon-sugar. Bake until filling is bubbling and biscuits are golden brown on top and cooked through, 15 to 18 minutes. Cool cobbler on wire rack 20 minutes and serve.

BLUEBERRY COBBLER WITH GINGERED BISCUITS

Follow recipe for Blueberry Cobbler, adding 3 tablespoons minced crystallized ginger to flour mixture and substituting an equal amount ground ginger for cinnamon in sugar for sprinkling on biscuits.

ALL-SEASON BLUEBERRY COBBLER (WITH FROZEN BLUEBERRIES)

Thawed berries shed a lot of flavorful liquid that must be reduced to a syrup on the stovetop before baking.

Thaw 36 ounces (about 6 cups) frozen blueberries (preferably wild) in colander set over bowl to catch juices. Transfer juices (you should have about 1 cup) to small saucepan; simmer over medium heat until syrupy and thick enough to coat back of spoon, about 10 minutes. Follow recipe for Blueberry Cobbler, mixing syrup with berries and other filling ingredients, increasing baking time for berry mixture to 30 minutes, and increasing biscuit baking time to 20 to 22 minutes.

TASTING: Blueberries in January?

When local berries are not in season, can you still make blueberry cobbler? Should you rely on fresh berries from South America or frozen berries? If you choose the latter, should you pick cultivated or wild frozen berries?

Last winter, the test kitchen tried fresh berries from Chile as well as five frozen brands. Easily beating the fresh imported berries as well as the other frozen contenders were Wyman's frozen wild berries. (Compared with cultivated berries, wild berries are smaller, more intense in color, firmer in texture, and more sweet and tangy in flavor.) The fresh imported berries tied for second place with Whole Foods frozen wild berries. While frozen cultivated berries trailed in the tasting, all but one brand received decent scores.

Flavor aside, the cost of frozen berries is $8 per cobbler versus $25 for the fresh South American berries. You could make three cobblers using the frozen berries for that price, and the money would also buy better quality.

Why did frozen wild berries beat fresh berries? The imported berries are picked before they have a chance to fully ripen to help them survive the long trip North. As a result, they are often tart and not so flavorful. Frozen berries have been picked at their peak—when perfectly ripe—and are then individually quick frozen (IQF) at -20 degrees. The quick freezing preserves their sweetness, letting us enjoy them year-round—and at a price just about anyone can afford. —E.M.

1st PLACE	Tied for 2nd PLACE	Tied for 2nd PLACE	3rd PLACE	4th PLACE	5th PLACE

WYMAN'S Frozen Wild
These small blueberries were intense in color and flavor, with a pleasing balance of sweetness and tanginess and a clean, fresh berry finish.

Fresh Blueberries (South American)
Imported fresh berries lacked that "picked at peak ripeness" flavor you get with local fresh berries, but they were still sweet/tart and juicy.

WHOLE FOODS Frozen Organic Wild
Juicy and complex in flavor, these wild berries were described by tasters as "sweet," "sour," and "slightly tannic."

CASCADIAN FARMS 100% Organic Frozen
This mix of berries includes "wild" blueberries. Berries had tart punch characteristic of wild berries and a pleasant "jammy" sweetness.

365 Grade A Fancy Frozen
These cultivated berries were very sweet, with just a hint of tartness. Compared with other brands, they lacked complexity.

SHAW'S Individually Quick Frozen Whole
This supermarket brand was the most disappointing. The berries were watery, bland, and flat tasting, with a mushy consistency.

Doritos Beats Boutique-Brand Tortilla Chips

How can a mass-market brand take first place, beating more expensive chips made from stone-ground, organic corn?

⇒ BY RAQUEL PELZEL ⇐

Now that salsa has overtaken ketchup as America's favorite condiment, it's only a matter of time before tortilla chips (with $3.9 billion in sales) say "hasta la vista" to potato chips (with $4.9 billion in sales) and take over the top spot in the snackfood competition. The growing popularity of tortilla chips is evident not only in sales reports but on supermarket shelves. Once there were only one or two varieties to choose from. Now there are a bevy of choices: red, white, blue, or yellow corn; circles, triangles, strips, or "minis"; baked or fried; organic or not; stone-ground or not; with sea salt or sprouted grains.

For our tasting, we decided to keep things simple. We stuck to chips made from white or yellow corn in the basic triangular shape. In addition, all of the chips we tasted were full fat, with salt. We tasted the chips solo, with salsa (testing each chip for its "scoopability"), and in nachos (testing the chips for durability and texture after being blanketed with cheese and toppings).

Masa Matters

Tortilla chips are basically made from just three ingredients—corn, oil, and salt—yet our tasters found a wide range of textures and flavors in the 10 brands we sampled. How could such simple ingredients yield such different results?

Tortilla chips begin with masa, or corn dough. Resembling cookie dough in texture, masa can be made from a number of different corn products, including corn flour, which has the texture of fine sand; stone-ground corn flour, which has a rougher, grittier texture; and stone-ground corn (made from softened whole corn kernels), which is very rough, like pebbly sand. Water is added to the corn product, and the dough is mixed. The masa gets flattened and goes through a contraption that looks something like a giant rolling pin that cuts the dough into triangles. The triangles are baked for less than a minute at up to 800 degrees, which dries out the dough so that it doesn't absorb too much oil when it gets fried. After being baked, the dough triangles look, feel, and taste like a corn tortilla.

Next the chips get cooled on a multilevel conveyor belt. This prevents puffing during the next phase—frying. The baked and cooled chips are flash-fried in 350-degree oil for only 1 minute; then the chips get cooled again in a cooling tunnel, salted, and bagged.

Even though this process is similar from producer to producer, the flavor and texture of the 10 brands we tasted varied dramatically. According to our results, tasters liked a corn presence, but not a sweet or tamale-like flavor. The chips needed to be crisp but not brittle and should not leave a slick or oily residue. I wanted to figure out what separates a great chip from a mediocre one.

Finer Texture Is Better

Based on our findings, we concluded that a masa made with stone-ground whole corn kernels results in a grittier, heartier chip than one made from a silky corn flour masa. Many manufacturers make a big deal out of their chips being made from stone-ground masa. A stone-ground corn chip, they say, has more texture, is stronger, and absorbs less oil.

While that all sounds good on paper, in reality, we found that tasters preferred finer and more fragile chips made with corn flour, like second-place Miguel's, described as "delicate," or third-place Newman's Own, called "crisp." (Frito-Lay, which manufactures our top-rated Doritos chips, would not comment on the ingredients in its masa. However, given the delicate texture of Doritos, it seems likely that corn flour is used here, too.) In contrast, two of the roughest, heartiest stone-ground chips, Nana's Cocina and Kettle Foods, ended up at the bottom of the scorecard. Their textures were described as "stale" and like "cardboard," respectively.

Another argument that enthusiasts of stone-ground corn flour make against the use of fine-ground corn flour is that it acts like a sponge, absorbing more oil. But in our tasting we didn't find that to be true. Both Miguel's and Newman's use fine flours, and neither was greasy. Yet the Nana's Cocina chips, which are made from whole corn kernels ground in lava stones, were called "slick" and "oily." In addition, despite differences in the texture of the masa and the chips, all of the chips we sampled contain similar amounts of fat—from 5.5 to 7 grams per 1-ounce serving.

Finally, we come to the flavor of the masa itself. We thought there might be a continental divide between those who preferred white or yellow corn tortilla chips, but we found that we liked both types of corn chips equally. We found white corn chips to be more subtly corn flavored, whereas yellow corn chips tasted "toasty" and "nutty."

In addition to the masa, salt has a big impact on tortilla chip flavor. Here the results of our tasting were quite clear. More salt makes a tastier chip. Among the top five brands, four have sodium levels between 110 and 120 milligrams per ounce. The sodium level in the five lowest-ranked brands ranges from 40 to 95 milligrams per ounce.

The Bag Tells a Story

Now that we understood more about masa and the effect of salt levels on flavor, we moved on to the oil. We thought that the success of our second favorite brand, Miguel's, might be due in part to the corn/oil combination. Miguel's pairs canola oil with its white corn masa chip. Because canola is a neutral-flavored oil, using it with the subtly flavored masa works well, as the flavor of the oil doesn't overwhelm that of the chip.

But then we came to Cape Cod chips. Like Miguel's, they are made with white corn masa and fried in canola oil. So why were Miguel's chips described as "toasted" and "authentic" tasting whereas Cape Cod chips were deemed "bland" and "unremarkable"? The most obvious difference right off the bat was in the packaging. Miguel's tortilla chips are packaged in a "metallized" bag, meaning that the bag's surface has been lined with a very thin film of aluminum.

Craig Mooney, vice-president of sales for Miguel's, says that the metal lining helps to ward off oxidation of the oil by blocking light. "Light can oxidize the product and cause it to go bad," he explained; the foil-lined bag "also creates a moisture barrier to help the chips stay crunchy." We observed that all of our top three chips—Doritos, Miguel's, and Newman's Own—are packed in metallized bags. Could a metal bag really prevent oxidation and be the reason for the strong performance of our three favorite chips?

According to Theron Downes, a packaging

TASTING TORTILLA CHIPS

We tasted the most popular brands of tortilla chips as well as several higher-priced "boutique" chips from specialty and natural foods stores. All the chips were tasted plain, with salsa, and in nachos (covered with cheese, salsa, guacamole, and sour cream—see page 15 for the recipe). The chips were sampled by 27 members of the *Cook's Illustrated* staff, who judged them for flavor, texture, durability, and size. Chips are listed in order of preference.

HIGHLY RECOMMENDED

Doritos Toasted Corn Tortilla Chips

➤ 13½ ounces, $3.29

Tasters loved Doritos' "fresh," "toasted corn" flavor and "crisp" texture. Many found them "just right" for dipping, although some tasters commented that the chips were "very flat," making it necessary to "dip from an angle." Doritos were also the top chip in the nacho tasting, where they were described as "still crispy." Available in Western states except California.

Miguel's Stowe Away White Corn Tortilla Chips

➤ 7 ounces, $2.95

Although these chips are "thick," they retained a "delicate crispness" that almost "flakes in your mouth." And they remained "crisp" even when covered with cheese in the nacho tasting. Miguel's flavor was subtle, with tasters calling it "toasted" but without an overwhelming amount of corn.

Newman's Own Organics Yellow Corn Tortilla Chips

➤ 8 ounces, $2.29

These chips tasted "home-fried," "clean," "simple," and "corny." Newman's were the thinnest chips tested, and its packages had a higher-than-average number of broken chips. However, when we found whole chips, they were judged "crisp" and the "perfect" size for dipping.

Bearitos Stone-ground Organic Yellow Corn Tortilla Chips

➤ 16 ounces, $2.79

While tasters found the size of these chips acceptable, many complained that the chips were "too hard" and that they "broke apart" into small pieces when eaten. Even so, tasters loved the "authentic," "coarse-ground" texture, with many firmly believing that these chips had the "best corn flavor."

RECOMMENDED

Santitas White Corn Tortilla Chips

➤ 18 ounces, $1.99

"Finally, a white tortilla chip that stands up to salsa," exclaimed one happy taster. Others agreed, calling this a "durable" but "crisp" chip that even stood up to our nacho test. Some commented that these chips "could use more corn flavor." Others contended that Santitas were on the "verge of being too large."

Cape Cod White Corn Tortilla Chips

➤ 9 ounces, $1.99

While tasters liked the crisp texture of the Cape Cod chips, they weren't very happy with the flavor, calling it "bland," "unremarkable," and reminiscent of "church communion." But when paired with cheddar cheese and salsa for our nacho tasting, Cape Cod ranked second, right behind Doritos.

Tostitos Restaurant-Style White Corn Tortilla Chips

➤ 13½ ounces, $2.29

"This is your basic Sunday football chip," said one taster. Another added, "If you want to taste the salsa more than the chip, this is a good choice." Others agreed that the chip was "too flimsy" in flavor and texture and didn't "hold up to heavy dipping."

NOT RECOMMENDED

Nana's Cocina Traditional Stone-ground Yellow Corn Tortilla Chips

➤ 16 ounces, $2.69

Many tasters thought these chips had a "fatty" mouthfeel that was "slick and oily." Tasters also felt that the chips were "thin" and somewhat "stale." And while some people liked the "tamale" flavor that Nana's brought forth in the nachos, the chips became "soggy" under the cheese.

Old Dutch Original Restaurant-Style Tortilla Chips

➤ 15 ounces, $3.19

These "thin" chips were deemed "too large" and "fell apart easily" when dunked in salsa. Several tasters picked up on an unwelcome "smoky," "popcorn" flavor. Old Dutch chips became very "soggy" in the nachos test.

Kettle Foods Five Grain Organic Yellow Corn Tortilla Chips

➤ 8 ounces, $1.99

In addition to stone-ground masa, these chips contain five sprouted grains: corn, barley, rye, sweet brown rice, and buckwheat. Tasters described these chips as being "strangely sweet," with a "stale," "old cornmeal" flavor. In the nachos tasting, Kettle came in last, being likened to "cardboard tamales."

---

professor with Michigan State University, "there are piles of evidence" that a metallized bag improves the shelf life of fried foods. In fact, Downes even refuses to purchase peanuts, a high-fat and light-susceptible food, packaged in clear bags since they go rancid from oxidation within a couple of weeks.

Of course, just because a chip tastes great doesn't mean it's the best choice for dipping into salsa or covering with cheese and other heavy nacho toppings. Although some manufacturers told us that the amount of fiber, and therefore the chip sturdiness, is increased by using stone-ground corn meal, we found chips made with corn flour masa to be just as strong. The only brands that were deemed unsuitable for scooping salsa were Tostitos and Old Dutch, which were both too large to dip and scoop in one swoop without breakage. For the nachos test, we liked Doritos, Cape Cod, and Miguel's the best (they all stayed crisp under pressure) and Kettle Foods, Nana's Cocina, and Old Dutch the least (they all became "soggy," "stale," and "greasy").

In the end, the results of our tasting were unexpected. Although many boutique brands make a big deal about the organically raised, stone-ground corn they use, it seems that the secret to a great tortilla chip isn't all that complicated. Just use fine corn flour (not coarse stone-ground), add plenty of salt, and then pack the chips in a foil-lined bag to keep the oil from oxidizing.

"Vegomatic" versus the Chef's Knife

Do late-night television choppers/slicers/shredders really work?
We tested eight models against a basic chef's knife to find out.

≥ BY ADAM RIED ≤

Every night owl, myself included, has seen the midnight infomercials advertising do-it-all food preparation devices that will "make superfresh salads, pizza, coleslaw, tacos, and more *in seconds!*" Testimonials from *real people* claim dramatically improved lives thanks to these gadgets, which quickly and effortlessly chop, mince, slice, dice, julienne, and shred.

Such gadgets would probably not tempt cooks with a sharp knife and passable skill in its use. But there are countless cooks with dull knives or limited time, interest, or facility who might well part with their hard-earned cash for the lure of easily and speedily dispatching all manner of foodstuffs. Wondering how well they'd be served by these devices, I gathered eight models—several of them courtesy of the toll-free number on my television screen—and repaired to the test kitchen to chop, mince, slice, and shred everything from garlic and parsley to cheese and potatoes. Could these machines really ease common kitchen burdens as promised?

Design and Intent

These eight models use a variety of designs. Of the five units intended to chop and mince, three—the Zyliss, Gemco, and Dalla Piazza—use a canister or chamber to contain the food and a pump-operated, rotating, zigzag-shaped blade that descends over the food to chop it. The first few pumps chop the food roughly; continued pumping chops it until finely minced. The New & Improved Quick Chopper operates like a hand-cranked food processor, with a blade spinning in a workbowl. The last of the five chopper models, the Kitchen Magic, combines a nonadjustable slicing blade mounted in the handle with a series of circular blades, which you roll back and forth over the slices you've made to chop them.

The remaining three models slice and shred.

Minced or Mashed?

Pieces of hand-chopped onion, at left, are uniform and discreet. The machine-chopped onions, right, are mashed and wet.

The Culinary 2000 Rocket Chef, like the Quick Chopper, is a hand-cranked manual food processor that includes slicing and shredding blades. The Presto Salad Shooter pushes food through a feed tube onto a rotating, cone-shaped slicing or shredding blade, and the Veg-o-Matic makes the cook push food through blades using a plunger and two hands.

Help or Hindrance?

In the course of running 11 separate tests on each unit, it didn't take long to reach the conclusion that this bunch of kitchen gadgets is unimpressive (see the chart on page 29 for more information). The shortcomings include uneven processing, whether chopping, shredding, or slicing; poor design in terms of rinsing, cleaning, and even safety; and lackluster manufacturing quality.

First, the cutting quality. Not one machine did a decent job on parsley, and several choked when I tried to chop nuts. In general, I found it best to process small amounts of food at one time because ½ cup of nuts or even a small onion brought several units to a halt. Speaking of onions, none of the units did better than a fair job of chopping them. The pieces usually came out bruised and wet because the onion was partly crushed rather than cleanly chopped (see photo below). This doesn't do any favors to the flavor of the food when cooked. We sautéed the machine-chopped onion and a hand-chopped onion and tasted them side by side, and the difference was dramatic. The machine-chopped onion tasted unpleasantly sharp (because many of its cells were crushed, more strong sulfuric compounds and enzymes were released), while the hand-chopped onion tasted sweeter and milder.

Cleaning or rinsing these units between runs through the dishwasher (so they could be used on different foods being prepared for the same meal) was no walk in the park. Most designs included numerous hard-to-reach nooks and crannies and multiple pieces. Only the Zyliss opened up to reveal the entire blade, which made it easy to clean. Cleaning became an issue largely because of residual food odors in the chambers, canisters, workbowls, and feed tubes. A quick rinse, or even a thorough hand-washing with hot, soapy water, was often not enough to eliminate food odors that plastic absorbs more readily than a metal knife blade.

Last, a brief word about structural integrity. Several models, including the New and Improved Quick Chopper, the Culinary 2000 Rocket Chef, and the Veg-o-Matic, felt so flimsy, unstable, or difficult to use that I was appalled.

A Little Help from My Friends

Since I am not the target consumer for these products—I have both a sharp knife and enough skill to use it comfortably—I expanded the testing to include four less experienced cooks who work in the production and accounting departments at the magazine. I asked each individual to finely chop an onion and to mince a knob of ginger, using both a freshly honed 8-inch chef's knife and the winning chopper.

It goes almost without saying that average onion-chopping times with the machine were much faster than those with the knife—one minute, 19 seconds, versus four minutes, 45 seconds, respectively. But, like me, three of the four testers were not pleased with the quality (fineness and evenness) of the chop, with one tester noting that he "had large onion chunks and onion slush at the same time." Another tester had several additional objections, saying that "although the chopper worked fast, it has to be cleaned, and cleaning it would take a lot more time than wiping off a knife blade." To be fair, the tester who took the longest to get through the onion and ginger with a knife was very enthusiastic about the chopper. In fact, she was ready to head out over her lunch hour *that day* to buy one. With her hectic daily schedule and rush to produce dinner for her family every evening, the chopper's time savings far outweighed any shortcomings in quality.

Final Recommendations

All in all, I would rather spend money on a decent chef's knife (which can be had for about $30; see "Weight Is Key for Inexpensive Chef's Knives," July/August 1999) and an adult education course in knife skills than on any of these machines. That said, if you are really averse to using a knife and think that one of these machines might help you out, the Zyliss is the one to go for.

RATING FOOD CHOPPERS AND SLICERS

RATINGS

★★★
GOOD

★★
FAIR

★
POOR

We rated eight food chopper/slicer/shredder devices and evaluated them according to the following criteria. All of the chopping and the slicing and shredding tests were conducted (to the extent possible) on every unit, but performance was based solely on the set of tests most appropriate for that unit's intended purpose. The devices are listed in order of preference within each category.

PRICE: Prices are those listed at Boston-area retail outlets, in national mail-order catalogs, or on Web sites, or are the manufacturer's suggested retail price.

OPERATION: The means by which the device is operated. All of the units except for the Presto were manually operated. We had no strong preference for any specific operating system.

DISHWASHER-SAFE: Notes whether the entire unit or its critical operating parts can be cleaned in the dishwasher. Units that are dishwasher-safe were preferred.

EASE OF USE: This rating accounts for relative ease of assembly for each use, as well as smoothness of operation and degree of hand and/or arm fatigue generated after average use. Models that required minimal assembly and that operated smoothly and comfortably were preferred.

EASE OF CLEANING: Assuming that many users would simply rinse the unit between uses with different ingredients, we assessed the ease with which residual food could be removed from the blades and assemblies. Many units posed notable risk of an accidental cut while trying to access the blades to clean them. Units that posed the least threat of an accidental cut and that offered the greatest access to the entire blade were preferred.

CHOPPING: To determine chopping performance, we conducted seven tests on routine ingredients, including garlic (in two amounts—two cloves and ¹/₂ cup cloves), fresh ginger, whole parsley leaves, 1-ounce chunks of baking chocolate, whole blanched almonds, dried apricots, and fresh onion. Units that made clean cuts easily, producing chopped and minced morsels of uniform size were preferred. Scores of good, fair, or poor were assigned for each test, and the average of those scores is what constitutes the overall chopping performance rating.

SLICING AND SHREDDING: To determine slicing and shredding performance, we conducted four tests on routine ingredients, including cheddar cheese, raw carrots, tomatoes, and potatoes. Units that produced neat, uniform slices, both thick and thin, or that shredded evenly and quickly, were preferred. Scores of good, fair, or poor were assigned for each test, and the average of those scores is what constitutes the overall slicing and shredding performance rating.

TESTERS' COMMENTS: Include observations about unusual or noteworthy aspects of the units' design and performance.

FOOD CHOPPERS

Brand	Testing Criteria		Testers' Comments
BEST CHOPPER			
Zyliss Comfort Food Chopper — Clever design and best performance by a wide margin make this a handy kitchen tool if you hate to use a knife.	PRICE: OPERATION: DISHWASHER-SAFE: EASE OF USE: EASE OF CLEANING: CHOPPING:	$19.99 Pump Yes ★★★ ★★★ ★★★	Comfortable handle, smooth pumping action, and clever design. By far the easiest of its kind to clean because body opens to expose blades. Parsley was the only test it failed miserably, as did every unit here.
RECOMMENDED WITH RESERVATIONS			
Gemco—The Chopper — Simple, cheap, and a bit flimsy, but it might be worth keeping around if you chop a lot of chocolate.	PRICE: OPERATION: DISHWASHER-SAFE: EASE OF USE: EASE OF CLEANING: CHOPPING:	$4.99 Pump Yes ★★★ ★★★ ★★	Easier than many of its ilk to clean, but it was difficult to remove the chopped food from its narrow jar. Uneven performance; great on chocolate and dried fruit, poor on garlic, ginger, nuts, and parsley.
Dalla Piazza Brushed Stainless Steel Food Chopper — Performance was acceptable in some cases, mediocre in most.	PRICE: OPERATION: DISHWASHER-SAFE: EASE OF USE: EASE OF CLEANING: CHOPPING:	$22.00 Pump Yes ★★ ★★ ★★	Irritating to assemble for each use because it's easy to put the blade guide plate in upside down. Did a surprisingly good job on almonds (though it choked when we tried ¹/₂ cup of them at once) and chocolate, and a terrible job on parsley.
NOT RECOMMENDED			
New & Improved Quick Chopper — Performance in key tests ranged from subpar to terrible.	PRICE: OPERATION: DISHWASHER-SAFE: EASE OF USE: EASE OF CLEANING: CHOPPING:	$14.95 Crank Yes ★★ ★★ ★	Difficult to hold steady and crank as we began to process foods. Food shot out of the hole in the lid if we didn't think to fit the egg separator into it. Bowl includes a molded pouring spout.
Kitchen Magic Chopper — Two words characterize this unit best: "dangerous" and "useless."	PRICE: OPERATION: DISHWASHER-SAFE: EASE OF USE: EASE OF CLEANING: CHOPPING:	$17.25 Rolling chopper Yes ★ ★★ ★	Handling this contraption, whether to clean it, slice with it, or just pick it up quickly to move it, feels dangerous because of the exposed twin blade that is mounted right in the handle. Performance was poor across the board.

FOOD SLICERS/SHREDDERS

Brand	Testing Criteria		Testers' Comments
NOT RECOMMENDED			
Presto 2972 Pro Salad Shooter Slicer/Shredder — Shredding is its strong suit; slicing performance is fickle.	PRICE: OPERATION: DISHWASHER-SAFE: EASE OF USE: EASE OF CLEANING: SLICING/SHREDDING:	$49.92 Electric/Power Yes ★★ ★★ ★★	There are four pieces to position and fasten before every use. Slicing performance is inconsistent; the neatness of the slices is based on how the food settles in the feed tube. The Salad Shooter does, however, do a good job of shredding, even with such unexpected foods as chocolate and dried fruit.
K-Tel Veg-o-Matic Food Cutter — Flimsy, unstable, and a disgracefully poor performer.	PRICE: OPERATION: DISHWASHER-SAFE: EASE OF USE: EASE OF CLEANING: SLICING/SHREDDING:	$22.35 Plunger Blades ★ ★★ ★	Makes very sloppy, thick slices, even when set up to slice thinly. Likewise, the julienne it produces, as for French fries, is too thick. Tomatoes must be cut in half to slice, and this tool won't work at all on raw carrots. Right at press time, we learned that this model will be discontinued.
Culinary 2000 New Rocket Chef & Supreme Ice Cream — The phrase "piece of junk" could have been coined for this unit.	PRICE: OPERATION: DISHWASHER-SAFE: EASE OF USE: EASE OF CLEANING: SLICING/SHREDDING:	$28.99 Crank No ★ ★★ ★	Claims to do it all—from slicing to shredding to chopping to beating to making ice cream—yet it arrived without instructions or information about the manufacturer. Frustrating to assemble, hard to crank, and flimsy.

⇒ BY BRIDGET LANCASTER ⇐

Crowd Pleaser

In the heat of summer, few things are as satisfying as a pile of smoky, juicy, baby back beauties. I don't know about you, but quite a few of us in the test kitchen have been known to polish off a whole rack without stopping for a breath. Unfortunately, a standard kettle grill has only enough real estate to hold two racks of ribs at a time, making it necessary to share with our fellow diners. That's why we were grateful to find the Weber BBQ Rib Rack. For gluttons like us (or if you're feeding a crowd), the Rib Rack fits twice as many racks of ribs on the grill (that's four baby backs). It's also handy for piling on the chicken parts. For availability, see Resources on page 32.

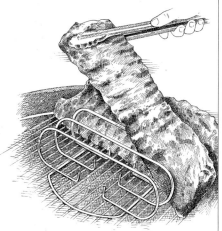

A rib rack rests directly on the grill grate. Four slots neatly hold four slabs of ribs upright.

The Sum of Its Parts

Fretting that your smoothie days are over because of that cracked blender jar? Have no fear: We've found a great resource that carries replacement parts for many of our most used (and abused) kitchen items. Culinary Parts Unlimited is in business just to make sure that your kitchen is never without the part you need. The company carries items from most of the big-name manufacturers, and, best of all, it usually ships within 24 hours. The company is easy to contact on the Web at www.culinaryparts.com, or call 800-543-7549.

In Hot Water

With many home cooks now counting meal preparation time in terms of minutes rather than hours, waiting for a pot of water to boil for pasta can seem like an eternity. To speed up the process, many of us now start with water that is hot from the tap, but a few still insist on cold tap water, claiming that it makes a difference to the flavor of the pasta. To see if this is really the case, we set up a taste test.

We brought 4 quarts each of hot and cold tap water to a boil and then added 1 tablespoon salt and 1 pound pasta to each. When the pasta was done, it was drained and tasted plain (no oil, no sauce). Tasters could not discern any difference in flavor. In fact, the only difference was in the time it took the pots to reach a boil—13½ minutes for the hot tap water and 15 minutes for the cold.

Before you turn on the hot tap, though, you might want to consider what the U.S. Environmental Protection Agency (EPA) has to say about cooking with hot tap water. According to the EPA, water hot from the tap can contain much higher levels of lead than cold tap water. In addition, even cold tap water should be run for awhile (until the water is as cold as it can get) to ensure that any lead deposits are "flushed" out of the system. All of a sudden that extra minute and a half doesn't seem quite so long.

Berry Nice

If fresh, plump berries are the crown jewels of summer, then a fresh fruit tart is the crown upon which they sit. Unfortunately, the crown will tarnish if dressed with crushed or bruised berries. In fact, a couple of bleeding berries can ruin the appearance of the tart (although we'd happily eat it just the same). Packaging is much to blame. It's simply shameful the way most berries are jammed (pun intended) in those pint containers. That's why we spread our summer berries in a single layer on a paper towel–lined baking sheet. The paper towels absorb any bleeding juices, and spacing the berries out allows us to pick and choose the prettiest ones (and to eat the others immediately).

TASTING: Greens-Span

We've all seen the pre-washed, packaged greens sold in supermarkets. OK, so maybe we've used them as well. But who can blame us? These pre-washed, pre-cut selections of leafy lettuces are the epitome of convenience, allowing us to enjoy a varied blend of greens without breaking a sweat.

But, honestly, how do they taste? Or look, for that matter? That's what we set out to learn when we gathered bushels of bagged lettuce from local

1st PLACE
PURE PACIFIC Certified Organic

2nd PLACE
READY PAC Organic Mesclun

supermarkets. The mixes were judged on the variety of greens and on overall freshness (the swimsuit competition was omitted).

Pure Pacific Certified Organic Spring Mix came out on top. Weighing in at 7 ounces and costing $3.69, this blend contains up to 10 varieties of baby lettuce. Tasters found this blend to be "delicate and moist" with a "good appearance." Tying for top billing was Ready Pac Organic Mesclun Blend (4½ ounces for $3.29). This blend of 14 different baby lettuces was described as "wonderful" and "varied."

After the top two, the quality dropped dramatically. The Dole Italian Blend (10 ounces for $2.99), which contains romaine and radicchio, was deemed "bland and tough." The Dole European Blend (10 ounces for $2.99), which contains iceberg, romaine, radicchio, endive, and unspecified "leaf" lettuces (how hard could it be to specify lettuces?), fared even worse. Described as "poorly cut coleslaw," this blend was little more than iceberg dotted with "leathery radicchio." The two least-favored mixes came from Stop and Shop. Stop and Shop Carmel Valley (7 ounces for $2.99), which consists of escarole, endive, and radicchio, was deemed similar to "cardboard." Stop and Shop Versailles (7 ounces for $2.99), a blend of green leaf lettuce, frisée, shredded carrots, and radicchio, garnered comments that were anything but kind—among them, "nasty," "sad," and "pale."

So it pays to shell out a little more money for the fresher taste and more interesting blends of greens in the organic mixes. It also pays to trust your own good judgment rather than the sell-by date when it comes to freshness. We found the date to be merely a gauge—by no means a guarantee—of freshness. For the freshest greens, only a careful inspection of the goods will do.

London (and Sydney) Calling

Well-known cookbook authors from Britain and Australia try to reach a new audience in America. Should we listen? BY CHRISTOPHER KIMBALL

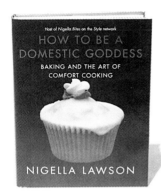

HOW TO BE A DOMESTIC GODDESS: BAKING AND THE ART OF COMFORT COOKING

Nigella Lawson

Hyperion, 374 pages, $35

➤ Nigella is England's sultry Martha Stewart: opinionated, sexy, and very smart. One gets the sense that she would be happy to move into your house, take over your kitchen, and tell you exactly what to do. Her prose style has tongue firmly planted in cheek, as when she refers to the book's reader as "Missus" or when she writes, "With mince pies, goes mulled wine. Don't fight it."

PROS: The book is gorgeous—the paper high-quality, the photos simple, and the typography clear, well designed, and to the point. The selection of recipes is also appealing, with many foods new to an American audience, including Ricciarelli (lozenge-shaped macaroons), Om Ali (an Egyptian bread and butter pudding), and Supper Onion Pie. You also get recognizable recipes, such as Cream-Cheese Brownies and Christmas Cupcakes, and some standard British fare, including several variations on trifle, Cornish Pasties, and Steak and Kidney Pudding.

CONS: If you like workmanlike prose, you may find Lawson's style off the mark. What is a "soft but firm" dough? Must we be exhorted to "tear greedily" at a loaf of bread with our "bare hands"?

RECIPE TESTING: Of the three books reviewed, this one had the least successful recipes. We tested 10 and only a handful passed muster. Cheese Blintzes were outstanding, Finnish Rye Bread was easy and delicious, Coconut Macaroons were fine but a bit sweet, the Gin and Tonic Gelatin Mold never set and unmolded sloppily but still tasted great, and the Buttermilk Birthday Cake was fine if a bit dense. Among the less successful efforts were The Essential White Loaf (too salty), Potato Bread (a snooze), Brownies ("some of the worst brownies I've ever tasted," said one test cook), and Garlic and Parsley Hearthbreads, which turned as hard as dog biscuits upon cooling.

OFF THE SHELF: COOKING FROM THE PANTRY

Donna Hay

William Morrow & Co., 192 pages, $25

➤ From Down Under comes Donna Hay's fifth book. Like two of her previous books—*New Food Fast* (Whitecap Books, 1999) and *Entertaining* (Whitecap Books, 1999)—*Off the Shelf* demonstrates a unique format and approach. The books are large, bright, and clean looking, and every recipe is photographed. The recipes themselves have short ingredient lists, employ an easy-to-follow shorthand when it comes to directions, and produce compelling taste and textural combinations. This is the sort of food served in hip Sydney restaurants these days, a blend of East and West with big, clean flavors.

PROS: Hay promises culinary nirvana and often delivers, as her combination of creativity and simplicity of approach is a winner. In addition to the recipes, Hay includes sections titled "Tricks and Tips" as well as "Short Order" recipes, each no more than a brief paragraph of directions and ingredients rolled into one.

CONS: What is gained in brevity is lost in execution. If a 2-pound pumpkin can't be found, what is the cook to use instead? Butternut squash? Exactly what does Hay mean by a "red chile"? Are "dried egg noodles" Chinese noodles or an Italian pasta? This is Outward Bound for home cooks—thrilling, and a serious test of one's culinary survival skills. Oh, one other thing. Hay uses too little salt, and cooking times are often inadequate. Fish, for example, often turns out rare.

RECIPE TESTING: We tested 17 recipes and 10 were worth a second go. We loved Garlic Chickpeas with Cumin-Fried Fish, Chickpea and Roast Pumpkin Soup (we had to add salt; it wasn't even listed as an ingredient), Chili Fish with Sweet Lemon Salad, Coconut Rice with Caramelized Banana (insanely sweet but delicious), and Creamy Polenta with Caramelized Fennel. There were a few problems, however. The Roast Lamb with Mustard Stuffing was mushy and too sweet, Pasta with Mushrooms was mediocre, the Noodle Salad with Crisp Tofu suggested shredding firm tofu (an impossibility,

unless what's actually called for is pressed tofu), and Seared Salmon on Coconut Spinach sounded good but was bland.

HOW TO COOK

Delia Smith

DK Publishing, 496 pages, $40

➤ This is the British equivalent of Julia Child's *The Way to Cook* (Knopf, 1989). It's big, and it's comprehensive. There are plenty of step-by-step photos, lots of color shots, and much discussion—the recipes are long and detailed.

PROS: *How to Cook* covers everything from how to whip egg whites to how to skin and bone fish. Smith has an easygoing, matter-of-fact tone; she is an excellent teacher—both patient and thorough—and she isn't trying to sell us a lifestyle.

CONS: This is British-style cooking—conservative, with few culinary surprises. Don't expect the cutting-edge recipes of Donna Hay or the more modern sensibility of the *Domestic Goddess*. Reading and cooking through *How to Cook* is like attending the Cordon Bleu; you're going to get solid, dependable, and trustworthy advice. Unfortunately, the recipe index is badly designed and hard to use.

RECIPE TESTING: Half of the 17 recipes tested were worth the effort, a respectable percentage. Winners included Perfect Rice, Toffee Bananas with Toasted Nuts, Gnocchi with Sage, Butter, and Parmesan (tasty, but the directions were a bit misleading), Classic Crème Caramel, Fast-Roast Pork with Rosemary and Caramelized Apples, and Perfect Mashed Potatoes. The Quick and Easy Flaky Pastry was a winner, but Chinese Stir-Fried Rice was an also-ran (greasy and dull-flavored), Penne with Wild Mushrooms and Crème Fraîche was pedestrian, and Cauliflower with Two Cheeses and Crème Fraîche was stringy and the sauce thin.

Most of the ingredients and materials necessary for the recipes in this issue are available at your local supermarket, gourmet store, or kitchen supply shop. The following are mail-order sources for particular items. Prices listed below were current at press time and do not include shipping or handling unless otherwise indicated. We suggest that you contact companies directly to confirm up-to-date prices and availability.

Food Chopper

After chopping pounds and pounds of nuts, garlic, onions, and dried fruit, the Zyliss Comfort Food Chopper came out head and shoulders above the rest of the field (see testing article on page 28). Its comfortable handle, fluid action, and clever design make prep work easy. Best of all, it's very easy to clean. The Zyliss Comfort Food Chopper, item #124537, is available for $20.95 from **Sur La Table (1765 Sixth Avenue, Seattle, WA 98134-1608; 800-243-0852; www.surlatable.com)**.

Frozen Blueberries

When the craving for blueberry cobbler hits in the off-season, frozen blueberries are your best bet. They are picked at the peak of freshness and quickly frozen, unlike the so-called fresh berries that are shipped unripe from South America and cost a small fortune. Our tasters ranked Wyman's frozen wild blueberries above four other brands (see page 25 for details). Wyman's blueberries are primarily distributed on the East Coast but are also available nationally in some markets, including parts of California, Arizona, New Mexico, and Illinois. Call the company's customer service number for a source close to you. The blueberries can also be ordered by the case directly from **Jasper Wyman and Son (P.O. Box 100, Milbridge, ME 04658; 800-341-1758; www.wymans.com)**. A dozen 12-ounce bags sells for $24, plus shipping.

Spices

Although the spices used in the rubs on page 20 are readily available at any market, we are fond of the offerings from **Penzeys Spices (19300 West Janacek Court, P.O. Box 924, Brookfield, WI 53008-0924; 800-741-7787; www.penzeys.com)**, noted by chefs and home cooks alike for their variety and freshness.

Salad Spinners

Nothing makes faster work of drying greens than a well-designed salad spinner. In our testing in the September/October 1999 issue of *Cook's*, salad spinners from Zyliss and Oxo Good Grips got the highest marks for speed, efficiency, and

design. The Zyliss was nominally faster, but we thought the Oxo was better designed, with such thoughtful extra features as a nonskid bottom and an ergonomically designed handle. Both spinners are available from **A Cook's Wares (211 37th Street, Beaver Falls, PA 15010; 800-915-9788; www.cookswares.com)**. The Zyliss, which comes with either a white top (item #7275) or a blue top (item #7275B), costs $20.95. The Oxo Good Grips, item #5965, sells for $25.99.

Pad Thai Ingredients

The ethnic food section in most grocery stores is expanding by leaps and bounds, but many markets don't carry the ingredients necessary for pad thai. While rice stick noodles and fish sauce should be easy to find, dried shrimp, tamarind paste, and salted radish may require some searching. We found everything we needed—without ever leaving the test kitchen—at the Web site for **Temple of Thai (104 Mosco Street, New York, NY 10013; 877-811-8773; www.templeofthai.com)**. The company carries an extensive line of Thai products, including sauces, noodles, cookbooks, and equipment. For the pad thai recipe (page 11), we found a pound of "oriental-style rice noodles" for $1.29, 8 ounces of "minced, salted, sweetened turnips" for $1.19 (salted radish and salted turnip are the same thing), a pound of tamarind paste without seeds for $2.99, 3½ ounces of dried shrimp for $4.99, and a 23-ounce bottle of Golden Boy fish sauce for $2.29.

Colander

Although often overlooked, a well-designed colander is a valuable kitchen tool—and essential for making the buttermilk coleslaw on page 21. In tests conducted for the September/October 2001 issue, we found that the best-designed strainers were thoroughly perforated, sturdily constructed, and firm-footed. The Endurance Pierced Colander/Strainer was our favorite. Its minute, mesh-like perforations drained quickly, and it sat squarely in the sink without tipping or sliding. It does a good job of draining salted cabbage for coleslaw, too. And at 5 quarts, the Endurance can hold a lot of cabbage. The colander, item #0656, is available for $24.99 from **Cook's Corner (836 S. 8th Street, Manitowoc, WI 54220; 800-236-2433; www.cookscorner.com)**.

Instant–Read Thermometer

Most any backyard grilling maestro will offer up a handful of techniques to determine the doneness of a steak (including the Tuscan steak on page 13), but there is only one surefire method:

a thermometer. An accurate reading prevents over- and undercooking and also spares the meat the invasive nicks made with a knife to check its color. Our favorite model, which easily surpassed many other models on the market when we tested them in July/August 1997, continues to be the Thermapen. It scored high marks for accuracy, response time, readability, and temperature range (from −50 to 572 degrees Fahrenheit). It provides a reading of the temperature within 10 seconds, just what's needed for checking fast-cooking meat and fish. And it's useful not only at the outdoor grill but by the kitchen stove, where it can be used to gauge the progress of baked goods, frying oil, and sugar syrup. At $79.95, the price is steep, but we think the Thermapen's performance is worth it. You can order the Thermapen, item #4325, from **The Baker's Catalogue (P.O. Box 876, Norwich, VT 05055-0876; 800-827-6836; www.bakerscatalogue.com)**.

Tuna Packed in Olive Oil

As we discovered during the recipe development of salade Niçoise, tuna packed in olive oil has little in common with conventional canned tuna. Deeply fishy—in a good way—and firmly textured, it is closer to fresh-cooked tuna and has a price tag to match, often costing three to four times as much as humble water-packed. In some cases, though—as with salade Niçoise, in which the tuna is only nominally dressed with a light vinaigrette—it is worth every penny. Tuna from Ortiz, a small Spanish processor with a long pedigree, swept the tasting for its big tuna taste and toothsome texture. The company uses only line-caught bonito del norte, a smallish tuna favored throughout Mediterranean Europe for its uniform coloring and pure flavor. **Angel Foods (467 Commercial Street, Provincetown, MA 02657; 508-487-6666; www.angelfoods.biz)** sells our three favorite tunas. The top choice, a 3.88-ounce can of "Ventresca," sells for $9.95. In second place was a tinned tuna, $3.99 for 3.95 ounces, and in third place a jarred tuna, $7.99 for 7.76 ounces. See the tasting results on page 9.

Rib Rack

If you are feeding a crowd and need to increase the recipe for ribs on page 7, you will need either two grills or one grill and a Weber BBQ Rib Rack. The Weber rack sits on the cool side of the grill and holds up to four racks of ribs vertically. Look for it at **Thegadgetsource.com (Calvert Retail, LP, 100 Lake Drive, Suite 6, Newark, DE 19702; 800-458-2616; www.thegadgetsource.com)**, item #3601, for $12.99.

RECIPES

July & August 2002

PHOTOGRAPHY: CARL TREMBLAY

http://www.cooksillustrated.com

If you enjoy *Cook's Illustrated* magazine, you should visit our Web site. Simply log on at http://www.cooksillustrated.com. Although much of the information is free, database searches are for site subscribers only. *Cook's Illustrated* subscribers are offered a 20 percent discount.

Here are some of the things you can do on our site:

Search Our Recipes: We have a searchable database of all the recipes from *Cook's Illustrated*.

Search Tastings and Cookware Ratings: You will find all of our reviews (cookware, food, wine, cookbooks) plus new material created exclusively for the Web.

Find Your Favorite Quick Tips.

Check Your Subscription: Check the status of your subscription, pay a bill, or give a gift subscription online.

Visit Our Bookstore: You can purchase any of our cookbooks, hardbound annual editions of the magazine, or posters online.

Subscribe to *e-Notes*: Our free e-mail companion to the magazine offers cooking advice, test results, buying tips, and recipes about a single topic each month.

AMERICA'S TEST KITCHEN

Join the millions of cooks who watch our show, *America's Test Kitchen*, on public television each week. Visit http://www.americastestkitchen.com for more information, including recipes from the show and a schedule of program times in your area.

Barbecued Baby Back Ribs, 7

French Potato Salad, 19

Salade Niçoise, 9

Pad Thai, 11

Grilled Tuscan Steak, 13

Spice Rubs for Grilled Chicken, 20

Creamy Buttermilk Coleslaw, 21

Cheesy Nachos, 15

Blueberry Cobbler, 24

Ice Cream Sandwiches, 23

Halford Cling Peach

Saturn (Donut) Peach

Babcock Peach

Honeydew Nectarine

Flamekist Nectarine

Arctic Rose Nectarine

Indian Blood Peach

Elberta Peach

PEACHES AND NECTARINES

NUMBER FIFTY-EIGHT

SEPTEMBER & OCTOBER 2002

COOK'S
ILLUSTRATED

Faster Lasagna
Ready to Bake in 30 Minutes

Salt Taste Test
Are Gourmet Salts Worth the Price?

Pan-Roasted Chicken
Quick Cooking and Crisp Skin

Rating Nonstick Skillets
Inexpensive Pans Perform Well

Tuscan Pork Loin
Not Dry, Not Tough

Best Corn Muffins
Tender, Moist, and Easy

Pear Almond Tart

Kung Pao Shrimp
Better Greek Salad
Homemade Applesauce
Creamy Dips
Crudités Done Right

www.cooksillustrated.com

$4.95 U.S./$6.95 CANADA

CONTENTS
September & October 2002

COOK'S ILLUSTRATED
Home of America's Test Kitchen
www.cooksillustrated.com

PUBLISHER AND EDITOR
Christopher Kimball
EXECUTIVE EDITOR
Jack Bishop
SENIOR EDITORS
Adam Ried
Dawn Yanagihara
EDITORIAL MANAGER
Barbara Bourassa
ART DIRECTOR
Amy Klee
TEST KITCHEN DIRECTOR
Erin McMurrer
SENIOR EDITOR, BOOKS
Julia Collin
SENIOR WRITERS
Bridget Lancaster
Sally Sampson
ASSOCIATE EDITOR
Matthew Card
COPY EDITOR
India Koopman
MANAGING EDITOR,
BOOKS AND WEB SITE
Rebecca Hays
TEST COOKS
Shannon Blaisdell
Keith Dresser
Meg Suzuki
CONTRIBUTING EDITOR
Elizabeth Germain
CONSULTING EDITORS
Shirley Corriher
Jasper White
Robert L. Wolke
KITCHEN ASSISTANT
Rochelle Rashotsky
TEST KITCHEN INTERNS
Rajeev Samantrai
Merrill Stubbs
Nina West
ASSISTANT TO THE PUBLISHER
Sumantha Selvakumar
PROOFREADER
Jana Branch
VICE PRESIDENT MARKETING
David Mack
RETAIL SALES MANAGER
Jason Geller
CIRCULATION RETAIL SALES MANAGER
Jonathan Venier
SALES REPRESENTATIVE
Shekinah Cohn
MARKETING ASSISTANT
Connie Forbes
CIRCULATION MANAGER
Larisa Greiner
PRODUCTS MANAGER
Steven Browall
DIRECT MAIL MANAGER
Robert Lee
CUSTOMER SERVICE MANAGER
Jacqueline Valerio
VICE PRESIDENT OPERATIONS
AND TECHNOLOGY
James McCormack
PRODUCTION MANAGER
Jessica Quirk
PRODUCTION COORDINATOR
Mary Connelly
PRODUCTION ASSISTANTS
Ron Bilodeau
Jennifer McCreary
SYSTEMS ADMINISTRATOR
Richard Cassidy
WEBMASTER
Nicole Morris
CHIEF FINANCIAL OFFICER
Sharyn Chabot
CONTROLLER
Mandy Shito
OFFICE MANAGER
Ruth Duncan
RECEPTIONIST
Henrietta Murray
PUBLICITY
Deborah Broide

For list rental information, contact The SpecialLISTS, 1200 Harbor Blvd. 9th Floor, Weehawken, NJ 07087; 201-865-5800; fax 201-867-2450. Editorial office: 17 Station Street, Brookline, MA 02445; 617-232-1000; fax 617-232-1572. Editorial contributions should be sent to: Editor, Cook's Illustrated. We cannot assume responsibility for manuscripts submitted to us. Submissions will be returned only if accompanied by a large self-addressed envelope. Postmaster: Send all new orders, subscription inquiries, and change of address notices to: Cook's Illustrated, P.O. Box 7446, Red Oak, IA 51591-0446. PRINTED IN THE USA.

SUMMER SQUASHES

SUMMER SQUASHES There are essentially two types of squash: summer and winter. What sets summer squash apart from winter squash is soft skin and tender, light-colored flesh. Summer squashes are harvested while still immature and can be eaten rind, seeds, and all. Crookneck squash and golden zucchini are two widely available varieties. Baby zucchinis with blossoms are not only beautiful but entirely edible. Pattypans—whether the familiar green, scallop-edged squash, the yellow "sunburst," or the striped "tiger eye"—are sweet and firm-textured. The globe squash, also called ronde de Nice, or round zucchini, is dense and heavy, and its nearly seedless flesh is juicy and meaty. Chayotes have a crunchy, pear-like texture and cucumber-like flavor. Unlike other summer squashes, they should be peeled before eating. The opo is an immature Asian bottle gourd with smooth, satiny flesh and a flavor akin to the white part of a watermelon rind. Beneath the ridged skin of the Chinese okra (also known as luffa) is very soft, spongy, mild-tasting flesh. Asian bitter melon is extremely bitter and definitely an acquired taste.

COVER (Pumpkin): ELIZABETH BRANDON, BACK COVER (Summer Squashes): JOHN BURGOYNE

THE ROAD TO AGADEZ

This is a true story about the summer of 1969. To be precise, it concerns only three days in late June when I drove across the Sahara desert with 18 other high school graduates, two English teachers, and a Harvard philosopher. We navigated our way across a 600-mile no man's land that ended in the town of Agadez in Niger. It was the beginning of the rainy season—when the track becomes impassable—in the southern Sahara, and, because of a late start, we had trouble getting permission from the embassy in Algiers to leave. There was no road to speak of, only a piste, which consists of the odd track and piles of stones, the only sign of human civilization a one-hut military outpost located smack dab in the middle. The road to Agadez turned out to be a long one.

The trip had begun in early June in London, where we picked up three new Land Rovers with special racks fitted for extra gas cans. After a couple of weeks driving through France and Spain, a dinner at heiress Barbara Hutton's palace in Tangiers (where one of my friends, Alfie, was sufficiently inebriated to entertain Ms. Hutton with an impromptu medley of Broadway show tunes), and a memorable meal of couscous on the cliffs overlooking Oran, we finally started on the road to Agadez. To our surprise, the desert was hauntingly beautiful and otherworldly. The huge sun pooled and melted into the horizon at sunset, the rocks were brightly colored (purple in one spot), and the stars at night were so crowded that it was hard work picking out the constellations.

The first night we came across an abandoned fort, the French Foreign Legion kind, and made camp there. Dinner was the usual execrable diet of canned sardines, deviled ham, and some sort of potted beef. Canned fruit was highly prized.

The next day we passed the halfway mark, a small hut inhabited by a handful of soldiers from Niger. One feature of this camp stood out. It was a large metal bathtub, full to the top, standing out from the surrounding terrain like a piece of space junk that had crash-landed on the moon. We took advantage of their hospitality, skinned off our clothes, and took turns sitting in a makeshift hot tub surrounded by a million acres of desert.

The next evening we ran into trouble. (We did most of our driving very early and very late to avoid the heat.) I was driving the first truck and lost sight of the track. The headlights picked up a carcass, then two, then a half dozen, all bloated, stiff-legged, and scattered about a cistern. We were soon stumbling over mummified camels, youthful shadows flitting in and out of headlights. Lost and for the first time doubting the possibility of reaching our next birthdays, we camped amidst the corpses and waited until morning.

At sunrise, our sober company circled and finally found the piste and headed south, but by noontime we hit a blinding sandstorm and turned the trucks downwind. One of them developed carburetor problems and had to be dismantled—a two-hour process—and rebuilt. It still ran poorly, the engine requiring constant gunning. Then we hit showers, and the road turned to mud every few miles. We winched the trucks through ruts so deep that the roofs of the Land Rovers were often below grade. We got stuck a dozen times, put our shoulders to the Rovers, and rocked them back and forth. It turned dark, the track was hard to follow, and we were down to a mere 1½ liters of gas. Finally, we saw a few lights far in the distance. We had finally found Agadez and the end of our Sahara adventure.

A few months ago, I came across a black-and-white photo of the Rovers in the Sahara. That small snapshot brought back the memory of an urgent need to travel, to move on through the desert, Central Africa, and then through Uganda to Kenya. We loved the trucks, the movement, the road ahead. We drove 10,000 miles that summer and didn't stop to wonder why some rocks are purple or who built the fort in the desert.

Last weekend, the kids and I piled into my red 1981 Ford F-150 and headed up the back road to Sherman's Country Store. It is a short drive and, for my kids, the destination is a penny-candy land: Sour Watermelon Slices, Cow Tales, Sugar Daddies, Round Up Candy, Robin's Eggs, Ring Pops, and Atomic Fireballs. They wanted me to hurry, excited by what was to come. For my part, I drove slowly and gazed out the window at a fallen crabapple tree, an alfalfa field that was a brilliant carpet of green, and the small billboard advertising the Church of Christ that reads, "If You Are Looking for a Sign, This Is It!" As we pulled up to the store, my kids spilled out of the truck, happy to have arrived. I sat a bit, thinking about that long drive from London to Nairobi, wondering if the journey and the destination are really the same thing. After those hard miles traveled, I had finally found a way back home through the scuffle of children pushing through the screen door at Sherman's, happy about the future that lies ahead.

FOR MORE INFORMATION

www.cooksillustrated.com

At the *Cook's Illustrated* Web site you can order a book, give a gift subscription to *Cook's Illustrated* magazine, sign up for our free e-newsletter, subscribe to the magazine, or check the status of your subscription. Join the Web site and you'll have access to our searchable databases of recipes, cookware ratings, ingredient tastings, quick tips, cookbook reviews, and more.

COOK'S ILLUSTRATED Magazine

Cook's Illustrated (ISSN 1068-2821) magazine is published bimonthly (6 issues per year) by Boston Common Press Limited Partnership, 17 Station Street, Brookline, MA 02445. Copyright 2002 Boston Common Press Limited Partnership. Periodical postage paid at Boston, Mass., and additional mailing offices, USPS #012487.

A one-year subscription is $29.70, two years is $55, and three years is $75. Add $6 postage per year for Canadian subscriptions and $12 per year for all other countries outside the U.S. To order subscriptions in the U.S. call 800-526-8442. Gift subscriptions are available for $24.95 each. Postmaster: Send all new orders, subscription inquiries, and change-of-address notices to *Cook's*

Illustrated, P.O. Box 7446, Red Oak, IA 51591-0446, or call 800-526-8442 inside the U.S. and 515-247-7571 outside the U.S.

COOKBOOKS

You can order the following books, as well as *The America's Test Kitchen Cookbook*, by calling 800-611-0759 inside the U.S. and 515-246-6911 outside the U.S.

➤ **The Best Recipe Series** Includes *The Best Recipe* as well as *Grilling & Barbecue, Soups & Stews, American Classics*, and *Italian Classics*.

➤ **The How to Cook Master Series** A collection of 25 single-subject cookbooks.

➤ **The Annual Series** Annual hardbound editions of the magazine as well as a nine-year (1993–2001) reference index.

AMERICA'S TEST KITCHEN Television Show

Look for our television series on public television. Go to http://www.americastestkitchen.com for program times in your area, recipes, and details about the shows, or to order the companion book to the second series, *The America's Test Kitchen Cookbook*.

Why One Cup of Flour Equals Five Ounces

In your baking recipes you provide some measurements in ounces as well as cups. What I don't understand is how 1 cup of flour can equal 5 ounces. The way I do math, 1 cup equals 8 ounces.

SUBMITTED BY
ONLINE READER

➤ You have confused volume measurements with weight. In baking, dry ingredients are most accurately and consistently measured by weight, and this is how professional bakers do it. Measures of volume can vary depending on what technique you use to get the flour in the cup and how aerated the flour is. (Sifting, for instance, aerates flour, so 1 cup of sifted flour weighs less than 1 cup of unsifted flour. All of our recipes call for unsifted flour unless indicated otherwise.) The technique we use to measure flour in the test kitchen is "dip and sweep": Dip the measure into the bag or canister of flour and fill it to overflowing, then sweep off the excess with a straight edge, such as the side of an icing spatula. When measured with dip and sweep, 1 cup of all-purpose flour weighs 5 ounces. The weight of flour varies with the protein content; the more protein, the heavier the flour. Bread flour, which is high in protein, thus weighs more cup for cup than cake flour, which is low in protein. The chart below shows the weights we rely on when measuring all-purpose, bread, and cake flours as well as the sweeteners we frequently use in baking recipes.

How Much Does It Weigh?

I cup of ...	Weighs ...
ALL-PURPOSE FLOUR	5 ounces
BREAD FLOUR	5½ ounces
CAKE FLOUR	4 ounces
GRANULATED SUGAR	7 ounces
PACKED BROWN SUGAR	7 ounces
CONFECTIONERS' SUGAR	4 ounces

When Grating Ginger, Grate Gingerly

Some recipes call for either minced or grated ginger. Can they really be substituted for one another, teaspoon for teaspoon? Do you recommend one technique over the other?

JANET PRIEST
CLEVELAND, OHIO

➤ To test the relative potency of minced and grated ginger, we made a simple chicken stir-fry with ginger sauce and a salad with ginger dressing. A whopping 4 tablespoons of minced ginger was called for in the stir-fry, and, when made with grated ginger, the ginger knocked out pretty much every other flavor in the dish. The dressing called for a more modest single tablespoon of minced or grated ginger. Here, too, however, we found that the dressing made with grated ginger packed a lot more ginger flavor. After experimenting a bit, we found we could use about half as much grated ginger as minced ginger and get just as much flavor. What's more, the flavor of grated ginger more completely permeates a dish, so you get a hit of ginger with every mouthful. Grating ruptures more of the root's cells than mincing and so releases both more juices and more flavor.

We tried grating ginger on a Microplane, our grater of choice for citrus zest and hard cheese, and on an official "ginger grater," this one a small, shallow ceramic bowl about 4 inches square with a raised center on which sit the "teeth" that do the grating. While a Microplane does a competent job, if given a choice, we would use a ginger grater. It creates a silkier pillow of ginger than the Microplane (with the ginger grater all of the root's tough strings are left behind in your hand; a Microplane breaks them down, and the effect is not quite as smooth), and it handily collects the flavor-packed ginger juice in its bowl. Williams-Sonoma carries a porcelain ginger grater that we like for $12 (look for item # 6-1130749 at www.williams-sonoma.com).

GINGER GRATER
The raised teeth break down the ginger, and the dish collects the flavorful juice.

A Better Feta

The feta cheese I buy at the supermarket is often dry and chalky. Is this the way the texture of the cheese is supposed to be?

HELEN RAPACZ
BERLIN, CONN.

➤ Feta cheese, a familiar presence on the Greek table, was originally made from sheep's milk or a mixture of sheep's and goat's milk. While many of the smaller, artisanal cheesemakers that have become increasingly popular in this country continue to observe this practice, the feta you find in the supermarket is almost certainly made by a large producer that uses pasteurized cow's milk. To make feta, the milk is curdled, shaped into a block, and steeped in brine.

To see how much of a difference we might find between supermarket and artisanal feta, we purchased some of both. At the supermarket we purchased two blocks, one sitting on a Styrofoam tray and wrapped in plastic, as is much of the feta sold in the supermarket, the other in a Cry-O-Vacked package that also contained a small amount of brine. Both were made from cow's milk. The artisanal cheese we purchased was made from sheep's milk and came sitting in a puddle of brine in a plastic container.

Much to our surprise, the tasters' favorite was the Cry-O-Vacked cheese. Far from being dry and chalky, it was moist, creamy, fresh-tasting, and tangy—all the qualities one would expect of a good feta. Tasters' next favorite was the artisanal cheese, which was slightly drier and also more salty. Coming in a very distant third was the feta placed on a Styrofoam tray and shrink-wrapped. It had a chalky consistency and was nearly flavorless.

What can be learned from our tasting? Packaging feta cheese with some of the brine is key to a moist texture. In the package of Cry-O-Vacked feta, we could see the moisture, and the cheese, when pressed, was somewhat soft and yielding rather than hard and crumbly. The quintessential feta should be creamy, tangy, supple, and moist, and you are not going to find these qualities in a block of cheese that has been left to sit high and dry on a Styrofoam tray. One final note: It's a good idea to rinse feta packed in brine just before serving to remove excess salt.

Vermouth versus White Wine

What is the difference between wine and vermouth? Can I use vermouth in place of white wine when cooking?

CAROL NEWMAN
BOSTON, MASS.

➤ Cooking vermouth, also called dry, or white, vermouth, is thought to have originated in early 19th-century France, which is why it is also sometimes called French vermouth. Sweet, or red, vermouth had a slightly earlier start in late 18th-century Italy and so is sometimes called Italian vermouth. Both types are now made in France and Italy as well as the United States.

No matter who makes it, dry vermouth starts out as a basic dry white table wine (several varieties are sometimes pooled, and they are often cheap). Traditionally, the wine was flavored with flowers, herbs, spices, and roots and then fortified with alcohol, bringing the total alcohol content up from the 12 to 13 percent typical of wine to about 18 percent. Today the process is much the same, although some large commercial producers use liquid concentrates rather than the botanicals themselves to achieve the characteristic flavor of a dry vermouth.

To see how dry vermouth would hold up in cooking against a modestly priced $10 bottle of dry white wine, we conducted two tests. We tried each in a simple risotto (the original recipe calls for white wine) and in the pan-fried chicken in this issue (which calls for dry vermouth; see page 6). We found that the dishes made with wine had a brighter, cleaner flavor, while those made with vermouth were more herbaceous and definitely more alcoholic.

Do we recommend one over the other? Our tests show that vermouth is a viable substitute for white wine, especially when the quantity called for isn't all that much (½ cup or less) and when the dish has other flavors that balance and dilute the flavor of the vermouth (both the risotto and the pan-fried chicken also called for chicken broth). Try substituting a bottle of vermouth for a bottle of Sauvignon Blanc when poaching pears, however, and you'll be sorry.

Considerations of flavor aside, vermouth has a couple of things going for it. First, at $5 or $6 for a 750-ml bottle, it is cheaper than most wines. Second, you're more likely to have an open bottle of vermouth on hand. When you don't want to open a bottle of wine just to obtain a small amount for a recipe, vermouth can be used as a substitute.

Taylor Oven Thermometer Update

Two years ago I purchased the Taylor Classic Oven Guide Thermometer that you picked as your favorite oven thermometer, and it looks just like the one recommended in the March/April 2002 issue of your magazine. Is there any reason I should purchase a new one? I was also wondering if it's safe to store the thermometer in the oven, which is what I've been doing.

STAN LIPOWITZ
BALTIMORE, MD.

➤ Although the Taylor Classic Oven Guide Thermometer that you'll find in stores today may look just like an older version of the thermometer, there is a difference. Owing to concerns about the toxicity of mercury, Taylor switched from a mercury-based thermometer to an alcohol-based thermometer in the year 2000, and beginning in 2001 it shipped only the newer model. Otherwise, however, the newer Oven Guide is just like its predecessor and even has the same item number.

You can tell if the thermometer you have is

WHAT IS IT?

I came across this pot at an estate sale. It's made entirely of copper, but, given its unusual rounded shape, I assume I can't use it on the stovetop and so have no idea what to do with it. Can you help?

MARCIA FERNALD
DANVERS, MASS.

➤ What you've come across is a beautiful copper pot designed for one thing only: the making of *zabaglione*, an Italian custard sauce fabled for its restorative powers. Occasionally also called *zabaione* in Italian and known as *sabayon* in French, the sauce is made by whisking egg yolks and sugar together until thick, pale yellow, and creamy, then adding Marsala wine and whisking still more over a barely simmering pot of water until the mixture is light, frothy, and at least doubled in volume.

The deep, bowl-like shape of the zabaglione pan is thought to facilitate whipping, and we were curious to see if this was true. We did find it much easier to whisk the eggs in a zabaglione pan than in a bowl or small saucepan. The custard also seemed to cook more evenly in the zabaglione pan than in the bowl or saucepan, both of which collected more bits of overcooked egg. We can only speculate as to why, but it may be that the custard is moved about so efficiently in the zabaglione pan that not one drop remains in one place long enough to overcook. The pan, made of unlined copper, is also an excellent conductor of heat, which is why it is so important to cook the custard over a very low, gentle flame.

A Cook's Wares sells a 1½-quart copper zabaglione pan, item #2090, made by Mauviel, for $55 (see www.cookswares.com).

alcohol- or mercury-based by the color of the fluid. If it's silver, you have the older mercury-based model; if it's blue or red, it's the newer model. According to Karen Yaggie, a marketing representative at Taylor, some retailers may have yet to refresh their inventory and so may still be carrying the older model. If you find that you have the older model and would prefer the newer one, just check the color of the fluid carefully before you buy it.

As for your question about storage, Yaggie told us that it is safe to store the thermometer in

the oven—whether warming a dish at 250 degrees or broiling a steak—except during its self-cleaning cycle. Some ovens reach 700 degrees or more during self-cleaning, and the thermometer is not designed to withstand such high temperatures.

To Strain or Not to Strain . . . Custard

I'm confused about the removal of chalazas from eggs. Though employed in the creation of the custard for your Chocolate Cream Pie (May/June 2001), this step is omitted in your recipe for Classic Crème Brûlée (November/December 2001). What criteria should be used to decide whether or not to remove the chalazas?

ELYSE GREENE
PLANTATION, FLA.

➤ The chalaza, a whitish, threadlike substance that anchors the yolk to the shell, turns hard, like an egg white, when cooked and so is undesirable in custards, which are in large part defined by their smooth texture. In the case of the chocolate cream pie, we removed each chalaza by hand by cracking open an egg, capturing the yolk in the palm of a hand, and letting the chalaza drop off along with the egg white (sometimes using our fingers for assistance if the chalaza was stubbornly stuck to the yolk). In the case of the crème brûlée, we did in fact remove the chalazas, just with a different technique: straining the cooked custard before allowing it to set. Straining better guarantees a smooth texture than does removing chalazas by hand. In the case of the pie, which has a bottom crust that adds crunch with every bite, a tiny bit of cooked chalaza here and there in the custard probably won't be noticed. With a crème brûlée, however, as senior editor Dawn Yanagihara explains, "a flawlessly silky texture is paramount."

Our recommendation is simple. For custards in which you don't want even the faintest trace of hardened white, straining is the technique of choice. Otherwise, the by-hand method of removing chalazas is fine and you don't need to dirty a strainer.

Erratum

➤ Our measurements were off for the Cajun Grill in our story about charcoal grills in the May/June 2002 issue. The chart on page 29 gives dimensions of 18 by 26 inches for a total of 442 square inches. The dimensions are in fact 17 (not 18) by 26 inches.

SEND US YOUR QUESTIONS We will provide a complimentary one-year subscription for each letter we print. Send your inquiry, name, address, and daytime telephone number to Notes from Readers, Cook's Illustrated, P.O. Box 470589, Brookline, MA 02447, or visit www.cooksillustrated.com

Quick Tips

Four Treats from One

A byproduct of the Poached Pear and Almond Tart recipe on page 24 is about 2½ cups of the fragrant liquid used to poach the pears. Loath to pour this elixir down the drain, we discovered that it can easily be made into any one of four frozen treats. Any flavorful poaching liquid can be handled the same way. In each case, use the poaching liquid just as it is.

Sorbet

Make sure the liquid is well-chilled and follow the freezing directions for your ice cream maker to make a smooth, refreshing sorbet. When the sorbet comes out of the machine, it will need about two hours in the freezer to firm up properly.

Granita

Granita, which is like Italian ice, can be made in one of two ways.
A. Freeze the liquid in ice cube trays until solid, place a single layer of cubes in the workbowl of a food processor, and pulse 10 or 12 times until no large chunks of ice remain. Scoop the crystals into individual bowls to serve, and repeat with any remaining cubes.
B. Alternatively, pour the liquid into a Pyrex deep-dish pie plate or 8-inch-square Pyrex baking dish and place in the freezer. To make a light and fluffy confection, stir the mixture once per hour with a dinner fork, using much the same motion you would to fluff a pot of freshly cooked white rice. Total freezing time should be three to four hours.

Flavored Ice Cubes

Freeze the liquid in ice cube trays until solid, and then use the cubes to chill a glass of sangría or iced tea.

Popsicles

Portion out the liquid among small paper drinking cups (such as Dixie), cover each cup with a small square of aluminum foil, and poke a wooden Popsicle stick or dinner spoon through the foil and into each cup. Freeze for several hours or until solid. Once frozen, remove foil and tear off the paper cups to serve the Popsicles.

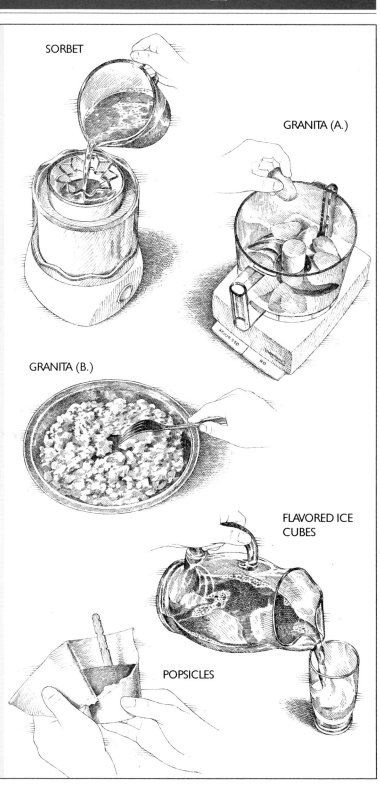

SORBET

GRANITA (A.)

GRANITA (B.)

FLAVORED ICE CUBES

POPSICLES

Mitigating Mixer Mess

Bakers who use a standing mixer know well the mess that scattered dry ingredients make if you add them to the mixer bowl too quickly. For cooks like Rose Kish of Beacon, N.Y., who are lucky enough to own a 5- or 6-quart KitchenAid mixer (the type that lifts the bowl up off the base with a crank, as opposed to smaller models, in which the bowl is fixed to the base), the mess is easy to control if you spread a kitchen towel out between the base and the bowl. This way, if dry ingredients scatter, they'll land on the towel instead of on the mixer base or counter.

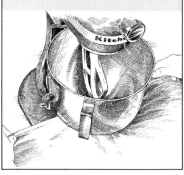

Shrimp Deveining Aide

Once removed from a shrimp, the vein can stick tenaciously to the tip of a paring knife, nail scissors, or other deveining tool of your choice. Instead of fighting to remove each vein from your utensil (as it fights to stay right where it is), try this method, submitted by Candace Steiner of Larchmont, N.Y.

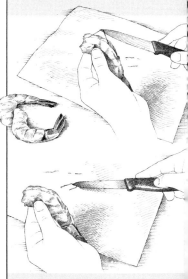

Place a sheet of paper towel flat on your work surface. Once you have freed the vein with the tip of the paring knife, just touch the knife to the paper towel and the vein will slip off the knife and stick to the towel. When you are through, toss the dirty towel into the trash.

Send Us Your Tip We will provide a complimentary one-year subscription for each tip we print. Send your tip, name, address, and telephone number to Quick Tips, *Cook's Illustrated*, P.O. Box 470589, Brookline, MA 02447 or visit www.cooksillustrated.com.

Bottle Opener Aide

When the small lid to a bottle of ketchup, Worcestershire or soy sauce, vinegar, salad dressing, or the like sticks and won't unscrew easily, take this advice from Eric Pryor of Brooklyn, N.Y., and enlist the services of a nutcracker.

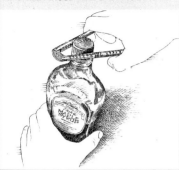

Making Small Amounts of Onion or Shallot Juice

Though the flavor of minced onion or shallot is essential in many dressings and sauces, some cooks, including Mildred Wilson of Township of Washington, N.J., find the texture gritty and unpleasant. To get the flavor without the bits and pieces, she juices small sections of onion or shallot by pressing them through a garlic press.

Extinguishing Kitchen Matches—For Sure

It is not unheard of for a kitchen fire to start from a casually extinguished match that was tossed into the trash. Elizabeth McCracken of Somerville, Mass., makes doubly sure to avoid this potential disaster by holding the head of the extinguished match under a running faucet (or dipping it into a water-filled dish in the sink) to douse it before putting it in the trash.

No-Fuss Flavoring

Garlic and herbs are oft-used flavorings in homemade soups, chowders, stews, and sauces. Two readers, Chris Cosentino of San Francisco, Calif., and Brian Linzie of St. Paul, Minn., offer methods for boosting these flavors while also cutting down on the work involved. Both use these ingredients almost whole, with great results.

A. When making bean soup, vegetable soup, or another such dish, you can boost and deepen the garlic flavor by adding a whole head. Just rub the papery outer layer of skin off an intact head of garlic, cut about ½ inch off the top to expose the flesh of the cloves, and throw the whole head into the soup pot. When the soup is done, remove the garlic head and either discard it or squeeze the softened garlic into the soup to further flavor and thicken it.

B. In recipes that call for thyme or rosemary, instead of stripping leaves off the branches and mincing them, simply throw the whole branch into the pan. Remember to remove the spent branch, as you would spent bay leaves, before serving. Rosemary is very strong, so you may want to keep it in the pot for only 15 minutes or so.

Instant Ice Water for Pastry

A plant mister is a terrific device for distributing a minimal amount of water evenly over a mixture of fat and flour when making pie dough. Emily Kikue Frank of Denver, Colo., fills a mister bottle with about ¼ cup water and stores it on its side in the freezer. When making pastry, she just grabs the bottle from the freezer and fills it with cold water, which quickly chills even further upon contact with the ice.

One Pan, Two Loaves

Pity the baker who owns but a single loaf pan but whose bread recipe yields enough dough to make two loaves. When faced with that very situation recently, Tim Kinnel of Boston, Mass., put his single loaf pan to unique—and very effective—use to bake both loaves. In testing, we found that this tip works particularly well with a Pyrex loaf pan matched with a Pyrex baking dish because their bottom edges share the same contours.

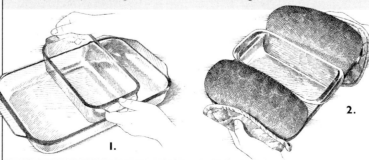

1. Place a single loaf pan across the center of a 9 by 13-inch baking dish.
2. Position one portion of shaped dough on either side of the loaf pan and bake. (You can even fill the loaf pan with a third portion of dough to bake three loaves.)

Short-Cutting Mashed Potatoes

When potatoes are destined for mashing, we prefer to boil them with their skins on to keep them from getting waterlogged (drier potatoes are able to absorb more melted butter and cream). There is no doubt, though, that peeling just-boiled potatoes is a painstaking job.

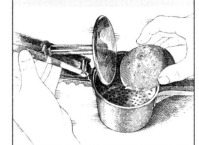

Here in the test kitchen we hold the potato with a fork and use a paring knife. If you have a ricer, you can avoid even this inconvenience, as does Doris Jensen-Futoma of Granger, Ind., who cuts each potato in half and then quickly places each half cut-side down in the ricer. This way the flesh is forced through the holes while the skin remains in the hopper.

Butter Shortcut

Sandra Spalding of Austin, Texas, suggests this small step to help streamline your cooking process.

When unwrapping a new stick of butter, cut it into tablespoons (using the markings on the wrapper as a guide) before placing it in a butter dish. This offers several advantages. First, you can grab as many tablespoons as you need without stopping to cut them when you're busy cooking. Second, if the recipe calls for softened butter, the smaller pieces will soften faster than an entire stick. Last, cut butter ensures that any new or inexperienced cooks in your home will get the right measure of butter without having to cut it themselves. Be sure to use the cut pieces of butter quickly or to keep them in a covered dish.

How to Pan-Roast Chicken

A restaurant technique promises superbly crisp skin on roast chicken
with just 20 minutes of cooking time. Is it too good to be true?

≥ BY DAWN YANAGIHARA ≤

To make a good basic roast chicken, some planning is required, and even then it can be a challenge to cook. For a moist, well-seasoned bird, you brine it; for the crispiest skin, you air-dry it; to coordinate the doneness of the thigh and breast, you flip the bird as it roasts. An hour or so later, the roast chicken emerges from the oven along with some drippings that, if not burnt, can be turned into a gravy or sauce before you dismantle the bird for serving.

In an effort to make roast chicken easier, I decided to investigate a technique found in several recent restaurant cookbooks: pan-roasting. This technique is used to cook cuts of meat, poultry, and fish that for reasons of size or thickness cannot be cooked exclusively on the stovetop without scorching the exterior. For pan-roasted chicken, the chicken is cut up (a slight variation, or cheat, if you must, on the roast chicken concept), browned on both sides on the stovetop, and then slid, skillet and all, into a hot oven to complete cooking. Pan-roasting means no iconic roast chicken to bring to the table, but I was hoping that it would deliver superior skin, shorter preparation time, and a rich, savory pan sauce to boot. The question was whether this technique was as simple as promised.

Water and Fire

Chicken first. I cut a 3½ - to 4-pounder into eight pieces, two each of drumsticks and thighs and four breast pieces. This arrangement meant that each serving could consist of a portion of both white and dark meat. The wings I discarded because they are the least favorite sections to eat and the 12-inch skillet was already full without them.

Brining (soaking in a solution of salt and sugar) has become customary in our test kitchen. When pan-roasted chickens were tasted side-by-side, we preferred brined birds for their moistness (which can act as a cushion against the effects of overcooking, if it happens) and for the agreeable saltiness that permeated the meat. However, I was forced to modify our all-purpose brine: I ousted the sugar because it led to uneven browning and burnt drippings. Because I was using a

Pan-roasting delivers crisp skin and flavorful drippings that can be used to make a quick sauce.

cut-up chicken, brining was expedited—just 30 minutes did the trick. Air-drying, which we have found necessary to produce ultra-crisp skin on roasted poultry, was not necessary. The hot skillet was crisping the skin quite well without adding hours to this weeknight recipe.

Medium-high heat was optimal for even browning. High heat was a tad furious and sometimes resulted in burnt pan drippings. The chicken could be browned in a skillet without any oil (it had sufficient fat that rendered as it cooked and prevented sticking), but the browning was spotty and not ideal. However, even a mere tablespoon of oil was too much; when the excess fat was poured off before sauce making, the drippings woefully went with it. A teaspoon of oil—the barest coating on the skillet's surface—did the job well.

I browned the chicken parts on both sides before sliding them into the oven. The burning question now was: When the chicken pieces go in the oven, should they be skin-side up or skin-side down? Skin-side up chicken did brown, but it was mottled and crisped in some spots, soft in others.

Skin-side down chicken was superior. The contact between the chicken skin and the hot metal of the pan produced a crackling crisp, darker, russet-toned skin. Both cast-iron and heavy-duty heat-conductive skillets performed well.

Suggested oven temperatures ranged from 375 all the way to 500 degrees. The winner was 450 degrees; 500 sometimes singed the drippings, and lower temperatures simply took longer to cook the chicken through. The lowest rack setting was best as it seemed better suited to maintaining even heat.

Pan-roasted chicken recipes recommend removing the breast pieces five to 10 minutes before the leg pieces because the breast is done when it reaches 160 degrees and the leg 175 degrees (the identical problem that plagues whole roasted poultry). However, the digital thermometer told me that the breast pieces—despite being cut into quarters—and the leg pieces were finishing at about the same time. It appeared that the thickness of the breast pieces made them cook more slowly than the flat, thin thigh pieces and slim drumsticks. Even if the breast pieces did overcook a smidgen, the brining cushion took effect.

Chicken Out

Once the chicken was removed from the skillet, the fond (brown bits on the bottom of the pan) was crusty and plentiful, so I needed only a handful of ingredients to turn it into a sauce, keeping the flavors honest and simple. Using a potholder and the utmost caution because the skillet handle was burning hot, I discarded most of the fat, sautéed minced shallots, and, in a step called deglazing, poured in chicken broth and vermouth, scraping the skillet to loosen the fond. A couple sprigs of thyme added a herbaceous note. The liquid simmered to about half its original volume as the chicken reposed. With the flavors of the sauce concentrated and its consistency slightly thickened, I added juices that the resting chicken had released and whisked in a few knobs of butter along with seasonings. A quick return to the skillet brought the chicken back up to serving temperature (this time skin-side up to keep the skin crisp).

Judging from the enthusiasm with which a plateful of pan-roasted chicken (and sauce) met, it was clear that this roast chicken was receiving high marks. Crisp-skinned roast chicken with an impressive sauce is suddenly possible on a weeknight.

PAN-ROASTED CHICKEN WITH SHALLOT AND VERMOUTH SAUCE

SERVES 4

Brining the chicken is optional but highly recommended. If you opt not to brine, use a kosher chicken if one is available (kosher chickens are salted during processing and have the moistness and flavor of brined chickens). This recipe requires a 12-inch ovenproof skillet. The handle will be blisteringly hot after being in the oven, so be sure to use a potholder or oven mitt to remove the skillet from the oven and when handling the skillet as you make the sauce. Dry white wine may be substituted for the vermouth.

Chicken

1 ½ cups kosher salt or ¾ cup table salt
1 chicken (3 ½ to 4 pounds), cut into 8 pieces (4 breast pieces, 2 thighs, and 2 drumsticks, wings discarded) and trimmed of excess fat
Ground black pepper
1 teaspoon vegetable oil

Shallot and Vermouth Sauce

1 large shallot, minced (about 4 tablespoons)
¾ cup canned low-sodium chicken broth
½ cup dry vermouth
2 sprigs fresh thyme
3 tablespoons unsalted butter, cut into 3 pieces
Salt and ground black pepper

1. Dissolve salt in 2½ quarts cold tap water in large container or bowl; submerge chicken pieces in brine and refrigerate until fully seasoned, about 30 minutes. Rinse chicken pieces under running water and pat dry with paper towels. Season chicken with pepper.

2. Adjust oven rack to lowest position and heat oven to 450 degrees.

3. Heat oil in heavy-bottomed 12-inch ovenproof skillet over medium-high heat until beginning to smoke, about 3 minutes; swirl skillet to coat evenly with oil. Brown chicken pieces skin-side down until deep golden, about 5 minutes; turn chicken pieces, and brown until golden on

Properly Browned Chicken

UNDERBROWNED　　NICELY BROWNED

An improperly heated pan produces chicken with pale, flabby skin (left). When the pan is heated until the oil smokes, the skin will crisp and brown (right).

Judging When the Pan Is Hot

Most home cooks do not properly preheat their skillets, which results in a lack of both crust and flavor development (see "Properly Browned Chicken," below). How do you know when your skillet is properly preheated? We began with the common cookbook advice of sprinkling water in the preheated pan. If the droplets immediately bead up and dance on the skillet's surface, the pan is hot enough. Not exactly. Beading and dancing occur even when the skillet is too cool. We held outstretched palms a few inches above the surface of the skillet, but this proved to be a very inaccurate measure. We put bread crumbs, bread slices, sugar, popcorn kernels, rice, salt, ice cubes, and measured amounts of water into cold skillets, turned on the heat, and waited for some sort of sign. Bread crumbs and slices charred and smoked much too soon. Sugar melted, began to caramelize, and made a mess. Popcorn and rice browned unevenly and erratically after a few minutes, before the skillet was hot enough. Salt was unresponsive. It showed no visible changes, even after the skillet was hotter than we cared for. Heated until every trace of water evaporated, ice cubes and measured amounts of water showed some promise, but given that boiling points vary with elevation, we thought the method a bit unreliable.

It was oil—smoking oil, to be exact—that held the answer. Measured into a cold skillet and heated for a few minutes, the oil gives off wisps of smoke that serve as a visual alarm that the skillet is hot and ready. We tested our theory with steaks, chicken (skin-on), and fish fillets and steaks. In each case, oil that had just begun to smoke was a good indicator that the skillet was hot enough to produce well-crusted, good-tasting, and good-looking food without overcooking.

That said, not every kind of oil is suitable for high-heat browning and searing. Unrefined oils, such as extra-virgin olive oil, should *not* be used because their smoke points are low. Refined oils like vegetable, canola, corn, and peanut (be careful of the unrefined peanut oil carried in some grocery stores) work well because their smoke points are high (above 400 degrees). A word to the wise: The just-smoking-oil heat indicator is good only for browning and searing in very little oil, no more than a couple of tablespoons. Smoking oil is simply too hot for pan-frying and deep-frying.

A few final words on browning and searing in a hot skillet. To minimize splattering and maximize browning, wick away excess moisture on the surface of the food with paper towels. For more serious splatter containment, use a splatter screen. And be prepared to turn on your exhaust fan or crack open a window. The light smoke that will waft from the skillet will dissipate more quickly with some ventilation.

As the oil heats in the pan, it goes through three stages—warm, hot, and very hot. Here's how to tell where the oil is in the process.
• When warm, the oil becomes more fluid but is inactive and still.
• When hot, the oil creates faint waves in web-like patterns, as shown above.
• When very hot, thin wisps of smoke lift from the skillet. The skillet and oil are now ready.

second side, about 4 minutes longer. Turn chicken skin-side down and place skillet in oven. Roast until juices run clear when chicken is cut with paring knife, or thickest part of breast registers about 160 degrees on instant-read thermometer and thickest part of thighs and drumsticks registers about 175 degrees, about 10 minutes longer. Using potholder or oven mitt to protect hands from hot skillet handle, remove pan from oven. Transfer chicken skin-side up to platter, and let rest while making sauce. (If not making sauce, let chicken rest 5 minutes before serving.)

4. Still using potholder or oven mitt, pour off most of fat from skillet, add shallot, then set skillet over medium-high heat; cook, stirring frequently, until shallot softens, about 1½ minutes. Add chicken broth, vermouth, and thyme; increase heat to high and simmer rapidly, scraping skillet bottom with wooden spoon to loosen browned bits. Simmer until slightly thickened and reduced to about ⅔ cup, about 6 minutes. Pour

accumulated chicken juices into skillet, discard thyme, and whisk in butter one piece at a time. Season sauce to taste with salt and pepper. Return chicken pieces skin-side up to skillet; simmer to heat through, about 1 minute. Serve immediately.

PAN-ROASTED CHICKEN WITH SHERRY-ROSEMARY SAUCE

Follow recipe for Pan-Roasted Chicken with Shallot and Vermouth Sauce, substituting dry sherry for vermouth and 2 sprigs fresh rosemary for thyme.

PAN-ROASTED CHICKEN WITH COGNAC-MUSTARD SAUCE

Follow recipe for Pan-Roasted Chicken with Shallot and Vermouth Sauce, substituting ¼ cup each white wine and Cognac or brandy for vermouth and 1 tablespoon Dijon mustard for an equal amount of butter.

Kung Pao Shrimp at Home

Tired of the dull, gloppy restaurant renditions of this Sichuan classic? With a few Asian pantry staples, you can make a spicy kung pao that puts most restaurant versions to shame.

⇒ BY ADAM RIED ⇐

Kung pao shrimp—or, as we have come to call it here in the test kitchen, kung P-O-W!!!!!—can be much more fun to say than to eat. This classic Sichuan stir-fry of shrimp, peanuts, and chiles in a rich brown sauce is a Chinese restaurant standard, yet the kung pao I sampled in half a dozen well-reputed spots around Boston was hopeless. The first one was dismal, with tough, tiny little shrimp drenched in a quart of pale, greasy, bland sauce, and things just got worse from there.

This sorry collection of kung pao renditions served as a not-so-subtle hint that I'd be better off making this dish at home. Like most stir-fries, kung pao cooks quickly, so it is well suited for a weeknight meal. Moreover, I thought that by carefully examining the key cooking issues—the type and preparation of both the shrimp and the nuts along with the composition and texture of the sauce—I could come up with something much better than what I'd encountered in restaurants.

Nuts over Shrimp

Most Chinese stir-fries go heavy on the vegetables, but kung pao dishes are different. The quantity of vegetables is limited, with the emphasis instead on the shrimp and the nuts. The restaurant versions I tried often included green pepper, and some added bamboo shoots, carrots, celery, scallions, and zucchini. I worked my way through these choices and more and settled on a modest amount of red pepper for sweetness and scallion for freshness, bite, and color. Kung pao needs nothing else from the vegetable kingdom.

Taking a step up the food chain, I looked at the shrimp next. Most restaurants use small to medium shrimp, which makes the dish seem skimpy. My tasters and I felt that larger shrimp made a more satisfying kung pao, and large shrimp were easier to peel, too. After checking out jumbo, extra-large, large, and medium, we selected extra-large (21/25 count) for their combination of succulence and generous appearance. (See "Size Matters" on page 9 to learn how shrimp are sized.)

The best way to prepare the shrimp was a matter of some debate. Traditionally, they are "velveted"—coated with egg white, cornstarch, and seasonings—and then fried in a generous quantity of oil. The idea here is to create a softly crisp coating that will help the sauce adhere. Though velveting did have its supporters, I was not

Extra-large shrimp, whole dried red chiles, peanuts, and a savory brown sauce are the hallmarks of great kung pao.

among them, for two reasons. First, the egg coating tended to cook up in unattractive clumps, which would later float about in the dish, and second, the two to three cups of oil required to deep-fry seemed both cumbersome and wasteful. Dealing with all that oil, from measuring it out to disposing of it later, edged the dish out of the realm of simple weeknight cooking. It would be much better, I felt, to quickly stir-fry the shrimp in a film of oil and to thicken the sauce slightly to help it coat the shrimp.

The nuts help define kung pao. In most of the restaurant dishes I tried, the flavor of the nuts was underdeveloped, so they acted more as a garnish than a key element. In contrast, I wanted to better integrate the nuts into the dish and to deepen their flavor. One move accomplished both goals. Whereas most recipes add the nuts near the end of the cooking time, I stir-fried them right along with the shrimp at the beginning. This way, they toasted briefly in the pan, intensifying in flavor, which they then contributed to the sauce. Most kung pao recipes rely on either peanuts or

cashews, and we appreciated the former for their savory flavor and crisp texture. By comparison, cashews seemed both sweet and a little soft.

Stir-Fry and Sauce

Luckily for me, the test kitchen has conducted extensive investigations into stir-frying technique, so I knew that a wide, heavy skillet, preheated until the oil smokes, is a better mate with the flat American stovetop burner than a deeply curved wok. With all that heat, though, it would be easy to overcook, and therefore toughen, the shrimp and to burn the aromatic garlic and ginger that are part of the sauce. With a little care, though, both problems are easy to avoid. First, I learned not to cook shrimp all the way through at first because they will finish cooking in the sauce later; an initial stay in the pan of just under two minutes was ideal. Second, while most stir-fry recipes add garlic and ginger near the beginning, at *Cook's* we prefer to add them near the end of cooking to prevent burning and preserve their fresh flavors.

When it came to the sauce, I pictured it deep brown, syrupy in texture, and glistening, with balanced elements of sweet, savory, salty, garlicky, and hot. I tried both chicken broth and water as a base and preferred the broth for the savory underpinning it provided. For a bit of sweetness I added sugar in amounts from 1 tablespoon down to 1 teaspoon, but even a mere teaspoon was overkill. Instead, I chose to add the classic Asian trio of hoisin sauce, oyster-flavored sauce, and sesame oil, all available (separately) in the supermarket and all good sources of color, flavor depth, and subtle sweetness. An ample supply of garlic—three cloves—gave the sauce authority, and ginger and rice vinegar added brightness. I liked Chinese black rice vinegar (called Chinkiang vinegar) even better because it was more complex—smoky, salty, plum-like, and slightly sweet—but it can be hard to come by. Cornstarch

TASTING: Putting the POW! into Kung Pao

Without spicy chile heat, it's not kung pao. The recipes I consulted, however, offered little agreement about the best source of that heat. For the sake of convenience and simplicity, I immediately ruled out exotic chili sauces that can be had only in ethnic markets. Instead, I hit the supermarket up the street and picked up the most oft-repeated contenders, including whole dried chiles (the traditional choice), crushed red pepper flakes, fresh chiles, chili oil, and two popular and widely available Asian chili sauces, Sambal and Sriracha. Thus outfitted to heat things up, I returned to the test kitchen and conducted a side-by-side kung pao tasting.

The exact formula for Sambal, a chunky chili-garlic paste, varies from maker to maker. Ours was seasoned with salt, sugar, and rice vinegar. Smoother Sriracha is a popular Thai chili sauce, and ours was seasoned with salt, sugar, garlic, and fish extract. Both Sambal and Sriracha are common Asian table condiments, but tasters gave them thumbs-down in the kung pao because they lacked depth and tended to taste too salty. Chili oil was also passed by because the one we used, actually a chili-flavored sesame oil, was judged too mild, and it made the sauce a bit greasy. The fresh chiles—jalapeños, to be exact—provided sharp heat, but the tasters did not appreciate the distinct green, vegetal notes. Crushed red pepper flakes provided a bright, direct heat that was utterly acceptable, but the tasters' favorite by a long shot was the whole dried chiles, which infused the kung pao with a round, even spiciness that offered a deep, toasty, almost smoky dimension as well.

This finding, of course, begged the question of whether one particular type of dried chile would be best, as there are many varieties. With my sights set on relatively small chiles (large chiles simply looked wrong in the dish), I returned to the market and gathered six varieties, including an unnamed Asian specimen from the bulk bin, Japones, Arbol, Guajillo, Costeño, and Cascabel. Tasters strained to detect distinctions between them in my kung pao. I concluded that any small whole dried red chiles will do quite nicely. —A.R.

SMALL WHOLE DRIED RED CHILES

CRUSHED RED PEPPER FLAKES

FRESH JALAPEÑO CHILES

CHILI OIL

SAMBAL SAUCE

SRIRACHA SAUCE

KUNG PAO SHRIMP
SERVES 4

You can substitute plain rice vinegar for the black rice vinegar (available in Asian markets), but we prefer the latter for its fruity, salty complexity. If you prefer roasted unsalted cashews over peanuts, substitute an equal amount. Do not eat the whole chiles in the finished dish.

- 1 pound extra-large shrimp (21 to 25 count), peeled and deveined
- 1 tablespoon dry sherry or rice wine
- 2 teaspoons soy sauce
- 3 medium garlic cloves, pressed through garlic press or minced (about 1 tablespoon)
- 1 piece (½-inch) fresh ginger, peeled and minced (about 2 teaspoons)
- 3 tablespoons peanut or vegetable oil
- ½ cup roasted unsalted peanuts
- 6 small whole dried red chiles (each about 1¾ to 2 inches long), 3 chiles roughly crumbled, or 1 teaspoon dried red pepper flakes
- ¾ cup canned low-sodium chicken broth
- 2 teaspoons black rice vinegar or plain rice vinegar
- 2 teaspoons Asian sesame oil
- 1 tablespoon oyster-flavored sauce
- 1 tablespoon hoisin sauce
- 1½ teaspoons cornstarch
- 1 medium red bell pepper, cut into ½-inch dice
- 3 medium scallions, sliced thin

---

is the thickener of choice for Asian sauces, and 1½ teaspoons reliably gelled the sauce to a soft, glazey, shrimp-coating consistency.

Eager to see if I could streamline the recipe by omitting an ingredient (or maybe two?), I systematically retested all of the sauce components. Alas, my tasters and I agreed that each one brought a distinct flavor dimension to the party; without any one of them, the sauce suffered a bit, inching its way back toward the dreaded

restaurant kung pao I was determined to outdo.

Spicy chile heat may be kung pao's true calling card. My tasters and I unanimously chose whole dried chiles (see above), which are traditional for this dish. I altered the technique with which they are generally used, however, by stir-frying them with the shrimp and peanuts at the beginning of the cooking. This extra bit of pan time toasted the chiles, deepening their flavor noticeably.

1. Toss shrimp with sherry and soy sauce in medium bowl; marinate until shrimp have absorbed flavors, about 10 minutes. Mix garlic, ginger, and 1 tablespoon oil in small bowl; set aside. Combine peanuts and chiles in small bowl; set aside. Mix chicken broth, vinegar, sesame oil, oyster-flavored sauce, hoisin sauce, and cornstarch in small bowl or measuring cup; set aside.

2. Heat 1 tablespoon oil in 12-inch skillet over high heat until just beginning to smoke. Add shrimp and cook, stirring about once every 10 seconds, until barely opaque, 30 to 40 seconds; add peanuts and chiles, stir into shrimp, and continue cooking until shrimp are almost completely opaque and peanuts have darkened slightly, 30 to 40 seconds longer. Transfer shrimp, peanuts, and chiles to bowl; set aside. Return skillet to burner and reheat briefly, 15 to 30 seconds. Add remaining 1 tablespoon oil, swirl to coat pan, and add red bell pepper; cook, stirring occasionally, until slightly softened, about 45 seconds. Clear center of pan, add garlic-ginger mixture, mash into pan with spoon or spatula, and cook until fragrant, 10 to 15 seconds; stir into peppers until combined. Stir broth mixture to recombine, then add to skillet along with reserved shrimp, peanuts, and chiles; cook, stirring and scraping up browned bits on bottom of pan, until sauce has thickened to syrupy consistency, about 45 seconds. Stir in scallions; transfer to serving plate and serve immediately.

Size Matters

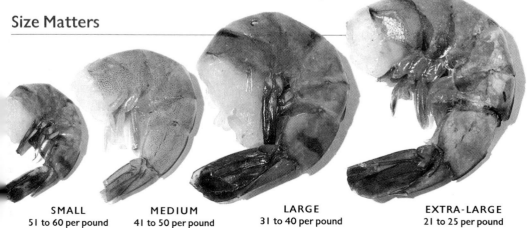

SMALL	MEDIUM	LARGE	EXTRA-LARGE
51 to 60 per pound	41 to 50 per pound	31 to 40 per pound	21 to 25 per pound

Shrimp are sold by size (small, medium, large, and so on) as well as by the number needed to make 1 pound, usually given in a range. Choosing shrimp by the numerical rating is more accurate than choosing by a size label, which varies from store to store. Here's how the two systems line up, with shrimp shown in actual sizes.

Tuscan-Style Roast Pork Loin

Perfumed with rosemary and garlic, this simple roast can turn out dry, tough, or bitter. We made more than 40 roasts to perfect this classic Italian recipe.

≥ BY ELIZABETH GERMAIN ≤

It's easy to fall in love with Tuscan-style roast pork, a famous dish with a history dating back to the 15th century. This roast pork loin is flavored with rosemary and garlic, served boneless, sliced thick, and often accompanied by pan juices. When properly made, the meat is succulent and the crust crisp. It works well as a showpiece roast or as an inexpensive family supper.

For such a simple roast, problems abound. The meat can be dry, tough, and unevenly cooked; the crust can be absent, resulting in a pale and unappealing roast; and the rosemary and garlic flavors can be either too bland or too harsh. For a seemingly straightforward recipe, research revealed that there is consensus on the cut of meat, the best way to flavor the pork, or the oven temperature at which to roast it.

When sliced, this huge roast reveals its secret ingredient—a potent paste made with rosemary and garlic.

Meat Matters

Among the recipes I looked at, the most common cut called for was a boneless, center-cut pork loin. I decided to test a wider range of choices. Imagine a pig and start from the shoulder, working your way back. First comes the blade roast, then the rib roast, next the loin roast, and, finally, the sirloin roast. I quickly eliminated the blade roast and the sirloin roast, both of which are composed of many separate muscles and fatty deposits. Tests showed that these cuts were difficult to cook evenly, flavor well, and carve.

That left the rib roast and the loin roast. Each of these roasts consists largely of the same single, uniformly shaped muscle, so I prepared them side-by-side. The rib roast provided not only the tastiest meat but also the ideal rack for cooking. Why was the meat better? The rib roast includes a protective cap of fat and muscle and is marbled more than the meat on the loin roast. The loin roast has less marbling, lacks the protective cap of fat and muscle, and does not have as many rib bones. As for the rack, the bones of the rib roast both protect the meat during roasting (boneless roasts had less flavor and were drier) and lift the meat up off the floor of the roasting pan, which allows for the circulation of air. This allows even

cooking and prevents mushy bottom meat. One last note. The backbone, called the chine bone, is sometimes attached to the rib bones, and it provides additional stability. After much testing, I concluded that the ultimate cut was a rib roast with the chine bone attached.

Purchasing a rib roast requires an understanding of the distinction between it and the loin roast because both of these roasts are often labeled "center-cut, bone-in, roast." (See photographs on

page 11.) Keep in mind that this is the same prized cut of meat that is sold as the rack of lamb or prime rib of beef.

Flavor Facts

With the cut of meat decided, I turned my attention to the traditional Tuscan flavors. Rosemary, garlic, and olive oil are strong characters, and I was determined to harness and marry their flavors so that the roast would be perfumed with their essence. Stuffing slivers of garlic with or without rosemary into slits on the outside of the roast failed to impress me. The flavors did not permeate deeply (even when the loin was refrigerated overnight before being cooked), and the garlic and rosemary were unpleasant. Garlic and rosemary rubbed on the outside tended to burn and become bitter. Rosemary sprigs tied to the outside looked appealing, but their flavor did not penetrate and the crust did not brown evenly. In an attempt to flavor the center of the meat, some recipes call for creating a hole in the middle of the loin and stuffing it, while other recipes suggest slitting open the loin and spreading a rosemary-garlic mixture on the inside.

I was convinced that using a paste and putting it in the center of the meat was the answer. I tried using a mini–food processor, but the garlic did not break down into small enough pieces. The bigger chunks were undercooked and sharp-tasting in the cooked pork. Making the paste by

---

TASTING: **Is Enhanced Pork Worth Trying?**

Our obsession with fat has prompted the pork industry to breed a leaner pig. Today's pork is 50 percent leaner than its counterpart in the 1950s, and less fat means less flavor and moisture. The industry has addressed this issue by introducing a product called enhanced pork, or meat injected with a solution of water, salt, and sodium phosphate. The idea is to both season the pork and prevent it from drying out. I wondered if I could skip brining and save time by using an enhanced pork roast.

In a side-by-side test, I compared roasts made with enhanced pork, unenhanced pork, and unenhanced pork that had been brined. The enhanced pork was salty and had a somewhat artificial flavor. The unenhanced pork that was not brined was dry and bland. The unenhanced pork that had been brined was juicy and well seasoned; it was the clear winner.

The benefits of brining pork are clear. First, you control the amount of salt and avoid any artificial aftertaste. Second, brining guarantees moist meat (as long as you don't overcook it). Finally, brining gives you a chance to add layers of flavor, like the rosemary and garlic in the Tuscan-style pork. During my research, I found a few supermarkets that carried only enhanced pork roasts. If you must buy an enhanced roast, skip the brining step in this recipe. —E.G.

hand with the help of a garlic press gave the best results. Equal parts rosemary and garlic were the most pleasing, and tests showed that the addition of olive oil helps heat and cook the paste, which in turn boosts flavor.

I was still having problems finding the best method for getting the paste into the meat for maximum flavor. I decided to try butterflying the roast, spreading the paste on the inside, and then tying it back together. This roast had flavor—too much flavor. Finally, I hit upon the solution. I cut the meat off the bones, slathered the bones with two-thirds of the paste, spread the rest on the cut in the meat, and then tied the meat back onto the bones. This technique worked like a charm. The rosemary and garlic flavors floated up into the meat, but most of the paste stayed on the bones when the roast was sliced and served. This technique produced one other major benefit. Simply cutting the twine after cooking made this bone-in roast as easy to slice and serve as the boneless roasts I had tried at the beginning. My search for flavor had served up convenience as well.

I still felt that the pork was a bit dry and lackluster in taste given the lean nature of commercial pork. (For more information on today's lean pork, see "Is Enhanced Pork Worth Trying?" on page 10.) I decided to try brining, soaking the roast in a saltwater solution, which gives it both moisture and seasoning that are retained during cooking. Sure enough, tests confirmed that this technique produced a roast that was better seasoned and more juicy. I added rosemary and garlic to the brine along with some brown sugar for depth and caramelization.

Temperature and Time

I was in the home stretch and ready to experiment with roasting methods. Older recipes called for cooking the loin until the internal temperature reached 160 degrees. Especially with today's lean pork, this much cooking produces a thumbs-down roast that is dry and gray. With concerns about the trichinosis parasite largely eliminated, the National Pork Board now recommends cooking pork until it is just slightly rosy in the center and registers 150 degrees on an instant-read thermometer. The *Cook's* test kitchen suggests a final temperature of 145 degrees. Because the internal heat will keep cooking the meat and cause the temperature to rise while the roast is resting, it should be removed from the oven at roughly 135 degrees.

Roasting at a constant temperature turned out not to be ideal. A low temperature (325 degrees or lower) produced the best meat, while high heat (temperatures of 400 degrees or higher) produced the best crust. I resisted dividing

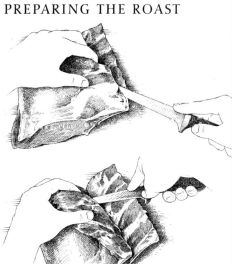

Position roast so bones are perpendicular to cutting board. Starting from far end and working toward you, make series of small, easy strokes with boning knife to gradually cut along curved rib bones down to backbone until meat is free of bones.

the cooking between the stovetop and the oven, trying every imaginable combination of high heat and low heat in the oven instead. But this approach also failed. The high heat dried out the meat and, even worse, occasionally sent billows of smoke pouring out of the oven from the pork fat.

Once I let go of my resolve to limit cooking to the oven, my problem was solved. Restaurant training had taught me that searing on the stovetop and then cooking in the oven is a failsafe method for producing an excellent crust and perfectly cooked meat. A constant 325-degree oven subsequent to stovetop searing gave the best results.

Finally, I had developed a recipe for a Tuscan-style roast pork that lived up to its reputation. The somewhat unusual method of boning the

Right Roast, Wrong Roast

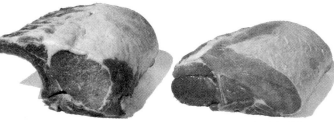

PORK RIB ROAST   PORK LOIN ROAST

Although both the rib roast (left) and the loin roast (right) may be labeled "center cut," they are not the same. The rib roast is the better choice. If you want to serve the ribs from the roast, make sure to ask the butcher to crack the chine bone between each rib. This makes it possible to slice through the ribs and serve them individually.

roast before cooking, brining the meat, spreading a paste on the bones, and then tying the meat back to the bone for roasting is the secret to this juicy, crisp-skinned roast. Maybe this recipe will last another 600 years.

TUSCAN-STYLE GARLIC-ROSEMARY ROAST PORK LOIN WITH JUS
SERVES 6 TO 8

The roasting time is determined in part by the shape of the roast; a long, thin roast will cook faster than a roast with a large circumference. Though not traditionally served, the ribs are rich with flavor. If you'd like to serve them or enjoy them for yourself, increase the oven temperature to 375 degrees, untie the roast and remove the loin as directed, then scrape off the excess garlic-rosemary paste from the ribs, set them on a rimmed baking sheet, and return them to the oven for about 20 minutes, until they are brown and crisp. Slice in between bones and serve.

Roast
- 2 cups kosher salt or 1 cup table salt
- 2⅓ cups (16 ounces) packed dark brown sugar
- 10 large garlic cloves, lightly crushed and peeled
- 5 sprigs fresh rosemary (each about 6 inches long)
- 1 bone-in, center-cut, 4-pound pork rib roast, prepared according to illustrations at left

Garlic-Rosemary Paste
- 8–10 garlic cloves, pressed through garlic press or minced to paste (1½ tablespoons)
- 1½ tablespoons finely chopped fresh rosemary leaves
- 1 teaspoon ground black pepper
- 1 tablespoon extra-virgin olive oil
- ⅛ teaspoon kosher salt or pinch table salt

- 1 cup dry white wine
- 1 teaspoon ground black pepper
- 1 medium-large shallot, minced (about 3 tablespoons)
- 1½ teaspoons minced fresh rosemary leaves
- 1¾ cups canned low-sodium chicken broth
- 2 tablespoons unsalted butter, cut into 4 pieces and softened

1. TO BRINE THE ROAST: Dissolve salt and brown sugar in 1½ quarts hot tap water in large stockpot or clean bucket. Stir in garlic and rosemary; add 2½ quarts cold water and submerge meat and bones in brine. Refrigerate until fully seasoned, about 3 hours. Rinse meat and ribs under cold water and dry thoroughly with paper towels.

2. FOR THE GARLIC-ROSEMARY RUB: While roast brines, mix together garlic, rosemary, pepper, olive oil, and salt in small bowl to form paste; set aside.

3. TO PREPARE THE ROAST: When roast is done brining, adjust oven rack to middle position

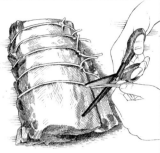

1. With fat side of roast down, slice through center of entire length of meat, stopping 1 inch shy of edge. Spread meat flat.

2. Rub one-third of rosemary mixture in even layer on one side of cut, leaving ½ inch on each end bare.

3. Spread remaining rosemary mixture evenly along bones from where meat was cut, leaving ½ inch on each end bare.

4. Fold meat back together and tie meat on bones exactly from where it was cut with 7 individual lengths of twine.

What about Dried Rosemary?

While our testing proved to us that dried rosemary is not an acceptable substitute for fresh rosemary in flavoring the roast pork loin (it tasted woody and bitter), we wondered if it might fare better in other applications, like soups or stews, in which it has a chance to fully hydrate and soften. Following an equivalency recommended by McCormick and Company, we pitted 2 teaspoons of fresh chopped rosemary against 1 teaspoon of whole dried rosemary, each simmered in chicken stock. Both versions were evaluated by tasters after 15 minutes and after one hour of cooking. After 15 minutes, tasters thought the fresh rosemary lent the stock a light, herbaceous note and piney aroma, while the dried rosemary had contributed little at all. After an hour, the tables had turned. The stock infused with fresh rosemary was unpalatably bitter, while the dried rosemary stock was pleasantly herby, albeit without much of a scent.

Our conclusion? Dried rosemary can be effectively used to flavor longer-cooked soups, stews, and braises, but with a caveat: It lacks the fresh herb's characteristic pungency and sweetness. For a fuller rosemary flavor and aroma, add minced, fresh rosemary within the last 15 minutes of cooking. Or, once the soup, stew, or braise is complete, add a whole sprig to the pot (off the stove), cover, and let it steep for 15 to 20 minutes. Then remove and discard the rosemary sprig. —Matthew Card

Fifteen Degrees of Separation

JUICY ROAST

DRIED OUT ROAST

At a final internal temperature (after resting) of 145 degrees, the meat is just slightly rosy at the center and moist (left photo). Let the roast reach an internal temperature of 160 degrees (as recommended in many older recipes) and the meat will be gray and dry (right).

and heat oven to 325 degrees. Heat heavy-bottomed 12-inch nonreactive skillet over medium heat until hot, about 4 minutes. Place roast fat-side down in skillet and cook until well-browned, about 8 minutes. Transfer roast browned-side up to cutting board and set aside to cool. Pour off fat from skillet and add wine; increase heat to high and bring to boil, scraping skillet with wooden spoon until browned bits are loosened, about 1 minute. Set skillet with wine aside.

4. Following illustrations above, make lengthwise incision in pork loin, rub with one-third of garlic-rosemary paste, rub remaining paste on cut side of ribs, and tie meat back to ribs. Sprinkle browned side of roast with 1 teaspoon pepper and set roast rib-side down in flameproof roasting pan. Pour reserved wine and browned bits from skillet in roasting pan. Roast, basting loin with pan drippings every 20 minutes, until center of loin registers about 135 degrees on instant-read thermometer, 65 to 80 minutes. (If wine evaporates, add about ½ cup water to roasting pan to prevent scorching.) Transfer roast to carving board and tent loosely with foil; let stand until center of loin registers about 145 degrees on instant-read thermometer, about 15 minutes.

5. While roast rests, spoon off most of fat from roasting pan and place over 2 burners at high heat. Add shallot and rosemary; using wooden spoon, scrape up browned bits and boil liquid until reduced by half and shallot has softened, about 2 minutes. Add chicken broth and continue to cook, stirring occasionally, until reduced by half, about 8 minutes. Add any accumulated pork juices and cook 1 minute longer. Off heat, whisk in butter; strain jus into gravy boat.

6. Cut twine on roast and remove meat from bones. Set meat browned-side up on board and cut into ¼-inch-thick slices. Serve immediately, passing jus separately.

TUSCAN-STYLE GARLIC-ROSEMARY ROAST PORK LOIN WITH ROASTED POTATOES

Instead of making a jus from the roasting pan drippings, use them to flavor roasted potatoes.

Follow recipe for Tuscan-Style Garlic-Rosemary Roast Pork Loin with Jus, reducing wine to ¾ cup and omitting shallot, rosemary, chicken broth, and butter. When pork has roasted 15 minutes, quarter 2 pounds 2½-inch red potatoes (about 14 potatoes total); toss with 2 tablespoons olive oil in medium bowl and season generously with salt and pepper. After pork has roasted 30 minutes, add potatoes to roasting pan; stir to coat potatoes with pan juices. After transferring roast to carving board, turn potato pieces with wide metal spatula and spread them in even layer. Increase oven temperature to 400 degrees and return potatoes to oven; continue to roast until tender and browned, 5 to 15 minutes longer. Serve potatoes with roast.

TUSCAN-STYLE GARLIC-ROSEMARY ROAST PORK LOIN WITH FENNEL

Fennel is a common addition to the classic garlic-rosemary flavored pork roast.

1. Trim 2 medium fennel bulbs of stalks and fronds; finely chop 2 teaspoons fronds. Cut each bulb lengthwise into eighths. Toss fennel with 1 tablespoon olive oil in medium bowl and season generously with salt and pepper.

2. Follow recipe for Tuscan-Style Garlic-Rosemary Roast Pork Loin with Jus, adding 1 teaspoon finely chopped fennel seeds and chopped fennel fronds to garlic-rosemary paste. Reduce wine to ¾ cup and omit shallot, rosemary, chicken broth, and butter. Add fennel to roasting pan along with wine. After transferring roast to carving board, return fennel to oven; continue to roast until tender, 5 to 15 minutes. Serve fennel with roast.

Creamy Dips for Crudités

Supermarket and homemade soup-mix dips have relegated the crudités platter to a bad memory. But the proper base and a few bold ingredients can bring it back.

⋑ BY SHANNON BLAISDELL ⋐

When I was young, mediocre vegetables and insipid soup-mix dips didn't phase me at all. Age and experience, however, have revealed the horror of pre-cut, dried-out vegetables surrounding a tub of gummy, musty, store-bought dip. For the crudités in this issue (see pages 16–17), I was determined to create dips with well-balanced, creamy bases and a few fresh and assertive ingredients that, with minimal effort, would draw a crowd.

My search began with the consistency of the dip. The word *creamy* can mean many things, so I polled my tasters. None of them was fond of the thick consistency of supermarket tub dips. As one of them put it: "If a carrot can stand straight up without moving, you know the dip is loaded with unsavory ingredients." My tasters wanted dips that were substantial enough to coat their vegetables without engulfing them.

I tested every potential combination of creamy ingredients imaginable, from the standard mayonnaise, sour cream, and yogurt to the not-so-obvious buttermilk, heavy cream, cottage cheese, and cream cheese. In the end, two combinations made it across the finish line: mayonnaise/sour cream and mayonnaise/yogurt. Mayonnaise contributes the body, richness, and perfectly velvety texture sought after in a creamy dip, while both sour cream and yogurt heighten flavor, the sour cream refreshingly cool and tangy, the yogurt bright and sharp. Yogurt has one problem, however. Right out of the container it is too slack and requires draining to thicken it. After testing timing and technique, I found that an overnight stay in the refrigerator in a fine-mesh sieve firmed up the yogurt perfectly.

Now it was time to turn my attention to dip flavors. I gathered up a battalion of flavor-charged ingredients—strong cheeses, fiery horseradish, spicy chili peppers, tangy citrus, and pungent herbs, to name a few—and got to work. I quickly discovered that boldness was required, as the flavorings were up against the deadening effects of rich dairy products. I also wanted simplicity, not a laundry list of ingredients. After going through a combined total of 4 gallons of mayonnaise, sour cream, and yogurt and 5 pounds of carrots and celery, I created five vibrant, singular dips with just the right combinations of texture and flavor. The crudités platter (and permission to double-dip) is finally back.

"CAESAR" DIP WITH PARMESAN AND ANCHOVIES
MAKES 1 1/2 CUPS

1	cup mayonnaise
1/2	cup sour cream
1/2	ounce grated Parmesan (1/2 cup)
1	tablespoon juice from 1 lemon
1	tablespoon minced fresh parsley leaves
2	medium garlic cloves, pressed through garlic press or minced (about 2 teaspoons)
2	anchovy fillets, minced to paste (about 1 teaspoon)
1/8	teaspoon ground black pepper

Combine all ingredients in medium bowl until smooth and creamy. Transfer dip to serving bowl, cover with plastic wrap, and refrigerate until flavors are blended, at least 1 hour; serve cold with crudités. (Can be refrigerated in airtight container for up to 2 days.)

CHIPOTLE-LIME DIP WITH SCALLIONS
MAKES 1 1/2 CUPS

1	cup mayonnaise
1/2	cup sour cream
3	scallions, sliced thin
2	medium garlic cloves, pressed through garlic press or minced (about 2 teaspoons)
3	small chipotle chiles in adobo, minced to paste (about 1 tablespoon), plus 1/2 teaspoon adobo sauce
1	teaspoon grated zest plus 1 tablespoon juice from 1 lime

Combine all ingredients in medium bowl until smooth and creamy. Transfer dip to serving bowl, cover with plastic wrap, and refrigerate until flavors are blended, at least 1 hour; serve cold with crudités. (Can be refrigerated in airtight container for up to 2 days.)

CREAMY HORSERADISH DIP
MAKES 1 1/2 CUPS

3/4	cup mayonnaise
3/4	cup sour cream
2	scallions, sliced thin
1/4	cup prepared horseradish, squeezed of excess liquid
1	tablespoon minced fresh parsley leaves
1/8	teaspoon ground black pepper

Combine all ingredients in medium bowl until smooth and creamy. Transfer dip to serving bowl, cover with plastic wrap, and refrigerate until flavors are blended, at least 1 hour; serve cold with crudités. (Can be refrigerated in airtight container for up to 2 days.)

GREEN GODDESS DIP
MAKES 1 1/2 CUPS

3/4	cup mayonnaise
3/4	cup sour cream
2	medium garlic cloves, pressed through garlic press or minced (about 2 teaspoons)
1/4	cup minced fresh parsley leaves
1/4	cup minced fresh chives
2	tablespoons minced fresh tarragon leaves
1	tablespoon juice from 1 lemon
1/8	teaspoon salt
1/8	teaspoon ground black pepper

Combine all ingredients in medium bowl until smooth and creamy. Transfer dip to serving bowl, cover with plastic wrap, and refrigerate until flavors are blended, at least 1 hour; serve cold with crudités. (Can be refrigerated in airtight container for up to 2 days.)

FETA-MINT DIP WITH YOGURT
MAKES ABOUT 1 1/4 CUPS

1	cup plain whole milk yogurt
1/2	cup mayonnaise
2 1/2	ounces feta cheese, crumbled (1/2 cup)
1/4	cup chopped fresh mint leaves
2	medium scallions, roughly chopped
2	teaspoons juice from 1 lemon

1. Place yogurt in fine-mesh strainer or cheese-cloth-lined colander set over bowl. Cover with plastic wrap and refrigerate 8 to 24 hours; discard liquid in bowl.

2. Process all ingredients in food processor until smooth and creamy, about 30 seconds. Transfer dip to serving bowl, cover with plastic wrap, and refrigerate until flavors are blended, at least 1 hour; serve cold with crudités. (Can be refrigerated in airtight container for up to 2 days.)

Faster Lasagna

Traditional lasagna takes the better part of a day to make. Could we get really good lasagna on the table in just 90 minutes?

⇒ BY SHANNON BLAISDELL ⇐

If your family is like mine, you have homemade lasagna once, maybe twice a year, on holidays (especially if you are Italian) or birthdays. Lasagna is not enjoyed more frequently because it takes the better part of a day to boil the noodles, slow-cook the sauce, prepare and layer the ingredients, and then finally bake it off. Although this traditional method does produce a superior dish, I was interested in an "Americanized" version, one that could be made in two hours or less from start to finish. I would have to sacrifice some of the rich flavors of my grandmother's recipe, but I was hoping to produce a lasagna good enough for a family gathering. A bland, watery casserole just wouldn't do.

I knew from the start that to expedite the lasagna-making process I would have to use no-boil lasagna noodles (see "No Boil, No Problem," page 15). For those unfamiliar or wary of them, relax. After a few initial tests, I discovered that the secret to success with no-boil noodles is to leave your tomato sauce a little on the watery side. The noodles can then absorb liquid without drying out the dish overall. With all this in mind, I got to work on the other components of the lasagna.

Getting Saucy

My grandmother builds her sauce from the meaty fond (brown bits) left in the pan from the meatballs and Italian sausages she cooks and later layers into the lasagna. By combining top-quality tomato products with a four-hour simmer, she makes a rich, thick, and complex-tasting sauce. I was after the same depth of flavor, but as time was of the essence, meatballs and a slow simmer were out of the question. I began by concentrating on different kinds of ground meat. Working with a base of sautéed aromatics—onions and garlic—I made an all-beef sauce that turned out one-dimensional and dull. Adding ground pork certainly made things more interesting, and the combination of beef and sweet Italian sausage (removed from its casing and browned with the beef) was even better, but my tasters were still left wanting. Finally, I turned to "meatloaf mix," a mix of equal parts ground beef, pork, and veal sold in one package at most supermarkets. Not only was it faster to buy a pound of pre-mixed

No-boil noodles and a quick meat sauce that cooks in just 15 minutes are the secrets to our streamlined lasagna recipe.

meats, but the flavor of the sauce it produced was robust and sweet. However, it was still too loose and taco-like. I wanted something richer, creamier, and more cohesive, so my thoughts turned to Bolognese, the classic three-hour meat sauce enriched with dairy. Borrowing the notion of combining meat and dairy, I reduced a quarter cup of cream with the meat before adding the tomatoes. The ground meat soaked up the sweet cream, and the final product was rich and decadent. Even better, at this point I had been at the stove for only 12 minutes.

Because no-boil noodles rely primarily on the liquid in the sauce to rehydrate and soften, I had to get the moisture content just right. If the sauce was too thick, the noodles would be dry and crunchy; too loose and they would turn flaccid, limp, and lifeless. I started building the sauce with two 28-ounce cans of pureed tomatoes, but tasters thought the sauce was too heavy for the lasagna, overwhelming the other flavors. Two 28-ounce cans of diced tomatoes yielded too thin a sauce. I settled on one can of pureed and one can of diced (drained). The combination yielded a luxurious,

saucy sauce, with soft but substantial chunks of tomatoes. I added the tomatoes to the meat mixture, warmed it through (no reduction necessary), and in just 15 minutes on the stove the meat sauce was rich, creamy, ultra-meaty, and ready to go.

More Cheese, Please

Most Americans like their lasagna cheesy. It was a given that I would sprinkle each layer with mozzarella—the classic lasagna addition—and, after a test of whole versus part-skim, I found that whole milk mozzarella is the best cheese for the job. It had a more intense flavor than its part-skim counterpart and nicer melting qualities, crucial for the dish. I also tested pre-shredded, bagged mozzarella, but because it has a very low moisture content, it melted oddly and was somewhat dry. Shredding a 1-pound block of whole milk mozzarella on a box grater or in the food processor (even faster) is the ticket.

Ricotta was the next cheese up for scrutiny. As it turned out, it made little difference whether I used whole milk or part-skim ricotta. They were characteristically creamy and rich, and tasters gave them both a thumbs-up. Grated Parmesan added a nice little kick to the mild, milky ricotta. An egg helped to thicken and bind this mixture, and some chopped basil added flavor and freshness. Tucked neatly between the layers of lasagna, this ricotta mixture was just what I was after.

Come Together

In my tests, I found that covering the lasagna with foil from the outset of baking prevented any loss of moisture and helped soften the noodles properly. Removing the foil for the last 25 minutes of baking ensured that the top layer of cheese turned golden brown. An oven temperature of 375 degrees proved ideal. By the time the top was browned, the noodles had softened.

I found that lasagna made with no-boil noodles takes a little longer in the oven than conventional lasagna. The real time savings is in the preparation. Start to finish, my meat and tomato lasagna took me about an hour and a half to make: 40 minutes prep time, 40 minutes in the oven, and 10 minutes to rest. Measuring the final product against my grandmother's authentic Italian lasagna may not be entirely fair, but having the time to make it on a weeknight, or whenever the craving strikes, is satisfying beyond compare.

1. Smear entire bottom of 9 by 13-inch baking dish with ¼ cup meat sauce. Place 3 noodles on top of sauce.

2. Drop 3 tablespoons ricotta mixture down center of each noodle. Level by pressing flat with back of measuring spoon.

3. Sprinkle evenly with 1 cup shredded mozzarella.

4. Spoon 1½ cups meat sauce evenly over cheese.

SIMPLE LASAGNA WITH HEARTY TOMATO-MEAT SAUCE
SERVES 6 TO 8

If you can't find meatloaf mixture for the sauce, or if you choose not to eat veal, substitute ½ pound ground beef and ½ pound sweet Italian sausage, casings removed, for the meatloaf mixture. The assembled, unbaked lasagna, if wrapped tightly in plastic wrap and then in foil, will keep in the freezer for up to 2 months. To bake, defrost it in the refrigerator for a day or two and bake as directed, extending the baking time by about 5 minutes.

Tomato-Meat Sauce
- 1 tablespoon olive oil
- 1 medium onion, chopped fine (about 1 cup)
- 6 medium garlic cloves, pressed through garlic press or minced (about 2 tablespoons)
- 1 pound meatloaf mix or ⅓ pound each ground beef chuck, ground veal, and ground pork (see note)
- ½ teaspoon salt
- ½ teaspoon ground black pepper
- ¼ cup heavy cream
- 1 can (28 ounces) pureed tomatoes
- 1 can (28 ounces) diced tomatoes, drained

Ricotta, Mozzarella, and Pasta Layers
- 15 ounces whole milk or part-skim ricotta cheese (1¾ cups)
- 2½ ounces grated Parmesan cheese (1¼ cups)
- ½ cup chopped fresh basil leaves
- 1 large egg, lightly beaten
- ½ teaspoon salt
- ½ teaspoon ground black pepper
- 12 no-boil lasagna noodles from one 8- or 9-ounce package (for brand preferences, see right)
- 16 ounces whole milk mozzarella cheese, shredded (4 cups)

1. Adjust oven rack to middle position and heat oven to 375 degrees.

2. Heat oil in large, heavy-bottomed Dutch oven over medium heat until shimmering but not smoking, about 2 minutes; add onion and cook, stirring occasionally, until softened but not browned, about 2 minutes. Add garlic and cook until fragrant, about 2 minutes. Increase heat to medium-high and add ground meats, salt, and pepper; cook, breaking meat into small pieces with wooden spoon, until meat loses its raw color but has not browned, about 4 minutes. Add cream and simmer, stirring occasionally, until liquid evaporates and only fat remains, about 4 minutes. Add pureed and drained diced tomatoes and bring to simmer; reduce heat to low and simmer slowly until flavors are blended, about 3 minutes; set sauce aside. (Sauce can be cooled, covered, and refrigerated for up to 2 days; reheat before assembling lasagna.)

3. Mix ricotta, 1 cup Parmesan, basil, egg, salt, and pepper in medium bowl with fork until well-combined and creamy; set aside.

4. Assemble first lasagna layer according to illustrations above. Repeat layering of noodles, ricotta, mozzarella, and sauce two more times. Place 3 remaining noodles on top of sauce, spread remaining sauce over noodles, sprinkle with remaining cup mozzarella, then with remaining ¼ cup Parmesan. Lightly spray a large sheet of foil with nonstick cooking spray and cover lasagna. Bake 15 minutes, then remove foil. Return lasagna to oven and continue to bake until cheese is spotty brown and sauce is bubbling, about 25 minutes longer. Cool lasagna about 10 minutes; cut into pieces and serve.

TASTING: No-Boil, No Problem

Over the past few years, no-boil (also called oven-ready) lasagna noodles have become a permanent fixture on supermarket shelves. Much like "instant rice," no-boil noodles are precooked at the factory. The extruded noodles are run through a water bath and then dehydrated mechanically. During baking, the moisture from the sauce softens, or rehydrates, the noodles, especially when the pan is covered as the lasagna bakes. Most no-boil noodles are rippled, and the accordion-like pleats relax as the pasta rehydrates in the oven, allowing the noodles to elongate.

No-boil lasagna noodles come in two shapes. The most common is a rectangle measuring 7 inches long and 3½ inches wide. Three such noodles make a single layer in a conventional 9 by 13-inch lasagna pan when they swell in the oven. Here in New England I found three brands of this type of no-boil lasagna noodle: Ronzoni (made by New World Pasta, which sells the same product under the American Beauty, Light 'n Fluffy, P&R, San Giorgio, Skinner, and Mrs. Weiss labels in other parts of the country), DeFino (made in the United States), and Barilla (imported from Italy). Italian noodles made by Delverde came in 7-inch squares. We made lasagnas with all four brands to see how they would compare.

Ronzoni and DeFino noodles are both thin and rippled, and although tasters preferred the Ronzoni for their flavor and the DeFino for their sturdiness, both brands worked well. Barilla noodles tasted great, but their texture was subpar. Two squares of Delverde noodles butted very closely together fit into a 9 by 13-inch pan, but when baked the noodles expanded and the edges jumped out of the pan and became unpleasantly dry and tough.

In the end, we rejected the Italian noodles in favor of the two American brands tested. At least when it comes to convenience, American pasta companies are the leaders. —S.B.

RONZONI
"Lightly eggy" flavor, and "perfectly al dente" texture. Ronzoni was the tasters' favorite.

PASTA DEFINO
These "fairly thick" noodles were praised for their "firm" texture and "mild" flavor.

BARILLA
"Like fresh pasta" but "a little too thin" and "slightly limp."

DELVERDE
"Unevenly cooked" with "hard, dry edges," but they did have a "good, clean" flavor.

Crudités Done Right

How to prepare vegetables that taste as good as they look.
BY JULIA COLLIN

We're all familiar with those black plastic trays from the supermarket displaying raw broccoli, cauliflower, celery, and carrots around a tub of commercial dip. But these boring vegetable trays are a poor representation of what crudités can be. With an extensive selection of vegetables now available year-round, crudités should be tempting, if not downright irresistible, with a colorful variety of flavors and textures. But the key to good crudités doesn't lie only in the selection and arrangement of good-looking vegetables. Vegetables that will actually taste good must be properly prepared. We found that 2 pounds of prepped vegetables are ample for a group of eight to 10 people, requiring about 1½ cups of dip (see page 13 for dip recipes).

(see page 13 for dip recipes)

BLANCHING PROTOCOL
The vegetables listed below are best prepared with a quick blanch before joining the rest on the platter. Blanch the vegetables in the order given below, which starts with the mildest and ends with the strongest.

CARROTS	15 seconds
SNOW/SNAP PEAS	15 seconds
CAULIFLOWER	1–1½ minutes
GREEN BEANS	1 minute
FENNEL	1 minute
BROCCOLI	1–1½ minutes
ASPARAGUS	30–60 seconds

BLANCH AND SHOCK

Not all vegetables are meant to be eaten raw (unless you're a rabbit), and many require a quick dunk in boiling, salted water—or blanching—before being added to the platter. This crucial step is often overlooked for the sake of convenience, but we found that it makes all the difference between great crudités and mediocre ones. Not only does blanching bring tough vegetables to a gentle crunch, but the salty water seasons the vegetables as they cook, enhancing their natural flavors. Below are three keys to successfully blanched vegetables.

First, to prevent carrots from tasting like asparagus or cauliflower from turning green, blanch each vegetable separately. Being mindful of the order in which you blanch the vegetables, begin with the bland and pale and finish with the bold and dark (see chart at right).

Second, use a large pot that allows the vegetables ample room to cook.

Third, once vegetables are crisp-tender, transfer them from the boiling water to an ice water bath immediately. This process (called shocking) will prevent residual heat within the vegetables from cooking them further and compromising their final color, texture, and flavor.

1. Bring 6 quarts of water to a boil in a large pot over high heat and season with 5 teaspoons salt. Cook the vegetables, one variety at a time, until slightly softened but still crunchy (crisp-tender), following the times recommended in the chart above.

2. Transfer the blanched vegetables to a bowl of ice water, and allow to soak until completely cool, about 1 minute. Place atop several layers of paper towels and pat dry.

PREPARATION TIPS FOR BLANCHED VEGETABLES

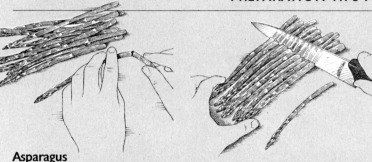

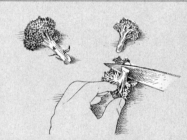

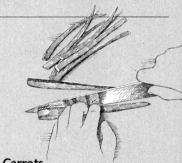

Asparagus
1. To efficiently trim a bunch of asparagus, gently bend one stalk from the bunch until the tough portion of the stem breaks off. **2.** Place this broken asparagus alongside the others, still untrimmed, and, using it as a guide, cut the tough ends off the remaining asparagus.

Broccoli and Cauliflower
To cut attractive, bite-sized florets, slice down through the main stem and out through the buds, producing 1-inch florets with 2-inch long stems.

Carrots
For long, elegant lengths of carrot, slice peeled carrots in half lengthwise. Then, with the cut-side flat to the board, slice each half into three long pieces.

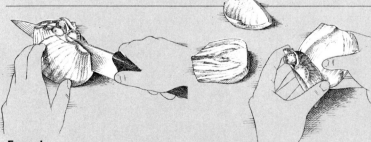

Fennel
1. After trimming the base and removing the upper stalks and fronds, slice the oval-shaped bulb in half lengthwise. **2.** Remove the layers of fennel from each half, then cut them into ½-inch-thick strips.

Green Beans
Instead of trimming the stems off one at a time, line up the beans and trim all the ends off with just one slice.

Snow and Snap Peas
Delicate peas taste best when rid of the fibrous string that runs along the straight edge of the pod. Using a paring knife, carefully remove this string.

PREPARATION TIPS FOR RAW VEGETABLES

Bell Peppers

1. To turn this unusually shaped vegetable into uniform pieces, first slice a ½-inch section off both the bottom and stem ends of the pepper. Make one slit in the trimmed shell, place the skin-side down, and lay the flesh flat onto the cutting board.

2. After removing the seeds and core, use a sharp knife to remove a ⅛-inch-thick piece of the tasteless membrane from the inside of the pepper. Then cut into ½-inch-wide lengths.

Celery

Celery often tastes harsh and vegetal. But its flavors can quickly turn sweet and mellow after its bitter skin and stringy fibers are removed with a vegetable peeler.

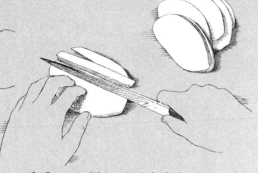

Endive

Gently pull the leaves off one at a time, continuing to trim the root end as you work your way toward the center.

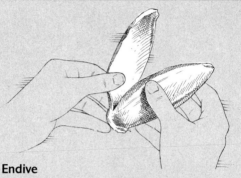

Jícama

1. After peeling the jícama, slice it into ½-inch-thick disks.

2. Cut each disk into ½-inch-thick strips.

Radishes

Choose radishes with their green tops still attached so that each half has a leafy "handle" for grasping and dipping. Slice each radish in half through the stem.

Zucchini, Summer Squash, and Daikon Radish

1. Though somewhat unusual for crudités, these vegetables can easily be added to the platter once cut into ⅛-inch-thick slices using a mandoline.

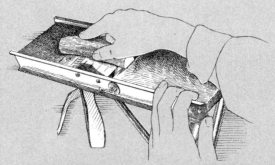

2. To make these thin slices easy to dip and eat, roll them into tidy cylinders and secure with toothpicks.

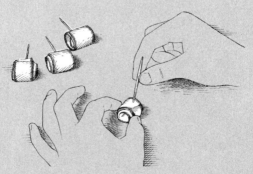

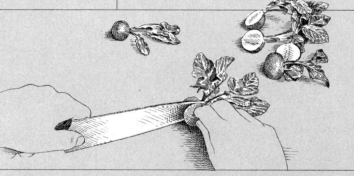

Seeing Green

Blanching not only makes certain vegetables taste better, it also makes them look better. Wondering why beans that are a peaked shade of green perk up to a vivid emerald after blanching, we consulted food scientist Robert Wolke, who offered a generally acknowledged explanation. As the vegetables cook, some of the air between their cells expands and bubbles off, bringing the cell walls closer together. As the cell walls become closer, the amount of chlorophyll per square inch is concentrated, producing a brighter green color. Yet this brilliance can be short-lived. If the vegetables continue to cook, the chlorophyll will convert to pheophytin, turning beans, for example, from a pretty emerald to an unattractive olive drab. By shocking the vegetables in ice water after blanching, the heat within the beans is immediately quelled, preventing this unfortunate transformation of the chlorophyll. Although many cooks believe that it is the salt that "sets" the green color, we found no difference in color between vegetables cooked in salted and unsalted water. —J.C.

Illustration: John Burgoyne

Simplifying Applesauce

Choose the right apple, don't peel it, and add nothing more than sugar and water. It's that simple.

⇒ BY ADAM RIED AND JULIA COLLIN ⇐

For the best flavor and texture, cook apples with the skin on and then puree them in a food mill.

The joys of homemade applesauce are subtle but persuasive. Compared with its jarred counterpart, which tends to be sweet, bland, and runny, homemade is noticeably fresh, with a deep apple flavor and a thick, supple texture. And it's simple to make. In fact, if you have a food mill nearby, you don't even need to peel the apples. Still, applesauce doesn't always come out perfectly. Often the tart, sweet, fruity, floral nuances of fresh apple flavor are lost to a heavy hand with sweeteners and spices, so the sauce ends up tasting like a bad pie filling. The texture, too, can vary from dry and chunky to loose and thin.

To us, preserving the taste of fresh apples was paramount. We wanted a pure, deep apple flavor that was neutral enough to swing both ways, either savory or sweet. For texture, we wanted a sauce that was soft, smooth, and thick, almost like a pudding.

The Big Apple

We kicked off this project with a massive tasting of 18 different apple varieties, each made into a simple applesauce. Following considerable post-tasting deliberation and discussion, we broke down the group into three categories: highly recommended, recommended, and not recommended for making sauce (see the chart at right.)

The flavor of the apples, more than their texture or color, influenced our judgment. Each of the apples that we recommend highly for sauce has distinctive individual flavor characteristics, yet each earned praise for its balance of sweet and tart, which many tasters interpreted as depth of flavor. The standouts in this group were the Jonagold, which garnered comments such as "delicate, spicy, fruity, and peachy" and the Pink Lady, which was described as "spicy, perfumed, and balanced." Jonagold's victory is good news for applesauce aficionados. According to a representative of the U.S. Apple Association, this variety is widely grown and readily available throughout the country during apple season. Pink Lady is included on the Apple Association's list of "up-and-coming" new varieties.

Apples that were not as well loved but still made acceptable sauce fell into the "recommended" category. The common thread among these varieties, including Golden Delicious, Rome, McIntosh, and Empire, was a milder flavor, with less dimension and depth than our absolute favorites. In short, these are fine choices in the absence of more interesting varieties. The apples in our "not recommended" category produced sauces that tasted either sour or flat.

We then decided to test combinations of apples. We were shocked when tasters flatlined in response to the first few blends. For instance, a McIntosh–Golden Delicious combination was judged to have a "muddy, indistinct" flavor. One taster thought that a mix of Cortland and Macoun tasted like jarred baby food. Based on the first few tests, tasters concluded that single-variety sauces had purer, stronger character. So rather than continue down this twisty path of combinations, we decided to leave well enough alone.

Getting the Best Flavor and Texture

In the recipes we tested, debate raged as to whether the apples should be cooked with or without their peels, and test results tipped the scales in favor of including peels. Most tasters thought this sauce tasted more complex than the skinless sauce, which was judged simple and straightforward. Cooking the apples with their peels has both advantages—it saves time and

effort—and disadvantages—a food mill is required for pureeing to separate the spent skins from the sauce. We opted in favor of the food mill because it is an easy, effective way to puree, and it produced a sauce with the smooth, thick, almost silky texture we considered ideal. We also tried running the apples through a food processor and blender, but these sauces were too runny, and the bits of skin left behind, though tiny, were unpleasant.

The Apple Varieties We Tested

We tested 18 apple varieties for our applesauce recipe. Apples are listed in order of preference.

HIGHLY RECOMMENDED

JONAGOLD
Fruity, spicy, honey-like, sweet/tart, balanced

JONATHAN
Complex, tangy, interesting, well rounded

PINK LADY
Spicy, assertive, sweet/tart, perfumed, balanced

MACOUN
Sweet/tart, deep, solid, round

RECOMMENDED

GOLDEN DELICIOUS: Sweet, solid, mainstream
EMPIRE: Mild, buttery, strawberry-like tones
MCINTOSH: Refreshing, tart, watery, balanced
ROME: Beautiful color, mild, generic

NOT RECOMMENDED

GRANNY SMITH: Mealy, mushy, tart
BRAEBURN: Odd, plasticky
CORTLAND: Mild, uninteresting, plasticky
BALDWIN: Chalky, bland, little flavor
IDARED: Dense, tart, vegetal
NORTHERN SPY: Sour, sour, sour, flat
STAYMAN/WINESAP: Gluey, sour, tart
SPARTAN: Gummy, mealy, dull
HONEYCRISP: Shallow, sour, citrusy
MUTSU/CRISPIN: Floury, potatoey, sour

A food mill is no longer a fixture in the American kitchen, but it is a terrific tool to have on hand. Think of it as part food processor (because it refines soft foods to a puree) and part sieve (because it separates waste such as peels, seeds, cores, and fiber from the puree as you go). And it accomplishes all of this with the simple turn of a crank, which rotates a gently angled, curved blade that catches the food and forces it down through the holes of a perforated disk at the bottom of the mill. The separation of unwanted material from the puree is the food mill's raison d'être, but another benefit is that it does not aerate the food as it purees, as do food processors and blenders, so you are able to avoid an overly whipped, lightened texture. A dense, more cohesive texture is often more desirable, especially, say, in an apple or tomato sauce.

Seeing that you can spend as little as $15 and as much as $90 on a food mill (some really large mills cost as much as $200), we wondered if some were better than others. We gathered five different models (Foley, Cuisipro, VEV Vigano, Norpro, and Moulinex) and tested them by making applesauce in each. Honestly, there was very little difference in the quality of the purees. They were all fine, smooth, and free of unwanted material. Consequently, for our evaluation of the mills we relied on other factors, such as how easy it is to turn a mill's crank, how efficiently a mill processes the apples, and whether a mill can be adjusted adequately to fit over bowls of various sizes.

The best mills in the group were the beautiful stainless steel Cuisipro, the VEV Vigano, and the white plastic Moulinex. Each one was efficient and easy to crank. Both the Foley and the Norpro were noticeably less efficient; their blades pushed the apples around in the mill instead of forcing them through the perforated disk. In addition, neither one offered additional disks for different textures; there was just one medium disk, fixed in place. The Cuisipro and VEV Vigano came with three disks, the Moulinex with two. —A.R.

CUISIPRO

MOULINEX

Of the five models tested, the top performer was the Cuisipro (top), but it costs $90. The $15 Moulinex (bottom) did nearly as well, so it became the pick of the pack for its combination of price and performance. The plastic is surely not as strong as the Cuisipro's stainless steel, but for occasional use it works just fine.

cinnamon, cloves, ground ginger, nutmeg, allspice, and vanilla, competed with the apple flavor. As far as the master recipe was concerned, any seasonings other than sugar and salt were out.

This applesauce is about as pure and as streamlined as they come. It may take a little more time than opening a jar, but once you taste the difference, you'll be dusting off the food mill and buying extra bushels of Jonagolds this fall.

SIMPLE APPLESAUCE
MAKES ABOUT 3 1/2 CUPS

If you do not own a food mill or you prefer applesauce with a coarse texture, peel the apples before coring and cutting them, and, after cooking, mash them against the side of the pot with a wooden spoon or against the bottom of the pot with a potato masher. Applesauce made with out-of-season apples may be somewhat drier than sauce made with peak-season apples, so it's likely that in step 2 of the recipe you will need to add more water to adjust the texture. If you double the recipe, the apples will need 10 to 15 minutes of extra cooking time.

4   pounds apples (8 to 12 medium), preferably Jonagold, Pink Lady, Jonathan, or Macoun, unpeeled, cored, and cut into rough 1 1/2-inch pieces
1/4 cup sugar
    Pinch salt
1   cup water

1. Toss apples, sugar, salt, and water in large, heavy-bottomed nonreactive Dutch oven. Cover pot and cook apples over medium-high heat until they begin to break down, 15 to 20 minutes, checking and stirring occasionally with wooden spoon to break up any large chunks.

2. Process cooked apples through food mill fitted with medium disk. Season with extra sugar or add water to adjust consistency as desired. Serve hot, warm, at room temperature, or chilled. (Can be covered and refrigerated for up to 5 days. Sauce will thicken slightly as it cools.)

To determine how the apples should be prepared, we tried cooking apples that had been broken down into both neat 1½-inch slices and rough 1½-inch chunks. Both the slices and the chunks cooked at about the same rate and resulted in no flavor differences, so we took the easier route and went with the chunks. Though we had been cooking the apples in a Dutch oven on the stovetop, we tried microwaving them, as suggested in several recipes. These apples tasted steamed and bland, so we stuck to the stovetop. We found that covering the Dutch oven accelerated the cooking time by up to 10 minutes, reducing it to a total of roughly 15 minutes.

Some of our initial tests produced applesauce that was too dry for our tastes, making it clear that a little extra liquid was necessary. So we tested various amounts of plain water, apple juice, cider, and sparkling cider and found that we preferred water for its invisibility. One cup, added at the beginning of cooking, was just right.

We tried the three sweeteners that we came across most often in recipes: granulated sugar, brown sugar, and honey. Plain white sugar earned unanimous approval because, like the water, it

did not compete with the flavor of the apples. The taste of both brown sugar and honey was too distinct. To decide how much sugar we wanted, we tried batches with 1 tablespoon up to 6 for our 4 pounds of apples. Four tablespoons of sugar enhanced the apple flavor of the sauce without oversweetening it. A pinch of salt added at the outset of cooking heightened the flavor even further, but all of the usual blandishments, including

---

Dressing Up Applesauce

Although we prefer our applesauce straight up, it takes well to a wide range of flavorings. We tested dozens of options and have listed our favorites below.

BUTTER: 2 tablespoons, unsalted—stir into finished sauce
CINNAMON: two 3-inch sticks—cook with apples and remove prior to pureeing OR 1/4 teaspoon ground—stir into finished sauce
CLOVE: 4 pieces, whole—cook with apples and remove prior to pureeing
CRANBERRY: 1 cup, fresh or frozen—cook and puree with apples
GINGER: three 1/2-inch slices fresh ginger, smashed—cook with apples and remove prior to pureeing
LEMON: 1 teaspoon zest—cook and puree with apples OR 2 tablespoons juice—stir into finished sauce
RED HOT CANDY: 2/3 cup—cook and puree with apples
STAR ANISE: 2 pieces, whole—cook with apples and remove prior to pureeing

Better Greek Salad

Iceberg lettuce, green peppers, tasteless tomatoes, bland feta, and canned olives. Sound familiar? We wanted a Greek salad that was worth eating.

≥ BY MEG SUZUKI ≤

My first college apartment was conveniently located across the street from a pizza parlor. Although our starving-student budgets didn't allow for many frills, my roommates and I would occasionally splurge by ordering pizza and salads. The establishment's version of a Greek salad consisted of iceberg lettuce, chunks of green pepper, and a few pale wedges of tomato, sparsely dotted with cubes of feta and garnished with one forlorn olive of questionable heritage. The accompanying dressing was loaded with musty dried herbs, and it was all packaged in an aluminum takeout container. While it was far superior to anything the college cafeteria produced, this salad was still pretty sad. Although years have gone by, my taste for Greek salad has not diminished. How could I make this pizzeria staple worthy of the dinner table?

Vim and Vinegar

What I wanted was a salad with crisp ingredients and bold flavors, highlighted by briny olives and tangy feta, all married together with a bright-tasting dressing infused with fresh herbs. I started by testing different vinaigrette recipes, with ingredients ranging from vinegar and lemon juice to yogurt and mustard. Tasters thought that the yogurt-based dressing overwhelmed the salad and that the mustard and cider vinegar versions were just "wrong." Lemon juice was harsh and white vinegar was dull, but a dressing that combined lemon juice and red wine vinegar had the balanced flavor I was looking for. There was no place for dried herbs in this salad. Fresh herbs typically used in Greek cuisine include dill, oregano, parsley, mint, and basil. Tasters loved the idea of mint and parsley, but they lost their zip when mixed with the vinaigrette. Oregano's bold flavor stood up well to the vinegar and lemon juice and was the clear favorite. Pure olive oil and extra-virgin olive oil worked equally well, and the addition of a small amount of garlic gave the dressing the final kick it needed.

It's All Greek to Me

The next ingredients up for scrutiny were the vegetables. Although lettuce is not commonly found in traditional Greek salad, it is a main ingredient in the American version. The iceberg lettuce had to go. Romaine, which has the body and crunch of iceberg but also more color and flavor, was the natural choice. Tomatoes were also essential, and only the ripest ones would do. Green bell peppers got a unanimous thumbs-down. Everyone preferred the sweeter red variety, which was improved even further by being roasted. In the interest of saving time, I also tried jarred roasted red peppers, which tasters liked even better. The jarred peppers are packaged in a vinegary brine and have more depth of flavor than freshly roasted peppers (for more information, see Kitchen Notes on page 30).

Onions were next. When the pungency of the raw onions sent some tasters running for breath mints, someone suggested soaking the onions in water to eliminate their caustic bite. I took that idea one step further: Why not marinate the onions in the vinaigrette? On a whim, I included some cucumbers as well. The results were striking. The cucumbers, which had been watery and bland just minutes before, were bright and flavorful, and the onions had lost their unpleasant potency.

Now the vinaigrette recipe was finalized and the vegetables selected, but there was still something missing. I returned to the mint and parsley that had been eliminated from the vinaigrette. Instead, I simply mixed them with the vegetables, tossed this mixture together with the marinated onions, cucumbers, and vinaigrette, generously sprinkled the salad with feta and kalamata olives, and offered it all to tasters. It was a hit. This was a Greek salad worthy of being served on china—not in an aluminum takeout container.

GREEK SALAD
SERVES 6 TO 8

Marinating the onion and cucumber in the vinaigrette tones down the onion's harshness and flavors the cucumber. For efficiency, prepare the other salad ingredients while the onion and cucumber marinate. Use a salad spinner to dry the lettuce thoroughly after washing; any water left clinging to the leaves will dilute the dressing.

Vinaigrette
- 3 tablespoons red wine vinegar
- 1½ teaspoons juice from 1 lemon
- 2 teaspoons minced fresh oregano leaves
- ½ teaspoon salt
- ⅛ teaspoon ground black pepper
- 1 medium garlic clove, pressed through garlic press or minced (about 1 teaspoon)
- 6 tablespoons olive oil

Salad
- ½ medium red onion, sliced thin (about ¾ cup)
- 1 medium cucumber, peeled, halved lengthwise, seeded, and cut into ⅛-inch-thick slices (about 2 cups)
- 2 romaine hearts, washed, dried thoroughly, and torn into 1½-inch-pieces (about 8 cups)
- 2 large vine-ripened tomatoes (10 ounces total), each tomato cored, seeded, and cut into 12 wedges
- ¼ cup loosely packed torn fresh parsley leaves
- ¼ cup loosely packed torn fresh mint leaves
- 6 ounces jarred roasted red bell pepper, cut into ½ by 2-inch strips (about 1 cup)
- 20 large kalamata olives, each olive pitted and quartered lengthwise
- 5 ounces feta cheese, crumbled (1 cup)

1. Whisk vinaigrette ingredients in large bowl until combined. Add onion and cucumber and toss; let stand to blend flavors, about 20 minutes.

2. Add romaine, tomatoes, parsley, mint, and peppers to bowl with onions and cucumbers; toss to coat with dressing.

3. Transfer salad to wide, shallow serving bowl or platter; sprinkle olives and feta over salad. Serve immediately.

COUNTRY-STYLE GREEK SALAD

This salad made without lettuce is known as "country" or "peasant" salad and is served throughout Greece. It's excellent with garden-ripe summer tomatoes.

Follow recipe for Greek Salad, reducing red wine vinegar to 1½ tablespoons and lemon juice to 1 teaspoon in vinaigrette. Use 2 medium cucumbers, peeled, halved lengthwise, seeded, and cut into ⅛-inch thick slices (about 4 cups) and 6 large tomatoes (about 2 pounds), each tomato cored, seeded, and cut into 12 wedges; omit romaine.

Moist, Tender Corn Muffins

Not just for breakfast, these quick, tender corn muffins rely on one simple method and one key ingredient.

⊃ BY ERIN MCMURRER ⊂

I have a love/hate relationship with corn muffins, and it seems to be getting harder to find any to love. Whether too coarse, dry, and crumbly, too sticky and sweet, or just too fluffy and cupcake-like, the majority of corn muffins on the market today just don't make the cut. What do I want? I want a muffin that won't set off sucrose alarms, and I want a pronounced but not overwhelming cornmeal flavor and a moist and tender crumb. And all of this goodness has to be capped off with a crunchy, golden, craggy muffin top.

I started by testing an assortment of recipes (see "Corn Raga-Muffins," page 22) from various cookbooks. Although their ingredient lists were similar, the end results were not. Some were too chewy, too short, and too puck-shaped, while others had too little corn flavor or were just plain too sweet or savory. Two recipes, however, stood out. One produced muffins that were tall and rustic; the other made muffins with a pleasant, wholesome cornmeal flavor. Working with these recipes as a starting point, I began to test variables.

To Cream or Not to Cream

After a bit of research, I learned that there are two basic methods used to mix muffins. The creaming method calls for beating softened butter and sugar together, adding eggs one at a time, then adding dry and wet ingredients alternately to complete the batter. In the quick-bread (or straight) method, the dry and wet ingredients are combined separately and then mixed together. First I tried creaming, which produced a high-rise muffin, but the crumb was too light and fluffy, much like a layer cake. (Air is whipped into the butter and sugar during creaming.) I then tried the quick-bread method, which turned out a muffin not only with good height but also a more substantial crumb. The quick-bread method, in its use of melted rather than creamed butter, apparently introduced less air to the batter, and the resulting muffin was less cupcake-like. Because I wanted a sturdy muffin, not an airy confection, this suited me just fine. As an added bonus, the quick-bread method was also both easier and quicker than creaming: Just melt the butter, pour, and stir.

Corn muffins are best served warm with a pat of butter.

Choosing a Cornmeal

With my mixing method down, it was now time to focus on the choice of cornmeal. I tested three brands: Quaker, Arrowhead Mills, and Hodgson Mill. Quaker cornmeal, the most common brand in supermarkets, is degerminated. During processing, the dried corn is steel-rolled, which removes most of the germ and husk. Because the germ contains most of the flavor and natural oils, this process results in a drier, less flavorful cornmeal. When baked into a corn muffin, Quaker offered an unremarkable corn flavor and, because of its dryness, an unpleasant "crunch."

Arrowhead Mills and Hodgson Mill are similar in that both are whole-grain cornmeals, made from the whole corn kernel. Hodgson Mill, which is stone-ground (the dried corn is ground between two stones), has a coarse, inconsistent texture, while Arrowhead Mills, which is hammer-milled (pulverized with hammers), has a consistent, fine texture. Both brands delivered a more wholesome and complex corn flavor than Quaker. However, the Hodgson Mill cornmeal made the muffins coarse, dry, and difficult to chew. Arrowhead Mills produced by far the best corn muffin, with a consistently fine texture and real cornmeal flavor. The conclusion? Use a whole-grain cornmeal in a fine grind, such as

Arrowhead Mills. (See "All Cornmeals Are Not the Same," page 22, for more information.)

The Mystery of the Moist Muffin

My muffins had the right texture and good flavor, but they were too dry. Some recipes suggest mixing the cornmeal with a hot liquid before adding it to the batter. This method allows the cornmeal to absorb the liquid while expanding and softening the grain. The other wet ingredients are then added to the mush and combined with the dry ingredients. This seemed like a good way to make a moister muffin—or so I thought. Unfortunately, testers found these muffins too dense and strong-tasting, more like cornbread than corn muffins, which should be lighter.

Back to square one. I made a list of the ingredients that might help produce a moist muffin: butter, milk, buttermilk, sour cream, and yogurt. I tried them all, using different amounts of each. My initial thought was "butter, butter, butter," with enough milk added to hit the right consistency. When tested, however, these muffins were lacking in moisture. I then tried using buttermilk in place of the milk. This muffin packed more flavor into each bite, but it was still on the dry side. What finally produced a superior muffin was sour cream paired with butter and milk. These muffins

TECHNIQUE

FILLING MUFFIN CUPS

Using an ice cream scoop or large spoon, divide the batter evenly among the muffin cups, dropping the batter to form mounds. Leave the batter mounded so that the baked muffins will be domed, not flat.

were rich, light, moist, and tender, but they were no dainty cupcakes, either. I was curious to see how a muffin made with whole milk yogurt would stand up to the muffin made with sour cream. The difference was slight. The muffin made with whole milk yogurt was leaner but still moist and delicious. Muffins made with low-fat yogurt, on the other hand, were too lean and dry. Based on these tests, I concluded that a moist muffin requires fat and the tenderizing effect of acidity, both of which are found in sour cream.

The leavener used in most muffins is baking powder and/or baking soda, and I found that a combination of 1½ teaspoons baking powder and 1 teaspoon baking soda delivered the ideal height. I tested temperatures from 325 to 425 degrees and found that 400 degrees delivered the crunchy, crispy, golden crust I was looking for.

So, with the right cornmeal and the addition of sour cream, butter, and milk, it is possible to bake a tender, moist, and delicious corn muffin. By decreasing the amount of sugar and adding a few savory ingredients, you can serve these muffins with dinner as well as for breakfast. Either way, they beat the coffee-shop variety by a country mile.

CORN MUFFINS
MAKES 12 MUFFINS

Whole-grain cornmeal has a fuller flavor than regular cornmeal milled from degerminated corn. To determine what kind of cornmeal a package contains, look closely at the label.

2	cups (10 ounces) unbleached all-purpose flour
1	cup (4½ ounces) fine-ground, whole-grain yellow cornmeal
1½	teaspoons baking powder
1	teaspoon baking soda
½	teaspoon salt
2	large eggs
¾	cup (5¼ ounces) sugar
8	tablespoons (1 stick) unsalted butter, melted
¾	cup sour cream
½	cup milk

1. Adjust oven rack to middle position and heat oven to 400 degrees. Spray standard muffin tin with nonstick cooking spray.

2. Whisk flour, cornmeal, baking powder, baking soda, and salt in medium bowl to combine; set aside. Whisk eggs in second medium bowl until well combined and light-colored, about 20 seconds. Add sugar to eggs; whisk vigorously until thick and homogenous, about 30 seconds; add melted butter in 3 additions, whisking to combine after each addition. Add half the sour cream and half the milk and whisk to combine; whisk in remaining sour cream and milk until combined. Add wet ingredients to dry ingredients; mix gently with rubber spatula until batter is just combined and evenly moistened.

SILHOUETTE PHOTOGRAPHY: VAN ACKERE

TASTING: **All Cornmeals Are Not the Same**

Cornmeal can vary greatly in texture (depending on how the corn kernels are ground) and flavor (depending on whether the kernels are whole grain or degerminated). We found that whole-grain Arrowhead Mills cornmeal (left) makes the best corn muffins. Its texture resembles slightly damp, fine sand. Whole-grain Hodgson Mill cornmeal (center) has great flavor, but the texture is coarser (akin to kosher salt), making muffins that are too coarse. Degerminated Quaker cornmeal (right) has a fine texture (similar to table salt) and makes muffins that are bland and dry.

Do not over-mix. Using an ice cream scoop or large spoon, divide batter evenly among muffin cups, dropping it to form mounds (see illustration on page 21). Do not level or flatten surface of mounds.

3. Bake until muffins are light golden brown and skewer inserted into center of muffins comes out clean, about 18 minutes, rotating muffin tin from front to back halfway through baking time. Cool muffins in tin 5 minutes; invert muffins onto wire rack, stand muffins upright, cool 5 minutes longer, and serve warm.

CORN AND APRICOT MUFFINS
WITH ORANGE ESSENCE

1. In food processor, process ⅔ cup granulated sugar and 1½ teaspoons grated orange zest until pale orange, about 10 seconds. Transfer to small bowl and set aside.

2. In food processor, pulse 1½ cups (10 ounces) dried apricots for ten 2-second pulses, until chopped fine. Transfer to medium microwave-safe bowl; add ⅔ cup orange juice to apricots, cover bowl tightly with plastic wrap, and microwave on high until simmering, about 1 minute. Let apricots stand, covered, until softened and plump, about 5 minutes. Strain apricots; discard juice.

3. Follow recipe for Corn Muffins, substituting ¼ cup packed dark brown sugar for equal amount granulated sugar and stirring ½ teaspoon

grated orange zest and strained apricots into wet ingredients before adding to dry ingredients. Before baking, sprinkle a portion of orange sugar over each mound of batter. Do not invert baked muffins; use a paring knife to lift muffins from tin one at a time and transfer to wire rack. Cool muffins 5 minutes longer; serve warm.

BACON-SCALLION CORN MUFFINS
WITH CHEDDAR CHEESE

Because these muffins contain bacon, store leftovers in the refrigerator wrapped in plastic. Bring them to room temperature or re-warm the muffins before serving.

1. Grate 8 ounces cheddar cheese (you should have 2 cups); set aside. Fry 3 slices bacon (about 3 ounces), cut into ½-inch pieces, in small skillet over medium heat until crisp and golden brown, about 5 minutes. Add 10 to 12 medium scallions, sliced thin (about 1¼ cups), ¼ teaspoon salt, and ⅛ teaspoon ground black pepper; cook to heat through, about 1 minute. Transfer mixture to plate to cool while making muffins.

2. Follow recipe for Corn Muffins, reducing sugar to ½ cup. Stir 1½ cups grated cheddar cheese and bacon/scallion mixture into wet ingredients, then add to dry ingredients and combine. Before baking, sprinkle a portion of additional ½ cup cheddar over each mound of batter.

Corn Raga-Muffins

Despite the simplicity of corn muffins, a lot can go wrong when making them. Here are some of the worst muffins we encountered in our testing, from left to right: (A) This flat muffin contains too much cornmeal and tastes like cornbread. (B) This pale muffin contains no butter and relies on egg whites as the leavener. (C) This hockey puck–like muffin starts with cornmeal mixed with hot water. (D) This cupcake-like muffin resembles many store-bought muffins and is made with too much sugar and leavener.

A. SQUAT AND CORNY **B. DENSE AND TOUGH** **C. SMALL AND WET** **D. FLUFFY AND CAKEY**

Poached Pear and Almond Tart

A soggy crust, sodden filling, and lackluster pears often afflict this French classic.
Made right, it's the perfect marriage of flavors and textures.

⇒ BY DAWN YANAGIHARA ⇐

A pear-almond tart has none of the glamorous superstar sophistication of a fresh fruit tart or an opera cake. It's more like the girl next door—wholesome and fresh-faced, with a quiet, classic beauty. Poached pears and almonds are such a natural pairing that imagining them wed in a dessert is hardly difficult: Satin-ribbon slices of tender, sweet, perfumed poached pears are embedded in a nutty, rich, fragrant, custard-cake almond filling (called frangipane in pâtisserie-speak), all contained in a crisp, buttery pastry.

As a dessert made from several components, however, a pear-almond tart invites havoc. A whole day of preparation is required, and the risks are great: a soggy crust, a coarse, wet frangipane heavy-handedly flavored with almond extract, and tasteless poached pears that either retain too much crunch or are soft to the point of listlessness. Unless each element is perfect, the tart's greatness is diminished.

Choosing and Baking the Crust

With a collection of recipes in hand, I began poaching, mixing, and baking. The first choice was the type of crust: a pâte brisée, with the flakiness of good American pie dough, or a pâte sucrée, with the sweetness and richness of a butter cookie. After the first tasting, the clear winner was pâte sucrée, with its fine, sandy-crisp texture that crumbles and melts in the mouth.

Unlike a pastry cream filling, which requires stovetop cooking, frangipane requires baking. The question therefore was whether the tart shell required prebaking and, if so, how much. At first, I filled a completely unbaked tart shell with frangipane, but it was no good. The bottom crust of the finished tart was soggy and pasty, and it tasted of raw flour, a common downfall of this tart. On the other hand, a fully prebaked pastry wound up a few degrees overbaked after the additional time in the oven with the filling. A partially baked pastry was deep golden and had a buttery shortbread-like texture in the finished tart. It was perfect.

The Perfect Pear

For a pear-almond tart, pear halves, not whole pears, are poached. Rock-hard pears never attained a tender texture no matter how long they simmered. But if the pears were too ripe, they

For a polished appearance, brush hot apple jelly over the pears in the just-baked tart.

were difficult to handle and easily cooked to mush. I found it imperative to use pears that were ripe yet firm; a knife should glide through them smoothly, as if they were baked custard, but they should not bruise against the cutting board. That meant buying them several days in advance of poaching and allowing them to ripen until they gave slightly when pressed with a finger. (See "From Pet Rock to Ripe Pear" on page 24 for more details on ripening pears.)

I tried the readily available pear varieties: Bosc, d'Anjou, Comice, and Bartlett. The favorites were the Bartlett, for its floral, honeyed notes, and the Bosc, because it tasted like a sweet, ripe pear should taste. The other two varieties were unremarkable in flavor and the least attractive in appearance, as they experienced some discoloration during poaching.

With pear varieties selected, I went about trying to bolster their flavor by testing different poaching mediums. The pears could be poached in a simple syrup of sugar and water or a sugar-sweetened white wine. The sugar-syrup pears were flat and dull, the wine-poached pears bright and spirited—the unanimous winner. A few spices added lush flavor: a cinnamon stick, black peppercorns, whole cloves, and, for those who like its seductiveness, a vanilla bean with its flecks of seeds.

Ripe pears poached in 10 minutes. Once the pears are tender, recipes often recommend that they be allowed to cool in their liquid. This, I found, was good advice. If the pears were plucked from the hot poaching liquid, the syrup did not penetrate to their insides, and their texture was dry. If left to cool in the liquid, the pears absorbed some syrup, took on a candied translucency, and became plump, sweet, and spicy.

Perfecting Frangipane

Much like pastry cream, frangipane serves as a filling in numerous types of pastries. Although it seems simple because it does not require stovetop cooking, frangipane can turn out coarse, eggy, wet, and overly sweet.

Frangipane begins with fresh almonds, not almond paste or marzipan. The nuts are ground finely in a food processor, and then one adds a combination of butter, sugar, eggs, and sometimes flour that has been beaten in a standing mixer. I quickly discovered that all of these ingredients could be added directly to the food processor without resorting to a mixer. After grinding the nuts and sugar, I incorporated the eggs and finally the softened butter until the mixture was thickly pourable.

Four ounces of nuts make the right amount of filling for an 11-inch tart shell with eight poached pear halves. I made the frangipane with unblanched sliced almonds (almonds sliced with hulls on), but this gave it a dark and impure appearance and a faintly bitter aftertaste. Whole blanched almonds worked better, but their large size refused to grind down to an even fineness. With a quick, rough chop by hand, they were more cooperative, but better yet were blanched slivered almonds, which yielded readily to a whirring blade. I processed them with the sugar ($\frac{1}{2}$ cup gave the right amount of sweetness),

The Wrong Tart Pan

Do not bake this tart in a 9-inch pan, as shown above. There is no room to place a pear half in the center of the tart, and the frangipane there does not brown on par with the edges and is often wet. This recipe requires an 11-inch tart pan with removable bottom.

which allowed them to be ground superfine without turning greasy as they broke down.

Flour—just a tablespoon or two—appeared in several frangipane recipes. I tried 1½ tablespoons. Astute tasters ferreted it out. Just that small amount made the frangipane not only drier and cakier but also starchier and pastier, so it was off the list. An overabundance of butter was lethal. Eight tablespoons made a greasy frangipane. With four it was too lean and the flavor fleeting. Six tablespoons were ideal. I noted that for the best-textured baked frangipane, the butter should be softened before it's added to the food processor. If too cold, it sometimes resisted incorporation and left pea-sized chunks that resulted in wet, oily pockets in the baked tart.

As for the eggs, I tested two whole eggs, one whole plus one yolk, one whole plus one white,

From Pet Rock to Ripe Pear

According to the Pear Bureau Northwest, pears are an uncommon type of fruit that do not ripen successfully on the tree. They must be harvested at maturity, but before they ripen, lest their texture turn gritty and granular. This explains why virtually all pears at the grocery store are more like pet rocks than edible fruit. I tested three methods for ripening: at room temperature, in a paper bag on the counter, and in the refrigerator.

The pears went into their respective corners on a Monday, and we tasted them each day to gauge their ripeness. By the end of the week, there was a clear loser. The pears kept in the fridge were only slightly riper and softer than when they were purchased. Those stored in a bag and those put in a basket on the counter ripened at the same speed; by Friday, they were both ready for poaching. —D.Y.

---

and so on. Yolk-heavy frangipanes were gluey. The version made exclusively with whole eggs was perfectly acceptable, but the whole-egg-plus-one-white frangipane was superior. It was cake-like without being dry, creamy without being wet. And it tasted of pure almond and sweet butter.

A pinch of salt and a half-teaspoon each of vanilla and almond extract were just right. Like the poached pears, the frangipane can be made in advance and refrigerated. It just needs a little softening outside the refrigerator before use to make sure it can be spread in the tart shell.

Assembling and Baking

For assembly, the pear halves are customarily cut into thin crosswise slices; the slices are kept together and the pear shape is intact, but the slices are fanned slightly toward the stem end. Then they are set in the frangipane like tiles in mastic. Another option is to place uncut pear halves in the frangipane. Though quicker to whisk into the oven, a tart prepared as such was not as stunning and eating it not so pleasurable (the force needed to cut through the pear with a fork tended to dislodge the fruit from the frangipane).

I discovered that it was important to dry the pears off after removing them from their liquid and before setting them on the frangipane. To that end, after slicing the pears, I wicked away excess moisture with paper towels. Otherwise, as they baked, they released moisture that turned the layer of frangipane immediately around them sticky and wet.

Three hundred and fifty degrees for about 45 minutes proved to be the best temperature and baking time. At the end of baking, the tart that had begun as monochromatically straw blond had a walnut-brown crust, frangipane with a nutty tan surface, and golden pears.

Even as it sits in its pan on the cooling rack, the humble pear-almond tart is radiant. But it was the juxtaposition of textures and flavors that made ardent admirers out of those who started as indifferent tasters (myself included). With each part perfected, this pear-almond tart was transcendent. And, unlike a fresh fruit tart, its good looks don't erode when the first slice is removed.

POACHED PEAR AND ALMOND TART
MAKES ONE 11-INCH TART, SERVING 10 TO 12

This tart has several components, but each can be prepared ahead, and the tart is baked several hours before serving. If you cannot find blanched slivered almonds, use whole blanched almonds, but chop them coarsely before processing to make sure they form a fine, even grind. The pears should be ripe but firm, the flesh giving slightly when gently pressed with a finger. Purchase the pears a few days ahead and allow them to ripen at room temperature (see box at left). If they ripen before you need them, refrigerate them and use them within a day or two,

---

or poach them and hold them in their syrup (they will keep for about 3 days). Many tasters liked the bright, crisp flavor of pears poached in Sauvignon Blanc. Chardonnay-poached pears had deeper, oakier flavors and were also well-liked. For ideas on using the strained poaching liquid, see page 4.

Poached Pears
- 1 bottle (750 ml) white wine
- ⅔ cup (about 4½ ounces) granulated sugar
- 2 tablespoons juice from 1 lemon plus 4 or 5 large strips zest removed with vegetable peeler
- 1 (3-inch) stick cinnamon
- 15 black peppercorns
- 3 whole cloves
- ⅛ teaspoon salt
- ½ vanilla bean, slit in half lengthwise (optional)
- 4 ripe but firm pears (about 8 ounces each), preferably Bosc or Bartlett

Tart Pastry (Pâte Sucrée)
- 1 large egg yolk
- 2 tablespoons heavy cream
- ½ teaspoon vanilla extract
- 1½ cups (7½ ounces) unbleached all-purpose flour
- ¾ cup (3 ounces) confectioners' sugar
- ¼ teaspoon salt
- 10 tablespoons (1¼ sticks) very cold unsalted butter, cut into ½-inch cubes

Almond Filling (Frangipane)
- 4 ounces (1 cup) blanched slivered almonds
- ½ cup (3½ ounces) granulated sugar
- ⅛ teaspoon salt
- 1 large egg plus 1 large egg white
- ½ teaspoon almond extract
- ½ teaspoon vanilla extract
- 6 tablespoons unsalted butter, cut into 6 pieces and softened to room temperature

Glaze
- ¼ cup apple jelly

1. TO POACH THE PEARS: Combine wine, sugar, lemon juice and zest, cinnamon, peppercorns, cloves, and salt in large, nonreactive saucepan. Scrape seeds from vanilla bean pod (if using), and add seeds and pod to saucepan. Bring mixture to simmer over medium heat, stirring occasionally to dissolve sugar. Meanwhile, halve, core, and peel pears (see illustrations on page 25). Slide pears into simmering wine; increase heat to high and return to simmer, then reduce heat to low and simmer, covered, until pears are tender (toothpick or skewer inserted into pear should slide in and out with very little resistance) and outer edges of pears have turned translucent, about 10 minutes, turning pears in liquid halfway through poaching time using wooden spoon or spatula. Off heat, cool pears in liquid, partially covered, until pears have turned translucent and are cool enough to handle, about 1 hour. (Pears

and liquid may be transferred to nonreactive bowl or container, cooled to room temperature, covered, and refrigerated for up to 3 days.)

2. FOR THE TART PASTRY: Whisk together yolk, cream, and vanilla in small bowl. Combine flour, sugar, and salt in food processor with four 1-second pulses. Scatter butter pieces over flour mixture; pulse to cut butter into flour until mixture resembles coarse meal, about twenty 1-second pulses. With machine running, add egg mixture and process until dough comes together, about 12 seconds. Turn dough onto sheet of plastic wrap and press into 6-inch disk; wrap with plastic wrap and refrigerate at least 1 hour or up to 48 hours.

3. Remove dough from refrigerator (if refrigerated longer than 1 hour, let stand at room temperature until malleable). Unwrap and roll out between lightly floured large sheets of parchment paper or plastic wrap (or piece 4 small sheets together to form 2 large sheets) to 15-inch round. (If dough becomes soft and sticky, slip onto baking sheet and refrigerate until workable, about 20 minutes.) Transfer dough to tart pan by rolling dough loosely over rolling pin and unrolling over 11-inch tart pan with removable bottom. Working around circumference of pan, ease dough into pan corners by gently lifting dough with one hand while pressing dough into corners with other hand. Press dough into fluted sides of pan, patching breaks or cracks if necessary. (If some edges are too thin, reinforce sides by folding excess dough back on itself.) Run rolling pin over top of tart pan to remove excess dough. Set dough-lined tart pan on baking sheet or large plate and freeze 30 minutes. (Frozen dough-lined tart pan can be wrapped tightly in plastic wrap and frozen up to 1 month.)

4. Meanwhile, adjust oven rack to middle position and heat oven to 375 degrees. Set dough-lined tart pan on baking sheet; lightly spray one side of 18-inch square heavy-duty extra-wide foil with nonstick cooking spray. Press foil, greased-side down, inside frozen tart shell, folding excess foil over edge of tart pan; fill with metal or ceramic pie weights. Bake until dry, pale gold, and edges have just begun to color, about 20 minutes, rotating halfway through baking. Remove from oven and carefully remove foil and weights by gathering edges of foil and pulling up and out. Set baking sheet with tart shell on wire rack and cool to room temperature, about 30 minutes.

5. FOR THE ALMOND FILLING: Pulse almonds, sugar, and salt in food processor until finely ground, about 25 two-second pulses; process until as finely ground as possible, about 10 seconds longer. Add egg and egg white, almond and vanilla extracts; process until combined, about 10 seconds. Add butter and process until no lumps remain, about 10 seconds. Scrape bottom and sides of bowl with rubber spatula and process to combine thoroughly, about 10 seconds longer. (Can be refrigerated in airtight

container up to 3 days. Before using, let stand at room temperature about 30 minutes to soften, stirring 3 or 4 times.)

6. TO ASSEMBLE, BAKE, AND GLAZE THE TART: Reduce oven temperature to 350 degrees. Remove pears from poaching liquid; set pears cut-side down on triple thickness paper towels and pat dry with additional paper towels. Follow illustrations 1 to 6, below, to spread frangipane in tart shell and slice and arrange pears.

7. Bake tart on baking sheet until crust is deep golden brown and almond filling is puffed, browned, and firm to the touch, about 45 minutes,

rotating baking sheet halfway through baking time. Cool tart on baking sheet on wire rack 10 minutes.

8. Bring jelly to boil in small saucepan over medium heat, stirring occasionally to smooth out lumps. When boiling and completely melted, brush glaze on pears. Cool tart to room temperature, about 2 hours. (Tart can be kept at room temperature longer but should be served the day it is made.)

9. Remove outer metal ring of tart pan, slide thin metal spatula between bottom of crust and tart pan bottom to release, then slip tart onto cardboard round or serving platter; cut into wedges and serve.

STEP-BY-STEP | PREPARING THE PEARS FOR POACHING

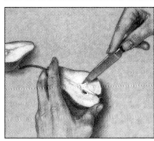

1. Cut each pear in half through stem and blossom ends. With tip of paring knife, cut out seed core from each pear half.

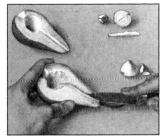

2. Remove blossom end of each pear half, then remove thin fibrous core and stem by making V-shaped incision along both sides of core.

3. Working quickly to avoid discoloration, peel cored pear halves with vegetable peeler.

STEP-BY-STEP | ASSEMBLING THE TART

1. Spread frangipane evenly into partially baked and cooled tart shell using offset icing spatula.

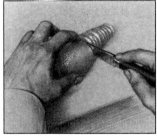

2. Cut one pear half crosswise into ³/₈-inch slices; do not separate slices, and leave pear half intact on cutting board. Pat dry with paper towels to absorb excess moisture.

3. Discard first 4 slices from narrow end of sliced pear half. Slide icing spatula under sliced pear and, steadying it with one hand, slide pear to center of tart.

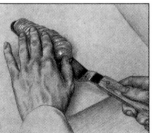

4. Cut and dry another pear half following step 2. Slide spatula under pear and gently press pear to fan slices toward narrow end.

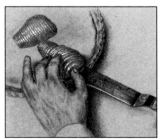

5. Slide fanned pear onto frangipane, narrow end toward center, making a flower-petal pattern off the center pear.

6. Repeat steps 2, 4, and 5 with remaining pear halves, spacing them evenly. If necessary, use spatula to push pears to space them evenly.

The Emperor's New Salt

Food magazines and celebrity chefs are touting the flavor of gourmet salts that cost up to $36 per pound. Do they really taste better?

≥ BY ANNA KASABIAN AND MEG SUZUKI ≤

Step into just about any gourmet shop and you will find sea salts from around the world in a variety of colors and textures. Most are pricey, up to 100 times the cost of table salt. American chefs have become big proponents of sea salt, pairing specific salts to specific dishes. Their passion can be infectious.

Paul Wildermuth, chef/partner at Chicago's acclaimed Red Light restaurant, uses kosher salt for seasoning things like stock and pasta water, but it's fleur de sel (the most expensive kind of sea salt) that is, in his opinion, the Rolls-Royce of salts. "It's a pure, beautiful product," he says. He particularly likes to use fleur de sel with shellfish, especially lobster, because of its clean flavor.

Bill Phillips, a chef/instructor at the Culinary Institute of America in Hyde Park, N.Y., also uses kosher salt at the stovetop but sprinkles Sea Star (a sea salt from Brittany) on finished dishes. "It's stunning, and smells like you're standing on the beach," he reports.

The food press has added to the hype, exalting exotic salts such as black sea salt from India and red sea salt from Hawaii as well as more common sea salts from France. We wondered if a pinch here or a smidgen there is really worth $36 a pound. Will your biscuits or steak taste better if you spend more money on salt?

And what about choosing an everyday salt for adding to pasta water or chicken stock? More home cooks are following the lead of chefs and keeping kosher salt (rather than table salt) next to the stove. Chefs have spread the word that these oversized grains of salt have a pure, clean flavor and that it's much easier to pick up these large crystals with your fingers. While the argument about crystal size is persuasive, we wondered if kosher salt really does taste better than table salt.

To answer these questions, we embarked on a two-month odyssey, testing nine brands of salt in five different kitchen applications. The results were, to say the least, surprising.

A Harvest of Salt

Salt is either mined from ancient seas that dried up millions of years ago or obtained by evaporating seawater. In their pure form—sodium chloride—salts from both locations taste the same. What distinguishes one salt from another in color and flavor are the type and amount of minerals (such as magnesium, calcium, and potassium) and/or clays attached to the crystals of sodium chloride. The size and texture of the crystals—whether big flakes, irregularly shaped large grains, or regularly shaped small grains—are largely determined by the way the salt is processed.

What is referred to as sea salt is obtained from seawater held in large, shallow ponds or large pans. As the water evaporates, coarse crystals of salt fall to the bottom. The crystals are then collected by raking. Maldon sea salt is made from seawater that is artificially heated. This process produces relatively large flakes. The white fleur de sel, or "flower of salt," is harvested by skimming off the thin film of salt that forms on the surface of the pans. As a result, it is extremely expensive. (The brand we tested costs $36 a pound.)

Table salt is usually obtained by pumping water into an underground salt deposit to dissolve the salt, pumping the brine to the surface, settling impurities, and vacuum-evaporating the clear brine. Rapid vacuum evaporation yields the tiny, regularly shaped grains that fit through the holes in a salt shaker. Some table salt is taken from the sea and then processed by vacuum evaporation to yield small crystals.

Kosher salt can be mined or harvested from the sea. Processing is designed to produce coarse, irregular crystals that will cling to meat for the purpose of koshering, in which the salt is applied to draw blood and juices out of just-butchered meats. Kosher salt is manufactured under rabbinical supervision, which, along with the large size of the crystals, is what distinguishes kosher salt from most other salts, especially table salt.

Unlike kosher salt and sea salt, most table salts contain additives. Iodized table salt contains potassium iodide, which protects against thyroid disease. Dextrose may be added to help stabilize the iodine, and calcium silicate or one of several other drying agents are often added to prevent caking. Many chefs claim these additives can impart an off flavor.

Tasting Results

To make sense of all these claims, we tasted two kinds of table salt (one iodized, one not), two brands of kosher salt, and five widely available sea salts. The price per pound of all the salts ranged from 36 cents to $36. Tests were divided into three categories: salt used at the table (we sprinkled each sample on roast beef), salt used in baking (we used a plain biscuit recipe), and salt dissolved in liquids (we tested each salt in spring water, chicken stock, and pasta cooking water).

Of the five tests run, we uncovered the most profound differences in our beef tenderloin test. Tasters loved the crunch of the large sea salt flakes or crystals when sprinkled over slices of roast tenderloin. Here, Maldon sea salt was the clear winner, followed by Fleur de Sel de Camargue and Light Grey Celtic sea salt.

Why did the sea salts win this test? According to Dr. Gary Beauchamp, director of the Monell Chemical Senses

What about Those Minerals?

To find out if sea salts are more nutritious than table salts, we had all of the salts we tasted analyzed for magnesium, calcium, and potassium, the three major trace minerals in salt. Although the sea salts did contain a lot more minerals than kosher and table salts, the actual amounts (listed in milligrams per teaspoon in the chart below) are still very, very small when compared with the Reference Daily Intakes (RDIs) of these minerals recommended by the Food and Drug Administration: 400 mg for magnesium, 1,000 mg for calcium, and 3,500 mg for potassium. (These are typical values and vary somewhat depending on gender and caloric intake.) You would have to eat 2 teaspoons of Esprit du Sel to equal the amount of magnesium in ¾ cup of cooked brown rice, 12 teaspoons of Maldon to equal the amount of calcium in ½ cup of skim milk, and 26 teaspoons of Esprit du Sel to equal the amount of potassium in a baked potato.

SALT	MILLIGRAMS PER TEASPOON		
	Magnesium	Calcium	Potassium
MALDON SEA	2.6	10.0	0.8
FLEUR DE SEL DE CAMARGUE	4.8	5.8	4.0
MORTON COARSE KOSHER	≤0.1	2.7	0.5
DIAMOND CRYSTAL KOSHER	0.1	1.6	0.4
LIGHT GREY CELTIC SEA	21.8	8.8	4.6
LA BALEINE SEA	13.4	2.1	0.8
MORTON IODIZED	≤0.1	1.3	1.0
ESPRIT DU SEL DE ÎLE DE RÉ	32.2	4.6	12.3
MORTON NON-IODIZED	0.1	0.9	1.1

TASTING SALT

Salts are listed in order of preference based on results in five tests, but the difference between the first- and last-place brands was small. The tests were as follows: Nine salts were dissolved in spring water, dissolved in chicken stock, dissolved in water used to cook pasta, baked in biscuits, and sprinkled onto pieces of roast beef tenderloin. For each test, we measured salt by weight rather than volume. Throughout the tests, we found that flavor differences were extremely subtle. Texture was a consideration in only the biscuit and tenderloin tests. Large, crunchy salt grains were preferred on the tenderloin but disliked in biscuits for their uneven, gritty consistency. For mail-order sources, see page 32.

Maldon Sea Salt MALDON, ENGLAND
➤ **$6.95 for 8.5 ounces** ➤ **$13.08 per pound**

These light, airy flakes resemble pyramids and are unique among the brands tested. This hand-harvested salt won the tenderloin test by a clear margin because tasters judged the delicately crunchy flakes to be a perfect match with meat. Available in gourmet stores and by mail.

Fleur de Sel de Camargue PROVENCE, FRANCE
➤ **$9.95 for 4.4 ounces** ➤ **$36.18 per pound**

The "great crunch" of this hand-harvested Mediterranean salt propelled it to second place in the tenderloin test. In the biscuit test, some tasters liked the "strong hits of salt," while others found it to be "gritty." Available in gourmet stores and by mail.

Morton Coarse Kosher Salt UNITED STATES
➤ **$1.69 for 48 ounces** ➤ **$0.56 per pound**

This "straightforward" salt performed well in the biscuit test, finishing in third place. Tasters generally also liked the crunch of these medium-sized grains on the tenderloin. Available in supermarkets nationwide.

Diamond Crystal Kosher Salt UNITED STATES
➤ **$1.99 for 48 ounces** ➤ **$0.66 per pound**

Tasters enjoyed the clean, sweet flavor of this salt on the tenderloin. The biscuits made with this salt were mild and buttery, though one taster detected "pockets of salt." Available in supermarkets nationwide.

Light Grey Celtic Sea Salt BRITTANY, FRANCE
➤ **$7.75 for 24 ounces** ➤ **$5.17 per pound**

This hand-harvested salt has the largest crystal size and a unique grayish hue because of its high mineral content. The coarse "pebbles" were too large in the biscuits (they also failed to dissolve in chicken stock) but were better suited to the tenderloin. Available in gourmet stores and by mail.

La Baleine Sea Salt Fine Crystals PROVENCE, FRANCE
➤ **$4.89 for 26.5 ounces** ➤ **$2.95 per pound**

This finely ground sea salt comes from the Mediterranean. Although it was judged to have a clean, sweet, mild flavor, tasters thought the powdery grains were "inappropriate for garnishing roasts." Available in supermarkets nationwide.

Morton Iodized Table Salt UNITED STATES
➤ **$0.59 for 26 ounces** ➤ **$0.36 per pound**

This salt won first place in the biscuit test but did not fare well in the tenderloin test, where it was deemed harsh and salty. Tasters unanimously thought the grains were too small, and one taster disliked the way it "dissolved into nothingness" on the meat. Available in supermarkets nationwide.

Esprit du Sel de Île de Ré BRITTANY, FRANCE
➤ **$9 for 8.8 ounces** ➤ **$16.36 per pound**

This hand-harvested fleur de sel from Brittany has a damp appearance and an irregularly coarse texture. Tasters thought the size of the grains was just right for tenderloin. In the biscuits, however, the large salt grains resulted in an unappealing, crunchy texture. Available in gourmet stores and by mail.

Morton Non-Iodized Table Salt UNITED STATES
➤ **$0.59 for 26 ounces** ➤ **$0.36 per pound**

This salt was described as "sharp and characterless" when sprinkled on tenderloin. However, as with the Morton's iodized salt, these small grains were thought to be perfect for biscuits. Available in supermarkets nationwide.

Center in Philadelphia and a leading expert on the science of taste and smell, flat crystals or crystals with holes cause a taste sensation different from that of regularly shaped small crystals. And, based on our testing results, it's clear that large crystals provided more pleasing sensory stimulation than fine table salt. In fact, tasters really objected to fine salts sprinkled on the beef, calling them "harsh" and "sharp." Tasters did like kosher salt on meat, but not as much as sea salts, which have larger crystals.

Does this mean that our tasters were reacting to the additives in table salt that the chefs had warned us about? It's possible, but given the results in our other tests, we are not convinced. In fact, the one fine-grained sea salt in our tasting (La Baleine) finished next-to-last in this test, and it does not contain any additives. It's hard to sprinkle fine-grained sea or table salt evenly over meat, and we think tasters may have been hitting pockets with a lot of salt and reacting negatively.

In the biscuit tests, Morton table salt was the winner, and most of the sea salts landed at the bottom of the ratings. The explanation here is simple. Small salt crystals are more evenly distributed in baked goods than large crystals, and tasters didn't like getting a big hit of crunchy salt.

In the spring water, chicken stock, and pasta cooking water, tasters felt that all nine salts tasted pretty much the same. Why didn't the fancy sea salts beat the pants off plain table salt in these tests? The main reason is dilution. Yes, sea salts sampled right from the box (or sprinkled on meat at the table) did taste better than table salt. And while crystal size did undoubtedly affect flavor perception in the tenderloin test, we suspect that our tasters were also responding favorably to trace minerals in these salts. But mineral content is so low in sea salt (by weight, less than 1 percent; see "What about Those Minerals?" on page 26) that any effect these minerals might have on flavor was lost when a teaspoon of salt was stirred into a big pot of chicken stock.

One final (and very important) point. Our results should not be taken to mean that all salts behave in the same way in the kitchen. For example, salts with a fine texture may seem saltier than coarse salts because of the way the crystals pack down in a teaspoon when measured (see Kitchen Notes on page 30 for more information).

What, then, can we conclude from the results of these tests? For one, expensive sea salts are best saved for the table, where their delicate flavor and great crunch can be appreciated. Don't waste $36-a-pound sea salt by sprinkling it into a simmering stew. If you like to keep coarse salt in a ramekin next to the stove, choose a kosher salt, which costs just pennies per pound. If you measure salt by the teaspoon when cooking, use table salt, which is also the best choice for baking.

Choosing an Everyday Nonstick Skillet

Most cookware sold in the United States is nonstick. When should you use it, when should you avoid it, and which inexpensive nonstick skillets are a best buy?

∋ BY ADAM RIED ∈

Much as I would love to drive a Porsche, the reality of my budget dictates a more modest conveyance. The same is true of the cookware that I (and most cooks) use at home. It would be great to have a battery of weighty, expensive, professional-grade pots and pans at my disposal, but most of what I use is, to be blunt, a lot cheaper. Does lower-cost cookware necessarily mean a big performance trade-off? I examined that question recently by conducting a full set of cooking tests on eight inexpensive nonstick skillets, all purchased at hardware or discount stores for no more than $50 a piece.

When to Choose a Nonstick Pan

Statistics reported by the Cookware Manufacturers Association indicate that 90 percent of all the aluminum cookware sold in the United States in 2001 was nonstick. The reasons to use nonstick are clear: It requires little or no fat to lubricate the food (and thereby prevent sticking), and cleanup is easy. Nonstick is terrific for extremely delicate, quick-cooking foods. Flaky white fish comes to mind, as do certain egg dishes, like omelets and eggs sunny-side up, the integrity of which would be destroyed if they stuck to the pan.

Those concerned with limiting their fat intake view the reduction of cooking fat as another significant benefit to nonstick. This makes sense if you want a simple sautéed fish fillet or chicken cutlet garnished with a wedge of lemon or lime. It may mean trouble, however, if you prefer to garnish your food with a pan sauce. Pan sauces rely on fond, the tiny caramelized bits of food that stick to the pan as its contents cook. When liquid is added to the pan (a process called deglazing), the bits of food dissolve to form the flavorful backbone of the sauce.

Because nonstick coatings prevent sticking, they also, in my experience, inhibit fond development. To test this notion, I sautéed skinless, boneless chicken breast cutlets in each pan and then deglazed the fond left behind with 1 cup of water, which I then boiled for one minute. I was looking for rich, dark brown liquid shaded deeply by the dissolved fond. What I got, in each and every case, more resembled dirty bathwater. Not a single sample was dark enough to offer much flavor to a sauce.

The chicken cutlet tests pointed to another drawback of nonstick cookware. Not only was the fond light, so was the chicken. The savory, caramelized crust that forms on the exterior of a piece of food as it sautés is the very reason to cook that way in the first place—the crust tastes great. None of the nonstick pans in our tests formed a crust on the lean chicken cutlets that would make us proud (or hungry).

Here in the test kitchen we choose nonstick when we want to cook lightly, keep flavors fresh, or ensure easy cleanup. If browning or fond are important to the dish, we reach for a traditional pan.

Slip-Sliding Away

The material used for nonstick coating—polytetrafluoroethylene, or PTFE—was developed by chemists at Dupont in the late 1930s. Trademarked originally as Teflon, the formula has evolved over the years, and now several companies in addition to Dupont supply PTFE to cookware manufacturers (many of which use individualized, proprietary, multicoat application processes to bond the coating to their pans). It is our understanding, however, that the majority of nonstick coatings today are the same basic substance.

The nonstick, nonreactive magic of PTFE is due, in large part, to one of the two types of atoms it contains—namely, fluorine. Robert Wolke, our resident science expert, reports that every PTFE molecule contains two carbon atoms and four fluorine atoms. In the atomic world, fluorine is highly resistant to bonding with other substances. That's why PTFE is so slippery.

And slippery it was. Every pan in the group received a good score in release ability and cleaning tests, the raisons d'être for nonstick. I tested both traits in a purposefully abusive manner by

The Skillets We Tested

RECOMMENDED

Farberware Millennium
Heaviest pan of the bunch, with the most solid construction.

RECOMMENDED WITH RESERVATIONS

T-Fal Ultrabase Royale Gala
It neither set a wrong foot forward nor blew us away with its performance. The price is right, though.

Wearever Concentric Air
Certainly not the last pan you'll ever have to buy, but a respectable performer nonetheless.

Innova Classicor Stainless Steel
Solid construction, but outperformed by less expensive pans.

NOT RECOMMENDED

Revere Polished Nonstick
The design of this pan, with its high sides, was our least favorite.

Bialetti Casa Italia
Slow sauté speed means food does not brown well: pale fish, pale chicken, and underdone eggs.

Meyer Commercial Weight II
Solid and heavy, but produces subpar browning when sautéing.

Simply Calphalon Nonstick
Most expensive pan in the group did not sauté to impress.

RATING INEXPENSIVE NONSTICK SKILLETS

RATINGS
★★★
GOOD
★★
FAIR
★
POOR

We tested and evaluated eight nonstick skillets (each rated with a 12-inch diameter—or as close to it as we could find in that manufacturer's line—available in open stock, and with a retail cost of less than $50) according to the following criteria. All stovetop cooking tests were performed over 10,000 BTU gas burners on the KitchenAid ranges in our test kitchen. The pans are listed in ascending price order within each category.

PRICE: Prices listed at Boston-area retail or national mail-order outlets. You may encounter different prices, depending on the outlet.

MATERIALS: The materials that go into the pan itself, as well as the handles. (In the chart, SS = stainless steel and AL = aluminum.)

WEIGHT: Measured without lids (none of the skillets had one) and rounded to the nearest ounce.

PERFORMANCE: To determine overall performance. we conducted three everyday cooking tasks that were especially well-suited to nonstick pans. We sautéed skinless, boneless chicken breast cutlets, seared salmon fillets, and prepared omelets. Scores of good, fair, or poor were assigned for each test, and the composite of those scores constitutes the overall performance rating for each pan. This factor was especially important in the overall ratings.

SAUTÉ SPEED: We started with a cold pan and sautéed 1½ cups chopped onions in 2 tablespoons olive oil over medium heat for 10 minutes. Pans that produced soft, pale gold onions with no burnt edges were rated good; pans that produced onions that were barely colored and retained notable crunch were rated fair.

CLEANUP/RELEASE ABILITY: To determine ease of cleaning, we intentionally burned oatmeal onto each pan, allowing it to cook unattended over high heat for 45 minutes. All the pans came clean with just a light washing with dish detergent and warm water and were rated good. All of the cooking tests, but most especially the omelet and oatmeal, helped determine the pans' release ability.

TESTERS' COMMENTS: These comments augment the information on the chart with observations about unusual or noteworthy aspects of the pans and their performance.

Brand	Price	Materials	Weight	Performance	Sauté Speed	Cleanup/ Release	Testers' Comments
RECOMMENDED **Farberware** Millennium 18/10 Stainless Steel 12" Nonstick Skillet	$29.99	SS with AL sandwich base, SS handle, Dupont SilverStone nonstick coating	3 lb. 6 oz.	★★★	★★★	★★★	Fantastic omelets, golden brown fish, and evenly sautéed onions. Only with chicken did this pan falter—and not much at that.
RECOMMENDED WITH RESERVATIONS **T-Fal** Ultrabase Royale Gala 12¼" Sauté Pan	$22.99	Enameled AL, phenolic handle, genuine T-Fal nonstick coating	2 lb. 2 oz.	★★★	★★	★★★	Cool, comfortable, ergonomic handle and plenty of interior space. Great job on omelets and salmon, decent job on chicken and onions.
Wearever Concentric Air Collection Super Slick Nonstick 12" Sauté Pan	$29.22	Enameled AL, phenolic handle, Maxalon nonstick coating	2 lb.	★★★	★★	★★★	Comfortable handle, but it came loose during testing. Sauté speed was slightly slow. Neat-freaks might find a little extra effort necessary to clean the shiny rim thoroughly.
Innova Classicor Stainless Steel Excalibur 12" Nonstick Frypan	$39.99	SS with AL sandwich bottom, SS handle, Excalibur nonstick coating	2 lb. 2 oz.	★★	★★★	★★★	Although this pan could not be faulted with any cooking disasters, it could not manage even browning with omelets, fish fillets, or chicken. Didn't care for the channel around the rim, which made it difficult to remove omelets neatly.
NOT RECOMMENDED **Revere** Polished Nonstick Open Skillet—12"	$19.99	SS with polished AL exterior, phenolic handle, Teflon nonstick coating	2 lb. 4 oz.	★★	★★	★★★	High sides make omelets a bit tricky. Browning on fish and chicken was unimpressive, and the handle loosened during testing.
Bialetti Casa Italia Hi-Base 11"	$19.99	AL, phenolic handle, Teflon Platinum nonstick coating	2 lb. 5 oz.	★★	★★★	★★★	Pan bottom is textured inside and out, a feature that does not produce any particular advantage as far as we could tell. Handle loosened slightly during testing.
Meyer Commercial Weight II 12" Nonstick Sauté Pan	$27.99	AL, phenolic handle, Dupont nonstick coating	3 lb. 2 oz.	★★	★★	★★★	Extra-thick, shiny rim requires extra elbow grease to come completely clean. Eggs were undercooked, and fish, chicken, and onions barely browned at all.
Simply Calphalon Nonstick 12" Omelette Pan	$49.99	Anodized AL, steel handle, Calphalon nonstick coating	2 lb. 8 oz.	★★	★★	★★★	Neither chicken nor onions browned sufficiently; fish was more successful. On the whole, it was outperformed by cheaper pans.

burning oatmeal onto the pans over high heat for 45 minutes. That kind of treatment would trash a traditional pan, but the scorched cereal slid out of the nonstick pans with no fuss, and they practically wiped clean.

The Pan to Pick

In their new, off-the-shelf condition, all of the pans turned in reasonable-to-good performances cooking the foods best suited to nonstick cooking—eggs and fish. In fact, every pan but the Revere produced evenly cooked omelets and released them with ease. The omelet made in the Farberware pan was especially impressive. The Farberware also did a particularly nice job searing salmon fillets to an even, crusty, medium brown. (Salmon is much higher in fat than skinless chicken cutlets and therefore browns more easily, even in a nonstick pan.)

Sauté speed is also an important measure of a pan's performance. I tested this by sautéing 1½ cups of hand-chopped onions over medium heat for 10 minutes, in the hope of ending up with pale gold onions that bore no trace of burning. And you know what? For the most part, I did. The Wearever, T-Fal, Innova, and Revere pans, which weigh less than the other pans, turned out the darkest onions, but they were still well within an acceptable color range. Onions sautéed in the Farberware, Meyer, Calphalon, and Bialetti were a shade lighter, indicating a slightly slower sauté speed. The Farberware onions, however, took top honors based on how evenly all the pieces colored.

Of course, construction quality is a concern with any piece of cookware but especially inexpensive models. Will the thing hold up, or will you have to replace it in six months? Based on my experience, you may well sacrifice a measure of construction quality with a budget pan. Pans with handles that were welded or riveted on to the pan body, including the Farberware, Innova, Meyer, and Calphalon, all felt solid and permanent. But the heat-resistant plastic (called phenolic) handles on the T-Fal, Revere, Bialetti, and Wearever pans were not riveted in place, and the last three of them came loose during testing. That does not bode well for their futures. (*Cook's* will report on how well these pans endure heavy test kitchen use in an upcoming issue.)

Of the pans tested, the $30 Farberware Millennium offered the best combination of good nonstick performance (in suitable applications), pleasing heft at almost 3½ pounds, and solid construction. It even beat out the priciest pan in the test, the Calphalon. The Farberware may not be the Porsche of my dreams, but then again, you can't make an omelet in a bucket seat, can you?

Beware of Greeks Bearing Peppers

Give us a fresh Greek salad any day, but hold the green peppers, please. Our preference is for red peppers, and the jarred variety at that. But are all jarred red peppers created equal? To find out, we collected a number of brands from local supermarkets and by mail order (see Resources on page 32). The contenders were Divina Roasted Sweet Peppers, Greek Gourmet Roasted Sweet Red Peppers, Lapas Sweet Roasted Peppers, Gaea Flame Roasted Red Peppers, and Peloponnese Roasted Florina Whole Sweet Peppers.

DIVINA	GREEK GOURMET
top choice of tasters	a close second

Three of these brands identified the type of pepper used (Divina, Gaea, and Peloponnese all use Florina peppers), and we wondered if a company's willingness to identify the variety of pepper it was selling would be an indicator of the quality of the pepper. In other words, would tasters prefer the clearly named Florina peppers over the generics (whose main ingredient was identified only as "peppers")? To more easily identify their preferences, tasters tried the peppers "as is" straight from the jar.

What we found was that tasters did not necessarily prefer the peppers labeled Florina. What counted was the flavor and texture of the pepper itself as well as the flavor of the brine.

The top two brands, Divina (roasted Florina pimento red peppers) and Greek Gourmet (fire

roasted peppers), were preferred for their "soft and tender texture" (the Divinas) and "refreshing," "piquant," "smoky" flavor (the Greek Gourmets). The other brands were marked down for their lack of "roasty flavor" and for the unpleasantly overpowering flavor of the brines. Some of these peppers tasted as if they'd been "buried under brine and acid." Others had a "pepperoncini-like sourness" or a "sweet and acidic aftertaste."

The conclusion? Tasters preferred peppers with a full smoky, roasted flavor, a spicy but not too sweet brine, and a tender-to-the-tooth texture.

Along Came a Spider

We don't mind finding a spider in our kitchen. Not the eight-legged variety, but the kitchen tool.

More often referred to as a mesh skimmer or strainer, this piece of equipment is invaluable when it comes to working with boiling water or hot oil. Compared with a slotted spoon, which generally retrieves only a few food items from the water or oil at a time, this not so itsy-bitsy spider has a wide basket made of open webbed (hence the name) mesh that can cradle asparagus by the bunch and allow excess water or oil to drain away quickly.

Cookware shops typically carry two types of spiders. One is made entirely of stainless steel and consists of a long handle with a wide, shallow basket welded to one end. The other, the bamboo spider, has a brass wire basket wired to the end of a bamboo handle. Of the two, we prefer the stainless model (see Resources on page 32), which is sturdier and has the added benefit of being dishwasher-safe.

How Much Salt Is in That Teaspoon?

Given their various crystal shapes and sizes, some brands of salt pack a lot less into every teaspoon when compared with regular table salt. To find out just how much less salt we might be using depending on the brand, we sent all nine salts tasted on page 27 to a laboratory to determine the exact weight of 1 teaspoon of each. As we learned, a teaspoon of Maldon sea salt contains only half the amount of salt that's in a teaspoon of Morton's table salt. The numbers on the far right in the table below indicate how many teaspoons of each brand are needed to equal 1 teaspoon of table salt.

Brand	Amount of Salt in 1 Tsp.	Amount to Equal 1 Tsp. Table Salt
MALDON SEA SALT	3.55 grams	2 teaspoons
DIAMOND CRYSTAL KOSHER SALT	3.60 grams	2 teaspoons
ESPIRIT DU SEL DE ÎLE DE RÉ SALT	5.30 grams	1 1/3 teaspoons
LIGHT GREY CELTIC SEA SALT	5.66 grams	1 1/4 teaspoons
MORTON COARSE KOSHER SALT	5.80 grams	1 1/4 teaspoons
FLEUR DE SEL DE CAMARGUE SALT	5.90 grams	1 1/4 teaspoons
MORTON TABLE (NON-IODIZED) SALT	7.15 grams	1 teaspoon
MORTON TABLE (IODIZED) SALT	7.15 grams	1 teaspoon
LA BALEINE SEA SALT	7.25 grams	1 teaspoon

Keep Your Cool

Should you finish a pan sauce with softened or cold butter? To put a longstanding debate to rest, we tested the use of softened versus cold butter in three different pan sauces. We made a lemony piccata pan sauce that was very acidic, a brandy cream pan sauce that included heavy cream, and a traditional red wine pan sauce. All sauces had the butter whisked in off heat.

The first strike against the softened butter was the foresight required to remove it from the fridge ahead of time—an extra step easily forgotten. The next strike against it was the fact that cold butter was much easier to control in the pan. The whisk would grab the top of the cold butter pat securely, making it easy to incorporate the butter into the sauce. Because the whisk could easily break apart the softened pat of butter, we found ourselves "chasing" little streaks of melting butter around the pan. The third and final strike against the softened butter was its inferior thickening ability. Cold butter helped to emulsify the sauce

and gave it a richer, more velvety mouthfeel. The melted butter would on occasion "break" upon contact with the sauce, creating a thinner, oily sauce.

Do You Know the Muffin Pan?

Do you prefer the muffin top or the cakey interior? To us, nothing beats the muffin top. In fact, the fluffy insides are merely a means of obtaining the crunchy, browned cap, which we pop off and eat first (although a few of us save the best for last). But until muffin shops pay attention and sell muffin tops alone (are you listening, bake shops of America?), we'll have to take care of the problem ourselves. Luckily, we found just the solution—a muffin top pan. This pan contains 6 cups that are only 1/2 inch deep but 4 inches in diameter. We found that each cup takes the same amount of batter as a cup in a standard muffin pan and that the baking time is cut by two minutes. Of course, this means that you will have to bake your muffins in batches (or buy two pans), but they are definitely worth the wait. (See Resources on page 32 for ordering information.)

Cookbooks from Collectives

Two cookbooks showcase the communal talents of Bay Area cooks. Both offer excellent recipes, but only one book speaks with a unique voice. BY CHRISTOPHER KIMBALL

Two of the great culinary collectives of Bay Area cookery are Chez Panisse, the culinary commune and restaurant founded by Alice Waters, and the Baker's Dozen, a group of 13 San Francisco–area bakers who meet informally to discuss weeping meringues and fallen cakes. Both have come out with new cookbooks that are, ostensibly, the result of collective efforts, although Alice is Chez Panisse while the Baker's Dozen are member artists without a conductor. Alice's new offering, *Chez Panisse Fruit*, reflects her soft-spoken, sometimes eclectic, French-inspired approach in which there is more emphasis on ingredients than technique. *The Baker's Dozen Cookbook* offers a sturdier, more mainstream style of American cookery.

CHEZ PANISSE FRUIT
Alice Waters
HarperCollins, 326 pages, $34.95

➤ This is one in a series of single-subject books from Chez Panisse, other titles having focused on vegetables; desserts; and pasta, pizza, and calzone. These are low-key, in-depth works with minimalist typography and nicely executed woodcuts. The informed, passionate tone of the copy marries nicely to the design, which could be described as both timeless and mature. There is no attempt to impress or cajole. As at Chez Panisse itself, the food is simply presented, and the taste alone is the seductress. There are no color photographs, celebrity snapshots, or cleverly designed charts or sidebars.

PROS: The recipes are very often both inspired and inspiring. Alice makes you think about the nature of the ingredients, keeping the combinations simple enough so as not to overwhelm the natural flavors. Fanny's Strawberry-Orange

Compote, for example, is an obvious but uncommon combination. In candying a bit of the orange peel, this simple recipe transcends its simplicity.

CONS: Alice is not a step-by-step cookbook writer. Although the directions are by no means sketchy, they are best suited for those with some kitchen experience. Beating egg yolks and sugar together "until thick" is a bit vague. The directions are not inaccurate; it's just that she assumes that you know your way around the kitchen. (For example, she often doesn't tell you whether to beat a mixture with a spoon, a whisk, or a standing mixer.) In addition, some of the recipes in the book are quite time-consuming.

RECIPE TESTING: Oddly enough, the recipe we had the most trouble with was the Pâte Sucrée (sweet pastry dough), where we wanted more specific directions. But all of the following were top-notch and, on occasion, revelatory: Raspberry Ice Cream; Calvados Apple Custard Tart; Spit-Roasted Pork with Onion-and-Apple Marmalade; Blueberry Buttermilk Pancakes; Ruby Grapefruit, Avocado, and Spring Onion Salad; Butternut Squash and Pear Puree; and Moroccan Preserved Lemons. Candied Grapefruit Peel tasted great but took a good part of two days to finish. As for excess, a Vin de Pamplemousse (grapefruit wine) required two huge containers (one at least 12 liters), six bottles of wine, and half a bottle of vodka. An ice cream recipe called for 2 cups of Armagnac, which is used to soak a mere half cup of prunes; then, to our surprise, only 2 tablespoons of the Armagnac is added to the ice cream. Never mind. The occasional recipe indulgence is a small price to pay for this luminous, inspired collection of recipes.

THE BAKER'S DOZEN COOKBOOK
Thirteen Bay Area Bakers
Morrow, 357 pages, $40

➤ The Baker's Dozen includes culinary headliners such as Flo Braker, Marion Cunningham, Carol Field, and Alice Medrich. (The book was edited by Rick Rodgers.) These big guns regularly get together to discuss and solve cooking problems. Marion Cunningham came up with the idea for a book, and the result is by nature a collaborative endeavor. The design is a no-frills black-and-white affair with one 32-page color signature.

The 135 recipes are, for the most part, likable American favorites such as butter cake and blueberry muffins, although the baking of Italy and France is also represented.

PROS: You are getting the collective wisdom of 13 top bakers all for the price of one. The recipe headnotes and the "Baker's Notes" that appear with most recipes convey a lot of information, and the collective test kitchen notion gives one the sense of well-researched recipes.

CONS: Collaborations in which various authors write different sections of a book are unpredictable; like committees, they are sometimes less than the sum of their parts. For one, it is hard to develop a unified voice or point of view—much like a symphony without a conductor. Second, great books, even cookbooks, should inspire, and that is usually easier to do with one voice than with 13. All of this, however, can be overcome with top-notch editing and packaging. Although most of the content in *The Baker's Dozen Cookbook* is first-rate, the material was assembled, designed, and packaged in a half-hearted manner. The typography is listless, only seven step-by-step photos are offered, and the tension between individual bakers and the Baker's Dozen collective is never fully resolved. In the right hands and with a committed publisher, this could have been a spectacular cookbook rather than a very good one. It's a bit like baseball's All-Star game. It's fun to see your favorite players on the field all at once, but it's not as satisfying as watching the well-orchestrated home team play.

RECIPE TESTING: A majority of these recipes were winners, although, out of 13 tested, we would not make five of them a second time. The usual suspects were nicely executed, including Our Favorite Butter Cake, Classic Meringue Buttercream, Chocolate Pots de Crème, Classic Rye Bread, and Meyer Lemon Chiffon Cake. We had a few minor quibbles with recipe directives, the chocolate chip cookies were fine but not spectacular, and the pie dough was on the heavy side. Two savory entries were disappointing. Artichoke and Potato Turnovers, after the addition of Worcestershire sauce and sour cream, were not worth the trouble, and the Popovers were made with olive oil (instead of butter) and vanilla, a combination that left us speechless. Pita, Bittersweet Chocolate Pudding Pie, and Apricot Streusel Bars were all winners. Despite some packaging flaws, simply put, this book is worth owning.

Most of the ingredients and materials necessary for the recipes in this issue are available at your local supermarket, gourmet store, or kitchen supply shop. The following are mail-order sources for particular items. Prices listed below were current at press time and do not include shipping or handling unless otherwise indicated. We suggest that you contact companies directly to confirm up-to-date prices and availability.

Splatter Screen

To keep mess to a minimum when browning chicken on the stovetop for the pan-roasted chicken on page 6, keep the skillet covered with a splatter screen. The fine-meshed cover will trap escaping grease without retaining steam (which can make for soggy skin) or affecting the cooking time. **Williams-Sonoma (P.O. Box 379900, Las Vegas, NV 89137-9900; 800-541-2233; www.williams-sonoma.com)** carries a heavy-duty splatter screen with a sturdy stainless steel handle. The screen comes in two sizes, 11½ inches and 13 inches. We prefer the latter—item #6-1279967, which sells for $18—because it easily spans a 12-inch skillet but can be used on smaller pans as well.

Roasted Sweet Peppers

Jarred, roasted sweet peppers are convenient when time is tight. And in some recipes, such as Greek salad (see page 20), they can be preferable to fresh, home-roasted peppers. The slightly sweet and sour brine in which the peppers are packed intensifies their flavor and adds a mild sharpness that nicely complements the salad. Divina brand sweet roasted peppers won our tasting of jarred peppers (page 30). **Whole Foods Market** stores across the country carry 13-ounce jars of Divina peppers for $3.99. To find a retailer near you, call **800-350-3411.** If Whole Foods does not have a store in your area, you can purchase the same jar for $4.39 from **GourmetFood4U.com (4481 Johnston Parkway, Cleveland, OH 44128; 888-468-7638; www.gourmetfood4u.com).**

Food Mills

A food mill worked wonders in our applesauce recipe (page 19), and it is also our favorite tool for making ultra-smooth mashed potatoes. We tested five different brands, and a gleaming stainless steel model from Cuisipro garnered top honors for its sharp design and smooth performance. It came with three disks, each with a different-sized perforation: fine, medium, and coarse. Such performance and sturdy craftsmanship do not come cheap, however. The Cuisipro, item #2067, retails for $89.95 at **Kitchen Arts (161 Newbury Street, Boston, MA 02116; 617-266-8701).** At a fraction of the cost—just $14.99—the Moulinex

plastic food mill came in a close second, performing nearly as well as the Cuisipro. Although it comes with just two disks (fine and medium), the Moulinex operated smoothly. If you plan on infrequent use, this food mill might be a better bet. The Moulinex, item #640086, is available from **Kitchen Etc. (32 Industrial Drive, Exeter, NH 03833; 800-232-4070; www.kitchenetc.com).**

Cornmeal

When developing the recipe for corn muffins (page 22) we were surprised to discover how much the flavor and grind can vary between different brands of cornmeal. Some had a barely perceptible corn flavor and a dusty texture, while others had a clean, pure flavor and gritty bite. Our tasters' top choice, Arrowhead Mills cornmeal, is hammer-milled from organically grown whole-grain corn and made a muffin with deep, resonant corn flavor and a delicate crumb. It is widely distributed in natural foods stores and many markets across the country. A 2-pound bag of Arrowhead Mills whole-grain yellow cornmeal is also available via mail order for $1.99, item #AHM47132, from **Akin's Natural Foods Market (7807 East 51st Street, Tulsa, OK 74145; 800-800-3133; www.akins.com).**

Pastry Tools

For the pear almond tart on page 23, a scalloped-edge, 11-inch tart pan with a removable bottom made for an attractive, well-defined crust and easy, safe removal once baked. **A Cook's Wares (211 37th Street, Beaver Falls, PA 15010; 800-915-9788; www.cookswares.com)** carries just such a pan, item #8436, for $9.

The raised handle of an offset icing spatula allowed us to spread the frangipane into an even, smooth layer without dragging our knuckles through the creamy filling or breaking the tart's edges. When slipped deftly under the pears, the spatula also aided in precisely positioning the fruit. **A Cook's Wares** sells a versatile 8½-inch model, item #6867, from Ateco for $5.

For glazing the pears on the just-baked tart, a narrow-tipped pastry brush is a must. Wide-headed, thick brushes made a mess of this close work. A 1-inch pastry/basting brush, item #8300, is available from **A Cook's Wares** for $7.

Sea Salt

While supermarket shelves are chockablock with numerous varieties of salt, our tasting (page 26) showed that in most instances there's not much difference between them all. For salt that's sprinkled on foods at the table, however, tasters preferred the coarser texture of sea salts over

everyday table salt. Maldon Sea Salt, which is hand-harvested on the southeastern coast of England, received high marks. Its uniquely jagged shape contributed crunchy texture to the foods tested. Tasters also appreciated the other top-shelf salts tested, including Fleur de Sel de Camargue, Celtic Light Grey Sea Salt, and Esprit du Sel de Île de Ré. **The Baker's Catalogue (P.O. Box 876, Norwich, VT 05055-0876; 800-827-6836; www.bakerscatalogue.com)** carries Maldon Sea Salt (8.5-ounce box, item #1105, $6.95), Fleur de Sel de Camargue (4.4-ounce bag, item #1108, $9.95), and Celtic Light Grey Sea Salt (24-ounce bag, item #1079, $7.75). **Williams-Sonoma** sells an 8.8-ounce jar of Esprit du Sel de Île de Ré, item #6-2083517, for $9.

Nonstick Skillet

The winner of our inexpensive nonstick skillet competition, page 28, was the Farberware Millennium 18/10 stainless steel 12-inch nonstick skillet. The pan's heft and solid construction—a stainless exterior sandwiching an aluminum core—made it a standout among the other pans tested. Aesthetically speaking, the highly polished stainless exterior belied its $29.99 price. As far as performance, the test kitchen proclaimed that it produced "fantastic omelets" and "golden brown fish." It also produced faultlessly browned onions. The Farberware skillet, item #677765, is available from **Kitchen Etc.**

Spider

Colorfully named, a spider is nothing more than a small, open-meshed strainer with a long handle. It is the best tool available for skimming vegetables or delicate stuffed pasta from boiling water and fried foods from blistering oil. We prefer spiders with fairly small heads because they are easily maneuvered in small pots and pans. While a variety of fancy models are on the market, our favorite is a simple affair, nothing more than thin-gauged tinned steel mesh affixed to a long handle. You can order a spider with a 5-inch diameter, item #BPDR-5, for $5.95, from **Bridge Kitchenware (214 East 52nd Street, New York, NY 10022; 212-688-4220; www.bridgekitchenware.com).**

Muffin–Top Pan

If you favor the crusty, browned top of the muffin over the delicate, crumbly bottom, a muffin-top pan might be for you. Almost flat, each of the pan's six muffin cups is just ½ inch deep, yielding flying-saucer-shaped muffins that are virtually all crispy brown top. Our favorite pan is made by Chicago Metallic, item #853606, and sells for $11.99 at **Kitchen Etc.**

RECINPES

September & October 2002

PHOTOGRAPHY: CARL TREMBLAY

Simple Applesauce, 19

Tuscan-Style Roast Pork Loin, 11

Pan-Roasted Chicken, 7

Simple Lasagna, 15

Greek Salad, 20

http://www.cooksillustrated.com

If you enjoy *Cook's Illustrated* magazine, you should visit our Web site. Simply log on to http://www.cooksillustrated.com. Although much of the information is free, database searches are for site subscribers only. *Cook's Illustrated* subscribers are offered a 20 percent discount.

Here are some of the things you can do on our site:

Search Our Recipes: We have a searchable database of all the recipes from *Cook's Illustrated*.

Search Tastings and Cookware Ratings: You will find all of our reviews (cookware, food, wine, cookbooks) plus new material created exclusively for the Web.

Find Your Favorite Quick Tips.

Check Your Subscription: Check the status of your subscription, pay a bill, or give a gift subscription online.

Visit Our Bookstore: You can purchase any of our cookbooks, hardbound annual editions of the magazine, or posters online.

Subscribe to *e-Notes:* Our free e-mail companion to the magazine offers cooking advice, test results, buying tips, and recipes each month.

Kung Pao Shrimp, 9

Green Goddess Dip, 13

AMERICA'S TEST KITCHEN

Join the millions of cooks who watch our show, *America's Test Kitchen*, on public television each week. For more information, including recipes from the show and a schedule of program times in your area, visit http://www.americastestkitchen.com.

Poached Pear and Almond Tart, 24

Corn and Apricot Muffins, 22

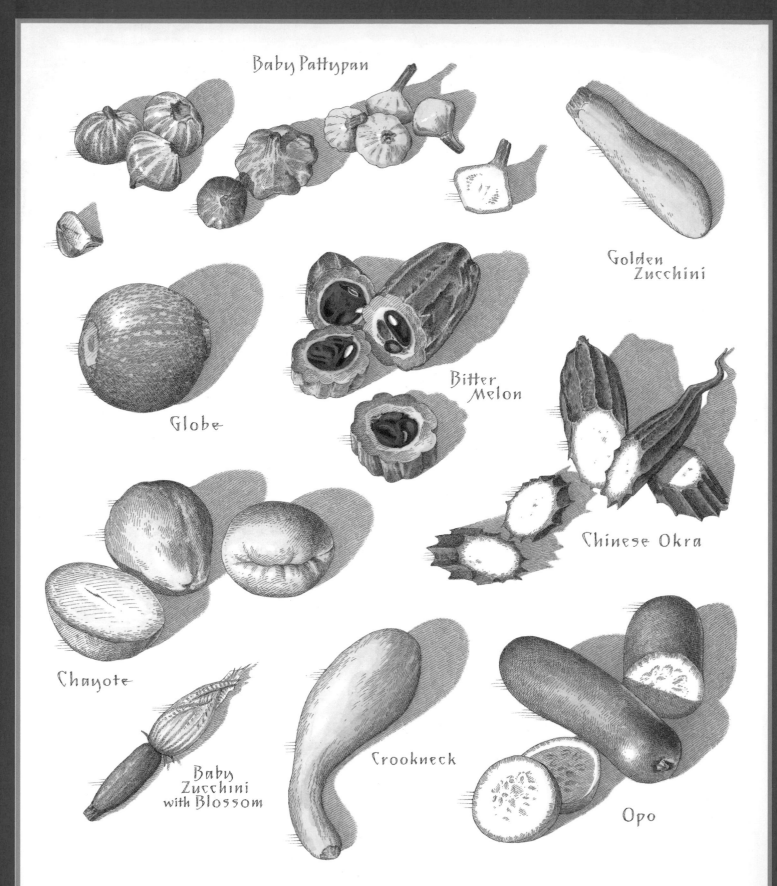

Baby Pattypan

Golden Zucchini

Globe

Bitter Melon

Chinese Okra

Chayote

Baby Zucchini with Blossom

Crookneck

Opo

SUMMER SQUASHES

NUMBER FIFTY-NINE

NOVEMBER & DECEMBER 2002

COOK'S
ILLUSTRATED

How to Roast a 20-Pound Turkey

Easy Chocolate Mousse Cake
Rich, Creamy, and Moist

Testing Chef's Knives
Does Price Matter?

Roast Beef and Yorkshire Pudding

Mashed Sweet Potatoes
New Stovetop Technique

Best Sugar Cookies
50 Batches Yield Winning Recipe

Rating Baking Chocolates

Sour Cream Coffee Cake

Smothered Pork Chops

Wild Rice Pilaf Perfected

Quick Pasta and Broccoli

www.cooksillustrated.com

$4.95 U.S./$6.95 CANADA

CONTENTS
November & December 2002

COOK'S
ILLUSTRATED
Home of America's Test Kitchen
www.cooksillustrated.com

FOUNDER AND EDITOR
Christopher Kimball
EXECUTIVE EDITOR
Jack Bishop
SENIOR EDITORS
Adam Ried
Dawn Yanagihara
DIRECTOR OF EDITORIAL OPERATIONS
Barbara Bourassa
ART DIRECTOR
Amy Klee
TEST KITCHEN DIRECTOR
Erin McMurrer
SENIOR EDITOR, BOOKS
Julia Collin
SENIOR WRITERS
Bridget Lancaster
Sally Sampson
ASSOCIATE EDITOR
Matthew Card
COPY EDITOR
India Koopman
MANAGING EDITOR,
BOOKS AND WEB SITE
Rebecca Hays
ASSISTANT TEST KITCHEN DIRECTOR
Meg Suzuki
TEST COOKS
Shannon Blaisdell
Erika Bruce
Keith Dresser
CONTRIBUTING EDITOR
Elizabeth Germain
CONSULTING EDITORS
Shirley Corriher
Jasper White
Robert L. Wolke
KITCHEN ASSISTANT
Rochelle Rashotsky
TEST KITCHEN INTERNS
Rajeev Samantrai
Merrill Stubbs
Nina West
ASSISTANT TO THE PUBLISHER
Sumantha Selvakumar
PROOFREADER
Jana Branch

VICE PRESIDENT MARKETING
David Mack
RETAIL SALES MANAGER
Jason Geller
CIRCULATION RETAIL SALES MANAGER
Jonathan Venier
SALES REPRESENTATIVE
Shekinah Cohn
MARKETING ASSISTANT
Connie Forbes
CIRCULATION MANAGER
Larisa Greiner
PRODUCTS MANAGER
Steven Browall
DIRECT MAIL MANAGER
Robert Lee
CUSTOMER SERVICE MANAGER
Jacqueline Valerio
CUSTOMER SERVICE REPRESENTATIVE
Julie Gardner

VICE PRESIDENT OPERATIONS
AND TECHNOLOGY
James McCormack
PRODUCTION MANAGER
Jessica Quirk
PRODUCTION COORDINATOR
Mary Connelly
PRODUCTION ASSISTANTS
Ron Bilodeau
Jennifer McCreary
PRODUCTION INTERNS
Yasmin Ali
Isabela Bermudez
SYSTEMS ADMINISTRATOR
Richard Cassidy
WEBMASTER
Nicole Morris
CHIEF FINANCIAL OFFICER
Sharyn Chabot
CONTROLLER
Mandy Shito
OFFICE MANAGER
Ruth Duncan
RECEPTIONIST
Henrietta Murray
PUBLICITY
Deborah Broide

For list rental information, contact The SpecialiSTS, 1200 Harbor Blvd. 9th Floor, Weehawken, NJ 07087; 201-865-5800; fax 201-867-2450. Editorial office: 17 Station Street, Brookline, MA 02445; 617-232-1000; fax 617-232-1572. Editorial contributions should be sent to: Editor, *Cook's Illustrated*. We cannot assume responsibility for manuscripts submitted to us. Submissions will be returned only if accompanied by a large self-addressed envelope. Postmaster: Send all new orders, subscription inquiries, and change of address notices to: *Cook's Illustrated*, P.O. Box 7446, Red Oak, IA 51591-0446. PRINTED IN THE USA.

SWEET POTATOES Tuberous root vegetables belonging to the same family of plants as the morning glory, sweet potatoes come in many shapes, sizes, and colors. Beauregard, Jewel, and Red Garnet are orange-fleshed, or "traditional," sweet potatoes, with Beauregards being the most widely available. When in doubt, you can bet you've bought a Beauregard. When cooked, all three have a decidedly loose, nonstarchy texture and sweet flavor. In most of the world, sweet potatoes have reddish skins and ivory-colored, starchy flesh. Varieties of white sweet potatoes sold in this country include the Japanese Sweet, White Sweet, and Batata (or Boniato). Of the three, Batatas are probably the most widely available, especially in markets serving Latino communities. Okinawa sweet potatoes have paper-thin tan skins and brilliant purple flesh. See page 15 for details about the flavor and textural characteristics of each variety.

COVER (*Pears*): ELIZABETH BRANDON, BACK COVER (*Sweet Potatoes*): JOHN BURGOYNE

A CHRISTMAS CAROL

Chef Scrooge was a mean cook, the type who would thin the chicken stock with dishwater if he could get away with it, the broad sweep of his chef's jacket a history of his desultory profession, the blotches of sauce faded not with time but as a reflection of their weak, underseasoned origins, penurious Scrooge having little truck with the best of ingredients—or any ingredients at all, if the truth be told. It was said that Chef Scrooge would be happiest making stone soup for not a farthing would be expended in the pursuit of taste; not a halfpenny's worth of pleasure could be extracted from its damnable origins, which suited Scrooge just fine since a shilling spent on good cheer and fellowship was a shilling wasted. Rumors of butter thinned with candle grease, chocolate bound with brick dust, and bread stretched with alum were no foreigners to the ears of Chef Scrooge, who plied his trade at the Marleybone Hotel to the great profit of his employers, who pocketed the fruits of his black, cold kitchen as one might pluck coins from the eyes of the dead.

So it was one Christmas Eve that Scrooge was busy extracting the maximum profit from a meager feast of mock turtle soup (could a faint undercurrent of horsemeat be detected by those with sensitive palates?) and squab pie (were there, as some had noted, fewer soot-dyed city pigeons in the area of the Marleybone?), with a great sack of boiled rice pudding for dessert. For the pudding, Scrooge needed sugar, an ingredient he guarded like a rat with a juicy morsel, trusting not even the hotel's head butler, Mr. Cratchit, with the keys to the larder.

It was there, in the dark recesses of his culinary vault, that Chef Scrooge was astonished to see the long-dead Chef Marley seated on a coarse three-legged stool. Here was his great mentor and benefactor, the man who had taught him the difference between pleasure and profit, who had threaded the needle so cleverly through the eye of the public's indifference to quality that Scrooge looked upon him as a minor deity, one who could sate the gross appetites of the rich and strip them of their wealth in the bargain.

"Scrooge . . . Scrooge," moaned Marley, his tremendous girth now reduced to a beggar's frame, the weight of shame having pulled the tallow skin of his bony face earthward, leaving two eyes burning bright in their sockets with visions of eternal purgatory. Chained to Marley's neck were the tools of his profession—

pots, pans, knives, whisks, rolling pins, a large chinois—the lot clanging loudly as he turned his head to speak once again.

"You will be visited this night by three ghosts. Take heed, Scrooge, and listen well, or you will be doomed to walk this earth like the man before you." Then Marley dissolved from sight, the last of him to fade being his eyes, which finally popped out like two snuffed candles leaving but a wisp of smoke.

Chef Scrooge quickly disregarded this incident in the larder as no more than a bit of undigested pudding, his greasy offering want to provide the customer with a nightmare or much worse long after the eating. It came as a quick shock, then, that at the stroke of midnight, as Scrooge was abed, he heard his name called out yet again.

"Scrooge, take my hand and we will visit Christmas Past," said a giant, dressed in green velvet, a wide red belt, and a soft crown of ermine and feathers. Suddenly, Scrooge was standing beside the dining table of his childhood, which was laid with a grand Christmas feast. Children scampered under the table, spirits were lively, and the scene softened Scrooge's fearsome countenance like that of a dog starved for affection. As Scrooge moved to take his place at the table, the ghost whisked Scrooge back to his cold, hard bed with a wave of his hand.

At the stroke of one, Scrooge was awakened a second time by the Ghost of Christmas Present who transported him to the dark, cheaply furnished dining room of the Marleybone, where couples sat without conversation, consuming sour joints of beef in an effort to dispose of hunger with the least expenditure of time or shillings. In an instant, this economy of pleasure, this triumph of hunger over soul, weighed heavily upon Scrooge, whose own thirst for the pleasures of the table had been rekindled.

Back in his bed, in a chilled sweat of fitful visions, Scrooge was awakened a third and last time by the Ghost of Christmas Future. There, where the Marleybone once stood, was a cheap, brightly colored storefront with a sign advertising "Marleybone Fish and Chips," with customers seated in molded plastic chairs, feeding

Christopher Kimball

on piles of greasy fried fish and chips, wrapped in yesterday's edition of the *Daily Sun*.

"Cannot the future be changed?" yelled Scrooge, the stench of old frying oil filling him with visions of Marley dragging his useless pots and pans into a heartless future. He at once drifted back into fitful sleep.

Chef Scrooge awoke unsure of his mortality. Had he died in his sleep, or had it all been just another long night of indigestion? He ran to the window, threw it open, and leaned out.

"You, boy, what day is this?" cried out Scrooge.

"Why, don't you know, sir? It is Christmas Day," replied the astonished young man.

"Well then, my fine fellow, run to the Poulterer's and buy me his three fattest geese and deliver them to the Marleybone Hotel. Here is three quid for your trouble and there are two more if you make it quick." Scrooge danced a little jig and raced off to the hotel.

Those lucky few who had Christmas dinner at the Marleybone that day would, even years later, become curiously wistful at the memory of it, as if the food itself had transported them to another, less earthbound, place. For some it was the skin of the goose—so crisp, thin, and perfectly roasted that it literally crackled between the teeth—and for others it was the desserts, fantasies of puddings so rich yet light that those who ate them said it recalled their childhood, each bite another warm memory of a mother's touch or a bedtime story.

To this day, it is said that Scrooge knew how to keep Christmas well because he discovered that those who cook for others are the richest among us, that the greatest profit margins are to be had not from thrift of spirit but from good fellowship and the gift of well-prepared food. Like a man humbled before the bench, Chef Scrooge would stand at the end of the feast and offer his guests a toast to a dark future that never came, to a life that was redeemed, and to the great tradition of the holiday table. Then, with an arm around the venerable butler, Mr. Cratchit, Scrooge would drain his punch, light the Christmas pudding, and say, with a happy twinkle in his eye, "God bless us, every one."

A Not So Salty Brine?

I've tried brining three or four times, and the meat always tastes much too salty for me. I don't use much salt in my cooking and was wondering if I should try brining with less salt.

KERRY TAYLOR
SUBMITTED VIA E-MAIL

➤ Our basic brining formula calls for ½ cup kosher salt (or ¼ cup table salt) and ½ cup sugar dissolved in 1 quart cold water (per pound of food), with food left to soak one hour per pound. We developed the formula with two goals in mind: to season the food through and through, such that even a 12-pound turkey would be seasoned right to the bone, and to provide a cushion of moisture that would keep the food from drying out as it cooked (or overcooked). With the exception of one editor, who, like you, thinks brined food is too salty and uses a very light hand with the salt shaker, everyone in the test kitchen likes the effect the brine has on flavor. For the sake of that editor and readers like yourself, however, we wanted to see if we could keep food moist without using so much seasoning.

We prepared two brines, one at the full strength of our basic formula and one at half strength. We brined 1 pound of shrimp, 1 pound of pork chops, and one whole chicken in the full-strength brine and did the same in the half-strength brine. We also cooked a batch of the same three foods with no brine at all as a baseline. Once the shrimp had been sautéed, the pork chops pan-fried, and the chicken roasted, we gathered around to check the results. What we found was that the foods brined in the half-strength solution were quite a bit less salty, but they were also quite a bit less moist than the foods brined at full strength. This was especially noticeable with the pork chops. While the chops treated with the half-strength brine were marginally more moist than unbrined chops, they were much drier and tougher than the chops brined at full strength. This is probably because the salt, and to some extent the sugar, acts not just to draw moisture into the food and provide seasoning but also to tenderize it by breaking down some of the proteins. The shrimp and chicken brined at half strength were a bit more juicy than the unbrined shrimp and chicken, but the difference was not enough for us to recommend that anyone take the trouble to brine at half strength; the results just aren't that impressive.

If you are very sensitive to salt, we recommend that you skip brining. Do take extra care not to overcook your food; in our experience, home cooks are more likely to overcook food than undercook it, and there's no better way to dry out a pork chop or a chicken breast than to overcook it.

What Is Vegetable Oil?

The instructions for frying taco shells in the May/June 2002 issue of the magazine call for corn, vegetable, or canola oil. Aren't corn and canola oils made from vegetables? How about safflower or peanut oil? In the same issue, you also list "vegetable oil" in the recipes for jambalaya and garlic-lemon potatoes. What is what with these different oils?

GORDON WALKER
ANAHEIM, CALIF.

➤ Loosely speaking, a vegetable oil is an edible oil made from any number of "vegetable" (as opposed to "mineral") sources, including nuts, grains, beans, seeds, and olives. In the more narrow confines of recipe writing, it usually refers to one of the more popular brands of cooking oil in the supermarket whose front label reads "Vegetable Oil" in large type; on closer inspection of the small type on the back label, you'll usually find that these generic vegetable oils consist of soybean oil. "Vegetable oil" is often the ingredient of choice in recipes that call for an oil with no flavor. All of the oils you mention, in addition to soybean oil, fall into this category, although some cooks would argue that corn and especially peanut oil have distinct flavors that should be kept in mind when used in any dish. In our taco recipe, as well as in the jambalaya and the garlic-lemon potatoes, any tasteless oil, including "vegetable" (that is, soybean) oil, canola oil, or safflower oil, would do just fine.

Boiling Potatoes

Your beef stew recipe (January/February 1996) calls for "boiling potatoes." What kinds of potatoes are classified as boiling potatoes?

MARY MCLANE
EAST HARWICH, MASS

➤ The most common boiling potatoes in the grocery store are round, thin-skinned red potatoes. (Boiling potatoes can also be white skinned.) These low-starch potatoes hold their shape well when cooked, and it is for this reason that we recommend them for use in stews as well as salads. The most popular variety is Red Bliss, and we generally use this boiling potato in the test kitchen. (In more recent recipes, we generally call for this potato by name or specify red-skinned potatoes and don't use the term *boiling potato*.) That said

FOR MORE INFORMATION

www.cooksillustrated.com

At the *Cook's Illustrated* Web site you can order a book, give a gift subscription to *Cook's Illustrated* magazine, sign up for our free e-newsletter, subscribe to the magazine, or check the status of your subscription. Join the Web site and you'll have access to our searchable databases of recipes, cookware ratings, ingredient tastings, quick tips, cookbook reviews, and more.

COOK'S ILLUSTRATED Magazine

Cook's Illustrated (ISSN 1068-2821) magazine is published bimonthly (6 issues per year) by Boston Common Press Limited Partnership, 17 Station Street, Brookline, MA 02445. Copyright 2002 Boston Common Press Limited Partnership. Periodical postage paid at Boston, Mass., and additional mailing offices, USPS #012487.

A one-year subscription is $29.70, two years is $55, and three years is $75. Add $6 postage per year for Canadian subscriptions and $12 per year for all other countries outside the U.S. To order subscriptions in the U.S. call 800-526-8442. Gift subscriptions are available for $24.95 each. Postmaster: Send all new orders, subscription inquiries, and change-of-address notices to *Cook's Illustrated*, P.O. Box 7446, Red Oak, IA 51591-0446, or call 800-526-8442 inside the U.S. and 515-247-7571 outside the U.S.

COOKBOOKS

You can order the following books, as well as *The America's Test Kitchen Cookbook*, by calling 800-611-0759 inside the U.S. and 515-246-6911 outside the U.S.

➤ **The Best Recipe Series** Includes *The Best Recipe* as well as *Grilling & Barbecue*, *Soups & Stews*, *American Classics*, and *Italian Classics*.
➤ **The How to Cook Master Series** A collection of 25 single-subject cookbooks.
➤ **The Annual Series** Annual hardbound editions of the magazine as well as a ten-year (1993–2002) reference index.

AMERICA'S TEST KITCHEN Television Show

Look for our television series on public television. Go to http://www.americastestkitchen.com for program times in your area, recipes, and details about the shows, or to order the companion book to the current season, *The America's Test Kitchen Cookbook*.

any red-skinned potato will do well in this stew. Note that baking potatoes, such as russets, are high in starch and tend to fall apart and become mealy if boiled or simmered in a stew. They do, however, take very nicely to melted butter and, if you're mashing them, to milk or cream, because they contain less moisture than boiling potatoes.

Baking Powder Failure

I made the carrot cake in your January/February 1998 issue, and it turned out more like a carrot brick. I suspect something was wrong with one of the ingredients. Does baking powder have a shelf life? If so, what is the best way to store it?

DIANE BUTLER
SUBMITTED VIA E-MAIL

➤ Baking powder generally has a shelf life of one to two years, and manufacturers stamp the can (often on the bottom) with a "use-by" date that tells you when its time is up. The enemies of baking powder are moisture and heat, according to Nita Livvix, laboratory supervisor at Hulman and Company, maker of Rumford and Clabber Girl baking powders. Both cause the leavening agents in baking powder to react and create the carbon dioxide gas that should have leavened your carrot cake. Livvix stressed that for maximum shelf life baking powder should be stored in a place that is cool and dry (the latter rules out the refrigerator, which is a source of moisture). If a can of baking powder is close to its expiration date, you can check the viability of the powder by adding ½ teaspoon to 1 cup of tap water. If it fizzes energetically, it's still active and usable.

Approximating Whole Milk

I frequently come across recipes calling for whole milk. However, my refrigerator is usually stocked with 2 percent milk and half-and-half (for my coffee). Is there a combination of these two that would be an adequate substitute for whole milk, and, if so, what is the ratio?

MICHELLE KALBAC
LOS ANGELES, CALIF.

➤ The fat content of dairy products is established by the U.S. Food and Drug Administration, with whole milk, half-and-half, light cream, and so on each requiring a minimum percentage of fat to qualify as what their label says. Whole milk must have a fat content of at least 3½ percent; half-and-half, which is equal parts light cream and whole milk, must have at least 10 percent. (Light cream must be at least 18 percent milk fat.) If your recipe calls for whole milk and all you have on hand is 2 percent milk and half-and-half, the goal is to get as close to 3½ percent fat as possible. A ratio of 3 parts 2 percent milk to 1 part half-and-half will give you a fat content of 4 percent, which puts you in the ballpark—close enough to work in just about any recipe

WHAT IS IT?

This rolling pin, which has 12 individual squared-off designs carved right into it, intrigued me when I saw it at an auction, and so I bid for it. I got it, along with another plain, hand-tooled rolling pin, for $25. I'd like to know first if there's a name for this fancier rolling pin and second if you think I got a good deal for it.

DIANA M. KELLY
BIG FLATS, N.Y.

This "fancy" rolling pin is designed to make springerle cookies, a holiday tradition in Germany and Switzerland, where the cookies are thought to have originated as early as the 15th century. The first springerle cookies were not made with rolling pins but with hand-carved molds made from flat pieces of wood. Like your rolling pin, some of the flat molds were divided into 12 or 16 pieces to create small square cookies, whereas others consisted of one large and often elaborate design. The cookies were often made to commemorate holidays, including Christmas, and were sometimes substituted for tithes by poorer members of the church. The designs on the cookies might reflect the occasion in religious themes or depict scenes from everyday life, such as a hunter with his kill or a woman at a spinning wheel. Farm animals and flowers were also popular. One of the earliest images carved into the wood was a leaping horse. In Old German, the word *springerle* is thought to mean "little horse" or "leaping horse."

The first springerle cookies were made from a stiff gingerbread-like dough consisting mostly of eggs, sugar, and flour. Over time the signature flavors of the cookie came to be anise and lemon, and most modern recipes include anise oil or seeds and lemon rind. To make the cookies, you first roll the dough out flat with a regular pin. You then run the springerle pin over the dough, pressing down to imprint the dough with the pictures on the pin. The dough is then cut into squares, as indicated by the arrangement of the pictures. The cookies are sometimes painted with colored icing, and, like gingerbread cookies, are sturdy enough to be used as ornaments for a Christmas tree.

Did you get a good deal on your springerle rolling pin? It sounds fair. We purchased one from www.cooking.com for $12.95. This site and others sell both pins and flat molds with different designs.

that calls for whole milk. Following are ratios for mixing skim or nonfat milk (milk fat less than ½ percent), 1 percent milk, and 2 percent milk with half-and-half to get an approximate equivalent of whole milk.

TO GET 1 CUP WHOLE MILK, COMBINE:
⅝ cup skim or nonfat milk with ⅜ cup half-and-half
⅔ cup 1 percent milk with ⅓ cup half-and-half
¾ cup 2 percent milk with ¼ cup half-and-half

Chili Powders

We were surprised to see "chili powder" listed as an ingredient for the tacos in your May/June 2002 issue with no further ado. "Chili powder" is one of those trick ingredients, no? It can refer either to pure ground chiles (what you might get from a specialty spice house) or to the standard supermarket blend, which tends to include cumin and oregano, among other ingredients. We'd love to hear your thoughts on this spice blurring.

CATHERINE NEWMAN AND MICHAEL MILLNER
EAST HAMPTON, MASS.

➤ Chili powder (or chile powder) is a tricky term, and, as you suggest, it is often applied to both the blend of ground ingredients that goes into the spice many Americans use to make a pot of chili *and* any powder made from a single type of chile, be it ancho, pasilla, or otherwise. In our recipe for beef tacos, our goal was to refresh a dish that had been processed to the point of concentrating all the flavors—not just the components of chili powder—in a single packet. At the same time, we wanted the recipe to be simple enough and the ingredients easy enough to find so that readers would have no trouble putting it together for a weeknight dinner. And so the chili powder available in every supermarket—often a blend of one or two ground red chiles as well as cumin and oregano and sometimes salt, garlic, paprika, and more—seemed the right spice for this recipe.

In general, recipes calling for a powder made from a single type of chile will specify the type—as in ancho chile powder. (As you suggest, powders made from single chiles are available from specialty spice houses, including Penzeys Spices, which can be accessed at www.penzeys.com.) If you see only "chili powder" in an ingredient list, you can be pretty sure it's the blend. That said, there are differences in the blends available, as we found in the chili powder tasting reported in our September/October 2000 issue. Spice Islands Chili Powder was the winner of that tasting.

SEND US YOUR QUESTIONS We will provide a complimentary one-year subscription for each letter we print. Send your inquiry, name, address, and daytime telephone number to Notes from Readers, *Cook's Illustrated*, P.O. Box 470589, Brookline, MA 02447, or visit www.cooksillustrated.com

Quick Tips

Edible Toothpicks for Hors d'Oeuvres

Any number of hors d'oeuvres—including small meatballs, crab cakes, marinated mushrooms, bits of semi-soft cheese, and squares of Spanish omelet—are served with toothpick skewers. Eric Pryor of Brooklyn, N.Y., adds a little salty crunch to the equation and avoids the problem of used toothpick disposal by spearing his hors d'oeuvres with slender pretzel sticks, which can be eaten right along with the tasty tidbit it has skewered.

Can Opener Cleanliness

Though they might not admit it, many cooks do not clean their manual can opener after each use. Of course, a trip through the dishwasher cleans it up well (though you may risk a bit of rust), but for regular cleaning and/or those without a dishwasher, Tom Saaristo of Chicago, Ill., suggests running a folded sheet of paper towel through the opener. The paper towel does a great job of cleaning both the blade and the gear.

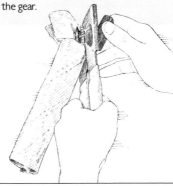

Easier Rinsing of Brined Poultry

Rinsing off the surface of brined poultry, as we did for the September/October 2002 recipe for pan-roasted chicken, is one way to ensure that the skin won't taste overly salty. Here is a method we discovered in the test kitchen to speed the rinsing process along.

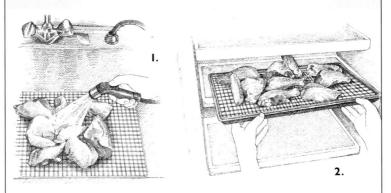

1. Place the chicken on a wire rack, set the rack in an empty sink, and use the sink sprayer to wash off the chicken. Then blot the chicken dry with paper towels.
2. If you plan to air-dry the chicken, simply set the rack with the towel-dried chicken pieces on a rimmed baking sheet or jelly roll pan and place the whole thing in the refrigerator.

Makeshift Dish-Drying Racks

Everyone dreads the huge pile of dishes that builds up after a dinner party or holiday gathering. In these situations, when the dishwasher and dish rack are full, drying space can be hard to come by. To create extra drying space for glasses and dishes, try one of the following tricks, suggested by readers Maria Mangano and her husband, Dan Read, of Durham, N.C., Marie Lambremont of Smyrna, Ga., and Alan Davison of North Falmouth, Mass.

A. Cooling racks used for baking are an ideal source of drying space, especially for delicate wine glasses. Place a towel underneath the rack to absorb the water that drips off the glasses.
B. Alternatively, set an oven rack over the sink. The air circulating on all sides of the rack will help dry dishes, glasses, and any other items placed on it.

Quick Dry for Baking Utensils

Most home bakers have just one piece of any given type of equipment, such as a strainer or sifter. Of course, these tools must be completely dry before you use them, but waiting for a just-washed strainer or sifter to dry fully can be frustrating, and it is easy to miss spots if you hand-dry with a dish towel. In the midst of a holiday baking bonanza, when in a rush to use her sifter, Donna Puorro of Framingham, Mass., came up with this way to dry it off quickly and completely.

Because the oven is on anyway, put the utensil in it to dry out. Set a timer for about two minutes to remind yourself that the utensil is in the oven. Just be sure that the utensil does not have any plastic parts that can melt. Because the utensil will be quite hot, use a mitt to protect your hand when you remove the utensil from the oven.

Preventing Sticky Jar Lids

Is there a cook out there who hasn't known the frustration of struggling with a sticky lid cemented to its jar? This problem is especially common when that jar is home to something sticky, such as maple syrup, molasses, honey, or flavored extracts. Sue Smialek of North Quincy, Mass., nips this problem in the bud with this easy tip.

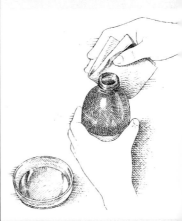

Dip a small piece of paper towel (or your impeccably clean fingertip) into a bit of vegetable oil and wipe the threads of the jar. The bare film of oil prevents the lid from sticking to the jar the next time you open it.

Send Us Your Tip We will provide a complimentary one-year subscription for each tip we print. Send your tip, name, address, and telephone number to Quick Tips, Cook's Illustrated, P.O. Box 470589, Brookline, MA 02447 or visit www.cooksillustrated.com

Getting a Clean Cut through Frozen Cookie Dough

With a roll of homemade cookie dough in the freezer, you can have hot, freshly baked cookies any time. Slicing through the frozen roll, however, can be a chore as the knife often drags, making sloppy cuts and producing mis-shapen cookies. Kerry Kresse of Madison, Wis., mini-mizes the sticky knife problem by dipping the blade in flour after each couple of cuts.

Heating Dinner Plates

Warm dinner plates make any meal special. David Johnson of Houston, Texas, warms all the plates and other dishes he needs (especially if the oven is in use) by running them through the dishwasher on the dry cycle.

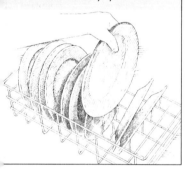

Getting Extra Use from Your Kitchen Torch

Crème brûlée aficionados use their kitchen torch to caramelize the sugar layer on their favorite dessert, but not for much else. Tired of extracting so little use from her torch, Sigrid Anderson of San Francisco, Calif., enlists it for extra browning of the already-baked meringue on meringue-topped pies, tartlets, and cakes.

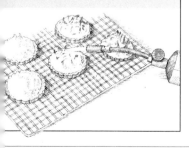

Keeping Cookies Separate as They Bake

Many types of cookies, including the sugar cookies on page 24, spread on the cookie sheet as they bake. If the balls of dough are placed too closely together on the sheet, they'll run into each other and fuse when they spread in the oven, resulting in cookies with odd shapes and soft edges. To give each cookie a little extra space without severely limiting the number of cookies baked in a batch, Hillary Noyes-Keene of Chilmark, Mass., arranges them as follows.

Instead of placing the dough balls in neat rows of three or four so that all the cookies line up, alternate the rows. For example, three cookies in the first row, two in the second, three in the third, two in the fourth, and so on.

Designated Serving Platters

Help transferring food to serving bowls and platters for a large dinner party or holiday meal is always welcome. But sometimes the host is busy cooking and unavailable to help match the food with his or her serving piece of choice. To get around this situation graciously and efficiently, Jenn Guille of Raleigh, N.C., labels the serving dishes and corresponding containers of food ahead of time with small Post-It notes to make it clear which foods and dishes go together.

Testing the Temperature of Leftovers

Judging the interior temperature of reheated leftovers such as lasagna or a casserole can be difficult. To avoid serving leftovers that are tepid at the center, try this trick from John Selen of Worcester, Mass.

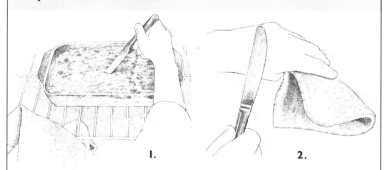

1.

2.

1. Before taking the casserole out of the oven, poke the center with the blade of a butter knife or dull dinner knife, and leave it in place for 15 to 30 seconds.
2. Remove the knife, and then touch the side of the blade very gently to the back of your hand. If the metal is hot, so, too, is the center of the casserole.

Alternative Turkey Tool

Some readers who tried our recipe for Crisp-Skin High-Roast Butterflied Turkey in the November/December 2001 issue reported some difficulty cutting the backbone out of a turkey. Shelley Sedwick of Glendale, Ariz., had trouble until she tried a clean (or new) pair of garden clippers. After cutting the bird's skin with a knife, she used the sturdy blades of her clippers to cut through the bones and wing tips, finding the clippers a good alternative to a dull knife.

Minimizing Sauté Splatter

When you are browning meat for a soup or stew, grease splatters on the stovetop and burners occasion a nasty mess and an unpleasant cleanup job. The stovetop is easy enough to wipe off, but cleaning the burners and burner plates is more involved. To keep unused burners from getting dirty in the first place, Constance Snyder of East Thetford, Vt., positions inverted disposable aluminum pie plates over them. The pie plates can be wiped clean and used again.

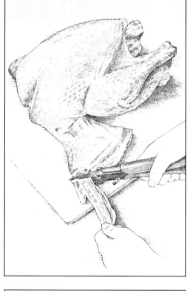

Sour Cream Coffee Cake

Forget about ersatz convenience-store cake. We set out to explore the secrets of the real thing: a dense, tender cake with a rich streusel topping.

≥ BY RAQUEL PELZEL AND BRIDGET LANCASTER ≤

offee cake has left home, abandoning grandma's kitchen for the industrial shelves full of supermarket ready-made pastries. Consisting of little more than a flat, dry, rectangular yellow cake topped with hard, pellet-like crumbs and nary a cinnamon swirl in sight, it is a far cry from the coffee cake of yesteryear—the sour cream coffee cake. This cake is distinguished by two indisputable facts. One: Hardly anyone makes it anymore (and that is a shame). Two: When it is made, it should be an ultra-moist cake, pleasantly rich and dense from the addition of sour cream.

That's not to say that there aren't some bad sour cream coffee cakes out there. They may be too dense and wet, too dry and tough, too sweet or too spicy, or just plain bland. The streusel inside the cake may be damp and pasty, and the streusel topping, if any, sometimes melts into the cake, while other times it stays sandy and granular.

After a first round of testing five different recipes, we came to a few conclusions. First, this is not a lean cake. Made from large amounts of sour cream, eggs, and butter, this cake is decadent. Second, we wanted to find a method of putting this cake together that was simple enough to tackle even before our first cup of coffee. Third, we love crispy, crunchy, yet melt-in-your-mouth streusel so much that we wanted not one but two layers of it on the inside, as well as a sizable amount on the cake top, and we knew that this would require a careful arrangement of sugar, flour, butter, nuts, and spices.

Lift and Structure

Cake flour is the norm in many sour cream coffee cake recipes, but this is a heavy cake that needs more structure, so we switched to the sturdier all-purpose flour. Brown sugar, a common coffee cake batter ingredient, had too much flavor, so we opted for the lower-profile granulated white sugar. We decided on four eggs, which produced the traditional buttery-yellow cake color and helped to provide for a tight crumb (we didn't want an open crumb, full of gaping, craggy holes). To give the cake tenderness and a capacity to remain moist for days, we relied on butter and, of course, sour cream. One-and-a-half sticks of butter and 1½ cups of sour cream produced the best flavor as well as a velvety mouthfeel. Quite a few recipes use both baking powder and baking soda

This classic breakfast cake comes together in about 30 minutes.

to lighten the cake's heavy load, and after testing a few cakes, we didn't disagree. (The baking soda, which reacts with acids to create lift, is necessary because of the quantity of sour cream used.) These recipes, however, used a mere ½ to 1 teaspoon of each, and we disliked the squat, dense cakes that were coming out of our oven. After increasing the amount of leavening bit by bit, we discovered that a hefty 1 tablespoon of baking powder along with ¾ teaspoon of baking soda would lift the cake to a nearly statuesque height.

For the mixing method, we started by creaming the butter and sugar (whipping them to incorporate air), a common cake-making technique. The resulting cake was pleasingly tall, but it also had a crumb that was airy and cakey instead of tight, as we wanted. We then tried a method used in our Rich and Tender Yellow Cake recipe, published in March/April 1999. This two-stage method starts out by taking slightly softened butter and, in our case, some of the sour cream and cutting them right into the dry ingredients, as is done for a pie dough. The liquid ingredients—in this case, eggs and more sour cream—are then mixed together, and added to the butter/sour cream/dry ingredient mixture. The batter is then beaten until aerated and pale in color. The result was a cake with a tight crumb and a tender texture, and, best of all, it was quick to put together.

Separate but Equal

The real joys of great sour cream coffee cake are its elegant streusel swirls and crunchy streusel topping. Starting with the sugar, we tried using solely brown sugar in the streusel, as many recipes dictate. We ended up preferring the appearance and flavor of a streusel made with both granulated and dark brown sugar. What we did not like was the way it melted and congealed into cement-like shards, so we took a cue from several recipes and added flour to prevent this from happening. Cinnamon, nutmeg, allspice, cloves, and even cocoa make regular appearances in streusel. In the end, cinnamon—and a potent 2 tablespoons of it at that—was the only spice needed to lend warmth to the streusel's flavor.

Our coffee cake was now well on the road to success, but some tasters objected to the use of nuts in the streusel to be used as filling. The answer? We blended the basic streusel ingredients—flour, granulated sugar, and brown sugar—together in the food processor, then removed some of the mixture to a bowl to use as filling. Nuts went into the food processor for the topping. Because butter made the interior layers of streusel pasty and mealy, we reserved it, along with the nuts, for the topping. We also found that we preferred the texture of streusel topping made by cutting cold butter into the dry ingredients; melted butter produced unsightly knobby chunks of streusel. As far as the interior streusel, we wanted it to be sweeter than the topping, so we added another ¼ cup of brown sugar. Even though the streusels get different treatments, they require little more work.

Bake Me a Cake

Now we had the cake, the streusel filling, and the streusel topping ready to go. All we had to do was bake. Easier said than done. Time after time we ended up with cakes that seemed underdone. We tried placing a cake in a hot 475-degree oven then immediately lowering the temperature. Unfortunately, this blast of heat was enough to burn the sugary streusel topping. We tried adding the streusel 30 minutes into the baking time, but this meant maneuvering a hot pan out of and into the oven—not the safest approach to baking

I. Using rubber spatula, spread 2 cups batter in bottom of prepared pan, smoothing surface.

2. Sprinkle evenly with ¾ cup streusel filling without butter or nuts.

3. Repeat steps I and 2 with 2 cups batter and remaining streusel without butter or nuts.

4. Spread remaining batter over, then sprinkle with streusel topping with butter and nuts.

coffee cake. We then realized that moving the oven rack might solve this problem. Baking the cake on the bottom oven rack at a steady 350 degrees for a full hour produced a cake that was cooked all the way through yet was still pleasingly tall. What's more, the streusel was perfectly browned. We found it best to let the cake cool in the pan for at least 30 minutes before unmolding to keep it from cracking. Best of all, if stored well, this cake actually improves with age.

SOUR CREAM COFFEE CAKE WITH BROWN SUGAR–PECAN STREUSEL
SERVES 12 TO 16

Refer to the illustrations above when layering the batter and streusel in the pan. A fixed-bottom, 10-inch tube pan (with 10-cup capacity) is best for this recipe. (See "The Right Pan," right.) Note that the streusel is divided into two parts—one for the inner swirls, one for the topping.

Streusel
- ¾ cup (3¾ ounces) unbleached all-purpose flour
- ¾ cup (5¼ ounces) granulated sugar
- ½ cup (3½ ounces) packed dark brown sugar
- 2 tablespoons ground cinnamon
- 2 tablespoons cold unsalted butter, cut into 2 pieces
- 1 cup pecans, chopped

Cake
- 12 tablespoons (1½ sticks) unsalted butter, softened but still cool, cut into ½-inch cubes, plus 2 tablespoons softened butter for greasing pan
- 4 large eggs
- 1½ cups sour cream
- 1 tablespoon vanilla extract
- 2¼ cups (11½ ounces) unbleached all-purpose flour
- 1¼ cups (8¾ ounces) granulated sugar
- 1 tablespoon baking powder
- ¾ teaspoon baking soda
- ¾ teaspoon salt

1. FOR THE STREUSEL: In food processor, process flour, granulated sugar, ¼ cup dark brown sugar, and cinnamon until combined, about 15 seconds. Transfer 1¼ cups of flour/sugar mixture to small bowl; stir in remaining ¼ cup brown sugar and set aside to use for streusel filling. Add butter and pecans to mixture in food processor; pulse until nuts and butter resemble small pebbly pieces, about ten 1-second pulses. Set aside to use as streusel topping.

2. FOR THE CAKE: Adjust oven rack to lowest position and heat oven to 350 degrees. Grease 10-inch tube pan with 2 tablespoons softened butter. Whisk eggs, 1 cup sour cream, and vanilla in medium bowl until combined.

3. Combine flour, sugar, baking powder, baking soda, and salt in bowl of standing mixer; mix on low speed for 30 seconds to blend. Add butter and remaining ½ cup sour cream; mix on low speed until dry ingredients are moistened and mixture resembles wet sand, with few large butter pieces remaining, about 1½ minutes. Increase to medium speed and beat until batter comes together, about 10 seconds; scrape down sides of bowl with rubber spatula. Lower speed to medium-low and gradually add egg mixture in 3 additions, beating for 20 seconds after each and scraping down sides of bowl. Increase speed to medium-high and beat until batter is light and fluffy, about 1 minute.

4. Using rubber spatula, spread 2 cups batter in bottom of prepared pan, smoothing surface. Sprinkle evenly with ¾ cup streusel filling (*without* butter or nuts). Repeat with another 2 cups batter and remaining ¾ cup streusel filling (*without* butter or nuts). Spread remaining batter over, then sprinkle with streusel topping (*with* butter and nuts).

5. Bake until cake feels firm to touch and long toothpick or skewer inserted into center comes out clean (bits of sugar from streusel may cling to tester), 50 to 60 minutes. Cool cake in pan on wire rack 30 minutes. Invert cake onto rimmed baking sheet (cake will be streusel-side down); remove tube pan, place wire rack on top of cake, and reinvert cake streusel-side up. Cool to room temperature, about 2 hours. Cut into wedges and serve. (Cake can be wrapped in foil and stored at room temperature for up to 5 days.)

LEMON-BLUEBERRY SOUR CREAM COFFEE CAKE

Toss 1 cup frozen blueberries with 1 teaspoon grated lemon zest in small bowl. Follow recipe for Sour Cream Coffee Cake with Brown Sugar–Pecan Streusel, sprinkling ½ cup blueberries over bottom and middle layers cake batter before sprinkling with streusel.

SOUR CREAM COFFEE CAKE WITH CHOCOLATE CHIPS

Follow recipe for Sour Cream Coffee Cake with Brown Sugar–Pecan Streusel, sprinkling ½ cup chocolate chips over bottom layer cake batter and additional ½ cup chocolate chips over middle layer cake batter before sprinkling with streusel.

APRICOT-ALMOND SOUR CREAM COFFEE CAKE

Follow recipe for Sour Cream Coffee Cake with Brown Sugar–Pecan Streusel, substituting 1 cup slivered almonds for pecans in streusel and ½ teaspoon almond extract for vanilla extract in batter. Measure ½ cup apricot jam; spoon jam in six 2-teaspoon mounds over bottom and middle layers cake batter before sprinkling with streusel.

The Right Pan

BUNDT PAN   TUBE PAN

Both Bundt and tube pans are used in coffee cake recipes. A Bundt pan bakes the cake upside-down, and, when flipped upright, the bottom becomes the top. We didn't care for the streusel topping baked in this pan. It never became crunchy, and it was compacted from the weight of the batter. The tube pan won hands down for presentation. We prefer a tube pan made from a single piece of metal, because it won't leak, as sometimes happens with a two-piece pan with a removable bottom. In a pinch you can use a tube pan with a removable bottom (also called an angel food cake pan). Set this pan on a large sheet of foil, then fold the foil up and around the sides of the pan before filling it with batter. If the pan springs small leaks during baking, the foil will catch the batter.

Smothered Pork Chops

Skip the condensed soup and thick-cut chops for deep flavor and tender meat.

≥ BY MATTHEW CARD AND ADAM RIED ≤

Smothered pork chops, a homey dish of chops braised in deeply flavored onion gravy, are a perfect counterpoint to the rarefied tastes of the holidays. Palates challenged by cocktail party canapés and plum pudding crave something hearty and simple, and smothered chops fit the bill—they are folksy, not fancy; denim, not worsted wool.

The cooking process seemed straightforward: Brown the chops, remove them from the pan, brown the onions, return the chops and cover them with the onions and gravy (hence the term *smothered*), and braise until tender. But initial recipe tests produced bland, dry pork and near-tasteless gravies with woeful consistencies ranging from pasty to processed to gelatinous to watery.

Poor texture and shallow flavor rob smothered pork chops of their savory-sweet glory. To get this recipe right, we knew we'd have to identify the best chop and the best way to cook it. And the gravy was no less important. We wanted a heady, multidimensional flavor, bold onion presence, and a satiny, just-thick-enough texture.

Chop Shopping

Some of the recipes we looked at specified sirloin chops, which are cut from the rear end of the loin. Our tasters found this cut a little dry, and in any case it's often unavailable. Blade chops, cut from the far front end of the loin, were juicier, but they suffer the same spotty availability. Of the two remaining types of chops, center-cut loin and rib, we found the latter to be the juiciest and most flavorful because it has a bit more fat.

We tried rib chops as thick as 1½ inches and as thin as ½ inch and were shocked when tasters unanimously chose the thin ½-inch chops. Thick chops overwhelmed the gravy, which we felt should share equal billing with the meat. Thin chops also picked up more onion flavor during cooking. While we were at it we tried boneless chops, but they turned out dry, so we decided to stick with bone-in for optimum juiciness.

The browned chops are covered with cooked onions and then "smothered" with a roux-thickened gravy.

Also in the service of juiciness (and thorough seasoning), we indulged our passion for brining by soaking the chops in a simple solution of salt, sugar, and water before cooking them. But brining turned out to be ill-suited to this dish for two reasons. First, the chops cook in a moist environment provided by the gravy, so why spend time instilling extra moisture to protect them from the harsh, dry heat of grilling, searing, or roasting? Second, no matter how we adjusted the salinity of the brine, the salt-infused meat caused the gravy to become intolerably salty.

Last we tackled the question of cooking time. Although we prefer to slightly undercook pork to ensure tenderness, this is one application in which further cooking was necessary, because we wanted to infuse the meat with the flavor of the gravy and onions. After their initial browning, the chops registered a rosy 140 degrees on an instant-read thermometer. They were cooked through and tender, but since they had yet to be smothered, they had none of the onion flavor we

were after. Fifteen minutes of braising in the gravy boosted the flavor but toughened the chops, which now registered almost 200 degrees. At that temperature, the meat fibers have contracted and expelled moisture, but the fat and connective tissue between the fibers, called collagen, have not had a chance to melt fully and turn into gelatin. It is this gelatin that makes braised meats especially rich and tender. Another 15 minutes of braising solved the problem. At this point, the chops registered 210 degrees, and the extra time allowed the fat and collagen to melt completely, so the meat was tender and succulent in addition to being oniony from the gravy.

Great Gravy

We wanted our gravy to build on the flavor of the browned pork chops. The canned, condensed soup called for in some recipes produced gravies that tasted processed. Water produced a weak, thin gravy, but chicken broth improved the picture, adding much needed flavor.

For liquid to morph into gravy, it must be thickened. Cornstarch is an easy solution, but it resulted in a gelatinous, translucent sauce that felt wrong. Next we tried flour, adding it in three different ways. Flouring the chops before browning turned their exteriors gummy and left the gravy with a chalky mouthfeel. Flouring the onions left the gravy tasting of raw flour. At last we called upon a roux, a common mixture of flour and fat (in this case, vegetable oil) cooked together. This occasioned the use of an extra pan, but the results were fantastic. The roux was easy to make, it thickened the sauce reliably without imparting the taste of raw flour, and it gave the gravy a smooth finish and another layer of flavor that was slightly nutty.

The roux was good, but we tried to improve it with two oft-used refinements. First, we fried a couple of slices of bacon and substituted the rendered fat for the vegetable oil in the roux. What a hit! The sweet/salty/smoky bacon flavor underscored and deepened all other flavors in the dish. Beyond that, we followed in the footsteps of those gravy masters who eke out even more flavor from their roux by browning it for five minutes to the shade of peanut butter. Cooking the flour unlocks a rich, toasty flavor that builds as the color of the roux deepens. Using bacon and cooking the roux in this way are widespread and justly popular techniques, and they turned out to be huge flavor builders.

Much Depends on Onions

The onions play a title role in the gravy. We tried them minced, chopped, and sliced both thick and thin. Thin-sliced onions cooked to a melting texture was our favorite. We tried different quantities of onions, from one to four, for four pork chops, and found that two worked best. We tried simply softening the onions until they were translucent rather than cooking them for a few minutes until their edges browned, a winning technique that accentuated their natural sweetness. Perhaps the most important test of onions that we conducted was trying different types, including standard-issue supermarket yellow onions, red onions, and sweet Vidalia onions. The yellow onions triumphed for their "deep brown hue" and "balanced flavor" when cooked. By comparison, tasters felt the red onions tasted harsh and looked ugly, and they thought the Vidalias tasted "bland" and looked "wan."

The onions cook in the same pan used to brown the chops. We wanted to make sure that the onions released enough moisture to dissolve (or deglaze) the flavorful, sticky, brown fond left in the pan by the chops, so we salted them lightly. The heat and salt worked together to jumpstart the breakdown of the onions' cell walls, which set their juices flowing. We also added 2 tablespoons of water to the pan for insurance.

Our last flavor tweak was an unusual one. We eliminated the salt we'd been using to season the chops themselves. Tasters agreed that the dish was adequately seasoned by the salt added to the onions, along with the naturally salty bacon and chicken broth and the garlic, thyme, and bay used to build extra flavor in the gravy. These chops were hearty, deeply flavored, and comforting enough to fortify you for the champagne and caviar of your next holiday party.

SMOTHERED PORK CHOPS
SERVES 4

Make sure to use low-sodium chicken broth in this recipe; regular chicken broth can result in an overseasoned sauce. Serve smothered chops with a starch to soak up the rich gravy. Simple egg noodles were the test kitchen favorite, but rice or mashed potatoes also taste great.

- 3 ounces bacon (about 3 slices), cut into ¼-inch pieces
- 2 tablespoons all-purpose flour
- 1¾ cups canned low-sodium chicken broth
  Vegetable oil
- 4 bone-in, rib-end pork chops, ½ to ¾ inch thick
  Ground black pepper
- 2 medium yellow onions, halved pole to pole and sliced thin (about 3½ cups)
  Salt
- 2 tablespoons water
- 2 medium garlic cloves, pressed through garlic press or minced (about 2 teaspoons)
- 1 teaspoon minced fresh thyme leaves
- 2 bay leaves
- 1 tablespoon minced fresh parsley leaves

1. Fry bacon in small saucepan over medium heat, stirring occasionally, until lightly browned, 8 to 10 minutes. Using slotted spoon, transfer bacon to paper towel–lined plate, leaving fat in saucepan (you should have 2 tablespoons bacon fat; if not, supplement with vegetable oil). Reduce heat to medium-low and gradually whisk flour into fat until smooth. Cook, whisking frequently, until mixture is light brown, about the color of peanut butter, about 5 minutes. Whisk in chicken broth in slow, steady stream; increase heat to medium-high and bring to boil, stirring occasionally; cover and set aside off heat.

2. Heat 1 tablespoon oil in 12-inch skillet over high heat until smoking, about 3 minutes. Meanwhile, dry pork chops with paper towels and sprinkle with ½ teaspoon pepper. Brown chops in single layer until deep golden on first side, about 3 minutes. Flip chops and cook until browned on second side, about 3 minutes longer. Transfer chops to large plate and set aside.

3. Reduce heat to medium and add 1 tablespoon oil, onions, ¼ teaspoon salt, and water to now-empty skillet. Using wooden spoon, scrape browned bits on pan bottom and cook, stirring frequently, until onions are softened and browned around the edges, about 5 minutes. Stir in garlic and thyme and cook until fragrant, about 30 seconds longer. Return chops to skillet in single layer, covering chops with onions. Pour in warm sauce and any juices collected from pork; add bay leaves. Cover, reduce heat to low, and simmer until pork is tender and paring knife inserted into chops meets very little resistance, about 30 minutes.

4. Transfer chops to warmed serving platter and tent with foil. Increase heat to medium-high and simmer sauce rapidly, stirring frequently, until thickened to gravy-like consistency, about 5 minutes. Discard bay leaves, stir in parsley, and adjust seasonings with salt and pepper. Cover chops with sauce, sprinkle with reserved bacon, and serve immediately.

SMOTHERED PORK CHOPS WITH CIDER AND APPLES

Follow recipe for Smothered Pork Chops, substituting apple cider for chicken stock and 1 large or 2 small Granny Smith apples, peeled, cored, and cut into ⅜-inch wedges, for one of the onions, and increasing salt added to onions to ½ teaspoon.

SMOTHERED PORK CHOPS WITH SPICY COLLARD GREENS

Follow recipe for Smothered Pork Chops, increasing oil in step 3 to 2 tablespoons, omitting one onion, and increasing garlic to 4 cloves. Just before returning browned chops to pan in step 3, add 4 cups thinly sliced collard greens and ½ teaspoon crushed red pepper flakes.

Develop Flavor in Every Step

FULL FLAVOR = BROWN ROUX + SEARED CHOP + BROWNED ONIONS

WEAK FLAVOR = BLOND ROUX + PALE CHOP + LIGHTLY COOKED ONIONS

Brown is good when it comes to flavor. Cooking each component fully contributes greater flavor to the finished dish. For instance, the blond roux (bottom left) is not particularly deep in flavor, whereas its counterpart (top left) is bronze and nutty. The well-browned chop (top center) tastes more savory than the poorly browned chop (bottom center). The onions with the brown edges (top right) are sweeter and softer than the light, crunchy onions (bottom right).

Mulled Wine Worth Drinking

To bring mulled wine into balance, use a modest amount of sugar,
toast the spices, and simmer (don't boil) for a full hour.

≽ BY REBECCA HAYS ≼

Mention mulled wine and most of us have visions of festive parties and cozy firesides. Yet the reality of the drink itself is more reminiscent of cough syrup—sickeningly sweet and overspiced, with a strong taste of alcohol. Other recipes produce a bitter, pithy brew that even additional sugar can't remedy. The holiday parties usually survive, but the mulled wine is often poured down the drain.

Sugar and Spice

Many recipes I researched called for 2 cups of sugar and two 750-ml bottles of wine. Knowing that this ratio must be out of balance, I decreased the sugar bit by bit and then finally settled on a dramatically reduced ½ cup sugar to 2 bottles of wine. Next, honey, brown sugar, and even grenadine syrup took a turn in the pot as possible sweeteners, but tasters preferred the clean, direct sweetness of white sugar.

I dug through our test kitchen spice cabinet and tried every whole spice that seemed even mildly appropriate (I learned early on that ground spices end up floating in a disturbing cloud on top of the wine). Tasters voted down obscure additions like star anise and coriander seeds, and I settled on a simple combination of cinnamon sticks, cloves, and allspice berries, throwing in a few black peppercorns for extra kick. In an effort to extract as much flavor as possible from the spices, I tried toasting them in a dry pan for a few minutes and infusing them in a sugar syrup as well as using them straight from the jar. Toasting proved to be the winning method, making mulled wine with deep but not overwhelming spice notes.

Fruit was next on my list. While limes and lemons tasted out of place, orange zest harmonized well with the hearty wine and spices I'd chosen. Citrus juice added too much acidity, and citrus slices imparted an unpleasant pithy taste. Diluting the wine with apple cider or cranberry juice produced a thin, weak mixture.

Mulling It Over

The term *body* can be used to broadly categorize red wines: The more body a wine has, the richer and more concentrated it tastes. Light reds are uncomplicated, fruity, and sometimes thin-tasting. Medium-bodied reds are smooth and lush, while full-bodied reds are often described as tannic, hearty, and robust. Nearly every recipe, reference book, and wine merchant I consulted recommended medium- to full-bodied reds for mulling, reasoning that light wines can't support heavy mulling spices and sugar. To test the validity of this theory, I made a working recipe with several medium- to full-bodied wines, but I also included a sampling of lighter wines. Each of the medium- and full-bodied wines had devotees; preference stemmed from personal taste. As predicted, mulled wine made with light-bodied red wine tasted, well, too light.

I quickly discovered that simmering, not boiling, was the way to go in creating a top-notch mulled wine. If the heat is too intense, fragile esters (flavor compounds) in the wine disintegrate, turning quickly from sweet and fruity to bitter and sour. I fiddled with the cooking time. A batch simmered for 15 minutes was raw-tasting, and even 30- and 45-minute simmers left a raw edge. A full hour was needed to achieve perfect balance. Some tasters complained that wine simmered for an hour lacked a boozy kick. I thought to stir in a few spoonfuls of alcohol off the heat. Adding some reserved raw wine made an odd-tasting drink. Ruby port was passable, but the sweet warmth of brandy hit the mark. Perfect mulled wine was finally mine.

MULLED RED WINE

MAKES ABOUT 1½ QUARTS, SERVING 8

The flavor of the mulled wine deteriorates if it is simmered for longer than 1 hour. It is best served immediately after mulling but will keep fairly hot off heat, covered, for about 30 minutes. Leftover mulled wine can be reheated in the microwave or in a saucepan on the stovetop.

3	sticks (3-inches each) cinnamon
10	whole cloves
10	black peppercorns
1	teaspoon (about 25) allspice berries
2	bottles medium- or full-bodied red wine (see "Red Wines for Mulling," right)
4	strips zest from 1 orange, removed with vegetable peeler, each strip about 2 inches long by ½ inch wide, cleaned of any white pith
½	cup plus 2 tablespoons sugar
2–4	tablespoons brandy

1. Toast cinnamon sticks, cloves, peppercorns, and allspice in medium heavy-bottomed non-reactive saucepan over medium-high heat until fragrant, about 2 minutes. Add wine, orange zest, and ½ cup sugar; cover partially and bring to simmer, stirring occasionally to dissolve sugar. Reduce heat to low and simmer 1 hour until wine is infused; do not boil.

2. Strain wine through fine-mesh strainer; return wine to saucepan and discard spices and orange zest. Stir 2 tablespoons brandy into wine; taste and add up to 2 tablespoons more sugar and 2 tablespoons more brandy, if desired. Ladle wine into small mugs; serve immediately.

MULLED RED WINE
WITH RAISINS AND ALMONDS

This variation is inspired by Scandinavian glögg.

Follow recipe for Mulled Red Wine, substituting 2 green cardamom pods, crushed, for allspice. Add ⅓ cup raisins and ⅓ cup whole blanched almonds to strained wine; omit brandy. Cover and let wine stand until raisins are plump, about 10 minutes; stir in 2 tablespoons vodka. Taste and add up to 2 tablespoons more sugar and 2 tablespoons more vodka, if desired. Ladle wine, raisins, and almonds into small mugs; serve immediately.

TASTING: Red Wines for Mulling
We tested a dozen inexpensive red wines and found that most were good candidates for mulling. That's not to say they all tasted the same. My advice? Use a medium- to full-bodied wine, including most Cabernets, Pinot Noirs, and Zinfandels, or choose from this list of our favorites, making your selection based on the flavors you like when drinking red wine. —R.H.

➤ **Domaine du Trillol, 1999,** CORBIÈRES, $9.95: "Tangy," "rich," and "juicy."
➤ **Rosemount Estate, 2001,** GRENACHE/SHIRAZ, $8.95: "Smooth" and "fruity."
➤ **Black Mountain Vineyard, Non-Vintage,** PINOT NOIR, $6.99: "Spicy," "piney," and "tannic."
➤ **Black Mountain Vineyard, Non-Vintage,** ZINFANDEL, $6.99: "Gentle" and "smooth."
➤ **Barefoot, Non-Vintage,** CABERNET SAUVIGNON, $4.99: "Complex" and "toasty."

Roast Beef and Yorkshire Pudding

We cooked more than 35 rib roasts to unlock the secrets of this forgotten classic.

⇒ BY ELIZABETH GERMAIN ⇐

England and America are very different places. The English take the extraordinary lightly ("Queen Mum Serves Doughnuts Amidst Rubble"), and Americans have a knack for turning the most mundane events into headline news ("Punxsutawney Phil Sees Shadow!"). This same dichotomy is evident when it comes to roast beef with Yorkshire pudding. The English make it on a Sunday afternoon with a cheap cut of beef from the shoulder or round. In America, we use an expensive rib roast and promote it as a special holiday recipe. Either way, I thought, it's worth making.

When I tested a half dozen sample recipes for this dish, however, I was disappointed. Too often the meat was dry, chewy, and unevenly cooked. The accompanying jus was bland, thin, and pale. The recipes for Yorkshire pudding seemed fickle: Sometimes the pudding failed to rise and its texture was too dense; other times it cooked unevenly. But I was steadfast (like a good Englishwoman) and quickly figured out what I wanted. I envisioned a roast beef with a browned, flavorful exterior complementing an evenly cooked, juicy, tender, and rosy red interior. The ideal jus, made from the beef drippings, would be rich in beef flavor and deep mahogany in color, with plenty of body. As for the perfect Yorkshire pudding, it would be dramatically high and have a crisp and lightly browned outer crust with a tender, moist, and airy interior. Although similar to a buttery popover, Yorkshire pudding is richly flavored with beef fat.

The Kindest Cut of All

Like a good American, I started with a fancy rib roast. Butchers tend to cut the whole roast—which consists of ribs 6 through 12—into two distinct cuts (see "Two Rib Roasts" on page 12). Wondering if one cut would be preferred over the other, I cooked them side by side. The answer was easy. Tasters liked best the more tender and regularly formed piece that comes from the loin end, often called the first cut.

Next to address was the issue of using a bone-in roast versus a boneless one. A blind taste test revealed the bone-in roast as the unanimous favorite. Tasters said this roast was juicier and had a beefier flavor. In comparison, the boneless roast was chewy and dry. I concluded that the bones must be protecting the non-fatty side of the meat, helping to retain the juices and bringing forth a meatier flavor. Discussing this discovery with my butcher, he suggested a way to have the best of

Brown the roast on the stovetop for good exterior color, and then roast the meat at a gentle 250 degrees for maximum juiciness and tenderness.

both worlds—the superior meat from cooking on the bone and the ease of serving a boneless roast. He cut the meat from the bones and tied it back on (most any butcher and many supermarkets will provide this service), and I cooked the whole thing. This was the first important step toward a great roast beef dinner, as I got the flavor I wanted along with quick and easy carving. Just snip the twine after roasting, set the bones aside, and start slicing.

Low and Slow Is the Way to Go

I realized that another key step to a successful roast would be an instant-read thermometer, which is essential to getting an accurate read from the middle of the roast. (It matters which type you buy; see "The Right Thermometer" on page 13.) Another revelation came to me by accident. Trying to squeeze in another test before the end of the workday, I took a shortcut and cooked one roast straight from the refrigerator. (I had been letting them sit at room temperature for a few hours before beginning to cook.) One hour into

roasting, the difference in temperature between the dead center of the meat and the center of the sides was 50 degrees, almost twice as much as in the room-temperature roasts. Consequently, when the center of this roast was cooked medium-rare, the sides were well-done. From now on I would not put any cold roasts into the oven.

I started my tests of oven temperature with a low 200-degree oven and then continued with nine more roasts at 25-degree intervals up to a high of 425 degrees. Each roast was cooked until the internal temperature of the meat reached 125 degrees. I wanted a combination of dark crust and tender meat, but no one temperature could deliver on this promise. Of more interest, and a real eye-opener for the test kitchen, was that the final internal temperature of the meat did not necessarily determine its juiciness or texture. The roasts cooked at 325 degrees and higher were dry and unevenly cooked (although higher oven temperatures did provide better exterior crusts), even though they were removed from the oven at an internal temperature of 125 degrees. The roasts cooked at 300 degrees and lower were juicier and had better internal flavor, but they lacked a flavorful, browned exterior.

When I carved the roast cooked at 250 degrees it was rosy pink from the surface to the center, and one bite convinced all tasters that the inner meat was incredible: juicy, tender, and with big flavors. The problem was its pale exterior. My first thought was to start the roast in a low oven and then finish with a blast of heat from a high oven (the classic textbook method), but this produced unevenly cooked meat, with the outer layer tough and dried out. The solution? I seasoned a roast with salt and pepper and seared it on the stovetop first. A minor obstacle appeared when the rendered beef fat weakened the twine that held the meat to the bones. I tried again, this time separating the meat from the bones and searing just the fatty top and sides of the meat. I let the meat cool briefly, tied it back onto the bones, and then roasted the meat. Finally, a perfectly prepared roast beef. The exterior was crusty, browned, and flavorful; the inside juicy, tender, evenly cooked, and brimming with beef flavor.

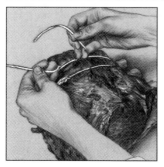

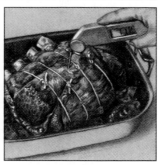

1. Position browned meat back on bones. Using four lengths of twine, tie meat back onto bones, exactly from where it was cut.

2. Place roast, bone-side down, (seared-side up) in center of roasting pan, pushing oxtails and onions to sides of pan.

3. To check temperature, insert thermometer through top of roast until you reach center.

Even so, I still had some problems to contend with. Slow roasting is so good at keeping the juices inside the meat that it was releasing no pan drippings for the jus and rendering no beef fat for the pudding. I tried using the fat rendered from searing on the stovetop, but it was overly seasoned, and the puddings were inedible. Seasoning the meat after searing, which would have produced usable fat, also failed because the low oven temperature did not dissolve the salt into the meat. I now had a perfectly cooked roast beef, but I also had to figure out where to find the flavor for the jus and the fat for the Yorkshire pudding.

The "Tail" of the Jus

Traditionally, a jus is prepared after a roast is cooked. The roasting pan is placed on the stovetop, and some liquid, typically wine, is added to deglaze the pan, a process in which all of the flavorful browned bits get lifted off the pan bottom. Broth is then added to the pan and reduced by simmering to concentrate the flavors and improve the texture. Vegetables and aromatics are often added to the pan prior to roasting to add flavor to a jus, so this is where I began my next batch of tests.

I threw onions, carrots, celery, and thyme in with the roast at the beginning of oven cooking.

The vegetables steamed, and the jus was terrible. (One taster likened this jus to dishwater.) Because browning brings out flavor, I considered using the time that the raw roast rests out of the refrigerator to roast the vegetables at high heat, using the same pan in which I'd cook the beef. This jus was better but too vegetal tasting. "Where's the beef?" asked one taster, thereby giving me an idea. I tossed in some oxtails (a readily available and inexpensive cut) with the vegetables in the next test. Oxtails are not only loaded with beef flavor, but they are also very fatty. I had struck gold! My search for flavor for the jus had also unearthed fat for the pudding.

It took a few more tests to determine that the jus was actually improved when I used oxtails and onions alone. I had eliminated the carrots and celery because they detracted from the rich beef flavor. The thyme proved more pleasing if I added it when making the jus on the stovetop. I tried another test, employing a technique used when roasting veal bones for stock: I rubbed the oxtails with a bit of tomato paste. "Wow, what did you do?" my tasters exclaimed. Not only was the rich beefy flavor more intense, but the jus was thicker and silkier. Now on a roll, I had one more idea to try. I snipped the twine on the cooked

roast and tossed the rib bones into the simmering jus. Perfection at last.

Finally, I used the fat from the oxtails to create the best Yorkshire pudding (see page 13). Now I had a superior recipe, albeit one that takes a bit more work than the standard English version. This is a dish worth serving on a special occasion, not just for Sunday dinner.

PRIME RIB ROAST BEEF WITH JUS
SERVES 10 TO 12

Ask the butcher to cut the meat off the ribs, but make sure to keep the ribs because the meat is tied back onto them for roasting. Letting the roast stand at room temperature for 2 hours before roasting helps it cook evenly. Plan on removing the roast from the refrigerator about 5½ hours before serving.

1	first-cut (ribs 9 through 12) beef rib roast (about 8 pounds), meat removed from bone, ribs reserved (see note), patted dry
1½	pounds oxtails
1	tablespoon tomato paste
3	medium onions, cut into eighths
3	tablespoons vegetable oil
	Salt, preferably kosher
2	tablespoons ground black pepper
1	cup medium-bodied red wine, such as Côtes du Rhône
1¾	cups canned low-sodium beef broth
1¾	cups canned low-sodium chicken broth
2	sprigs fresh thyme

1. Remove roast and ribs from refrigerator and let stand at room temperature 2 hours. After an hour, adjust oven rack to lowest position and heat oven to 400 degrees. Rub oxtails with tomato paste and place in heavy-bottomed, burner-safe roasting pan. Toss onions with 1 tablespoon oil, then scatter onions in roasting pan. Roast until oxtails and onions are browned, about 45 minutes, flipping oxtails halfway through cooking time. Remove from oven and set roasting pan with oxtails aside; reduce oven temperature to 250 degrees.

2. When roast has stood at room temperature 2 hours, heat heavy-bottomed 12-inch skillet over medium heat until hot, about 4 minutes. Meanwhile, rub ends and fat-side of roast with remaining 2 tablespoons oil, then sprinkle with 1½ teaspoons kosher salt (or ¾ teaspoon table salt) and pepper. Place roast fat-side down in skillet and cook until well-browned, 12 to 15 minutes; using tongs, stand roast on end and cook until well-browned, about 4 minutes. Repeat with other end. Do not brown side where ribs were attached. Place roast browned-side up on cutting board and cool 10 minutes. Following illustration 1 above, tie browned roast to ribs. Set roast bone-side down in roasting pan (see illustration 2), pushing oxtails and onions to sides of pan. Roast 1 hour, then

---

Two Rib Roasts

A whole rib roast consists of ribs 6 through 12. Butchers tend to cut the roast in two. We prefer the cut further back on the cow, which is closer to the loin (See pages 16-17 for more information). This cut is referred to as the first cut, the loin end, or sometimes the small end. The first cut can include anywhere from two to four ribs. We like a large roast for the holidays and prefer four

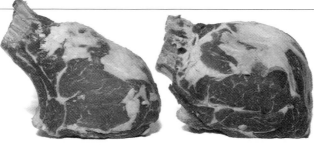

FIRST CUT   SECOND CUT

ribs. When ordering, be sure to specify the first four ribs from the loin end—ribs 9 through 12—to receive the first cut. This cut is more desirable because it contains the large, single rib-eye muscle. The less desirable cut, which is still an excellent roast, is closer to the chuck (or shoulder) end and is sometimes called the second cut. The closer to the chuck, the less tender the roast becomes. —E.G.

SILHOUETTE PHOTOGRAPHY: VAN ACKERE, ILLUSTRATION: YEVGENIY SOLOVYEV

remove from oven and check internal temperature; center of roast should register about 70 degrees on instant-read thermometer. (If internal temperature is higher or lower, adjust total cooking time.) Return roast to oven, and prepare Yorkshire pudding batter now (if making), and cook 1¼ to 1¾ hours longer, until center of meat registers about 122 degrees for rare to medium-rare or about 130 degrees for medium-rare to medium (see illustration 3). Transfer roast to cutting board and tent loosely with foil. Increase oven temperature to 450 degrees for Yorkshire pudding.

3. While roast rests, spoon off fat from roasting pan, reserving 3 tablespoons for Yorkshire puddings; set roasting pan aside while preparing puddings for baking. While puddings bake, set roasting pan over 2 burners at high heat. Add wine to roasting pan; using wooden spoon, scrape up browned bits and boil until reduced by half, about 3 minutes. Add beef broth, chicken broth, and thyme. Cut twine on roast and remove meat from ribs; re-tent meat. Add ribs, meaty side down, to roasting pan and continue to cook, stirring occasionally, until liquid is reduced by two-thirds (to about 2 cups), 16 to 20 minutes. Add any accumulated beef juices from meat and cook to heat through, about 1 minute longer. Discard ribs and oxtails; strain jus through mesh strainer into gravy boat, pressing on onions to extract as much liquid as possible.

4. Set meat browned-side up on board and cut into ⅜-inch-thick slices; sprinkle lightly with salt. Serve immediately, passing jus separately.

EQUIPMENT:
The Right Thermometer
Beyond the type of display—digital or dial-face—an important element in the design of an instant-read thermometer is the location of the temperature sensors. On a digital thermometer, which we recommend, the sensors are located at the very tip of the stem. On a dial-face thermometer, the sensors are located roughly 1½ inches up from the tip. The placement of the sensors is essential to an accurate internal temperature reading of the roast beef. The sensors on the dial-face thermometer are so far up from the tip that this thermometer will not give you a reading from the true center of such a big roast. (See Resources for more information on our favorite digital thermometer, the Thermapen, shown here at left.) A digital "timer-thermometer" is also ideal for this recipe. It allows you to monitor the temperature of the roast as it cooks without opening the oven door. (See Resources for more information.)—E.G.

DIGITAL   DIAL-FACE

Will Yorkshire Pudding Rise to the Occasion?

Yorkshire pudding is made with flour, salt, eggs, milk, and fat rendered from the roast beef, which gives it flavor and distinguishes it from the popover, which is generally made with butter. The eggy batter rises dramatically in the oven, and, as this happens, the center becomes airy and custardy and the crust crisps and browns.

Yorkshire pudding is often prepared in a roasting pan and then cut into individual pieces. Initial tests revealed that pieces from the center of the pan were squat and lacking in the delectable browned crust, while those from the edges were missing a pleasing amount of the tender, soft interior. My tasters and I were smitten by individual puddings. They are uniform in shape, consistent in contrasting components, and much easier to serve. Because a popover pan serves only six and most people do not have one, I tried a muffin pan and got excellent results.

With the baking vehicle settled, the biggest challenge was getting the right height and texture. Yorkshire pudding can be notoriously fickle, rising beautifully sometimes and other times falling flat. I started my tests by leaving the batter lumpy (a common recipe directive). When this approach failed, I tried the less popular instruction: whisking the ingredients until smooth. These puddings rose a bit higher, and the texture became more airy.

Next I tried the common practice of using room-temperature ingredients and letting the batter rest before baking. The former gives the batter a bit of a head start when it enters the oven, having to rise up from a base temperature of about 70 degrees rather than a chilly 40 to 50 degrees. The latter gives the gluten in the batter time to relax so it will have more "give" in the oven. Sure enough, a rested, room-temperature batter enhanced the height and inner texture of the puddings.

I obtained the best results by starting with a hot oven (450 degrees) and then lowering the heat about halfway through baking (to 350 degrees).

If the batter does not rest to give the gluten time to relax or if the oven door is opened during baking, the puddings will fall (left). Proper mixing and resting of the batter and undisturbed baking ensure huge crowns with crisp, golden brown exteriors and tender, moist, airy interiors (right).

The intense 450-degree heat not only browned the puddings nicely but quickly turned the moisture in the batter to steam, causing the batter to expand. The interior then cooked through at 350 degrees.

Following through on the idea that an initial blast of heat is good, I also tried preheating the greased muffin tin. The beef fat was smoking hot, and the batter sizzled when it hit the tin. This worked like a charm. I thought I was done until I noticed that the leftovers fell slightly as they sat. I pierced the next batch of puddings with a skewer as soon as they came out of the oven. This allowed the steam to escape instead of condensing inside the puddings and turning the interiors soft and overly moist, which causes collapse.

As for flavor, recipes for Yorkshire Pudding are remarkably consistent in terms of using beef fat, although amounts vary. I prepared a batch using 4 tablespoons of fat from the rendered oxtails. Although these puddings were flavorful, they were dripping in fat. Three tablespoons proved ideal. —E.G.

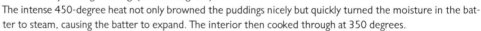

INDIVIDUAL YORKSHIRE PUDDINGS
SERVES 12

Prepare the Yorkshire pudding batter after the beef has roasted for 1 hour, then, while the roast rests, add beef fat to the batter and get the puddings into the oven. While the puddings bake, complete the jus. An accurate oven temperature is key for properly risen puddings, so check your oven with an oven thermometer before making this recipe. Work quickly to fill the muffin tin with batter, and do not open the oven door during baking.

- 3   large eggs, at room temperature
- 1½   cups whole milk, at room temperature
- 1½   cups (7½ ounces) unbleached all-purpose flour
- ¾   teaspoon salt
- 3   tablespoons beef fat

1. Whisk eggs and milk in large bowl until well-combined, about 20 seconds. Whisk flour and salt in medium bowl and add to egg mixture; whisk quickly until flour is just incorporated and mixture is smooth, about 30 seconds. Cover batter with plastic wrap and let stand at room temperature for at least 1 hour or up to 3 hours.

2. After removing roast from oven, whisk 1 tablespoon of beef fat into batter until bubbly and smooth, about 30 seconds. Transfer batter to 1-quart liquid measuring cup or other pitcher.

3. Measure ½ teaspoon of remaining 2 tablespoons beef fat into each cup of standard muffin pan. When roast is out of oven, increase temperature to 450 degrees and place pan in oven to heat for 3 minutes (fat will smoke). Working quickly, remove pan from oven, close oven door, and divide batter evenly among 12 muffin cups, filling each about ⅔ full. Immediately return pan to oven. Bake, without opening oven door, for 20 minutes; reduce oven temperature to 350 degrees and bake until deep golden brown, about 10 minutes longer. Remove pan from oven and pierce each pudding with skewer to release steam and prevent collapse. Using hands or dinner knife, lift each pudding out of tin and serve immediately.

Mashed Sweet Potatoes

Bake, boil, or steam? None of these methods is the right one for the best texture and flavor.

⇒ BY JULIA COLLIN ⇐

For the holidays, mashed sweet potatoes are often overdressed in a Willie Wonka–style casserole topped with marshmallows and whipped cream. But this candied concoction doesn't hold a candle to an honest sweet potato mash in terms of flavor. With a deep, natural sweetness that doesn't require much assistance, the humble sweet potato, I thought, would taste far better if prepared using a modicum of ingredients.

Yet even with a simple recipe, mashed sweet potatoes would pose some problems. Nailing a fork-friendly puree every time is a form of cooking roulette. Mashed sweet potatoes often turn out overly thick and gluey or, to the other extreme, sloppy and loose. I also found that most recipes overload the dish with pumpkin pie seasonings that obscure the potato's natural flavor. I wanted a recipe that would push that deep, earthy sweetness to the fore and that would produce a silky puree with enough body to hold its shape while sitting on a fork. Focusing first on the cooking method, I figured I could then test the remaining ingredients, from butter to heavy cream, and, finally, fiddle with the seasonings.

Bake, Boil, or Steam?

To determine the best cooking method, I tested a variety of techniques: baking potatoes unpeeled, boiling potatoes whole and unpeeled, boiling them peeled and diced, steaming them peeled and diced, and microwaving them whole and unpeeled. Adding a little butter and salt to the potatoes after they were mashed, I found huge differences in texture, flavor, and ease of preparation.

The baked potatoes produced a mash with a deep flavor and bright color, but the potatoes took more than an hour to bake through, and handling them hot from the oven was a precarious endeavor. I also found that sweet potatoes range drastically in size, altering their baking times by as much as 30 minutes. Boiling whole sweet potatoes in their skins turned out a wet puree with a mild flavor. In using a fork to monitor the potatoes as they cooked, I made holes that seem to have let the flavor seep out and the water seep in. Steaming and boiling pieces of peeled potatoes produced the worst examples,

A unique (and simple) method—braising and mashing sweet potatoes in the same pot—turns out to be the best.

with zero flavor and a loose, applesauce-like texture. The microwave, although fast and easy, was also a disappointment. The rate of cooking was difficult to monitor, and the difference between undercooked and overdone was only about 30 seconds. Over-microwaving the potatoes, even slightly, produced a pasty mouthfeel and an odd plastic flavor. By all accounts, this first round of testing bombed. Yet it did end up pointing me in a promising direction.

I had certainly learned a few things about cooking sweet potatoes. First, their deep, hearty flavor is surprisingly fleeting and easily washed out. Second, the tough, dense flesh reacts much like winter squash when it's cooked, turning wet and sloppy. I also found it safer to peel the sweet potatoes when they were raw and cold rather than cooked and hot. Taking all of this into account, I wondered if braising the sweet potatoes might work. If cut into uniform pieces and cooked over low heat in a covered pan, the sweet potatoes might release their own moisture slowly and braise themselves.

Adding a little water to the pan to get the

process going, I found the sweet potatoes were tender in about 40 minutes. I then simply removed the lid and mashed them right in the pot. To my delight, they were full of flavor because they had essentially cooked in their own liquid. I tried various pots and heat levels and found that a medium-sized pot (accommodating two or three layers of potatoes) set over low heat worked best. Higher heat levels cooked the potatoes unevenly and, in some cases, burned them. I also noted that the potatoes cooked quickly when cut into thin slices rather than chunks.

The Supporting Cast

Up to this point, I had been adding only butter to the mash but wondered what the typical additions of cream, milk, or half-and-half would do. Making four batches side by side, I tasted mashes made with only butter, with butter and milk, butter and half-and-half, and butter and heavy cream. Tasters found the butter-only batch tasted boring, while milk turned the mash bland and watery. The batch made with half-and-half came in second, with a heartier flavor and fuller body, but the heavy cream stole the show. Two pounds of potatoes tasted best when blended with 4 tablespoons of unsalted butter and 2 tablespoons

"Yam I Am"

What is the difference between a yam and a sweet potato? It depends on where you live. In U.S. markets, a "yam" is actually a mislabeled sweet potato. If you can get a glimpse of the box they're shipped in, you'll see the words "sweet potato" printed somewhere, as mandated by law. In other parts of the world, "yam" refers to a true yam, a vegetable having no relation to the sweet potato. Sold under the label "ñame" (pronounced ny-AH-may) or "igname" here in the United States, a true yam has a hairy, off-white or brown skin and white, light yellow, or pink flesh. This tuber is usually sold in log-shaped chunks that weigh several pounds each. A true yam is bland tasting and has an ultra-starchy texture. —J.C.

SWEET POTATO

TASTING: **Beauregards and Batatas**

Ranging in color from pale white to shocking purple, sweet potatoes are available in numerous varieties (see back cover), many of which are misleadingly sold as "yams" (see "Yam I Am," page 14). Having developed my recipe for mashed sweet potatoes with the conventional orange-fleshed variety found at our local grocery store, I wondered what difference, if any, these other hard-to-find varieties would make.

Sampling seven varieties of mashed sweet potato side by side, my tasters and I found the differences in flavor and texture astounding. Of the orange varieties, **Beauregard** (usually sold as a conventional sweet potato) was favored for its "standard sweet potato flavor" and perfect texture; **Jewel** (sold as a "yam") was found to be "moderately sweet," with a wetter consistency; and **Red Garnet** (sold as a "yam") was downright "savory" and "loose." In the non-orange category, the white-fleshed **Japanese Sweet** was "unbelievable," with a "buttery," "chestnut" flavor unlike anything we had ever tasted. By comparison, the similar but less potent flavor of the **White Sweet** was considered "nice" and "creamy," but the flavor was "fleeting." Ranking at the bottom were the off-white **Batata**, with its mild flavor and "Play-Doh-like" texture, and the purple **Okinawa**, which produced a "dry," nutty-flavored mash with an intense violet hue that was "a bit scary to look at." —J.C.

of heavy cream. Although this may seem like a minuscule amount of cream, more simply ran over the sweet potato's delicate flavor. I found 1/2 teaspoon of salt was plenty and noted that a bit of sugar did wonders to bolster flavor. Common sweet potato seasonings, such as nutmeg, vanilla, allspice, and cinnamon, were simply distracting.

As I had made this recipe many times by now, an oversight finally became obvious. Why didn't I replace the small amount of water used to cook the potatoes with the butter and heavy cream? I was gratified when this streamlined technique produced the ultimate texture. The potatoes stood up on a fork, with a luxurious texture that was neither loose nor gluey. And, with the water out of the picture, the sweet potato flavor was more intense than ever.

These mashed sweet potatoes are truly a one-pot wonder. When paired with flavors borrowed from other sweet potato–loving countries—coconut milk from Thailand or garam masala from India—they make a far more stunning addition to the holiday table than any Willy Wonka wonder.

TESTING EQUIPMENT: **Modern Mashers**

There are two classic styles of potato masher: the wire-looped masher with a zigzag presser and the disk masher with a perforated round or oval plate. Modern mashers, as it turns out, are simply variations of these two original designs. I tested a total of eight mashers to see which would have the most comfortable grip and the most effective mashing mechanism.

When I wrapped up my mash-fest, I concluded that the wire-looped mashers were second-rate. The space between the loops made it hard to achieve a good, fast mash, and most of the potato pieces escaped between the loops unscathed. One model, the Exeter Double Masher ($9.99), is worth mentioning, however, because it is spring-loaded and uses a double-tier set of wire loops for mashing. It took some muscle to use this masher, but it was the fastest of all the mashers that I tested.

In general, the disk mashers outperformed the wire-looped models, and the Profi Plus ($15.99) was our favorite. With its small holes, this oval-based masher turned out soft and silky spuds. Its rounded edges snuggled right into the curves of the saucepan, enhancing its efficacy, and its round handle was easy to grip. The runner-up, the Oxo Smooth Masher ($9.99), has an oval metal base and rectangular perforations. The larger perforations allowed a bit more potato through, so it took longer to get the job done; still, this squat device with its cushiony handle was very easy to use. I did not like the all-plastic Oxo Good Grips Masher—it has an awkward grip and ineffective mash—so shop carefully if buying this brand. —Shannon Blaisdell

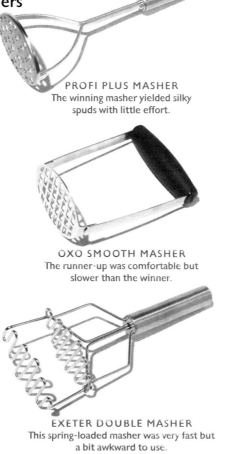

PROFI PLUS MASHER
The winning masher yielded silky spuds with little effort.

OXO SMOOTH MASHER
The runner-up was comfortable but slower than the winner.

EXETER DOUBLE MASHER
This spring-loaded masher was very fast but a bit awkward to use.

MASHED SWEET POTATOES
SERVES 4

Cutting the sweet potatoes into slices of even thickness is important in getting them to cook at the same rate. A potato masher will yield slightly lumpy sweet potatoes; a food mill will make a perfectly smooth puree. The potatoes are best served immediately, but they can be covered tightly with plastic wrap and kept relatively hot for 30 minutes. This recipe can be doubled in a Dutch oven; the cooking time will need to be doubled as well.

- 4 tablespoons unsalted butter, cut into 4 pieces
- 2 tablespoons heavy cream
- 1/2 teaspoon salt
- 1 teaspoon sugar
- 2 pounds sweet potatoes (about 2 large or 3 medium-small potatoes), peeled, quartered lengthwise, and cut crosswise into 1/4-inch-thick slices
- Pinch ground black pepper

1. Combine butter, cream, salt, sugar, and sweet potatoes in 3- to 4-quart saucepan; cook, covered, over low heat, stirring occasionally, until potatoes fall apart when poked with fork, 35 to 45 minutes.

2. Off heat, mash sweet potatoes in saucepan with potato masher, or transfer mixture to hopper of food mill and process into warmed serving bowl. Stir in pepper; serve immediately.

MAPLE-ORANGE MASHED SWEET POTATOES

Follow recipe for Mashed Sweet Potatoes, stirring in 2 tablespoons maple syrup and 1/2 teaspoon grated orange zest along with black pepper.

INDIAN-SPICED MASHED SWEET POTATOES WITH RAISINS AND CASHEWS

Follow recipe for Mashed Sweet Potatoes, substituting dark brown sugar for granulated sugar and adding 3/4 teaspoon garam masala to saucepan along with sweet potatoes. Stir 1/4 cup golden raisins and 1/4 cup roasted unsalted cashews, chopped coarse, into mashed sweet potatoes along with black pepper.

GARLIC-SCENTED MASHED SWEET POTATOES WITH COCONUT MILK AND CILANTRO

Shake the can of coconut milk before opening to combine the coconut cream with the liquid beneath.

Follow recipe for Mashed Sweet Potatoes, substituting 1/2 cup coconut milk for butter and cream and adding 1/4 teaspoon red pepper flakes and 1 small garlic clove, minced, to saucepan along with sweet potatoes. Stir in 1 tablespoon minced fresh cilantro along with black pepper.

An Illustrated Guide to Beef Roasts

Supermarkets carry many kinds of roasts, often with confusing labels. Here's how to know what you are buying, and how best to cook it. BY SHANNON BLAISDELL

Choosing a beef roast can be an exasperating and confusing endeavor. To help make this job easier, we identified the roasts most often found in the supermarket (as well as their aliases), cooked them in the test kitchen, and evaluated each on a range of qualities, from tenderness to fattiness. We also rated each roast for flavor (★★★★★ being best) and cost ($$$$$ being most expensive).

Our thanks go out to Christopher Radley, sales manager of John Dewar & Co., and Mike Lewis, butcher extraordinaire at Star Market. These meat experts helped to guide us through this process.

By definition, a roast is a thick cut of meat that is suitable for cooking by dry heat (roasting) or moist heat (braising or pot-roasting). Tender cuts with little connective tissue respond well to dry-heat cooking. Tougher cuts, which generally come from heavily exercised parts of the animal, such as the shoulder and rump, respond best to braising (being cooked in a relatively small amount of liquid in a closed container for a long period of time). The primary goal of braising is to melt the collagen in the connective tissue, thereby transforming a tough piece of meat into a tender one.

CHARACTERISTICS OF PRIMAL CUTS

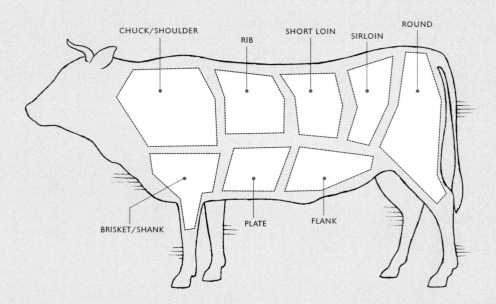

Butchers refer to the first, basic cuts made to an animal as primal cuts. In a cow, there are eight primal cuts, and beef roasts generally come from five of these, listed below.

Chuck The chuck section includes ribs 1 through 5 (the ribs are numbered from the head to the tail) as well as the shoulder blade bone. Roasts from the chuck contain a lot of connective tissue and generally require moist heat cooking to become tender.

Rib The rib section contains ribs 6 though 12. A full 7-bone rib roast, or a whole standing rib roast, can tip the scales at more than 16 pounds, so butchers divide the rib into two distinct cuts. Both are very tender, very expensive, and generally cooked by dry heat.

Short Loin This part of the cow is usually cut into premium steaks. The tenderloin is the most common roast from the short loin. It is very tender and is usually roasted.

Sirloin The sirloin is sometimes referred to as the hip area. The meat from the sirloin is not as tender as that from the short loin, but these cuts are still generally roasted.

Round Cuts from the steer's butt and leg are tender enough for roasting (though not nearly as tender as the cuts from the rib or the short loin), but they are often braised.

Illustration: John Burgoyne

Top Blade Roast
Alternate Names: Chuck Roast First Cut, Blade Roast, Top Chuck Roast

FLAVOR	★★★★
COST	$$
BEST WAY TO COOK	Braise

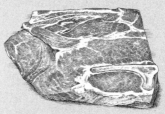

This broad, flat cut was far and away the best chuck roast we tasted—flavorful, juicy, and tender. Its connective tissue is unattractive but not unpleasant to eat.

Chuck 7-Bone Roast
Alternate Names: Center-Cut Pot Roast, Chuck Roast Center Cut

FLAVOR	★★★★
COST	$$
BEST WAY TO COOK	Braise

A bone shaped like the number seven gives this cut its name. We enjoyed the deep flavor of this thin cut, which needed less liquid and less time to cook than other cuts from the chuck.

Chuck-Eye Roast
Alternate Names: Boneless Chuck Roll, Boneless Chuck Fillet

FLAVOR	★★★
COST	$$
BEST WAY TO COOK	Braise or Roast

This boneless roast is cut from the center of the first five ribs (the term *eye* refers to any center-cut piece of meat). It is very tender and juicy but was criticized for its excessive fat content.

Under Blade Roast

Alternate Names: Bottom Chuck Roast, California Roast

FLAVOR ★★★
COST $$
BEST WAY TO COOK **Braise**

We found this roast's flavor to be quite similar to the 7-bone roast, but it had a bit more connective tissue. It also had a fair amount of fat, which enhanced the flavor but made the meat fall apart when carved.

Chuck Shoulder Roast

Alternate Names: Chuck Shoulder Pot Roast, Chuck Roast Boneless

FLAVOR ★★
COST $$
BEST WAY TO COOK **Braise**

Our tasters thought this roast had an unpleasantly chewy, almost bouncy texture and relatively mild flavor.

RIB ROASTS

Rib Roast, First Cut

Alternate Names: Prime Rib, Loin End, Small End

FLAVOR ★★★★★
COST $$$$$
BEST WAY TO COOK **Roast**

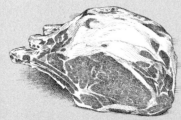

This cut consists of ribs 9 through 12, toward the back of the rib section,

closer to the loin of the animal. It contains the large rib-eye muscle and was judged to be extremely tender and flavorful. The clearest way to indicate what you want when you order a rib roast is to ask for "the first four ribs from the loin end."

Rib Roast, Second Cut

Alternate Name: Large End

FLAVOR ★★★★
COST $$$$$
BEST WAY TO COOK **Roast**

The large end of the rib roast is cut from ribs 6 though 9. Though it is still an excellent roast, we thought this cut was fattier, a little less tender, and slightly more irregularly formed than the first cut rib roast.

SHORT LOIN AND SIRLOIN ROASTS

Tenderloin

Alternate Name: Whole Filet

FLAVOR ★★★
COST $$$$$
BEST WAY TO COOK **Roast**

The tenderloin sits just under the spine of the steer, so it gets no exercise and is the most tender piece of beef you can buy. Our tasters found its flavor to be pleasantly mild, almost nonbeefy. Unpeeled tenderloins, which come with an incredibly thick layer of exterior fat still attached, also come with a tremendous amount of waste (the fat should be removed) and cost more (in both time and money) than peeled roasts, which have scattered patches of fat that need not be removed. Even peeled roasts, however, usually come with some silver skin, a sheath of thin, opalesque membrane that must be trimmed.

Top Sirloin Roast

Alternate Names: Top Butt, Center-Cut Roast

FLAVOR ★★★★
COST $$
BEST WAY TO COOK **Roast**

This cut has big beefy flavor. Aside from the vein of gristle that runs through it, which we found slightly unpleasant to eat, the roast was tender and juicy.

Sirloin Tri-Tip Roast

Alternate Name: Triangle Roast

FLAVOR ★★
COST $$
BEST WAY TO COOK **Roast**

This cut is popular out West, but butchers on the East Coast usually cut it up into sirloin tips or "steak tips." This small, triangular roast is moist but has a strange, spongy texture and mild flavor.

ROUND ROASTS

Top Round Roast

Alternate Names: Top Round First Cut, Top Round Steak Roast

FLAVOR ★★★
COST $
BEST WAY TO COOK **Braise or Roast**

This affordable roast is the most common choice in supermarkets. Our tasters liked it, commenting that it was very similar to the top sirloin

roast, with good flavor, texture, and juiciness. We like the top round roast sliced thin because it can be overly chewy if sliced thick.

Bottom Round Rump Roast

Alternate Names: Round Roast, Bottom Round Pot Roast, Bottom Round Oven Roast

FLAVOR ★★
COST $
BEST WAY TO COOK **Braise or Roast**

For the money, we think this cut makes a juicy, relatively beefy roast. It was slightly less tender than the top round roast and should be sliced thin for serving.

Eye-Round Roast

Alternate Names: Round-Eye Pot Roast

FLAVOR ★
COST $
BEST WAY TO COOK **Braise or Roast**

This boneless roast had mediocre flavor and was considerably less juicy than any other roast.

Bottom Round Roast

Alternate Names: None

FLAVOR (no stars)
COST $
BEST WAY TO COOK **Braise or Roast**

This cut was the tasters' least favorite. It was essentially devoid of flavor and had a rubbery, chewy texture. This roast is not worth even the little that it costs.

Roasting the Big One

If you have but one oven and a long guest list for Thanksgiving, only a gargantuan turkey will do. Here's what we learned about successfully roasting "the big one."

⇒ BY SALLY SAMPSON ⇐

Most food magazines, including this one, suggest roasting 12- to 14-pound turkeys, a size that is easy to handle and that delivers, according to many tasters, superior flavor. But what if you have more than 10 people coming to dinner? Roasting two turkeys is not an option for most home cooks. This "silent majority"—of which I am one—opts for the massive bird to feed the multitudes because we have but one oven to dedicate to the turkey. Welcome to real home cooking.

Working with a 20-pound plus bird has its drawbacks. How was I to find a container large enough for brining, a technique that our test kitchen finds essential to great Thanksgiving turkey? I was also concerned about turning the bird in the oven, another important step to turkey perfection. This pumped-up Tom was going to be hot, heavy, and dangerous to move halfway through roasting. Uncompromising in my goals, however, I still wanted the Norman Rockwell picture of perfection: a crisp, mahogany skin wrapped around tender, moist meat.

My first step was to select the right brand at the market. Two years ago the test kitchen conducted a turkey taste test and came up with an interesting—and totally unexpected—result. The frozen Butterball finished ahead of the fresh Butterball entry as well as more than one fresh premium brand. The reason? Frozen Butterball turkeys are injected with a salt solution—in other words, they are brined. Although the flavor of the meat was a bit on the bland side, many tasters commented that this bird "tastes just like Thanksgiving." I performed another taste test just to be sure and found that the meat was, indeed, moist and tender. So now I had a turkey that had been brined for me, eliminating a step that would be all but impossible with a huge bird.

Other techniques had to be eliminated from the start, given the size of the bird. I chose not to air-dry (another favored *Cook's* technique that would be unworkable with a huge bird) or stuff the turkey (which would add to the already long cooking time). Finally, I wanted to keep this bird as traditional as possible, so I opted not to rub it with spices or massage it with flavored butter.

My next task was to determine the proper cooking temperature. I roasted it, per the instructions included with the Butterball, at 350 degrees until the thigh registered 170 to 180 degrees, approxi-

A no-fuss recipe yields a beautiful bird that will please everyone around the crowded holiday table.

mately 4½ hours. Although the breast meat was tender, the dark meat was surprisingly fatty and the skin a tad blond and springy. Next I cooked a turkey at 400 degrees. I began with it breast-side down and, after an hour, flipped it breast-side up, hoping for a deeply browned showstopper. (This technique yields great results for smaller turkeys. As the fat renders out of the dark meat it flows down into and bastes the breast.) Although it looked great, the breast meat turned out chalky and parched, as if it had spent the day at the beach.

Because high temperature had yielded a prettier bird and low temperature a more tender one, I decided to try a combination of both. After roasting a dozen birds or so, I finally hit on the right combination of temperatures for a large turkey: 425 degrees for the first hour (breast-side down) and 325 degrees thereafter (with the breast up). The breast meat was firm and juicy, the dark meat rich and tender, and the skin a breathtakingly rosy mahogany brown.

After I had cooked and turned 200 pounds of turkey, a test cook pointed out to me that her mother would never be able to rotate a turkey of

this weight. I tried yet another turkey, with the same combination of high and low heat, but I kept the turkey breast-side up the entire time. It was slightly inferior to the turned bird but still good enough to eat, so those not up to the task can skip this step. (I also tried this same method breast-side down, and the skin turned out mottled and undercooked.)

Although I had opted not to stuff the bird, I wondered if a simple aromatic mix in the cavity might add flavor to the meat. I started with the classic onion, carrot, and celery combination, and, while this turkey was better, something was still missing. Lemon added freshness to the meat closest to the bone and gave the pan juices a cleaner taste. Sprigs of fresh thyme added the scent of Thanksgiving. More vegetables went into the roasting pan to flavor the drippings. I added a little water to ensure that the vegetables didn't dry out.

After roasting trussed and untrussed several birds, I concluded that trussing added a fussiness I didn't want as well as an unwelcome 15 to 20 minutes in cooking time. (To fully cook the inner thigh, which is hidden by trussing, you inevitably overcook the white meat.) I also investigated the best way to treat the skin, leaving it as is versus brushing it with unsalted butter, olive oil, or vegetable oil. The difference was not appreciable, but the turkey with the butter tested better and—more, well, buttery. The next question was whether regular basting is worth the effort. It turned out that basting actually makes the skin soggy, so I simply brushed the turkey with melted butter once prior to cooking.

Tenting the turkey either during or after roasting was also abandoned: The foil traps the steam and softens the skin. Instead, letting the roasted bird sit at room temperature, uncovered, for 35 to 40 minutes allows the juices, which rise to the surface during cooking, to flow back into the meat. This was more successful than the usually recommended 20 minutes, probably because of the size of the bird.

For those who can't bring themselves to buy a Butterball, I wondered if this method would work on another brand of turkey. I tested an organic turkey, which wasn't injected, and a kosher turkey, which is essentially brined by the koshering process. All the testers preferred the Butterball for its juicier meat. The kosher bird came in second, and the organic turkey took last place because the meat was dry. If you prefer to avoid a frozen, injected bird, try a kosher brand.

Thirty-five turkeys later, I had come up with a simple method that turns out a superior Thanksgiving turkey for a crowd with a modicum of fuss. Yes, I opted for a frozen Butterball, but the roasted bird looked just like one from a Norman Rockwell Thanksgiving, and it tasted good, too.

TURKEY FOR A CROWD
SERVES 20 TO 24

You can use any roasting pan to roast the turkey, even a disposable one, but make sure to use a V-rack to keep the bird elevated. Be careful to dry the skin thoroughly before brushing the bird with butter; otherwise it will have spotty brown skin. Rotating the bird helps produce moist, evenly cooked meat, but for the sake of ease, you may opt not to rotate it. In that case, skip the step of lining the V-rack with foil and roast the bird breast-side up for the entire cooking time. Because we do not brine the bird, we had the best results with a frozen Butterball (injected with salt and water) and a kosher bird (soaked in saltwater during processing). See Kitchen Notes, page 30, for tips on defrosting a frozen turkey.

- 2   medium onions, chopped coarse
- 2   medium carrots, chopped coarse
- 2   celery ribs, chopped coarse
- 1   lemon, quartered
- 2   sprigs (3 to 4 inches each) fresh thyme
- 1   frozen Butterball or kosher turkey (18 to 22 pounds gross weight), neck, heart, and gizzard reserved for gravy, if making (recipe follows), turkey rinsed and thoroughly dried with paper towels
- 4   tablespoons unsalted butter, melted
- 2   teaspoons kosher salt or 1 teaspoon table salt
- 1   teaspoon ground black pepper

1. Adjust oven rack to lowest position; remove remaining racks. Heat oven to 425 degrees. Following illustration above, line large V-rack with heavy-duty foil and poke holes in foil; set V-rack in 15- by 12-inch roasting pan.

2. Toss onions, carrots, celery, lemon, and thyme in medium bowl; set aside. Brush turkey breast with 2 tablespoons butter, then sprinkle with half of salt and half of black pepper. Set turkey breast-side down on V-rack. Brush with remaining 2 tablespoons butter and sprinkle with remaining salt and black pepper. Fill cavity with half of onion mixture; scatter rest in roasting pan and pour 1 cup water into pan.

3. Roast turkey 1 hour; remove roasting pan with turkey from oven. Lower oven temperature to 325 degrees. Using clean dishtowel or 2 potholders, turn turkey breast-side up; return roasting pan with turkey to oven and continue to roast until legs move freely and instant-read thermometer inserted into thickest part of thigh registers 170 to 180 degrees, about 2 hours longer. Transfer turkey to carving board and let rest, uncovered, 35 to 40 minutes. Carve and serve.

GIBLET PAN GRAVY
MAKES ABOUT 2 QUARTS

To eliminate the rush to make gravy once the turkey emerges from the oven, this gravy is brought close to completion while the turkey roasts. (If you prefer, prepare the gravy through step 2 one day in advance, refrigerate the gravy, and then bring it back to a simmer as the turkey nears completion.) Once the bird is out of the oven, the gravy is enriched with defatted turkey drippings and heated through.

- 1   tablespoon vegetable oil
    Reserved turkey neck, heart, and gizzard
- 1   onion, unpeeled and chopped medium
- 6   cups canned low-sodium chicken broth
- 3   cups water
- 2   sprigs fresh thyme
- 8   parsley stems
- 5   tablespoons unsalted butter
- 1/4 cup plus 2 tablespoons all-purpose flour
- 1 1/2 cups dry white wine
    Salt and ground black pepper

1. Heat oil in large heavy-bottomed saucepan over medium-high heat until shimmering but not smoking; add turkey neck, heart, and gizzard and cook, stirring occasionally, until browned, about 5 minutes. Add onion and cook, stirring occasionally, until softened, about 3 minutes. Reduce heat to low; cover and cook, stirring occasionally, until turkey parts and onion release their juices, about 20 minutes. Add chicken broth, water, and herbs; increase heat to medium-high and bring to boil, then reduce heat to low and simmer, uncovered, skimming any scum that rises to surface, until broth is rich and flavorful, about 30 minutes. Strain broth (you should have about 8 cups), reserving heart and gizzard; discard neck. When cool enough to handle, remove gristle from gizzard; dice heart and gizzard and set aside.

2. Heat butter in large heavy-bottomed saucepan over medium-low heat; when foam subsides, whisk in flour. Cook, stirring constantly, until nutty brown and fragrant, about 10 minutes; gradually and vigorously whisk in giblet broth and wine. Increase heat to medium-high and bring to boil, then reduce heat to medium-low and simmer, stirring occasionally, until slightly thickened and flavorful, about 30 minutes; set aside until turkey is done.

3. While turkey is resting on carving board, spoon out and discard as much fat as possible from roasting pan, then strain drippings into saucepan with gravy, pressing on solids in strainer to extract as much liquid as possible. Stir in reserved giblets; return to simmer to heat through. Adjust seasonings with salt and pepper; serve with turkey.

TECHNIQUE
PREPARING THE RACK

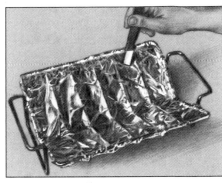

A V-shaped rack lifts the bird off the roasting pan bottom and ensures crisp skin. However, the bars on the rack will form ribbed impressions in the skin on the breast. To prevent this from happening, line the rack with foil and then use a paring knife or skewer to poke 20 to 30 holes in the foil so juices can drip down into the pan as the bird roasts.

TASTING: **Can You Buy Good Gravy?**
Is store-bought gravy worth the time saved? After sampling six supermarket gravies, we unequivocally say no.

HEINZ Fat Free Roasted Turkey Gravy: "Strange vegetable flavor," "foul," "metallic."
HEINZ Home Style Roasted Turkey Gravy: "Lemony," "vegetal," "gummy."
FRANCO-AMERICAN Slow Roast Turkey Gravy: "Pasty," "gooey," "metallic," sour."
FRANCO-AMERICAN Turkey Gravy: "Awful," "harsh," "muddy color."
McCORMICK Turkey Gravy Mix: "Salty," "chemical-y," "slimy."
KNORR Gravy Classics Roasted Turkey Gravy Mix: "Bland," "thin," "scary aftertaste."

Pasta and Broccoli

We set out to rescue this classic Italian pairing and avoid the inevitable bowl of lackluster, overcooked broccoli married to underseasoned pasta.

➢ BY SHANNON BLAISDELL ⫷

The Italians were the first to recognize that broccoli and pasta make a handsome pairing. The crisp texture and hearty vegetal flavor of broccoli marry well with the mild wheaty tones and tender texture of pasta. The problem is figuring out how to properly cook the broccoli. Generally, we are subjected to broccoli's extremes: mushy, overcooked, and dull, or undercooked, unyielding, and bland. I set out to find broccoli's happy medium—crisp, sweet, and tender.

First I tried boiling the broccoli in the pasta water. Picking the vegetables from the water was a bit awkward and beat up the broccoli quite a bit, so I rejected that option. Next I steamed the broccoli in a steaming basket, then sautéed it with extra-virgin olive oil and lots of garlic. The results were good, but working with the two pans was a bother. I wondered if I could simply sauté the florets and stalks in a frying pan with oil, but I found that the relatively dry heat took a while to penetrate and cook the vegetables. I was able to speed things up by adding water to the pan. When the cold water hit the hot pan, it turned into steam, and the moisture quickly turned the broccoli bright green and tender. The combination of both dry and moist heat did the trick.

As far as flavorings go, broccoli has an affinity for garlic and anchovies but also works well with heartier combinations such as sausage and peppers or olives and feta.

SPAGHETTI WITH BROCCOLI, GARLIC, AND ANCHOVIES
SERVES 4 TO 6 AS A MAIN DISH

In these recipes, begin cooking the broccoli immediately after putting the pasta into boiling water. When cut into small pieces, the broccoli takes only a few minutes to cook through.

> Salt
> 1 pound spaghetti
> 4 tablespoons extra-virgin olive oil
> 5 anchovy fillets, minced to paste (2 teaspoons)
> 9 medium garlic cloves, pressed through garlic press or minced (3 tablespoons)
> ½ teaspoon red pepper flakes
> 2 pounds broccoli, cut according to instructions at right
> 3 tablespoons chopped fresh parsley leaves
> 1 cup (2 ounces) grated Parmesan cheese

1. Bring 4 quarts water to rolling boil, covered, in stockpot. Add 1 tablespoon salt and pasta, stir to separate, and cook until al dente. Drain and return to stockpot.

2. While pasta is cooking, combine 2 tablespoons oil, anchovies, garlic, pepper flakes, and ½ teaspoon salt in 12-inch nonstick skillet; cook, stirring constantly, over medium-high heat until fragrant, about 3 minutes. Increase heat to high; add broccoli and ½ cup water, then cover and cook until broccoli begins to turn bright green, 1 to 2 minutes. Uncover and cook, stirring frequently, until water has evaporated and broccoli is tender, 3 to 5 minutes longer. Add broccoli mixture, remaining 2 tablespoons oil, parsley, and Parmesan to pasta in stockpot; toss to combine. Serve immediately.

ORECCHIETTE WITH BROCCOLI, SAUSAGE, AND ROASTED PEPPERS
SERVES 4 TO 6 AS A MAIN DISH

> Salt
> 1 pound orecchiette
> 4 ounces sweet Italian sausage, casing removed
> 9 medium garlic cloves, pressed through garlic press or minced (3 tablespoons)
> 1 cup (8 ounces) roasted red peppers, cut into ½-inch squares
> ½ teaspoon ground black pepper
> 2 pounds broccoli, cut according to instructions at right
> 1 tablespoon extra-virgin olive oil
> 1 cup (2 ounces) grated Pecorino Romano cheese

1. Bring 4 quarts water to rolling boil, covered, in stockpot. Add 1 tablespoon salt and pasta, stir to separate, and cook until al dente. Drain and return to stockpot.

2. While pasta is cooking, cook sausage in 12-inch nonstick skillet over medium-high heat, breaking it into small pieces with spoon, until browned, about 5 minutes. Stir in garlic, roasted peppers, ½ teaspoon salt, and pepper; cook, stirring constantly, until fragrant, about 2 minutes. Increase heat to high; add broccoli and ½ cup water, then cover and cook until broccoli begins to turn bright green, 1 to 2 minutes. Uncover and cook, stirring frequently, until water has evaporated and broccoli is tender, 3 to 5

minutes longer. Add broccoli mixture, oil, and cheese to pasta in stockpot; toss to combine. Serve immediately.

FARFALLE WITH BROCCOLI, OLIVES, AND FETA
SERVES 4 TO 6 AS A MAIN DISH

> Salt
> 1 pound farfalle
> 4 tablespoons extra-virgin olive oil
> 9 medium garlic cloves, pressed through garlic press or minced (3 tablespoons)
> 1 tablespoon grated zest plus 2 tablespoons juice from 1 lemon
> ½ teaspoon ground black pepper
> 2 pounds broccoli, cut according to instructions below
> ½ cup pitted and quartered kalamata olives
> ½ cup chopped fresh parsley leaves
> 4 ounces feta cheese, crumbled (about ¾ cup)

1. Bring 4 quarts water to rolling boil, covered, in stockpot. Add 1 tablespoon salt and pasta, stir to separate, and cook until al dente. Drain and return to stockpot.

2. While pasta is cooking, combine 2 tablespoons oil, garlic, lemon zest, ½ teaspoon salt, and pepper in 12-inch nonstick skillet; cook, stirring constantly, over medium-high heat until fragrant, about 2 minutes. Increase heat to high; add broccoli and ½ cup water, then cover and cook until broccoli begins to turn bright green, 1 to 2 minutes. Uncover and cook, stirring frequently, until water has evaporated and broccoli is tender, 3 to 5 minutes longer; stir in olives and parsley. Add broccoli mixture, remaining 2 tablespoons oil, and lemon juice to pasta in stockpot; toss to combine. Serve immediately, sprinkling feta over individual servings.

Cutting Broccoli for Sauce

The florets should be cut into bite-sized 1-inch pieces. The stalks (right) should be peeled, halved lengthwise, and then cut into ¼-inch thick pieces.

Perfect Wild Rice Pilaf

Too often, this American grain resembles mulch and has a taste to match. We figured out how to tame the flavor and turn out properly cooked rice every time.

⇒ BY MATTHEW CARD ⇐

Like a couture evening gown, wild rice is slinky black, demurely elegant, and exorbitantly pricey. But like the dress, the rice's inky sheath is no guarantee of what lies underneath. More often than not, that sleek ebony coating masks a chewy interior tasting of little but the marsh from whence the rice came. The question before us was how to make wild rice taste as good as it looks.

Properly cooked wild rice is a study in contrasts: chewy yet tender and cottony—like popcorn. Ideally, the cooked grains remain discreet, doubling to quadrupling in size from their uncooked state. Undercooked rice is tough and, quite literally, hard to chew. At the other end of the spectrum, overcooked wild rice is gluey.

To find the best cooking method, I first tried steaming and boiling, but both methods produced poorly cooked wild rice. (Technically speaking, wild rice is not rice at all but a grain harvested from a variety of marsh-growing grass.) Research revealed the best approach to be slow simmering, although the timing varied from batch to batch. The key is to stop the cooking process at just the right moment; otherwise the texture goes quickly from tough to gluey. The solution? Once the rice had simmered for 35 minutes, I checked it for doneness every couple of minutes.

Finding good flavor was another story. Plain water made for distinctly bad-tasting rice, and the addition of wine only accentuated the off flavor. Beef broth was overwhelming, but chicken broth was a revelation. Mild yet rich, the chicken broth tempered the rice's muddy flavor to a pleasant earthiness and affirmed its subdued nuttiness. Bay leaves and thyme added finesse and complexity.

Although it was now perfectly cooked, tasters found the wild rice alone to be overwhelming. Perhaps it could be better appreciated if complemented by a mellower grain, such as brown or white rice. Brown rice offered too little contrast, so I quickly settled on white. Cooking both rices in the same pot (adding the white rice midway through the simmer) caused the texture of the white rice to suffer, so an additional pot was called for. To make the most of this second saucepan, I decided to add flavoring ingredients in the style of a pilaf (see "Exploring Rice Pilaf," March/April 2000), a simple technique that guarantees flavorful, fluffy rice. Aromatics are first softened in oil or butter, and then the rice is lightly toasted in the pan, after which the liquid is added (in a smaller amount than for conventional cooking) and the rice steamed until tender. The winning pilaf ingredients turned out to be onions, carrots, dried cranberries, and toasted pecans.

Finally, the secret to perfect wild rice pilaf: Simmer it in plenty of chicken broth and combine it with white rice. The marriage of flavors and textures makes it taste as good as it looks.

WILD RICE PILAF WITH PECANS AND DRIED CRANBERRIES
SERVES 6 TO 8

Wild rice goes quickly from tough to pasty, so begin testing the rice at the 35-minute mark and drain the rice as soon as it is tender. See Kitchen Notes on page 30 for information about buying wild rice.

- 1 ¾ cups canned low-sodium chicken broth
- 2 bay leaves
- 8 sprigs thyme, divided into 2 bundles, each tied together with kitchen twine
- 1 cup wild rice, rinsed well and picked over
- 1 ½ cups long-grain white rice
- 3 tablespoons unsalted butter
- 1 medium onion, chopped fine (about 1 ¼ cups)
- 1 large carrot, chopped fine (about 1 cup)
  Salt
- ¾ cup sweetened or unsweetened dried cranberries
- ¾ cup pecans, toasted in small dry skillet over medium heat until fragrant and lightly browned, about 6 minutes, then chopped coarse
- 1 ½ tablespoons minced fresh parsley leaves
  Ground black pepper

1. Bring chicken broth, ¼ cup water, bay leaves, and 1 bundle thyme to boil in medium saucepan over medium-high heat. Add wild rice, cover, and reduce heat to low; simmer until rice is plump and tender and has absorbed most liquid, 35 to 45 minutes. Drain rice in mesh strainer to remove excess liquid. Return rice to now-empty saucepan; cover to keep warm and set aside.

2. While wild rice is cooking, place white rice in medium bowl and cover with 2 inches water; gently swish grains to release excess starch. Carefully pour off water, leaving rice in bowl. Repeat about 5 times, until water runs almost clear. Drain rice in mesh strainer.

3. Heat butter in medium saucepan over medium-high heat until foam subsides, about 2 minutes. Add onion, carrot, and 1 teaspoon salt; cook, stirring frequently, until softened but not browned, about 4 minutes. Add rinsed white rice and stir to coat grains with butter; cook, stirring frequently, until grains begin to turn translucent, about 3 minutes. Meanwhile, bring 2¼ cups water to boil in small saucepan or in microwave. Add boiling water and second thyme bundle to rice; return to boil, then reduce heat to low, sprinkle cranberries evenly over rice, and cover. Simmer until all liquid is absorbed, 16 to 18 minutes. Off heat, fluff rice with fork.

4. Combine wild rice, white rice mixture, pecans, and parsley in large bowl; toss with rubber spatula. Adjust seasonings with salt and pepper to taste; serve immediately.

Getting the Texture Right

UNDERCOOKED   **PERFECTLY COOKED**   **OVERCOOKED**

Undercooked wild rice is tough and hard to chew. At the other end of the spectrum, overcooked wild rice bursts, revealing the pasty starch concealed beneath the glossy coat. Perfectly cooked wild rice is chewy but tender, the individual grains plumped but intact.

Rediscovering Chocolate Mousse Cake

Chocolate mousse cake runs the gamut from fluffy, insubstantial layer cake to a dense-as-a-brick, fudge-like slab. Could we make one that maintained the qualities of a perfect chocolate mousse—rich, creamy, and full of chocolate flavor?

⇒ BY MEG SUZUKI ⇐

Chocolate mousse is comfort food dressed up for company, like pudding for grownups. Less familiar to most home cooks is the chocolate mousse cake. After investigating local bakeries, I discovered that this dessert has two distinct styles. One was a fancy, fluffy chocolate sponge layer cake, brushed with syrup, with mousse sandwiched between the layers. The other was essentially chocolate mousse baked in a cake pan, almost cheesecake-like in density. Before deciding on one style, I'd have to make both of them.

The sponge cake/mousse combination was incredibly time-consuming (make the cake, cool the cake, cut the cake, make the syrup, soak the cake, make the mousse, assemble the cake, chill the cake—whew). An enormous sinkful of dishes and several grueling hours later, I tasted the cake. Its elegant appearance couldn't make up for its lack of chocolate flavor. This cake was a dud—all show and no substance. Although I could work on improving the flavor, I decided not to try. This cake was simply too much work for the home cook.

The baked mousse was much simpler—a major benefit—but it came out of the oven a dense, homely mess. Texture and appearance aside, however, this ugly duckling showed promise. The flavor was excellent: fudgy, chocolatey, and very, very rich. With a more mousse-like texture and a bit of a facelift, this cake could be a winner.

Choosing Ingredients

The ingredient list for chocolate mousse cake is short: chocolate, sugar, butter, eggs, vanilla, and salt. I tackled the most important ingredient first: the chocolate. I tried grocery-store brands as well as a few high-end boutique chocolates and determined that Hershey's Special Dark made a great cake with nicely balanced chocolate flavor. Baker's Bittersweet Chocolate was less successful, having an artificial aftertaste that tasters rejected. Other, more expensive brands worked, but I

Lightly sweetened whipped cream balances the rich texture and flavor of this cake.

decided to stick to the more widely available Hershey's, which had also done well in a previous tasting of bittersweet chocolates (see the September/October 2001 issue). But bittersweet chocolate alone didn't bring the intensity I was looking for. I tried adding unsweetened cocoa, but it gave the cake a sour flavor. After some experimentation, I found that adding a mere ounce of unsweetened chocolate to 12 ounces of bittersweet provided a deep, chocolatey taste and a darker, slightly more sophisticated quality.

Butter and egg yolks are the ingredients that give this cake its melt-in-your-mouth texture. Twelve tablespoons was the perfect amount of butter. Any more made the cake unpalatably greasy; less made it dry. As for egg yolks, I made cakes using as few as four and as many as 10. The 10-yolk version remained a little too damp in the middle, even when thoroughly baked. Eight was the magic number. Adding some vanilla and a pinch of salt heightened the chocolate flavor even more. The vanilla does double duty: It rounds out the smokiness of the chocolate, giving the cake slightly fruity overtones, while taming the egginess of the yolks.

The final ingredient in this cake is beaten egg whites, which are folded into the batter just before it goes into the oven. But folding the beaten egg whites into the chocolate mixture was proving problematic. The delicate whites collapsed under the weight of the chocolate, giving the cake a dense, brick-like texture. Was there anything I could do to make the whites sturdier? I tried beating the egg whites further, until they were almost rigid. That wasn't the answer; it just made the cake unappealingly dry. Maybe beating the whites less was the answer. No such luck. That made the cake even more dense. I looked again at the mousse cake recipes I had found in my initial research. All of them called for the sugar to be added to the yolks and chocolate. I decided to add the sugar, along with a pinch of cream of tartar, to the whites instead. (Sugar creates a thicker, more stable egg foam, and acids, such as cream of tartar, help prevent egg foams from collapsing.) Finally, I had uncovered the secret to the perfect texture. This method produced a creamy meringue that held up well when folded into the chocolate mixture and produced a baked mousse cake that was moist, rich, and creamy.

Final Touches

I tried baking the cake at 350 degrees, the standard temperature for most cakes. Not for this one. It turned into a giant mushroom that collapsed after cooling. A more gentle heat was clearly necessary. I tried lowering the temperature, but even at 300 degrees the outside of the cake was overdone while the center remained raw. Baking the mousse cake in a water bath—an extra complication I had hoped to avoid—might do the trick. I placed the mousse-filled springform pan in a roasting pan, filled the roasting pan with hot water, and put it all in the oven. Once again, I tried 350, 325, and 300 degrees. The cake baked at 325 degrees was perfect. It rose evenly and had a velvety, creamy texture throughout. That extra step was definitely worth the effort.

Now I had a cake with great texture, but there was still something missing. The chocolate flavor was intense but still a little too sweet and one-dimensional. Perhaps reducing the sugar was the answer. Not so. It only made the cake slightly bitter. On a whim, I tried using light brown sugar

TESTING EQUIPMENT:
Springform Pans

A springform pan is essential to the recipe for chocolate mousse cake. To see if there was a superior (9-inch) springform pan on the market, we baked chocolate mousse cakes and cheesecakes in six, ranging in price from $9 to $32.

An ideal pan, we thought, would release a cake from the sides and bottom effortlessly. All six pans tested had acceptable side release, but dislodging a cake from the bottom was trickier. Here the top pans were the Kaiser Bakeware Noblesse and the Frieling Glass Bottom, each of which has a rimless bottom. The other pans tested have rimmed bottoms that can get in the way of cake removal.

TOP CHOICE: This Kaiser Bakeware Noblesse pan delivered superior results in all tests.

RUNNER-UP: Although very expensive, this Frieling pan has handles that come in handy when lifting the pan out of a water bath.

To test leakage, we baked cheesecakes in a water bath tinted with green food coloring, our theory being that the less secure the seal of the pan, the more water would seep through, and the greener the cheesecake would be. This was a tough test. Even the best-performing pan, the Kaiser Noblesse, showed an edge of green around one-third of the cake. The worst performers were the Kaiser Bakeware Tinplate and the Cuisipro Tall Tinned pan, in which the green made a complete circle around the cake. Of all the pans tested, these two also had the flimsiest construction and were cheapest, priced at $8.99 and $9.99, respectively. The Frieling pan as well as the Roshco Commercial ($12.99) and the Exeter Non-Stick ($11.49) showed decent performance in this test. We recommend wrapping the bottom of a pan with foil when baking in a water bath.

The two pans we really liked—the Kaiser Noblesse ($19.80) and the Frieling Glass Bottom ($31.95)—are the priciest of the lot, but each is also solidly constructed and well designed.
   —India Koopman and Meg Suzuki

instead of granulated white sugar. The flavor was fabulous, with just the right amount of sweetness and a tiny hint of smokiness from the molasses. Brown sugar offered an additional bonus. The molasses in brown sugar is slightly acidic, eliminating the need for cream of tartar (another acid) to stabilize the egg whites. When beaten together, the whites and brown sugar turned into a glossy, perfect meringue.

My chocolate mousse cake was rich and creamy, with tremendous chocolate flavor, and was relatively easy to make to boot. What more could a chocoholic ask?

BITTERSWEET CHOCOLATE MOUSSE CAKE
MAKES ONE 9-INCH CAKE, SERVING 12 TO 16

Because it is available in most supermarkets and has scored highly in past tastings, Hershey's Special Dark is the chocolate of choice in this recipe. Other bittersweet chocolates will work, but because amounts of sugar and cocoa butter differ from brand to brand, they will produce cakes with slightly different textures and flavors. When crumbling the brown sugar to remove lumps, make sure that your fingers are clean and grease-free; any residual fat from butter or chocolate might hinder the whipping of the whites. If you like, dust the cake with confectioners' sugar just before serving or top slices with a dollop of lightly sweetened whipped cream.

12	tablespoons (1 1/2 sticks) unsalted butter, cut into 12 pieces, plus 1 teaspoon softened butter for greasing pan
	Flour for dusting pan
12	ounces bittersweet chocolate (such as Hershey's Special Dark), chopped
1	ounce unsweetened chocolate, chopped
1	tablespoon vanilla extract
8	large eggs, separated
1/8	teaspoon salt
2/3	cup (4 1/2 ounces) packed light brown sugar, crumbled with fingers to remove lumps (see note)

1. Adjust oven rack to lower-middle position and heat oven to 325 degrees. Butter sides of 9-inch springform pan; flour sides and tap out excess. Line bottom of pan with parchment or

Beating Egg Whites

The egg whites and brown sugar should be beaten together until they appear smooth and creamy. When the beater is lifted out of the bowl, the egg whites should hold a soft peak (right). If the egg whites are beaten too long, they will look dry and grainy and will begin to separate (far right).

waxed paper round. Wrap bottom and sides of pan with large sheet of foil.

2. Melt 12 tablespoons butter and chocolates in large bowl over large saucepan containing about 2 quarts barely simmering water, stirring occasionally, until chocolate mixture is smooth. Cool mixture slightly, then whisk in vanilla and egg yolks. Set chocolate mixture aside, reserving hot water, covered, in saucepan.

3. In clean bowl of standing mixer fitted with whisk attachment, beat egg whites and salt at medium speed until frothy, about 30 seconds; add half of crumbled brown sugar, beat at high speed until combined, about 30 seconds, then add remaining brown sugar and continue to beat at high speed until soft peaks form when whisk is lifted (see photo, below), about 2 minutes longer. Using whisk, stir about one-third of beaten egg whites into chocolate mixture to lighten it, then fold in remaining egg whites in 2 additions using whisk. Gently scrape batter into prepared springform pan, set springform pan in large roasting pan, then pour hot water from saucepan to depth of 1 inch. Carefully slide roasting pan into oven; bake until cake has risen, is firm around edges, center has just set, and instant-read thermometer inserted into center registers about 170 degrees, 45 to 55 minutes.

4. Remove springform pan from water bath, discard foil, and cool on wire rack 10 minutes. Run thin-bladed paring knife between sides of pan and cake to loosen; cool cake in springform pan on wire rack until barely warm, about 3 hours, then wrap pan in plastic wrap and refrigerate until thoroughly chilled, at least 8 hours. (Cake can be refrigerated for up to 2 days.)

5. To unmold cake, remove sides of pan. Slide thin metal spatula between cake and pan bottom to loosen, then invert cake onto large plate, peel off parchment, and re-invert onto serving platter. To serve, use sharp, thin-bladed knife, dipping knife in pitcher of hot water and wiping blade before each cut.

CHOCOLATE-ORANGE MOUSSE CAKE

Follow recipe for Bittersweet Chocolate Mousse Cake, reducing vanilla extract to 1 teaspoon and adding 1 tablespoon orange liqueur and 1 tablespoon finely grated orange zest to chocolate mixture along with vanilla and egg yolks.

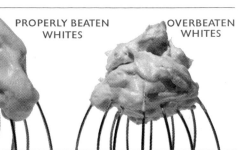

PROPERLY BEATEN WHITES   OVERBEATEN WHITES

The Best Sugar Cookies

Is it possible to make sugar cookies that have a perfect balance of texture and flavor?
After 50 batches and 1,200 cookies, we know the answer.

⇒ BY MEG SUZUKI ⇐

In the lineup of classic American cookies, sugar cookies are the Plain Janes of the bunch. They lack the smoky sophistication of molasses spice cookies, the heartiness of oatmeal raisin, and the decadence of chocolate chip. They can be dry, tasteless, pasty, and boring, and they are usually the last ones left on the holiday cookie platter. Why have a sugar cookie when you can have anything else?

What I wanted was a rich, buttery sugar cookie with a crackling sugar exterior—not the thin, cut-out butter cookies that are more fun to decorate than to eat but a chewy cookie with a big vanilla flavor. It should be able to stand on its own without having to rely on garish decorations or cloyingly sweet frosting for its appeal. Could I make the kind of cookie that would leap off the holiday cookie tray?

A little brown sugar gives these soft, chewy cookies a hint of nuttiness.

A Wrong Turn

Assuming that the sugar cookie's blandness must come from its lack of interesting ingredients, I started by testing recipes that called for sour cream, cream cheese, milk, and heavy cream and pitted them all against a no-frills version that included only the basics: butter, sugar, flour, egg, vanilla, salt, and baking powder. "Is this a muffin top?" a taster asked, after trying the cookies made with sour cream. The heavy cream version was greasy, and the cookies made with milk were flat in terms of both texture and flavor. Cream cheese made a dense, sour cookie, which reminded one taster of "a yellow cake that someone forgot to leaven." The only cookie that even came close to what I was looking for was the no-frills version. It was bland, but it had none of the off flavors of the others. After trying them all, I reached a conclusion: Strange ingredients make strange sugar cookies. I went back to square one. If I wanted the perfect sugar cookie, I would have to concentrate on basic ingredients.

Back to Basics

During my initial research, I had come across many recipes that used both shortening and butter. Cookies made using this combination were dry and flavorless; an all-butter cookie was clearly the only way to go. Most baking recipes call for butter and sugar to be creamed together until fluffy. Looking for shortcuts, I tried using melted butter, thinking that the dough would be easier to mix. However, creaming the butter and sugar proved to be key (see "Getting Creamed," page 25, for details).

For flour, I chose all-purpose. Both bleached and unbleached flours worked equally well, though a few tasters detected a minor metallic aftertaste in the bleached flour. Having a chewy cookie meant having only a small amount of leavening; too much and the cookies turned into fluffy little cakes. One-half teaspoon of baking powder did the trick, giving the cookies just the right amount of lift.

What about eggs? I tried one egg, two eggs, and various yolk-and-white combinations in between. One whole egg plus one yolk made the cookies spongy, two eggs made them even fluffier. Using just one whole egg was the answer. With the addition of a little salt and a healthy dose of vanilla, this recipe was on the right track.

Finishing Touches

On to the sugary outer crunch. Simply rolling the dough in sugar wasn't enough. The sugar crystals were not sticking readily to the dough, and the cookies weren't nearly as sparkly as I wanted. I tried dipping the balls of dough in beaten egg whites, then rolling them in the sugar. No luck. This process made a huge mess and resulted in cookies with an odd, meringue-like coating. The solution was to form the balls of dough using slightly dampened hands. The small amount of water kept my hands from sticking to the dough and ensured that enough sugar remained on the cookies. Because I wanted a thick, substantial cookie, I rolled the dough into 1½-inch balls and then flattened them slightly with the bottom of a drinking glass.

Now the dough was ready for the oven. Proper baking times and temperatures could make or break these cookies. I tried baking them at 350, 375, and 400 degrees. Cookies baked at 350 degrees never browned enough. Four hundred degrees was more than the cookies could handle, turning them into cookie brûlée on the outside and leaving them pasty and underdone on the inside. A more moderate 375 degrees was just right. The cookies emerged from the oven with pale golden centers and toasty browned edges. I

The Secret to Evenly Baked Cookies

Does your oven turn out trays of baked cookies that vary in color and texture (like those pictured here)? Are some cookies a bit burnt around the edges while others on the same baking sheet are not quite done? Most ovens cause such uneven baking because their temperature varies from back to front, side to side, and top to bottom. The solution is simple. At the halfway mark in the baking time, rotate the cookie sheet so that the back side faces front. If you have two cookie sheets in the oven, also switch their position so that top goes to bottom and bottom goes to top.

eagerly tried one. The edges tasted as toasty as they looked, but the centers were disappointingly bland. What were they missing? I knew that additions such as sour cream or cream cheese weren't the answer. Was there something else that would enhance the flavor of the cookies without making them taste like some other kind of cookie?

I looked at an ingredient that I had taken for granted: the sugar. I had assumed that granulated white sugar was the obvious choice for this cookie. What would happen if I were to use a different kind? I made a batch of cookies with just 1 tablespoon of light brown sugar added to the dough. The resulting cookies were perfect; the brown sugar gave the cookies just a hint of nuttiness and brought out the deep, rich tones of the vanilla.

Now I had a sugar cookie that both looked and tasted great. This was a cookie that deserved to be eaten first, not left behind on the holiday cookie platter.

SOFT AND CHEWY SUGAR COOKIES
MAKES 2 DOZEN COOKIES

The cookies are softer and more tender when made with unbleached flour that has a protein content of about 10.5 percent. Pillsbury or Gold Medal works best; King Arthur flour has a higher protein content (around 11.7 percent) and will result in slightly drier, cakier cookies. Do not discard the butter wrappers; they have just enough residual butter on them for buttering the bottom of the drinking glass used to flatten the dough balls. To make sure the cookies are flat, choose a glass with a smooth, flat bottom. Rolled into balls, the dough will keep in the freezer for up to 1 week. The baked cookies will keep in an airtight container for up to 5 days.

    2   cups (10 ounces) unbleached all-purpose flour,
         preferably Pillsbury or Gold Medal
    1/2 teaspoon baking powder
    1/4 teaspoon salt
    16   tablespoons unsalted butter (2 sticks), softened
         but still firm (60 to 65 degrees)
    1   cup (7 ounces) granulated sugar, plus 1/2 cup
         (3 1/2 ounces) for rolling dough
    1   tablespoon light brown sugar
    1   large egg
    1 1/2 teaspoons vanilla extract

1. Adjust oven racks to upper- and lower-middle positions; heat oven to 375 degrees. Line two large baking sheets with parchment paper. Whisk flour, baking powder, and salt in medium bowl; set aside.

2. In standing mixer fitted with paddle attachment or with hand mixer, beat butter, 1 cup granulated sugar, and brown sugar at medium speed until light and fluffy, about 3 minutes, scraping down sides of bowl with rubber spatula as needed. Add egg and vanilla; beat at medium

---

Getting Creamed

I am, by far, the laziest cook in the test kitchen. If there's a shortcut to be discovered or a step that can be eliminated, I will find it. Most cookie recipes tell you to soften the butter and cream it together with the sugar. Is this really necessary? Why not just melt the butter and mix all the ingredients together?

To find out, I made a batch of sugar cookies with melted butter. The result? Flat cookies that spread into giant, crispy disks—not exactly what I was going for. If I wanted thick and chewy cookies, then creaming was an essential step.

Creaming together butter and sugar accomplishes two things. First, it makes the butter malleable, allowing the other ingredients to be easily mixed together. Second, the tiny sugar crystals act like extra beaters, helping to incorporate air into the butter. These pockets of air, along with the air produced by the baking powder, expand when baked, giving the cookie lift. To achieve the perfect texture, the butter should be softened slightly until it's cool but pliable (about 60 to 65 degrees).

I wondered how long I needed to cream the butter and sugar. Using an electric mixer, I tested creaming for 45 seconds, three minutes, and 12 minutes (see the results at right). Although undercreaming did not bring on disaster, I had the best results when I creamed the butter and sugar until the mixture was pale yellow and fluffy, about three minutes. Creaming butter and sugar for too long turned out to be a big mistake. The extra beating warms up the mixture. Butterfat begins to melt at 68 degrees, and as the temperature increases, the emulsion of butterfat and whey separates. Because liquefied butter doesn't have the ability to hold air bubbles, the resulting cookies were flat.

For best results, use butter that's at the right temperature, and cream it with the sugar until fluffy but not warm. –M.S.

CREAMED 45 SECONDS
The butter and sugar were yellow and dense, and it was hard to incorporate the egg and other ingredients. Baked cookies were pretty good.

CREAMED 3 MINUTES
The butter and sugar were pale yellow and fluffy, and other ingredients were easily added. When baked, these cookies won the taste test.

CREAMED 12 MINUTES
The butter and sugar turned almost stark white and appeared greasy. The baked cookies were flat.

---

speed until combined, about 30 seconds. Add dry ingredients and beat at low speed until just combined, about 30 seconds, scraping down bowl as needed.

3. Place sugar for rolling in shallow bowl. Fill medium bowl halfway with cold tap water. Dip hands in water and shake off excess (this will prevent dough from sticking to your hands and ensure that sugar sticks to dough). Roll heaping tablespoon dough into 1 1/2-inch ball between moistened palms; roll ball in sugar, then place on prepared baking sheet. Repeat with remaining dough, moistening hands after forming each ball and spacing balls about 2 inches apart on baking sheet (you should be able to fit 12 cookies on each sheet). Using butter wrapper, butter bottom of drinking glass; dip bottom of glass in remaining sugar and flatten dough balls with bottom of glass until dough is about 3/4 inch thick.

4. Bake until cookies are golden brown around edges and just set and very lightly colored in center, 15 to 18 minutes, reversing position of cookie sheets from front to back and top to bottom halfway through baking time. Cool cookies on baking sheet about 3 minutes; using wide metal spatula, transfer cookies to wire rack and cool to room temperature.

GINGERED SUGAR COOKIES

In food processor, process 1/2 cup sugar for rolling and 1 teaspoon grated fresh ginger until combined, about 10 seconds. Follow recipe for Soft and Chewy Sugar Cookies, adding 2 tablespoons finely chopped crystallized ginger to creamed butter and sugars along with egg and vanilla, and using ginger sugar for coating dough balls in step 3.

SUGAR COOKIES WITH LIME ESSENCE

In food processor, process 1/2 cup sugar for rolling and 1 teaspoon grated lime zest until zest is evenly distributed, about 10 seconds. Follow recipe for Soft and Chewy Sugar Cookies, adding 2 teaspoons grated lime zest to creamed butter and sugars along with egg and vanilla, and using lime sugar for coating dough balls in step 3.

LEMON-POPPYSEED SUGAR COOKIES

Follow recipe for Soft and Chewy Sugar Cookies, whisking 1 tablespoon poppy seeds into dry ingredients and adding 1 tablespoon grated lemon zest to creamed butter and sugars along with egg and vanilla.

Are Expensive Unsweetened Chocolates Worth the Money?

Scharffen Berger costs three times more than Baker's. Is it that much better?

⇒ BY SALLY SAMPSON ⇐

Like Hollywood, the world of chocolate has celebrities, some of whom earn their fame through stellar performances, while others simply coast on favorable publicity. We wanted to see if all the fuss over premium chocolates is based on quality or hype. We selected unsweetened chocolate (rather than semi- or bittersweet) because it is a building-block ingredient in countless desserts, most notably brownies and chocolate cake. Not for nibbling, it is pure, unadulterated chocolate, or solidified chocolate liquor, produced without added sugar or flavorings (see "Chocolate Glossary" for more definitions). Seven brands were rated: the four American supermarket standbys, Baker's, Ghirardelli, Hershey's, and Nestlé; the premium American brand, Scharffen Berger; and two brands used largely by candy makers and pastry chefs, Callebaut from Belgium and Valrhona from France. We conducted a blind tasting with 20 *Cook's* staffers and four pastry chefs, sampling a classic American brownie and a chocolate sauce.

Our assumption going into this tasting (based on prior taste tests) was that, in general, the more expensive brands would prevail. In fact, this was the outcome. However, we found a surprising range of taste differences from one brand to the next. If unsweetened chocolate is pure chocolate, how could one brand be so different from another? We spent weeks searching for the answer to this question, encountering red herrings, unhelpful company spokesmen, and conflicting stories along the way.

The Beans Matter

The first thing we learned was that most chocolate companies don't like to talk about their product in detail. With the exception of Scharffen Berger, the companies we contacted were distinctly vague. The response from Marie Olson of Nestlé said it all: "Most of what we do is proprietary. Nestlé has established a certain flavor profile, and we blend beans from various sources based on availability and cost to match our profile."

We turned to outside experts to uncover the trade secrets of chocolate manufacturers. One was Maricel Presilla, a cacao and chocolate expert and the author of *The New Taste of Chocolate: A Cultural and Natural History of Cacao with Recipes* (Ten Speed Press, 2001). "Normally," she told us, "companies use a lower-priced bulk bean—from Malaysia, Indonesia, the Dominican Republic, or the Ivory Coast—for their unsweetened. I would not use a company's unsweetened as a barometer for the quality of any brand. With a few notable exceptions, that is not where a company uses their best beans." A cacao trader who sells to most of the major chocolate companies and wished to remain unnamed agreed. "They don't use their best beans for unsweetened. After all, you don't put your best burgundy in a coq au vin." The irony of this practice is that there is more chocolate in unsweetened than in any other type, so the quality of the beans may matter more, not less.

Every expert we contacted told us that the flavor of unsweetened chocolate is largely determined before it gets to the chocolate processor. Country of origin and specific bean blend are the most critical factors. In fact, the above-mentioned cacao trader said, "If you gave Scharffen Berger Nestlé's beans and they put it through their process, the chocolate would taste like Nestlé." Scharffen Berger cofounder Robert Steinberg concurred, adding, "A processor can ruin a good bean but cannot make good chocolate from an inferior one." Both comments underscore a simple fact: When it comes to making chocolate, you have to start with good ingredients. If this is the case, however, then why don't all companies purchase the highest quality beans?

Cacao beans mainly come from West Africa, Indonesia, Brazil, and Malaysia, with smaller amounts coming from other South American countries and the Caribbean. Each region has diverse outputs and characteristics. If a flavor profile includes, say, the taste of coffee, a company would select West African beans; for floral notes, Ecuadorian arriba; for fruity flavor, beans from Venezuela and Trinidad; and for citrus flavor, beans from Madagascar.

Scharffen Berger's Steinberg allows that taste is his company's priority when it comes to buying beans, and they are willing to pay more to secure that taste. "Without exception," he said "we are paying above-market prices for our beans." But some companies can't afford the luxury of buying the best-flavored beans, and it's not necessarily because of the price. Large companies may use 10,000 tons of beans per year, so what is most important to them is supply. They need to buy chocolate from a region that consistently produces a large amount, such as West Africa. For example, they cannot risk a short supply from Venezuela, which produces a tiny amount of some of the best beans.

We concluded that the really big players in the unsweetened chocolate business use a more limited mix of beans because their volume demands exclude smaller suppliers, and this in turn may make the flavor profile of their product less interesting.

Blending, Roasting, Conching

If the quality of a bean is one important determinant of flavor, the blend of beans selected is another. "One great bean can give you a flat taste, whereas a blend of many can give you

---

Chocolate Glossary

Cacao Beans: Seeds harvested from fleshy yellow pods that grow on cacao trees.

Nibs: The meat of cacao beans, which get ground into chocolate liquor.

Chocolate Liquor: The thick, nonalcoholic liquid that results when the roasted, hulled beans (nibs, see above) are ground.

Cocoa Butter: The fat that can be extracted from chocolate liquor. It is not a dairy product.

Cocoa Powder: The solids that remain after the cocoa butter is extracted. When the solids are dried, they are processed and then either "Dutched" (treated with alkali) or left as is.

Unsweetened Chocolate: Solidified pure chocolate liquor that contains between 50 percent and 60 percent cocoa butter.

Bittersweet/Semisweet Chocolate: Chocolate that contains at least 35 percent chocolate liquor. The remainder is sugar, vanilla, and/or lecithin.

Milk Chocolate: Chocolate made primarily from sugar, at least 10 percent chocolate liquor, milk solids, vanilla, and/or lecithin.

TASTING UNSWEETENED CHOCOLATE

Because unsweetened chocolate, which does not contain sugar or milk solids, is an ingredient that is not eaten in its raw form, we tested it in brownies and in chocolate sauce. We rated the brownies and sauce for flavor and texture and gave each an overall rating from 1 to 10. The chocolates are listed in order of preference based on the combined results of these two tests. Scharffen Berger, a relative newcomer, ranked first overall. Scharffen Berger came in first in the sauce test, while Ghirardelli came in first in the brownies.

RECOMMENDED

SCHARFFEN BERGER Unsweetened Pure Dark Chocolate

➤ $8.95 for 275 grams ($14.78 per pound)

Scharffen Berger chocolate is made in small batches from high-quality beans from small producers with refurbished vintage equipment from Europe. Tasters described this chocolate as "fruity" and "nutty," with a "deep, caramelized flavor."

CALLEBAUT Unsweetened Chocolate

➤ $11.95 for 1 kilogram ($5.43 per pound)

Belgian Callebaut is the number one chocolate manufacturer in the world and a favorite of pastry chefs. In both tests, our tasters ranked this chocolate second and described it as "nutty," with hints of "cinnamon" and "cherry." One devotee called it "spicy," while another said it had "deep, chocolate flavor."

GHIRARDELLI Unsweetened Chocolate Baking Bar

➤ $2.19 for 4 ounces ($8.76 per pound)

Tasters described it with the terms "coffee," "rich," and "earthy." Brownie was described as "normal" and won that test.

VALRHONA Cacao Pâte Extra

➤ $25 for 1 kilogram ($11.36 per pound)

A French chocolate available in unsweetened only in bulk. Often elicited the words "cherry," "fruity," "wine," and "rich." One detractor said it "tasted more like flowers than chocolate," while another found it "dull."

NESTLÉ Unsweetened Baking Chocolate Bars

➤ $1.99 for 8 ounces ($3.98 per pound)

The only chocolate in the group processed with alkali, our lab found it significantly higher in pH (or lower in acidity). Its fat content was the highest at 58.42 percent. A basic chocolate that fans called "earthy" and "nutty" and detractors described as "scorched" or "dull."

NOT RECOMMENDED

BAKER'S Unsweetened Baking Chocolate Squares

➤ $2.39 for 8 ounces ($4.78 per pound)

This chocolate was considered "acidic" and "bitter," but a few fans found it "rich" and "earthy." One taster described it as "dry and mealy," while another said it "didn't have much chocolate flavor."

HERSHEY'S Unsweetened Baking Chocolate

➤ $2.19 for 8 ounces ($4.38 per pound)

Hershey's adds cocoa to its unsweetened chocolate, which came in last in both tastings. Tasters found it "acidic," "muted," and "chemical-y." One panelist generously wrote, "plain and dull."

---

more depth," said the cacao trader. Greg Ziegler, associate professor of food science at Penn State University, agreed, pointing out that roasting is yet another key step in the process. Of most interest, according to Ziegler, is whether a company roasts bean types individually or together.

Other experts agree that roasting varieties of beans separately allows the roaster to be more selective and to both preserve and concentrate flavor. Beans vary in size, moisture content, and acidity, and as a result they require different roasting temperatures and times. "If you mix everything together," said Presilla, "you're not doing justice to any bean; you destroy the nuances. Beans should be roasted independently." Of the companies whose chocolate we tasted, Scharffen Berger is the only one that would confirm that it roasts beans separately by type. Although many experts vouch for roasting independently, our tasting results suggest it's not the only way to produce a high quality

chocolate. In fact, a spokesperson for third-placed Ghirardelli noted that the company roasts their beans together.

One final production issue is conching, which aerates and homogenizes the chocolate, thereby mellowing the flavor and making its texture smooth and creamy. While eating chocolates are always conched, only Scharffen Berger and Valrhona conch their unsweetened chocolate, and these chocolates finished first and third in our chocolate sauce tasting, where smooth texture was an important consideration.

What About Fat?

We sent all of the chocolates in our tasting to a laboratory to measure fat content as well as pH (acidity), thinking that the higher-fat chocolates would rate better and that the acidity of each chocolate might also have a role to play. The results were mixed. While three of the four top-rated chocolates—Scharffen Berger, Callebaut, and Valrhona—did have slightly

more fat than most of the other brands, fifth-place Nestlé had the highest fat content of all. As for pH, there was no correlation at all with the results of our tasting.

What do we recommend? The more expensive chocolates—Scharffen Berger, Callebaut, Ghirardelli, and Valrhona—were all well liked and received similar scores. If you are willing to buy in bulk by mail, Callebaut turns out to be a best buy. Of the three mass-market brands (Nestlé, Baker's, and Hershey's), Nestlé received more positive comments and significantly higher scores. In fact, there were so many negative comments about Baker's and Hershey's that we cannot recommend either chocolate. It's important to remember, though, that chocolate, much like coffee, is a matter of personal preference, so consider each brand in order to find a chocolate that suits your palate. The gamut of flavors runs from "nutty" and "cherry" to "smoky," "earthy," and "spicy."

The $90 Chef's Knife Meets the $30 Upstart

Can a chef's knife with a stamped blade hold its own against a heavy, forged model?

≥ BY ADAM RIED ≤

When purchasing a chef's knife, traditional kitchen wisdom has its dictates: Buy a knife with a forged, not a stamped, blade; buy one that's heavier rather than lighter; and buy one with a bolster, that piece of metal between the handle and the blade that both protects your fingers and provides extra weight for better balance. Given that knives, like most cookware, have undergone advances in design, we wondered if traditional wisdom still held true. To find out we rounded up eight popular 8-inch chef's knife models, covering a range of styles and prices (from $30 to $112). We then put them to the test in an extensive battery of everyday cutting tasks, from mincing parsley to butchering chickens. We sought the participation of testers who have different levels of skill with a knife and different hand sizes, in the hope of uncovering the best all-purpose chef's knife.

Forged versus Stamped

The weight and balance of a chef's knife is said to depend on how the blade was manufactured. Forging, which involves pounding a relatively thick, red-hot billet of steel into shape under extreme pressure using a forging hammer and die, produces a slightly thicker, heavier blade. A forged knife also has a bolster, the thick piece of metal between the blade and the handle. A bolster adds weight, is said to improve the balance between the blade and handle, and can protect your fingers by separating them from the cutting edge. Among the knives we tested, both Wüsthofs, both Henckels, the Global, and the KitchenAid have forged blades.

The Forschner and Oxo knives have stamped blades, which began life as thin sheets of steel called ribbons. Blade-shaped blanks are punched out of the ribbon in a huge press, almost like cookies being cut from rolled dough. Manufacturing techniques now allow bolsters to be attached to knives with stamped blades, which is the case with the Oxo knife.

So, were the forged knives the hands-down winners? Well, it turned out that impressions of weight and balance are highly subjective. Regardless of whether they were doing heavy chopping or light mincing, some cooks appreciated the maneuverability and quick moves of the lighter knives in the group, including the stamped, bolster-less Forschner as well as the Wüsthof Grand Prix, Oxo, and Henckels 4-Star. They all weigh about 7 or 8 ounces. Other testers, however, preferred the heavier forged and/or bolstered knives, weighing 9 to 10 ounces, noting that the weight of the knife made heavy chopping tasks slightly easier. In the rankings, though, the lighter knives came out slightly ahead. In our tests, then, stamped blades were at no disadvantage to the forged blades.

In addition, evidence did not suggest that a bolster necessarily improves balance. There was not a single complaint about the balance of the bolster-free Forschner, whereas a couple of testers noted that the Wüsthof Culinar, which had a bolster, felt handle-heavy.

"Ergonomic" Handles and Sharp Blades

Twenty-five years ago, the basic choice in handle material was wood versus a wood-plastic composite. Now consumers have quite a few more choices. There is stainless steel as well as many kinds of molded plastic handles, including textured, smooth, flat-sided, rounded, straight, curved, and "ergonomic." Most of our test kitchen staff prefers molded plastic handles, which six of the eight knives have. The other two, the Wüsthof Culinar and the Global, have stainless steel handles. These two handles are also notable for their shapes, the Culinar curved in profile with a squared grip, and the Global straight in profile with a rounded grip. Though each of these handles had one fan among the testers, most testers gravitated toward molded plastic handles.

That is not to say that each and every one of the molded handles earned high regard. One in particular, the ergonomic handle on the Henckels Twinstar, was universally disliked for its excessive girth; it was a poor fit in all the testers' hands, be they large, medium, or small. The hard black handle on the KitchenAid knife swung too far in the other direction. While it was not considered outright uncomfortable by anyone, testers called it "skinny," "shallow," and "small." Simply shaped molded plastic handles, without exaggerated curves, bulges, and long flat planes, were clear winners.

All but one of our knives had impressively sharp cutting edges fresh from the box. In fact, not one of them earned a single "poor" mark in any of the individual tests. However, testers did form a distinct impression of each knife's sharpness. Most notable were the Global, which was perceived as the sharpest of the lot, and the Henckels Twinstar, which was thought to be the least sharp.

All blades curve gently from the heel to the tip, but the more pronounced that curve, the more easily a knife will rock on a cutting surface. This rocking action is especially useful for fine mincing because it allows you to use the length of the blade. In general, blades that rocked easily drew more positive responses. Among the knives tested, the two Wüsthofs had the greatest curvature and were therefore the rocking champs. Forschner and Oxo followed close behind. In contrast, the Global had the least curvature and was therefore more difficult to rock.

What Should You Buy?

First of all, let it be said that all of the knives in our testing did a perfectly good job even after we butchered 30 chickens and cut up the same number of butternut squash. Our testers were divided into two camps: those who prefer a lighter knife (7 to 8 ounces) and those who like the power of the heavier models (9 to 10 ounces). (However, based on prior testing, we don't recommend that you buy a knife that weighs less than 7 ounces—it will be too lightweight for many tasks.) As for forged versus stamped, it simply doesn't matter, nor does the existence of a bolster. And as for the handle, it has to fit your hand much like a glove. Before you buy a chef's knife, pick it up and see how it feels. Most folks preferred a softer, textured plastic handle to either steel or hard plastic but, once again, we discovered testers who were exceptions to the rule.

If you prefer a lighter (and less expensive) knife, look to either the Forschner or the Oxo (about $30). For those who insist on a heavier blade (with a forged blade and bolster), the Wüsthof Grand Prix or Henckels Four Star are great bets, and at $87 and $70, respectively, both are less expensive than some of the more esoteric brands we tested.

RATING CHEF'S KNIVES

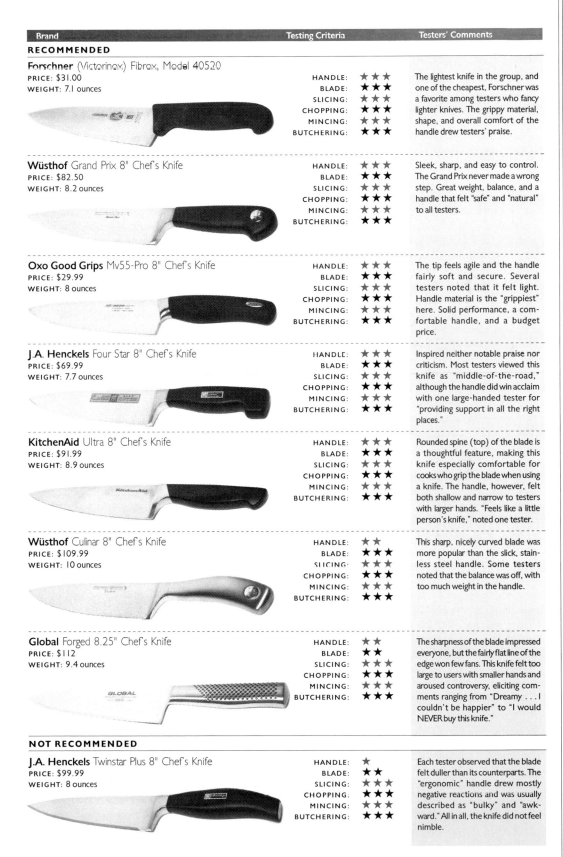

RATINGS

★★★ GOOD

★★ FAIR

★ POOR

Seven everyday cooking tasks, including slicing tomatoes and bacon, chopping butternut squash and onions, mincing parsley and ginger, and butchering whole chickens into 10 serving pieces, were performed by four members of the kitchen staff with each of the knives. Like tasks are grouped into four general categories, detailed below, and ratings in a given category reflect the average score on the tests included in that category. The final numerical tallies for the knives were very, very close. Among the recommended models, scores varied by only a few hundredths of a point. The knives are listed in order based on descending numerical scores.

PRICE: Prices are those listed at Boston-area retail outlets, in national mail-order catalogs, or on Web sites. Because cutlery prices are often heavily discounted, you may encounter different prices for the same item where you shop.

WEIGHT: No preference was given to heavy or light knives.

HANDLE: Handles that formed a tight, secure seal in users' hands and that resisted slipping out of wet or greasy hands were preferred.

BLADE: Blades with a very sharp factory edge and sufficient curvature were preferred.

SLICING (tomato and bacon): Knives capable of making superthin, even tomato slices and cutting easily through bacon stacked four slices high were preferred.

CHOPPING (hard butternut squash and onion): Knives requiring minimal force on squash and capable of cutting onion evenly and accurately were preferred.

MINCING (parsley and fresh ginger): Knives that were capable of fine, even cuts, a good rocking motion, and the capacity to slice through ginger fibers with minimal effort were preferred.

BUTCHERING (whole chicken): Knives that felt well controlled and maneuverable and required minimal force to work through joints and bone were preferred.

TESTERS' COMMENTS: General observations, including comfort, balance, perceived solidity and construction quality, and promotion of hand fatigue.

Brand	Testing Criteria		Testers' Comments
RECOMMENDED			
Forschner (Victorinox) Fibrox, Model 40520 PRICE: $31.00 WEIGHT: 7.1 ounces	HANDLE: BLADE: SLICING: CHOPPING: MINCING: BUTCHERING:	★★★ ★★★ ★★★ ★★★ ★★★ ★★★	The lightest knife in the group, and one of the cheapest, Forschner was a favorite among testers who fancy lighter knives. The grippy material, shape, and overall comfort of the handle drew testers' praise.
Wüsthof Grand Prix 8" Chef's Knife PRICE: $82.50 WEIGHT: 8.2 ounces	HANDLE: BLADE: SLICING: CHOPPING: MINCING: BUTCHERING:	★★★ ★★★ ★★★ ★★★ ★★★ ★★★	Sleek, sharp, and easy to control. The Grand Prix never made a wrong step. Great weight, balance, and a handle that felt "safe" and "natural" to all testers.
Oxo Good Grips Mv55-Pro 8" Chef's Knife PRICE: $29.99 WEIGHT: 8 ounces	HANDLE: BLADE: SLICING: CHOPPING: MINCING: BUTCHERING:	★★★ ★★★ ★★★ ★★★ ★★★ ★★★	The tip feels agile and the handle fairly soft and secure. Several testers noted that it felt light. Handle material is the "grippiest" here. Solid performance, a comfortable handle, and a budget price.
J.A. Henckels Four Star 8" Chef's Knife PRICE: $69.99 WEIGHT: 7.7 ounces	HANDLE: BLADE: SLICING: CHOPPING: MINCING: BUTCHERING:	★★★ ★★★ ★★★ ★★★ ★★★ ★★★	Inspired neither notable praise nor criticism. Most testers viewed this knife as "middle-of-the-road," although the handle did win acclaim with one large-handed tester for "providing support in all the right places."
KitchenAid Ultra 8" Chef's Knife PRICE: $91.99 WEIGHT: 8.9 ounces	HANDLE: BLADE: SLICING: CHOPPING: MINCING: BUTCHERING:	★★★ ★★★ ★★★ ★★★ ★★★ ★★★	Rounded spine (top) of the blade is a thoughtful feature, making this knife especially comfortable for cooks who grip the blade when using a knife. The handle, however, felt both shallow and narrow to testers with larger hands. "Feels like a little person's knife," noted one tester.
Wüsthof Culinar 8" Chef's Knife PRICE: $109.99 WEIGHT: 10 ounces	HANDLE: BLADE: SLICING: CHOPPING: MINCING: BUTCHERING:	★★ ★★★ ★★★ ★★★ ★★★ ★★★	This sharp, nicely curved blade was more popular than the slick, stainless steel handle. Some testers noted that the balance was off, with too much weight in the handle.
Global Forged 8.25" Chef's Knife PRICE: $112 WEIGHT: 9.4 ounces	HANDLE: BLADE: SLICING: CHOPPING: MINCING: BUTCHERING:	★★ ★★ ★★★ ★★★ ★★★ ★★★	The sharpness of the blade impressed everyone, but the fairly flat line of the edge won few fans. This knife felt too large to users with smaller hands and aroused controversy, eliciting comments ranging from "Dreamy . . . I couldn't be happier" to "I would NEVER buy this knife."
NOT RECOMMENDED			
J.A. Henckels Twinstar Plus 8" Chef's Knife PRICE: $99.99 WEIGHT: 8 ounces	HANDLE: BLADE: SLICING: CHOPPING: MINCING: BUTCHERING:	★ ★★ ★★★ ★★★ ★★★ ★★★	Each tester observed that the blade felt duller than its counterparts. The "ergonomic" handle drew mostly negative reactions and was usually described as "bulky" and "awkward." All in all, the knife did not feel nimble.

⇒ BY BRIDGET LANCASTER ⇐

Wild about Rice

Just as use of the word *rice* in wild rice isn't correct (it's an aquatic grass), the use of *wild* usually isn't accurate, either. Cultivated wild rice—grown under regulated conditions in man-made paddies—is the standard offering in most supermarkets. True to its name, real wild rice is grown in the wild. Hand-harvested from lakes and rivers in Minnesota and Canada, true wild rice can be very expensive, as much as $9 per pound. (Cultivated wild rice costs $3 to $5 per pound.) Should you spend more money on "wild" wild rice when combining it with white rice to make our pilaf recipe on page 21? To find out, we simmered each type of rice in chicken stock (per our recipe) and tasted them. The hand-harvested wild rice had a pale appearance, a smoky flavor, and a light, tender texture. So that's the rice for our pilaf, right? As it turned out, we preferred the cultivated rice for its deep, ebony color and resilient texture, especially when contrasted with the tender white rice used in the pilaf. Although the flavor of cultivated wild rice is slightly less robust than that of the real thing, when it comes to pilaf, we'll save our pennies and go for the cultivated rice.

Safer Seasoning

Although the trips to and from the sink are tedious, washing your hands each time you handle raw meat, poultry, or fish is safe food handling practice. To avoid contaminating our salt box or pepper mill when seasoning raw meat, poultry, and fish, we crack fresh ground pepper into a small bowl or ramekin, and then mix it with kosher salt (a ratio of 1 part pepper to 4 parts salt is ideal). This way we can keep reaching into the bowl to season the meat without having to wash our hands every time we touch the meat. After using the seasoning, the meat goes into the pan (or oven), and the bowl goes into the dishwasher.

Dicey Business

Dicing an onion can be tricky if your chef's knife is dull. We know there is no substitute for regular knife sharpening and honing, but we've found that the tips of our knives—the first 2 inches of the blades, which are usually used to make entry cuts in onions—are often a little dull. We have much better results when we start each horizontal and vertical cut with the middle part of the blade, which is about 4 inches from the tip. This part of the knife is usually sharper.

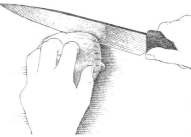

The middle of the blade is usually sharper than the tip and is your best bet when dicing an onion.

The Big Chill

We had excellent results when roasting a frozen Butterball turkey (page 18), but without allowing sufficient time for defrosting, this iceberg of a bird can sink your Thanksgiving dinner faster than you can say, "Titanic." It's best to defrost the turkey in the refrigerator, figuring 1 day of defrosting for every 4 pounds of turkey. That means a frozen 20-pound turkey should go into the refrigerator on Saturday morning if it's to be ready to cook on T-Day (Thursday).

There is a faster (and more tedious) means of defrosting the turkey if you find yourself on Wednesday morning with a frozen bird. Place the turkey, still in its original wrapper, in a bucket of cold water for about 10 hours (or 30 minutes per pound), and change the water every half hour. Yes, every 30 minutes you will be handling this gargantuan bird, a step necessary to guard against bacterial growth.

Since babysitting a turkey is not our idea of fun, if faced with a frozen turkey that late in the game, we'd go out and buy a fresh bird.

Parsley Wars

Here in the test kitchen, we always use flat-leaf parsley over curly-leaf parsley. Recently, a well-known Boston chef challenged our parsley predilection. We decided to put our partiality aside, chop up bushels of both kinds (finely chopped, so each type was less easily identifiable), and hold a taste test. When tossed with hot pasta and garlic, we found little flavor distinction between the two types of parsley. In fact, the test kitchen was filled with a quiet shame because tasters couldn't pick their preconceived favorite. It wasn't until the chopped parsley was tasted alone that tasters noted differences. On its own, the flat-leaf parsley was preferred for its "fresh," "grassy" flavor and "tender" texture, while some found the curly-leaf parsley to be "bitter" or "tough." The moral of the story? If you're making a dish in which parsley gets star billing, go for flat-leaf. However, if you're sprinkling a little parsley into a stew or onto pasta, don't worry if your local supermarket carries only the curly stuff.

When Good Nuts Go Bad

The holiday season is full of nuts. Pecan pie, almond torte, nut crescents . . . But improper storage and a harsh kitchen environment (think hot, bright, and humid) are enough to make a good nut go bad. To prevent an outbreak of rancid nut bread, the test kitchen stores all shelled nuts in the freezer. Sealed in a freezer-safe, zipper-lock storage bag, the nuts will stay fresh-tasting for months. By the way, there's no need to defrost nuts. Frozen nuts chop up just as easily as (if not moreso than) fresh.

Equipment Update: Blenders

In the May/June 2000 issue, we rated blenders and found the Oster Designer 12-Speed Osterizer Blender, Model 6663, to be our favorite. We've now used this blender (almost daily) for more than two years, and it still sails through smoothies and produces perfect purees. That is, unless the feeder cap (the hard plastic piece at the center of the rubber jar lid) falls into the blender during use, as it has on several infuriating occasions. Immediately we turned to the instruction booklet to see what might be going wrong and discovered that the dishwasher could be to blame. According to Oster, only the glass blender jar is dishwasher-safe; none of the other blender parts qualify, including the lid. The plot thickened, however, when an Oster technician working the company's product hotline thought it unlikely that the dishwasher was causing our problem. Instead, the rep thought that the cap was simply worn down, which is not much of a surprise given the intense use our test kitchen equipment sees. Oster offered to ship a brand new feeder cap, gratis. When it arrives, we'll press it into duty and wash it by hand—just in case.

This Oster was rated best blender two years ago and is still going strong, except for the feeder cap, which has shown signs of aging.

New Ways to Cook

Have Sally Schneider and Gray Kunz really delivered a window into the future? Our kitchen tested 35 of their recipes to find out. BY CHRISTOPHER KIMBALL

Every few years, a cookbook author proclaims that he or she has invented a new way of cooking: fewer ingredients, healthier recipes, a more eclectic "modern" style, or even an entirely new aesthetic regarding the combination of tastes and textures. Have Sally Schneider and Gray Kunz delivered on their promises? We went into the test kitchen to find out.

A NEW WAY TO COOK
Sally Schneider
Artisan, 739 pages, $40

➤ Sally Schneider is also the author of *The Art of Low-Calorie Cooking* (Steward Tabori & Chang, 1990), in many ways a fitting precursor to *A New Way to Cook* (about 25 recipes have been repeated), where in the introduction she swerves into the ditch of cancer rates and animal fats, the sort of thing one would find in one of those passionate but dreadful "healthy" cookbooks. However, Schneider finally comes to her senses and sides with moderation, refusing to exclude fat, animal or otherwise, in the pursuit of healthy but flavorful food. In this impressive tome, the author is aiming for a seminal reference work, a *How to Cook Everything* (by Mark Bittman) that has been heavily influenced by the vegetarian worldview of Deborah Madison and the appealing taste combinations of Jamie Oliver's *The Naked Chef*.

PROS: The first thing one notices about *A New Way to Cook* is that it is thick and heavy and has a well-designed, classic look. The next appealing feature is that the recipes sound interesting but not silly. Greek Garlic Sauce, Berry Elixir, or Carrots in Chermoula sound fresh but not forced. We particularly like her emphasis on improvising variations on recipes using both ingredient options and improvising notes. Most of all, this cookbook is packed with ideas—how to use leftovers, how to quickly add flavors—that should appeal to any serious cook.

CONS: Once in a while, the need to be either healthy or different gets the better of Schneider, and this results in a recipe that is worse than its precursor. (Is mushroom meatloaf better than the real thing? Our answer is no.) Other times her lower-fat approach is simply that: lower fat, which results in less flavor or more work or both. For example, to save a few tablespoons of butter in a biscuit recipe, she has to add sour cream and rosemary to boost flavor. You don't

end up with a basic all-purpose recipe, you have to find two extra non-pantry ingredients, and you save only a handful of calories. Seems like wasted effort to us.

RECIPE TESTING: We tested 21 recipes from *A New Way to Cook,* and a majority would be worth making again, even though many of the recipes were underseasoned or utilized techniques that were not particularly successful. Clear winners included Brown Butter Orzo "Risotto," Ginger-and-Cilantro Crab Cakes, Braised Fish Fillets with Their Own Pan Sauce, Carrots in Chermoula, and Fruits in Fragrant Wines. The "no thanks" recipes included the aforementioned Meat Loaf with Wild Mushrooms, an overwrought duck breast recipe, Crispy Salmon with Warm Lentils and Balsamic Essence (higher heat would have delivered crispier skin but would have required more fat for sautéing), and three recipes that worked just fine but tasted a bit bland: Yogurt Sauce with Toasted Spices, Lime Zest, and Basil; Everyday Vinaigrette; and Basic Vanilla Bean Syrup. Many recipes are quite good, but we found that the ideas in this book are sometimes better than the execution. If you agree with the basic principle of healthy eating (and are willing to sacrifice some small degree of flavor to this end), you will bless Schneider's latest work. If taste is everything in your culinary world, we still heartily recommend *A New Way to Cook,* but be prepared to tweak, alter, and boost flavors as you go.

THE ELEMENTS OF TASTE
Gray Kunz and Peter Kaminsky
Little, Brown and Company, 261 pages, $40

➤ Like a few other top-notch New York chefs, Kunz is a master of blending and opposing flavors, making poetry out of the simplest combinations. In *The Elements of Taste,* Kunz sets out to categorize and explain the method to his madness so that home cooks can think about taste and textural combinations in a fresh, more organized manner.

PROS: For anyone interested in the theory of cooking, reading about Kunz's 14 elements of taste is like discovering Dostoevsky after ingesting a lifelong diet of dime-store novels. This is heady stuff and forces one to see recipes in an entirely new light. Although an imperfect book in many respects, Kunz's intellectual approach to food is eminently appealing to anyone who takes

food seriously. For examples, he divides tastes into those that push (salty, sweet, and picante), pull (tangy, vinted, bulby, floral herbal, spiced aromatic, and funky), and punctuate (sharp/bitter) as well as into taste "platforms," which refer to vegetables, meat, fish, and starches.

CONS: *The Elements of Taste* is not an approachable book for home cooks. The recipes are often better suited for restaurant than home cooking, the ingredient lists are often long and fussy, and there is a precious quality to the whole endeavor. "Our Taste Notes"—brief discussions of why Kunz chose the flavor combinations in a particular recipe—are interesting but, after a bit, take on the high-minded style of a German opera critic. Is this art or is this dinner?

RECIPE TESTING: Unfortunately, the recipes in this book received low marks from our test kitchen. All five test cooks who made sample recipes would not recommend buying this book. For one thing, the construction of the recipes was often confusing, so it is not clear in what order to proceed. (The Pork Tenderloin with Bourbon Mustard Brine and Tangy Pears starts off with instructions for the pears before one even brines the pork, an overnight process.) As with many chef recipes, one finds silly ingredients such as 2 tablespoons of diced leeks. So what do I do with the rest of it? Let it also be said that the recipes are often inordinately complicated. Cauliflower Fricassee with Cilantro Raita and Pea Sprouts has 26 ingredients (and, to make matters worse, the end result was badly received since it was over-spiced). There are winners here, such as the Oven-Crisped Chicken with Maple Vinegar Sauce, and many of the flavor combinations are indeed brilliant, but the recipes are overwrought and undertested. *The Elements of Taste* is a great read, one that we can recommend to anyone interested in how a great chef develops recipes, but, unfortunately, a poor cookbook.

Most of the ingredients and materials necessary for the recipes in this issue are available at your local supermarket, gourmet store, or kitchen supply shop. The following are mail-order sources for particular items. Prices listed below were current at press time and do not include shipping or handling unless otherwise indicated. We suggest that you contact companies directly to confirm up-to-date prices and availability.

Digital Thermometers

We don't like the idea of ruining an expensive cut of meat, such as our Prime Rib Roast Beef (page 12), just because we can't get a good read on the temperature. We think a digital thermometer is a much safer bet than a dial thermometer. In the former, the sensor is positioned at the very tip, so it is easy to gauge the temperature of a roast at dead center and a steak's doneness without skewering it horizontally.

Two digital thermometers that we have tested extensively and endorse are the Electronic Remote Thermometer-Timer made by Polder and the Thermapen. The Polder device is a two-piece model—a plastic unit and a metal probe joined by a 43-inch cord—that acts as a thermometer and timer. The design allows you to program the temperature at which the food will be done and to leave the probe in the food as it cooks; an alarm sounds when the programmed temperature is reached. The cord is long enough so that the plastic unit, which displays the time elapsed and the temperature of the food, can be set on a countertop or affixed to the stove by means of a magnet. One word of caution: The metal probe gets quite hot and should not be held by hand, and the cord dangles treacherously. But for the price—just $27.99—this device does a lot of work. The Polder Electronic Remote Thermometer-Timer, item #2999, is available from **A Cook's Wares (211 37th Street, Beaver Falls, PA 15010; 800-915-9788; www.cookswares.com).**

While the Thermapen costs more than the Polder device, we think it is well worth the investment. It has a long probe, a comfortable handle, and a rapid reaction time: It reads the temperature within 10 seconds, while the Polder takes 30 seconds. For fast-cooking foods, such as certain cuts of meat and fish, reaction time can make the difference between perfectly done and overdone. The Thermapen's temperature range is also impressive, accurately reading from −50 to 550 degrees Fahrenheit—clearly beyond the needs of most home cooks but impressive nonetheless. The Thermapen, item #4325, sells for $79.95 in **The Baker's Catalogue (P.O. Box 876, Norwich, VT 05055-0876; 800-827-6836; www.bakerscatalogue.com).**

Extra-Large Turkey Rack

We prefer to roast poultry on a V-rack because it helps to ensure crackling crisp, golden brown skin. A behemoth 20-pound turkey (page 18) overwhelms a standard rack, but **Williams-Sonoma (P.O. Box 379900, Las Vegas, NV 89137-9900; 800-541-2233; www.williams-sonoma.com)** carries a rack that easily accommodates its girth. The rack's stout steel ribs are Teflon coated, which makes cleanup a snap. In addition to holding big birds, the rack can support large cuts of beef or pork. The Williams-Sonoma Large Teflon Roasting Rack sells for $22.

Potato Mashers

Our favorite masher, the Profi Plus by WMF, impressed us right from the start with its sturdy stainless steel construction and solid heft. The Profi Plus, item #744004095906, is available from **thegadgetsource.com (Calvert Retail, LP, P.O. Box 302, Montchanin, DE 19710; 800-458-2616; www.thegadgetsource.com)** for $15.99.

The eccentrically shaped runner-up came from Oxo. The Oxo Good Grips Smooth Masher has a conventional gridded stainless steel mashing head, but the handle consists of a comfortable rubberized grip positioned parallel to the head rather than perpendicular to it, which is the usual position. The Oxo masher, item #619221, sells for $9.99 at **Kitchen Etc. (32 Industrial Drive, Exeter, NH 03833; 800-232-4070; www.kitchenetc.com).**

The Double Potato Masher from Exeter came in third place. It is a conventionally shaped, stainless steel coil model that sports an unconventional second, spring-loaded head that effectively cut work time in half. The Double Potato Masher, item #783597, sells for $9.99 at **Kitchen Etc.**

Chef's Knives

The pleasant surprise of the knife test (page 28) was the strong showing by the budget knives, which took first and third place, outperforming knives costing up to three times as much. The Forschner/Victorinox Fibrox won us over with its keen edge, fine balance, and comfortable handle. For those favoring svelte knives, this was the lightest of the bunch. **Professional Cutlery Direct (242 Branford Road, North Branford, CT 06471; 800-859-6994; www.cutlery.com)** carries the Forschner, item #2CICF, for $31. A close second, the Wüsthof-Trident Grand Prix, is slightly stouter than the Forschner but was nonetheless described as sleek, sharp, and easy to control. All the testers noted its natural feel in their hands. **Professional Cutlery Direct** carries the Grand Prix, item #2CICW, for $82.50. With its uniquely grippy handle and light weight, the third-place

Oxo Pro MV-55 chef's knife proved agile and adept at any task. It is available for $29.99 at **Kitchen Etc.**

Tube Pan for Sour Cream Coffee Cake

For dense, high cakes like our Sour Cream Coffee Cake (page 6), a tube pan (sometimes called an angel food cake pan) is essential. The center tube helps conduct heat to the middle of the cake, allowing for even cooking and a stable structure.

After trying several different brands with our coffee cake recipe, we found that the one-piece Calphalon Commercial Nonstick Angel Food Cake pan did a great job. It is surprisingly heavy, constructed of thick aluminum with an impressively stout bottom, and coated with a nonstick surface. The pan, item #181810, sells for $24.95 at **Cooking.com (Guest Assistance, 2850 Ocean Park Boulevard, Suite 310, Santa Monica, California 90405; 800-663-8810; www.cooking.com).**

Springform Pans for Mousse Cake

After making both chocolate mousse cakes (page 22) and cheesecakes in six different 9-inch springform pans, we were most impressed by the Kaiser Noblesse and the Frieling Handle-It Glass Bottom Spring Form Pan. The Kaiser's solid construction and exceptionally tight-fitting bottom made for easy use and excellent results. The pan, item #6512, sells for $19.80 from **A Cook's Wares**. Definitely unique, the Frieling won accolades for the handles that sprout from the pan's sides and allow for easy maneuvering, especially in and out of a hot oven or water bath. The pan also sports a perfectly smooth glass bottom so that cakes can slide right off. The Frieling pan, item #157723, sells for $31.95 at **www.cooking.com.**

Chocolate

Three out of the four top-ranked chocolates in our tasting—Scharffen Berger, Callebaut, and Valrhona—can be hard to find outside of specialty stores and high-end markets, but they can easily be had by mail order. American-made Scharffen Berger took top honors in the tasting and is available in 275-gram (9.7-ounce) bars from **Chocosphere (5200 SE Harney Drive, Portland, OR 97206; 877-992-4626; www.chocosphere.com)** for $8.95. Chocosphere also sells our fourth-place chocolate, French-made Valrhona Cacao Pâte Extra, for $25 per kilogram (2.2 pounds). Belgian-produced Callebaut came in second. A 1-kilogram chunk of Callebaut unsweetened, item #97217, can be bought for $11.95 from **Sweet Celebrations (P.O. Box 39426, Edina, MN 55439-0426; 800-328-6722; www.sweetc.com).**

RECIPES
November & December 2002

Wild Rice Pilaf, 21

Prime Rib, 12, and Yorkshire Pudding, 13

PHOTOGRAPHY: CARL TREMBLAY

Mulled Red Wine, 10

Turkey for a Crowd, 19

Smothered Pork Chops, 9, and Mashed Sweet Potatoes, 15

http://www.cooksillustrated.com

If you enjoy *Cook's Illustrated* magazine, you should visit our Web site. Simply log on at http://www.cooksillustrated.com. Although much of the information is free, database searches are for site subscribers only. *Cook's Illustrated* subscribers are offered a 20 percent discount.

Here are some of the things you can do on our site:

Search Our Recipes: We have a searchable database of all the recipes from *Cook's Illustrated*.

Search Tastings and Cookware Ratings: You will find all of our reviews (cookware, food, cookbooks) plus new material created exclusively for the Web.

Find Your Favorite Quick Tips.

Check Your Subscription: Check the status of your subscription, pay a bill, or give a gift subscription online.

Visit Our Bookstore: You can purchase any of our cookbooks, hardbound annual editions of the magazine, or posters online.

Subscribe to *e-Notes:* Our free e-mail companion to the magazine offers cooking advice, test results, buying tips, and recipes about a single topic each month.

Orecchiette with Broccoli, 20

Sour Cream Coffee Cake, 7

AMERICA'S TEST KITCHEN

Join the millions of cooks who watch our show, *America's Test Kitchen,* on public television each week. For more information, including recipes from the show and a schedule of program times in your area, visit http://www.americastestkitchen.com.

Bittersweet Chocolate Mousse Cake, 23

Sugar Cookies, 25

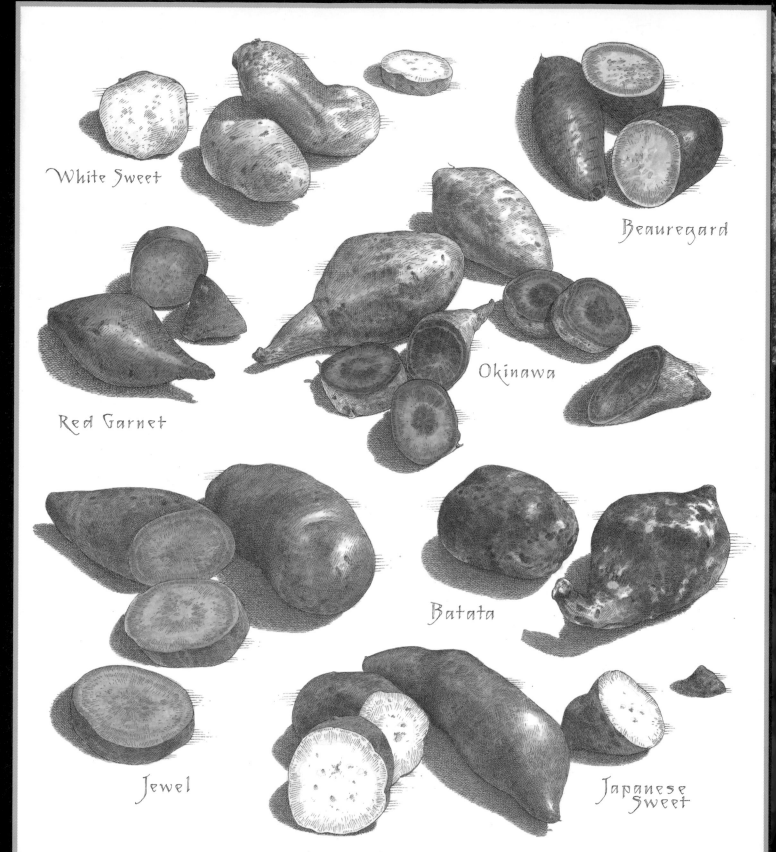

White Sweet

Beauregard

Red Garnet

Okinawa

Jewel

Batata

Japanese Sweet

SWEET POTATOES